Employer's Liability at Common Law

By the same author:

The Law of Quasi Contracts
The Technique of Advocacy
Damages for Personal Injuries

Employer's Liability
at Common Law

ELEVENTH EDITION

By John Munkman, LL B
of the Middle Temple and North-Eastern
Circuit, Barrister

Butterworths
London, Dublin, Edinburgh
1990

United Kingdom	Butterworth & Co (Publishers) Ltd, 88 Kingsway, LONDON WC2B 6AB and 4 Hill Street, EDINBURGH EH2 3JZ
Australia	Butterworths Pty Ltd, SYDNEY, MELBOURNE, BRISBANE, ADELAIDE, PERTH, CANBERRA and HOBART
Canada	Butterworths Canada Ltd, TORONTO and VANCOUVER
Ireland	Butterworth (Ireland) Ltd, DUBLIN
Malaysia	Malayan Law Journal Sdn Bhd, KUALA LUMPUR
New Zealand	Butterworths of New Zealand Ltd, WELLINGTON and AUCKLAND
Puerto Rico	Equity de Puerto Rico, Inc, HATO REY
Singapore	Malayan Law Journal Pte Ltd, SINGAPORE
USA	Butterworth Legal Publishers, AUSTIN, Texas; BOSTON, Massachusetts; CLEARWATER, Florida (D & S Publishers); ORFORD, New Hampshire (Equity Publishing); ST PAUL, Minnesota; and SEATTLE, Washington

A CIP Catalogue record for this book is available from the British Library.

ISBN 0 406 18100 4 0168 9 IX

Typeset by Phoenix Photosetting, Chatham
Printed by Mackays of Chatham PLC, Chatham, Kent

Foreword

This edition has involved a large amount of new material—larger perhaps than any previous edition—and extensive re-writing.

The most important item is the manufacturer's strict liability for products under the Consumer Protection Act 1987. I have included a full explanation of this.

There are several new codes of safety regulations, many of which apply to all places of work. The Control of Substances Hazardous to Health Regulations 1988 replace numerous existing safety codes for various substances, in particular all those relating to dust and fumes of any kind, and to such things as spraying in agriculture. There are in addition:

The Control of Asbestos at Work Regulations 1987;

The Ionising Radiation Regulations 1985;

The Electricity at Work Regulations 1989.

Then there are new codes for particular places of work:

The Docks Regulations 1988;

The Loading and Unloading of Fishing Vessels Regulations 1988;

The Mines (Safety of Exit) Regulations 1988 which supersede sections of the Mines and Quarries Act;

The Quarries (Explosives) Regulations 1988;

Merchant Shipping (several sets of regulations, including means of access, machinery, lifting apparatus and electricity).

I have given a full explanation of the Animals (Scotland) Act 1987 which is, as so often, an improvement on the English legislation. One of my colleagues frequently advises injured postmen and it is surprising how many are bitten by dogs and other animals—one was even attacked by a sheep.

There has been a vast amount of case-law, much of it from Scotland, mostly on points of detail such as the Construction Regulations. Perhaps the only case of major importance is the decision of the House of Lords in *McDermid*, which re-stated in strong terms the employer's non-delegable duty not only to establish a safe method of work but *to put it into operation.*

Case-law starts with a clear statement of principle, but with the incessant overlay of new cases it is liable to become muddled and inconsistent. Where this happens, it is important to unravel the tangled web and set out the general effect in an orderly and consistent pattern. Where there is inconsistency, I have never hesitated to say what I think is the better opinion. I have re-written several passages on these lines. For example, I have torn to pieces the whole section on 'Safe Means of Access' (pp 289–299) and re-drafted it on a clearer plan.

I now add some personal comments on the present state of the law, which those who are not interested may ignore.

I find it ironic that absolute liability has been introduced for manufactured products, a long way off from the consumer, when there is no such liability for things close at hand such a bricks falling from a scaffold or moving machinery—apart from the accident that some breach of statutory duty may apply which has not itself been eviscerated by reading into it the uncertain test of 'foreseeability'.

This new product liability has not resulted from a logical and reasoned approach to law reform, such as we might expect to be undertaken by a full-time Law Commission. It is merely a response to fashionable pressure groups, starting in the USA and taken up by the EEC. I would prefer to see a wider approach to the whole law of tort.

I have always felt that absolute or strict liability, as in the old law of Trespass to the Person, and in the rule in *Rylands v Fletcher*, is more in line with the traditions of the common law than the uncertain and arbitrary working of the fashionable law of negligence. Trespass was formerly available for every injury directly caused by the defendant. 'In trespass the defendant shall not be excused without unavoidable necessity, which is not shown here': *Dickenson v Watson* (1682) T Jo 205. In *Weaver v Ward* (1616) Hob 134 crimes were distinguished because absence of intention was an excuse: ' . . . yet in trespass which tends to give damages only according to hurt or loss, it is not so'. In other words, the law of tort is about compensation for infringing other people's rights. It was not until the nineteenth century that theorists such as Bentham and Pollock lost sight of this and started to treat it as a code of moral behaviour; and it is only since 1945 that the law of trespass to the person has been so devitalised that a plaintiff is now required to prove negligence. The principle of *Rylands v Fletcher*—that a defendant is liable for dangerous things within his control which he allows to escape—is a natural extension of trespass, from which it developed. But some influential lawyers—from a conviction that the law of tort is a code of moral behaviour—have entertained such a fierce and bitter hatred for *Rylands v Fletcher* that they have qualified it and watered it down to a very minor role. Yet imaginative law reformers could have extended the principle to make defendants liable for any risk they have created or installed—such as those I instanced of bricks on a scaffold or moving machinery—unless damage is caused by circumstances beyond their control (Act of God, or of a third party, to quote the old exceptions). Liability for negligence would then be limited to cases where there was *mutual* exposure to risk, as with collisions of vehicles. There could be a defence of contributory *causation*—as distinct from contributory negligence.

Distaste for the older traditions of the common law is largely due to the extraordinary adulation of the law of negligence which became fashionable in the post-war years, especially the 1960s. 'Negligence' came to be looked upon as a supreme and perfect test of liability to which everything else should give way. It is difficult to understand why, except for the fallacy that no one should be liable for causing damage unless he is morally blameworthy. The flaw in negligence is that it is a matter of opinion and degree, and therefore inherently uncertain. The uncertainty was accentuated by importing from the USA the test of 'foreseeability'. This meant that the court had to assume the stance of a prophet and gaze at the unknown future. But of course everybody foresees different things. Some strain at a gnat; others swallow a camel; some can do both at the same time. Unfortunately, too, this vague 'foreseeability' test has been transposed to the meaning of 'safe' and 'dangerous' in the context of such things as means of access and machinery under the Factories Act, which should have been looked upon as questions of pure fact. In many cases it is impossible to predict what a court will decide. There are some who think that negligence is as real and recognisable as a brick. I do not share this view.

There is concern at present about the delay in bringing injury cases to trial. No one seems to have made the point that this is largely due to the uncertainty of the law of negligence. Plaintiffs in a weak case go slow in the hope of extracting at any rate some payment; defendants in a strong case spin out the defence to get a reduced settlement. Reforms in court procedure make little impact on this. What is needed is reform of the law itself.

John Munkman
February 1990

Extract from Foreword to Fourth Edition

The aim of this book is to give the legal profession a reliable and comprehensive text-book on liability for accidents at work: at the same time special efforts have been made to keep the text clear and intelligible for readers who are not expert in legal terminology, and by express request there is a short glossary of legal terms—including Latin phrases—in Appendix I.

Contents

Table of statutes

References in this Table to *Statutes* are to Halsbury's Statutes of England (Fourth Edition) showing the volume and page at which the annotated text of the Act may be found.

Table of Cases

xxix

PAGE

C

PAGE

M

McAlister (or Donoghue) v Stevenson. See M'Alister (or Donoghue) v Stevenson

PAGE

U

V

W

Chapter 1
The historical development of employer's liability law

1 Introductory

The meaning of employer's liability

Employer's liability—in the most restricted sense of the term—means the liability of an employer to pay damages to his employees (who are conveniently described by the common law as 'servants', however exalted their status and whatever their type of work) for personal injuries which they have sustained in the course of their employment.

An employer may incur such a liability in more than one way. In the first place, he is liable if an accident is due to his own act or default, for example if he carries out dangerous operations without establishing a safe method of work. This is the employer's *personal liability*. But he is also responsible for the acts of his servants in the course of their employment, as where one workman injures another by operating a crane carelessly. This is *vicarious liability*. The employer has always been liable to his servants for his own personal acts; and employers have for many years been held liable to the outside world for the acts of their servants. Formerly, however, under the rule known as the doctrine of 'common employment', an employer was not liable to his own servants for the negligence of their fellow-servants, as this was considered to be one of the risks of the employment, which a servant agreed to accept. This doctrine was abolished by the Law Reform (Personal Injuries) Act 1948. There are still some differences between personal liability and vicarious liability, and for certain purposes they must be kept distinct. In general, however, the effect of the Act of 1948 is that the employer's personal liability and his vicarious liability have been integrated into a single general duty. The employer, acting personally or through his servants or agents, must take reasonable care for the safety of his workmen and other employees. Liability of this broad and general kind is a *common law liability*, i.e. it arises under the ordinary law of the land as interpreted by the courts and does not depend upon an Act of Parliament. As a rule, proof of negligence is required to establish liability at common law. But there is, in addition, liability for *breach of statutory duty*, i.e. for a failure to comply with a duty imposed by an Act of Parliament or by regulations, such as the obligation under s. 14 of the Factories Act 1961 to fence dangerous machinery. Liabilities of this type are absolute, in the sense that it is not necessary to prove negligence, and the only question to be decided by the court is whether the statutory duty has been performed or not.

Under the earlier legislation, statutory duties were usually imposed on the employer not so much in his capacity as employer but as the person in control of the place of work. Under the Factories Act 1961, the person liable is the occupier of the factory, and under the Mines and Quarries Act 1954, it is the owners who are responsible: and they are responsible to all persons working in the factory or mine, whether employed by them or not. Under more modern safety regulations, such as those for the building industry and docks, the main duty for the safety of his own employees specifically rests on the employer, but duties are also imposed on associated contractors and on suppliers of equipment and materials.

It would, therefore, be inconvenient to restrict the scope of this subject to cases where a workman claims against his own employer. Accordingly, this book is concerned with employer's liability in the widest possible sense, i.e. with the rights of an injured workman both against his own employer and against other persons, either at common law or for a breach of statutory duty; or, to put it another way, with the liability of an employer to other workmen as well as to his own[1]. To some extent also, though only incidentally, reference is made to the liability of those in control of industrial establishments to the general public, for example their liability as occupiers to those who enter their premises,

---

1   For convenience, the term 'workman' is used frequently throughout the text as synonymous with 'servant' or 'employee' generally, since the great majority of cases arise out of accidents in industry.

and their duties under safety legislation which in many cases extend beyond employees to other persons at risk from their activities.

The historical background

If the present law is to be properly understood, it is necessary to have some knowledge, in outline at least, of its origins and history: for, to give just one illustration, modern statutes and case-law contain references to obsolete rules such as the doctrine of common employment, or the rule that a workman 'accepts the risk' when he undertakes a dangerous task.

Every branch of the law is influenced to a certain degree by the social and economic surroundings (including current beliefs as well as facts) in which it grows up: and this applies with special force to a subject like employer's liability, which is closely related to the life and welfare of ordinary people. It would be wrong, of course, to suppose that the common law (as distinct from legislation) is shaped entirely, or even mainly, by economic forces, since the primary aim of the courts is to reach an objective standard of justice[2]. Nevertheless, it often happens that there is a conflict between two or more different interests. So, in the field of employer's liability, the right of the community to have industry carried on in the most efficient manner, although this may create some risk, is in conflict with the right of the workman to integrity of life and limb; and the adjustment between the two interests is a matter of degree rather than of principle, in which the facts and theories accepted at any given time have great weight.

The recorded history of employer's liability does not start until 1837, and during the next hundred years three phases can be distinguished. First there was the early nineteenth century, dominated by the economic theory of laissez-faire, according to which the welfare of the community was best served by leaving each individual free to pursue his own interests. This theory was reflected in the courts, where the prevailing

2   'I am most firmly convinced by all my experience and study of and reflection upon the law that its principal purpose is the quest of justice': per Lord Wright in *Interpretations of Modern Legal Philosophers*, p. 794. The word 'justice' is not used by the law in a sentimental sense: it simply means the vindication and protection of a person's legal rights. *Suum cuique tribuere*, as Roman law said—'Give to each man that which is his *right*'. The importance and value of a system of law with definite rules is that it defines the extent of each right, with qualifications which take into account the rights of other individuals and of the community as a whole.

mood was that each workman should look after himself and that if he entered a dangerous employment he accepted its risks. Towards the middle of the century there was a change of view: it began to be recognised that workmen needed special protection against dangerous conditions of work, and while Parliament imposed minimum standards of safety in mines and factories, a more humane tone also crept into the decisions of the courts. The latest phase has simply carried the same policy farther. Dangerous industries have been regulated in minute detail, and the safety standards have been raised continuously. At the same time the right to recover damages at common law has been greatly enlarged, partly by statute and partly by a series of decisions in the House of Lords. The chief innovation of the twentieth-century legislators is the scheme of national insurance against various incidents of life, which includes, as a major component, insurance against industrial injuries and diseases; but this does not supersede the right to damages at common law, though to a limited extent benefits received under the scheme are taken into account in assessing the damages.

At the present day, therefore, the law is favourable to the injured workman. He receives insurance benefits whether he was to blame for his accident or not. In addition, he is entitled to damages at common law if the accident was caused by the fault of his employer, of his fellow-workmen, or of third parties; and if the workman's own negligence contributed to the accident, the effect is not to defeat his claim but to reduce the damages in proportion to his fault.

Apart from the background of social doctrine, the general state of the law at the beginning of the nineteenth century must also be taken into account: and two matters in particular call for special notice. First, how far was an employer liable at that date for the acts of his servants? Secondly, in what circumstances could a plaintiff recover damages for personal injuries?

(i) Vicarious liability[3]

Early law did not in general recognise the principle, now so firmly established, that a master was liable for the torts of his servants. The master was responsible only in certain special cases, as where the act was expressly ordered, or where the master took some benefit from it. As a further special case, the Admiralty Court held that the master of a ship,

3   See Holdsworth *History of English Law*, Vol. 8, pp. 472–482.

and later, the owners, were liable for the acts of the crew towards passengers and third parties. The first formal recognition of vicarious liability *as a general principle* was contained in the judgment of Holt C J, in *Boson v Sandford* (1690) 2 Salk 440, where he said:

> 'Whoever employs another is answerable for him, and undertakes for his care to all that make use of him.'

After this dictum, the doctrine crept in gradually, but many different opinions were expressed as to its real justification. Two quotations will indicate the final rationalisation arrived at in the nineteenth century. Lord Brougham said in *Duncan v Findlater* (1839) 6 Cl & Fin 894 at 910:

> 'The rule of liability and its reason I take to be this: I am liable for what is done for me and under my orders by the men I employ . . . and the reason I am liable is this, that by employing them I set the whole thing in motion.'

To a similar effect are the words of Chief Justice Shaw in the American case of *Farwell v Boston and Worcester Rly Road Corpn* (1842) 4 Metcalf, 49:

> 'This rule is obviously founded on the great principle of social duty, that every man in the management of his own affairs, whether by himself or by his agents or servants, shall so conduct them as not to injure another; and if he does not, and another thereby sustains damage, he shall answer for it.'

The point to be noted here is that the doctrine of vicarious liability was set up to protect the interests of *strangers*, on the basis that, in the eyes of an *outsider*, master and servant are one. Thus, in approaching the question of the liability of a master for injuries caused by one servant to another, the courts had to consider whether they should *extend* vicarious liability. They decided against any extension, as we shall see, and so the doctrine of common employment was born. But it is wrong to suppose that, *prima facie*, the master was liable for the torts of his servants towards both outsiders and insiders, and that the courts established an exception as regards insiders, on the ground that they had agreed to accept the risk: though this was the view taken by the courts after the doctrine became established.

(ii) Liability for personal injuries
When personal injuries *directly* resulted from the defendant's act, there
was a remedy at common law in the action of Trespass. Where they
resulted *indirectly* from some earlier action or omission on the part of the
defendant, as would usually happen in employer's liability cases, there
might or might not be a remedy in Case[4]. In deciding whether or not an
action in Case should succeed, the courts had grown into the habit of
considering whether due care had been shown. But the notion of an
independent tort of negligence, depending on a positive duty of care
between two persons standing in a close relationship, had not yet arisen.
A common law action was wholly defeated by the defence of *contributory
negligence*, where the plaintiff's own negligence contributed to cause his
injuries.

2 The doctrine of common employment

It is curious that, before 1837, no case can be traced in the English law
reports where a servant sued his employer for injuries sustained in the
course of his employment. The first case of the kind is *Priestley v Fowler*
(1837) 3 M & W 1.

In *Priestley v Fowler* the plaintiff was employed by a butcher, and was
carried on the butcher's van in the course of his employment. The van
was overloaded, one of the wheels gave way, and the plaintiff was
injured. He sued his master, the butcher, in Case, alleging that it was the
defendant's duty to have the van in a proper state of repair and carry
passengers safely. Thus he claimed, in effect, to have much the same
rights as a passenger on a stage coach would have. Lord Abinger CB
said:

> 'It has been objected . . . that from the mere relation of master and
> servant no contract, and therefore no duty, can be implied on the part
> of the master to cause the servant to be safely and securely carried, or
> to make the master liable for any damage to the servant, arising from

4   Historically, the action on the case grew out of Trespass. Trespass was available
     when there was a *direct* injury to the person, and by analogy the courts extended it
     by degrees, one step at a time, to allow an action of Trespass 'on the case' for an
     indirect injury. Thus there always was, and indeed still is, an element of discretion
     in allowing a claim of a type which has not been allowed before.

any vice or imperfection, unknown to the master, in the carriage, or in the mode of loading and conducting it.'

Moreover the plaintiff had not alleged that the defendant knew of the overloading, or of the defect in the vehicle. Therefore, said Lord Abinger, to hold him liable would mean that a master was responsible for all the acts of his servants to one another, for the act of the chambermaid in putting damp sheets in the bed, of the upholsterer in providing a rickety bed, or of the butcher in supplying bad meat. Lord Abinger could not bring himself to sanction such an indefinite extension of vicarious liability: the consequences seemed to him to be unpredictable. One cannot help feeling that Lord Abinger's thoughts were dwelling on his own extensive pre-Victorian household, and the liabilities to which he himself might be subjected[5].

Towards the end of the judgment there is an important passage, which suggests vaguely the sort of personal negligence for which a master might be held liable:

'In truth, the mere relation of the master and the servant never can imply an obligation on the part of the master to take more care of the servant than he may reasonably be expected to do of himself. He is, no doubt, bound to provide for the safety of his servant in the course of his employment, to the best of his judgment, information and belief.'

Here the age of laissez-faire is speaking: the servant must look out for himself. But there is at least a hint of general duty resting on the employer to take reasonable care for the safety of his servants.

At all events, *Priestley v Fowler* laid down for the first time the doctrine of common employment: that a master was not liable to his servant for an injury caused by the negligence of a fellow-servant, with whom he was engaged in a common employment. In *Farwell v Boston and Worcester Rail Road Corpn, supra*, which was decided a few years later, the American courts reached a similar conclusion.

The doctrine of common employment had not yet finally triumphed, and the whole question was argued again in *Hutchinson v York, Newcastle and Berwick Rly Co* (1850) 5 Exch 343. In that case two trains belonging to the same railway company had collided, and the plaintiff, a railway

5 'These instances seem to show personal apprehension, rather than any principle': per Lord Wright in *Radcliffe v Ribble Motor Services Ltd* [1939] AC 215 at 239, [1939] 1 All ER 637 at 651. Lord Abinger was the owner of Inverlochy Castle near Ben Nevis.

employee travelling on duty in one of the trains, brought his action against the company alleging negligence on the part of both engine-drivers. The company pleaded that both engine-drivers were fellow-servants of the plaintiff and were fit and competent persons. The plea was held good. Thus the court, after full argument, upheld the doctrine of common employment, and explained its scope more clearly. It had been suggested that the plaintiff was in common employment with his fellow-servants in the *same* train, but not with the engine-driver on the *other* train. The court rejected this argument, saying in effect that any fellow-servant was in 'common employment' with the plaintiff if the risk arising from his negligence was incidental to the plaintiff's employment. Alderson B re-stated the law as follows (the italics are not in the original):

> 'This principle upon which a master is in general liable to answer for accidents resulting from the negligence or unskilfulness of his servants is that the act of his servant is in truth his own act. . . . Equally clear it is, that though a *stranger* may treat the act of the servant as the act of his master, yet the servant himself, by whose negligence or want of skill the accident has occurred, cannot. . . . The difficulty is as to the principle applicable to the case of several servants employed by the same master, and injury resulting to one of them from the negligence of another. In such a case, however, we are of opinion that the master is not in general responsible, *when he has selected persons of competent care and skill*.'

It will be noted that Alderson B considered that at all events it was the master's duty to select competent persons. He continued:

> 'They have both engaged in a common service, the duties of which impose a certain risk on each of them; and in case of negligence on the part of the other, the party injured knows that the negligence is that of his fellow-servant and not of his master. He knew, when he engaged in the service, that he was exposed to the risk of injury, not only from his own want of skill or care, but also from the want of it on the part of his fellow-servant; and he must be supposed to have contracted on the terms that, as between himself and his master, he would run this risk.'

The point of this reasoning will be missed unless it is appreciated that Alderson B is contrasting the position of a servant with that of a stranger. The stranger has no inside knowledge. To him, master and servants form a single organisation, and he must therefore have the benefit of vicarious liability. But the servant has inside knowledge of what is done by the master and what is done by fellow-servants, and contracts with the knowledge that he can only hold the master accountable for his own acts. The reasoning is, of course, somewhat flimsy; but it is not foolish or perverse, as modern critics with the preconceptions of their own century have supposed.

Finally Alderson B said:

> 'This must be taken with the qualification that the master shall have taken due care not to expose his servant to unreasonable risks.'

Thus it was conceded that a vague duty of care rested on the master, though, as in *Priestley v Fowler*, its details were left undefined.

3 Personal duties of the master: developments in Scotland

Meanwhile the Scottish courts had taken on the more positive task of formulating the personal duties of the master. The Scottish cases are interesting, because they were ultimately adopted by English law, and indeed in employer's liability law we owe a great debt to Scotland.

In *Sword v Cameron* (1839) 1 D 493, blasts were fired in a quarry, but warning was not given quickly enough to allow workmen to move to a safe distance. One of the workmen was injured, and the Court of Session held that the master was liable on the ground that it was his duty to provide a safe method of work.

Paterson v Wallace & Co (1854) 1 Macq 748 was a Scottish case which reached the House of Lords. There a miner who was working in the main road of a mine complained of a large stone which was hanging over his place of work. At last two men were sent to remove the stone, but they stood by until the miner finished his work, and in the meantime the stone fell and killed him. The defence alleged that the miner had brought about his own death by his rashness in staying to finish his work. The House of Lords sent the case back for re-trial on the ground of misdirection by the judge, who had placed too much emphasis on the workman's 'rashness'. The Lord Chancellor said, however:

> 'The law of Scotland is admitted on all hands to be this—and I
> believe it to be entirely conformable to the law of England also—that
> where a man is employing a servant in a work, particularly work of a

dangerous character, he is bound to take all reasonable precautions that there shall be no extraordinary danger incurred by the workman.'

He gave as an example the use of a defective rope in a pit shaft. Lord Brougham added that if this duty were entrusted to a manager, the company would be responsible for the manager's negligence.

In *Brydon v Stewart* (1855) 2 Macq 30, miners insisted on leaving the pit before their work was finished, as they were dissatisfied with the bad ventilation of the mine and the lowness of their wages. In the course of the ascent of the pit shaft, a stone fell from the side of the shaft, and one of them was killed. The cage was open at the top. The judge had misdirected the jury by saying that the owners were not liable if the miners had left their work without excuse. The House of Lords directed judgment to be entered for the pursuers, since, according to the findings of the jury, the pit was in an unsafe condition. In the *Bartonshill* case, *infra*, Lord Cranworth said that *Brydon v Stewart*

> 'turned . . . on a point established by many preceding cases, namely, that when a master employs his servant in a work of danger, he is bound to exercise due care in order to have his tackle and machinery in a safe and proper condition, so as to protect the servant against unnecessary risks.'

Up to this point, then, the line of cases had settled that a master has a personal duty to take care for the safety of his servants, and that this extends to the place of employment, to the machinery and tackle, and to the system of work. It had also settled that if these fundamental duties were entrusted to a manager, the master remained responsible for his negligence.

In *Dixon v Ranken* (1852) 14 D 420 the Court of Session had rejected the doctrine of common employment, on the ground that the 'recent English cases', if they were correct, depended on a foreign system of jurisprudence; and the liability of an employer under the law of Scotland for fellow-servants was defined as follows by Lord Hope L J-C:

> 'For their careful and cautious attention to duty, for their neglect of precautions by which danger to life may be caused, he is just as much responsible as for such misconduct on his own part, if he were actually working or present.'

But this decision was now challenged on appeals to the House of Lords from Scotland in the *Bartonshill* cases.

4 The Bartonshill cases

Bartonshill Coal Co v Reid (1858) 3 Macq 266 was a remarkable case. It was heard by a single Lord (Lord Cranworth), who deferred judgment for a period of two years. In the meantime *Bartonshill Coal Co v McGuire* (1858) 3 Macq 300 was argued before three Law Lords—it arose out of the same accident—and judgment in both cases was delivered simultaneously.

In these cases a party of miners was being drawn up the mine-shaft in the pit cage, and the engine-man failed to stop the cage, with the result that it was upset, and both Reid and McGuire were killed.

Here it could not be alleged that the machinery was defective. Liability could be based only on the negligence of the engine-man. Thus the case raised the question whether the doctrine of common employment was good law in England, and whether it also applied to Scotland. Lord Cranworth decided both points in the affirmative. After referring to the principle of vicarious liability, and saying that it was based on public policy, he continued:

> 'But do the same principles apply to the case of a workman injured
> by the want of care of a fellow-workman engaged together in the same
> work? I think not. When the man contracts to do work of any particular
> sort, he knows, or ought to know, to what risk he is exposing himself.
> He knows, if such be the nature of the risk, that want of care on the
> part of a fellow-workman may be fatal or injurious to him, and that
> against such want of care his employer cannot by possibility protect
> him.'

In *McGuire's* case the argument had taken the rather different form that the engine-man and the men in the cage were in different departments of duty, and that common employment did not exist. Lord Chelmsford LC conceded that common employment did not apply to servants engaged in 'different departments of duty', but did not agree that this position was established in this case, as the safety of the miners depended, in the ordinary course of things, on the care and skill of the engine-man.

Lord Cranworth recognised the validity of the principles applied in *Sword v Cameron, Paterson v Wallace & Co* and *Brydon v Stewart*. However, the dominant fact was that common employment had now been riveted on the law of both England and Scotland, and this completely overshadowed the earlier decisions, which did not regain their full force until 1937.

One more development followed. Scottish law had never taken kindly to common employment, and the Court of Session now developed the doctrine that a manager or other superior person was not in common employment with the workman under him, and that for the negligence of such a person, at any rate, the master was liable. This doctrine came up for review by the House of Lords in *Wilson v Merry* (1868) LR 1 Sc & Div 326.

In this case a temporary scaffold had been erected to drive a level in a new seam in a coal mine. The platform caused a temporary obstruction to the free circulation of air in the mine. There was an accumulation of fire damp, and an explosion followed in which the appellant's son was killed. The owners took no personal part in the erection of the platform, which was carried out under the superintendence of their underground manager. The judge directed the jury that it was the duty of the owners to have a safe system of ventilation in their mine, and that if they had delegated the whole of their reponsibility to the underground manager, they were responsible for his negligence. The House of Lords held that this direction was wrong. Lord Cranworth said (p. 334):

'Workmen do not cease to be fellow-workmen because they are not all equal in point of station or duty.'

Lord Cairns LC said (p. 332):

'But what the master is, in my opinion, bound to his servants to do, in the event of his not personally superintending and directing the work, is to select proper and competent persons to do so, and furnish them with adequate materials and resources for the work. When he has done this he has, in my opinion, done all that he is bound to do. And if the persons so selected are guilty of negligence, this is not the negligence of the master.'

There is a touch of Victorian complacency in the speech of Lord Colonsay (p. 343):

'The constantly increasing scale on which mining and manufacturing establishments are conducted, by reason of new combinations and applications of capital and industry, has necessarily called into existence extended organisations for management—more gradations of servants, more separation and distribution of duties, more delegation of authority, and less of personal presence or interference of the master. The same personal superintendence by owners or masters, common and beneficial in some minor establishments, is in many cases unattainable, and, even if attained, would not be beneficial. The principles of the law, however, have sufficient elasticity to enable them to be applied, notwithstanding such progressive changes in the manner of conducting business[6].'

All the same, careful reading of the opinions shows that in accordance with the earlier cases their Lordships recognised that the employer had certain fundamental duties for which he would be responsible though he had delegated them to a subordinate. For instance, Lord Colonsay thought that the employer would be liable if the system of ventilation in the pit as a whole was defective: but here there was only a temporary obstruction in one part of the system.

It is not surprising, however, if the case left the false impression (which was not corrected until 1937, in *Wilsons and Clyde Coal Co v English* [1938] AC 57, [1937] 3 All ER 628) that the employer's only duty, if absent from his undertaking, was to appoint competent managers. Common employment thereupon became an almost insurmountable difficulty in the way of an injured workman. In the few cases where personal negligence by the employer could be proved, the workman might encounter a further difficulty: for if he had been guilty of negligence contributing to the accident, this was a complete bar to his right to recover damages.

5 The Employers' Liability Act 1880

The first breach in the doctrine of common employment was made by the Employers' Liability Act 1880 which, however, gave only a partial and incomplete remedy to the workman. Under this Act the workman could succeed if, speaking very broadly, he could prove that the accident resulted from a defect in 'the ways, works, machinery or plant', or from the negligence of some person placed in a position of superintendence or whose orders the workman had to obey, or, in the case of a railway,

6   These remarks are curious because the law, far from having 'sufficient elasticity', had not adapted itself at all to the changes mentioned by Lord Colonsay. It would have adapted itself only if the employer was made liable for the default of the delegated management, which is precisely the opposite of what the House decided. But critics of Victorian complacency should take it as a warning against similar complacency in our own time, e.g., the belief in the supreme excellence of 'negligence' and 'foreseeability' in determining liability for hazards which our ancestors never dreamed of.

from the negligence of a signalman or engine-driver. Lord Watson said in *Smith v Baker & Sons* [1891] AC 325:

> 'The main, although not the sole, object of the Act of 1880 was to place masters who do not upon the same footing of responsibility with those who do personally superintend their works and workmen, by making them answerable for the negligence of those persons to whom they entrust the duty of superintendence, as if it were their own. In effecting that object, the Legislature has found it expedient in many instances to enact what were acknowledged principles of the common law.'

The defence of common employment was excluded *pro tanto* in the limited categories of cases which fell within the Act. But to counterbalance the concession, the amount of damages recoverable was restricted to three years' wages, at the most.

The Act applied to railway servants and also to manual workers generally. Plaintiffs were not bound to proceed under the Act, with its limited degree of liability, but remained free to sue at common law in cases where common employment did not apply. The limitation of liability under the Act shows the extreme nervousness of nineteenth-century legislators in imposing burdens which, in their view, might have weakened the stability of industry[7].

During the currency of the Act of 1880 an attempt was made to defeat its object by introducing the doctrine of common employment under another form, viz. the defence of *volenti non fit injuria*, the plea that the workman had voluntarily assumed the risk of dangerous work, and thereby released his employer from liability. This defence was raised in *Smith v Baker & Sons* [1891] AC 325, a case which arose out of a typical nineteenth-century accident, where a gang of navvies were clearing a railway cutting. Heavy stones were being slung by crane over their place of work, and though protests were made the system was not altered. Finally one of the stones fell and injured the plaintiff. It is curious that the plaintiff did not bring his action at common law, as he might well have done, pleading an unsafe system of work and relying on the authority of *Sword v Cameron*: perhaps proceedings under the Act of 1880 were taken on the ground of cheapness, as they could be brought in the county court. At any rate the jury found in favour of the plaintiff

---

7 Again, modern critics should not be too supercilious. In this century, when industry is more vulnerable, we have fallen into the opposite error of supposing that it can carry unlimited burdens.

that there had been negligence. Furthermore, in reply to a question from the county court judge, 'Did the plaintiff voluntarily undertake a risky employment with knowledge of its risks?' the jury said 'No'. In the House of Lords the defendants argued that, as a matter of law, there was no evidence to support the answer of the jury, that the plaintiff had taken the risk of injury with his eyes open, and that therefore he could not succeed.

The House of Lords rejected this argument. They said that it was not enough that the plaintiff, knowing of the risk, carried on with his work: it must be shown that he consented to take the risk upon himself without compensation. A feature of interest in the case is the dissenting judgment of Lord Bramwell, who, in the following extract, puts the law as high as it could possibly be pitched in favour of the employer:

> 'It is said that to hold the plaintiff is not to recover is to hold that a master may carry on his work in a dangerous way and damage his servant. I do so hold, if the servant is foolish enough to agree to it. This sounds very cruel. But do not people go to see dangerous sports? Acrobats daily incur fearful dangers, lion-tamers and the like. Let us hold to the law. If we want to be charitable, gratify ourselves out of our own pockets.'

Fortunately this hard view did not prevail.

6 The Workmen's Compensation Acts

The Employers' Liability Act proved to be inadequate, and in 1897 the first Workmen's Compensation Act was passed. This was based on an entirely new principle. Liability did not depend on the negligence of the employer or of any of his servants. Compensation became payable automatically whenever a workman met with an accident in the course of his employment and was incapacitated for work. The compensation took the form of a weekly payment during incapacity, roughly representing half the wages which the workman was earning. If he caused the accident by his own misconduct, he could not claim compensation for minor accidents: but if he was permanently disabled, he could claim compensation in spite of his own misconduct. If a workman was killed, his dependants could claim a small lump sum.

In this scheme, of course, common employment had no place: but the compensation was, in most cases, much smaller than damages would have been at common law. It was really a scheme of insurance under which the employer insured the workman against half the loss of his wages as a result of an accident: the workman had to bear the other half of the loss himself.

The Act of 1897 applied only to a limited group of industries. A new Act was passed in 1906 which extended to all wage earners within a certain financial limit. Finally, after a series of amendments, the law was consolidated in the Workmen's Compensation Act 1925. In its final form the scheme gave compensation for industrial diseases as well as for accidents.

The Workmen's Compensation Acts undoubtedly fulfilled a useful need. The procedure for enforcing claims was cheap, as there was a special arbitration procedure in the county court. Workmen were usually supported by their trade unions and employers by their insurance companies, so debatable points were often fought out, and an immense volume of case-law grew up.

However, the Workmen's Compensation Acts did not modify the rules of the common law, which continued to exist side by side with the new system. Where the workman was in a position to claim either at common law or under the Workmen's Compensation Acts, he had to elect between the two; he could not enforce both claims (Workmen's Compensation Act 1925, s. 29). This question of 'election' raised many difficulties, and the cases were not easy to reconcile. Eventually it was settled that if a workman knew of his right to elect, and yet accepted weekly payments, knowing that they were paid to him under the Workmen's Compensation Act, he was precluded from raising a claim at common law: *Young v Bristol Aeroplane Co Ltd* [1946] AC 163, [1946] 1 All ER 98.

Section 29 of the Workmen's Compensation Act 1925, which required the workman to elect between compensation and damages at common law, also stated that the employer was not to be liable at common law except for his own 'personal negligence or wilful act'. For a long period it was not clear whether this section cut down the common law rights of the workman where, for instance, some personal or statutory duty was imposed on the employer but its performance had been delegated to a subordinate[8].

8   For the ultimate decision on the point, see p. 21, *post*.

7 Breach of statutory duty

While these developments were taking place, a broad new stream of common law liability had arisen, and flowed around the obstacle of common employment. This was liability for breach of statutory duty.

The nineteenth century saw a great wave of legislation for the improvement of safety and health in factories and mines. The factory laws started with the Health and Morals of Apprentices Act 1802. They began to take a modern form in the Factories Act 1844, which contained, for example, the requirement that dangerous machinery must be fenced while in motion. This, with a number of amending Acts, was consolidated in the Factory and Workshop Act 1878, later replaced by the Factory and Workshop Act 1901. As regards coal mines, the first Act was passed in 1842, but this was mainly concerned with prohibiting the employment of women and children underground. An Act for the inspection of mines was passed in 1850. This was extended by the Coal Mines Act 1855, which laid down a number of general rules to be observed in all mines: in particular there had to be a proper system of underground ventilation to prevent the accumulation and explosion of firedamp gas. The Act of 1855, after various amendments, was followed by the Coal Mines Regulation Act 1872, a comprehensive Act imposing a series of detailed obligations to ensure the safety of the miners: this in its turn was superseded by the Coal Mines Regulation Act 1887[9]. Then, after further amendments, the law was consolidated in the Coal Mines Act 1911, which continued in force until 1957.

Now it was established law that if a statute conferred rights (or what comes in this case to the same thing, imposed duties), but gave no special remedy, a person injured by breach of the statute could bring an action for damages at common law. But the Acts for regulating factories and mines were enforced, primarily, by penalties in the criminal courts. At first sight, therefore, as there was this special remedy, it might appear that injured persons had no right of action.

In spite of this apparent difficulty, actions were brought under the Factories Act of 1844, which were based, in part at any rate, on the failure to fence machinery as required by statute. *Coe v Platt* (1851) 6 Exch 752 (later proceedings (1852) 7 Exch 460, 923) turned partly on the exact scope of the enactment, i.e. whether it was for the protection of

9   22 Halsbury's Statutes, 3rd Edn., 42.

workers generally, as Parke B thought, or only for the protection of young persons working near the machinery. The case failed in the end on the ground that the machinery was not alleged to have been in motion at the time of the accident, and the Act required machinery to be fenced only while in motion. In *Clarke v Holmes* (1862) 7 H & N 937, the fencing had broken, and the employer had promised to replace it. There was, accordingly, an element of personal negligence, and the case was decided on this ground. In these and other early cases, breach of statutory duty seems to have been relied on as evidence of negligence, rather than as an independent cause of action.

In *Wilson v Merry* (1868) LR 1 Sc & Div 326 the question was raised incidentally whether an action for damages lay for not providing proper ventilation in a mine in accordance with the Coal Mines Acts. The point was not decided, as it was not raised by the pleadings: but Lord Chelmsford expressed the opinion that no right of action was conferred by this statute, and that, even if it was, it would extend only to the personal acts of the employer.

Nevertheless, in *Baddeley v Earl of Granville* (1887) 19 QBD 423, it was taken for granted that an action lay for breach of the Coal Mines Regulation Act 1872. In that case a banksman was not in attendance at the pit shaft, as required by statutory regulations, to control the movements of the cage, and an accident happened because a signal to lower the cage was given prematurely by an unauthorised person. The deceased miner had known that no banksman was present, and the defendant set up *volenti non fit injuria* as a defence. The court held that *volenti non fit injuria* cannot be pleaded as a defence to breach of statutory duty; it would be against public policy for a workman to agree to waive the requirements of an Act of Parliament.

The validity of the cause of action for breach of statutory duty was finally fought out before the Court of Appeal in the case of *Groves v Wimborne (Lord)* [1898] 2 QB 402, where the plaintiff had been injured through the failure of the defendant to have dangerous machinery fenced, as required by the Factory and Workshop Act 1878. The court accepted that, where penalties or other special remedies are provided in a statute, this is a *prima facie* indication that the right of action for damages is excluded. However, this was not in itself conclusive: it was necessary to consider the whole purview of the statute. As the Factory and Workshop Act was passed for the benefit of the workmen, and penalties received by the Crown could not compensate them for their injuries, it must be accepted that a breach of the Act gave rise to an action for damages. The court declined to follow the dictum of Lord Chelmsford to the contrary effect in *Wilson v Merry*.

The court also held that common employment is not a defence in such an action. Rigby L J said at p. 413:

> 'There has been a failure in the performance of an absolute statutory duty, and there is no need for the plaintiff to allege or prove negligence on the part of anyone in order to make out his cause of action. That being so, the doctrine of common employment is out of the question.'

From 1898 onwards, therefore, it was firmly established that the workman had a remedy whenever his injuries resulted from a breach of the Factories Acts or similar legislation: and to such a claim neither common employment nor *volenti non fit injuria* afforded a defence.

In this way a new and extensive field of remedies was opened to the injured workman, and the field widened as special safety regulations were imposed in all the major industries. Moreover, the new remedies had the advantage of simplicity: it was not necessary to prove negligence, but simply a breach of the statute causing an accident.

8 The final development of common employment

At this stage it is convenient to explain the form finally taken by the doctrine of common employment before it was abolished by statute.

The defence was excluded in cases depending on breach of the employer's personal duties at common law, or his statutory duties. In other cases the following points had to be proved to establish the defence:

(i) that the injured man and the fellow-servant who injured him were employed by the same master;

(ii) that they were in 'common employment'.

As to point (i), it made no difference that the two men were working on a common task if they worked for different masters. Thus, in *Johnson v Lindsay & Co* [1891] AC 371, two contractors were engaged in building the same house, and a servant of one dropped a bucket on to a servant of the other. It was held that the injured man could recover damages from the master of the negligent man.

As to point (ii), it was not necessary that the two men should be engaged on the same task: thus the drivers of two separate railway trains on the same line were in common employment. But it was necessary to show that the two servants were so related that the negligence of one towards the other was an ordinary risk of the employment, as distinct from a risk of ordinary life. In *The Petrel* [1893] P 320, it was held that the crews of two ships owned by the same company were not in common employment, at any rate as regards collisions in a river like the Thames, or on the high seas: for, though they might collide with one another, they might equally collide with any other ship. Following this, the House of Lords held in *Radcliffe v Ribble Motor Services Ltd* [1939] AC 215, [1939] 1 All ER 637 that the drivers of motor coaches, though travelling in convoy, were not in common employment when out in the streets. Similarly, in *Glasgow Corpn v Bruce* (or *Neilson*) [1948] AC 79, [1947] 2 All ER 346, the drivers and conductors of different motor buses were not in common employment. On the other hand, the drivers and conductors of different tramcars were: *Graham* (or *Miller*) *v Glasgow Corpn* [1947] AC 368, [1947] 1 All ER 1; for tramcars, like trains, are confined to a single set of lines.

Common employment had its last fling in a case where these two series of decisions converged, with the result that the House of Lords was divided. This was *Lancaster v London Passenger Transport Board* [1948] 2 All ER 796, where a trolley-bus injured a man on a tower-wagon who was repairing the overhead wires. The majority decision was against common employment, on the ground that the plaintiff might equally well have been injured by any other tall vehicle[10].

9 Later trends in case-law and legislation: the abolition of common employment

Modern case-law, especially in the House of Lords, has been as much in favour of the workman as the case-law of the early nineteenth

---

10 Where, under the dock labour scheme, men were employed by a Labour Board and allocated to stevedores, they were employed by the stevedores and in common employment with other men allocated to the same firm: *Powell v Docks and Inland Waterways Executive* (1950) 83 L1 L Rep 107, CA: *Kelly v Spencer (James) & Co* 1949 SC 143.

century was against him[11]. It will be useful to mention a few landmarks.

In *Lochgelly Iron and Coal Co Ltd v M'Mullan* [1934] AC 1 the House of Lords gave the weight of their authority to the action for breach of statutory duty, and held that it was equivalent to 'personal negligence' in s. 29 of the Workmen's Compensation Act 1925[12], so that the workman's action was not barred by that section.

In *Caswell v Powell Duffryn Associated Collieries Ltd* [1940] AC 152, [1939] 3 All ER 722 it was finally held, after some doubts had been expressed, that contributory negligence is a defence to an action for breach of statutory duty. At the same time the House adopted the observation of Lawrence J in an earlier case:

> 'It is not for every risky thing which a workman in a factory may do in his familiarity with the machinery that a plaintiff ought to be held guilty of contributory negligence.'

Finally, in the most important case of all, *Wilsons and Clyde Coal Co v English* [1938] AC 57, [1937] 3 All ER 628 the House of Lords rescued from oblivion the old Scottish cases on the personal duty of the employer to take reasonable care for the safety of his workman. This duty, they decided, is threefold: it requires him to provide safe plant and machinery, a competent staff and a safe system of work—to which other authorities have added a safe place of work. The decision was followed by a vast number of cases in which an unsafe system was made the foundation of the claim.

The principle enunciated by the House of Lords in *English's* case was this: that within the wide area covered by the employer's duties, he could not relieve himself from liability by delegating performance of the duties to fellow-servants, and so the defence of common employment did not arise. This was not an innovation, since it merely re-instated the law declared in the oldest authorities, and restricted the defence of common employment to acts of personal carelessness by fellow-servants. However, the earlier law had been so completely forgotten, at any rate in England, that 'common employment' had come to be regarded as a

---

11 Lord Wright (67 L.Q.R. 534) refers to 'a long established tradition of the English common law for the protection of workers'. It might be added that this tradition has been particularly strong in the House of Lords, at any rate since *Smith v Baker & Sons* [1891] AC 325.

12 See p. 16, *ante.*

defence to every common law action against an employer. By restricting it to its proper place, as a defence only where the action was founded on true vicarious liability, the decision in *English's* case proved to be a more important turning point in the law than the final abolition of the defence by statute.

Many changes have been made by legislation: partly by steady extension of the safety codes, partly by Law Reform Acts which eliminated unsatisfactory rules of the common law.

The factories legislation was consolidated by the Factories Act 1961, and is in the main a clear and satisfactory code. In many cases it renders the employer absolutely liable for defects in machinery: see *Galashiels Gas Co Ltd v O'Donnell* (or *Millar*) [1949] AC 275, [1949] 1 All ER 319. Mining law was modified by the Mines and Quarries Act 1954. The Offices, Shops and Railway Premises Act 1963 was modelled on the simpler requirements of the Factories Act. The last part of the title is misleading, as it applies only to a limited class of railway premises.

There was also special legislation for safety in agriculture and forestry.

Finally, the Health and Safety at Work Act 1974 generalised the safety legislation and imposed safety obligations on all employers in every kind of work, not merely in factories, mines and other particular workplaces. As most employments were already covered, the practical effect of the extension was at first small: but the administration of the safety laws is centralised in a single authority and has been simplified. Gradually, new codes of regulations under the 1974 Act are replacing the various special Acts: in the meantime they remain in force within the framework of the Act.

One innovation of the 1974 Act is that it creates duties towards outsiders who are affected by industrial activities.

By the Law Reform (Contributory Negligence) Act 1945[13], contributory negligence lost most of its force as a defence. Previously a workman who was found guilty of contributory negligence could recover nothing. Now, under the 1945 Act, the effect of such a finding is to reduce the damages in proportion to the degree of fault. The tendency of judges to circumvent the Act in some cases by holding that the plaintiff was the 'sole cause' of his accident was checked by the House of Lords in *Stapley v Gypsum Mines Ltd* [1953] AC 663, [1953] 2 All ER 478 and *Boyle v Kodak Ltd* [1969] 2 All ER 439.

---

13 23 Halsbury's Statutes, 3rd Edn., 789.

The Law Reform (Personal Injuries) Act 1948 abolished the doctrine of common employment, and an employer is now liable for the negligence or other torts of his servants (in the course of their employment) to insiders and outsiders alike; the Employers' Liability Act 1880, and the Workmen's Compensation Act 1925, were repealed, and a workman is no longer under the disagreeable necessity of making his election between compensation and damages. The Workmen's Compensation Acts were replaced by a state insurance scheme, originally the National Insurance (Industrial Injuries) Act 1946, which gave benefits during incapacity, and to which employer and workman both contribute. In view of the fact that the employer is paying for part of the cost of this scheme, the Law Reform (Personal Injuries) Act 1948 directs that in certain cases damages at common law are to be reduced by half the estimated value of the insurance benefits to be received by the workman. Industrial injuries benefits have since been absorbed into the general social security scheme.

Some interesting facts have come to light since the final abolition of the doctrine of 'common employment'. If this reform had occurred at the end of the nineteenth century—when it was already overdue—it would have been a change of immense importance, for industrial operations were then of a simpler kind and safety depended in direct and obvious ways on the acts of fellow-servants. But the Act of 1948 had no great effect on litigation: it was little more than a ripple on the surface of the tide. After all, only a small proportion of persons run down by negligent drivers are likely to be fellow-servants. And on the railways (leaving aside accidents to whole trains due to negligent driving or signalling, where most of the injured are likely to be passengers) a man who performs such duties as shunting, or driving on a main line, is not generally able to look out for stray fellow-servants: the working rules still require railwaymen in positions of danger to look out for their own safety, and if this system is challenged it can only be on the ground of unsafe method of work. There have, on the other hand, been many successful claims against negligent crane-drivers; and numerous claims have been made for negligence in the manhandling of loads.

The striking fact, however, is that many accidents seem to be due to impersonal causes: this is true not only of the cases which are reported, but also of the much greater number encountered in everyday practice. Generally there is some undiscovered fault in plant or machinery, or a failure to set up proper safety measures. The forecast of Viscount Simon in *Bristol Aeroplane Co v Franklin* [1948] WN 341, that allegations of 'unsafe system' would lose much of their importance, has proved to be mistaken. Frequently fault cannot be attributed to any individual, but only to the organisation as a whole, that is to say to the employer who owns it.

During the same period the workings of the concept of 'negligence' have been brought into the open, because, with the disuse of juries in civil actions, the verdict is now given by a judge who has to disclose his reasons. 'Negligence' as the criterion of liability involves the further test of 'reasonable foreseeability', which has been shown up as vague, capricious and subjective when applied to anything much more complex than bows and arrows, or horses and carts. Some judges are able to foresee very little; others, by taking a complex succession of events step by step, are able to foresee almost anything. This difference of mental approach may be seen even when cases reach the House of Lords. Thus the common law is in the position which used to be a standing reproach to courts of equity, where justice varied 'according to the length of the Chancellor's foot'[14]. It may be doubted, indeed, whether the question of fault or blame has any legitimate place in the law of compensation for civil injuries: it is a concept which is properly associated with punishment for wrongdoing, and therefore belongs to the criminal law. The more natural approach, in accord with the English law up to the eighteenth century, is that *prima facie* a man is responsible for the consequences of his activities, but that a more lenient standard is admissible in activities—such as traffic on highways—where there has to be 'give-and-take' on all sides. Scots law has always favoured a 'fault' approach to liability, but it is a fallacy to regard this as meaning 'moral', or subjective, fault. 'Fault' in other systems of law, and for that matter in earlier English law, has overtones of 'responsibility' in the sense of being the cause of damage, rather than being blameworthy for not foreseeing it.

Hazards such as fast-moving machinery and electricity have greatly increased both in industry and in ordinary life in the last century. The natural direction of law reform at the present time would be to impose strict liability, without proof of negligence, for hazards like these created

14 I expressed these views to visiting American lawyers a few years ago; they were much amused, and said their own experience was similar. In fact, the use of the subjective test of foreseeability was due to American influence, largely through the mediation of the late Sir Arthur Goodhart who had a foot in both camps.

by an enterprise and involving danger to others. Such a reform is likely to be delayed, however, because lawyers have at present the same exaggerated respect for the law of negligence as their predecessors had for the doctrine of 'common employment'.

In any case, this is a matter which affects the law of tort generally and is not peculiar to employer's liability. In fact a workman who meets with an accident such as an electric shock, which cannot be traced to the fault of any individual, is often in a stronger position than a member of the public because he can rely upon the breach of an absolute statutory duty. Probably the inadequacy of the law of negligence would not have been tolerated so long if strict liability had not established itself in this indirect form, which, however, is highly capricious because statutory duties vary from one industry to another, and in many cases do not exist at all[15].

In New Zealand, following a Royal Commission under the chairmanship of Mr. Justice Woodhouse, DSC, the law of damages for liability in tort has been replaced by a state insurance scheme. In the United Kingdom, a Royal Commission on Civil Liability and Personal Injuries, under the chairmanship of Lord Pearson, recommended in 1978 that in the case of road accidents the law of tort should cease to apply and be replaced by a state insurance scheme. They did not recommend any immediate change for accidents at work, except that state insurance benefits should be deducted from damages in full, and not in part only as at present.

The Consumer Protection Act 1987 imposed strict liability on manufacturers for unsafe products; although this was due to pressure to make pharmaceutical firms liable for the side effects of drugs, it applies equally to materials and equipment for use at work.

The Employers' Liability (Compulsory Insurance) Act 1969 introduced compulsory insurance against an employer's liability to his own employees for damages.

---

15 See further an article in (1957) 107 Law Journal 659, on 'Strict Liability in the Law of Tort'. My view of strict liability differs from the fashionable one. I do not favour an insurance scheme but would prefer to see English law revert to the *Rylands v Fletcher* principle in the case of hazardous activities. I find it absurd that, because of unbalanced populist agitation—which started in the U.S.A. and was imitated here—the manufacturer, who is a long way off, is subjected to strict liability, whereas those who create risks close at hand are still liable only for negligence unless there is a statutory duty.

10 The present law

In this book, the law is explained in the following order:

In the first place there is an account of the liability at common law apart altogether from breach of the Factories Act or any other statute. This starts with an explanation of the general principles of negligence, and particularly of the standard of care required in industrial operations. Next there is an account of the employer's general duty to take care for the safety of his servants in the course of their employment, and of his liability for the acts of fellow-servants. Lastly, there is a chapter on the rights of the injured workman against third parties.

After this the major part of the book is taken up with liability for breach of statutory duty—first of all an examination of the general principles of this type of liability, then a detailed explanation of the particular statutes and regulations which contain the safety codes for various provinces of industry—factories, mines, docks, railways and so forth.

Thirdly, there is a group of chapters in which the possible defences are discussed at some length. The most important of these is contributory negligence[16]. Finally, there is a chapter on some questions of practice and procedure.

---

16 I have considered the point made by one reviewer that contributory negligence should be treated earlier. There are, of course, numerous ways in which a book of this kind could be planned, and some would prefer to see the details of the statutes put after everything else. I, however, regard the statutes as an integral part of the law on liability, and have decided not to alter the original order—liability first, defences afterwards.

Chapter 2

The general principles of negligence as applied to injuries at work

1 The tort of negligence

Before setting out in detail the duty of an employer towards his employees—and the duties of other persons who are brought into contact with them in the course of their work—it is necessary to explain the general principles of liability for negligence, of which these duties are particular examples.

In English law (and Scottish law) negligence or careless conduct which injures another does not automatically establish legal liability. It must first be shown that, in the circumstances of the case, there was a legal duty to take care to avoid injury to the other person. Lord Wright said in *Lochgelly Iron & Coal Co v M'Mullan* [1934] AC 1 at 25:

> '... negligence means more than heedless or careless conduct, whether in omission or commission: it properly connotes the complex concept of duty, breach of duty and damage thereby suffered by the person to whom the duty was owing.'

So the tort of negligence has three elements: a duty of care, a negligent breach of the duty and consequent damage.

The necessity for a positive duty of care is obvious enough where the negligence consists of an 'omission', a failure to do something, as is commonly the case with industrial accidents. It is not obvious in the case of a positive act which directly causes injury. In these cases the old action of 'Trespass to the Person' was available at common law, and under the old authorities a defendant was liable unless he was 'wholly without fault', which probably meant that the accident was beyond his control, as where an archer's arm was jogged as he was firing. But in modern times this has been re-interpreted to mean that there must be intention or negligence: moreover the onus of proof has been reversed so that the plaintiff has to prove this: *Fowler v Lanning* [1959] 1 QB 426, [1959] 1 All ER 290. So for practical purposes this old action has been absorbed into the tort of negligence.

2 The legal duty to take care

The existence of a duty of care is decided by the court as a question of law, but the court may inform its mind by evidence as to the relationship of the parties and the dangers likely to arise in given circumstances. In many of the everyday relationships of life the existence of a duty of care has been recognised by the law over a long period. Examples may be found in the duties of users of the highway and of navigators at sea to avoid collisions, of occupiers of buildings to prevent damage from dangers on the premises, and of employers for the general safety of their work-people. The extent of these and other duties—and in particular the kind of dangers against which they are intended to give protection—has been defined by the law, and those which affect an employee in the course of his employment are explained in detail in the next few chapters.

However, situations of a novel kind may arise, and it is then open to the court to hold that a duty to take care exists, although there is no exact precedent. A modern example is the duty of a manufacturer of equipment or articles which are to be used without independent examination, a duty which was considered by the House of Lords in *Donoghue v Stevenson* [1932] AC 562. In this case Lord Macmillan said (at p. 619) that 'The categories of negligence are never closed.' When problems of this sort arise, it is now usual for the courts to refer to a well-known passage in the speech of Lord Atkin, in the same leading case of *Donoghue v Stevenson*, where he said (at pp. 579–80):

> 'The duty which is common to all the cases where liability is established must logically be based upon some element common to the cases where it is found to exist. . . . There must be, and is, some general conception of relations giving rise to a duty of care, of which the particular cases found in the books are but instances. . . . You must

take reasonable care to avoid acts or omissions which you reasonably foresee would be likely to injure your neighbour. Who, then, in law is my neighbour? The answer seems to be—persons who are so closely and directly affected by my act that I ought reasonably to have them in contemplation as being so affected when I am directing my mind to the acts or omissions which are called in question.'

This passage does not lay down a fixed and universal rule of law: it is rather a matrix-principle or guide, which is followed in deciding whether a duty of care exists unless there is good reason to the contrary. But there is not one universal duty of care, there are different categories of duty whose nature and extent varies according to the type of situation[1]. Lord Wilberforce said in *Anns v Merton London Borough* [1977] 2 All ER 492 at 498:

'First one has to ask whether, as between the alleged wrongdoer and the person who has suffered damage, there is a sufficient relationship of proximity or neighbourhood such that, in the reasonable contemplation of the former, carelessness on his part may be likely to cause damage to the latter, in which case a *prima facie* duty of care arises. Secondly . . . it is necessary to consider whether there are any considerations which ought to negative, or to reduce or limit the scope of the duty or the class of person to whom it is owed or the damages to which a breach of it may give rise . . .'

Lord Keith of Kinkel said in *Peabody Donation Fund (Governors) v Sir Lindsay Parkinson & Co Ltd* [1984] 3 All ER 529 at 534, [1984] 3 WLR 953 at 960:

'A relationship of proximity in Lord Atkin's sense must exist before any duty of care can arise, but the scope of the duty must depend on all the circumstances of the case.'

In *Yuen Kun Yeu v AG of Hong Kong* [1987] 2 All ER 705 at 710, Lord Keith made these further comments, which have been accepted in a

---

1 See *Hedley Byrne & Co Ltd v Heller & Partners Ltd* [1964] AC 465 at 524, [1963] 2 All ER 575 at 607, per Lord Devlin (negligent statement causing financial loss); *Home Office v Dorset Yacht Co Ltd* [1970] 2 All ER 294 at 297, 304, 311, 321, 325–6 (allowing escape of Borstal trainees who damaged boat); also the Canadian case *The Ogopogo* [1970] 1 Lloyd's Rep 257 at 261 per Schroeder JA (rescue of passenger fallen from pleasure boat: the Supreme Court of Canada eventually held—[1971] 2 Lloyd's Rep 410—that the owner of a pleasure steamer owes a duty of reasonable care to his guests which extends to rescue if they fall overboard, but on the facts there was no negligence). See also Chapter 5 for the application of the principle to the duties of persons other than employers.

series of House of Lords decisions as a correct statement of the law (the italics have been added to emphasise the key passage):

> '... the two-stage test formulated by Lord Wilberforce for determining the existence of a duty of care has been elevated to a degree of importance greater than it merits, and greater perhaps than its author intended. Further, the expression of the first stage ... carries ... a risk of misinterpretation ... there are two possible views of what Lord Wilberforce meant. The first ... is that he meant to test the sufficiency of proximity simply by the reasonable contemplation of likely harm. The second ... is that Lord Wilberforce meant the expression "proximity or neighbourhood" to be a composite one, importing the whole concept of necessary relationship between plaintiff and defendant described by Lord Atkin ... In their Lordships' opinion the second view is the correct one ... *it is clear that foreseeability does not of itself, and automatically, lead to a duty of care* ... the ... cases referred to by Lord Wilberforce each demonstrate particular sets of circumstances ... adjudged to have the effect of bringing into existence a relationship apt to give rise to a duty of care. Foreseeability of harm is a necessary ingredient of such a relationship but it is not the only one. Otherwise there would be liability in negligence on the part of one who sees another about to walk over a cliff with his head in the air and forbears to shout a warning.'

Lord Keith went on to say that the second stage can rarely arise: it arises only when, though there is a relationship of proximity, public interest outweighs it and makes the imposition of legal liability unreasonable. An example is *Hill v Chief Constable for West Yorkshire* [1989] AC 53, [1988] 2 All ER 283 where it was held that though the police have a *public* duty to detect dangerous criminals, it is wholly unreasonable that they should have a *private* duty which would make them liable to any potential victim.

So the two factors which, *prima facie*, give rise to a legal duty of care (and determine its extent) are these:

(i) there must be a close and direct relationship between the defendant and the plaintiff—as, e.g. between employer and employee, or the occupier of premises and a visitor[2]; and

(ii) the defendant must 'contemplate', or visualise, that there is a real risk of injury to the plaintiff if he, the defendant, does not

---

2   To be more accurate, the close and direct relationship is not so much between the defendant and the plaintiff as between the defendant's operations, or property under his control, and the plaintiff. The point that a duty of care arises because the defendant is carrying out some *activity* is well brought out in South African case-law, e.g. *Joffe & Co Ltd v Hoskins* (1941) App D 431 at 451–2.

conduct his operations, or manage his property, with due care.

Injury need not be foreseen as certain to happen, while on the other hand a fanciful possibility may be ignored. The older authorities spoke of 'likelihood' of damage, but this does not mean 'more probable than not', it simply means that there is a real possibility that sooner or later injury or damage will occur. Lord Reid has said in several cases that a reasonable man should not disregard any risk unless it is extremely small: e.g. *The Wagon Mound (No. 2)* [1967] 1 AC 617, [1966] 2 All ER 709 (risk of heavy oil being set on fire was remote but spilling could easily be avoided). If the risk is slight, and the cost of eliminating it is out of all proportion, there will be no negligence in failing to take expensive measures, but this does not mean there is no duty of care. The degree of risk is therefore more relevant to the extent of the duty in various circumstances, i.e. to what (if anything) reasonable care requires. The cases are summarised in the next section[3].

What can be foreseen depends on knowledge: either what the defendant actually knows, or what a reasonable man in his position should know (e.g. what a chemical manufacturer should know about the

3 The necessity of determining, as a fact, whether an event was 'foreseeable' becomes less formidable when it is remembered that foresight must always depend on past experience: either normal human experience, of which the court may take judicial notice—such as the fact that knives cut, so that an exposed and fast-moving knife is liable sooner or later to cut off the fingers of an operator who works beside it—or special experience, which must be proved by evidence. Thus the common law claims failed in *Nicholls v Austin (Leyton) Ltd* [1946] AC 493, [1946] 2 All ER 92, where a piece of wood flew out of a machine, and in *Carroll v Barclay (Andrew) & Sons* 1947 SC 411 (approved in the House of Lords [1948] AC 477, [1948] 2 All ER 386), where a belt broke and struck someone outside its enclosure, because—per Lord Wright in the former case—such accidents were 'outside normal experience'. An illuminating example of how 'foreseeability' should be approached is to be found in the speech of Lord Reid in *Carmarthenshire County Council v Lewis* [1955] AC 549 at 564-5, [1955] 1 All ER 565 at 571-2, where each element in the situation is taken step by step and it is shown that the result could easily have been *foreseen by a man who took the trouble to think about it*. The fact remains that as a test of liability 'foreseeability' is uncertain. Because it is vague and subjective, its application varies from judge to judge, as can be seen even in the House of Lords. There seem to be two modes of thought: one is bluff and 'practical', and believes in getting on with the job without looking for imaginary snags; the other believes in pausing for a minute and deliberately considering the safety implications of the job (e.g. Lord Reid). Nor is this cleavage peculiar to judges. It also exists among foremen on the job. If Lord Reid's approach is generally adopted—and that seems to be the present tendency—there will be less variation between one case and another.

behaviour of chemicals). If with such knowledge no risk can be foreseen, there is no duty[4].

The extent of the duty

The extent of the duty is often enough more important than its existence, and, like the latter, it depends partly on the nature of the relationship giving rise to the duty and partly on the foreseeability of damage. The extent of a duty of care involves three questions:

(i) Against what dangers must care be exercised?
The answer to this question varies greatly with the relationship of the parties and the sort of danger likely to arise. The dangers for which a person is responsible are in general those which originate from his activities or are in some way under his control. An employer, for instance, must safeguard his workmen against defects in his own premises, but (with certain reservations) he is not responsible for the collapse of the building of a third party to which the employees are sent in the course of their employment: for the structure of such a building is not under the employer's control. While (as the authorities now stand) any real genuine risk of injury to others gives rise to a *duty* of care, the degree of risk is critical in deciding whether the defendant was negligent in failing to take measures against it.

An example of the 'fanciful' possibility which a reasonable man should ignore altogether is to be found in the Scots case where a cow entered an open door, walked upstairs, turned on the taps and flooded the floor below: *Cameron v Hamilton's Auction Marts* 1955 SLT (Sh Ct) 74[5].

4   And there will be no negligence in not taking measures against the unknown risk. The existence of a different risk from the same source, itself too slight to justify expensive measures, does not alter the position; e.g. *Tremain v Pike* [1969] 3 All ER 1303 (farm infested with rats, danger of catching Weil's disease unknown; even if known the cost of exterminating would be out of proportion, *a fortiori* out of proportion to risk of bites or scratches); *Doughty v Turner Manufacturing Co Ltd* [1964] 1 QB 518, [1964] 1 All ER 98 (negligible risk of splash from lid falling into molten metal; explosion occurred from unexpected chemical reaction between lid and metal).
5   Yet a German cow has since had a similar experience at an inn in Hanover: *Times*, 28 July 1970.
    Quaere whether (as Viscount Dunedin said) it is a 'fantastic' possibility that a big

The 'real' possibility of injury, which is nevertheless exceedingly unlikely, is well-illustrated by *Bolton v Stone* [1951] AC 850, [1951] 1 All ER 1078 where a batsman made a quite exceptional hit over the boundary of a cricket ground, clearing a 17 foot fence and going some way beyond, where the ball struck a lady in a quiet suburban road. Here there was a doubly remote contingency, not just the remarkable stroke but the coincidence of someone being in line with it. The House of Lords held that the cricket club were not negligent (as there was already a fence, in order to eliminate all risk they would have had to stop using the ground); some of the speeches suggest there is no *duty* to take care unless an accident is likely rather than a possibility. Lord Reid (himself a party to the decision) has explained that this is a misunderstanding; the decision was that because of the slightness of the risk, there was no negligence in failing to take measures which would involve great sacrifice or cost (Lord Radcliffe's speech is best on the point); but (said Lord Reid) it is negligent to allow even a small risk to arise if it can easily be avoided. In *The Wagon Mound (No 2.)* [1967] 1 AC 617, [1966] 2 All ER 709 (where this explanation was given) it was held negligent to spill fuel oil into the waters of a harbour, though the chance of such oil catching fire is exceedingly remote, and a conflagration occurred only through the coincidence of smouldering rags on the water which acted as a wick. The point is that avoidance was easy.

Similarly the fact that blind persons may walk along city streets near excavations is 'reasonably foreseeable', though they are so few in comparison with others, and account should be taken of them in protecting the excavation if undue expense is not involved: *Haley v London Electricity Board* [1965] AC 778, [1964] 3 All ER 185 (there was just a long hammer placed in a sloping position in front of the trench; a

---

dog locked in a car might break the window and injure a passer-by with a glass splinter: *Fardon v Harcourt-Rivington* (1932) 146 LT 391. The decision is best supported on the ground that the risk was so slight that it was not negligent to leave the dog in the car: a duty of care but no breach. A genuine case of a 'fantastic' possibility, at any rate to a person without great technical knowledge, was *Woods v Duncan* [1946] AC 401, [1946] 1 All ER 420 where the blocking with paint of a tiny hole in the mechanism of a submarine led to the sinking of the vessel. (The main cause of the catastrophe was the unexplained opening of the bow cap on a torpedo tube: but if the hole had not been blocked, water would have come through and given warning; an example, like *Bolton v Stone*, of two remote possibilities coinciding.)

blind man would have a better chance of feeling the usual barrier with his stick).

It is not necessary that the precise manner in which an accident happens should be foreseeable, so long as the general nature of the danger can be foreseen: see *Harvey v Singer Manufacturing Co Ltd* 1960 SLT 178 (where a demonstrator met with an unexplained accident from the very danger in a machine of which he was giving warning) and *Hughes v Lord Advocate* [1963] AC 837, [1963] 1 All ER 705.

Within the limits of what is foreseeable, human behaviour must be taken into account. This includes the possibility that danger may be brought on or magnified by the negligence of another person, 'when experience shows such negligence to be common': *London Passenger Transport Board v Upson* [1949] AC 155 at 176, [1949] 1 All ER 60 at 72; but (in contrast to such cases) it is legitimate to assume that the statutory codes of regulations for safety in industry will be observed, when in practice they are strictly enforced: *Grant v Sun Shipping Co Ltd* [1948] AC 549 at 567, [1948] 2 All ER 238 at 247, per Lord du Parcq.

A fortiori, an employer of labour ought to expect that, when a dangerous process or operation is continually repeated, there will be mistakes or accidental slips due to wavering attention or the urgency of completing the work, and 'have in mind not only the careful man but also the man who is inattentive to such a degree as can normally be expected': *Smith (or Westwood) v National Coal Board* [1967] 2 All ER 593, per Lord Reid. Lord Oaksey said in *General Cleaning Contractors Ltd v Christmas* [1953] AC 180 at 189–190, [1952] 2 All ER 1110 at 1114–1115:

> 'It is . . . well known to employers . . . that their work-people are very frequently, if not habitually, careless about the risks which their work may involve[6].'

An employer must also taken into account the possibility that a workman may have a sudden attack of illness, e.g. that a scaffolder may have a sudden attack of giddiness when working at a height: *Holtum v W J Cearns Ltd* (1953) Times, 23 July, CA.

(ii) Who are the persons to whom a duty is owed?

A duty may be owed to one person but not to another: here again the test

---

6   Cf. *Baynes v Union S.S. Co of New Zealand Ltd* [1953] NZLR 617 (tarpaulin spread on top of uneven cargo with gaps—foreseeability of workmen walking over carelessly).

is partly the relationship, partly the foreseeability of injury. In general a duty is owed only to those persons who are within the ambit of probable danger. On this ground a motorist involved in a collision owed no duty to a bystander who suffered nervous shock but was outside the range of likely danger: *Hay* (or *Bourhill*) *v Young* [1943] AC 92, [1942] 2 All ER 396. But the law develops, and the House of Lords subsequently held that a duty of care may be owed to a person who foreseeably suffers shock from being told of an accident or seeing its effects though not on the scene at the time: *McLoughlin v O'Brian* [1983] 1 AC 410, [1982] 2 All ER 298 (mother was told of disastrous accident to family and went to hospital). There are other cases where shock to the persons on the scene, though not otherwise injured, was foreseeable: *Dooley v Cammell Laird & Co Ltd* (1951) 1 Lloyd's Rep 271 (shock to crane driver when sling broke and load fell); *Chadwick v British Transport Commission* [1967] 2 All ER 945 (shock of rescuer at bad railway accident brought on neurosis). In Australia, shock and resulting neurosis from seeing an injured husband in hospital after an accident was held to be actionable: *Jaensch v Coffey* (1984) 54 ALR 417. Shock may be foreseeable from other things besides the sight of injuries, such as the destruction of the plaintiff's home by fire: *Attia v British Gas PLC* [1988] QB 304, [1987] 3 All ER 455. Injury from a startled reaction to a loud noise may also be foreseeable: *Slatter v British Rlys Board* (1967) 1 KIR 336 (examiner, known to be in vicinity, jumped at crash of shunting and right hand was cut off); *Colvilles Ltd v Devine* [1969] 2 All ER 53 (man scared by explosion jumped off platform: Lord Donovan said the likelihood was too obvious to require 'positive proof' of foreseeability). Liability was established in all these cases.

The duty of an employer to his workmen may include within its scope such a person as a doctor, who is called to a well where men have been overcome by dangerous fumes and endeavours to help them: *Baker v T. E. Hopkins & Son Ltd* [1958] 3 All ER 147. Hitherto, it has been the firm view of English law that there is no cause of action where, because of injury to one person or his property, damage is caused to a third person—indirect or consequential damage—and there is no good reason for departing from this rule[7]. The case of a rescuer does not

7 *Weller & Co v Foot and Mouth Disease Research Institute* [1966] 1 QB 569, [1965] 3 All ER 560 (cattle infected: no liability to auctioneer because markets not held); *Electrochrome Ltd v Welsh Plastics Ltd* [1968] 2 All ER 205 (water supply damaged, no liability to factory for supply cut off). The decision to the contrary in

contravene it because he is directly injured by the same hazard which threatened the workman[8].

When a duty is owed to a class of persons—as by an employer towards his employees—it is owed to each of those persons as an individual, and must take into account individual peculiarities which are known to the defendant, such as the fact that a man with one eye runs a greater risk of blindness than a normal person: *Paris v Stepney Borough Council* [1951] AC 367, [1951] 1 All ER 42[9].

In the same way more care is owed to a man who is less experienced: *Byers v Head Wrightson & Co Ltd* [1961] 2 All ER 538; and conversely, less to one who is fully experienced and conversant with the dangers: *Quintas v National Smelting Co Ltd* [1961] 1 All ER 630 at 639.

(iii) What is the degree or standard of care?
A fully concrete duty involves a certain degree or standard of care, that is to say, an obligation to take particular measures to avoid the anticipated danger. The standard of care is discussed in detail under the heading of 'Negligence' in the following section.

There is of course a strict correlation between the extent of the duty on the one hand, and negligence (the breach of duty) on the other. Both depend on the degree of risk foreseeable.

SCM (U.K.) Ltd v W.J. Whittal & Sons Ltd [1971] 1 QB 337 (claim of factory for interruption to electricity by damage to the electricity authority's cable) seems with respect to overstep this line and could lead to a grossly excessive enlargement of liability, e.g. if a whole town's electricity were cut off, or a firm in South America did not receive a cable, not to mention the familiar case of a partner who loses money through injury to his colleague. The Court of Appeal did, however, hold that there is no claim for purely financial loss where no physical damage occurs, and the same view has been taken in Scotland: *Dynamco Ltd v Holland and Hannen and Cubitts (Scotland) Ltd* 1972 SLT 38.

8   And where the defendant is not to blame for this hazard arising, he is not liable to the rescuer: *The Ogopogo* [1971] 2 Lloyd's Rep 410. A person who negligently puts himself in danger also owes a duty to a rescuer: *Harrison v British Rlys Board* [1981] 3 All ER 679 (guard pulled off train by man he was trying to help on); but this extends, as always, only to foreseeable risks: *Crossley v Rawlinson* [1981] 3 All ER 674 (no liability when A.A. patrolman tripped and fell when running to lorry on fire).

9   *Aliter*, in general at any rate, if the peculiarity is not known to the master: *Clayton v Caledonian Stevedoring Co Ltd* (1948) 81 Ll L Rep 332 (sensitive skin).

3 Negligence: the standard of care

To fall below the standard of care—in other words, to omit to exercise the degree of care necessary in the circumstances—is negligence: and the accepted definition of negligence is that set out in the judgment of Alderson B in *Blyth v Birmingham Waterworks Co* (1856) 11 Exch 781 at 784, where he says:

> 'Negligence is the omission to do something which a reasonable man, guided upon those considerations which ordinarily regulate the conduct of human affairs, would do, or doing something which a prudent and reasonable man would not do.'

Thus the conduct of a hypothetical 'reasonable man'—an imaginary being who is neither imprudent nor over-cautious—determines the standard of care. The outcome of this legal fiction is explained by Lord Macmillan in *Glasgow Corpn v Muir* [1943] AC 448 at 457, [1943] 2 All ER 44 at 48:

> 'The standard of foresight of the reasonable man is in one sense an impersonal test. It eliminates the personal equation and is independent of the idiosyncrasies of the particular person whose conduct is in question. Some persons are unduly timorous and imagine every path beset with lions; others, of more robust temperament, fail to foresee or nonchalantly disregard even the most obvious dangers. The reasonable man is presumed to be free both from over-apprehension and from over-confidence.'

To complete the background it must be added that where a man is in a position calling for special knowledge and skill, a failure to have or to exercise such knowledge or skill will amount to negligence. This rule has frequently been applied to doctors and other professional men. On principle it applies with equal force to those who control or manage a large industrial undertaking such as a foundry or a mine: such persons are expected to have skilled knowledge required by their position, including knowledge of safety methods. This is one reason why a higher standard of care may be expected from employers than is (in general) expected of their employees, whose duty it is to carry out their work according to the methods they are told to follow[10]. But an employee too is required to use the skill and knowledge which his work demands,

---

10 Cf. *General Cleaning Contractors Ltd v Christmas* [1953] AC 180 at 189–190, [1952] 2 All ER 1110 at 1114, 1115.

e.g. 'to use that degree of care which an ordinary, prudent crane-driver would have used': *Stavely Iron & Chemical Co Ltd v Jones* [1956] AC 627 at 638, [1956] 1 All ER 403 at 405.

Of course, even an expert may be entitled to rely on a specialist with greater knowledge: *Investors in Industry Commercial Properties Ltd v South Bedfordshire District Council* [1986] QB 1034, [1986] 1 All ER 787, CA.

In general, an employer is expected to keep reasonably abreast of current knowledge concerning dangers arising in trade processes, and should be acquainted with pamphlets issued by the Health and Safety Executive and other safety organisations drawing attention to risks which have come to light and means of avoiding them: *Wright v Dunlop Rubber Co Ltd and I.C.I. Ltd* (1972) 13 KIR 255 (substances added in processing rubber to prevent rotting caused bladder cancer after 20 years' exposure: full discussion in Court of Appeal on when this ought to have been known); *Cartwright v G. K. N. Sankey Ltd* (1973) 14 KIR 349 (arc welder's lung disease: special risk of fumes at close quarters even though general ventilation good). These cases show that a large organisation like I.C.I., with its own medical and scientific research sections, may be expected to know considerably more than a small employer, and must ensure that information affecting safety is brought to the notice of executive authorities with power to decide. An employer is not, of course, expected to know of scientific and medical matters known only in specialist circles[11]. Thus a building firm is not expected to have *medical* knowledge of the risks of dermatitis from cement and brick dust: *Riddick v Weir Housing Corpn* 1971 SLT 24. The court added that as knowledge diffused more widely, a point would come when they ought to know. This point, where knowledge has ceased to be specialist but may not be generally known, is a matter of fact, which must depend to some extent on the size and resources of a firm. In *Thompson v Smiths Shiprepairers (North Shields) Ltd* [1984] QB 405, [1984] 1 All ER 881, the shipbuilders were aware of the possible damage to hearing caused by excessive noise, but there was no easy or obvious remedy, and the question was at what stage they ought to have become aware that ear-muffs of a satisfactory design were available. It was said that in the flood of printed material employers cannot be expected to see every

---

11 See *Wallhead v Ruston and Hornsby Ltd* (1973) 14 KIR 285. The dictum that an employer need only 'acquire information commonly known in the trade' is, however, inconsistent with the later decisions above and sets too low a standard.

small item, but a stage was reached when references to protective devices were common and they should have known about them, and in any case there were organisations available to give advice. The question to be answered was this:

> 'From what date would a reasonable employer, with proper but not extraordinary solicitude for the welfare of his workers, have identified the problem of excessive noise in his yard, recognised that it was capable of solution, weighed up the potential advantages and disadvantages of that solution, decided to adopt it, acquired a supply of the protectors, set in train the programme of education necessary to persuade the men and their representatives that the system was useful and not potentially deleterious, experimented with the system, and finally put it into full effect?'

As Mustill J said, the choice of date does not admit of a precise answer. It is a matter of degree.

The issue of warning pamphlets by the Health and Safety Executive may be decisive: the *Cartwright* case shows that the courts expect these pamphlets to be read carefully by a person with authority, not skimmed over quickly.

If an employer who took reasonable care to keep in touch with current information would not have been aware of any danger, there is no liability: *Graham v C. W. S. Ltd* [1957] 1 All ER 654 (mahogany dust as cause of dermatitis); *Tremain v Pike* [1969] 3 All ER 1303 (farmer not expected to know of Weil's disease carried by rats, no warning having been issued by health authorities)[12]. The employer must act promptly when there is a real risk and not neglect reasonable precautions because of interference with production: *Stokes v Guest Keen and Nettlefold (Bolts and Nuts) Ltd* [1968] 1 WLR 1776 (scrotal cancer due to overalls being soaked in oil: factory doctor knew of risk but feared 'turmoil' if warnings and checks were made).

In general, since the standard of liability for negligence is an objective one, it is no defence to say that the defendant's failure was due to some personal incapacity or lack of knowledge and experience: *Roberts v Ramsbottom* [1980] 1 All ER 7, [1980] 1 WLR 823 (elderly motorist liable to sudden stroke); *Nettleship v Weston* [1971] 2 QB 691 at 699 F, G, [1971] 3 All ER 581 at 586 b to c (learner driver). This principle would apply equally to employers, or those acting on their behalf, if they

12 It is, however, more widely known today.

undertake responsibilities without the necessary knowledge and experience[13].

At one time the issue of negligence or no negligence was decided by a jury, and the decision of twelve average men reflected very adequately the standards of the reasonable man. Questions of negligence are now decided by a single judge, with the consequence that it is less easy to keep the standard objective. Fortunately, there are three useful factors which help to maintain objectivity, and stand out more and more solidly as the courts give reasons for their decisions: these are the magnitude of the risk, the practical possibilities, and the general practice of competent persons.

The magnitude of the risk

In the sort of situation which has to be visualised, the imaginary 'reasonable man' is conducting operations, or controlling property, which may endanger other persons: and it is his duty to take reasonable precautions to avert the danger. It is plain that the precautions to be taken are a question of fact and degree. The degree of care, the amount of effort taken and money expended, will depend chiefly on the magnitude of the risk. At one end of the scale, where there is only a 'fantastic possibility' of injury, no precautions at all need to be taken: though a risk ought not to be disregarded 'unless it is extremely small': see the cases at pp. 31–33, *ante*. At the other end of the scale, 'an exacting standard of care is incumbent on manufacturers of explosive shells' and other persons engaged in ultra-hazardous activities: per Lord Macmillan in *Read v Lyons (J) & Co Ltd* [1947] AC 156 at 171.

---

13 *'Error of judgment'*. Defendants have sometimes sought to exonerate themselves—especially where expert knowledge or skill is involved—by saying that there was an 'error of judgment' but not negligence. The distinction is a false one: *Whitehouse v Jordan* [1981] 1 All ER 267. It is true that there may be genuine and reasonable differences of expert opinion on the right course to take, in which case it is legitimate to take either course if it is supported by a reputable body of opinion: *Maynard v West Midlands Regional Health Authority* [1985] 1 All ER 635, [1984] 1 WLR 634; also there are matters of degree in which exact judgment is impossible and reasonable latitude has to be allowed, and all the circumstances have to be taken into account, such as the need to take a quick decision in an emergency or to concentrate on some more important factor. But a mistake which falls below the reasonable level of care and competence does not cease to be negligent by being described as an 'error of judgment'.

'The law in all cases exacts a degree of care commensurate with the risk created': ibid. at 173. Where there is a grave risk to life which cannot otherwise be avoided, reasonable care may involve great expense and trouble, e.g. the dismantling of a furnace in a dangerous condition: *Henderson v Carron Co* (1889) 16 R 633[14].

The magnitude of the risk depends partly on the probability of an accident occurring but partly also on the gravity of the results if it does occur. 'There are two factors in determining the magnitude of a risk— the seriousness of the injury risked, and the likelihood of the injury being in fact caused': *Salmond on Torts* (10th Edition), p. 438[15]. In *Paris v Stepney Borough Council* [1951] AC 367; [1951] 1 All ER 42, where this statement of the law was approved by the House of Lords, it was held that in the carrying out of a task where metal particles may strike the eye, goggles may have to be provided for a one-eyed workman, though for a normal workman the risk could be ignored: for total blindness is a much graver injury than the loss of one eye. Lord Morton sums up the matter as follows:

> 'There are occupations in which the possibility of an accident
> occurring to a workman is extremely remote, while there are other
> occupations in which there is constant risk of accident. Similarly, there
> are occupations in which, if an accident occurs, it is likely to be of a
> trivial nature, whilst there are other occupations in which . . . the result
> . . . may well be fatal . . . there is in each case a gradually ascending
> scale between the two extremes . . . the more serious the damage
> which will happen if an accident occurs, the more thorough are the
> precautions which an employer must take.'

Finally, the magnitude of the risk has to be weighed against other factors, and particularly against the expense and effort involved in safety measures, and the necessity of carrying out the work in hand[16]. Lord Reid said, for example, in *Morris v West Hartlepool Steam Navigation Co Ltd* [1956] AC 552, [1956] 1 All ER 385, that:

14 'As the danger increases, so must [the] precautions increase': *Lloyds Bank Ltd v Railway Executive* [1952] 1 All ER 1248 at 1253, per Denning LJ.
15 This has been accepted law in Scotland for many years: *Mackintosh v Mackintosh* (1864) 2 Macph (CT of Sess) 1357. In England it did not arise until the *Paris* case.
16 This factor has been recognised more explicitly in the U.S.A. According to the *American Re-statement of the Law of Tort: Negligence*, para. 291, the standard of care is determined by the magnitude of the risk and the social utility of the work being done.

'It is the duty of an employer, in considering whether some precaution should be taken against a foreseeable risk, to weigh, on the one hand, the magnitude of the risk, the likelihood of an accident happening and the possible seriousness of the consequences if an accident does happen, and, on the other hand, the difficulty and expense and any other disadvantage of taking the precaution.'

If, for instance, equipment is being used which (through no fault of the employer) is not entirely satisfactory, and involves some extra risk, a reasonable man, though taking such precautions as are possible, is not bound to bring his operations to a standstill because of the extra danger: see the comment of Asquith L J in *Daborn v Bath Tramways Motor Co Ltd* [1946] 2 All ER 333 at 336[17]. Again, an employer cannot in general be expected to close down a factory or department of a factory because, as an aftermath of a violent storm, oily cooling liquid has been washed out of ducts and has left the floor in an abnormally slippery and dangerous state: *Latimer v A. E. C. Ltd* [1953] AC 643, [1953] 2 All ER 449. And it is not necessary that the current should be cut off for every minor repair on electric railway lines, because this 'would immobilise the electric railways of this country': per Pilcher J in *Hawes v Railway Executive* (1952) 96 Sol Jo 852. However, while in general it is true that operations ought not to be stopped or slowed down to an unreasonable extent merely because there is some unavoidable risk, there may be occasions when the danger is so great that work ought to be suspended or stopped altogether: see *Latimer v A.E.C. Ltd, supra*, at 659 per Lord Tucker. Some of these cases have attracted the attention of Parliament: for example, the use of white phosphorus in making matches is prohibited; and coal mines in a gassy or fiery state may have to be closed down for a time. Other examples where the danger is of equal gravity occasionally come to the notice of the courts, e.g. the addition of certain chemicals to rubber was so liable to cause cancer that its continued use was negligent: *Wright v Dunlop Rubber Co Ltd and I.C.I. Ltd* (1972) 13 KIR 255. (The same substances are now prohibited by the Hazardous Substances Regulations—see Chapter 8.) On the other hand, risks may have to be accepted where an important object is in view such as the saving of life: *Watt v Hertfordshire County Council* [1954] 2 All ER 368 (fire brigade used unsafe vehicle in emergency).

17 This case involved the use in war-time of an American motor vehicle with left-hand drive and a notice on the back giving the warning 'No Signals'.

Practicability

The question of practicability has already been touched upon in the preceding paragraph, where it is pointed out that the due degree of care—which includes the expense and effort of safety measures—is in proportion to the magnitude of the risk, and that cases seldom arise where it is reasonable to stop an operation altogether or to retard it to such an extent that it becomes uneconomic.

Apart from these rare cases, a defendant cannot be held blameworthy for carrying on processes where it is impossible to institute any effective safety measures. The law does not compel a man to do the impossible.

It sometimes happens that a safety method carries with it both advantages and disadvantages. In such circumstances a reasonable man cannot normally be held negligent in deciding that the disadvantages outweigh the advantages where they are evenly balanced, but he must always apply his judgment; and the small risk, for instance, to seamen engaged in erecting a rope round an open hatchway at sea may be altogether outweighed by the risk to persons moving near the hatchway if it were left unguarded in poor light: *Morris v West Hartlepool Steam Navigation Co Ltd* [1956] AC 552, [1956] 1 All ER 385. This observation applies with particular force where a device or a method is new. While employers in technical trades may be expected to keep in touch with current improvements, they are not bound to adopt them until their advantages and practicability have been investigated. Where the new method appears to be practicable, however, and meets an obvious and substantial danger, it would *prima facie* be negligent to delay in adopting it. A good illustration is the miner's safety lamp; when this was first introduced it furnished such an evident answer to the perils of inflammable gas that delay in ordering the lamps and putting them into service would clearly have been blameworthy[18]. Conversely, an illustration of legitimate failure to adopt a new method is to be found in *Whiteford v Hunter* [1950] WN 553, where a surgeon was charged with negligent diagnosis in failing to use a new instrument; it was proved that this instrument, although used in the United States, was very difficult to obtain in England, and that skilled surgeons in this country did not

18 This may be an over-confident assertion! New inventions do not always work well at first, and old-timers may have preferred to keep the time-honoured device of canaries in cages.

generally use it. The House of Lords held that the surgeon was not negligent.

Safety measures are obviously of less value if they will give only a limited and partial protection. In gypsum mines a rare geological phenomenon known as 'slickenside' gives rise to dangerous falls of rock: but systematic propping of the roof will not stop the falls, as the rock will still fall, in smaller pieces, around the props. It has been held that systematic propping in every part of such a mine is not 'reasonably practicable': *Marshall v Gotham Co Ltd* [1954] AC 360, [1954] 1 All ER 937. *A fortiori*, failure to prop would not be negligent. Similarly it is not negligent to fail to provide barrier cream as protection against dermatitis, where the evidence shows that there are doubts as to the value of such protection: *Brown v Rolls-Royce Ltd* [1960] 1 All ER 577.

Where an employer is aware of a risk and has after careful investigation fixed a reasonable standard for exposure to it, it is not in general negligent to fail to give warning or arrange medical examinations or other special precautions for employees who may be unusually sensitive to the risk even within the approved standard; at any rate where injury to them is unlikely to occur: *Sloan v British Rlys Board* 1981 SLT 239 (hearing of diesel train driver affected by noise); *Murphy v Lord Advocate* 1981 SLT 213; *Joseph v Ministry of Defence* (1980) Times, 4 March (numbness of fingers—a progressive disease known as 'whitefinger'—caused by the vibration in one case of a chain saw and in the other of a pneumatic drill). In *Joseph's* case it was said that a warning could cause unnecessary alarm to all the employees for the sake of the exceptional vulnerable one who could avoid the risk only by giving up the job.

To summarise the whole matter, therefore, it is first necessary to decide what safety measures are feasible in the light of current knowledge. Then, to determine what is reasonable, it is necessary to balance the disadvantages of safety measures on the one hand—the effort and expense, the possible frustration of important activities, and the possibility that the precautions will be futile—against the magnitude of the risk on the other hand. If the disadvantages of safety measures altogether outweigh the risk involved, those measures need not be taken.

The question what precautions (if any) ought to be taken in a given case is always a question of *fact*, to be answered by a jury or by a judge acting as a jury: it is not a matter of law to be governed by decisions in other cases where the evidence may have been different: *Qualcast (Wolverhampton) Ltd v Haynes* [1959] AC 743, [1959] 2 All ER 38 (employers not bound as a matter of law to urge or require employees to wear safety spats against splashes of molten metal). Such cases, including those cited above, should be regarded as illustrations only.

'General and approved practice' as a criterion

General practice has always been taken into account in determining the standard of care, but it is not conclusive, because 'no one can claim to be excused for want of care because others are as careless as himself': per Cockburn C J in *Blenkiron v Great Central Gas Consumers' Co* (1860) 2 F & F 437. It is easily seen that general practice may go wrong: motorists quite often go round blind corners on the wrong side of the road, or take risks in overtaking, and yet such acts are negligent. Indeed, it is not so much the uniform *behaviour* of mankind in a particular field to which the law gives weight, as the *standard of conduct*, whether uniformly followed or not, which is generally accepted as correct: such a recognised standard of conduct, for example, is contained in the Highway Code, or in the Regulations for Preventing Collisions at Sea[19]. The Health and Safety at Work Act 1974, s. 16, authorises the issue of 'codes of practice' for any matter affecting health and safety at work and these will have a similar value.

Recognised practice has greater force in specialised departments of life, such as medical practice, or the management of an engineering works or a coal mine. The reason is that expert knowledge and judgment are required to assess (i) the magnitude of the risks involved, and (ii) what safety measures are practicable—i.e. what measures are physically possible, how effective they are likely to be, and how much expense, trouble and restraint upon useful activity they will involve. If informed opinion is in agreement, it is almost conclusive, and yet not quite, for the court, after inquiring into the grounds of informed opinion, may find that too little emphasis has been put on safety, and too much on the expense of ensuring it. In particular it has been said that evidence of

---

19 Cf. *Thomas Stone Shipping Ltd v Admiralty (The Albion)* [1953] P. 117, [1953] 1 All ER 978 (collisions at sea rules represent proper standard of care for naval vessels, which are not technically bound by them).

general practice is of little value unless it is shown to have been followed *without mishap* for a sufficiently long period and in similar circumstances: per Lord Reid in *Morris v West Hartlepool Steam Navigation Co Ltd* [1956] AC 552, [1956] 1 All ER 385.

These principles are concisely expressed in the dictum of Lord Alness in *Vancouver General Hospital v McDaniel* (1934) 152 LT 56 (which related to the methods of preventing infection in a hospital):

> 'A defendant . . . can clear [himself] if he shows that he acted in accordance with general and approved practice.'

This dictum has been followed in other medical cases[20]. It will be noticed that according to this statement of the law the practice relied on must not only be general, but also be 'approved', which means primarily approved by those qualified to judge, but also approved, in the last resort, by the court itself. The courts have not hesitated to turn a searchlight on an established system and to judge for themselves, with the aid of expert evidence, whether it is reasonably safe; and sometimes they have held an established system to be insufficient. In *Lloyds Bank Ltd v Savory (E. B.) & Co* [1933] AC 201 a bank was charged with negligence in accepting cheques which a clerk had stolen from his employers. There was an established system under which the bank inquired into the circumstances of each person opening an account, and made inquiries when he paid in cheques drawn by his employers; but this system broke down when cheques were paid in at one branch for credit at another branch. Thus there was an evident loophole in the system itself, and the bank was held negligent. Lord Wright said at p. 232:

> 'It is argued . . . that a bank is not negligent if it takes all precautions usually taken by bankers. I do not accept that . . . when the ordinary practice of bankers fails in making due provision for a risk fully known to those experienced in the business of banking.'

In *Markland v Manchester Corpn* [1934] 1 KB 566 a burst pipe had flooded a road, and the flood water had remained undetected for three days when it froze over and caused an accident. The water authority had carried out checks every seven days (in accordance with general

20 *Marshall v Lindsey County Council* [1935] 1 KB 516 at 540; *Mahon v Osborne* [1939] 2 KB 14 at 43, [1939] 1 All ER 535 at 556; *Whiteford v Hunter* [1950] WN 553.

practice) but there was evidence that on the average fifty bursts a week occurred in the area. The authority were held liable because they 'failed to take reasonable precautions against an obvious and known danger': per Slesser L J at p. 582. It was further held by the Court of Appeal in this case that it was not necessary for the plaintiff to show what exact precautions ought to have been taken, and this was expressly approved when the case went to the House of Lords: [1936] AC 360 at 364. In *General Cleaning Contractors Ltd v Christmas* [1953] AC 180, [1952] 2 All ER 1110, the general practice in the window-cleaning trade was held to be negligent in that no precautions were taken to protect the men against loose window-sashes, and it was again held that the plaintiff is not required to show exactly what the correct practice should be. Perhaps the strongest decision of all is *Barkway v South Wales Transport Co Ltd* [1950] AC 185, [1950] 1 All ER 392, where an omnibus had crashed owing to a burst tyre, and though the omnibus company had followed the established practice in all respects, they were yet held negligent by the House of Lords because they had not instructed their drivers to report incidents which might cause an unusual type of tyre fracture.

These decisions show that an established practice is not sacrosanct where there is a danger—not always an obvious one—for which it does not provide adequately[1].

The Dunedin test—'folly' to omit precautions: its doubtful value

Negligence may consist either of acts or of omissions. It is usually easy to see whether an *act* is negligent: in practice, it is the question whether the *failure* to do something is negligent which gives rise to difficulty. A test to be applied in such cases was formulated by Lord Dunedin in *Morton v Dixon (William) Ltd* 1909 SC 807. This test was adopted in many cases

---

1   Cases where the established practice has (after examination) been approved by the court are *Wright v Cheshire County Council* [1952] 2 All ER 789 (gymnastics in school); *Sexton v Scaffolding (Great Britain) Ltd* [1953] 1 QB 153, [1952] 2 All ER 1085 (dismantling of scaffold); *Hawes v Railway Executive* (1952) 96 Sol Jo 852 (electricity not switched off for minor repairs to rails). The general practice in shipbuilding of painting from the steep altar courses of a dry dock without some such precaution as a safety belt was found to be negligent in *Hurley v J. Sanders & Co Ltd* [1955] 1 All ER 833.

in Scotland, and subsequently quoted in the House of Lords, where, however, it was much qualified. It has now become clear that it does not lay down any proposition of law (see *Brown v Rolls-Royce Ltd* [1960] 1 All ER 577) and contains some rhetorical overstatement. What Lord Dunedin said was this:

> 'Where the negligence of the employer consists of what I may call a fault of omission, I think it absolutely necessary that the proof of that fault of omission should be one of two kinds—either to show that the thing which he did not do was a thing which was commonly done by other persons in like circumstances, or to show that it was a thing which was so obviously wanted that it would be folly in anyone to neglect to provide it.'

In *Bristol Aeroplane Co Ltd v Franklin* [1948] WN 341, *Barkway v South Wales Transport Co Ltd* [1950] AC 185, [1950] 1 All ER 392 and *Paris v Stepney Borough Council* [1951] AC 367, [1951] 1 All ER 42, Lord Normand referred to this passage with approval, while pointing out that there was some rhetorical exaggeration, and in the last mentioned case he added:

> 'It contains an emphatic warning against a facile finding that a precaution is necessary when there is no proof that it is one taken by other persons in like circumstances, but it does not detract from the test of the conduct and judgment of the reasonable and prudent man.'

There was a sharp reaction to these comments in *Gallagher v Balfour Beatty & Co Ltd* 1951 SC 712—where the court overruled the finding of a jury that a tunnel in the course of excavation should be systematically supported by means of props and re-affirmed the strict rule as stated by Lord Dunedin. Lord President Cooper said, at p. 718:

> 'We are still entitled and bound to direct juries in every suitable case that the usual and ordinary practice is the primary guide and the normal test of liability, that it is only in the extreme case where it is obvious that some precaution is needed and inexcusable or folly to omit it that they are entitled to apply their own judgment unguided by practice, and that it is not for juries, any more than it is for the House of Lords, to lay down safety codes for the conduct of technical industrial processes.'

Lord Cooper expressly disagreed with the words of Lord Normand in the *Franklin* case, *supra*, that the respondent must prove that the need for a precaution 'was so obvious that no employer of ordinary prudence, if it is not presumptuous to substitute a milder phrase for [Lord Dunedin's] forcible language, would have rejected it.'

English law has approached the problem from the rather different angle of 'general and *approved* practice', always reserving the right to say, with the aid of expert evidence, whether general practice is sound or not[2]. The House of Lords has now made it clear in a series of cases that the strict view taken by Lord Cooper is wrong. For example, Lord Tucker said in *General Cleaning Contractors Ltd v Christmas* [1953] AC 180 at 195, [1952] 2 All ER 1110 at 1117, 1118 that the correct principle is simply this:

'long-established practice in the trade, although not necessarily conclusive, is generally regarded as strong evidence in support of reasonableness.'

The matter was finally settled by the majority decision of the House of Lords in *Morris v West Hartlepool Steam Navigation Co Ltd* [1956] AC 552, [1956] 1 All ER 385 where it was held to be negligent to fail to fence hatchways left open between decks in a grain ship at sea, notwithstanding evidence of a general custom that hatches are never fenced at sea[3]. Lord Morton (dissenting) was in complete agreement with the language of Lord Cooper, but Lord Reid said:

'Lord Dunedin's statement of the law must now be read with Lord Normand's gloss, and it is important to see what it was that the House of Lords held to be "folly" in *Paris's* case.'

And in *Cavanagh v Ulster Weaving Co Ltd* [1960] AC 145, [1959] 2 All ER 745 the House of Lords held that a jury was entitled to find negligence in the method of carrying cement on a roof although this method was in accordance with normal building practice. Lord Keith (who sat in the Court of Session when the *Gallagher* case was decided)

2   The phrase 'general and approved practice' was, it is believed, first used by another Scottish judge, Lord Alness, in a medical case in the Privy Council, p. 46, *ante*.
3   For a full analysis of this case, see an article in (1956) 106 L Jo 198. The decisive factor with the majority was that grain ships differ from other ships in that the holds are opened and got ready at sea, and men may have to go near the openings. A recent example of a long-standing practice held to be insufficient is *Ross v Tennant Caledonian Breweries* 1983 SLT 676n (system of lowering kegs of beer loosely roped though followed for 17 years without accident failed to allow for keg slipping out and striking someone).

said that there is 'no magic' in the word 'folly', which is simply used with rhetorical forcefulness to underline the danger of saying too readily that common practice is wrong.

> 'The ruling principle is that an employer is bound to take reasonable care for the safety of his workmen, and all other rules or formulas must be taken subject to this principle.'

Lord Tucker said that 'folly' means no more than 'unreasonable or imprudent'. 'Folly' has obviously acquired a strained meaning in this context: it includes failure to provide goggles for a one-eyed man working under a motor vehicle: *Paris v Stepney Borough Council* [1951] AC 367, [1951] 1 All ER 42; failure to provide wedges for window-cleaners to keep sashes from closing: *General Cleaning Contractors Ltd v Christmas* [1953] AC 180, [1952] 2 All ER 1110; failure to instruct coach-drivers to report incidents which might damage a tyre: *Barkway v South Wales Transport Co Ltd* [1950] AC 185, [1950] 1 All ER 392; failure to rig up a guard rail where a seaman who asked for it 'would probably be laughed at': *Morris v West Hartlepool Steam Navigation Co Ltd* [1956] AC 552, [1956] 1 All ER 385; and allowing the use of wet rubber boots on a crawling ladder: *Cavanagh v Ulster Weaving Co Ltd* [1960] AC 145, [1959] 2 All ER 745. 'Folly' was not established in *Quinn v Cameron and Roberton Ltd* [1958] AC 9, [1957] 1 All ER 760 (precautions against dust) but since the danger of silicosis from invisible dust was not recognised at the time, there was no negligence by any standards. In *Potec v Edinburgh Corpn* 1964 SC (HL) 1 the pursuer stood on a platform at a refuse depot over a deep trench in which he had to keep the refuse moving with a long pole. He fell into the trench, and contended that there should have been a guard rail; but such rails were not provided at other depots and the overwhelming evidence was that they would impede the use of the pole. Lord Guest said 'the non-existence of a practice does not by itself in law absolve employers. But . . . it places a very heavy onus . . . to show that a practice not adopted by other employers in like circumstances is one which a reasonable employer would regard as obviously necessary.' A jury could not apply their own standard without support from technical evidence. A verdict for the pursuer was set aside as contrary to the evidence under the Jury Trials Amendment (Scotland) Act 1910. In *Martin v Greater Glasgow Health Board* 1977 SLT (Notes) 66 there was no negligence where a nurse at a nurses' home fell over banisters which (at 34½ inches high) were no lower than at similar institutions.

Conversely, the fact that an employer does *not* follow general practice in some matter (e.g. in providing cream as a protection against dermatitis) does not show conclusively that he is negligent: *Brown v Rolls-Royce Ltd* [1960] 1 All ER 577. But—as was said in that case—it may well be *sufficient* evidence of negligence unless there is evidence which throws in doubt the value of the protection.

The effect of the actual decisions can be summed up as follows: *General and approved practice in an industry is the primary guide in determining the standard of care; but it is not inflexible and may be departed from when there is a failure to take account of some proved danger.* This way of stating the law was approved by Edmund Davies L J in *Brown v John Mills & Co. (Llanidloes) Ltd* (1970) 8 KIR 702 (unsafe practice to polish, with emery paper held in hand, brass components revolving in lathe: no excuse that it was common practice condoned by most employers). In Scotland, too, it is now accepted that where a precaution is shown to be reasonably practicable, it is not necessary to prove a practice elsewhere: *Macdonald v Scottish Stamping and Engineering Co* 1972 SLT (Notes) 73.

The way in which this principle is phrased is of some importance: in all industrial enterprises, economical working is a paramount objective, and there may be a tendency at times to lean more towards economy than towards safety. Therefore, it would be quite wrong if recognised practice were accepted as conclusive[4].

Again, there are many occasions when the appeal to general practice cannot be made. On the one hand there may be diversity of methods within the industry, even in matters which arise every day: on the other hand, the circumstances may be such as do not often occur, as in the *Paris* case, where the House of Lords had to consider whether goggles

4   Lord Dunedin's test is criticised by Fair ACJ in a forceful dissenting judgment in *Donohue v Union S.S. Co of New Zealand Ltd* [1951] NZLR 862 at 879, where he says:

'An ordinarily prudent employer does not provide only against obvious dangers. If he is an employer, particularly if he is the employer of a large business with intricate technical processes, or extensive and varied operations, it is his duty to take thought for the safety of his workmen, and take such precautions as reasonable consideration of the probable dangers would suggest. It is not only the obvious he has to guard against, nor has it been generally stated that he is to be judged by the standard of what it would be foolish not to do. In my view, the word "foolish" understates his duty.'

In the U.S.A., as in England, 'the fact that the master uses customary methods does not prove conclusively that he has not been negligent': *Restatement, Agency,* § 493 *(c).*

should be provided for a one-eyed man in a process where metal splinters might be thrown out. On these occasions the court must use its own judgment, having regard to the magnitude of the risk and to the question of what is practicable.

It will be clear that nothing in Lord Dunedin's dictum or the various cases which have commented on it can now be regarded as establishing a strict rule of law: what they establish is rather a guide in the evaluation of evidence of negligence.

Statutory codes and official leaflets as a guide

A statutory code of regulations may be referred to as showing the proper precautions to be taken, although it does not apply of its own force to the circumstances in which a workman was injured, but only to a similar process carried on in similar circumstances: *Franklin v Gramophone Co Ltd* [1948] 1 KB 542, [1948] 1 All ER 353 (dry grinding of metal). Similarly, the Health and Safety Executive leaflets may be used as a guide to the standard of care and the nature and extent of a danger, although they have no statutory force: *Clifford v Charles H Challen & Son Ltd* [1951] 1 KB 495, [1951] 1 All ER 72 (dermatitis from handling synthetic glue), *Dickson v Flack* [1953] 2 QB 464, [1953] 2 All ER 840 (woodworking machinery). It is wrong, however, to spell out common law duties on the analogy of a code of regulations which imposes arbitrary requirements, e.g. that a plank at a certain height above the ground must be of a certain width, and to argue that a plank which is nearly at that height must be of a similar width: *Chipchase v British Titan Products Co Ltd* [1956] 1 QB 545, [1956] 1 All ER 613. The use of regulations appears to be admissible as a guide to the existence of known dangers and of practicable safety measures, but not as a guide to what is reasonable protection against an ordinary and known risk. Generally, information which is widely circulated, whether by the Health and Safety Executive or others, must be relevant evidence of what an employer 'ought' to know.

Conversely, a statutory duty may be so detailed and exhaustive that where it does apply and has been performed, the common law duty of care does not require any further precaution: *Franklin v Gramophone Co Ltd, supra.* But a statutory code does not supersede the common law duty; and even an exhaustive code, like that which regulates shot-firing in a coal mine, may still leave room for a residual duty of care: *Nicol v National Coal Board* (1952) 102 L Jo 357; *Matuszczyk v National Coal Board* 1953 SC 8. While compliance with a statutory code has 'evidential value' there is no presumption that it is sufficient, and the court must form an independent judgment of what is required for a safe method of work: *Bux v Slough Metals Ltd* [1974] 1 All ER 262 ('provision' of goggles satisfied regulations: but employers should have taken measures to encourage wearing).

The Health and Safety at Work Act 1974, s. 16, authorises the issue of 'codes of practice' on health and safety matters. Under s. 17 failure to comply with such a code is *prima facie* evidence in *criminal* proceedings against an employer or other person for failure to carry out safety obligations to which the code is relevant. Although the Act does not say so, such a code must also be admissible in an action for negligence on the principles explained above, just as official leaflets on such matters as dust suppression and handling of loads are admissible.

Three useful questions on the issue of negligence

In the New Zealand courts three questions have been formulated which give a convenient and simple approach to the issue of negligence. They are set out in the judgment of Callan J in *Fletcher Construction Co Ltd v Webster* [1948] NZLR 514 at 518:

'(a) What dangers should the [defendant], exercising reasonable foresight, have foreseen?
(b) Of what remedies, applying reasonable care and ordinary knowledge, should [he] have known?
(c) Was the remedy, of which [he] should have known, for the danger [he] should have foreseen, one [he] was entitled to reject as unreasonably expensive or troublesome?'

While, however, these questions certainly resolve the issue into its simplest terms, they cannot be answered correctly without an appreciation of the factors explained in the foregoing paragraphs.

4 Negligence as the cause of damage

In English law, unlike some systems such as the Roman-Dutch law, damage is a necessary part of the right of action for negligence. The question arises how closely the damage must be connected with the negligence, particularly when the results are unexpected, and a discussion of this topic revolves round two controversial leading cases in which different views have been taken. It seems best to set out these cases first, and then assess their results.

In *Re Polemis and Furness Withy & Co Ltd* [1921] 3 KB 560 a plank was negligently allowed to fall in a ship, struck a spark, ignited petrol vapour and set the ship on fire. The defendants were held liable for the whole loss. The Court of Appeal said that damage is recoverable if it is the 'direct' consequence of the negligent act although 'not the exact kind of damage one would expect' (per Scrutton L J). More generally, following Lord Sumner's remarks in an earlier case, they said that foreseeability is the test for liability, but once liability is decided it is not the text for determining what damage is recoverable.

In an Australian appeal to the Privy Council, *Overseas Tankship (U.K.) Ltd v Morts Dock and Engineering Co Ltd, The Wagon Mound* [1961] AC 388, [1961] 1 All ER 404, conveniently referred to as *The Wagon Mound (No.* 1), a ship which was taking on fuel oil in Sydney harbour negligently spilt some of it into the water. The evidence was that there is no risk that fuel oil spread on water will ignite. In fact molten metal fell near it and lit a rag, with the unforeseen result that there was a serious conflagration which damaged a wharf. The Judicial Committee disagreed with *Re Polemis*, and decided that foreseeability is the test for the range and type of damage recoverable as well as for liability. Therefore, although trivial damage to the jetty by fouling with oil was foreseeable, so that some liability in negligence was established, the damage by fire, a different risk, which on the findings of fact was not foreseeable, could not be recovered. It was not questioned that where damage of a certain kind is foreseeable, there is liability for 'more extensive damage of the same kind'. The opinion of the Judicial Committee was in somewhat sweeping terms, which suggested that all former law on causation had been superseded, and that foreseeability was the only criterion for all purposes: it seemed that this might produce startling results, for example striking a person with an abnormally thin skull would establish liability for no more than bruising, although the injured man died. Controversy followed throughout the English legal world, reaching indeed to Pretoria and Dublin[5].

5   The subject was controversial before *The Wagon Mound*. Dr. A. L. Goodhart always criticised *Polemis*, and *The Wagon Mound* is perhaps the result of his sustained advocacy. Another Oxford scholar, A. M. Honoré, summarises the

Decisions in the English courts, while accepting and following *The Wagon Mound*, have now qualified it considerably. In *Hughes v Lord Advocate* [1963] AC 837, [1963] 1 All ER 705 injury by burns from a lamp left at a street excavation was foreseeable, damages were recoverable though the accident was due to an unforeseeable explosion when the lamp was knocked over. Lord Reid said 'a defender is liable although the damage may be a good deal greater in extent than was foreseeable. He can only escape liability if the damage can be regarded as differing in kind from what was foreseeable', and again 'This accident was caused by a known source of danger, but caused in a way which could not have been foreseen, and in my judgment that affords no defence.' In *Smith v Leech Brain & Co Ltd* [1962] 2 QB 405, [1961] 3 All ER 1159 it was said that *The Wagon Mound* does not alter the rule that a defendant takes a plaintiff as he finds him (e.g. with a thin skull or an abnormal tendency to bleed) and in any event is liable where damage of a foreseeable kind is more extensive than expected or spreads in an unexpected way (burn on lip turned to cancer).

Finally, *The Wagon Mound (No. 2)* [1967] 1 AC 617, [1966] 2 All ER 709 came up for decision, a claim for damage to a ship in the same fire as *Wagon Mound (No. 1)*. In this second case the evidence of fact was

---

decision as a licence to be negligent at other people's expense: *Canadian Bar Review*, May 1961, p. 267. Very great names in English law have supported *Polemis*—e.g. Lords Wright, Porter and Sumner and Scrutton LJ, the first two having been counsel for the unsuccessful party. There is also much Scottish support for *Polemis*, contrary to what is sometimes said: see D. M. Walker, *Law of Damages in Scotland* (1955), pp. 536–8; T. B. Smith, *Short Commentary on the Law of Scotland*, pp. 713–16, both of whom substantially agree with it and quote authorities. For a South African dissent from *The Wagon Mound*, in a learned judgment quoting continental and American law, see *Alston v Marine and Trade Insurace Co* [1964] 4 SA 112. Both Hiemstra J in this case, and the American law, are in line with *Polemis* in so far as they treat the consequences as recoverable unless there is a 'superseding cause' (*nova causa interveniens*). A possible view is that there is a misunderstanding on both sides of the controversy, and that *The Wagon Mound* and *Polemis* are not in real conflict: *The Wagon Mound* rightly says that only a certain range of damage is recoverable but defines it too narrowly; *Polemis* assumed that the damage to the ship was within the acceptable range ('not the *exact* kind' said Scrutton LJ but by implication near enough) and was a decision on causation. Dicta in both cases are too sweeping. *The Trecarrell* [1973] 1 Lloyd's Rep 402 is an interesting illustration, on facts reminiscent of *Polemis*, of how the law has now settled down. A drum of inflammable lacquer for coating ship's tanks was dropped carelessly by ship repairers: cable severed, spark, fire, ship destroyed. Held by Brandon J fire hazard being foreseeable, immaterial how it was brought about.

different, and led to the conclusion that it was foreseeable for engine oil in water to be set alight, though the possibility was remote. The Judicial Committee held that even a small risk is sufficient to come within the range of foreseeable damage unless a reasonable man would disregard it, e.g. on the ground that the effort or expense of eliminating the risk was out of proportion; and in that event it is a case of no negligence, rather than being outside the foreseeable range[6].

In working out the result of the cases, there are three distinct issues which are not to be confused:

(1) What kind of damage establishes liability in negligence?
(2) Was the damage caused by the negligence?
(3) Was the causal connection too 'remote'?

(1) No liability for damage unless within the range of the duty of care

The Wagon Mound (No. 1) establishes the rule that damage is not recoverable in an action for negligence unless it is within the range of the duty of care, i.e. is the type of damage which, by being reasonably foreseeable in the circumstances, gave rise to the duty.

So understood, it is the counterpart of the well-known rule on liability for breach of statutory duty, the rule in *Gorris v Scott* that when a statute requires measures to be taken for one purpose, there is no liability for a totally different matter: thus the absence of pens to prevent the spread of disease among sheep on board ship created no liability for sheep swept overboard. 'Totally different' deserves emphasis[7]. The cases summarised above show that a difference in extent of damage is not

---

6 *Doughty v Turner Manufacturing Co Ltd* [1964] 1 QB 518, [1964] 1 All ER 98 seems out of line with *Hughes v Lord Advocate*; injury was foreseeable by a splash of molten liquid from a cover of asbestos cement falling into a cauldron, but a violent eruption caused by an unforeseen chemical reaction when the cover fell in was held to be a totally different risk, outside the range of liability. Yet it was only a larger splash caused in a different way, factors which according to the House of Lords are irrelevant. The decision can however be justified on the ground that the foreseeable risk was so slight and so difficult to prevent that there was *no negligence*.
7 I take it from *Donaghey v Boulton and Paul Ltd* [1968] AC 1, [1967] 2 All ER 1014 where Lord Reid treated the two rules as counterparts. The suggestion in *Evans v Sanderson and Newbould Ltd* (1968) 4 KIR 115 that the *Wagon Mound* applies to statutory duty, as well as *Gorris v Scott*, seems to be a misunderstanding.

enough, nor a difference in causation. It is therefore not legitimate to limit the scope of recoverable damage by the manner in which it is caused. It is arguable that *The Wagon Mound* (*No. 1*) takes too narrow a line, and that a duty to take care against damage to property is wide enough to include any kind of damage to property though not, e.g. damage to reputation. Below the generality of, say, 'damage to vessels and property in the harbour', distinctions almost inevitably turn on how the damage was *caused* (by fouling, choking, burning, explosion). In statutory duty cases the courts have taken a broad view. Thus in *Grant v National Coal Board* [1956] AC 649, [1956] 1 All ER 682 (breach of statutory duty to keep the roof of a mine secure) where stone fell from the roof of a mine and a vehicle bumped into it, the duty was held to be intended to give protection against personal injury in any form, not just injury by the fall of a roof on a person; in *Donaghey v Boulton & Paul Ltd* [1968] AC 1, [1967] 2 All ER 1014 a regulation requiring crawling boards above fragile roofs was held wide enough to cover a fall through a hole, without breaking the roof, the broad object being to prevent falls from the roof in whatever way.

Examples of cases where the injury fell outside the scope of the duty are *Reid v Sir Robert McAlpine & Son Ltd* 1986 SLT 108 where a building worker fell into an unguarded drop while investigating a fire, and the fall was held to be outside the fire risk; and *Bell v Scottish Special Housing Association* 1987 SLT 320 where a boy was electrocuted by faulty wiring (caused by damp) when investigating a leaking ceiling, and this was held to be outside the landlords' liability for disrepair. On the other hand, where a sprain to the wrist was foreseeable, tenosynovitis was also within the risk though due to continuing wear and tear rather than a sudden injury: *Rowark v National Coal Board* [1986] CLY unreported appeal No. 42.

(2) The negligence must be a cause of the damage

Although in *The Wagon Mound* (*No. 1*) Lord Simonds visualised the complete elimination of 'the never-ending and insoluble problems of causation', the question of causation cannot be avoided; one may foresee all kinds of possibilities without being causally responsible for them, and, as Lord Atkin said in *Caswell v Powell Duffryn Associated Collieries Ltd* [1940] AC 152 at 165, [1939] 3 All ER 722 at 730:

'whether you ask whose negligence was responsible for the injury, or
from whose negligence did the injury result, or adopt any other phrase
you please, you must in the ultimate analysis be asking who "caused"
the injury; and you must not be deterred because the word "cause"
has in philosophy given rise to embarrassments which in this
connection should not affect the judge.'

To eliminate causation would involve overruling numerous House of
Lords decisions, and make it impossible to deal with the question
whether the defendant was the *sole* cause of the damage or only one
contributory cause. But in inquiring into the cause of an accident, the
law accepts common sense standards, and is not concerned with the
explanations of causation put forward by scientists or philosophers:
Caswell v Powell Duffryn Collieries Ltd [1940] AC 152 at 165, [1939] 3
All ER 722 at 730 per Lord Atkin; *Yorkshire Dale SS Co v Minister of
War Transport, The Coxwold* [1942] AC 691 at 706, [1942] 2 All ER 6 at
14–15 per Lord Wright. According to common sense standards, the
cause of a happening is that which actively brings it about. It is the
answer to the question: What (or who) did it? or (with an omission) Who
let it happen? For it must be remembered that negligence may consist
either of an act or of an omission, and the two are governed by rather
different considerations. One big difference is that an 'act' causes the
results it brings about, irrespective of whether the act is an actionable
tort: but an 'omission' is not a cause at all unless there was a duty to do
the thing omitted[8].

(i) Proof of causation
The onus of proving that the defendant's negligence caused the injury is
always on the plaintiff, though, as in all civil actions, it will be sufficient if
he proves a causal connection on the balance of probability. If there are
several possible causes (as often happens in medical cases, or where
disease is produced by exposure to adverse conditions), and none is
more probable than the others, the onus of proof is not discharged and
the claim fails: *Wilsher v Essex Area Health Authority* [1988] AC 1074,

8 *Who did it?* is a sensible question whether the act was blameworthy or not. *Who let
it happen?* does not make sense unless someone should have stopped it. The reason
for this is that the only real causation is by acts done: but in order that liability for
failure to exercise control may be apportioned to responsible persons, the artificial
notion of causing a result by an omission is established by analogy: just as in
mathematics negative numbers are introduced by analogy to positive numbers (or
imaginary numbers by analogy to real ones).

[1988] 1 All ER 871, HL; *Kay's Tutor v Ayrshire and Arran Health Board* [1987] 2 All ER 417, HL. In particular there is no presumption, or legitimate inference, that negligence is the cause (if it has occurred) rather than any other competing cause, nor is there any legal liability for negligently creating a 'risk' to another person's health (which may be merely statistical) unless the risk has materialised. However, if increased exposure to a risk is shown to involve increased risk of harm (as with exposure to asbestos dust) the increased risk, even if statistical rather than cumulative, may be sufficient on a balance of probability to show that the additional exposure has caused the damage: *Bryce v Swan Hunter Group plc* [1988] 1 All ER 659. (See also Chapter 6, section 4 on causation by breach of statutory duty.)

(ii) A negligent act as a cause

A negligent act as the cause of an accidental injury presents little difficulty: it falls exactly within the common sense notion of an agency which actively brings about a definite result, as, for example, where one workman carelessly strikes the hand of another workman with a hammer. In *Boy Andrew (Owners) v St Rognvald (Owners)* [1948] AC 140, [1947] 2 All ER 350—a case of a collision between two ships, which was held to have been caused by both of them—Lord Porter remarked that one of the ships 'was always an active party in the final result', and that as to her liability at least there could be no question.

It is evident, however, that the causal efficacy of a negligent act may be carried far beyond its immediate consequences. It may set up a dangerous and continuing state of affairs, and an accident arising out of this continuing danger may still be due to the original act of negligence. Thus if, by a negligent act, defective lifting tackle is attached to a crane, this negligence is the cause of a subsequent accident due to the breakage of the tackle. So, too, a road collision may be caused, wholly or in part, by negligence in leaving a lorry across the road, and it is no answer to say that the lorry was in a static position where it could do no harm unless someone ran into it: *Harvey v Road Haulage Executive* [1952] 1 KB 120.

(iii) A negligent omission as a cause

An omission cannot, like an act, be a cause in the sense of exercising an active influence. Nevertheless, if the omitted act had been performed, some positive factor—such as a safety device—would have been interposed. If that safety device would have prevented the accident, then the failure to put it there is a cause of the accident. It is enough, indeed, to show a probability that the accident would have been prevented.

> 'It may often be impossible to say that, if a man had done what he omitted to do, the accident would certainly have been prevented. It is enough in my judgment, if there is a sufficiently high degree of probability': per Lord Reid, in *Stapley v Gypsum Mines Ltd* [1953] AC 663 at 682, [1953] 2 All ER 478 at 486.

In general, a negligent omission to take safety measures entails a continuing state of danger for which the negligent person is responsible. The failure to fence a machine is an excellent example. If the fence had been fixed, it would have interposed an effective barrier between the machine and the workman: and injuries which would not have been sustained if such a barrier had been present are caused by the omission to fence[9]. Conversely, if the injuries would have been sustained whether or not a barrier was there, they are not caused by the omission to fence[10]. Another example is where the guard on a machine was faulty in that it left too wide a gap over the cutters; but the accident happened because the guard had been replaced loosely by the plaintiff himself, and would have happened just the same with an adequate guard: *Lineker v Raleigh Industries Ltd* (1980) ICR 83, CA.

(iv) 'Causa causans' *and condition* 'sine qua non'
There is an important distinction between the preconditions of an accident, or conditions *sine qua non*—the whole collection of existing

---

9 See e.g. *Biddle v Truvox* [1951] 2 TLR 968 at 970 (failure to case unsafe machinery was a cause of the accident though plaintiff came into contact through the act of another man); *Cork v Kirby Maclean Ltd* [1952] 2 All ER 402 (unsafe scaffold a contributory cause though man fell in epileptic fit). In *Shepherd v J. and J. White Ltd* (1954) 105 L Jo 106 a man slipped and fell into a vat, which was not fenced or covered as required by regulations. The Court of Session (Lord Migdale) held that there was 'no causal connection' between the breach and the accident. But this, with respect, is surely wrong: see the remarks of Lord Wright in *Caswell v Powell Duffryn Associated Collieries Ltd* [1940] AC 152 at 170, 172 [1939] 3 All ER 722 at 734–5 on unfenced machinery. It is in each case the absence of the safeguard which creates *exposure* to danger. Cf. *A/S Rendal v Arcos Ltd* [1937] 3 All ER 577 at 588 (ship exposed to danger by absence of ice-breakers).

10 Where the omission consists of a failure to supply a safety belt or other device which a workman might or might not use at his opinion the action will fail if it is shown positively or on a balance of probability that the workman would not have used the device: *Qualcast (Wolverhampton) Ltd v Haynes* [1959] AC 743, [1959] 2 All ER 38 (protective spats in foundry). For a full discussion of this and other examples of causal connection in cases of omissions, see Chapter 6, section 4.

circumstances without which it would not have occurred, or would not have had the same result—and the operative causes which, either by act or by omission, actually bring about the accident.

This distinction is elusive, and difficult to formulate: sometimes it looks unreal, but the chief reason for this is that cases are not argued before the courts unless they lie on the uncertain borderline between the two conceptions. At all events it has frequently been recognised that a condition *sine qua non* is not the same thing as a cause—e.g. in the speech of Viscount Simon in *Boy Andrew (Owners) v St. Rognvald (Owners)* [1948] AC 140, [1947] 2 All ER 350[11].

Causes and conditions *sine qua non* are alike in that they precede the accident. Conditions *sine qua non*, however, are no more that the setting of the stage, so to speak, while the causes are the actors on the stage: that is to say, they are the factors, whether of a dynamic or a static character, which bring about the accident.

> 'Two causes may both be necessary preconditions of a particular result . . . yet the one may, if the facts justify that conclusion, be treated as the real, substantial, direct or effective cause, and the other dismissed as at best a *causa sine qua non* and ignored for purposes of legal liability': per Lord Asquith in *Stapley v Gypsum Mines, Ltd* [1953] AC 663 at 687, [1953] 2 All ER 478 at 489.

There is a well-known case where a vehicle ran into a donkey tethered in the middle of the highway, in broad daylight: *Davies v Mann* (1842) 10 M & W 546. Certainly the donkey would not have been run over if it had not been there: but the sole cause of the accident was held to be negligent driving. In the somewhat similar case of *Anglo-Newfoundland*

---

11 *Cause and condition* sine qua non. The distinction is taken from classical logic, and a denial of its validity involves the fallacy *post hoc ergo propter hoc*. A condition *sine qua non* is *not* correctly described as a cause. Cf. Denning LJ in *Jones v Livox Quarries Ltd* [1952] 2 QB 608 at 616: 'causes are different from the circumstances in which, or on which, they operate'; and again in *Minister of Pensions v Chennell* [1947] KB 250, [1946] 2 All ER 719: 'not a *cause*, but only part of the history'. Lord Simonds' reference in *The Wagon Mound*, to 'scholastic theories of causation and their ugly and barely intelligible jargon' seems unduly harsh. In fact what he is criticising is Greek logic, not medieval scholars who merely rediscovered it through Arab sources and handed it on. But in any case an English lawyer should know better than to despise medieval scholars. They are part of the same talented culture which founded English law in the 13th century, founded the universities and built the great cathedrals: not to mention the craft guilds which, unlike their modern counterpart, were as much concerned about the quality of their work as about their pay.

Development Co Ltd v Pacific Steam Navigation Co [1924] AC 406 a ship lay athwart a narrow channel, but there was sufficient room to pass it: and an approaching vessel, which had seen the obstruction in ample time to manoeuvre safely, was held to be the sole cause of the resulting collision. Where, however, a lorry was left in a dangerous position across the highway, and an oncoming motor-cyclist had only a few seconds to avoid it, the dangerous position of the lorry was held to be one of the causes of the accident: *Harvey v Road Haulage Executive* [1952] 1 KB 120. Plainly it may be a question of degree whether—as in the *Anglo-Newfoundland* case—a given factor has so far sunk into the background that it is only a part of the setting of the stage: and if there is any doubt the court will tend to hold that any dangerous element in the situation is a cause rather than a condition *sine qua non*.

Reduced to its simplest terms, the question in each case is this: What factors actually *brought about* the accident?—as distinct from factors which merely *led up* to it.

(3) The damage must not be too remote

In the light of subsequent cases, it now seems plain enough that *The Wagon Mound (No. 1)* (whether narrowly or widely interpreted) declares a rule on the extent of liability for negligence, not on causation: for, having decided what *occurrences* give rise to liability, you still have to work out how far the consequences of those occurrences are recoverable—let us say if the oil that fouled the jetty had also corroded it, or lay on harbour steps where someone slipped.

Now one thing springs from another, and consequences spread out indefinitely like ripples from a pebble thrown into a lake, and the line has to be drawn somewhere. This is the true question of remoteness of damage, distinct from the question in *The Wagon Mound* whether the type of damage is within the scope of the duty of care. To a great extent this is a 'practical' matter, i.e. a matter of fact and degree, as Lord Wright said in *Liesbosch. Dredger v Edison SS (Owners)* [1933] AC 449. Hitherto damage had not been considered remote if it was either (i) a direct consequence of the occurrence, i.e. the automatic physical effects on things as they stood before some new factor intervened, or (ii) although indirect, it was a foreseeable consequence. The fact that English law accepts a dual test appears from the speech of Lord Porter in *Morrison SS Co Ltd v Cargo in Greystoke Castle* [1947] AC 265 at 295, [1946] 2 All ER 696 at 709:

> 'One method of ascertaining the damages in an action of tort is to ask what loss would a reasonable man anticipate as a result of the wrongful act. To this the *Polemis* case added a further liability, viz. damage consisting of the direct physical consequences of the tortious act, whether they could reasonably be anticipated or not.'

There are good historical reasons for this dual test[12].

Scots law on causation does not seem fundamentally different. In *McKillen v Barclay Curle & Co Ltd* 1967 SLT 41 (where a claim that a rib injury reactivated tuberculosis was negatived on the facts) Lord President Clyde said that under the law of Scotland reasonable foreseeability applies only in determining liability. Once a man injures another by his negligence 'he is liable for all the damage to the injured man which naturally and directly arises out of the negligence'; such damages (per Lord Kinloch in *Allan v Barclay* (1863) 2 M 873) 'as naturally and directly arise out of the wrong done; and such therefore as may reasonably be supposed to have been in the view of the

---

12 It is an error to suppose that the notion of damage 'directly' caused was a novelty introduced by *Re Polemis*. It goes back to the old days of the common law, the distinction between the forms of action in Trespass and Case. Blackstone says (*Commentaries*, 17th Edn., Vol. III, p. 122):

> 'And it is a settled distinction, that where an act is done which is in itself an immediate injury to another's person or property, there the remedy is usually by an action of trespass *vi et armis*; but where there is no act done, but only by a culpable omission; or where the act is not immediately injurious, but only by consequence and collaterally; there no action of trespass *vi et armis* will lie, but an action on the special case, for the damages consequent on such omission or act.'

This surely puts it beyond doubt that there was always a remedy in trespass for damage directly inflicted (such as striking a man with a thin skull) and trespass included a negligent injury if direct: *Leame v Bray* (1803) 3 East 593. Trespass also included the type of case where there was an automatic sequence of events without deliberate human intervention: see *Scott v Shepherd* (1773) 2 Wm Bl 892, when a lighted squib was thrown in a market-house and persons in danger threw it away from themselves, as an automatic reaction. This is what the *Polemis* case means by 'direct', as a slight extension of 'immediate'. (De Grey CJ in the squib case said it was 'direct and immediate'.) But where the damage is *indirect*, it could be remedied only by an action on the case, and it was in this action that the alternative test of foreseeability grew up. Hence (as Lord Porter says) damage became recoverable if it was either (i) direct or (ii) indirect but foreseeable.

It is arguable that in *The Wagon Mound* the damage was not 'direct' at all but caused by the intervention of a new factor, molten metal.

wrongdoer'[13]. (Lord Migdale, in a minority, thought that foreseeability was the sole criterion for causation but is wide enough to involve unknown physical weaknesses.)

(i) Direct consequences are not too remote
While *Polemis* is discredited as a test of liability, it does not seem to be wrong as a test of causation. The 'thin skull' cases, the spread of the cancer in *Smith v Leech Brain*, and the explosion of the lamp in *Hughes v Lord Advocate* were all unexpected, and therefore could be recoverable only on the basis that they were direct results. In *Polemis* Scrutton L J said that a consequence ceases to be direct if it is due to 'the operation of independent causes having no connection with the negligent act, except that they could not avoid its results': but it is direct if it results from the steady working out of a single train of consequences, one flowing automatically from another. In short, what is required to establish liability is not so much immediate causation as *a direct sequence of events*, arising out of existing circumstances whether known or unknown, and not interrupted or diverted by a new active agency.

Human intervention will normally mean that the results become indirect, unless, for example, it is reflex or automatic as in *Scott v Shepherd* (1773) 2 Wm Bl 892 (squib in market place thrown in self-defence from one point to another by persons endangered). Human intervention more than anything else requires the alternative test of foreseeability.

(ii) Natural and probable consequences are not too remote, even if indirect
This test has been acted upon in scores of cases, especially where some human agency intervenes between the negligence and the damage. If the defendant ought to have foreseen such an intervention as likely, he

---

13 This can include both consequences in the course of nature and others (such as human intervention) which are foreseeable. As to Scottish support for *Polemis* in causation (as distinct from liability) see the works mentioned in footnote 5, p. 55. Criticisms by some Scottish judges seem to be based on misunderstandings, e.g. *Hay (or Bourhill) v Young* [1943] AC 92, [1942] 2 All ER 396 (extent of *liability*: did not extend to shock to bystander in traffic accident); *Malcolm v Dickson* 1951 SC 542 (man had heart attack in trying to retrieve his property in a fire—a deliberate human act is never a 'direct' consequence). Scots law uses the maxim *causa directa non remota spectatur*. As to Lord Migdale's dissent, if you must take a man as you find him, why not take a ship as you find it with inflammable vapour in the hold?

cannot avoid liability by saying that the result was indirect: see, e.g. *Haynes v Harwood* [1935] 1 KB 146 where a policeman sustained injuries through intervening to stop a runaway horse. Similarly a defendant is liable if his act puts the plaintiff in a position where an error of judgment may result in further damage: *Baron Vernon SS v SS Metagama* 1928 SC (HL) 21 (error of judgment in mooring stranded ship); *Rubens v Walker* 1946 SC 215 (error in medical diagnosis); *Robinson v Post Office* [1974] 2 All ER 737 (doctor injected serum against tetanus, which caused brain injury: although negligent not to make full tests of sensitivity, these would have made no difference as reaction would not have occurred in time). Or he may be liable for a second accident due to weakness from the original injury: *McKew v Holland and Hannen and Cubitts (Scotland) Ltd* [1969] 3 All ER 1621 (on the facts the accident was due to the injured man's own imprudence in going down steep steps without a stick or a helping hand). To make a defendant liable for damage done by an intervening human act, such an act must be foreseeable as a likely thing to happen, and not only that, it must be foreseeable as a *consequence* of the defendant's tort: it is not enough that he has merely created an occasion or opportunity which he was under no duty to prevent: *Home Office v Dorset Yacht Co Ltd* [1970] 2 All ER 294 at 298–9 (liability of Borstal officer for damage by escaping detainee to boat in vicinity); *Lamb v London Borough of Camden* [1981] QB 625, [1981] 2 All ER 408, CA (burst pipe caused house to subside and be left vacant: no liability for irruption of squatters and consequent damage).

(iii) Novus actus interveniens
The chain of causation is broken by what is described as a *novus actus interveniens*, that is to say, a new independent cause which could not reasonably be foreseen. This proposition is a corollary from points (i) and (ii) above, since the new cause is neither a direct nor a probable consequence. Usually—but not always—it will be a deliberate human act which supervenes in this way: but even a deliberate act may not break the sequence if it is not done with full knowledge of the danger: *Philco Radio and Television Corpn of Great Britain v Spurling (J.) Ltd* [1949] 2 All ER 882.

> 'It must always be shown that there is something which I will call ultroneous, something unwarrantable, a new cause coming in disturbing the sequence of events, something that can be described as either unreasonable or extraneous or extrinsic. I doubt very much

whether the law can be stated more precisely than that' (Lord Wright in *The Oropesa* [1943] P 32 at 39, [1943] 1 All ER 211 at 215, where the death of a seaman owing to the capsizing of a life-boat was held to be a consequence of the collision damaging his ship).

In general, the chain of causation is not broken where an accident occurs through the inadvertent or automatic acts of a workman, or partly through his own negligence: in particular it is not broken when a workman takes a risk (even if ill-judged and outside the scope of his ordinary duty) to protect his employer's property: *Steel v Glasgow Iron and Steel Co Ltd* 1944 SC 237, *Hyett v Great Western Rail Co* [1948] 1 KB 345, [1947] 2 All ER 264. Similarly it is not a *novus actus* if a doctor risks his own life to save the life of a workman in danger through an unsafe method of work: *Baker v T. E. Hopkins & Sons Ltd* [1959] 3 All ER 225. Even suicide is not automatically a *novus actus interveniens.* If there is an injury to the head which results in a disturbed mental state, not necessarily amounting to insanity, suicide may be a foreseeable consequence of the accident: *Pigney v Pointer's Transport Services Ltd* [1957] 2 All ER 807 (not, with respect, a direct consequence as was said); *Farmer v Rash* [1969] 1 All ER 705. *Aliter*, where suicide resulted from brooding over an injury which had no direct effect on the mental condition, for such a result is neither direct nor foreseeable: *Cowan v N.C.B.* (1958) SLT (Notes) 19.

In general, on the other hand, a free human act is a *novus actus* which separates the original wrongdoer from subsequent damage, even though he has created the opportunity for it; but this is not so when the wrongdoer ought to have foreseen harmful intervention by a third party *as a consequence of his own act or neglect*, nor where the plaintiff or his advisers have had to make a choice (which has turned out to be an error of judgment) in difficult circumstances. Negligence, if foreseeable as a consequence, is not necessarily a *novus actus*, and may (as in the common cases of contributory negligence and joint tortfeasors) be a concurrent cause of the harm resulting in division of liability. There is no reason in principle why this should not include negligence in medical treatment, but normally the first defendant would then obtain full indemnity.

An omission or failure of duty by a third person may nevertheless be decisive enough to be a *novus actus*, as in *Taylor v Rover Co Ltd* [1966] 2 All ER 181 where the manufacturer's liability for a badly made chisel came to an end when the purchasers, after discovering its brittle condition, failed to take it out of use in their factory. A good example of the supervening negligence of a third party as a *novus actus* is *Knightley v Johns* [1982] 1 All ER 851, [1982] 1 WLR 349. A motorist who negligently overturned his car and blocked a road tunnel was not liable for a subsequent accident which occurred because the police inspector failed to close the tunnel promptly and sent a police motor-cyclist riding back the wrong way. This was something which went beyond the normal consequences foreseeable from the original accident.

The plaintiff's own act in taking a risk which increases the damage may be a *novus actus*: *McKew v Holland and Hannen and Cubitts (Scotland)* Ltd [1969] 3 All ER 1621 (man with weak knee chose to walk down steep steps without stick or help). As Lord Reid said in this case, the fact that a defendant can foresee a *novus actus* does not make him liable: it is not a foreseeable *consequence* of his own act because it interrupts the causal sequence. Also refusal to have a surgical operation may be a *novus actus* which exonerates the defendant from liability for consequences which could have been avoided: and the onus of proving that refusal was reasonable is on the plaintiff: *Selvanayagam v University of West Indies* [1983] 1 All ER 824, [1983] 1 WLR 585.

Concurrent causes and sole causes

In an action for damages for negligence, it is never necessary to show that the defendant's conduct was the whole cause, or even the principal cause, of the accident. It is enough to show that it made a material contribution. Thus there have been a number of cases where the plaintiff sustained pneumoconiosis as a result of exposure to invisible fractured silica dust: and, although most of the dust came from sources of which no complaint could be made, the fact that a relatively small part arose from negligence or breach of statutory duty was sufficient to establish liability: *Bonnington Castings Ltd v Wardlaw* [1956] AC 613, [1956] 1 All ER 615; *Quinn v Cameron and Roberton Ltd* [1958] AC 9, [1957] 1 All ER 760; *Nicholson v Atlas Steel Foundry and Engineering Co Ltd* [1957] 1 All ER 776. In the *Bonnington* case Lord Reid said:

> 'What is a material contribution must be a question of degree. A contribution which comes within the exception of *de minimis non curat lex* is not material, but I think that any contribution which does not fall within that exception must be material.'

This rule that a 'material contribution' is sufficient to substantiate a claim also applies to factors succeeding one another in time, e.g. where a disease has been contracted through exposure to dust over a number of years, some of which are outside the time limit for bringing action: *Clarkson v Modern Foundries Ltd* [1958] 1 All ER 33. It does not follow, of course, that there is liability for all the damage, and where negligence or breach of statutory duty has supervened (as in the case of deafness) after much of the damage has already occurred, the liability will be limited to the further deterioration: *Thompson v Smiths Shiprepairers (North Shields) Ltd* [1984] QB 405, [1984] 1 All ER 881.

Leaving aside this type of case, where only one party is at fault, it frequently happens that several factors 'lead up' (to use a neutral term) to the occurrence of an accident, and are, in a very broad sense, among its causes. The question may then arise—both as between plaintiff and defendant, and as between two or more defendants—whether they are *concurrent causes*, or whether one factor can be singled out as the *sole cause* of the accident. If the plaintiff's conduct was the sole cause, then his action fails, because the defendant is not responsible. If the defendant's conduct was the sole cause, he is liable in full. If, on the other hand, the plaintiff and defendant were concurrent causes, the plaintiff's damages are reduced in proportion to the degree of responsibility: Law Reform (Contributory Negligence) Act 1945. If two or more defendants were concurrent causes, they, as between themselves, must share the liability in proportion to the degree of responsibility: Civil Liability (Contribution) Act 1978. There may, of course, be causal factors which are not in a legal sense blameworthy, including purely physical factors such as fog causing a road accident, or that part of the cloud of dust in the *Bonnington* case which was unavoidably present. For the purpose of legal liability, all factors must be eliminated unless they can be traced to human conduct which is blameworthy as being either negligent (or wilful) or a breach of statutory duty.

We may mark off at once two classes of cases where it is clear that one person is the sole cause of an accident. First, it frequently happens that only one person was at fault, as in *Judson v British Transport Commission* [1954] 1 All ER 624, where a railwayman, in breach of the rules, moved from one line on to an adjoining line to avoid an oncoming train, and was injured by a train coming up on the second line. Secondly, there are cases where two persons were undoubtedly at fault in a legal sense, but the conduct of one is merely a condition *sine qua non*, which has set the scene for entirely independent and unconnected fault of the other: see *Norris v Moss (William) & Sons Ltd* [1954] 1 All ER 324, where defendant employers were in breach of reg. 10 of the Building Regulations because the upright of a scaffold was out of the vertical, and the plaintiff came on the scene, saw that the upright was out of position, and attempted to put it right by an unsafe method, with the result that he fell. Here the breach of reg. 10 was merely an antecedent circumstance which, though prompting the plaintiff to interfere, did not in any sense bring about the accident. Similarly in *Moir-Young v Dorman Long (Bridge and Engineering) Ltd* (1969) 7 KIR 86, an impatient workman explored dark places where, as it turned out, he had no business to be, and this was the sole cause of the accident, the employer's technical breach of regulations being only an attendant circumstance. In *Quinn v Burch Brothers (Builders) Ltd* [1966] 2 QB 370, [1966] 2 All ER 283 a breach of contract to supply plant to a sub-contractor was not a 'cause' of the sub-contractor being injured by using makeshift equipment, but just the 'opportunity' or 'occasion'.

At the other extreme is the model case of concurrent causes, where two or more parties are at fault, quite independently, up to the moment of the accident. Typical examples are to be found in head-on collisions in the middle of the road, or in such cases as *Jones v Livox Quarries Ltd* [1952] 2 QB 608 where a man riding in a dangerous position on the back of a vehicle was struck by another vehicle.

The really difficult problems arise where causal factors are successive, often interdependent, and closely mixed up with one another. The classical exposition of the law on this subject is to be found in *Admiralty Commissioners v Volute, S.S.* [1922] 1 AC 129 (a case of a collision at sea). The essence of the principle expounded by Viscount Birkenhead LC in this case is that where first one party is negligent, then another, you cannot say that the party guilty of the last act of negligence must bear the whole responsibility; where the acts of negligence are closely 'mixed up' together, both must be treated as contributory. Nevertheless, in some cases 'a clear line' can be drawn and the negligence of one party may be 'subsequent and severable' so as to make him the sole cause of the accident. In *Sigurdson v British Columbia Electric Rail Co Ltd* [1953] AC 291 it was argued that, where there are successive acts of negligence, knowledge of the prior negligence in time to avoid its effects is the decisive factor. This argument was rejected. Lord Tucker said:

'Time and knowledge may often be decisive factors, but it is for the
. . . tribunal of fact to decide whether . . . the existence of one of these
factors results or does not result in the ascertainment of that clear line
to which Viscount Birkenhead referred—moreoever, their Lordships
do not read him as intending to lay down that the existence of
"subsequent" negligence will alone enable that clear line to be found.'

The fact that the injured person was aware of the risk, and being
perfectly free, decided to take it, does not make him the sole cause of the
accident: *A. C. Billings & Sons Ltd v Riden* [1958] AC 240, [1957] 3 All
ER 1. The question in such a case is whether the injured person acted
reasonably, which will mean, generally, whether there were other
circumstances which outweighed the risk.

There was a tendency at one time, in employer's liability cases, to
single out one party as having taken a decisive step which made him the
sole cause of the accident. This tendency was arrested by the House of
Lords in *Stapley v Gypsum Mines Ltd* [1953] AC 663, [1953] 2 All ER
478 where it was held that the principle is just the same as it is in
collision cases: when negligent acts are 'mixed up' together, there
cannot be a finding that one factor was the sole cause unless a clear line
can be drawn so as to make that factor 'subsequent and severable'. In
Stapley's case two men were told to bring down an unsafe roof in a mine,
found the task too difficult, gave it up, and went away. Later one of the
men came back to work under the unsafe roof and was killed by a fall of
rock. The Court of Appeal held that the deceased, by returning under
the roof, was the sole cause of the accident. The House of Lords (by a
majority) rejected this view and held that the prior failure to make the
roof safe was a contributory cause. In *National Coal Board v England*
[1954] AC 403, [1954] 1 All ER 546 the plaintiff was assisting a
shotfirer in a coal mine, and contrary to regulations he coupled up the
cable to the detonator (the coupling should be done by the shotfirer
personally): the shotfirer then broke the regulations by firing the shot
without making sure that the plaintiff was clear. The House of Lords
reversed the decision of the Court of Appeal that the shotfirer was the
sole cause of the accident, and held that the plaintiff and the shotfirer
were both contributory causes.

Where two or more men of more or less equal status join together in
disobeying the employer's instructions, or even statutory regulations,
they are concurrent causes of the accident, and the disobedience cannot
(like joint estates in the law of property) be treated as something

indivisible which is to be imputed in full to each of the men: so the employers may be vicariously liable to some extent to one of the men for the negligence or breach of duty of the others unless they have some special defence such as *volenti non fit injuria: Stapley v Gypsum Mines Ltd (supra); Imperial Chemical Industries Ltd v Shatwell* [1965] AC 656, [1964] 2 All ER 999 (Viscount Radcliffe dissenting).

It is still occasionally alleged, and even held, that a man who is injured in an unfenced machine and has mishandled the machine in some way is the 'sole cause' of his injuries as in *Rushton v Turner Brothers Asbestos Co Ltd* [1959] 3 All ER 517 where the man put his hand inside a moving machine to clean it. Such decisions are inconsistent with later authorities, notably the decisions of the House of Lords discussed in Chapter 23, section 6. As a matter of principle failure to fence a machine, with continuing exposure to danger, must be a contributory cause of injury *unless*, of course, it is shown that even if there had been a fence the man would have removed it. In a case where a demonstrator put his hand into a dangerous gap, *Harvey v Singer Manufacturing Co Ltd* 1960 SLT 178, Lord Thomson L J-C said:

> 'I do not see how it could be said that the sole cause of the accident was the negligence of the pursuer, since the accident would not have occurred but for the continued existence of the nip.'

In *Stocker v Norprint Ltd* (1970) 10 KIR 10 (hand caught in unfenced machine by trying to collect articles coming out) the Court of Appeal said that it is impossible to hold that the employer is under no liability where there is a breach of his statutory duty not caused by the workman.

At any rate, whenever causal factors are closely mixed up together, *prima facie* they are concurrent causes and responsibility is shared. It will require a strong case to throw the whole liability on to one side. It is not enough to say that there was full knowledge and freedom to choose, for the decision may be made under the shadow of the prior negligence, as in *Stapley*'s case. It is not enough to say that the effect of the earlier negligence could have been avoided. In *Hartley v Mayoh & Co* [1954] 1 QB 383, [1954] 1 All ER 375 a fireman called to a factory was electrocuted owing to failure to turn off the current. The manager had pointed out the wrong switch as the main switch: but this switch would still have turned off the current, if the wires had not been transposed by the electricity authority. Both mistakes were held to be concurrent causes of the accident.

Good examples of subsequent and severable negligence are given by Lord Atkin in *Caswell v Powell Duffryn Associated Collieries Ltd* [1940] AC 152 at 164–5, [1939] 3 All ER 722 at 729, 730 where he says that:

> 'no cause of action arises . . . if out of bravado [the plaintiff] puts his hand into moving machinery or attempts to leap over an unguarded cavity.'

The principle that, to make one party the sole cause, his negligence must be subsequent and severable so that a clear line can be drawn, is exactly the same (from a different angle) as the rule that damage does not become too remote unless something 'ultroneous' intervenes, i.e. a *nova causa interveniens*.

5 Evidence of negligence

The onus of proving negligence on the case as a whole always rests upon the plaintiff, though the temporary onus of producing evidence, e.g. to show why trade practice has not been followed, may shift from time to time during the trial: *Brown v Rolls-Royce Ltd* [1960] 1 All ER 577.

Evidence of negligence is to a great extent a matter of procedure (and of the practical preparation of a case for trial), but it has a close connection with the substantive law, and there are two questions which the courts have frequently had to consider:

(i) Is there 'evidence of negligence', i.e. is there *sufficient* to support a finding in favour of the plaintiff? This is always a question of law: so, if a court or jury finds in favour of the plaintiff where, in contemplation of law, there is not sufficient evidence, the judgment or verdict may be set aside on appeal.

(ii) Granted that there is 'evidence of negligence', i.e. just sufficient evidence, what weight should be given to it? This is a pure question of fact. The court may not find the evidence convincing, or may find that it is outweighed by the evidence for the defence. Such a decision relates to the weight of the evidence, and cannot in general be reversed if it was given by a jury, or by a judge whose decision on the facts is not subject to appeal.

The question whether there is sufficient evidence of negligence—with which alone we are concerned—has two main aspects.

(i) The facts of the accident

There must be evidence of *how the accident was caused*. If there were eyewitnesses of the accident—even if the plaintiff himself was the only witness and his evidence is contested by the defence—this requirement is always satisfied. It is, therefore, in the case of fatal accidents which no one saw that a plaintiff is faced with a difficulty—e.g. when a man has been drowned in a dock basin, or found dead on a line of rails where trucks were being shunted, with no evidence of how he got there: *Mersey Docks and Harbour Board v Procter* [1923] AC 253; *Jones v Great Western Rail Co* (1930) 144 LT 194. In these difficult cases, nevertheless, there may be facts of a circumstantial nature which point to the accident having occurred in one way rather than another. The court has no right to make a 'conjecture', that is to say, a guess unsupported by the facts; but it has every right to make proper inferences from the proved facts. If there are proved facts from which a reasonable person could draw an inference in favour of the plaintiff—facts which show, on balance, that the plaintiff's version of the accident is *more likely* than the defendant's—then there is sufficient evidence to support a finding for the plaintiff; and this is so even when the inference is not of a compelling character. Provided that the inference is one which can reasonably be made, it is for the judge of fact to decide whether he is satisfied that it ought to be made. This, in effect, is the principle explained by the House of Lords in *Jones v Great Western Rail Co, supra*, distinguishing between unsupported conjecture on the one hand and legitimate inference on the other.

(ii) The standard of care

Besides proof of the facts of the accident, there must be some evidence from which it can be inferred that the defendant has fallen below the proper standard of care. A good illustration of the minimum degree of proof necessary under this head is *Vella v Llanberis S.S. Co Ltd* (1950) 84 Ll L Rep 140 where ship-repairer's men had access to their staging by means of a Jacob's ladder, which they left at night in a safe position: but on coming back the next day they found that it had been moved, and the ladder came away from its support when one of the men started to go down it. The Court of Appeal held that, on these facts, it could properly be inferred that the shipowners ought to have made a daily inspection of the safety of the means of access, and that they had failed to do so. It was pointed out that if the shipowners thought that this was impracticable, they could have called evidence to that effect.

A case on the other side of the line is *Flaherty v Smith Coggins (A. E.) Ltd* [1951] 2 Lloyd's Rep 397 where a load fell and injured the plaintiff though it was handled according to a proper and safe system, and the Court of Appeal held that there was no evidence from which it could be inferred that there was negligence in carrying out the system.

In general, there ought to be evidence directed specifically to the standard of care. Such evidence may relate to the general and approved practice in the industry[14]; but it should be noted that the evidence must relate to *general* practice alone, and not to what is done at some particular factory or factories: *Boldron v Widdows* (1824) 1 C & P 65. Failing this, the facts proved may show—as in *Vella v Llanberis S.S. Co Ltd, supra*— that there was some danger of which the defendant ought to have been aware, and which (so far as is known) he did nothing to prevent; in such a case, the plaintiff is not required to show what kind of precautions the defendant ought to have taken: *Manchester Corpn v Markland* [1936] AC 360; *General Cleaning Contractors Ltd v Christmas* [1953] AC 180, [1952] 2 All ER 1110.

Res ipsa loquitur

There is a class of cases where, as a Latin maxim says, 'The thing speaks for itself'—*Res ipsa loquitur*—and the happening of the accident is in itself evidence of negligence. In the leading case of *Scott v London Dock Co* (1865) 3 H & C 596, where the plaintiff, a customs officer, was injured by bags of sugar which fell from a crane, Erle C J said:

> 'There must be reasonable evidence of negligence. But where the thing is shown to be under the management of the defendant or his servants, and the accident is such as in the ordinary course of things does not happen if those who have the management use proper care, it affords reasonable evidence, in the absence of explanation by the defendant, that the accident arose from want of care.'

Similar cases are *Byrne v Boadle* (1863) 2 H & C 722, where a barrel rolled out of the upper floor of a warehouse without warning; and *McPherson v Devon Area Health Authority* [1986] CLY unreported appeal No. 44, where a pot of boiling water fell off a tray as it was put down.

Res ipsa loquitur is not a rule of law, it is no more than a rule of

14 Fully discussed at pp. 45–52, *ante.*

evidence based on common sense[15]: but it raises a presumption of fact, in the absence of any other evidence or explanation, that the defendant has been negligent. If this presumption is not displaced, in one way or another, the plaintiff has established his case: see, for instance, *Cassidy v Ministry of Health* [1951] 2 KB 343, [1951] 1 All ER 574; *Moore v R. Fox & Sons* [1956] 1 QB 596, [1956] 1 All ER 182; *Swan v Salisbury Construction Co Ltd* [1966] 2 All ER 138 (presumption raised by collapse of crane, rebutted by positive finding employers not negligent). It does more, therefore, than raise a probable inference which the court is free to accept or reject. Before the presumption can arise, it must be shown that the case really is one where 'The thing speaks for itself'.

There are three ways in which the presumption may be displaced or rebutted:

(i) Alternative explanation not involving negligence
The defendant may offer an alternative explanation—even without proving it—of a way in which, *equally probably*, the accident could have happened without negligence on his part. 'If the defenders can show a way in which the accident may have occurred without negligence, the cogency of the fact of the accident by itself disappears, and the pursuer is left as he began, namely, that he has to show negligence': per Lord Dunedin in *Ballard v North British Rail Co* 1923 SC (HL) 43 at 54. For, unless the happening itself—the *res ipsa*—points to negligent management as the explanation more likely than any other, the maxim does not *begin* to apply[16]. Thus it does not apply on the occurrence of a fire, for which there are many possible causes: *Flannigan v British Dyewood Co Ltd* 1970 SLT 285. But once the maxim applies, a defendant cannot exonerate himself by hypothetical suggestions as to detailed causes: *Moore v R. Fox & Sons* [1956] 1 QB 596, [1956] 1 All ER 182. He must give evidence of facts showing at least a likely explanation—without necessarily proving it—but *this explanation must be*

15 *Lloyde v West Midlands Gas Board* [1971] 2 All ER 1240 at 1246–7, per Megaw LJ.
16 This statement of the law was questioned in *Moore v R. Fox & Sons, supra,* on the ground that it was contained in a dissenting opinion (though the dissent was not on this point): and it was stated that the presumption can be displaced only by (i) proof that the defendant exercised all due care or (ii) proof that the accident was due to a cause not involving negligence on his part. In *Moore v R. Fox & Sons,* the accident was an explosion due to a gas apparatus not functioning correctly: the defendants, without giving evidence, sought to avoid liability by suggesting possible theoretical explanations of how the apparatus went wrong, and this was held insufficient.

one which involves no negligence on his part: *Colvilles Ltd v Devine* [1969] 2 All ER 53 (explosion of oxygen fed to furnace probably due to impurities in pipe, but negligence was not excluded as defenders had not examined filters); *Pearce v Round Oak Steel Works Ltd* [1969] 3 All ER 680 (piece fell off old machine due to metal fatigue: no proof of reasonable examination on purchase of machine second-hand).

(ii) Positive disproof of negligence
The defendant may prove by positive evidence that he exercised all reasonable care, though he cannot show how the accident happened: see *Woods v Duncan* [1946] AC 401, [1946] 1 All ER 420 n (unexplained sinking of submarine); *Walsh v Holst & Co Ltd* [1958] 3 All ER 33 (brick fell off scaffold, but proof that regular inspection carried out) and *Turner v National Coal Board* (1949) 65 TLR 580 (unexplained breaking of wire rope in colliery which had been inspected regularly and found to be in good order). Or he may show what caused the accident, and that it was not due to his negligence[17].

(iii) Complete evidence of facts
The facts leading to the accident may be put before the court in detail. The maxim has then no application: the court has to decide, on the proved facts, whether the defendants were negligent. This is the effect of *Barkway v South Wales Transport Co Ltd* [1950] AC 185, [1950] 1 All ER 392 where an omnibus crashed as the result of a tyre burst; the defendants gave evidence of their methods of inspecting and maintaining tyres, and, since the detailed facts were available, *res ipsa loquitur* ceased to have any application.

In employer's liability cases, the maxim *res ipsa loquitur* may have to be applied rather cautiously. It does not apply where the operation (or equipment) was not under the sole control of the employer: *Corrigan v Mavisbank Rigging Co Ltd* 1983 SLT 316n (ladder collapsed). If the plaintiff himself took any part in the operation which 'speaks for itself' as being negligently conducted, there is always the possibility that his own negligence was one of the causes of the accident. Before 1948, the possibility that it might be due to the negligence of fellow-workmen would also have defeated him; but with the abolition of the defence of

---

17 Cf. *Birchall v J. Bibby & Sons Ltd* [1953] 1 All ER 163 (proof that rope had been cut deliberately by unknown person displaced *res ipsa loquitur*).

common employment, *res ipsa loquitur* may now apply to any operation, even where the plaintiff was personally engaged, always provided that the plaintiff's own negligence is clearly excluded: *Moore v R. Fox & Sons, supra.*

The special application of the maxim to plant and machinery is examined in a later chapter (pp. 123–124, *post*).

6 Liability without proof of negligence

The foregoing paragraphs have traced in some detail the principles to be applied when liability is founded on negligence. But are there any cases where a plaintiff, who sustains injuries in the course of his work, can claim damages, either against his employer or against a third party, without proof of negligence?

For the moment, cases of breach of statutory duty may be left aside; there is certainly absolute liability for injuries due to a breach of the duties imposed by statute in factories, mines and other undertakings, but this important matter is taken up at length in a later chapter. Moreover, with a few exceptions breach of statutory duty is a species of 'fault', or 'statutory negligence', in which the standard of care is laid down in exact terms by the statute, instead of being left to the vague tests of the common law: *Lochgelly Iron and Coal Co Ltd v M'Mullan* [1934] AC 1.

Apart, then, from breach of statutory duty, there are three cases where the common law recognises an absolute or strict liability:

   (i) Liability for the escape of fire (not being a fire which started accidentally) from the defendant's premises.

   (ii) Liability for injuries caused by wild animals (or domestic animals known to be of ferocious disposition).

   (iii) Liability for damage caused by the escape of things that the defendant has brought on to his land, which are likely to do mischief if they escape, either by reason of their inherent nature or because they have been accumulated in quantity; this liability does not arise unless the defendant has brought the dangerous thing on to his land in the course of an artificial change in its natural use, in which case he is bound at his peril to prevent the 'escape' of the thing: *Rylands v Fletcher* (1868)

LR 3 HL 330 (escape of water accumulated in an artificial reservoir)[18].

These liabilities are explained in general textbooks on the law of tort, and it is enough to say here that although negligence need not be proved, the defendant may excuse himself by showing that the escape and consequent damage were caused by the Act of God (i.e. some violent catastrophe of nature), or by the act of a third party, or by the act of the plaintiff[19]. Liability for fire and under *Rylands v Fletcher* depends on the 'escape' of something—the fire or dangerous substance or accumulation—from the premises where it is kept. Provided that there is some 'escape' from other premises to the premises where a man is working, there seems no reason why he should not be able, if injured, to claim damages, although in the House of Lords it is an open question whether the principle of *Rylands v Fletcher* applies to personal injuries as distinct from damage to property: see *Read v Lyons* [1947] AC 156[20]. In the same case Lord Porter said (at pp. 178, 480) that the 'escape' which is necessary under the principles of *Rylands v Fletcher* 'must be escape from a place over which a defendant has some measure of control to a place where he has not'.

Liability for animals depended at common law not on escape but on the mere 'keeping' of an animal of a wild species (*ferae naturae*) or the keeping of a domestic animal (*mansuetae naturae*) after knowledge that the particular animal had vicious propensities. The English law has been codified in the Animals Act 1971. Liability (s. 2) still depends on the mere keeping of the animal, and no more need be proved if it is of a 'dangerous species'. This means—s. 6 (2)—that it is either a species 'not normally domesticated' in the United Kingdom or one which can cause severe damage when fully grown (this could include animals such as deer as well as the obvious elephant). For animals *not* of a dangerous species, it has to be shown that the damage was of a kind natural to the

---

18 Cf. the Scottish case of *Kerr v Orkney (Earl)* (1857) 20 D 298.
19 In Scotland an Act of God is referred to as *damnum fatale*: *Caledonian Rly Co v Greenock Corpn* 1917 SC (HL) 56.
20 Actions for personal injuries under *Rylands v Fletcher* succeeded in *Shiffman v Venerable Order of the Hospital of St. John of Jerusalem* [1936] 1 All ER 557, *Hale v Jennings Bros* [1938] 1 All ER 579 and *Miles v Forest Rock Granite Co (Leicestershire) Ltd* (1918) 34 TLR 500, CA, but failed in *Howard v Furness Houlder Argentine Lines Ltd* [1936] 2 All ER 781—escape of steam on a ship—on the ground that the 'escape' was within the premises, not to a place outside. See also *Perry v Kendricks Transport Ltd* [1956] 1 All ER 154.

species or due to characteristics (known to the animal's keeper) not normally found in animals of that species, or not normally found except at particular times or circumstances. These known characteristics need not involve a tendency to violence; it is sufficient that they are not normally found, for example the fact that a particular horse is 'unpredictable': *Wallace v Newton* [1982] 2 All ER 106, [1982] 1 WLR 375[21]. They would also, more obviously, include the specially dangerous characteristics due to an animal being tethered as a guard dog: *Cummings v Granger* [1977] 1 All ER 104.

Apart from this absolute liability, there could always be liability for negligence in controlling animals and this is not altered by the Act, which merely replaces the old absolute liability: see s. 1.

Under the old law the keeper of the animal was deemed to accept the inherent risks and there was no liability, for instance, to a farm hand injured by a bull unless the employer was negligent: *Rands v McNeil* [1955] 1 QB 253, [1954] 3 All ER 593. Under the 1971 Act, s. 5(2), voluntary acceptance of a risk excludes liability but by s. 6(5) an employee who 'incurs a risk incidental to his employment' is *not* 'treated as accepting it voluntarily'. Liability is however excluded under s. 5(1) where injury is 'due wholly to the fault of the person who suffers it'; and a trespasser cannot complain of injury from an animal such as a guard dog kept for protection where such keeping is 'not unreasonable': s. 5(3).

In Scotland, the former rules about strict liability for animals are replaced (where the injury occurs after 8 June 1987) by the Animals (Scotland) Act 1987. Under the Act, liability is imposed on the person who was the 'keeper' at the time of the injury: s. 1(1)(a). This means— s. 5—the person who owned the animal or had possession of it, but if this was a child under 16 liability is imposed on the parent or other person having care and control of the child. The keeper continues to be liable for an animal which has escaped or been abandoned until someone else becomes the 'keeper' by assuming ownership or taking possession: but a person who detains an animal temporarily as a stray, or for safety reasons, is not liable as a 'keeper'.

To fall within the Act, an animal must belong to a species, or subdivision of a species, which by its 'physical attributes' or 'habits' is likely, if not controlled, to 'injure severely or kill persons or animals':

21 Or aggressiveness in guarding its territory: *Curtis v Betts* [1990] 1 All ER 760.

s. 1(1)(b). For this purpose a species may be subdivided in any way which is relevant to its behaviour, for instance sex (as with a ram or bull) or age: s. 1(2); so a mature rutting stag may be within the Act though a fawn or hind would not. The reference to 'severe injury' does not exclude small animals, because even a shrew may inflict a nasty injury. Under s. 1(3) all dogs are automatically deemed to satisfy the criteria; and so are animals listed in the Schedule to the Dangerous Wild Animals Act 1976, which, it may be noted, includes some birds and reptiles such as the ostrich and viper. Section 7 of the 1987 Act specifically excludes bacteria and other microbes, so presumably insects such as swarming bees and poisonous spiders are covered.

Liability under the Act extends only to injury due to the 'physical attributes' or 'habits' which bring the animal within the Act. In particular under s. 1(4) there is no liability for transmitting disease unless (in substance) it is incidental to a type of injury within the Act, e.g. rabies from a monkey bite.

There are three exceptions to liability. The first—s. 2(1)(a)—is where the injury was *wholly* due to the fault of the injured person. (If partially due, contributory negligence applies.) The second is where he voluntarily accepted the risk: s. 2(1)(b). The third—s. 2(1)(c) and (2)—is broadly where he trespassed on the land where the animal was kept; but if the animal was kept for guard purposes, it must be shown that it was reasonable to do so—a lion or crocodile would hardly be reasonable in Scotland—and if it was a guard dog s. 1 of the Guard Dogs Act must be complied with (controlled by a dog handler *or* chained, and in either case a warning notice displayed).

There was an alternative liability under the previous Scottish law for actual negligence in the management of an animal: *Henderson v John Stuart (Farms) Ltd* 1963 SC 245. This is not affected by the 1987 Act.

'Ultra-hazardous' activities

In the leading case of *Read v Lyons (J.) & Co Ltd* [1947] AC 156, [1946] 2 All ER 471, a bold attempt was made to establish absolute liability upon a much wider basis. In this case the plaintiff was employed by the Ministry of Supply to inspect the filling of shell-cases in an explosives factory operated by the defendants, and while working there she was injured by the explosion of a shell. Since there was no 'escape' of the shell from the factory, the case did not fall within the four corners of *Rylands v Fletcher*. It was nevertheless contended that *Rylands v Fletcher*, and the other strict liabilities quoted above, were simply exemplifications of a wider principle that if any person carries on 'ultra-hazardous' activities, such as the manufacture of explosives, he is liable for all damage due to the risks thereby created. This contention was rejected by the House of Lords. An 'ultra-hazardous' activity, therefore, does not give rise to an absolute liability: but it does call for 'a high degree of care'[1].

There is absolute liability by statute for injury caused by nuclear radiation from atomic installations and similar matters: Nuclear Installations Act 1965, ss. 7–16[2]. This legislation is too detailed and specialised to be analysed here at length.

---

1 It is unfortunate that the common law has not been left free to enlarge the field of absolute liability; such an enlargement is surely inevitable, sooner or later, and the amendment of the law of tort by Act of Parliament has rarely yielded satisfactory results. There is nothing ethically admirable or inflexible in the principle 'No liability without personal negligence', especially if, in *Rylands v Fletcher* cases, there is absolute liability for damage to property but not for personal injuries. Explosives are a greater public danger than mad dogs: and a resolute application of the maxim, *Qui sentit commodum, sentire debet et onus*, would justify the conclusion that, when an ultra-hazardous activity creates an exceptional risk, a man should pay for the consequences of the risk created for his own interest. There are analogies in other systems of law. In France and Quebec there is liability for risks created by things under one's control: *Quebec Railway etc. Co Ltd v Vandry* [1920] AC 662. In the early Soviet Civil Code for the R.S.F.S.R., Art. 404, there is liability for activities bound up with increased danger to others; under the Mexican Civil Code, Art. 1913, persons using mechanisms, instruments, apparatus, or materials dangerous in themselves or by reason of their speed, explosive nature, etc., are answerable except when the injured person was himself at fault. See these and other citations in F. H. Lawson, *Negligence in the Civil Law* (Oxford, 1950). In the U.S.A. (from which the term 'ultra-hazardous' is borrowed) there is also a trend towards absolute liability in these cases; see the discussion by Scott LJ in *Read v Lyons (J.) & Co Ltd* [1945] KB 216 at 225–233, [1945] 1 All ER 106 at 108–112. See further 'Strict Liability in the Law of Tort' (1957) 107 L Jo 659.

2 Amended by the Nuclear Installations Act 1969 and Part II of the Energy Act 1983.

Chapter 3

The employer's duty of care

1 General nature of the duty

It is the duty of an employer, acting personally or through his servants or agents, to take reasonable care for the safety of his workmen and other employees in the course of their employment. This duty extends in particular to the safety of the place of work, the plant and machinery, and the method and conduct of work: but it is not restricted to these matters. Lord Wright said in *Wilsons and Clyde Coal Co Ltd v English* [1938] AC 57 at 84, [1937] 3 All ER 628 at 644:

> 'The whole course of authority consistently recognises a duty which rests on the employer, and which is personal to the employer, to take reasonable care for the safety of his workmen, whether the employer be an individual, a firm or a company, and whether or not the employer takes any share in the conduct of the operations.'

Lord Oaksey said in *Paris v Stepney Borough Council* [1951] AC 367 at 384, [1951] 1 All ER 42 at 50:

> 'The duty of an employer towards his servant is to take reasonable care for his servant's safety in all the circumstances of the case.'

And, to add one more quotation, Parker LJ said in *Davie v New Merton Board Mills Ltd* [1958] 1 QB 210 at 237–8, [1958] 1 All ER 67 at 82:

> 'The duty owed by a master to his servant at common law can be stated in general terms as a duty to take reasonable care for the safety of his servants . . . if the master delegates . . . the performance of that

duty to another he remains liable for the failure of that other to exercise reasonable care ... this principle holds good whether the person employed[1] by the master is a servant, a full-time agent or an independent contractor.'

This duty exists whether the employment is inherently dangerous or not: *Speed v Thomas Swift & Co Ltd* [1943] KB 557, [1943] 1 All ER 539 per Goddard LJ; *Colfar v Coggins and Griffith (Liverpool) Ltd* [1945] AC 197, [1945] 1 All ER 326 per Viscount Simon LC.

The law has sometimes been stated in the alternative form that the employer must not expose his employees to 'unnecessary' risk, or 'unreasonable' risk: *Street v British Electricity Authority* [1952] 2 QB 399 at 406, [1952] 1 All ER 679 per Singleton LJ[2]. This is an older way of stating the law, and may be found, for example, in *Hutchinson v York, Newcastle and Berwick Rail Co* (1850) 5 Exch 343; *Bartonshill Coal Co v Reid* (1858) 3 Macq 266; *Smith v Baker & Sons* [1891] AC 325 at 362 (per Lord Herschell). In *Wilsons and Clyde Coal Co v English, supra,* the House of Lords used these earlier dicta as the foundation of their decision that the employer's duty extends to providing a safe system of work, and evidently regarded this as the better way of stating the law. In subsequent cases the House of Lords have generally treated the employer's duty as a simple duty to exercise reasonable care, adding, where appropriate, a reference to method of work, place of work, or

1   I.e. 'employed' as the employer's delegate to carry out his personal duty—not the 'person employed' to whom the duty is owed.

2   Cf. *Latimer v A.E.C. Ltd* [1952] 2 QB 701 at 708, [1952] 1 All ER 1302 at 1305; *Harris v Bright's Asphalt Contractors Ltd* [1953] 1 QB 617 at 626, [1953] 1 All ER 395 at 397; *Drummond v British Buildings Cleaners Ltd* [1954] 3 All ER 507 at 512; *Rands v McNeil* [1955] 1 QB 253 at 257, [1954] 3 All ER 593 at 595; *Morris v West Hartlepool Steam Navigation Co Ltd* [1956] AC 552 at 576, [1956] 1 All ER 385 at 400. This formula that the employer must not subject (or expose) his employees to unnecessary (or unreasonable) risks throws no real light upon any problem and is liable to cause confusion. If 'unnecessary risks' means risks which can be avoided by the exercise of reasonable care—the only legitimate meaning today—it is merely a roundabout way of saying that the employer must exercise due care. On the other hand, the phrase can be misunderstood as implying that the employer has no liability at all for the 'necessary', i.e. inherent, risks of the employment. This is exactly what some of the older cases meant, but is in flat contradiction to the present law. The resuscitation of obsolete phrases involves the risk of resuscitating, unintentionally, obsolete law. But the words used by Parker LJ in *Wilson v Tyneside Window Cleaning Co* [1958] 2 QB 110, [1958] 2 All ER 265—'The master's duty is general, to take all reasonable steps to avoid risk to his servants'—overcome this ambiguity.

plant, as in *English's* case[3]. The last word on the subject is in *Cavanagh v Ulster Weaving Co Ltd* [1960] AC 145, [1959] 2 All ER 745 where Lord Keith said:

> 'The ruling principle is that an employer is bound to take reasonable care for the safety of his workmen, and all other rules or formulas must be taken subject to this principle.'

Employer responsible though duty delegated

An employer remains liable if he delegates to another person—whether a manager, foreman, charge hand or outsider—responsibilities which involve his own primary duty for the safety of his employees. This usually arises in connection with the system of work or plant maintenance. So in *McDermid v Nash Dredging and Reclamation Co Ltd* [1987] AC 906, [1987] 2 All ER 878, HL, the employers were liable when the plaintiff was put under the orders of a tug-boat captain belonging to an associated company, who failed to put into operation a safe warning system when starting the engines. The High Court of Australia reached a similar conclusion in *Kondis v State Transport Authority* (1984) 55 ALR 225 where independent contractors engaged by the employers to assist with a crane failed to establish a safe system. In *Donnelly v Ronald Wilson (Plant Hire) Ltd* 1986 SLT 90, employers were liable for the default of an independent contractor who failed to make his regular inspection of plant, so that a steering defect was missed.

Inherent risks of the employment

At one time the courts had a tendency to say that an employee accepts the risk of the inherent dangers of the employment, and must rely, at any rate mainly, upon his own skill and nerve for his safety: cf. *Thomas v*

---

3   E.g. *Latimer v A.E.C. Ltd* [1953] AC 643, [1953] 2 All ER 449; *General Cleaning Contractors Ltd v Christmas* [1953] AC 180, [1952] 2 All ER 1110; *Richard Thomas and Baldwins Ltd v Cummings* [1955] AC 321, [1955] 1 All ER 285; *Carroll v Andrew Barclay & Sons Ltd* [1948] AC 477, [1948] 2 All ER 386; *Davie v New Merton Board Mills Ltd* [1959] AC 604, [1959] 1 All ER 346; *Qualcast (Wolverhampton) Ltd v Haynes* [1959] AC 743, [1959] 2 All ER 38.

Quartermaine (1887) 18 QBD 685; *Smith v Baker & Sons* [1891] AC 325 per Lord Bramwell (a rather harsh personal view in a dissenting opinion: see p. 15, *ante*). This is not now the law, if it ever was. If one employment is more dangerous than another, a greater degree of care must be taken: *Paris v Stepney Borough Council* [1951] AC 367, [1951] 1 All ER 42 per Lord Morton. If the employer is not able to eliminate the risk, he must at least take reasonable care to reduce it as far as possible: *General Cleaning Contractors Ltd v Christmas* [1953] AC 180, [1952] 2 All ER 1110; *Ellis v Ocean S.S. Co Ltd* [1955] 2 Lloyd's Rep 373, CA. These cases show that where a man is exposed to an unavoidable danger, as by working in a high place as a window-cleaner, or at a place near a ship's side where there is no rail, it is not sufficient for the employer to say that the employee must rely upon his own skill and judgment: the employer must take (and plan in advance where necessary) such safety measures as are practicable.

If, however, all due care has been exercised, and yet the workman sustains injury through an inherent risk of the employment, he cannot recover damages against the employer, because the employer is not liable in the absence of negligence: see, e.g. *Rands v McNeil* [1955] 1 QB 253, [1954] 3 All ER 593 (farm worker injured by bull); *Watt v Hertfordshire County Council* [1954] 2 All ER 368 (unsuitable lorry used by fire brigade in emergency); *Michie v Shenley* (1952) Times, 19 March (nurse injured by mental patient). In a hazardous occupation such as deep-sea fishing where risks are always present, it is not necessarily negligent to misjudge the risks, as where a skipper kept the men at work clearing the fish-deck in rough seas, and one of them was injured by an exceptionally heavy wave: *Saul v St. Andrew's Steam Fishing Co Ltd, The St Chad* (1965) 109 Sol Jo 392[4].

In a number of cases decided in the nineteenth century it was held that an employee could not succeed in an action for damages if he had knowledge of the danger. All these cases are now obsolete[5]. The employee's knowledge is always relevant, however, in determining whether he was guilty of contributory negligence, or in the rare cases where it is said that he voluntarily assumed a risk for his own purposes, so that the defence of *volenti non fit injuria* can be invoked.

---

4   The House of Lords refused leave to appeal in this case.
5   They were in substance overruled by *Smith v Baker & Sons* [1891] AC 325. For these cases see the 2nd edition of this book, pp. 60–61.

Liability rests upon tort rather than on contract[6]

Under the general law of tort, a duty of care arises when two persons are so closely and directly related that the activities of one of them may involve appreciable risk of injury to the other: *Donoghue v Stevenson* [1932] AC 562. Such a close and direct relationship exists between employer and employee. The employer invites the employee to enter his premises, to use his machinery and to follow his methods of work. Thus, under the ordinary principles of tort, the employer owes a duty of care and is liable for negligence.

Many of the earlier cases were decided before the law of negligence had been developed, and it was therefore said that the duties of the employer rested upon the contract of employment, for example, by Lord Herschell in *Smith v Baker & Sons* [1891] AC 325 at 362. But even before *Donoghue v Stevenson, supra*, the view had been expressed that the employer's liability could be based upon the ordinary law of negligence: see *Baker v James* [1921] 2 KB 674. This is now supported by the wording of s. 2 of the Crown Proceedings Act 1947, which includes, under the heading 'Liability of the Crown in tort', 'breach of those duties which a person owes to his servants or agents at common law by reason of being their employer'.

There is also a number of cases where it has been held that the employer's duty extends to persons who are not employed by him, such as a doctor who has come to the assistance of an injured workman, as well as to workers who are unpaid or on temporary loan. These decisions imply that the duty arises under the law of tort and not under a contract; and in *Davie v New Merton Board Mills Ltd* [1959] AC 604, [1959] 1 All ER 346 liability was regarded as arising in tort, though Viscount Simonds said that it might also be based on implied terms in a contract of employment. But in *Matthews v Kuwait Bechtel Corpn* [1959] 2 QB 57, [1959] 2 All ER 345, CA, a workman under an English contract, injured abroad, was held entitled to base his claim on contract

---

6   This passage in an earlier edition was criticised in the Court of Appeal so far as it implied that there is no liability in contract: *Matthews v Kuwait Bechtel Corpn* [1959] 2 QB 57, [1959] 2 All ER 345, CA. But it is now generally accepted that employer's liability finds its natural and logical place in the law of tort—see the *Davie* case—and this textbook can claim some credit for helping to establish this view. The text has, of course, been revised to show that, as the Court of Appeal held, liability can still be based on contract where there is some advantage in doing so.

to bring it within the jurisdiction of the English courts. It therefore appears that (at any rate where there is employment under contract, not just unpaid service or a temporary loan) it is optional to claim in either tort or contract: but contract would not normally be relied upon unless there are special advantages, and it would apparently (per Viscount Simonds in the *Davie* case) be necessary to allege the implied terms (safe plant, place of work and system) as was customary before the abolition of the defence of common employment. In Scotland, a seaman's claim has been treated as a claim in tort for the purpose of deciding the law applicable to an injury sustained in foreign territorial waters: *Mackinnon v Iberia Shipping Ltd* 1955 SC 20, 1955 SLT 49, [1954] 2 Lloyd's Rep 372. The alternative of claiming in contract was not discussed, and there seems no reason why the Scottish courts should not accept the decision in the *Kuwait Bechtel* case.

Whether the duty is based on tort or on contract, the employer is not under an absolute duty to ensure safety, and negligence must always be proved. There is no warranty that the machinery and plant are safe, or that the system of work will be free from risk: *Weems v Mathieson* (1861) 4 Macq 215, 149 PR 322 per Lord Wensleydale: *Wilsons and Clyde Coal Co v English, supra*, per Lord Wright; *General Cleaning Contractors Ltd v Christmas, supra*, per Lord Tucker; *Davie v New Merton Board Mills Ltd, supra*[7].

The Health and Safety at Work Act 1974 has now imposed on employers a general *statutory* duty for the safety of persons employed. Failure to comply with this may result in a prosecution but does not give rise to liability for damages. The common law duty is left unaltered, and the wording of the new statutory duty is largely based upon it (see Chapter 7).

2 The persons to whom the duty is owed: regular servants, temporary servants and volunteers

The duty to take care depends upon the existence of the relationship of master and servant, i.e. the relationship which exists between an

---

7 While this is certainly the law, there is no compelling reason why it should be so, and there would be good sense in an implied warranty that plant is fit for its purpose. This would overcome difficulties about defective tools where the maker cannot be traced.

employer and his workmen or other employees. It is usually created by a contract of service or employment (e.g. an agreement to work for a weekly wage). Exceptionally it may arise from the loan of a servant to a temporary master, or when one person volunteers to work for another without payment.

In general the relationship of master and servant exists when the master has the right to tell the servant not only what to do but also *how to do it*. If a man is employed to do work, but can decide for himself how to do it—a window-cleaner or repairer for example—he is not an employee or servant but an independent contractor. An employer does not owe any general duty of care to an independent contractor: the latter carries out his work in his own way, and if, for instance, he borrows an item of equipment such as a cement mixer it is his own responsibility to see that it is properly fenced: *Jones v Minton Construction Ltd* (1973) 15 KIR 309. Similarly the duties under the Factories Act and regulations are in general owed only to 'persons employed', but under the Health and Safety at Work Act 1974 duties may also be imposed for the safety of the 'self-employed'[8]. The

8   *Distinction between employed person and independent contractor.* The view taken in the text—which certainly has the support of the House of Lords—is that the right of 'control' (even if it is the sort of control which can be exercised only through a specialist) is the decisive criterion for common law liability. However, a large number of cases (e.g. *Market Investigations Ltd v Ministry of Social Security* [1969] 2 QB 173, [1968] 3 All ER 732) have been decided on the meaning of 'employed person' for the purpose of the National Insurance Acts which say that the court must have regard to several different criteria, not only control and method of payment, but whether the worker is part of the employer's organisation or has his own little organisation, whether paid by wages or otherwise, whether he provides the tools and materials. Since, unfortunately, none of these factors is decisive and they often point in different directions, the result in borderline cases is quite arbitrary. This is not satisfactory in the different context of the Factories Act. Nevertheless, these cases were applied in *Maurice Graham Ltd v Brunswick* (1974) 16 KIR 158 to a prosecution for breaches of regulations under the Factories Act where two men were employed on piecework remuneration which they could divide as they pleased: it was held that, since it was a borderline case, the justices were entitled to find as a fact that they were 'persons employed'. Where men were said to be engaged as a 'lump labour force' but hired and fired, told what to do and supplied with tools like employees, it was held that to describe them as self-employed sub-contractors was contrary to the facts and they were 'employed': *Ferguson v Dawson & Partners (Contractors) Ltd* [1976] 3 All ER 817. When, however, the facts could fit either alternative, an agreement to be 'self-employed' is effective: *Massey v Crown Life Insurance Co* [1978] 2 All ER 576. A man working on his own as a rough-caster on a building site, remunerated not at a basic rate but for work actually done, and paying his own tax and insurance was held to be self-employed and the employer owed no duty to him in that capacity (nor, on the facts, in any other capacity): *Poliskie v Lane* 1981 SLT 282.

Diving Regulations are a notable example where such a duty has been imposed. In some cases a duty of care may be owed to an independent contractor for the safety of the place of work or of plant he is allowed to use: see generally Chapter 5.

On the other hand, if there is in the last resort a right to control the way in which the work is done, it does not matter how highly skilled or professional the character of the work may be, nor is it material that the employee is allowed in practice to act entirely in accordance with his own judgment: he is still in law a 'servant'. For example, a surgeon on a full-time engagement at a hospital is the servant of the hospital authority: *Cassidy v Ministry of Health* [1951] 2 KB 343, [1951] 1 All ER 574. The test to be applied was clearly stated by Lord Porter in *Mersey Docks and Harbour Board v Coggins and Griffith (Liverpool) Ltd* [1974] AC 1 at 17, [1946] 2 All ER 345 at 351:

> 'It is not enough that the task to be performed should be under his [the master's] control, he must also control the method of performing it. It is true that in most cases no orders as to how a job should be done are given or required. The man is left to do his own work in his own way, but the ultimate question is not what specific orders, or whether any specific orders, were given, but who is entitled to give the orders as to how the work should be done.'

It is this right, in the last resort, to exercise detailed control, which gives rise to the two chief legal consequences of the relationship:

(i) the master is liable for the acts and omissions of his servants in the course of the employment;

(ii) as explained in the preceding section, he owes a duty to the servants themselves to exercise reasonable care for their safety.

Temporary loan of servant

The relationship may arise upon a temporary basis, if a workman is lent by his permanent employer to a temporary employer. There is, however, a distinction between lending a workman on the one hand, and merely making available the benefit of his services, on the other hand. In the former case, the temporary master has the right of control; in the latter case, control remains with the permanent employer.

It is only in rare and exceptional cases that the right of control over an employee is transferred to a temporary master, and the burden of proving such a transfer is a heavy one: *Mersey Docks and Harbour Board v Coggins and Griffith (Liverpool) Ltd* [1947] AC 1, [1946] 2 All ER 345. In particular, as that case shows[9], it is not usually discharged where a man is lent together with valuable equipment such as a crane, or as an expert: *Savory v Holland Hannen and Cubitts (Southern) Ltd* [1964] 3 All ER 18 (shotfirer): nor even when a driver is on *permanent* loan with his lorry, the arrangement being that the hirers can tell him what to do but not how to do it: *O'Reilly v I.C.I. Ltd* [1953] 3 All ER 382: but transfer of control may be inferred more readily when a man is lent on his own, without equipment, especially an unskilled man: *Garrard v A. E. Southey & Co and Standard Telephones and Cables Ltd* [1952] 2 QB 174, [1952] 1 All ER 597 (electrician lent and placed under orders of foreman of temporary employers); *Denham v Midland Employers' Mutual Assurance Ltd* [1955] 2 QB 437, [1955] 2 All ER 561 (labourer lent by brickfield company to assist contractors drilling on brickfield, under orders of contractors' foreman). A fitter sent to do work on machinery at a papermill, who was simply told what the job was and not supervised in any way, remained under the control of his own employers, who were liable when he dropped part of the machine: *Moir v Wide Arc Services Ltd* 1987 SLT 495. There is not necessarily transfer of control where a man is lent, with others, under the supervision of a foreman lent by his general employers: *Johnson v A. H. Beaumont Ltd* [1953] 2 QB 184, [1953] 2 All ER 106 (trimmers for unloading ship): in such a case the question must be whether the foreman is under the control of the temporary employer in matters of detail, or is answerable to his permanent employers. In *Brogan v William Allan Smith & Co Ltd* 1965 SLT 175, where a party under a chargehand were lent as a unit to do electrical work and paid for on a time basis, the customer's foreman simply pointing out what had to be done, the normal employers were liable to an apprentice in the party for negligence by the chargehand. Where dock labourers had regularly worked for stevedores for many years, though the dock board were their nominal employers and paid their wages, it was held that the stevedores were in the position of

9   And as the House of Lords again emphasised in *John Young & Co (Kelvinhaugh) Ltd v O'Donnell* 1958 SLT (Notes) 46, (1958) Times, 25 July. See also *Boyle v Glasgow Corpn* 1975 SC 238 (no transfer of craneman hired with crane); *Park v Tractor Shovels* 1980 SLT 94 (workman at steel site engaged on repair of site vehicles, assisted by workman of another employer using lifting machine: certainly no transfer of second man to employer of first).

temporary employers so as to be liable for an unsafe system of work: *Gibb v United Steel Companies Ltd* [1957] 2 All ER 110. But it must be shown that 'entire and absolute control' has been taken by the temporary employer, and the assignment of a gang of stevedores to do a ship, although the tasks they do will be indicated by the ship's officers, is not sufficient: *Bhoomidas v Port of Singapore Authority* [1978] 1 All ER 956.

Once the right of control is transferred, the temporary master is subject to all the ordinary liabilities of an employer, and owes the employer's ordinary duty of care to the temporary servant: *Holt v W. H. Rhodes & Son Ltd* [1949] 1 All ER 478 (unsafe method of work); *Garrard v Southey, supra* (unsafe plant): *Denham v Midland Employers' Mutual Assurance Ltd, supra* (law stated in general terms by Denning LJ *obiter*: 'The right of control carries with it the burden of responsibility'): where there is no transfer of control, the employee simply has the ordinary common law rights, against other persons concerned: *O'Reilly v ICI Ltd, supra*; *Leckie v Caledonian Glass Co Ltd* 1958 SLT 25. It was said in *Savory v Holland Hannen and Cubitts (Southern) Ltd* [1964] 3 All ER 18 that transfer is no longer important, because as occupier or contractor the temporary user of services has the same duty of 'reasonable care in the circumstances'. This seems dubious: 'the circumstances' can only mean those relevant to the particular duty, which is not the same for an employer as for an occupier, or for a head contractor who is not the man's employer. It cannot be assumed that a person who is not the employer is responsible for a safe method of work or for providing assistance, although he may have such duties where he assumes control as an employer; see further below, 'Volunteers' and 'Persons analogous to employers'[10].

Most of these cases about the 'temporary' loan of an employee have turned on which of the employers, the permanent or the temporary one, was vicariously liable for the acts of the employee on loan when some third party was injured. They do also show that a 'temporary' employer who takes full control assumes the full duty of care towards the employee. This does not necessarily mean that the general employer is exonerated. His duty is a personal one, for which he remains responsible though he may delegate the performance of it, for example in arranging a safe method of work, to some other person.

10 Thus in *Poliskie v Lane* 1981 SLT 282, no duty was owed by anyone to a self-employed man on a building site.

Volunteers

In principle, the relationship of master and servant is also created, and all the usual consequences follow, where a plaintiff has volunteered to do work without pay under the orders of another person. It is, of course, essential that the master should have given his consent to the creation of the relationship, and where a volunteer has been invited to assist workmen in their tasks, the question will arise whether the workmen were authorised by their master to invite assistance.

The authorities on this subject are discussed in Chapter 24 on Voluntary Assumption of Risk.

The employer's duty of care extends to a doctor called to assist workmen who have been put in a position of danger by the employer: *Ward v T. E. Hopkins & Son Ltd, Baker v T. E. Hopkins & Son Ltd* [1959] 3 All ER 225 (men poisoned by fumes in well); and similarly to a volunteer rescuer in a railway accident: *Chadwick v British Transport Commission* [1967] 2 All ER 945.

Persons analogous to employers

Since the employer's duty of care, particularly as to method of work, springs from the fact of control, an analogous duty may fall on a person with similar authority, such as the Chief Constable of a police force: *Robertson v Bell* 1969 SLT 119 (safety at road blocks): or the authorities at a technical school: *Butt v Inner London Education Authority* (1968) 66 LGR 379 (unfenced printing machine). So too where anyone exercises a limited degree of control or supervision, there is a duty of care to the same extent: as at a prison: *Ferguson v Home Office* (1977) Times, 8 October (prisoner not instructed how to use machine saw safely.)

Safety consultants engaged by contractors owe a duty of care to the contractors' employees: *Driver v William Willet (Contractors) Ltd* [1969] 1 All ER 665. Principal contractors, or building owners acting as principal contractors, who supervise and co-ordinate the activities of different sub-contractors, are responsible for arranging safety measures so far as the activities of sub-contractors may endanger one another's men: *McArdle v Andmac Roofing Co* [1967] 1 All ER 583 (this duty, however, unlike an employer's, could be discharged by giving adequate instructions to sub-contractors and where necessary providing materials: the judgment of Edmund Davies LJ is valuable on the extent of the duty in such a case). An architect does not in general exercise control or supervision over how work is done, but merely indicates what work is required to comply with the contract: *Clayton v Woodman & Son (Builders) Ltd* [1962] 2 QB 533, [1962] 2 All ER 33. But if an architect positively intervenes about the way in which work is to be done—as the court of first instance held in the *Clayton* case, [1961] 3 All ER 249—or the essential plan does not take safety into account, he may be liable. In *Clay v A. J. Crump & Sons Ltd* [1964] 1 QB 533, [1963] 3 All ER 687 the Court of Appeal held that an architect planning a demolition and construction operation owed a duty of care to workmen when the question arose whether a certain wall could safely be left standing, and was liable (together with the contractors) for failing to investigate the wall sufficiently. The chain of causation was not broken by the intervening opportunities of the contractors to inspect. Where a fishing boat was run on a profit-sharing basis between the owner and the crew, the owner's duty was to provide reasonably safe gear for the joint adventure: *Parker v Walker* 1961 SLT 252. When a sub-contractor without equipment of his own undertakes work, it may be an implied contractual term that reasonably safe equipment will be supplied within a reasonable time after request, but if the sub-contractor injures himself by using makeshift equipment the damage will be too remote: *Quinn v Burch Brothers (Builders) Ltd* [1966] 2 QB 370, [1966] 2 All ER 283.

Duty owed to each individual

The employer's duty of care is owed to each workman or employee as an individual: *Paris v Stepney Borough Council* [1951] AC 367, [1951] 1 All ER 42. Therefore, it must take into account any special weakness or peculiarity of a workman which is (or ought to be) known to the employer, such as the fact that he is one-eyed: *Porteous v National Coal Board* 1967 SLT 117[11]. Also, a lower duty may be owed to a workman who is experienced and familiar with the dangers: *Qualcast (Wolverhampton) Ltd v Haynes* [1959] AC 743, [1959] 2 All ER 38; and a

---

11 *Aliter* if the employer neither knows nor ought to know of the peculiarity: *Clayton v Caledonian Stevedoring Co Ltd* (1948) 81 Ll L Rep 332 (sensitive skin); *James v Hepworth and Grandage Ltd* [1968] 1 QB 94, [1967] 2 All ER 829 (illiterate man unable to read warning notice).

higher duty to a workman who has not sufficient experience for his task and needs help and supervision: *Byers v Head Wrightson & Co Ltd* [1961] 2 All ER 538.

3 Liability for the negligence of fellow-servants and independent contractors

As indicated above (section 1), an employer always remains liable when he delegates responsibilities which involve his own primary duties. If they do not, he is vicariously liable for his own employees but not—in general—for others.

(1) Fellow-servants

It is a general rule in the law of tort that an employer is liable for the acts or omissions of his servants in the course of their employment. Formerly, under the doctrine of common employment, this rule did not apply where one servant was injured as a result of the negligence of a fellow-servant: but this doctrine was abolished by s. 1 (1) of the Law Reform (Personal Injuries) Act 1948, which reads as follows:

> 'It shall not be a defence to an employer who is sued in respect of personal injuries caused by the negligence of a person employed by him, that that person was at the time the injuries were caused in common employment with the person injured.'

By s. 1 (3) of the Act, any agreement in a contract of service or apprenticeship, or any collateral agreement, is declared to be void so far as it would have the effect of excluding or limiting the liability of the employer for the negligence of fellow-servants. In *Smith v British European Airways Corpn* [1951] 2 KB 893, [1951] 2 All ER 737, an airways employee, while being carried in an aircraft, was killed in a collision due to the negligence of his fellow-servant, the pilot. He had entered into a pension scheme, collateral to his contract of service, and one of the terms of the scheme was that the employers were not to be liable for damages or any other payment except the benefits under the scheme. This clause was held to be void. An agreement in a seaman's contract that Norwegian law should apply was also held void because Norwegian law excluded liability for a fellow-servant: *Brodin v A/R Seljan* 1973 SLT 198. Under the Unfair Contract Terms Act 1977, s. 1(1) (or s. 16 under Scottish law) liability for negligence causing injury or death cannot now be excluded by any contract or notice disclaiming liability.

An employer, therefore, is now liable for the negligence of his servants towards one another in the same way as he is liable for their negligence towards the world at large: he is liable, in other words, provided that the negligence occurs in the course of their employment.

Before this change was made in the law, the employer's duty of care extended only to the fundamental conditions of the employment—the safety of the plant, the premises and the method of work—and where there was negligence by fellow-servants in these matters, it was treated as the personal negligence of the employer for which he was responsible. Now he is also liable for the negligence (and other torts) of one workman towards another in routine matters: and the two liabilities have to be integrated together, 'statute law and common law should be integrated as one law', so that the employer's duty is, quite generally, to take reasonable care for the safety of his servants: see *Broom v Morgan* [1953] 1 QB 597, [1953] 1 All ER 849, per Denning L J. The employer is liable for a casual act of negligence in the course of the work, as where one workman, who was hammering a piece of steel held by another workman, accidentally struck him: *Lindsay v Connell & Co* 1951 SC 281: though (somewhat surprisingly) the fact that one workman accidentally hits another with a hammer in such a case has been held not to be sufficient evidence of negligence: *Baxter v Colvilles Ltd* 1959 SLT 325. But vicarious liability has still to be kept distinct from personal liability. In cases of vicarious liability, the only question to be answered is, was the fellow-servant negligent? If he was, the employer is vicariously liable: *Stavely Iron & Chemical Co Ltd v Jones* [1956] AC 627, [1956] 1 All ER 403 per Lord Morton. And the employer is still liable, although, on personal grounds, e.g. because he is the plaintiff's husband, the fellow-servant is immune from being sued: *Broom v Morgan, supra.*

As regards 'the course of the employment', the servant is acting in the course of his employment whenever he is doing the employer's work. He may be doing it negligently instead of diligently, or fraudulently instead of honestly, but the employer is still liable for his acts. Thus in *Century*

Insurance Co Ltd v Northern Ireland Road Transport Board [1942] AC 509, [1942] 1 All ER 491 a driver, who was delivering petrol in bulk, stood by while the petrol was flowing from the lorry to the tank, began to smoke, and threw the match down, with the result that a fire was started. The employers were held liable on the ground that smoking while delivering petrol in bulk was negligence in the discharge of the duty of delivery.

Similarly if a storekeeper exposes a naked light while in charge of a store where petrol is kept, it is negligence in his capacity as storekeeper: *Dunk v Hawkes, Sanders Ltd* (1953) Times, 27 October, CA; when a fork-lift driver, finding a lorry in his way, got in to move it although not authorised to drive a lorry, that also was in the course of his employment: *Kay v I.T.W. Ltd* [1968] 1 QB 140, [1967] 3 All ER 22. It is often found that when a workman did the act which caused injury, he was acting in contravention of orders—possibly orders issued under an Act of Parliament, possibly orders emanating from the employer. In such circumstances, recourse must be had to a distinction established by *Kerr v Dunlop (James) & Co* [1926] AC 377 and other authorities interpreting the words 'course of the employment' in the Workmen's Compensation Acts: that is, the distinction between *orders which limit the scope of the employment*, and orders which merely regulate the methods to be used. In the mining industry it is a strict rule—imposed by statute—that shots must not be fired except by an authorised person: and this prohibition clearly has the effect that these duties are altogether removed from the province of the ordinary miner. Therefore, in *Alford v National Coal Board* [1952] 1 All ER 754, where an unauthorised person took it upon himself to fire a shot, it was held that the act was outside the scope of his employment and the employers were not liable for this act. But where, in the course of his work, an apprentice, though not authorised to drive, took it upon himself to move a van out of his way, the employers were held liable: *Mulholland v Wm. Reid & Leys Ltd* 1958 SLT 285[12]. Where, as on a building site, it is the accepted practice that employees of different contractors will give one another occasional assistance, such assistance is in the course of their employment: *Park v Tractor Shovels* 1980 SLT 94.

12 In *Iqbal v London Transport Executive* (1974) 16 KIR 329, on the other hand where, as a bus was about to leave a depot, the driver asked the conductor to get someone to move another bus which was in the way, it was held that the conductor had clearly moved outside his authorised duties when he moved it himself.

A case of a different type is *Smith v Crossley Bros Ltd* (1951) 95 Sol Jo 655, where two apprentices, by way of a practical joke, injected compressed air into the body of a third apprentice: here they were clearly acting (as an old case puts it) 'on a frolic of their own', and the employers could not be held responsible. The apprentices were not carrying out authorised duties in an unauthorised manner, but were doing an act which was not part of their work at all[13]. Similarly, miners who retired to a quiet part of the waste to smoke, in disregard of strict regulations, were doing something outside the scope of their employment: *Kirby v National Coal Board* 1959 SLT 7; and where demolition workers were permitted to use the employer's van for refreshment during the lunch hour, the workman driving the van was not acting in the course of the employment: *Hilton v Thomas Burton (Rhodes) Ltd* [1961] 1 All ER 74. But men authorised to tell a boy what to do were acting in the course of their employment when they misused their authority to play a practical joke by telling him to put his hand in the aperture of a machine: *Chapman v Oakleigh Animal Products* (1970) 8 KIR 1063, and when a man pushed a truck just a little off course to knock the plaintiff's duck-board as a practical joke, it was not so divergent from his work that it ceased to be part of it: *Harrison v Michelin Tyre Co Ltd* [1985] 1 All ER 918. When a workman, having finished his work, cycled to another part of the premises where he had to collect his pay, it was held that he was cycling in the course of his employment: *Staton v National Coal Board* [1957] 2 All ER 667; and employers were held vicariously liable when workmen stampeded down stairs at the end of work: *Bell v Blackwood Morton & Sons Ltd* 1960 SC 11. Where two men travelled to a distant work site in the car of one of them, and were paid wages for the time spent in doing so—and not just travelling allowances—the driving was in the course of their employment: *Smith v Stages* [1989] AC 928, [1989] 1 All ER 833, HL.

But where a fire brigade operated a 'go-slow' and arrived too late to put out a fire, the employers were not liable because the men were not

---

13 Cf. *O'Reilly v National Rail and Tramway Appliances Ltd* [1966] 1 All ER 499 (man tempted another to hit live shell among scrap metal). *Coddington v International Harvesters of Great Britain Ltd* (1969) 6 KIR 146 (men lit tin of paint thinners for warmth; man passing kicked it over as a joke); *Wood v Duttons Brewery* (1971) 115 Sol Jo 186 (fellow-employee induced to drink caustic soda from cask in belief it was beer: employers not at fault for failing to label in anticipation of such an accident).

performing their ordinary duty—to drive *expeditiously* to a fire—'going slow' could not be described as a mode of doing it at all: *General Engineering Services Ltd v Kingston and St. Andrew Corp* [1988] 3 All ER 867, [1989] 1 WLR 69.

The cases discussed above are all cases of negligence. Other torts by a fellow-servant are not often encountered in practice, but must be mentioned briefly. As a matter of principle, an employer is liable for all torts committed by the fellow-servant in the course of the employment, including, for example, assault and libel[14]. But if the tort is of the kind which, like negligence, consists of a breach of duty, it must be shown that the duty, as well as the breach, arose in the course of the employment: *Twine v Bean's Express Ltd* [1946] 1 All ER 202 (lift given by driver to workman without employer's permission: no liability)[15].

It is established that fellow-servants owe a duty to take reasonable care for one another's safety, and it may be negligence even if workmen merely agree with one another not to carry out orders (e.g. to make the roof of a mine safe) or decide to unload cargo by an unsafe method which saves trouble: *Stapley v Gypsum Mines Ltd* [1953] AC 663, [1953] 2 All ER 478; *Williams v Port of Liverpool Stevedoring Co Ltd* [1956] 2 All ER 69. A workman who consents to such an agreement will, of course, have his damages reduced in proportion to his share of the blame, and in some cases the defence of *volenti non fit injuria* (see Chapter 24) may succeed.

The standard of care required from a workman is that appropriate to his status and duties, e.g. to act as a reasonable and prudent crane-driver: and it is not correct (in the context of liability for an employee's

---

14 In the U.S.A. violent quarrels in the course of work seem to be quite common and there are numerous authorities on the subject of assaults.

15 In recent years there has been a controversy, which is not yet finally settled, about the nature of the employer's vicarious liability. One view is that the employer is liable for the servant's *liability*: *Young v Edward Box & Co Ltd* [1951] 1 TLR 789. The other view is that he is liable for the servant's *act*: *Broom v Morgan* [1953] 1 QB 597, [1953] 1 All ER 849, per Denning LJ: this implies that the employer is not liable unless the servant's act is a breach of the employer's personal duties, and would limit the employer's liability to cases of negligence and breaches of statutory duty imposed directly on the employer. The true view, surely, is that the employer is liable for the servant's act, but that where the act is in itself a tort, the tortious quality of the act is also imputed to the employer. At any rate, the theory that an employer's liability for negligence arises on the ground that the servant's conduct is a breach of the employer's duty of care is no longer tenable since *Staveley Iron & Chemical Co Ltd v Jones* [1956] AC 627, [1956] 1 All ER 403. See also a valuable article by Prof. F. H. Newark in 17 Mod LR 102 and one by the present author in (1955) 105 L Jo 437.

negligence) to say that everyday acts of carelessness or inadvertence in a factory cannot amount to negligence, or to apply an especially lenient standard of conduct in a case where workmen are collaborating together and working in a team: *Stavely Iron & Chemical Co Ltd v Jones* [1956] AC 627, [1956] 1 All ER 403. Thus an experienced building workman should know that a masonry nail is hard and brittle, and refrain from hitting it with a heavy hammer when a fellow-workman is near enough to be struck by fragments: *Bowden v Barbrooke Brothers* (1973) 15 KIR 232. Many everyday tasks are simple, requiring no more than *attention to what is being done* and holding something firmly or moving something in the right direction. A mistake in such a task is, therefore, a strong indication of want of care. Yet in Scotland, somewhat surprisingly, it has been held that where one workman accidentally hits another with a hammer, or lets go of a barrel which he and another are lifting, that is not in itself evidence of negligence: *Baxter v Colvilles Ltd* 1959 SLT 325; *Dillon v Clyde Stevedoring Co Ltd* 1967 SLT 103[16]. In New Zealand, more sensibly, where a man tripped and sent the garbage can he was carrying through a window, it was held that tripping is not neutral: it calls for an explanation, and the maxim *res ipsa loquitur* applies in the absence of an explanation: *Frederic Maeder Proprietary Ltd v Wellington City* [1969] NZLR 222. Another example of negligence in the ordinary actions of life is *O'Connor v State of South Australia* (1976) 14 SASR 187, where a judge opened the door into a brother-judge's room and struck that judge's secretary in the back (she, however, was 50 per cent to blame for standing in the 'danger zone'!). In the English Court of Appeal it was held to be *res ipsa loquitur* where a heavy panel fell while several men were moving it, and in the absence of any rebutting evidence by the defendants, the claim succeeded: *Bennett v Chemical Construction (G.B.) Ltd* [1971] 3 All ER 822. It was likewise *res ipsa loquitur* when a pot of hot water fell off a tray as it was put down: *McPherson v Devon Area Health Authority* [1986] CLY unreported appeal No. 44. This approach receives strong support from *McCann v J. R. McKeller (Alloys) Ltd* 1969 SC (HL) 1;

---

16 Reference was made to English cases similarly decided on the facts: *Sowerby v Maltby* [1953] 1 Lloyd's Rep 462; *O'Leary v Glen Line Ltd* [1953] 1 Lloyd's Rep 601; *Sims v T. and J. Harrison* [1954] 1 Lloyd's Rep 354 (dropping, or letting go of, a bag of sugar, a bale of rubber, the tail of a tent). This line of cases seems, to say the least, pedantic. At least, one would think, to hit another man's hand with a hammer, or drop one end of a load without warning, calls for an explanation such as 'his hand was too close', 'it was too heavy,' or even 'a wasp stung me'—and such explanations may well indicate an unsafe system of work.

there the House of Lords sustained the verdict of a Scottish jury that it was negligent for a workman to drop his end of a heavy steel ingot, although he excused himself by saying that his hand was suddenly 'jagged' or 'pricked' by a sharp edge[17]. In *Hill v James Crowe (Cases) Ltd* [1978] 1 All ER 812, where a badly nailed packing case collapsed, the inference was drawn that one of the employees of the maker had been negligent.

Breach of statutory duty has given rise to difficult questions where the duty is imposed directly on the servant, for example, the statutory duties which have to be observed by shotfirers in coal mines. If the duty arises in the course of the employment, the employers ought in principle to be liable for a breach of the duty if the breach also arises in the course of the employment. On the other hand, it has been argued that a statutory duty which is imposed on the servant personally does not flow from the master's orders and does not concern him. Lord MacDermott said in *Harrison v National Coal Board* [1951] AC 639 at 671, [1951] 1 All ER 1102 at 1120:

> 'To my mind this, as a general proposition, finds no support in principle or authority. Vicarious liability is not confined to negligence. It arises from the servant's tortious act in the scope of his employment.'

Nevertheless the House of Lords have left the question open, both in *Harrison v National Coal Board* and in subsequent cases: see *Stapley v*

---

17 This case, being decided on the facts, has not been reported in England. The pursuer alleged negligence in failing to grip firmly, or give warning before letting go. The fellow-workman gave evidence that he was pricked suddenly by the sharp edge and dropped his end 'automatically' without time to give warning. The decision of the House was that on the evidence the jury were entitled to give a verdict of negligence which could not be disturbed. Lord Guest said that the fact that an action was 'automatic and instinctive' did not mean it was not negligent—it was no more than saying 'he jerked his hand away without thinking'. Lord Denning said that the dropping of the ingot was 'some evidence of negligence': the jury might have rejected the explanation either because they did not believe it, or because they thought the prick was not severe enough to excuse letting go. Lord Upjohn said that a sudden injury may excuse dropping a thing involuntarily, but 'it all depends on the degree of pain and . . . unexpectedness . . .' He thought there could only have been a pinprick. Lord Diplock said the jury could have found that the hand was not pricked at all, or the prick was not severe enough to justify dropping without warning. Lord Donovan (who alone dissented) said that the happening of the accident 'raises no presumption of negligence—otherwise much existing authority would have to be overruled'. The result of the case seems to be that the authorities in footnote 16, p. 99, *supra*, are indeed overruled: it supports entirely the comment in that note.

Gypsum Mines Ltd [1953] AC 663, [1953] 2 All ER 478; *National Coal Board v England* [1954] AC 403, [1954] 1 All ER 546[18].

In Scotland it has been expressly held that an employer is liable for breach of a statutory duty imposed on a servant in the performance of his work: *Nicol v National Coal Board* (14 May 1952), Ct of Sess per Lord Guthrie (noted in 102 L Jo 357). But there is no liability for a breach of regulations occurring outside the course of the employment, as where miners went to smoke in a quiet part of the waste: *Kirby v National Coal Board* 1959 SLT 7.

Employers are not relieved from liability for the negligence of a servant by the fact that they are not allowed to do the work themselves, but are compelled by statute to employ a qualified person: *Wilson and Clyde Coal Co Ltd v English* [1938] AC 57, [1937] 3 All ER 628 (manager of mine).

(2) Independent contractors

A person is not in general liable for the negligence of independent contractors—or agents—to the same extent as he is liable for the negligence of servants. Thus he is not liable for 'casual' acts of negligence by contractors, such as dropping an object from a structure they are erecting on his behalf. But it is a general rule of law that:

> 'a person causing something to be done, the doing of which casts on him a duty, cannot escape from the responsibility attaching on him of seeing that duty performed by delegating it to a contractor': per Lord Blackburn in *Dalton v Angus* (1881) 6 App Cas 740 at 829.

The employer's duty of care falls into this special category. In *Davie v New Merton Board Mills Ltd* [1959] AC 604; [1959] 1 All ER 346 Lord Tucker said:

> '. . . the employer may delegate the performance of his obligations in this sphere to someone who is more properly described as a contractor

---

18 Curiously, no reference was made in these cases to *Alford v National Coal Board* [1952] 1 All ER 754, where the decision to remit the case to the Court of Session turns on the necessary basis that the employers would be vicariously liable if breach of statutory duty were proved. In Australia it has apparently been decided that there is no vicarious liability for breach of statutory duty: *Darling Island Stevedoring & Lighterage Co v Ling* (1957) 31 ALJ 208 (but the author has only seen a short note of the case).

than a servant, but this does not affect the liability of the employer, he will be just as much liable for his negligence as for that of his servant. Such a contractor is entrusted by the employer with the performance of the employer's personal duty.'

Employers have therefore been held liable for the failure of a tug-boat captain employed by an associated company, under whose orders the plaintiff was working, to put into operation a safe system of work: *McDermid v Nash Dredging and Reclamation Co Ltd* [1987] AC 906, [1987] 2 All ER 878; similarly in Australia for the failure of independent contractors assisting with a crane to establish a safe system: *Kondis v State Transport Authority* (1984) 55 ALR 225; for the failure of contractors to install sufficient insulation in an electrical kiosk: *Paine v Colne Valley Electricity Supply Co Ltd and British Insulated Cables Ltd* [1938] 4 All ER 803; for the failure of contractors to make a regular inspection of plant as stipulated: *Donnelly v Ronald Wilson (Plant Hire) Ltd* 1986 SLT 90; and in the Supreme Court of Canada employers have been held liable for the failure of contractors to follow a safe method in operating machinery at a farm: *Marshment v Borgstrom*, [1942] SCR 374. More generally, it was held in *Wilsons and Clyde Coal Co Ltd v English* [1938] AC 57, [1937] 3 All ER 628 that the employer's personal duty cannot be delegated so as to divest him of responsibility, at any rate so far as it concerns plant, place of work and method of work, and although the case concerned liability for superior employees the principle applies with equal force to independent contractors.

In practice the difficulty is to determine how far the personal duty of the employer extends, and whether the negligent person was acting as the delegate of the employer. It is not necessary that the duty of care should be expressly delegated: it is enough that the employer should engage the contractor to do work, such as construction of a scaffold, in which the employer's own duty of care is involved. But there is no vicarious liability, under common law principles, for a person who is not in any true sense the delegate or agent of the employer. In *Davie v New Merton Board Mills Ltd* [1959] AC 604, [1959] 1 All ER 346, the House of Lords held that where a tool (or other plant) is bought from a reputable supplier, who in turn bought from the manufacturer, the latter cannot be regarded as a person to whom the employer's duty is delegated, and the employer is not liable for his negligence in the course of manufacture. The House also said that it makes no difference if the article is bought direct from the manufacturer, and overruled the decision to the contrary in *Donnelly v Glasgow Corpn* 1953 SC 107. Similarly where trucks had been hired by a ship for the use of an employer's workmen in provisioning the ship, the owners of the trucks were not the delegates of the employer and he was not liable for their negligence in supplying defective trucks: *Sullivan v Gallagher and Craigh* 1960 SLT 70. Where a large store was being modernised and at the same time kept open as a store, the owners were treated as having delegated their duty for the safety of their employees to the various contractors, so as to be liable for the negligence of the latter; but not for the negligence of the manufacturer of defective cable: *Sumner v William Henderson & Sons Ltd* [1964] 1 QB 450, [1963] 1 All ER 408.

The Employer's Liability (Defective Equipment) Act 1969 has overruled some of these cases and made the employer liable for defects in *equipment* due to the negligence or other tort of a manufacturer or other third party: see Chapter 4, section 1, where the Act is summarised.

Apart from this Act, an employer is not liable for the negligence of third parties who are not his agents, although he may be using their premises or equipment. For example, the employer of a window-cleaner is not liable for the negligence of the occupier of a house who has allowed the windows to fall into a dangerous state of disrepair: *Wilson v Tyneside Window Cleaning Co* [1958] 2 QB 110, [1958] 2 All ER 265.

4 The limits of the employer's duty: the course of the employment

It is evident that the employer's duty does not extend to every moment of the workman's life, and equally evident that it cannot be restricted to the period when the workman is actually inside the factory or other place of work, since his duties may take him outside. The employer must still take reasonable care for the workman's safety when he is working at the premises of other persons: see *General Cleaning Contractors Ltd v Christmas* [1953] AC 180, [1952] 2 All ER 1110 (window-cleaner); but the extent of the precautions to be taken upon other persons' premises must take into account the fact that the employer has no control over the structure: *Thomson v Cremin* [1953] 2 All ER 1185 at 1192 (stevedores on ship).

The employer's duty, therefore, is 'to provide for the safety of his servant *in the course of his employment*', as was said by Lord Abinger CB in *Priestley v Fowler* (1837) 3 M & W 1.

The course of the employment has been used as a test for determining the vicarious liability of the employer to the world at large, and the phrase was also used and defined in numerous cases under the Workman's Compensation Acts. For present purposes, a somewhat broader view is taken, and decisions in other branches of the law will not necessarily apply: see *National Coal Board v England* [1954] AC 403, [1954] 1 All ER 546. Lord Cranworth LC said in *Brydon v Stewart* (1855) 2 Macq 30:

> '[A master] is only responsible while the servant is engaged in his employment: but whatever he does in the course of his employment, according to the fair interpretation of the words—*eundo, morando et redeundo*—for all that the master is responsible.'

In the above case the employer was held liable for the unsafe condition of the pit shaft which resulted in an accident when the workmen were leaving the pit. The Latin phrase *eundo, morando et redeundo* may be translated freely as meaning 'while at his place of employment, and while entering and leaving it'. The employer's duty therefore extends to matters arising while the workmen are coming to the place of work, or leaving it, at any rate while they are on the employer's premises, for example on the stairs on the way out: *Bell v Blackwood Morton & Sons Ltd* 1960 SC 11: but it does not extend to the safety of transport arrangements to take the men home: *Ramsay v Wimpey & Co Ltd* 1951 SC 692 (accident due to disorganised rush of men for transport).

The duty is not confined to the actual performance of work, but also applies when the servant is doing something reasonably incidental to work, as where the plaintiff had gone to wash a tea-cup when she slipped on an oily duck-board and injured herself: *Davidson v Handley Page Ltd* [1945] 1 All ER 235.

> 'The obligation of the employer extends to cover all such acts as are normally and reasonably incidental to a man's day's work': per Lord Greene MR, ibid. p. 237.

Difficult questions may arise where a man strays to a part of a factory or ship where his duties do not require him to be, and there encounters some danger. If, however, the workman is doing his employer's work, he does not cease to be acting in the course of his employment by the fact that he is working in a place where he is forbidden to go, even by statutory orders: see *Rands v McNeil* [1955] 1 QB 253, [1954] 3 All ER 593 (entry into shed where dangerous bull was kept); *Stapley v Gypsum Mines Ltd* [1953] AC 663, [1953] 2 All ER 478 (working under roof which was not secure); *Laszczyk v National Coal Board* [1954] 3 All ER 205 (trainee miner at coal face contrary to regulations). Likewise, disobedience to orders does not necessarily mean that the workman has moved out of the course of the employment, even when he arrogates to himself duties which he is not employed to perform and is forbidden by statute to perform: *National Coal Board v England* [1954] AC 403, [1954] 1 All ER 546 (miner coupled up cables, which should be done by shotfirer personally)[19]. All these cases have the common feature that the plaintiff, however foolishly or misguidedly, was doing the employer's work. Probably the reason why the court has taken a broader view of the course of employment in this connection is that the fault of the plaintiff can always be taken into account to reduce the damages. See also the cases on the course of employment in section 3(1) of this chapter, which to some extent cover the same ground in connection with vicarious liability.

5 The main branches of the employer's duty

Before the doctrine of common employment was abolished, the responsibility of the employer was restricted to such fundamental matters as the safety of the plant, the place of work and the method of work. Now his responsibility is general and unrestricted: but the authorities which explain the various branches of his duty are still important, if only for illustrative purposes[20]. In many cases it cannot be shown that any particular person did a negligent act, and it is then

19 The decision in *Bloor v Liverpool Derricking and Carrying Co Ltd* [1936] 3 All ER 399, CA, that a man who went to assist a fellow-workman doing a different job 'accepted the risk', and that no duty was owed to him, is inconsistent with these decisions and clearly obsolete.

20 'Within this general duty, and exemplifying it, the courts have defined several categories of obligation in broad terms': *Smith v Howdens Ltd* [1953] NI 131 per Lord MacDermott LCJ. Cf. Birkett LJ (with regard to safe system) in *Buckingham v Daily News Ltd* [1956] 2 QB 534: 'It is not an enlargement . . . but an illustration of the nature of the common law duty.'

necessary to rely on the employer's personal responsibility for the fundamental conditions of work. It is sometimes said that the employer's personal duty can be divided into three main branches—plant, place of work, method of work—but the selection and supervision of fellow-servants may also be important.

Parker LJ said in *Wilson v Tyneside Window Cleaning Co* [1958] 2 QB 110 at 116:

> 'The master's duty is general, to take all reasonable steps to avoid risk to his servants. For convenience it is often split up into different categories, such as tools, or safe system of work, but it always remains one general duty.'

The branches of the duty have been expressed in different cases with a varying degree of emphasis. Lord Wright said in *Wilsons and Clyde Coal Co v English* [1938] AC 57 at 78, [1937] 3 All ER 628 at 640, quoting from Lord McLaren in *Bett v Dalmeny Oil Co* (1905) 7 F 787:

> 'The obligation is threefold, "the provision of a competent staff of men, adequate material, and a proper system and effective supervision".'

And Lord Maugham in the same case, at pp. 86 and 645, summed up the course of the common law decision as follows:

> 'In the case of employments involving risk . . . it was held that there was a duty on the employer to take reasonable care, and to use reasonable skill, first, to provide and maintain proper machinery, plant, appliances, and works; secondly, to select properly skilled persons to manage and superintend the business, and, thirdly, to provide a proper system of working.'

These observations may be supplemented by the dictum of Scott LJ in *Vaughan v Ropner & Co Ltd* (1947) 80 Ll L Rep 119, when he said at p. 121:

> 'The three main duties [of the employer] are (1) to provide proper premises in which, and proper plant and appliances by means of which, the workman's duty is to be performed; (2) to maintain premises, plant and apparatus in a proper condition; (3) to establish and enforce a proper system of working.'

This way of putting the matter has the advantage of bringing out the continuing obligation to *maintain*, and also makes it clear that the duty extends to premises as well as plant. It has further been said that the duty is to take care for the workman's '*health* and safety': per Glyn-Jones J in *Crookall v Vickers-Armstrong Ltd* [1955] 2 All ER 12 (a case of silicosis). It is, for example, the duty of the owners of a ship to provide medical equipment to mitigate the effects of injuries occurring on board: *Smith v Howdens Ltd* [1953] NI 131. There are many employments today where employees should be 'monitored' against exposure to such things as radioactivity, dust, poisons or (for hospital staff) infectious diseases. The need to give protection against injury to the hearing by noise is now well recognised: *McCafferty v Metropolitan Police District Receiver* [1977] 2 All ER 756.

Where employees work overseas and a war situation or other serious danger arises, the employer's duty may extend to evacuating them or advising them to leave: but this is a matter of degree, depending on how imminent and how serious the danger is: *Longworth v Coppas International (UK) Ltd* 985 SLT 111.

An employer has no duty to protect the *financial* welfare of an employee, either at home or abroad, for instance by taking out insurance in a country where road accidents are not compensated, or advising the employee to take it out himself: *Reid v Rush & Tompkins Group plc* [1989] 3 All ER 228, CA[1].

The effect of the abolition of common employment has been to add a new branch to the employer's liability, though not to his personal duty. His servants must now carry out routine operations safely, and he is vicariously liable if they negligently fail to do so: *Staveley Iron and Chemical Co Ltd v Jones* [1956] AC 627, [1956] 1 All ER 403.

All these branches of the duty are illustrated in detail in the next chapter.

6 What constitutes negligence?

What sort of facts have to be established, to show that an employer has negligently failed to perform his duty? This depends on the

---

1   See also the note in Appendix II on liability—or rather non-liability—for loss of property.

circumstances of the case, and on the principles with regard to the standard of care and evidence of negligence which were explained in Chapter 2, pp. 37–53 and pp. 72–77, *ante*. Nevertheless, some general remarks may be useful at this stage.

First of all, it may be that the employer has done nothing at all to carry out his obligations. This is likely to happen, above all, with the system of work. Sometimes an operation is conducted in so haphazard a fashion that it is impossible to say that there is any system at all. But there may also be a total failure to provide proper appliances. In *Williams v Birmingham Battery and Metal Co* [1899] 2 QB 338, the workman had to descend from an elevated tramway, for which no ladder was provided, and in trying to make his way down he fell and killed himself. A. L. Smith LJ observed:

> 'This is not the case where a master has provided proper appliances and done his best to maintain them in a state of efficiency. . . . This is the case of no proper appliances having been supplied by the master at all.'

In the second place the employer may have been informed of a defect or danger, but done nothing to remedy it. This was the case in *Clarke v Holmes* (1862) 7 H & N 937 where the employer had been told that the fencing round a dangerous machine was broken, but had failed to replace it.

Thirdly, the employer, knowing of a defect in his plant or premises, or of a danger in the course of the work, may have taken inadequate measures to eliminate or reduce the risk. There may, for example, have been excessive delay: see *Paterson v Wallace & Co* (1854) 1 Macq 748, cited at p. 9, *ante*.

Fourthly, though the employer does not know that anything is wrong, it may be that he ought to know—that is, he could have found out by reasonable care. Thus Cockburn CJ said in his direction to the jury in *Webb v Rennie* (1865) 4 F & F 608 at 612:

> 'Although in general an employer was not liable unless he knew of the danger, yet it was his business to know if, by reasonable care and precaution, he could ascertain whether the apparatus or machinery were in a fit state or not.'

This raises the question how far periodical inspections of plant and premises are necessary. To this the common law can only answer that inspections should be made when it is reasonable to make them. It is largely a question of evidence, depending on the experience of the industry and expert opinion.

At all events, the employer is not liable for latent defects which he had no means of discovering. Lord Campbell said in *Weems v Mathieson* (1861) 4 Macq 215, 149 RR 322 where a cylinder had fallen owing to weakness in the supporting machinery, that it had to be proved that the weakness:

> 'did not arise from any inherent secret defect, and that it was known, or might by the exercise of due skill and attention have been known, to the defendant, who was the employer of the deceased'[2].

Evidence of the general practice of good employers in similar circumstances may always be given in proof or disproof of negligence. The law on this matter is explained at length in Chapter 2, pp. 45–52, *ante*, and here it is only necessary to say that general practice is particularly important in connection with (i) methods of inspection and maintenance of plant and premises and (ii) safe methods (or systems) of carrying out dangerous operations. On principle it is also permissible to give evidence of information in general circulation in the trade, for example, of dangers from materials in use or methods of preventing various types of accident. A reasonable employer cannot be expected to know everything but he should at least take some notice of information from the Health and Safety Executive and other public organisations which exist to help him.

---

2 This dictum must be qualified as regards onus of proof. If a defect in plant is proved, decisions in Scotland suggest that, even apart from *res ipsa loquitur*, the onus is on the employer to show that the defect could not reasonably be discovered: see p. 123.

Chapter 4

Illustrations of the employer's duty: plant, place of work, method of work

1 Plant and machinery

One branch of the employer's duty is that he must take reasonable care to provide and maintain proper plant and machinery. 'Plant' is used in this context as a convenient general term to denote all manner of things employed in the course of the work. It comprises, for example, such widely divergent objects as scaffold-poles and cart-horses.

The first question, logically, is whether particular plant is required at all. A reasonable employer has to decide whether equipment is required and, if so, to make a choice of type. The provision of plant was 'especially within the province of the master' even under the old law before the abolition of common employment: *Toronto Power Co Ltd v Paskwan* [1915] AC 734.

Next, the plant must be kept in good order. Lord Wright said in *Wilsons and Clyde Coal Co Ltd v English* [1938] AC 57 at 84, [1937] 3 All ER 628 at 644:

> 'The obligation to provide and maintain proper plant and appliances is a continuing obligation. It is not, however, broken by a mere misuse of, or failure to use, proper plant and appliances, due to the negligence of a fellow-servant, or a merely temporary failure to keep in order or adjust plant and appliances.'

So the original responsibility of the employer was to provide plant, and set up a regular system of maintenance. Since the abolition of common employment he has in addition been vicariously responsible for the negligence of fellow-workmen in routine maintenance, such as careless and haphazard inspection, delay in carrying out repairs, or badly executed repairs. He is also liable if a fellow-servant negligently fails to use equipment which is available, or selects the wrong equipment for a particular task.

Formerly the duty to take reasonable care in the provision of equipment did not make the employer liable for negligence by a manufacturer or other supplier, since these were not persons to whom he delegated his duty. The employer's liability depended on whether he exercised reasonable care in purchase or hire, and if plant of apparently good quality was bought or hired from a reputable manufacturer or supplier, the employer was not liable for unknown defects: *Davie v New Merton Board Mills Ltd* [1959] AC 604, [1959] 1 All ER 346; *Sullivan v Gallagher and Craig* 1960 SLT 70.

The law was changed by the Employer's Liability (Defective Equipment) Act 1969. This makes an employer liable in all cases where an employee sustains 'personal injury' in the course of his employment 'in consequence of a defect in equipment provided by his employer for the purposes of the employer's business', if 'the defect is attributable wholly or partly to the fault of a third party (whether identified or not)': s. 1(1). Equipment includes 'any plant and machinery, vehicle, aircraft, and clothing'. At one extreme it has been held to include an entire ship: *Coltman v Bibby Tankers Ltd, The Derbyshire* [1988] AC 276, [1987] 3 All ER 1068, HL; at the other extreme it includes soap: *Ralston v Greater Glasgow Health Board* 1987 SLT 386. 'Business' includes 'activities carried on by any public body'. 'Employee' means any person employed under a contract of service or apprenticeship for the purposes of the employer's business. 'Personal injury' includes death, physical or mental impairment, and disease. The Act binds the Crown, persons in the service of the Crown being treated as employees: s. 1(4). Any agreement to exclude or limit the employer's liability under the Act is void: s. 1(2). The employer's rights to set up contributory negligence, or claim indemnity or contribution, are not affected.

The Act takes an awkward and anomalous form. It does not create a true vicarious liability for agents of the employer, since it covers third parties with whom he may have had no contact.

There is a penumbra of cases where the Act does not apply. It applies only to employment in a business, or under a public authority: so employment for non-business purposes or by a private organisation or club is excluded. There must be a contract: *de facto* service is not enough. There must be a 'defect' in equipment: unsuitability or inadequacy is not enough, though in a Scottish case the fact that soap was 'materially more irritant than other soaps', and therefore liable to cause dermatitis, was held to be a defect: *Ralston v Greater Glasgow Health Authority, supra.* There must be 'fault' by a third party—defined as negligence, breach of statutory duty or other tort. This may cause difficulty where the third party does not know what the equipment will be used for, or for some other reason owes no duty to the injured person, or a duty less than an employer's. Lastly the equipment must be 'provided' by an employer, but this must include what is 'provided' under his authority, even if casually borrowed from someone else by a foreman or chargehand. An example of the operation of the Act is *Yuille v Daks Simpson Ltd* 1984 SLT 115n where ventilation ducts gave way owing to negligent choice of inadequate supports by the heating engineers, and both they and the employers were held liable.

Where the Act does not apply, the old rule will still operate that the employer is liable for an independent contractor where the contractor is carrying out the employer's duty of 'providing' or 'maintaining', but not for the negligence of a manufacturer, hirer or other supplier not acting on the employer's behalf.

Broadly, then, an employer is now liable for the negligence of himself, his servants and agents in the provision, maintenance and selection of plant, and in many cases is under an extended liability for the negligence of manufacturers, repairers and other third parties. But he does not 'warrant' the plant and is not liable for latent defects not discoverable by the exercise of reasonable care: *Weems v Mathieson* (1861) 4 Macq 215, 149 RR 322. It follows that, when defects arise after installation, liability must depend on whether they have been brought to notice, or ought to have been discovered by proper methods of inspection and testing. A 'merely temporary failure' to learn of a fault, or to rectify it at once, will not constitute negligence unless the delay is unreasonable.

(1) The provision of plant

The provision of plant may be considered under three heads.

(i) Total failure to provide necessary plant
Accidents sometimes occur because necessary equipment was totally wanting, and unsafe improvised methods have been used. These cases

overlap the employer's duty to establish safe method and conditions of work, because it is these which decide whether equipment (or equipment of some particular design) is required. The deficiency may be so glaring that no further evidence is required: *Mellors v Shaw* (1861) 1 B & S 437; *Williams v Birmingham Battery and Metal Co* [1899] 2 QB 338 (no ladder to overhead tramway, elderly workman had to scramble up by improvised holds); *Lovell v Blundells and Crompton & Co Ltd* [1944] KB 502, [1944] 2 All ER 53 (staging needed to overhaul ship's boiler, no planks supplied, workman left to forage and used unsound one); *Garrard v Southey & Co and Standard Telephones and Cables Ltd* [1952] 2 QB 174, [1952] 1 All ER 597 (told to look round and find trestle); *Kyle v Salvesen* 1980 SLT (Notes) 18 (no safety net under ship's gangway: drunken seaman fell off).

More often some evidence is required of the risks likely to arise without the equipment. Examples are *Bright v Thames Stevedoring Co* [1951] 1 Lloyd's Rep 116 (light for bogie on uneven dock surface); *Bradford v Robinson Rentals Ltd* [1967] 1 All ER 267 (car-heater for television engineer on long journey in severe weather); *Roy v Co-ordinated Traffic Services* (1969) 6 KIR 102 ('jolodas', i.e. sliding strips on lorry floors to elevate loads, liable to stick as employers knew; driver overbalanced in using improvised hook to free; proper appliances should have been provided); *Busby v Robert Watson & Co* (*Constructional Engineers*) *Ltd* [1972] 13 KIR 498 (loose ash made unsafe footing on platform: no brush available to clear it away)[1].

(ii) Failure to provide sufficient plant

An employer may be liable for failing to provide sufficient plant, as e.g. in *Machray v Stewarts and Lloyds Ltd* [1964] 3 All ER 716 (some chain blocks were provided on a large building site: rigger requiring them for an urgent job made a search but could not find any and had to use rope blocks which were less safe). A ship at sea should carry enough spares to last the voyage: *Vaughan v Ropner & Co Ltd* (1947) 80 Ll LRep 119 (no wire rope available when rope on ship's hoist damaged, accident due to makeshift rope of odd pieces of fibre).

---

1   But in *Baker v Harvey Farms* (*Thorpe*) *Ltd* (1961) Times, 26 October it was held that wirecutters need not be provided for farm workers repairing barbed wire fences, as cutting the wire by a blow from a hammer created no foreseeable risk of fragments flying off. This finding seems to fly in the face of common sense.

(iii) Providing defective or dangerous equipment

In general an employer is not liable unless he (or some person for whom he is responsible) knew or ought to have known of the defect or danger, as in *Yarmouth v France* (1887) 19 QBD 647 and *Bowater v Rowley Regis Corpn* [1944] KB 476, [1944] 1 All ER 465 (horses known to be unsafe). Knowledge of a defect which a fellow-servant has acquired in a temporary task is not necessarily to be imputed to the employer: *Maclean v Forestry Commission* 1970 SLT 265 (fellow-servant aware of horse's uncertain temper when using it temporarily but was not in charge of horses).

An employer who has designed apparatus himself must take reasonable care that the design is safe: *McPhee v General Motors Ltd* (1970) 8 KIR 885.

If the employer bought new equipment such as hand tools from a reputable supplier, or direct from the manufacturer, he was formerly entitled to rely upon the manufacturer and was not expected to carry out an independent examination and test for latent defects before taking the equipment into use: *Mason v Williams and Williams Ltd and Thomas Turton & Sons Ltd* [1955] 1 All ER 808 (steel chisel was too hard and splintered). (Second-hand equipment, however, might well require thorough checking at the time of purchase: *Pearce v Round Oak Steel Works Ltd* [1969] 3 All ER 680.) In *Davie v New Merton Board Mills Ltd* [1959] AC 604, [1959] 1 All ER 346 (overruling *Donnelly v Glasgow Corpn* 1953 SC 107) the House of Lords held that the manufacturer was not a person to whom the employer has delegated performance of his own duty, so as to make the employer vicariously liable for latent defects due to negligence in manufacture; and this was so even if equipment was bought direct from the manufacturer to special order, like the chassis of the omnibus in *Donnelly's* case (but the employer could be liable for negligence in his own specification). It was accepted that the employer is liable for the negligence of any person to whom he 'entrusts' the performance of his duty to provide plant. The difficulty was in saying that the duty is 'entrusted' to a manufacturer with whom the employer may have no direct relations, or to any manufacturer at all, since the employer's duty is not to *make* but only to *provide* plant. Similarly the employer was not liable for latent defects in plant *hired* from a reputable source: *Sullivan v Gallagher and Craig* 1960 SLT 70 (trucks, in this case not hired directly by the employer but by the ship which he was loading).

These decisions are now superseded by the Employer's Liability

(Defective Equipment) Act 1969 which, as explained at p. 111, above, makes the employer liable for defects due to the negligence of other persons.

In the case of machinery, defects or dangers may be of many kinds. The design of a machine may be faulty, or there may be something wrong with its construction: the defect may cause the machine to work in an erratic or unexpected manner, or may cause it to break or even (if it is a badly-constructed boiler, for instance) to explode.

Many types of plant and machinery are dangerous in their ordinary working, and where this is the case it is the duty of the employer to install any necessary safety device with the machine. Thus in *Watling v Oastler* (1871) LR 6 Exch 73 it was held to be negligent to set up dangerous machinery in a factory without a proper fence. The fencing of machinery is now largely governed by statute, but there are still occasions when it is important to appreciate that failure to fence may be negligence at common law: see, e.g. *Jones v Richards* [1955] 1 All ER 463 (farm machinery); *Close v Steel Co of Wales Ltd* [1962] AC 367, [1961] 2 All ER 953 (machinery liable to throw out fragments, not required to be fenced under Factories Act).

The duty to minimise dangers which are inherent in the plant is not confined to machinery. In *Naismith v London Film Productions Ltd* [1939] 1 All ER 794 the plaintiff, as a crowd extra in a film studio, had to wear material which was highly inflammable and caught fire. Lord Greene MR said:

> 'if [the employers] supplied equipment which was dangerous, that would impose upon them . . . the further duty to take whatever steps were reasonable and proper to ensure that that danger should be minimised . . .'

This case perhaps falls more logically under the heading of safe system of work, but it rests on the same principle as cases where there has been a failure to provide a safety device.

(iv) No obligation to provide latest improvements

An employer is not bound to adopt the latest improvements, and the fact that his machine or plant is less safe than those generally in use is not in itself evidence of negligence (*Dynen v Leach* (1857) 26 LJ Ex 221; *Parkes v Smethwick Corpn* (1957) 121 JP 415, 55 LGR 438—ambulance not fitted with retractable gear for stretcher). However, the absence of modern safety devices must be taken in conjunction with the other circumstances of the case, because on the particular facts it may have been negligent not to adopt the improvement. In *Toronto Power Co Ltd v Paskwan* [1915] AC 734 the deceased was killed by a block falling from a travelling crane. The accident was caused by the overwinding of the chain which hoisted the block. Evidence was given that there was in existence a safety device which would have prevented this overwinding, but that the defendants had not adopted this device, although a similar accident had occurred before. The jury found the defendants negligent, and the Privy Council held that their verdict was supported by the evidence.

This question must be approached from a common sense angle: if an improvement would result in greatly increased safety, an employer taking reasonable care would usually adopt it. As a Canadian case puts it (*Reed v Ellis* (1916) 27 OWR 490):

> 'A master is not bound to provide all the latest devices for the care or benefit of those he employs; he *is* bound to take reasonable means to protect them from injury in his service'[2].

Where there is a quantity of equipment which cannot all be replaced at once, it is not necessarily negligent to keep some obsolete equipment in use, although it is not as safe as the later types: *O'Connor v British Transport Commission* [1958] 1 All ER 558, CA (railway van).

(2) The maintenance of plant

It is the duty of the employer to take reasonable care to maintain his plant and machinery in proper condition. He is liable for the negligence of his servants; and he is also liable for the negligence of independent contractors to whom the maintenance of machinery is entrusted: *Rodgers v Dunsmuir Confectionary Co* 1952 SLT (Notes) 9; for instance if a contractor fails to make his regular visit of inspection and a fault is overlooked: *Donnelly v Ronald Wilson (Plant Hire) Ltd* 1986 SLT 90.

It will be profitable to inquire what sort of methods of maintaining plant and machinery are likely to be followed by an employer exercising reasonable care. The primary guide, no doubt, is 'general and approved

2   See also pp. 38–45, *ante*.

practice' (pp. 45–53, *ante*), which will vary greatly according to the nature of the equipment. If it is machinery of a complex character, there ought usually to be some form of planned servicing. An illustration may be taken from the operation of aircraft—a case where safety is extremely important, and the duty of care stands at its highest. Here there is a daily inspection and test, to check that the mechanism is in running order; at regular intervals there are major and minor inspections, involving a more or less complete overhaul; the inspections are supplemented by defect reports, which are rendered whenever the machine runs in a faulty, erratic or peculiar manner, or has been subjected to a special strain; and if any serious defect is disclosed, the machine is marked unserviceable until the defect has been remedied. On a less intricate level, such items as scaffold-poles, ropes and chains, which wear out more or less rapidly in the course of use, require to be inspected and tested at regular intervals, and, if found to be worn out, should be condemned and put out of the way. Where plant is neither complex nor liable to wear and tear—for example a ladder which is not in constant use—it may be reasonable to take no action unless a defect is reported. In this context, negligence is very much a question of fact and degree, and careful maintenance may involve, according to the circumstances, any or all of the following measures: (i) regular inspection and testing; (ii) calling for defect reports; (iii) discarding worn-out equipment; (iv) carrying out repairs and servicing without undue delay; to which may be added (v) the cleaning of plant liable to become covered with oil, or otherwise slippery or dangerous.

This general outline of good modern practice will serve to indicate the points to which evidence should be directed, and will help to complete the gaps between the decided cases, to which we must now turn.

(i) Failure to remedy known facts
Liability is conspicuously clear when the employer has received notice of a defect and has failed to do anything to remedy it, and there are numerous cases which illustrate the point. In *Clarke v Holmes* (1862) 7 H & N 937 the plaintiff was employed to oil a machine. The fencing broke, and he reported it to his employer, who promised to carry out repairs, but did nothing: and the employer was held liable for the subsequent accident. In *Monaghan v Rhodes (W. H.) & Son* [1920] 1 KB 487 a stevedore's labourer fell off an unsafe rope ladder leading to the

hold: one of the heads of the firm had seen that the ladder was dangerous, but gave no instructions for its replacement, and the firm were held liable. Similarly, in *Abbott v Isham* (1920) 90 LJKB 309 the managers of a school were held liable to its headmaster for the bursting of a boiler after he had repeatedly warned them that it was unsafe, and in *Baker v James* [1921] 2 KB 674 a commercial firm were held liable to one of their travellers for a defect in the starting gear of a motor car which he had reported to them.

In all these cases the employers had ample time to put matters right: the position would be different if, in the circumstances, the delay was reasonable.

(ii) Discovery of unknown defects: inspection and testing

Where an accident has been caused by a defect whose existence was unknown until the accident happened there is no liability if the defect could not have been discovered by the exercise of reasonable care. There is in general a duty to inspect and test the plant, but the frequency and method of inspection and testing are questions of fact to be decided according to the evidence. What defects are 'discoverable with reasonable care' does not set any absolute standard, as older decisions about simple things like timber suggest. It depends on the position and duty of the person inspecting and the knowledge and techniques he ought to have: inspection of a Rolls-Royce engine by the maker is different from an overhaul even by a large garage, and *a fortiori* from a check by the employer's own mechanic or driver.

In *Webb v Rennie* (1865) 4 F & F 608 a scaffolding had been erected for shipbuilding, and the poles had been left in the ground for two years. The plaintiff, with other workmen, was ordered to dismantle the scaffolding, and in the process one of the poles snapped at its base and fell upon him. Cockburn CJ in his direction to the jury said:

> 'The servant had a right to expect . . . that the machinery or apparatus about which he is to be employed, and out of which danger arises, shall be attended to with reasonable care, to ensure its being in a fit state to be worked without undue or extraordinary dangers . . . ; and although in general an employer was not liable unless he knew of the danger, yet it was his business to know if, by reasonable care and precaution, he could ascertain whether the apparatus or machinery was in a fit state or not. . . . Thus in the case of a manufacturer employing machinery which might be attended with danger to the persons employed about it . . . the master must either ascertain the state of the

machinery or apparatus himself; or employ some competent person to do so[3].'

He continued that it was a question of fact for the jury whether the defendant had been negligent in not examining the poles, taking into account the evidence on the experience and practice of the shipbuilding industry; and the jury returned a verdict for the plaintiff.

In *Murphy v Phillips* (1876) 35 LT 477 a worn-out chain had broken. Evidence was given as to the standard methods of testing chains, none of which had been used by the employers. Kelly CB said at p. 478:

'The defendant was bound from time to time, as the occasion might require, to have the chains used in his business . . . properly and duly examined and tested.'

Even such ordinary articles as chairs should be checked when they have been in use for some time, and in an organisation of any size there should be some system to ensure that this is done: *Baxter v St. Helena Group Hospital Management Committee* (1972) Times, 14 February, CA.

But there are cases where inspection, or at any rate frequent inspection, is not obligatory. An obvious example is simple protective equipment such as boots issued to employees for slippery conditions: employers were not liable for worn-down treads when they had not been told about them: *Smith v Scot Bowyers Ltd* [1986] IRLR 315, CA. In *Pearce v Armitage* (1950) 83 Ll L Rep 361 a safety device known as a 'lazy band', attached to a chute for the discharge of cargo from a ship, had been removed or loosened. The Court of Appeal held that, having regard to the custom of the trade, the employer was entitled to rely upon the tipper to report the fault, which was of an obvious character and rendered the continuance of work dangerous: per Singleton LJ at p. 369. It has been said that it is not necessary at any stage to examine such items as tools purchased from a reputable manufacturer, unless some defect becomes apparent: *Mason v Williams and Williams Ltd and Thomas Turton & Sons Ltd* [1955] 1 All ER 808, approved in *Davie v New Merton Board Mills Ltd* [1959] AC 604, [1959] 1 All ER 346[4]. But in the case of complex apparatus such as an oxy-acetylene burner, it is not justifiable to rely upon the workman operating the apparatus to

3 Under the present law, the employer is, of course, liable for negligence on the part of the 'competent person' he employs.
4 Contrast *Taylor v Rover Co Ltd* [1966] 2 All ER 181 (employers liable for continuing to use chisel after defect appeared).

inspect it and report defects: *Shotter v Green (R. and H.) and Silley Weir Ltd* [1951] 1 Lloyd's Rep 329. Where a part of a hand drill of reputable make flew out due to a loosened screw, it was held negligent not to have had regular inspection, the more so as the drill was subject to vibration: *Bell v Arnott and Harrison Ltd* (1967) 2 KIR 825.

The necessity to supplement inspection by requiring defects reports to be rendered is illustrated by *Barkway v South Wales Transport Co Ltd* [1950] AC 185, [1950] 1 All ER 392, an action by the widow of a passenger against an omnibus company where an accident had been caused by a tyre burst. The House of Lords examined the system of inspection and testing and found it excellent: but they held the company liable because they had failed to instruct their drivers to report incidents which might have caused a hidden tyre fracture. The case is noteworthy, because there was no general practice that such reports should be rendered. A reasonable system may require that defect reports should be properly recorded in writing, rather than made casually by word of mouth when they may be forgotten: *Franklin v Edmonton Corpn* (1965) 109 Sol Jo 876, Times, 27 October (tipper lorry). The maintenance system should also take into account any history or use of the plant which may require special overhaul: *Henderson v Henry E. Jenkins & Sons and Evans* [1970] AC 282, [1969] 3 All ER 756 (part of hydraulic brake system on lorry corroded, normally safe for many years: defendants failed to show there was no history of corrosive loads or similar risks and were held liable).

(iii) Failure or delay in carrying out repairs etc
According to the dictum of Lord Wright in *English's* case, 'a merely temporary failure to keep in order or adjust plant or appliances' does not establish a breach of duty. An employer cannot be held liable unless he has had time and opportunity to remedy the defect after it came (or ought to have come) to his knowledge. In all the cases quoted above (heading (i)) there was unreasonable delay: there was also unreasonable delay in *Paterson v Wallace & Co* (1854) 1 Macq 748 (p. 9, *ante*).

In some cases it may be legitimate to rely on the workman himself to rectify simple defects in the plant which he is using, and in such circumstances there is no negligence on the part of the employer. In *Bristol Aeroplane Co v Franklin* [1948] WN 341 the House of Lords thought that it was proper to allow a skilled workman to repair his own tools; and in *Pearce v Armitage* (1950) 83 Ll LRep 361 the Court of

Appeal thought it reasonable that even an unskilled workman should be expected to tighten a slack rope on a safety device.

A point which has not been explicitly considered is whether plant should be marked unserviceable and put out of use pending repairs. Certainly this course should be taken if continued operation will be dangerous[5]. Similarly, where ropes and similar articles have been condemned as worn-out, it is reasonable that they should be put out of the way so that they cannot be taken into use by mistake[6]. If it is alleged that equipment was not examined frequently enough, the *onus* may lie on the employer to show that no better arrangements were practicable: *McDonald v British Transport Commission* [1955] 3 All ER 789 (goods wagons neglected during busy season).

Where plant is liable to become covered with oil or other substances, so as to render it slippery or otherwise dangerous, it is the duty of the employer to keep it in a safe condition so far as practicable. In *Davidson v Handley Page Ltd* [1945] 1 All ER 235, there were duck-boards on the floor which were liable to get covered with suds and become slippery. The plaintiff slipped and injured herself, and the Court of Appeal held the defendants liable.

(iv) Selection of plant
The selection of safe plant for the work in hand is now the responsibility of the employer, whether he makes the choice personally or acts through his servants. In *Fanton v Denville* [1932] 2 KB 309 (selection of properties for stage play) and *Wigmore v Jay* (1850) 5 Exch 354 (use of unsound pole for scaffolding) the plaintiff's claim failed on the ground of common employment, the selection having been made by a fellow-servant, but both claims would succeed under the present law.

If, however, the selection of equipment was properly left to the plaintiff himself, being a competent and experienced man, the employer cannot be held negligent: *Johnson v Croggon & Co Ltd* [1954] 1 All ER 121 (plaintiff chose light fruit-picking ladder for building operation); *Richardson v Stephenson Clarke Ltd* [1969] 3 All ER 705 (foreman rigger chose unsafe shackle when ample equipment was available)[7]. Similarly

5   See *Latimer v A.E.C. Ltd* [1952] 2 QB 701 at 708, [1952] 1 All ER 1302 at 1303 per Singleton LJ *obiter*.
6   In *Johnstone v Clyde Navigation Trustees* (1949) 82 Ll LRep 187 HL the system of 'inspection and discarding from use' was investigated but found in order.
7   In this case Nield J quoted with approval the statement of the law in the text.

in *Bristol Aeroplane Co v Franklin* [1948] WN 341 the House of Lords held that no blame was imputable to the employers when a skilled workman, who was allowed to repair his own tools, selected brittle material from the stores. Three further cases, all of which involved the accidental use of worn-out articles, are *O'Melia v Freight Conveyors Ltd and Rederiaktiebolaget Svenska Lloyd* [1940] 4 All ER 516 (a workman used a defective rope belonging to a third party instead of the sound rope provided); *Johnstone v Clyde Navigation Trustees* (1949) 82 Ll L Rep 187, HL (a tray used for loads, which had been condemned, was accidentally brought back into use); and *Woodman v Richardson and Concrete Ltd* [1937] 3 All ER 866 (an invitor-invitee case, where a discarded ladder was brought back by an unknown person from a rubbish dump).

The selection of unsuitable equipment is not necessarily negligent. If the task to be performed is sufficiently urgent, it may be reasonable to use plant which is not entirely suitable: *Watt v Hertfordshire County Council* [1954] 2 All ER 368 (fire brigade used unsuitable lorry for saving life in emergency); and a skilled person may be expected to adapt himself to the circumstances: *Prince v Ministry of Defence, The Praia de Adrage* [1965] 1 Ll L Rep 354 (awkward for pilot to pass from ship to Admiralty tug with high bulwark: should have waited till it was flat alongside). But where there is a choice between two items of equipment, one safer than the other, the wrong choice is sufficient evidence of negligence in the absence of an explanation: *Ralston v British Railways Board* 1967 SLT (Notes) 105 (jack to replace train on rails). It was negligent for employers, who knew that the pursuer had back trouble, to give him a barrow which was too narrow to do the task safely: *McDonald v Whiteford & Robertson Ltd* 1980 SLT (Notes) 2.

(v) Duty to maintenance men
Men sent to repair apparatus are not required to suspect every aspect of its working. The duty of care is owed to them as to other employees and they should be warned of any danger, e.g. where the known erratic working of a machine may have affected a safety device: *McPhee v General Motors Ltd* (1970) 8 KIR 885.

(3) Evidence of negligence

The nature of the evidence which is ordinarily required in an action based on defective plant—and in particular the necessity for proof of correct practice in such matters as inspection and testing—will be apparent from the foregoing paragraphs. It is necessary, however, to distinguish between the cases where *res ipsa loquitur* does and does not apply.

(i) Where res ipsa loquitur *applies*

The maxim *res ipsa loquitur* has been discussed at length at pp. 74–77. It applies where an accident is of such a character that it would not normally happen without negligence on the part of the person in charge: but not where the accident is equally consistent with the absence of negligence on the part of any person: per Lord Dunedin in *Ballard v North British Rly Co* 1923 SC (HL) 43 at 53, (Lord Dunedin was dissenting, but not on this point). *Prima facie*, the maxim applies to such cases as a tyre burst, the breaking of a rope, and an explosion: *Barkway v South Wales Transport Co Ltd* [1950] AC 185; [1950] 1 All ER 392; *Turner v National Coal Board* (1949) 65 TLR 580; *Moore v R. Fox & Sons* [1956] 1 QB 596, [1956] 1 All ER 182.

In the *Barkway* case the House of Lords decided that there is no scope for the application of the maxim where all the facts of the accident are proved in evidence and its cause is known: the court has then to assess, on the proved facts, whether the defendants were negligent. Where the maxim does apply, we are left with an unexplained occurrence which on the face of it is negligent: and (provided that any negligence on the part of the plaintiff himself is excluded) there is a presumption of negligence by the defendants or their servants, which can be rebutted only by express proof that either (i) the defendants and their servants exercised all reasonable care or (ii) there is a likely explanation which does not connote negligence on the part of the defendants.

(ii) Where res ipsa loquitur *does not apply*

A number of Scottish decisions have a bearing on the subject. In *Gavin v Rogers* (1889) 17 R 206 it was held in uncompromising terms that positive proof must be given that (a) a defect or fault existed and (b) it would have been detected on reasonable examination. This certainly goes too far. A Scottish judge of high authority has also said:

> 'provided that it is proved that some defect in the machinery or plant caused the accident, it is not necessary to show the precise nature of that defect, and an onus is thrown upon the master to show that the defect was one for which he was not to blame.'

i.e., to show that it could not have been discovered by the exercise of reasonable care: per Lord Moncrieff LJ-C in *Macfarlane v Thompson* (1884) 12 R 232, approved by Lord Dunedin in *Ballard v North British Rail Co* (1923) SC (HL) 43 at 53. The remarks of Lord Moncrieff were based on *Fraser v Fraser* (1882) 9 R 896 where a rope supporting a steeplejack broke, and, on proof that there was probably a 'nip' or kink in the centre which might have been detected by feel, it was held that an employer who had not carried out any examination could not be allowed to say that he would not have discovered it; also on the similar case of *Walker v Olsen* (1882) 9 R 946 (stevedore's tackle broke). Both these cases may be regarded as examples of *res ipsa loquitur*, and it is doubtful whether Lord Moncrieff's statement of the law applies in other cases. In *Macfarlane v Thompson, supra,* the actual decision was that the occurrence of an accident does not in itself prove a defect in the manner of rigging up plant (metal casing fell from top of boiler). There does not seem to have been an actual breakage. Perhaps all breakages and failures are examples of *res ipsa loquitur,* unless the equipment is of such a kind that breakage or failure at times is a normal incident of operation which cannot be met by regular inspection and replacement. In *Pearce v Round Oak Steel Works Ltd* [1969] 3 All ER 680 the maxim was applied when a piece of old machinery broke off due to metal fatigue in a bolt. In *Henderson v Henry E. Jenkins & Sons and Evans* [1970] AC 282, [1969] 3 All ER 756, a disastrous lorry crash due to brake failure, a pipe had corroded at a place not accessible to normal inspection. Because the evidence showed that the pipe ought to last a long period without inspection, the House of Lords held that the defendants could not discharge themselves without positive proof of due care, which would include evidence of the history of the vehicle and precautions taken on exposure to corrosion. *Res ipsa loquitur* was not mentioned, but the case is best explained on that basis[8].

---

8   I.e. the brake failure and crash raised *res ipsa loquitur*. Lord Pearson says 'a *prima facie* inference' which is much the same. The defendants excused themselves by saying that the part was not one which should be opened up and inspected, but if this was correct then the corrosion was abnormal, and the defendants failed to explain it in a way which *excluded* negligence on their part.

2 The place of work

The employer's responsibility for the place of work is very similar to his responsibility for plant and machinery; and the two earliest decisions in the House of Lords turned on the duty to take reasonable care for the safety of the place of work. Both related to accidents in coal mines. In *Paterson v Wallace & Co* (1854) 1 Macq 748 there was a large stone liable to fall from the roof of the mine. In *Brydon v Stewart* (1855) 2 Macq 30 the pit shaft was so unsafe that a lump of rock fell down on to the cage as it was bringing up the miners. Neither case contains a detailed analysis of the liability: but *Brydon v Stewart* makes it clear that the liability, such as it is, extends not only to the actual place of work but to the means of access to and from it. If there are alternative means of access, it is normally sufficient if one of them is safe: *Brodie v British Railways Board* 1986 SLT 208.

It would be sufficient, at the present day, to say that the employer's general duty, limited as it always is to the exercise of reasonable care, applies to the place of work as it does to all the other circumstances of the employment: but some reference must be made to the earlier case-law, although much of it is now obsolete.

Thus *Seymour v Maddox* (1851) 16 QB 326 where a chorus-girl fell into a hole at the back of the stage, and the court held that the employers owed no duty to her, is not now good law. Nor is the *obiter dictum* of Pickford LJ in *Cole v De Trafford* (No. 2) [1918] 2 KB 523 that the employer's duty was 'to take reasonable care to maintain premises free from any concealed danger of which she was aware or ought to have been aware'. It cannot be right to limit the duty to 'concealed' dangers: the large stone in *Paterson v Wallace & Co, supra*, was not concealed. Since *English's* case it is the duty of the employer to take care, by himself or by his servants or agents, to provide a safe place of work. Scrutton LJ had already said in *Cole v De Trafford (No. 2), supra*, at p. 535:

'[The master] is bound to use reasonable care to provide safe premises and appliances for his servants to work in and with, and to use reasonable care to keep them safe.'

In *Paine v Colne Valley Electricity Supply Co Ltd and British Insulated Cables Ltd* [1938] 4 All ER 803 it was held that the duty of care is not fulfilled merely by employing a skilled contractor. In that case an electrical kiosk had been set up without proper insulation, and the plaintiff was electrocuted. (For the general question of liability for independent contractors, see Chapter 3.)

In *Latimer v A.E.C. Ltd* [1953] AC 643, [1953] 2 All ER 449 a factory was flooded in an exceptional storm, and the floor was rendered slippery by a mixture of oil and rainwater. A workman having slipped while wheeling a trolley, Pilcher J held that the employers were negligent in not sending the men home until the condition of the floor improved. The Court of Appeal reversed this decision on the ground that the danger was not grave enough to justify the stoppage of work, but said that it would be different if (e.g.) the structure were rendered unsafe by a fire.

In the House of Lords the case turned mainly upon the Factories Act 1937, s. 25. However, the House upheld the decision of the Court of Appeal holding that there was no liability at common law: but Lord Tucker said that, if the danger is sufficiently grave, such a drastic step as closing down the factory may be necessary.

In many cases, of course, the danger cannot be removed, and the employer is not expected to make the premises safe in all circumstances. His duty is to take reasonable precautions for the safety of the employees; this may require, for example, thorough inspection of a quarry face (not a cursory glance) before work is done beneath, especially after rain or other circumstances liable to affect the face: *Sanderson v Millom Haematite Ore and Iron Co Ltd* [1967] 3 All ER 1050; a safety rail for work on a ledge over a steep drop: *Bath v British Transport Commission* [1954] 2 All ER 542; a handrail on a flight of steps which, though short, is steep and irregular: *Kimpton v Steel Co of Wales Ltd* [1960] 2 All ER 274; or where there is a foreseeable risk of slipping: *Halsey v South Bedfordshire District Council* (1984) Times, 18 October; a handhold on a roof crawling ladder used for carrying buckets: *Cavanagh v Ulster Weaving Co Ltd* [1960] AC 145, [1959] 2 All ER 745; a line of demarcation—a 'safety line'—on a roof over which a ropeway runs: *Quintas v National Smelting Co Ltd* [1961] 1 All ER 630; a safety belt or rope for work which involves moving over steep and slippery altar courses in a dry dock: *Hurley v J. Sanders & Co Ltd* [1955] 1 All ER 833; a safety net under a ship's gangway in case anyone falls off: *Kyle v Salvesen* 1980 SLT (Notes) 18; the re-siting of a points lever which may endanger a person riding on the footboard of a railway engine: *Hicks v British Transport Commission* [1958] 2 All ER 39; warning of the presence of debris which blocks a route between a bank and railway *track: Smith (or Westwood) v National Coal Board* [1967] 2 All ER 593; altering the lay-out of a private line which is too close to an adjacent railway line, or fencing it off: *Braithwaite v South Durham Steel Co Ltd* [1958] 3 All ER 161; or even the fencing of an open hatchway between decks at sea, where the seamen may go near the edge: *Morris v West Hartlepool Steam Navigation Co Ltd* [1956] AC 552, [1956] 1 All ER 385; but not a fence on the edge of a sloping roof: *Regan v G. and F. Asphalt Co Ltd* (1967) 2 KIR 666.

Where a man has to work out of doors in rough country, the employer cannot be expected to protect him against ordinary natural risks: *McGinley v Nuttall Sons & Co Ltd (London) Ltd* (1956) Times, 29 December, Ct of Sess (Inner House) (man slipping on frozen burn in Scottish Highlands when going to inspect rain gauge). But protective clothing or other equipment may be required: *Bradford v Robinson Rentals Ltd* [1967] 1 All ER 267. The duty of an employer *may* (but does not necessarily) extend to warning and evacuation of employees in a foreign country if war risks are likely: *Longworth v Coppas International (UK) Ltd* 1985 SLT 111.

Other cases on general conditions of work (e.g. traffic danger) are mentioned under system of work.

Evidence of negligence

In *Paterson v Wallace & Co* and *Brydon v Stewart* little turned on evidence of negligence, as this had been established by findings of the jury. Presumably negligence was proved by the obviously unsafe condition of the pit. In *Brydon's* case the pit shaft was obviously unsafe; in *Paterson's* case the miner himself had called attention to the stone overhanging his place of work, and there had been unreasonable delay in removing it. *Mellors v Shaw* (1861) 1 B & S 437 was a case very like *Brydon v Stewart*: the pit shaft was unsafe, and a stone fell down it and injured the plaintiff. Blackburn J said that the 'sides of the shaft were *in such a state as to be evidence of negligence*'. On the other hand in *Morton v Dixon (William) Ltd* 1909 SC 807 where a piece of coal fell between the cage and the side of the shaft, striking a miner at the pit bottom, and in *Sneddon v Summerlee Iron Co Ltd* 1947 SC 555 where a block of ice fell from the wall of the shaft on to the cage, the employers were held not liable on the ground that they had taken all measures deemed necessary in accordance with usual mining practice[9].

If, then, it is proved that there is a defect of a dangerous character, so conspicuous that no one could fail to see it, the employer may be held negligent if he delays in remedying it, at least where there is a known remedy. But difficulties arise when injuries are caused by a hidden defect. Here it is a question of fact whether the employer ought to have discovered the defect; and if it is contended that inspections should have been made, this must be supported by evidence. In the case of a ship, for example, it could be proved that regular inspections are necessary and customary: but in the case of an ordinary private house, there is no rule of law which requires the master to look for defects, at any rate by making regular inspections where there is no sign of anything wrong: see *Cole v De Trafford* (No. 2) [1918] 2 KB 523 (chauffeur employed in private house, injured by glass which fell out of garage door, though this had appeared safe).

Just as the degree of care to be taken in discovering latent defects is a question of fact, so also, in the case of known dangers, it is a question of fact whether the defendant ought to have taken special precautions, or whether those he has taken were sufficient. Thus, as Bowen LJ said in *Thomas v Quartermaine* (1887) 18 QBD 685, it would be going too far to say that a builder cannot be employed on a roof unless a parapet is put round it. *Thomas v Quartermaine* is not now regarded as good law. It was a case where there was a narrow passage between two vats of hot liquid and the plaintiff, in pulling a board from underneath one vat, overbalanced and fell back into the other. There was a parapet round the vat, but it was not high enough to prevent this unusual accident. A majority of the Court of Appeal decided that there was no evidence of negligence. Clearly, however, it was a question of fact whether, by erecting this low parapet, the defendant had taken reasonable care; and a jury might have decided the issue either way. In *McIlhagger v Belfast Corpn* [1944] NI 37 where a workman fell into an unfenced tank at a sewage-pumping station the employers were held liable.

9   It may be argued that the Scots courts were too strict in the latter case at any rate, and gave undue weight to general practice; but Scots law has in the past tended to be strict on this point (see p. 47).

3 Premises and plant of a third party

The duty of an employer is to take reasonable care for the safety of his workmen throughout the course of their employment. This duty does not come to an end because the workmen are sent to work at premises which do not belong to the employer: see *General Cleaning Contractors Ltd v Christmas* [1953] AC 180, [1952] 2 All ER 1110 (window-cleaners); *Thomson v Cremin* [1953] 2 All ER 1185 (stevedores); *Smith v Austin Lifts Ltd* [1959] 1 All ER 81 (lift engineers)[10].

The degree of care to be taken by the employer in such cases is quite another matter. 'The duty is there, whether the premises are in the occupation of the master or of a third party . . . but what reasonable care demands in each case will no doubt vary': per Parker LJ in *Wilson v Tyneside Window Cleaning Co* [1958] 2 QB 110, [1958] 2 All ER 265. In the Scottish case of *M'Quilter v Goulandris Bros Ltd* 1951 SLT (Notes) 75, ship-repairers' men had to go along an unlighted deck, and one of them tripped over a ring-bolt, fell into an uncovered hatchway, and was killed. The employers were held liable. Lord Guthrie said:

> 'The fact that the work had to be carried out on the premises of a third party did not absolve an employer from his duty of exercising reasonable care for the safety of his workmen. The duty must still be fulfilled, although its scope is circumscribed by the fact that the work was being done on premises not within the possession and control of the employer. As the structure of the premises is outwith his control, and any defects therein beyond his power to rectify, his care for his men could only be exercised within the limits imposed by those circumstances. But he was still under the duty of exercising reasonable care to safeguard them against dangers which he should anticipate and which he had power to avert.'

An important factor in this case was that lighting could have been provided.

The custom of the trade may allow the employer to rely, to a certain extent, upon the diligence of a third party. The House of Lords have

10 Such cases as *Hodgson v British Arc Welding Co Ltd and B. & N. Green and Silley Weir Ltd* [1946] KB 302, [1946] 1 All ER 95 (staging on ship provided by other contractors), *Taylor v Sims and Sims* [1942] 2 All ER 375 (repair of bomb-damaged house), and *Cilia v H. M. James & Sons* [1954] 2 All ER 9 (plumber sent to private house), if, and so far as they decide that the employer has *no duty* to safeguard his workmen against dangers arising from the state of the premises of third parties, are inconsistent with the authorities in the House of Lords cited in the text.

held that stevedores are in general entitled to rely upon the shipowners for safety: *Thomson v Cremin* [1953] 2 All ER 1185, approving *M'Lachlan v The Peverill S.S. Co Ltd and MacGregor and Ferguson* (1896) 23 R 753. Lord Wright said at p. 1192:

> '[The stevedore] is *prima facie* entitled to assume that the shipowner has discharged his duty of care in regard to the safety of the premises ... [he] has in the ordinary course no right to interfere with the structure, permanent or temporary ... No doubt, if there are apparent indications which he observes, or ought to observe, that the structure is defective, he owes a duty to take reasonable measures for the protection of his men[11].'

Similarly, in the shipbuilding trade, it is not practicable for every sub-contractor to insist upon making an independent check of the staging: *Hodgson v British Arc Welding Co Ltd and B and N. Green and Silley Weir Ltd* [1946] KB 302, [1946] 1 All ER 95; ship-repairers are entitled to assume that a reputable ship will be reasonably safe: *Mace v R. and H. Green and Silley Weir Ltd* [1959] 2 QB 14, [1959] 1 All ER 655; an employer of a man sent to do repairs from a platform beneath the funnels of a ship was not required to inspect the safety rail (which gave way): *Shepherd v Pearson Engineering Services (Dundee) Ltd* 1981 SLT 197; and contractors in a coal mine may rely on the judgment of the Coal Board as regards support of the roof: *Szumczyk v Associated Tunnelling Co Ltd* [1956] 1 All ER 126. So, too, the employer of a plumber or a window-cleaner who is sent to a private house is not expected to make a preliminary visit of inspection: *Cilia v H. M. James & Sons* [1954] 2 All ER 9; *Wilson v Tyneside Window Cleaning Co* [1958] 2 QB 110, [1958] 2 All ER 265. But where men are sent to a site such as a showground, preliminary inspection for any dangers may be necessary: *McDowell v F.M.C. (Meat) Ltd* (1968) 3 KIR 595 (high voltage line near flagpole); a builder undertaking a substantial task such as a demolition must take all reasonable measures, e.g. by shoring up unstable brickwork: *Knight v Demolition and Construction Co Ltd* [1954] 1 All ER 711n; a demolition contractor should make a preliminary inspection for anything such as an unstable chimney which may endanger either his employees or the public: *Glasgow v City of Glasgow District Council* 1983 SLT 65; sub-contractors on a building site

---

11 Applied in *Durie v Main & Sons* 1958 SC 48 (handrail left insecure). See also *Gibson v Skibs A/S Marina* [1966] 2 All ER 476 (stevedores not liable for hair-line crack in ship's winch regularly inspected by crew).

which is badly obstructed and dangerous should take up the matter with head contractors: *Smith v Vange Scaffolding and Engineering Co Ltd* [1970] 1 All ER 249; and window-cleaners must take precautions against recognised dangers such as loose window-sashes: *General Cleaning Contractors Ltd v Christmas* [1953] AC 180, [1952] 2 All ER 1110; but they need not give repeated warnings against loose handles to experienced employees aware of such dangers: *Wilson v Tyneside Window Cleaning Co, supra.* In *Smith v Austin Lifts Ltd* [1959] 1 All ER 81 employers were held negligent when, after several reports of disrepair in the access to a lift, they took no steps to have it made safe. Failure to have electricity turned off while repair or decoration is going on may be negligent: *Fisher v C.H.T. Ltd (No. 2)* [1966] 2 QB 475, [1966] 1 All ER 88.

The employer's duty of care extends to the means of access to the place of work where it crosses the property of a third party: but when the employer's premises were on a dock estate, and were approached by a private road and also by a short cut across which shunting might be in progress, the employer's duty was sufficiently discharged by giving warning of the risk of shunting: *Ashdown v Samuel Williams & Sons Ltd* [1957] 1 QB 409, [1957] 1 All ER 35.

The principle of these cases applies also to the use of plant belonging to third parties. In *Fryer v Short Bros and Harland Ltd* (reported in *The Scotsman* 6 May 1949 and 99 LJo 328), Lord Mackintosh held the employers liable when they were using scaffolding loaned by a third party (the R.A.F.) on the express terms that they were responsible for inspection and maintenance[12]. Whether there is a duty to inspect or not depends on the circumstances. In *Bott v Prothero Steel Tube Co Ltd, Dainty (L.) Ltd* [1951] WN 595 a ladder was placed against a crane belonging to a third party, and the crane—which had no parking brake—moved unexpectedly and threw the ladder down. It was held by the Court of Appeal that the employers had done their duty by asking the third parties to confirm that their plant was safe. Where an experienced slaughterman was sent by his employers to a municipal slaughterhouse, the employers were held to be entitled to rely upon the judgment of the corporation and of their own employee as to the safety and suitability of

---

12 In such a case the workman has of course no rights under the contract between his employer and the third party: but it is suggested that the *de facto* division of responsibility, under the contract, is part of the *res gestae* determining the extent of the duty in tort.

the equipment: *Gledhill v Liverpool Abattoir Utility Co Ltd* [1957] 3 All ER 117.

An employer may be liable if, through his own failure to make proper equipment available, the workmen are left to find equipment for themselves which proves to be unsound. He may also be liable if a negligent selection is made, by a fellow-servant of the plaintiff, out of equipment made available by a third party: see the cases cited at pp. 121–122, *ante.*

4 Competent staff and personnel management

The duty to provide competent staff is of little importance, as the employer is now liable for the negligence of fellow-servants, but there may still be cases where it applies. For instance, a skilled employee may hold all necessary qualifications and act with reasonable care, but may be deficient in experience to meet situations which the employer ought to have foreseen. A case in point is *Butler (or Black) v Fife Coal Co Ltd* [1912] AC 149. There carbon monoxide had escaped into a coal mine, and poisoned one of the miners. Under the Coal Mines Regulation Act 1887[13], it was the statutory duty of the manager and fireman to withdraw the men in such a case until the matter had been investigated; but, under the terms of the Act, the owners were not liable for the breach of this duty if they could prove that it occurred without negligence on their part. Although, therefore, the case turned on statutory duty, it is an illustration of common law negligence. It was proved that the manager and the fireman had no previous experience of carbon monoxide emanations, which, however, the owners knew to be a possible danger in their pit. These two officials were properly qualified; but as they lacked this necessary experience, the House of Lords held that the owners were negligent in appointing them. Lord Shaw of Dunfermline said at p. 170:

'My Lords, it is extremely difficult to understand how, in such a situation, men could be supposed to be competent who had no knowledge of the dangerous properties of the gases in these pits, or of

13 22 Halsbury's statutes, 3rd Edn., 42.

the peril to human life involved in the non-withdrawal or re-admission of workmen in the circumstances described.'

There is, of course, no warranty that the staff are competent. The question in each case is whether the employer has taken reasonable care to select competent staff.

In a number of cases in the United States, actions have succeeded against employers, especially shipowners, for recruiting vicious or dangerous fellow-servants who have injured the plaintiff. In the only English case of this kind, *Smith v Ocean S.S. Co Ltd* [1954] 2 Lloyd's Rep 482 a ship's officer was stabbed by a native labourer, but the claim failed because the defendants had no reason to expect danger from the employment of native labour[14].

In *Hudson v Ridge Manufacturing Co Ltd* [1957] 2 QB 348, [1957] 2 All ER 229, a fellow-workman persistently indulged in 'skylarking', such as tripping up other workmen, and had taken no notice of the foreman's reprimands. Streatfield J held that:

'if . . . a fellow-workman . . . by his habitual conduct is likely to prove a source of danger to his fellow-employees, a duty lies fairly and squarely on the employers to remove the source of danger.'

by dismissal if necessary. Reprimands, unaccompanied by threat of dismissal, were not enough. Employers are not liable where they have no reason to think that a man would do anything dangerous, even if he is given to mild practical jokes: *Coddington v International Harvesters of Great Britain Ltd* (1969) 6 KIR 146.

A topic allied to the provision of competent staff is the duty to give adequate supervision—so far as this can be distinguished from the system of work. In *Smith v Crossley Bros Ltd* (1951) 95 Sol Jo 655, two apprentices mischievously injected compressed air into a third, but the Court of Appeal held, on the evidence, that such an action could not reasonably be foreseen, and that there was no failure in the duty of supervision.

Where a seaman who had become insane went overboard, the employers were negligent in not putting him ashore earlier: *Ali v Furness Withy (Shipping) Ltd* [1988] 2 Lloyd's Rep 379.

---

14 In the United States proof of negligence is not required in such a case, because the warranty of 'seaworthiness' is given a very wide scope and is considered to be broken if a member of the crew is dangerous.

5 A proper system or method of working

A very important branch of the employer's duty is that he must take reasonable care to establish and enforce a proper system or method of work. The earliest case in which this principle can be traced is *Sword v Cameron* (1839) 1 D 493 where men were working in a quarry in which blasting operations were being carried out. The men were not given sufficient time to get clear before an explosion took place, and one of them was injured. The Court of Session held the employers liable for failing to have a proper method of giving warning. Similarly in *Smith v Baker & Sons* [1891] AC 325 the House of Lords held (although it was not the main question before the House) that it was an unsafe system for heavy stones to be swung by a crane, without warning, over the heads of workmen drilling in a railway cutting.

In Scotland it has consistently been recognised that an employer might be held liable for a faulty system: in England—in spite of *Smith v Baker*—the possibility of a claim along these lines was hardly recognised until modern times. In both countries the law was decisively settled by the decision of the House of Lords in *Wilsons and Clyde Coal Co v English* [1938] AC 57, [1937] 3 All ER 628 where it was held that it is the personal duty of the employer to see to the safety of the system of work, and that he cannot escape liability by delegating performance of the duty to someone else—even though, as in the case of coal mines, delegation of the management to a qualified official is required by law. In this case a miner on the morning shift was leaving the pit when the haulage plant was put into operation, and he was crushed against the side of the road by the hutches before he had time to reach a refuge hole: the employers—who had delegated their duties to a qualified manager— were held liable on the basis of a finding by the jury that it was an unsafe system for the haulage plant to be operated while the morning shift was leaving work. Since *English's* case there have been a large number of decisions on the employer's duty to provide a safe system of work: some of these may have gone a shade too far, but the extent and limits of the duty have now become fairly clear. Since the doctrine of common employment was abolished, the employer has become responsible not only for establishing a safe method of work in advance, but also for the safe conduct (through his servants) of all working operations. This does not mean that the duty to establish a safe method of work has become obsolete[15]. The importance of 'safe system' is that it stresses the obligation to plan the work in advance with due regard to safety:

'It is the duty of an employer to give such general safety instructions as a reasonably careful employer *who has considered the problem presented by the work* would give to his workmen': per Lord Oaksey, *General Cleaning Contractors Ltd v Christmas* [1953] AC 180 at 189, [1952] 2 All ER 1110 at 1114.

What amounts to a safe system is in all cases a question of fact, to be decided by the judge as if he were a jury: there is no doctrine of precedent which requires cases to be followed where the facts are similar: *Qualcast (Wolverhampton) Ltd v Haynes* [1959] AC 743, [1959] 2 All ER 38.

(1) Meaning of system of work

In *Winter v Cardiff Rural District Council* [1950] 1 All ER 819 at 822 Lord Oaksey said:

'There is a sphere in which the employer must exercise his discretion and there are other spheres in which foremen and workmen must exercise theirs.'

It has already been seen that the state of the premises and plant, and the choice and supervision of personnel, fall especially within the employer's province. In adding as a further component the system of work, the law does no more than adopt and clarify a distinction accepted

15 In *Bristol Aeroplane Co v Franklin* [1948] WN 341 Viscount Simon said: 'Now that the Law Reform (Personal Injuries) Act 1948 has passed into law, we may expect that, in cases arising from the injury of a workman when at his work, the allegation against the employer of negligence in not providing a proper system of working will lose much of its importance. There is no doubt about the validity of such an allegation when the evidence really makes it out. But resort to this allegation largely arose from efforts to get the injured man compensation in an action at law, where he might otherwise have been defeated by a plea of common employment.' But, as later cases have shown, 'safe system' is a great deal more than a gloss on common employment, it is a substantive duty of fundamental importance. In Scotland the duty was recognised consistently before, independently of, and after common employment; that it did not follow a similar course in England was due to a premature ossification of English law. On its restoration to its true place in 1937, it may have been stretched a little, but not, it is thought, to excess.

In the U.S.A. the duty extends to 'working conditions', including the 'general plan of work': *Restatement, Agency*, §§492, 506.

in everyday life. The employer is responsible for the general organisation of the factory, mine or other undertaking; in short, he decides the broad scheme under which the premises, plant and men are put to work. This organisation or 'system' includes such matters as co-ordination of different departments and activities; the lay-out of plant and appliances for special tasks; the method of using particular machines or carrying out particular processes; the instruction of apprentices and inexperienced workers; and a residual heading, the general conditions of work, covering such things as fire precautions. An organisation of this kind is required—independently of safety—for the purpose of ensuring that the work is carried on smoothly and competently: and the principle of law is that in setting up and enforcing the system, due care and skill must be exercised for the safety of the workmen. Accordingly, the employer's personal liability for an unsafe system—independently of the negligence of fellow-servants—is not founded on an artificial concept, but is directly related to the facts of industrial organisation. The Lord Justice Clerk (Lord Aitchison) said in the Court of Session in *English's* case, 1936 SC 883 at 904:

> 'What is system and what falls short of system may be difficult to define . . . but, broadly stated, the distinction is between the general and the particular, between the practice and method adopted in carrying on the master's business of which the master is presumed to be aware and the insufficiency of which he can guard against, and isolated or day to day acts of the servant of which the master is not presumed to be aware and which he cannot guard against; in short, it is the distinction between what is permanent or continuous on the one hand and what is merely casual and emerges in the day's work on the other hand.'

In *Speed v Swift (Thomas) & Co Ltd* [1943] KB 557 at 563, [1943] 1 All ER 539 at 542 Lord Greene MR cited this passage and continued:

> 'I do not venture to suggest a definition of what is meant by system. But it . . . may include . . . the physical lay-out of the job—the setting of the stage, so to speak—the sequence in which the work is to be carried out, the provision in proper cases of warnings and notices and the issue of special instructions. A system may be adequate for the whole course of the job or it may have to be modified or improved to meet circumstances which arise; such modifications or improvements appear to me equally to fall under the head of system.'

It appears from these extracts that questions of system may arise where the work is of a settled and permanent character, or where it varies from time to time, or possibly even for a single isolated task: and something must be said about each of these cases. But, in all cases alike, the issue is 'whether adequate provision was made for the carrying out of the job in hand under the general system of work adopted by the employer or under some special system adapted to meet the particular circumstances of the case': per Lord Porter, in *Winter v Cardiff Rural District Council* [1950] 1 All ER 819 at 822[16].

In planning the system of work, the employer must take into account the fact that workmen become careless about the risks involved in their daily work. In *General Cleaning Contractors Ltd v Christmas* [1953] AC 180 at 189, [1952] 2 All ER 1110 at 1114, Lord Oaksey said:

> 'It is . . . well known to employers . . . that their workpeople are very frequently, if not habitually, careless about the risks which their work may involve. It is . . . for that very reason that the common law demands that employers should take reasonable care to lay down a reasonably safe system of work. Employers are not exempted from this duty by the fact that their men are experienced and might, if they were in the position of an employer, be able to lay down a reasonably safe system of work themselves. Workmen are not in the position of employers. Their duties are not performed in the calm atmosphere of a board-room with the advice of experts. They have to make their decisions on narrow sills and other places of danger and in circumstances where the dangers are obscured by repetition.'

Lord Reid said in the same case (pp. 194, 1117).

> 'Where a practice of ignoring an obvious danger has grown up I do not think that it is reasonable to expect an individual workman to take the initiative in devising and using precautions. It is the duty of the employer to consider the situation, to devise a suitable system, to instruct his men what they must do and to supply any implements that may be required[17].'

---

16 The duty is limited to the system of *work*, and does not extend (e.g.) to the safety of transport arrangements to take the men home: *Ramsay v Wimpey & Co Ltd* 1951 SC 692.

17 Cf. *Velekou v Daniell Ltd* [1954] NZLR 513 (duty to protect workmen against own inadvertence); reversed on other grounds]1955] NZLR 645 (the question was whether the bench was too near to a saw, having regard to foreseeable movement of the saw-mill hand: the Court of Appeal held that the lay-out of the apparatus was not a matter of system for the employers but a matter of routine for the foreman).

(i) Permanent organisation

The primary application of these principles is to be found in undertakings such as factories and mines, for 'a system of working normally implies that the work consists of a series of similar or somewhat similar operations': per Lord Reid, in *Winter's* case, *supra*, at p. 825. When an operation or process is constantly repeated, and involves some element of danger, it is evidently the duty of the employer to establish a standard method of carrying out the operation or process, which will eliminate the danger as far as practicable. Such a standard method is necessary if the danger, although it does not arise upon every occasion, does arise from time to time:

> 'The danger in this case is one which is constantly found, and it calls for a system to meet it': per Lord Reid, in *General Cleaning Contractors Ltd v Christmas*, *supra*, at pp. 94, 1117 (risk of loose window-sash to window-cleaner gripping it).

Lord Green said in *Speed v Swift, supra* (at pp. 563, 541 in the respective reports):

> 'Where the work to be performed is regular and uniform as in the ordinary factory or mine, provision of a safe system for the type or class of work and provision of a safe system for the individual job will in general be the same, although a particular occurrence or emergency may call for special precautions.'

The necessity for system in the conduct of an isolated and exceptional task—as distinct from the general running of the factory—depends on the considerations mentioned in para. (iii), *infra*.

(ii) Industries where the nature of the task varies from day to day

There are many important occupations where the nature of the task to be performed is constantly varying. This is the case, for example, in the building trade, in constructional engineering, in shipbuilding yards, and, most of all, in the loading and unloading of ships. In *Speed v Swift*, *supra*, the Court of Appeal held that in industries of this kind it is the employer's duty to establish a proper system for each new task. Lord Greene said:

> 'But in many kinds of work there is no . . . regularity or uniformity, and what is a safe system can only be determined in the light of the actual situation on the spot at the relevant time . . . It is the master's

duty to decide what the lay-out of the job shall be and in doing so he must pay proper regard to the safety of his men.'

This case arose out of the loading of a ship, a type of work which varies from day to day and even from hour to hour, according to the type of ship and cargo and the apparatus available. At the particular time when the accident happened, a ship was being loaded from a barge, and two of the ship's derricks were working together in 'married gear', that is, the falls of both derricks were joined together to lift the same load. One derrick arm was fixed in an outward position of the barge, to enable the load to be lifted vertically, and after the load had been lifted it was swung over towards the hold by the other derrick. During one of its return journeys the empty hook caught the ship's rail and dislodged it, together with an adjacent piece of timber, into the barge below, with the result that the plaintiff, who was working in the barge, sustained injuries. Evidence was given that the ship's rail is not normally removed when married gear is used, but that on this particular occasion, since the rail was loose and timber was lying beside it, the rail ought to have been removed. The Court of Appeal held that the system of work—the 'lay-out' of the apparatus—was unsafe, and the employer was liable. While this decision was essentially a finding of fact, the case is noteworthy as showing that, when a proper system has to be established for a particular operation, attention must be given to any special circumstances which may give rise to danger—such as the looseness of the ship's rail and the presence of the timber on this occasion.

The principles explained in *Speed v Swift* were approved by the House of Lords in *Colfar v Coggins and Griffiths (Liverpool) Ltd* [1945] AC 197, [1945] 1 All ER 326 where, however, Viscount Simon LC was of the opinion that the case carried the employer's personal duty to its extreme limit. In *Colfar v Coggins*, which also concerned the lay-out of apparatus in ship-loading, the employers were held not liable, because the accident was not due to improper lay-out but to the negligence of a fellow-workman in failing to fasten a guy-rope properly. (This was before the abolition of 'common employment'.)

(iii) Isolated tasks requiring organisation
The concept of a proper system of work finds its primary application in the permanent organisation, and is extended, of necessity, to the many industries where the nature of the task is constantly varying. The further

application of system to isolated tasks was at one time considered exceptional, but it is doubtful whether that view would now be taken. In *Winter v Cardiff Rural District Council* [1950] 1 All ER 819 at 825 Lord Reid said:

> 'The conception of a system of working is not easily applied to a case where only a single act of a particular kind is to be performed. Recently, however, this obligation has been extended to cover certain cases when only a single operation is involved . . . the justification for this is that, where an operation is of a complicated or unusual character, an employer, careful of the safety of his men, would organise it before it was begun . . . Where such organisation is called for an employer must provide it . . . but . . . it has never even been suggested that such an obligation arises in every case where a group of the employer's servants are doing some work which may involve danger if negligently performed.'

In *Rees v Cambrian Wagon Works Ltd* (1946) 175 LT 220 (approved by the House of Lords in *Winter's* case) a machine was being dismantled, and a heavy cog wheel was being removed by means of a plank and a sloping wedge: owing to the insufficiency of the wedge, the wheel overbalanced and injured one of the workmen. The Court of Appeal held that 'the operation was one which required proper organisation and supervision', and that the employers were liable. On the other hand, in *Winter's* case itself, where a heavy voltage regulator was being carried on a lorry, but had not been tied to it, and the regulator fell off, carrying the plaintiff with it, the House of Lords held that the manner of loading the lorry was a routine matter within the discretion of the chargehand, and that the employers were not required to establish a proper system for such a routine task.

The dividing line between these two decisions is a very narrow one, especially as the wheel in *Rees'* case and the regulator in *Winter's* case were both about the same weight of 15 cwt. The fact that the operation is dangerous is no criterion—for the handling of any heavy load is dangerous—nor is the fact that a number of men are involved—for a chargehand or foreman should be able to co-ordinate their efforts. It must be shown—in Lord Reid's words—that the operation was 'complicated or unusual', so as to necessitate special organisation.

In cases of this kind, the employer is now liable for the negligence of the person in charge of the operation, and it will rarely be necessary to rely upon absence of safe system, unless, of course, the operation

involved expert planning and supervision which was beyond the capacity
of the man in charge.

(iv) Allowance for infirmities or inexperience of individual workmen
The concept of system received a surprising extension in *Paris v Stepney
Borough Council* [1951] AC 367, [1951] 1 All ER 42, on the ground that
the employer owes a duty to each workman individually and must take
into account his known peculiarities. In this case a one-eyed workman
was engaged in hammering a rusty bolt on a motor vehicle when a chip of
metal flew into his eye and blinded him. The trial judge held that—
having regard to the risk of total blindness—protective goggles ought to
have been provided for this workman, although it was not the practice to
provide them for normal two-eyed workmen engaged in similar work.
The House of Lords, by a majority, declined to set aside this finding of
fact.

It follows that, in planning the method of carrying out particular
processes, the employer ought to take into account the known infirmities
of individuals: but it does not follow that special measures will in every
case be necessary[18].

The same variation of duty applies from one workman to another
where their experience is different: thus a man ought not to be given a
task to carry out, without supervision, where it is beyond his
competence: *Byers v Head Wrightson & Co Ltd* [1961] 2 All ER 538. But,
conversely, an experienced man may not need warning and advice about
risks with which he is familiar: *Qualcast (Wolverhampton) Ltd v Haynes*
[1959] AC 743, [1959] 2 All ER 38.

(v) Duty to establish and enforce system: 'casual departure'
Under the terms of the employer's personal duty as it existed before
1948, the employer was required to establish and maintain a safe

---

18 An employer will not be liable for the consequences of an infirmity or weakness of
   which he neither knows nor ought to know, and is not normally under any duty to
   have employees medically examined to see if they are fit for the work: *Parkes v
   Smethwick Corpn* (1957) 121 JP 415, 55 LGR 438 (ambulance man); or to refuse
   employment to persons liable to dermatitis: *Withers v Perry Chain Co Ltd* [1961] 3
   All ER 676; or to inquire, on putting up a safety notice, whether any of the men are
   illiterate: *James v Hepworth and Grandage Ltd* [1968] 1 QB 94, [1967] 2 All ER 829.
   See also the cases cited at p. 44, *ante*, as to warning or medical checks not being
   required where a minority of employees may be susceptible to some hazard below
   the accepted level of tolerance.

system, but was not liable for negligence by a fellow-workman which was 'a casual departure from the system' (Lord Wright in the *English* case)[19]. Now, after the abolition of common employment, he will be vicariously liable for his own employees: but the distinction is still important because the casual negligence may be that of a third party or his employees.

In *McDermid v Nash Dredging & Reclamation Co Ltd* [1987] AC 906, [1987] 2 All ER 878, the House of Lords made it clear that the duty is not merely to devise a safe system but to put it into operation and maintain it in operation. A tug captain employed by an associated company, who was in charge of the operation, arranged to give a signal when he was about to start the engine, so that the rope could be cast off safely. He failed to give the signal, and the House of Lords held that the employers were liable. The captain was the man in charge on behalf of the employers and had failed to put into operation his own system. His negligence could not be dismissed as the 'casual' negligence of an employee (for which the employers would not have been responsible as he belonged to another company).

It is not always easy to draw a clear line between the employer's failure to enforce a system, and a servant's casual departure from it. Where the employers told an electrician to read the Electricity Regulations but did nothing further to ensure that he was aware of the dangers and complied with the regulations, and in fact the senior electricians were following a dangerous method contrary to the regulations, it was held that no system had been established or enforced: *Barcock v Brighton Corpn* [1949] 1 KB 339, [1949] 1 All ER 251. In general, if a system has been set up on paper but never put into regular operation, or has been allowed to lapse, it would be the fault of the employer: but if it is shown that the system has been followed regularly, then a single deviation, once in a while, would be a 'casual departure'. Where a dangerous method of using a machine is actually taught by or on behalf of the employers, it is a clear case of liability: *Herton v Blaw Knox Ltd* (1969) 6 KIR 35 (too much of workpiece protruding from lathe).

Since the abolition of the defence of 'common employment', the employer has become liable for the casual departure of one of his servants from a proper system, provided that the casual departure amounted to negligence by the servant. Where—as is quite possible—the servant has not been negligent, there is no liability: accordingly the distinction

---

19 See the passages cited at pp. 106 and 110.

between enforcement of a system, and a casual departure from it, may still be important, even in the case of the employer's own men. It may also be important if the workman who has deviated from the system has been injured.

In *Clifford v Charles H. Challen & Son Ltd* [1951] 1 KB 495, [1951] 1 All ER 72 the employers were held liable for failing to insist on the use of protective cream against dermatitis, but this is rather an extreme case which would probably be decided differently since *Qualcast (Wolverhampton) Ltd v Haynes, supra.* The employers in such a case are not expected to keep a constant eye on mature and experienced workmen to make sure that they do as they are told: *Woods v Durable Suites Ltd* [1953] 2 All ER 391 (another case of protective cream). They must take all reasonable measures, including warning of the dangers, and persuasion: *Crookall v Vickers-Armstrong Ltd* [1955] 2 All ER 12 (use of masks against dust causing silicosis):

> 'But if he [the employer] does all that is reasonable to ensure that his safety system is operated he will have done all that he is bound to do': per Lord Reid, *General Cleaning Contractors Ltd v Christmas* [1953] AC 180 at 194, [1952] 2 All ER 1110 at 1117.

There is no duty to order or exhort experienced steel erectors to wear safety belts when many steel erectors reasonably believe there are disadvantages in wearing them: *Cummings (or McWilliams) v Sir Wm. Arrol & Co Ltd* [1962] 1 All ER 623. In *Nolan v Dental Manufacturing Co Ltd* [1958] 2 All ER 449, there was serious risk to the eyes in grinding tools, but the toolsetters generally were not willing to wear goggles. It was held that strict orders should have been given to wear goggles, and enforced by supervision. In *Bux v Slough Metals Ltd* [1974] 1 All ER 262, where the eyes were at risk when pouring molten metal, it was held insufficient merely to provide goggles, the practice of wearing them should have been insisted on or at least encouraged more. In *James v Hepworth and Grandage Ltd* [1968] 1 QB 94, [1967] 2 All ER 829 it was sufficient to post a notice that spats were available as protection against metal splashes although the plaintiff was illiterate and could not read it. (It was right for spats to be optional as on one view they might retain metal and be more dangerous.)

If employers, after careful investigation, fix a standard level of tolerance for some hazard such as noise or vibration, they are not in general required to give warning that some employees may be specially susceptible to harm even below that level, or to arrange medical checks to discover susceptible persons; see the cases cited at p. 44, *ante*.

All these cases are decisions on the facts, and lay down no general rule of law. In *Qualcast (Wolverhampton) Ltd v Haynes* [1959] AC 743, [1959] 2 All ER 38 Lord Radcliffe said:

> 'Though indeed there may be cases in which an employer does not discharge his duty of care towards his workmen merely by providing an article of safety equipment, the courts should be circumspect in filling out that duty with the much vaguer obligation of encouraging, exhorting or instructing workmen or a particular workman to make regular use of what is provided[20].'

(2) Illustrations of defective system

The cases on defective system may be grouped conveniently under the following headings, which, however, are not necessarily exhaustive. All these cases should be treated as *illustrations*, rather than authorities: for the decision that a particular system is unsafe is essentially a finding of fact, dependent on the evidence, and this is especially true where reliance is placed on the practice of the industry: *Qualcast (Wolverhampton) Ltd v Haynes* [1959] AC 743, [1959] 2 All ER 38; *Brown v Rolls-Royce Ltd* [1960] 1 All ER 577.

(i) Faulty co-ordination of departments or branches of work, where one may endanger the other
English's case is an instance of this: the haulage system was being run while the workmen on the morning shift were leaving the pit. *Sword v Cameron* is another example: blasting operations were carried out before the men had time to get out of the way. In *Smith v Baker & Sons* a crane was swinging stones over a cutting where men were drilling, without any warning being given.

In *English's* case a proper system would have been to stop the haulage

---

20 There is, however, some reason for holding as a fact that the duty goes beyond provision in some cases. The Chief Inspector of Factories has said (1961) that one of the major problems is to find ways of persuading workmen to use protective equipment, which would prevent many accidents. This applies especially to such things as goggles and ear-muffs which may be uncomfortable but in some cases should clearly be compulsory.

system at certain times. In *Smith v Baker & Sons* either the crane should have been swung over another route, or warning should have been given. Likewise in *Sword v Cameron* the remedy would have been a prompt warning.

The warning system was also at fault in *Dyer v Southern Rail Co* [1948] 1 KB 608, [1948] 1 All ER 516, where railwaymen were working on the permanent way, and a look-out man, who had been posted to give warning, saw a train coming from one direction, but failed to see another coming from the opposite direction. The line was a busy one, and Humphreys J held on the facts that the system was unsafe; there ought to have been two look-out men, one to watch in each direction.

Other cases are *Calvert v London Transport Executive* [1949] WN 341 (a cleaner of trolley-buses in a depot was struck by a parking vehicle, owing to the absence of a white line to ensure it did not come too close); *Kerr v Glasgow Corpn* 1945 SC 335 (vehicles parked in depot so as to create artificial blind corner and endanger testers); *Spencer v Green (R. and H.) and Silley Weir Ltd* (1947) 80 Ll LRep 217, CA (man painting door of workshop was thrown from ladder by unexpected opening of door to another department).

(ii) Planning for a specific task, especially lay-out of plant[21]
Lord Green describes this as 'the setting of the stage'. *Speed v Swift (Thomas) & Co Ltd, supra,* was a case of this kind, where the ship's rail was not removed as required by the circumstances of the particular operation. *Porter v Port of Liverpool Stevedoring Co Ltd* [1944] 2 All ER 411 was another ship-loading case where lifting tackle, quite suitable for one task, was not altered to meet the needs of the next operation. In *Grantham v New Zealand Shipping Co Ltd* [1940] 4 All ER 258, yet another ship-loading case, where a crate of cheese rolled over the ship's side into a barge (the ship's rail having been removed), it was held as a fact that spars or rope should have been rigged up when the ship's rail was taken away. In *Braithwaite & Co (Structural) Ltd v Caulfield* (1961) Times, 5 May, HL a 'Spanish windlass' (double wire with lever at right angles to twist and tighten it, thereby pulling up the end of a bar inserted in brickwork) was held unsafe in a confined space high on a building where the lever was liable to be knocked out. Where a train shunted through a bridge with narrow clearance and went tender first so that

21 See also the cases at p. 121 on selection of plant.

look-out was difficult, the system was held unsafe and it was not for the plaintiff to say whether he should have been routed differently, or had a better engine, or the tender behind: *McArthur v British Railways Board* (1969) 6 KIR 40.

(iii) Method of using particular machines or performing particular processes
There is old authority for regarding the method of using machines as a question of system. Lord Wensleydale said in *Weems v Mathieson* (1861) 4 Macq 215 at 226 that the master was liable for default on his part 'in not providing good and sufficient machinery and not seeing to it being properly used'. And Lord Watson said in *Smith v Baker & Sons* [1891] AC 325 at 353:

> 'A master is no less responsible to his workmen for personal injuries caused by a defective system of using machinery than for injuries caused by a defect in the machinery itself.'

Thus a dangerous machine may require to be fenced, quite independently of statute: *Thurogood v Van den Berghs and Jurgens Ltd* [1951] 2 KB 537, [1951] 1 All ER 682 (electric fan under test in workshop); *Jones v Richards* [1955] 1 All ER 463 (farm machinery). In *Kilgollan v Wm. Cooke & Co Ltd* [1956] 2 All ER 294 it was held that a machine which threw out small fragments and had caused numerous small accidents ought to be fenced to keep in the fragments. So too where a sharp metal ribbon stripped off and curled as steel was fed into a machine, some means should have been provided to cut off the coils: *Littley v Fairey Engineering Ltd* (1965) 109 Sol Jo 512. Where a fence has to be adjusted for particular tasks, it may be a proper system to leave a skilled workman to make the adjustments himself: *Beal v E. Gomme Ltd* (1949) 65 TLR 543.

It may be a dangerous system for an adult to clean machinery in motion, although the express statutory prohibition (Factories Act 1961, s. 20) is confined to women[1] and young persons: *Murray v Donald Macdonald (Antartex) Ltd* 1968 SLT 10; but a system of turning rollers by an inching button and cleaning them when stationary is not rendered unsafe because a man saves himself trouble by holding a rag against the parts in motion: *Finnie v John Laird & Son Ltd* 1967 SLT 243. It is a dangerous system to polish a rapidly revolving article in a lathe by emery paper held in the hand: *Brown v John Mills & Co (Llanidloes) Ltd* (1970) 8 KIR 702.

---

1   'Women' now omitted: Employment Act 1989, s. 9(4).

Similarly goggles or other special protection may be required in dangerous processes, as in *Finch v Telegraph Construction and Maintenance Co Ltd* [1949] 1 All ER 452, where the plaintiff was engaged in grinding metal when a fragment flew into his eye[2]. Special protection is not required for a slight and remote risk: *Hay v Dowty Mining Equipment Ltd* [1971] 3 All ER 1136. Where a miner was breaking stone with a hammer, there was no duty to tell him to use goggles (which had in fact been provided): the usual practice of looking away or closing the eyes when the blow was struck was considered sufficient: *Fletcher v National Coal Board* 1982 SLT 345. In other cases where there is some risk, it may be sufficient to make goggles available on request: if the risk is greater, as where the plaintiff's work was at any part of a large site and involved risk to the eyes, the goggles ought to be given to him and held personally: *Crouch v British Rail Engineering Ltd* [1988] IRLR 404, CA; it is not generally necessary to tell the employee what they are for: *Coe v Port of London Authority* (1988) Times, 16 May, CA; or to instruct or encourage him to wear them: *McKinley v British Steel Corpn* 1988 SLT 810. Where the employee does not know of some risk (in this case from dermatitis) he should be told when gloves are issued that they are to give protection against it: *Campbell v Lothian Health Board* 1987 SLT 665. In extreme cases where the risk is high if protective equipment is not used, it is not *necessarily* sufficient to provide equipment: it may be necessary to advise or educate the workmen to use it: or to make its use compulsory by a rule of the factory: *Nolan v Dental Manufacturing Co Ltd* [1958] 2 All ER 449 (goggles in grinding tools). The courts should be circumspect in extending the employer's duty beyond provision of safety equipment to such vague obligations as exhorting or instructing the workmen to use it: *Qualcast (Wolverhampton) Ltd v Haynes* [1959] AC 743, [1959] 2 All ER 38; nevertheless there are cases where systematic encouragement, instruction and supervision are necessary: *Bux v Slough Metals Ltd* [1974] 1 All ER 262 (goggles near molten metal liable to splash). *Paris v Stepney Borough Council*, [1951] AC 367, [1951] 1 All ER 42 shows that in some circumstances goggles may have to be provided for a one-eyed man where they would not be necessary in the ordinary course. Shatter-proof glasses should have been provided for a man who wore spectacles and was at risk

2　For fragments from a bit in an electric drill, see *Birkby v Jackson Bros Ltd* (1964) Times, 10 March (Rees J drew the attention of industry to this danger for future consideration). Most dangerous processes are covered by the Protection of Eyes Regulations: Chapter 12, section 9.

when using a wrench: *Pentney v Anglian Water Authority* [1983] ICR 464.

In many cases instructions ought to be given as to the method of carrying out a process or operation: see, e.g. *Barcock v Brighton Corpn* [1949] 1 KB 339, [1949] 1 All ER 251 (electrician should have been told not to remove safety screen when testing switchboard); *Gallagher v Dorman, Long & Co Ltd* [1947] 2 All ER 38 (unsafe system to set men to work on crane without proper instructions on limits of loading capacity); *Lewis v High Duty Alloys Ltd* [1957] 1 All ER 740 (oiling of machinery in motion should have been forbidden); *Quinn v Horsfall & Bickham Ltd* [1956] 2 All ER 467 (hood-guard on machine tool should have been kept down unless machine switched off); *Dimmock v British Railways Board* (1965) Times, 1 July (plaintiff should have been instructed to use soft hammer on case-hardened metal); *Payne v Peter Bennie Ltd* (1973) 14 KIR 395 (inexperienced labourer put on job involving striking broken link near hard steel pin: risk of hard steel splintering not common knowledge, should have been warned to avoid pin or wear goggles).

In like manner instructions may have to be given to window-cleaners as to the safe method of dealing with various types of window: *General Cleaning Contractors Ltd v Christmas* [1953] AC 180, [1952] 2 All ER 1110 (use of wedges where window-sash is gripped and may be loose); *Drummond v British Building Cleaners Ltd* [1954] 3 All ER 507 (attachment of safety belt to transom). But it is not necessary to give repeated warnings to experienced men of dangers such as loose window handles which they know may be encountered: *Wilson v Tyneside Window Cleaning Co* [1958] 2 QB 110, [1958] 2 All ER 265. Nor is it necessary to tell ordinary workmen how to clean slippery fluid from a factory floor without slipping on it themselves: *Vinnyey v Star Paper Mills Ltd* [1965] 1 All ER 175.

It may be necessary to plan in advance the right method of handling a dangerous animal: *Rands v McNeil* [1955] 1 QB 253, [1954] 3 All ER 593 (bull on farm)[3].

It is negligent to allow men to go down a well which contains dangerous fumes, or to fail to give a warning sufficiently urgent to impress the danger on them: *Ward v T. E. Hopkins & Sons Ltd, Baker v T. E. Hopkins & Son Ltd* [1959] 3 All ER 225.

---

3   Cf. *Henderson v John Stuart (Farms) Ltd* 1963 SC 245 (Friesian bull in loose box); *Sneddon v Baxter* 1967 SLT (Notes) 64 (bringing Friesian bull in from field).

A system under which bottles had to be carried across the tiled floor of a dairy, which for hygienic reasons was always wet, was held to be unsafe: *Gay v St Cuthbert's Co-operative Association* 1977 SC 212.

(iv) Handling heavy loads
Where heavy loads are handled on a single occasion, the operation will not require organisation unless it is complex or unusual: see *Winter*'s case and *Rees'* case (p. 140, *ante*). The position where the employers habitually allow loads to be handled in a dangerous manner may well be different[4]. In *Larmour v Belfast Corpn* [1945] NI 163, CA it was held to be negligent to allow a workman at a gasworks to go up a vertical ladder with a heavy damper which caused him to overbalance[5]. In *Ross v Tennant Caledonian Breweries Ltd* 1983 SLT 676n a system of lowering beer kegs in use for 17 years was held to be unsound when a keg escaped. In *Fricker v Benjamin Perry & Sons* (1973) 16 KIR 356, though a load did not exceed the maximum safe weight for two men to lift, there was a foreseeable risk that the load would be shared unevenly if it jammed, and this had not been allowed for.

(v) Not enough men for task
In *Williams v B.A.L.M. (N.Z.) Ltd* (No. 3) [1951] NZLR 893 it was held to be an unsafe system to fail to give standing instructions that barrels should be moved by two men, when they were too heavy to be moved by one man on his own. Similarly, employers were liable for not providing a plumber with a mate to help in carrying a bath upstairs: *Hardaker v Huby* (1962) Times, 11 April, CA. But where the task is not obviously dangerous for one man to do himself, it may be reasonable to leave it to the man himself to ask for help: *Johnson v Pressed Steel Co Ltd* (1963) Times, 15 March (lifting heavy guard off machine)[6].

4 Experienced ambulance man need not be told exactly how to lift a patient out of an ambulance: *Parkes v Smethwick Corpn* (1957) 121 JP 415, 55 LGR 438.
5 Factory Dept. pamphlet 16 deals with 'Weight Lifting by Industrial Workers'. It shows very clearly the importance of a proper system for the habitual lifting and handling of heavy loads. Large numbers of accidents (41,100 in factories during 1957) are due to manhandling of loads, and the Industrial Welfare Society runs special courses to train foremen in safe methods.
6 For other cases of a task too heavy for one man, see *Sayer v Stephenson Clarke Ltd* [1961] 1 Lloyd's Rep 271; *Kinsella v Harris Lebus Ltd* (1963) 108 Sol Jo 14, CA (*not* reasonable with awkward load of 145 lbs to leave man to ask for help, where it was not readily available and requests for help were discouraged); *Peat v N. J. Muschamp & Co Ltd* (1970) 7 KIR 469 (a man may be left to ask for help when necessary if it is then available).

(vi) The use of dangerous materials and contact with disease
In *Clifford v Charles H. Challen & Son Ltd* [1951] 1 KB 495, [1951] 1
All ER 72, Denning LJ said that when an employer

> 'asks his men to work with dangerous substances, he must provide
> proper appliances to safeguard them, he must set in force the
> necessary system by which they use the appliances . . . and he must do
> his best to see that they adhere to it.'

Accordingly, in an occupation where the handling of synthetic glue gave
rise to a risk of dermatitis, it was the duty of the employer to have
protective cream available on the spot in the workshop, and see that it
was used. But in another case there was held to be no duty even to
provide protective cream, doubts being raised by the evidence as to its
value: *Brown v Rolls-Royce Ltd* [1960] 1 All ER 577. No precautions
were practicable in handling oil-covered screws as gloves would
puncture quickly and cream have to be applied repeatedly: *Darvill v C.
& J. Hampton Ltd* (1972) 13 KIR 275. Elbow-length gloves may be
necessary where there is a known risk of dermatitis from splashing with
detergents: *Voller v Schweppes (Home) Ltd* (1970) 7 KIR 228.

This obligation is of some importance where disease-producing
materials are handled, but the onus is on the plaintiff to show that a
special risk of disease exists: *Coleman v Harland and Wolff Ltd* [1951] 2
Lloyd's Rep 76[7].

Special care may likewise be necessary in the storage and issue of
such things as flammable spirits or explosives: *Smedley v Moira Colliery
Ltd* [1948] WN 467. Employers were not liable for a live shell in scrap
metal where no person in authority knew of its presence: *O'Reilly v
National Rail and Tramway Appliances Ltd* [1966] 1 All ER 499
(workman found it and induced another to kick it).

Periodic checks by X-ray are required by normal practice where
nurses are in close contact with active tuberculosis patients but not for
occasional contacts in a mental defective institution: *Sorman v Royal
Scottish National Institution Board of Management*, 1961 SLT 217.
Regular tests and warnings may be required for other cases of exposure

---

7 Employers are not liable if they cannot reasonably be expected to know that the
   substance is dangerous: *Harman v Mitcham Works Ltd* (1955) Times, 12 June
   (beryllium poisoning); *Graham v Co-operative Wholesale Society Ltd* [1957] 1 All ER
   654 (mahogany wood dust causing dermatitis); *Riddick v Weir Housing Corpn* 1970
   SLT (Notes) 71 (cement, etc. on building site causing dermatitis).

to disease, e.g. scrotal cancer through soaking overalls in oil: *Stokes v Guest Keen and Nettlefolds (Bolts and Nuts) Ltd* [1968] 1 WLR 1776 (medical officer wrong to decide checks would cause fear disproportionate to risk). But when employers, after reasonable investigation, have fixed the level above which exposure to some hazard such as noise or vibration is likely to be harmful, they are not in general required to give warning that specially susceptible persons may sustain harm at a lower exposure, or to institute medical checks to discover such persons: see the cases cited at p. 44, *ante*. There is no duty when a workman goes to a works surgery with some medical trouble to inquire whether it is due to his work and put him on other duties: *Kossinski v Chrysler United Kingdom Ltd* (1973) 15 KIR 225.

If there is a risk that materials may produce serious disease, their use may have to be discontinued: employees who have been at risk should be told: *Wright v Dunlop Rubber Co Ltd and I.C.I. Ltd* (1972) 13 KIR 255.

(vii) Instruction and supervision of workers
There is an old authority for the employer's duty to instruct an inexperienced workman. In *Grizzle v Frost* (1863) 3 F & F 622 a girl lost her arm in revolving rollers in a rope factory; in *Cribb v Kynoch Ltd* [1907] 2 KB 548 a girl was injured by a cartridge which exploded while she was testing it; and in *Young v Hoffman Manufacturing Co Ltd* [1907] 2 KB 646 a boy was injured by a circular saw. In all of these cases the accident was due to insufficient instructions, or at any rate to the instructions not being emphasised sufficiently. Under the old law of 'common employment' which was then applied, the employer carried out his duty by establishing a system of instruction and appointing a competent foreman but was not liable for the latter's negligence in giving instruction. Even under the old law the employer was liable if a bad method of work was in use and was taught to employees: *Olsen v Corry and Gravesend Aviation Ltd* [1936] 3 All ER 241 (starting of aircraft engines).

These older cases related to young persons, but there is a similar duty to an inexperienced man, e.g. to warn him of risks inherent in the work, such as a fall of earth: *Blake v Thompson* [1949] NZLR 659; also instruct him in the working of a machine: *Cummings v Reister and Anderson* (No. 2) [1948] 2 WWR 260.

As to supervision, it may be negligent to give even a fairly experienced man a task beyond his competence: *Byers v Head Wrightson & Co Ltd*

[1961] 2 All ER 538 (moving heavy machine over trench); to fail to supervise such a man and make sure that he knows the safety requirements: *Jenner v Allen West & Co Ltd* [1959] 2 All ER 115 (work without crawling boards over fragile roof); to employ a disabled man on work which involves special risk to him: *Porteous v National Coal Board* 1967 SLT 117 (one-eyed man labouring in trench, eye caught by twig: some limitation should have been placed on outdoor work suitable for him); to allow a youth to work a circular saw merely on his assurance that he knows how to do it: *Kerry v Carter* [1969] 3 All ER 723; to permit a man to use a grinding machine in a hospital workshop without checking that he was 'competent' to use it, or giving him instruction: *Bromwich v National Ear, Nose and Throat Hospital* [1980] 2 All ER 663, [1980] I CR 450.

(viii) General conditions of work

This is a residual heading. The general conditions under which work is carried on must, so far as reasonable care can ensure, be such as are consistent with safety.

The following are examples.

Ventilation.   See the cases on coal mines discussed under 'Place of Work', p. 125, *ante*; also *Franklin v Gramophone Co Ltd* [1948] 1 KB 542, [1948] 1 All ER 353 (pneumoconiosis due to abrasive dust from dry grinding near place of work); *Crookall v Vickers-Armstrong Ltd* [1955] 2 All ER 12 (masks for protection against dust); *Quinn v Cameron and Robertson Ltd* [1958] AC 9 [1957] 1 All ER 760 (no liability for invisible dust in foundry not known at that time to cause silicosis).

Lighting.   *Garcia v Harland & Wolff Ltd* [1943] 1 KB 731, [1943] 2 All ER 477 (inadequate light near open hatchway); *Russell v Criterion Film Productions Ltd* [1936] 3 All ER 627 (excessive light in film studio injured crowd extra's eyes).

Fire precautions.   *D'Urso v Sanson* [1939] 4 All ER 26 (furnace installed and fed so as to involve fire risk); *Bain v Moss Hutchison Line Ltd* (1948) 81 Lloyd LR 515 (failure to hold fire drills at sea).

Access to work.   *Ramsey v Wimpey & Co Ltd* 1951 SC 692 (employers not liable for disorganised rush for transport outside place of work, though provided by them); *Trznadel v British Transport Commission* [1957] 3 All ER 196n (not wrong to allow railway workers to walk along track to work);

Brodie v British Railways Board 1986 SLT 208 (where a trackman was able to follow a safe route, there was no liability because another route was blocked); *O'Keefe v John Stewart & Co Shipping Ltd, The Yewkyle* [1979] 1 Lloyd's Rep 182 (ladder in ship's hold was only lightly fastened and 'footed' by man at bottom, unsafe when man at foot had to climb to rescue the other: should have been securely lashed).

Traffic conditions. *Maher v Hurst* (1969) 6 KIR 95 (barriers not essential for road workers); *Robertson v Bell* 1969 SLT 119 (safety of police at road block).

Natural hazards. *Hutchinson v London County Council* [1951] 2 Lloyd's Rep 401 (drowning); *Bradford v Robinson Rentals Ltd* [1967] 1 All ER 267 (frostbite).

Attack by criminals. *Houghton v Hackney Borough Council* (1961) 3 KIR 615 (rent collector at makeshift office; sufficient *inter alia* to have porter within call); *Williams v Grimshaw* (1968) 3 KIR 610 (club stewardess with night's takings, sufficient to have man accompanying); *Charlton v Forrest Printing Ink Co Ltd* [1978] IRLR 559 (manager robbed while collecting wages: negligent in view of known risks in particular case not to employ security firm).

Disease. *Tremain v Pike* [1969] 3 All ER 1303 (farm infected by rats, but no liability as risk of Weil's disease unknown).

Scalding shower in crew accommodation on ship. *Foulder v Canadian Pacific Steamships Ltd* [1969] 1 All ER 283 (not properly adjusted).

Noise. *Berry v Stone Manganese Marine Ltd* (1972) 12 KIR 13 (where noise level—pneumatic hammers—so high as to hurt, and endanger hearing, ear-muffs should be provided and warning given of danger of not wearing); *McCafferty v Metropolitan Police District Receiver* [1977] 2 All ER 756 (police officer employed on gun testing—room should have been soundproofed and ear-muffs provided).

Washing facilities. *McGhee v National Coal Board* [1972] 3 All ER 1008 (showers should be provided at end of work involving heavy exposure to abrasive dust).

Vibration. *White v Holbrook Precision Castings* [1985] IRLR 215, CA (risk of damage to nerves of hand from using grinding machinery, which could not be avoided: employee should be warned of risk if he did not know, but once he knew no further liability).

6 The safe conduct of working operations

The last branch of the employer's liability is that he is responsible for his own personal negligence and the negligence of his servants in failing to carry out his routine working operations safely[8]. An employer has always been liable for his own personal carelessness in the course of routine work: since the Law Reform (Personal Injuries) Act 1948, he has become liable for the negligence of fellow-servants in the course of their routine work. In effect, therefore, the employer, acting through his servants, must exercise reasonable care in the conduct of routine operations. The negligence of a fellow-servant is measured, for this purpose, by the normal standard of the reasonable man in his position, for example, the standard of 'an ordinary, prudent crane-driver': it is not correct to 'apply an especially lenient standard of conduct in a case where workmen are collaborating together and working in a team', or to say that everyday acts of carelessness in a factory do not amount to negligence: *Stavely Iron and Chemical Co Ltd v Jones* [1956] AC 627, [1956] 1 All ER 403. See further p. 99, *ante*. (A more lenient standard is however applied for *contributory* negligence: see Chapter 23, section 4).

Numerous examples could be given of negligence in the course of routine work. Where possible, the illustrations quoted below are taken from cases decided since the Law Reform (Personal Injuries) Act 1948. Where no case is cited, they are based upon cases decided before that Act in which the plaintiff was defeated by reason only of the defence of common employment.

---

8   Perhaps in time a formula may be found which will combine the duty to establish in advance a safe method with the duty to carry out routine work safely. With great respect to the distinguished judges who, *obiter*, have thought otherwise, the revival of the old phrase, 'so to carry on the operations that the workmen are not exposed to unnecessary risks', does not meet the case. For the difficulties in this phrase, see p. 83, *ante*.

OCCUPiERS LiABiLiTY

Sec 0 (i)

Some illustrations

(a) Traffic accidents due to the careless driving of vehicles on the highway or at the place of work—especially on large building and engineering sites, where such accidents have been frequent. The employer has been held liable where he arranged for the plaintiff to be carried by a fellow-servant on his own motor-cycle to do a repair job, although the accident happened when they had left the job for the lunch-break: *Harvey v R. G. O'Dell Ltd* [1958] 2 QB 78, [1958] 1 All ER 657.

(b) Railway accidents. This extends to the negligence of signalmen, guards and other railway servants, as well as the engine-driver. There are limits to an engine-driver's ability to avoid accidents, because he has to keep to fixed tracks and watch signals, and cannot stop quickly: *Trznadel v British Transport Commission* [1957] 3 All ER 196; but drivers and guards must still exercise care and keep a good look-out so far as they are able: *Braithwaite v S. Durham Steel Co* [1958] 3 All ER 161.

(c) Negligent navigation of ships and aircraft, e.g. *Holman v F T Everard & Sons Ltd, The Jack Wharton* [1986] 2 Lloyd's Rep 382 where the master ordered anchoring at an unsafe time and the chief officer on the forecastle was hit by a heavy wave.

(d) Negligent handling of machinery or tools, e.g. *Staveley Iron and Chemical Co Ltd v Jones* [1956] AC 627, [1956] 1 All ER 403 (crane-driver failed to pause to check security of load before lifting); *Wattson v Port of London Authority* [1969] 1 Lloyd's Rep 95 (crane moved back at time when no look-out posted); *Lindsay v Connell & Co Ltd* 1951 SC 281 (workman accidentally struck with hammer another workman who was holding steel for him).

(e) Negligently handling or dislodging objects liable to fall, e.g. by a thoughtless movement which dislodges a piece of timber or a brick from a scaffold.

(f) Disobedience to safety instructions. Frequently these are statutory regulations, but disobedience to the employer's own orders is equally negligent. Examples are *Stapley v Gypsum Mines Ltd* [1953] AC 663, [1953] 2 All ER 478 (failure to obey order to make roof of mine secure);

National Coal Board v England [1954] AC 403, [1954] 1 All ER 546 (firing shot in mine without clearing adjacent area, contrary to statutory orders).

(g) Negligent creation of static dangers, e.g. *Broom v Morgan* [1953] 1 QB 597, [1953] 1 All ER 849 (fellow-servant left trap-door open).

(h) Negligent supervision of the work of subordinates, e.g. by allotting work which is too heavy or otherwise unsuitable, or by failing to give sufficient instruction in the method of doing the work, especially to young or inexperienced workers; not exercising sufficient oversight: *Kendrick v Cozens and Sutcliffe Ltd* (1968) 4 KIR 469 (foreman saw workman had moved off ladder to work from fragile roof and failed to check him).

(i) Negligent maintenance of plant[9].

(j) Negligent selection of plant.

(k) Negligent rigging up of plant, e.g. failure to tie a rope securely as in *Colfar v Coggins and Griffith (Liverpool) Ltd* [1945] AC 197, [1945] 1 All ER 326.

(l) Misuse of plant, e.g. *Barry v Black-Clauson International Ltd* (1967) 2 KIR 237 (guard rail with defective base gave way when used as support for rope pulling up cable: on the facts it was not wrong to use the rail though not designed for the purpose).

(m) Negligently adopting an unsafe method of work, e.g. where a gang of dock workers, disregarding the instructions of the foreman, agreed to unload cargo in a manner which was dangerous but less troublesome; *Williams v Port of Liverpool Stevedoring Co Ltd* [1956] 2 All ER 69.

Some of these examples overlap the duty of the employer to provide and maintain safe plant and machinery, but they are also mentioned here in order to give a comprehensive picture of the possible cases of negligence by fellow-workmen.

9   See cases under 'Maintenance of plant', pp. 116–122, *ante*.

Chapter 5

The liability of third parties to an injured workman

1 General

In the course of industry it is often found that several employers, with their workmen, are engaged on a common task, or are working on the same premises or at any rate in the same vicinity. Thus in building or engineering operations, or in shipbuilding—which are important and characteristic examples—there may be a principal contractor and several sub-contractors, and in addition there will be the occupiers of the site or of the ship, as the case may be. It follows, then, that a textbook on employer's liability will be incomplete unless it takes into account the rights of an injured workman against 'third parties'—by which is meant, in this context, all persons other than the workman's own immediate employer and his fellow-workmen. This involves an extension—not, on practical grounds, an undue extension—of the meaning of the term 'employer's liability': it involves, besides, the exploration of several branches of the law of tort which used to be obscure but are now much clearer. Within a single chapter it is not possible to quote all the detailed case-law, which relates, of course, to other situations as well as accidents occurring in the course of work. Attention is, therefore, concentrated on: (i) the leading principles—as established and explained by the cases, and, in the case of dangers on premises, the statutes which have now replaced them—and (ii) the subsidiary cases which illustrate the specific orientation of the law towards injuries sustained by workmen in the course of their employment.

All forms of liability set out in this chapter are examples of the tort of negligence, that is to say of the breach of a duty to take reasonable care.

For the exceptional cases of absolute liability without proof of negligence, such as liability as the keeper of animals, or for the escape from the defendant's premises of fire and of other things likely to do mischief if they escape, reference should be made to Chapter 2, section 6. The starting point in defining any duty of care is now the general principle of Lord Atkin in *Donoghue v Stevenson* [1932] AC 562, that a duty is owed to those persons who are 'so closely and directly affected by my act that I ought reasonably to have them in contemplation' (see Chapter 2). This does not mean that everyone owes a duty to everyone else to exercise reasonable care in all the circumstances of the case. Another well-known remark in that case was that 'the categories of negligence are never closed', which implies that there are different categories of duty according to the relationship of the parties. Otherwise everyone would owe the same high duty as an employer[1]. It is not enough that a risk should be foreseen if there is no responsibility for preventing it. In *Hedley Byrne & Co Ltd v Heller and Partners Ltd* [1964] AC 465, [1963] 2 All ER 575 Lord Devlin said:

> 'It is not in my opinion a sensible application of what Lord Atkin was saying for a judge to be invited on the facts of any particular case to say whether or not there was "proximity" between the plaintiff and the defendant. That would be a misuse of a general conception and it is not the way in which English law develops. What Lord Atkin did was to use his general conception to open up a category of cases giving rise to a special duty. It was already clear that the law recognised the existence of such a duty in the category of articles that were dangerous in themselves. What *Donoghue v Stevenson* did may be described either as the widening of an old category or as the creation of a new and

1 The view that there is not one overriding duty of care, but duties of varying scope, whose extent the court has to define according to the type of situation in which they arise, is confirmed by *Home Office v Dorset Yacht Co Ltd* [1970] 2 All ER 294 especially at pp. 304, 325, and now in *Peabody Donation Fund (Governors) v Sir Lindsay Parkinson & Co Ltd*, [1984] 3 All ER 529, [1984] 3 WLR 953. There are dangers in the notion of a duty of care which is infinitely variable from case to case. To a judge who does not look beyond the confines of his list, it may seem desirable to do perfect justice on the unique facts of each case. But this is not what 'the common law' has traditionally meant—it means a *common* standard, not one man's opinion: and that means rules which are known and can be relied on in thousands of cases which never reach court or even the issue of a writ. 'Reasonableness' in the common law is 'reason' applied to determine rules. (For example, the old duty of the invitor as defined by Willes J.) Chief Justice Coke opposed King James I when the latter wished to sit in court, on the ground that legal knowledge was essential. If it were only a matter of deciding what is 'reasonable in the circumstances', it would hardly be necessary to have legally qualified judges.

similar one. The general conception can be used to produce other categories in the same way.'

In *Home Office v Dorset Yacht Co Ltd* [1970] 2 All ER 294 at 326 Lord Diplock took a similar view of Lord Atkin's principle:

'Used as a guide to characteristics which will be found to exist in conduct and relationships which give rise to a duty of care this aphorism marks a milestone in the modern development of the law of negligence. But misused as a universal it is manifestly false.'

In *Peabody Donation Fund (Governors) v Sir Lindsay Parkinson Ltd*, [1984] 3 All ER 529, [1984] 3 WLR 953, Lord Keith of Kinkel said:

'The true question in each case is whether the particular defendant owed to the particular plaintiff a duty of care having the scope which is contended for . . . A relationship of proximity in Lord Atkin's sense must exist before any duty of care can arise, but the scope of the duty must depend on all the circumstances of the case.'

Thus a head contractor on a building site does not have the same responsibility to men working on the site, but not employed by him, as their own employer has; though he may have duties of another kind, e.g. as occupier of premises or supplier of plant[2]. In applying Lord Atkin's principle, we must remember that some relationships are more 'close and direct' than others, also we must consider what the 'act' is which is said to give rise to a duty. Lastly in the *Hedley Byrne* case, *supra*, which turned on liability for misleading information, not on physical damage, the House of Lords thought that a key factor in establishing a duty of care was the *reliance* placed by one person on another, and this may be important also where plant is supplied by a third party.

In general, third parties do not stand in the same close relationship to a man as his own employer, who has power to control every detail of his work. Accordingly their duty towards him is hardly ever so high, at any rate over so wide a field. If a third party has a direct interest in the work going on, that naturally gives him greater responsibility than if he were a detached bystander. Similarly the duty of a man who makes a gratuitous loan may be less onerous than the duty of a contractor who has undertaken express responsibility for supplying equipment.

In *Membery v Great Western Rail Co* (1889) 14 App Cas 179 Lord

---

2 Or of course under statutory regulations, which likewise generally limit his responsibility to things he provides or controls.

Herschell, considering the case of work done on premises for the benefit of the occupiers, suggests that the duty of the occupiers falls under three heads:

    (i) 'machinery, appliances or tackle' which they have provided for the workman's use,

    (ii) the condition of their premises,

    (iii) dangerous activities carried out in the course of their business.

Liabilities may attach, of course, to other persons besides the occupiers of the premises where a man is doing work; for example to the manufacturers and repairers of plant and the suppliers of materials used in a factory. These other cases, however, can be all fitted into the threefold classification made by Lord Herschell, which is therefore taken as the framework of this chapter.

The Consumer Protection Act 1987 introduced into English law, under an E.E.C. Directive, the new concept of 'product liability' derived from American law, under which a manufacturer is liable for unsafe products without proof of negligence.

Liability as occupier of premises now depends on the Occupiers Liability Act (for England or Scotland as the case may be). There are numerous cases on defective or dangerous plant, many of them still good law, others subject to reconsideration in the light of *Donoghue v Stevenson.*

As to active operations, Lord Herschell said that in the *Membery* case there was a duty to take care not to

> 'do any act (I emphatically use the word "act") which would endanger the safety of persons . . . employed.'

There is of course no doubt that a person is liable for injury due to negligence in carrying out his own active operations such as running cranes or vehicles. The difficulties in saying whether there is a duty of care usually arise when there has been a mere failure to do something, e.g. to establish a safe method of work or maintain plant efficiently. The *Membery* case decided that in general a third party, unlike an employer, is under no positive obligation to establish a safe method of work, even when the work is done on his premises and for his benefit. In this case a railway company had engaged an independent contractor to carry out shunting operations in their yard. The man sent to do the work sustained injury while shunting trucks single-handed, and he alleged that the company had negligently failed to provide him with assistants.

There was no fault in the plant or the premises, and the plaintiff's injuries were not due to any operations of the defendants, but to the way in which he had performed his own task; and it was held that the circumstances disclosed no cause of action.

Yet if a third party—such as a building owner, superior contractor, safety consultant or architect—intervenes in the control of operations, or assumes responsibility for the method of carrying them out, he is under a duty of care similar to an employer, dependent on the extent of his intervention. The cases are summarised in Chapter 3, section 2, under 'Persons analogous to employers'. An example is *McArdle v Andmac Roofing Co* [1967] 1 All ER 583 where a person in the position of building owner or occupier, who (in the absence of a main contractor) was co-ordinating the activities of sub-contractors, was liable for failure to allocate safety responsibilities when the operations of one sub-contractor endangered the workmen of another[3]. In *Kealey v Heard* [1983] 1 All ER 973, [1983] 1 WLR 573 a building owner of a small property accepted no responsibility to supervise, but simply employed separate contractors to do the various jobs, including erection of a scaffold. He was nevertheless held liable to a self-employed plasterer injured in the collapse of the scaffold on the ground he had a duty to take care that the equipment to be used by those who came on to the land to work there was fit for the purpose, and he had failed to provide any superintendence at all. Similarly a farmer was held liable for supplying an unsuitable ladder to a self-employed 'labour only' bricklayer: *Wheeler v Copas* [1981] 3 All ER 405.

The Health and Safety at Work Act 1974 imposes a series of general safety duties on various persons, in addition to the duty imposed on an employer (s. 2) to his own employees. Thus duties, variously defined, are owed:

By employers and self-employed persons to others *not* in their employment (s. 3);

By persons in control of premises (s. 4);

By manufacturers and designers of articles and substances used at work (s. 6).

---

3 Sellers and Davies LJJ treated the duty as one arising from the fact of supervision and control: Edmund Davies LJ (quoting from Lord Herschell's words in the *Membery* case) treated it as a duty created by a dangerous activity initiated through sub-contractors; if they had instructed the sub-contractors to attend to safety matters and provided equipment (the sub-contractors being for labour only) it might have been sufficient, but they did nothing.

These duties are modelled on the common law duties of care, but they do not replace these duties or give rise to an action for damages: failure to perform them is an offence liable to prosecution. Their wording may, nevertheless, help to crystallise the common law duties where these are at present ill-defined.

2 Product liability

(1) Product liability: Consumer Protection Act 1987

Liability for faults in products supplied to an employer by third parties will now usually depend on Part I (ss. 1–9) of the Consumer Protection Act 1987, which was passed to give effect to a Directive of the European Economic Community and came into force on 1 March 1988[4]. There is no liability for a defect in a product which was 'supplied'—and passed out of the control of the producer—before that date, although it causes injury later: s. 50(7) of the Act.

Under this Act a manufacturer or other supplier may be absolutely liable for personal injury and (within limits) damage to property if caused by a 'defective' product, subject to a number of statutory exceptions. Liability cannot be excluded by agreement, notice or otherwise: s. 7. The Act does not affect liability under the existing law—s. 2(6)—so it will be possible to fall back on common law liability, mainly for negligence, in cases where the Act does not apply. It does not, of course, apply to common law jurisdictions outside the United Kingdom though they may have similar legislation. Accordingly a full account of the pre-existing English and Scottish law on a manufacturer's liability is retained in the next section.

The Act contains precise definitions of the persons liable, of the 'products' within the Act, and of what is meant by a 'defect'; to establish

---

4   However, 'product liability' is an American invention, initiated by the courts which implied a fictitious warranty by the manufacturer. This started with the motor car, where the warranty was first held to run down to the purchaser, and then to members of the public injured by a faulty vehicle. The same concept was applied to aircraft. There have, of course, been strong consumer pressure groups in the U.S.A., and it has become fashionable to imitate them elsewhere. In the United Kingdom they have chiefly directed their agitation against the manufacturers of drugs which have had unexpected side effects.

liability in any case it must be brought within the four corners of these definitions.

(i) Persons liable

(a) The 'producer' of the product (s. 2(2)(a))   This means, primarily, the 'person who manufactured it': s. 1(2)(a). But if it is a substance—coal for example—which has not been manufactured but 'won or abstracted', the producer is the person who won or abstracted it: s. 1(2)(b). There is a third alternative. If it has not been 'manufactured, won or abstracted', but 'essential characteristics' have been given to it by 'an industrial or other process', the producer is the person who applied that process: s. 1(2)(c). This is vague enough to cover many situations. Flour milling, oil refining and fruit canning are obvious examples.

The 'producer' includes not only the manufacturer of the completed product, but also those who have contributed material or components. This will become clearer from the definition of 'product'.

(b) An ostensible producer (s. 2(2)(b))   This means a person who 'held himself' out as the producer by using (i) his name (ii) his trade mark or (iii) some other distinguishing mark on or in relation to the product. It would include, apparently, such firms as Marks & Spencer who use the certification trade mark 'St. Michael' on their goods, and supermarkets with 'own brands', and is likely to apply chiefly to 'consumer' goods.

(c) Importers: but only if they have imported the product into an E.E.C. state from outside the E.E.C., and have done so in order to supply it in the course of business: s. 2(2)(c).

(d) Suppliers (s. 2(3))   This includes *any* person in the line of supply between the manufacturer of a 'product'—which includes any component or material incorporated in a later product—and the ultimate user. A 'supplier' therefore includes an intermediate manufacturer who has used components from elsewhere, though the only fault is in these. The liability of a supplier is of a secondary character: he is not liable unless, on a request within a reasonable time by an injured person (or in death cases—s. 6(2)—his representatives, dependants or relatives), he fails to identify the producer or importer liable under head (a), (b) or (c) above.

A person who supplies a product in which other products are incorporated (whether as components, raw materials 'or otherwise') is not treated as the supplier of the components by reason only of supplying the main product: s. 1(3). In other words he can exonerate himself by giving information about the producer or importer of the main product without going further back.

(e) More than one person liable   Where two or more persons are liable under these rules, their liability is joint and several: s. 2(5). This would not, of course, include a supplier who has exonerated himself by giving information. But in some cases the manufacturer of a finished product and the maker of components may both be liable, though one of them may be exonerated under the special statutory exception which applies in such cases.

(2) What are 'products'?

This term means 'any goods', and also 'electricity': s. 1(2). It includes a product comprised in another product as (a) a component or (b) raw material or (c) otherwise. 'Goods' include growing crops and things attached to land, also any ship, aircraft or vehicle: s. 45(1). But there is no liability for a defect in 'game or agricultural produce' (which includes fishery produce) unless it has been treated by an industrial process.

(3) What is a 'defect'?

The term 'defects' has been much used in English law, but it is always vague and unsatisfactory, and the definition (s. 3) includes other vague concepts which are matters of opinion and degree. However, the defect must be related to 'safety'; and this in turn includes risks to property, as well as risks of injury and death: s. 3(1). The standard of safety is such as 'persons generally' are 'entitled to expect'. In deciding what they are entitled to expect—s. 3(2)—all the circumstances are taken into account, in particular the purpose for which the product has been marketed, its get-up and markings, and any instructions and warnings; also what might be expected to be done with or in relation to the product. But the fact that a product has since been made safer is not, by itself, proof that it was unsafe before.

(4) Who may claim?

In the United States questions have arisen whether liability is to the user only or extends to bystanders. Under this Act, there is no limitation on the persons who may claim. The only requirement is that 'damage' has been caused by a 'defect': s. 2(1). 'Damage' includes 'death or personal injury': s. 5(1); and all the usual law on such things as contributory negligence, contribution between tortfeasors and death claims applies: s. 6. The Act was intended primarily for the benefit of the consumer of such articles as drugs, though it has an enormously wider scope. Claims for damage to property are restricted to private property where the loss exceeds £275. Liability under the Act must of course extend to products which cause accidents when being used or handled at work, such as faulty tools, but in such cases there is unlikely to be a claim for damage to property other than clothing and personal possessions.

(5) Exceptions to liability

The statutory exceptions to liability are listed in s. 4. The onus of proving these is on the defendant. Some of them may be dismissed briefly:
  (a) the defect was due to complying with a legal requirement;
  (b) the defendant never 'supplied' the product; or
  (c) he did not supply it 'in the course of business' or with a view to profit.
The other three exceptions require full analysis.

(i) Defect did not exist at 'relevant time' (s. 4(1)(d))
The relevant time depends on the status of the particular defendant. If he came within s. 2(2) as 'producer' or 'importer', it was the date when he supplied it. If he came within s. 2(3) as a 'supplier' only, it was the date when the last 'producer' or 'importer' supplied it. The Act does not impose liability on the supplier for defects arising while the product was in his possession: it is aimed at the manufacturer or importer, and the supplier's liability is similar to that of a guarantor, secondary to theirs.
  In the case of *electricity*, the relevant point of time is when it leaves the

generator. Presumably the only 'defect' in electricity could be excessive voltage or current.

(ii) State of knowledge at 'relevant time' (s. 4(1)(e))
This means that 'scientific and technical knowledge' at the relevant time was not sufficient to enable a producer of similar products to discover the defect while the product was still under his control. Similar problems of how far a manufacturer must keep abreast of the latest knowledge have arisen in connection with negligence (see p. 38). Under the statute the test is the same in the case of a small manufacturer as it is in the case of a monster firm with a large scientific staff. However, it must be a question of fact and degree what the general 'state' of knowledge is at any particular time. Knowledge takes time to filter through, and the state of knowledge cannot include every tentative hypothesis which is not yet generally accepted, or at any rate taken seriously, by other scientists. Curiously, too, the test is whether the defect could have been 'discovered'. The important question in many cases is whether there was an unknown risk in a product (e.g. tobacco) which was once considered safe. If, however, we give a free interpretation to s. 3 and translate the inept word 'defect' to mean 'danger', the test will extend to such cases.

(iii) Special case of components (s. 4(1)(f))
This clause applies where there is a fault in the main product, and gives an opportunity to suppliers of components or materials to exonerate themselves. They can do this by showing that the fault was *wholly* attributable to (a) the design of the main product or (b) compliance by the component producer with the instructions of the main producer. In case (a) there is nothing wrong with the component itself. In case (b) there may be something wrong; but this is entirely due to complying with the main manufacturer's specification.

It seems that in any case a component manufacturer would not be liable unless there is something wrong with his own product; this would include, of course, under s. 3(2)(a), supplying it without adequate instruction or warnings. On the other hand, the maker of the main product is not liable if the only fault was in the component and he exonerated himself by supplying information about the maker or importer of the component: ss. 1(3), 2(3).

(6) General

The Act binds the Crown, to the extent of its liability under the Crown Proceedings Act (Chapter 25). There are special rules about limitation periods in Sch. 1, amending the English and Scottish Limitations Acts. In general the period is the same as for other personal injuries claims; but there is a maximum of ten years from the date of the last supply by a producer or importer, after which claims are extinguished.

3 Dangerous machinery, plant, loads and materials: the common law liability

In *Griffiths v Arch Engineering Co (Newport) Ltd* [1968] 3 All ER 217 the view was expressed that there is now only one category of duty in all cases where the plant of a third party is used, the general duty under *Donoghue v Stevenson*, and that older cases are obsolete or of illustrative value only[5]. The decisions of the House of Lords quoted at the beginning of this chapter show that this was an undue simplification. The actual decision in the *Griffiths* case, referred to later, is a valuable decision and unquestionably right. Certainly many of the older cases are obsolete—the decision in *Donoghue v Stevenson* itself now expresses a manufacturer's liability too narrowly. But the fact that excessively narrow distinctions have been drawn is not a good reason for saying that there are no distinctions at all and that all types of cases are alike. First of all, plant cases are very varied in comparison with occupier's liability for premises, where the occupier is in continuous control, while plant passes through different hands. Starting with a manufacturer or repairer, he has made or repaired the article, so he is the author of any defect which has arisen in the process. A subsequent purchaser may have no knowledge of a hidden defect, and no duty towards a stranger to find out, unless he has assumed responsibility for providing an article in good condition. On the other hand—in spite of academic derision of those who still refer to things 'dangerous in themselves'—anyone in charge of poisons, explosives or acids is normally aware of their

---

5 A view also expressed by Denning LJ, *obiter*, in *Hawkins v Coulsdon and Purley Urban District Council* [1954] 1 QB 319, [1954] 1 All ER 97 at 104.

inherently dangerous nature: it is not a hidden defect which has to be discovered.

Finally, it is unreasonable that where a wholly gratuitous loan is made—e.g. where a tradesman asks an ordinary householder for the loan of a step-ladder—the lender should be liable for not maintaining it properly. In *Fraser v Jenkins* [1968] NZLR 816, the New Zealand Court of Appeal thought that the cases which impose a lower duty for a gratuitous loan are still good law—at any rate on lending a circular saw which was unfenced, a deficiency which was obvious, there was no duty to give instructions on the safe method of working[6].

The broad types of case seems to be as follows.

(1) The duty of a manufacturer or repairer

It used to be thought that a manufacturer owed no duty to the persons who ultimately used the plant, machinery or materials which he had manufactured, except when he had entered into a contract with those persons; such a contract would not help an injured workman, since it would be made with his employer, and the workman could not sue for breach of a contract to which he was not a party.

Eventually, in the leading case of *Donoghue v Stevenson* [1932] AC 562 it was held in the House of Lords, by a majority, that the manufacturer does owe a duty to take care for the safety of the ultimate user of his products, though at that stage, the starting point for subsequent development of the law, the duty was limited to rather special circumstances. In that case (a decision given on a point of law, heard before the action went to trial) the facts were assumed to be as follows. The pursuer bought a bottle of ginger beer, which had been manufactured by the defenders; the bottle was of dark glass, so that its contents could not be seen before they were poured out, and it was sealed, so that it could not be tampered with until it reached the ultimate consumer; when the pursuer poured out the ginger beer, the remains of a decomposed snail floated out into her glass, and not unnaturally the pursuer was taken ill (she had already drunk part of the bottle). The

---

6 In the English case of *Jones v Minton Construction Ltd* (1973) 15 KIR 309 it was held on similar facts that no duty was owed in lending a cement mixer with a visibly defective guard to self-employed bricklayers.

House of Lords held that if these facts were established at the trial—and if the presence of the snail was due to the defenders' negligence in the process of manufacture—the defenders would be liable.

The essential foundation of the duty established in this case was that the defenders, by using a sealed and opaque bottle, had *intentionally excluded all intermediate interference* between themselves and the ultimate consumers; thus, they had deliberately brought themselves into a direct and immediate relationship with the consumers, and owed them a duty to take care. But at first no duty was considered to arise when the manufactured article was to be examined by some intermediate person, or by the injured person himself. In *Farr v Butters Brothers & Co* [1932] 2 KB 606 a crane was supplied in parts, including gear wheels which fitted badly. It was the duty of a skilled workman to examine the parts and erect the crane, and, though noticing the defects, he erected the crane and afterwards sustained injury in using it. The Court of Appeal held that he had no remedy.

Donoghue v Stevenson broke new ground in holding that a manufacturer owed a duty of care in the limited range of cases where interference was excluded. Since then the wider concept of negligence has been so universally accepted that it is taken for granted that a manufacturer owes a duty to the ultimate consumer. Where there is or should be intermediate examination, the tendency now is to reject claims because the damage is too remote, rather than on the ground of no duty. Older cases which decided that the mere possibility or opportunity of inspection excludes liability are now obsolete[7]. The reasonable probability that an article will be used without examination was taken as the test in *Grant v Australian Knitting Mills Ltd* [1936] AC 85 (manufacturers of pants containing injurious chemicals liable to purchaser who sustained dermatitis through wearing them without washing them); *Herschthal v Stewart and Ardern Ltd* [1939] 4 All ER 123 (sale of re-conditioned motor car for immediate use); and *Haseldine v Daw & Son Ltd* [1941] 2 KB 343, [1941] 3 All ER 156 (lift in building).

7   E.g. *Dransfield v British Insulated Cables Ltd* [1937] 4 All ER 382, disapproved in *Haseldine v Daw, supra*. In *Eccles v Cross and M'Ilwham* 1938 SC 697 the pursuer, in addition to suing the manufacturer, averred that another defender had the opportunity and duty to inspect, and it was held that in view of this averment he could not succeed against the manufacturer (doubted in *Miller v S. Scotland Elec. Board* 1958 SLT 229). But in Scotland, as in England, a mere opportunity to inspect does not exonerate the manufacturer: *Donnelly v Glasgow Corpn* 1953 SC 107.

Since the probability of an examination of the product excludes the manufacturer's liability, *a fortiori* it is excluded if, as in *Farr v Butters Brothers & Co, supra*, the injured man knew of the defect before he sustained injury (and see *Gledhill v Liverpool Abattoir Utility Co Ltd* [1957] 3 All ER 117). Moreover, in the case of an article which ought to be examined from time to time, though not necessarily at once, an injury after a lapse of time may be too remote: *Evans v Triplex Safety Glass Co Ltd* [1936] 1 All ER 283. But in *Mason v Williams and Williams Ltd and Thomas Turton & Sons Ltd* [1955] 1 All ER 808 manufacturers who had supplied a chisel to employers were held liable to a workman who used the chisel, and was injured because the steel was too hard and a piece flew out, on the ground that it is not the duty of an employer to examine tools supplied by reputable manufacturers: this was approved by the House of Lords in *Davie v New Merton Board Mills Ltd* [1959] AC 604, [1959] 1 All ER 346. The manufacturer's liability ceases, however, if the employer after discovering the dangerous condition of such a tool chooses to keep it in use: *Taylor v Rover Co Ltd* [1966] 2 All ER 181.

These decisions negativing liability where the defect is known, or could reasonably have been discovered, are best regarded as decisions on causation, rather than inherent limitations of the manufacturer's liability. In some cases knowledge of a defect may not break the causal connection, or for other reasons both manufacturer and employer may be liable: e.g. *Hadley v Droitwich Construction Co Ltd* (1967) 3 KIR 578 (crane inaccurately adjusted by manufacturers, users failed to check and maintain, crane collapsed, both equally liable).

Where a part of the process of manufacture is carried out by an independent contractor, it is that contractor who owes the duty of care so far as any defect arises in the course of his process: and the manufacturer is entitled to rely on a reputable contractor: *Taylor v Rover Co Ltd, supra* (faulty hardening of chisel).

In *Haseldine v Daw & Son Ltd, supra*—an accident due to improper repair of hydraulic lift—the Court of Appeal, approving earlier cases, held that a repairer, who does not contemplate a further examination of the repaired plant or article after it has left his hands, is under the same duty as a manufacturer to the ultimate user.

The principle of *Donoghue v Stevenson*, at any rate as originally decided, has certain limits. It does not apply to articles which are 'dangerous in themselves', which fall under a different line of cases (sub-heading (3), *post*). It applies where there is a defect in the particular article, which the consumer or user cannot see for himself, and which will make it dangerous for him to use it, either because the article will break or because it will work in an erratic or unexpected way. It ceases to apply as soon as the user has full knowledge of the danger, or when, in the ordinary course of affairs, the article is examined and tested before being taken into use. Within these limits the duty of the manufacturer or repairer is to take reasonable care that no defect or danger shall arise; and the duty applies to every kind of article—not only to machinery and plant, but also to materials. Suppliers of materials for use in a manufacturing process, so far as they are aware of the nature of the process, owe as high a duty of care as the employer in assessing and eliminating the risks: they should at least give warning of any risks, and if it becomes clear that the materials are too dangerous to be used at all they should stop supplying them: *Wright v Dunlop Rubber Co Ltd and ICI Ltd* (1972) 13 KIR 255 (chemicals added to rubber to prevent rotting caused cancer of the bladder). But the manufacturer will not be liable if the article, or material, is put to a use which could not have been expected, and gives rise to a danger which the manufacturer could not foresee: *Davie v New Merton Board Mills Ltd* [1957] 2 All ER 38.

Strictly speaking, the maxim *res ipsa loquitur* does not apply in these cases: *Donoghue v Stevenson* [1932] AC 562 at 622; *Mason v Williams and Williams Ltd and Thomas Turton & Sons Ltd* [1955] 1 All ER 808. Since, however, the process of manufacture or repair is under the defendant's control, the presence of some substance or dangerous defect which ought not to be there may give rise to an inference of negligence, which will be sufficient evidence in the absence of a good explanation, and the plaintiff is not required to prove exactly what went wrong in the course of manufacture: *Lockhart v Barr* 1943 SC (HL) 1.

(2) Plant or materials delivered for use or handling, where reliance is placed on the person delivering them

In this type of liability there are three essential characteristics: delivery for immediate use, some material interest to the defendant, and reliance by the plaintiff on the defendant's care (and particularly on inspection by the defendant)[8]. Subject to these requirements being satisfied, it is the duty of the defendant to take reasonable care for the safety of those who are in his contemplation as users of the plant or article, and his liability is not confined to known defects, but extends also to defects of which he ought to know. In the leading case of *Heaven v Pender* (1883) 11 QBD 503, staging was supplied by a dock company for the use of shipowners (who would, of course, pay the usual dock charges, so that the supply was not a gratuitous loan). The staging was used by painters, one of whom was injured owing to a defect in construction. The Court of Appeal held the dock-owners liable, stressing mainly the fact that the plant was supplied for immediate use by workmen such as the plaintiff. In *Caledonian Rail Co v Mulholland* [1898] AC 216 at 227 Lord Herschell was careful to point out the element of material advantage which was present in *Heaven v Pender*: the staging, he said, was 'part of the appliances supplied by the dock company for purposes connected with the carrying on of their business'.

On similar grounds it has been held that shipowners are liable to stevedores' workmen for failing to take reasonable care for the safety of the ship's winches, and other equipment used in loading and unloading: *Butler v Hogarth Shipping Co Ltd* (1947) 80 Ll LRep 84; *Norwegian Shipping and Trading Mission v Behenna* (1943) 169 LT 191; and building owners who accept no responsibility for supervision nevertheless owe a duty to independent contractors engaged to do work for them to take reasonable care for the safety of plant and equipment which is on the land for their use: *Wheeler v Copas* [1981] 3 All ER 405 (farmer lent flimsy fruit ladder to 'labour only' bricklayer); *Kealey v Heard* [1983] 1 All ER 973, [1983] 1 WLR 573 (scaffold erected by another contractor collapsed under self-employed plasterer: building owner did nothing at all to supervise or check safety). (But a building owner was not liable when a ladder placed against scaffolding by a self-employed workman moved, the latter being virtually alone on the site and in sole control: *Poliskie v Lane* 1981 SLT 282: there appears to have been no fault in the equipment.)

---

8   In analysing the authorities in the earlier editions of this book, it seemed to the author that 'reliance' on the defendant's care was a key factor: it may be a better way of putting the law to say that the circumstances must be such that the defendant would not expect a further examination to be made. The House of Lords, however, has used the test of reliance in the case of statements causing damage, so perhaps the original suggestion was right: *Hedley Byrne & Co Ltd v Heller & Partners Ltd* [1964] AC 465, [1963] 2 All ER 575.

The use of equipment for mutual convenience in a joint operation (which is really a special example of material interest to the defendant) is illustrated by *Oliver v Saddler & Co* [1929] AC 584. In this case stevedores were raising bags of grain from the hold of a ship to the deck, and at the deck a portage company took over and transferred the loads to the quayside by means of a crane. The stevedores provided rope slings which they fitted to the load down in the hold, and it was a matter of mutual convenience that the same slings should be used throughout the two phases of the operation. The stevedores provided a man to examine the slings and reject defective ropes: the portage company relied on the stevedores to do this. On these facts the House of Lords held the stevedores liable when a defective sling broke and the load fell on to a workman employed by the portage company. The case brings out the important point that there must be reliance by the injured workman upon proper care being taken by the third party[9].

In *Griffiths v Arch Engineering Co Ltd* [1968] 3 All ER 217 where a grinding wheel not properly set up was hired out to a firm carrying out work on a dock, and they in turn lent it (without charge) to a man working for another firm of contractors, both the owners and the hirers were held liable. The owners owed a duty of care to all who might be expected to use it, and loan of tools between contractors working on a project is a common practice for mutual convenience, not a purely gratuitous loan. But where a house builder lent an unfenced circular saw to a sub-contractor's workman, the New Zealand Court of Appeal held that it was a gratuitous loan and, the deficiency being obvious to both parties, the lender was under no liability for failing to warn about the risks in using the saw unless he knew the borrower did not appreciate them: *Fraser v Jenkins* [1968] NZLR 816.

The decision of the House of Lords in *Caledonian Rail Co v Mulholland* [1898] AC 216 is not easily reconciled with the modern trend of the law. In this case a railway company allowed a wagon with a faulty brake to go on to the lines of another company, where a servant of the second company sustained injury by reason of the defect. It was held that the first company owed no duty once the wagon had left their lines.

9   The necessity for proof of 'reliance', express or implied, on inspection or testing by the third party, may mean that it is sometimes more difficult to establish liability against an immediate supplier than against a maker or repairer. If so, this is not unreasonable, for the maker or repairer is the author of the defects, which may be unknown to the immediate deliverer.

Perhaps the case is best distinguished on the ground that no special reliance was placed on inspection of the wagon by the despatching railway, as the receiving railway could equally well have made a check when the wagon reached their lines. A further case which illustrates the importance of some reliance being placed on the third party is *Marshall v Cellactite and British Uralite Ltd* (1947) 63 TLR 456, CA. There contractors were carrying out work in a factory, and were given a general permission to use the factory plant. A defect in a ladder belonging to the factory caused injury to one of the contractor's men, but it was held that, as the contractors had used their own judgment in selecting the ladder, the owners of the factory were not liable.

All the foregoing cases relate to the plant and equipment used in the course of work: but in *Denny v Supplies and Transport Co Ltd* [1950] 2 KB 374 the Court of Appeal extended the same principles of law to third parties who prepare loads to be discharged by the workmen of another employer. A firm of stevedores had unloaded timber from a ship and stacked it negligently on a barge, in such a manner that unloading would be dangerous. The plaintiff was a labourer employed by a second firm, who helped to unload the barge at the quayside and sustained injury in handling the timber. The Court of Appeal held the stevedores liable to the plaintiff, and Sir Raymond Evershed MR remarked that it was a matter of practical necessity to unload the timber as it stood, even though the risk might be apparent. *Denny's* case was distinguished in *Twiss v Rhodes (W. H.) & Son Ltd and Mersey Docks and Harbour Board* [1951] 1 Lloyd's Rep 333, which was also a case of cargo badly stowed on a barge, on the ground that it was the duty of the plaintiff's employer to inspect the load and decide upon a safe system of unloading. It must be supposed that in this latter case it was possible to devise a safe method of unloading, whereas in the former case it was not: even so, the line of distinction between the two cases is very slender.

Similar in principle is *Sammays v Westgate Engineers Ltd* (1962) 106 Sol Jo 937, Times, 15 November, CA (liability to dustman for leaving cardboard carton with sharp glass sticking out).

(3) Things dangerous in themselves

It has long been recognised, both in English and in Scots law, that a special duty of care arises in connection with 'things dangerous in themselves'. Thus in *Dominion Natural Gas Co Ltd v Collins and Perkins* [1909] AC 640 at 646 Lord Dunedin said:

> 'It has, however, again and again been held that in the case of things dangerous in themselves, such as loaded firearms, poisons, explosives, and other things *ejusdem generis*, there is a peculiar duty to take precaution imposed upon those who send forth or install such articles where it is necessarily the case that other persons will come within their proximity.'

In *Donoghue v Stevenson* [1932] AC 562 at 611–612 Lord Macmillan regarded this type of case 'as a special instance of negligence where the law exacts a degree of diligence so stringent as to amount practically to a guarantee of safety': this, however, seems to be a rhetorical overstatement, because there is no question here of the sort of absolute liability which arises under the rule in *Rylands v Fletcher* (pp. 77–78, *ante*).

Perhaps, as some judges have thought, the distinction between things which are dangerous *per se*, and those which are dangerous by reasons of some defect or improper use, is an illogical one, because both classes of things may be equally harmful. Nevertheless, it cannot be questioned that some things are lethal by nature, and one consequence is that the person in possession of these articles must know that they are dangerous, whereas he is not in general aware of a danger arising from defective condition. In practice the class of things recognised as dangerous *per se* is quite small, and is limited to such articles as loaded guns, explosives, poisons, acids, chemicals and inflammable substances.

The cases establish three duties, or perhaps one should say recognised standard precautions, in connection with things dangerous in themselves.

(i) They must not be delivered to an irresponsible person
In *Yachuk v Oliver Blais Co Ltd* [1949] AC 386, [1949] 2 All ER 150, for instance, the defendants were held liable for supplying gasoline (petrol) to children, who started a bonfire and burnt themselves. More commonly, the defendant is held liable to a third party, as in *Dixon v Bell* (1816) 5 M & S 198 where a servant girl, who had been sent to fetch a loaded gun, pointed it playfully at the plaintiff and shot him.

Such cases may occur in workplaces, if something specially dangerous is put in the hands of an irresponsible apprentice or juvenile worker.

(ii) They must not be delivered even to a responsible person without due warning
The older authorities are *Farrant v Barnes* (1862) 11 CB (NS) 553 where a carboy of acid was delivered to a carrier without warning of its nature and the acid burnt the carrier's servant while being carried on his back; and *Bamfield v Goole and Sheffield Transport Co Ltd* [1910] 2 KB 94 where fumes from a poisonous cargo, delivered to a bargee without warning of its nature, poisoned the bargee's wife. In both these cases the action was successful, but the decisions turned in part on the special duty owed to a common carrier.

A more recent example is *Philco Radio and Television Corpn of Great Britain Ltd v Spurling (J.) Ltd* [1949] 2 All ER 882 where defendants were held liable for delivering inflammable celluloid scrap to the wrong place without any indication or warning of the danger. Other cases of the same kind are *Anglo-Celtic Shipping Co Ltd v Elliot and Jeffrey* (1926) 42 TLR 297 and *Macdonald v MacBrayne (David) Ltd* 1915 SC 716.

(iii) They must not be left in a situation where they may be tampered with
Liability has been established under this head for leaving about such things as a loaded firearm, or phosphorus: *Sullivan v Creed* [1904] 2 IR 317; *Williams v Eady* (1893) 10 TLR 41.

Under this rule the owner of an industrial establishment may be liable if dangerous substances like petrol, acids, explosives or injurious chemicals are left in an accessible place instead of being stored under proper control: *Smedley v Moira Colliery Ltd* [1948] WN 467. Contractors working on a ship have similarly been held liable for leaving a cylinder of gas in a place where it might be tampered with and endanger the workmen of other contractors: *Beckett v Newalls Insulation Co Ltd* [1953] 1 All ER 250.

(4) Articles supplied gratuitously, and other residual cases

If articles are not dangerous in themselves, and do not come under any other of the foregoing heads, then it is thought still to be good law that the only duty of a third party who supplies them is to give warning of any danger which is actually known to him. In particular it was held in *Coughlin v Gillison* [1899] 1 QB 145, and repeated by the House of

Lords in *Oliver v Saddler & Co* [1929] AC 584, that the duty of a gratuitous lender of equipment is simply to give warning of known defects. The same duty exists between buyer and seller where, in the circumstances, no stricter duty can be established: *Clarke v Army and Navy Co-operative Society* [1903] 1 KB 155. If, in such a case, the article is safe when properly used, but dangerous unless special precautions are taken, it is the duty of the supplier to give warning of the special precautions which are necessary: *Holmes v Ashford* [1950] 2 All ER 76. Where materials which are potentially dangerous in this way are supplied to an industrial establishment, it will be sufficient to send proper instructions to the persons in charge of the establishment, and it is their duty to see that the instructions are followed: *Holmes v Ashford, supra*. If it becomes clear that materials supplied for an industrial process are too dangerous to be used at all, supply should be stopped: *Wright v Dunlop Rubber Co Ltd and I.C.I. Ltd* (1972) 13 KIR 255 (chemicals added to rubber to prevent rotting caused cancer of bladder).

In Scotland, a contractor who gratuitously lends equipment to the workmen of another contractor is under no duty to inspect it for defects: *Leckie v Caledonian Glass Co* 1957 SC 89 (board lent by joiner to glazier). (But see the cases on loans between contractors discussed under subheading (2), *ante*.)

4 Dangerous premises

An important branch of the law of tort is concerned with liability for dangerous premises, that is to say with liability to persons who enter land, buildings or other structures and are injured by defects or dangers which they encounter there. The first possibility which arises is the liability of a builder or repairer for any danger which is due to him. It was formerly held in English law that a builder or repairer owed no duty to anyone except the customer who had contracted with him. A similar view was, of course, taken of the liability of manufacturers of movable property until *Donoghue v Stevenson* [1932] AC 562 when a majority of the House of Lords overturned the old law and held that there was liability for negligence towards other persons who ought to be in the contemplation of the manufacturer as being at risk from his product. In 1932 and for many years afterwards the new principle was not thought to apply to land and buildings. But in *Dutton v Bognor Regis United Building Co Ltd* [1972] 1 QB 373, [1972] 1 All ER 462 it was held that it does apply to land and buildings. This new departure was later approved by the House of Lords: *Anns v Merton London Borough* [1978] AC 728 [1977] 2 All ER 492. The claims in these cases were by subsequent purchasers for damage to the building due to faulty foundations, but once it is accepted that a duty of care arises, it must at least cover injury due to collapse of the building or other faults in it. In fact, the House of Lords have since said that the basis of the decisions is the risk to safety and health: *Peabody Donation Fund (Governors) v Sir Lindsay Parkinson & Co Ltd* [1984] 3 All ER 529, [1984] 3 WLR 953; *D. and F. Estates Ltd v Church Comrs for England* [1989] AC 177, [1988] 2 All ER 992, HL. (However, liability extends to physical damage caused by a faulty part such as foundations, though not to the faulty part itself or to financial loss.) The liability of a builder may extend to subsidence due to the choice of an unsuitable site: *Batty v Metropolitan Property Realizations Ltd* [1978] 2 All ER 445; *Bowen v Paramount Builders (Hamilton) Ltd* [1977] 1 NZLR 394. There may also be liability for negligent design or planning of a building: *Rimmer v Liverpool City Council* [1984] 1 All ER 930, [1984] 2 WLR 426 (fragile glass in council flat). Questions of remoteness would arise, as they have done for motor vehicles and other equipment, once a defect has become apparent so that there has been an opportunity to put it right, or where a long time has elapsed since the work was done and the fabric should have been checked for normal wear and tear (pp. 169–171, *ante*).

The Defective Premises Act 1972 was passed mainly as the result of pressure for 'consumer protection': it makes builders and other contractors liable for defects in dwelling houses to the original purchaser and subsequent purchasers. This, however, concerns damage to the property rather than personal injury. It is in any case excluded where approved guarantees for repairs (NHBRC Certificate) are provided on the sale. Section 3, on the other hand, links with the duty of care owed by a person doing 'construction, repair, maintenance or demolition' to persons who may be affected by defects in the state of the premises. It does not define or create such a duty, but merely assumes that it exists at common law, and enacts that it shall not be 'abated' by disposal or letting of the premises by the person who owed the duty unless this took place—or there was a contract or option for value—before the Act came into force. This section applies to 'premises' generally[10].

Section 4 relates to a landlord's liability to persons generally when he is responsible for repairs. It replaces s. 4 of the Occupiers' Liability Act 1957 and is considered in connection with that Act.

It may now also be possible for a person injured by a structural defect in a building to claim against the builder or other contractor for breach of the Building Act 1984 and the Building Regulations 1985 (S.I. No. 1065)[11]. These regulations are not to be confused with the Construction Regulations under the Factories Act for the protection of building workers. They replace the Building Regulations 1976 made under the Health and Safety at Work Act 1974. These in turn replaced the building bye-laws which for many years were made and enforced by local authorities under the Public Health Acts, chiefly to prevent unhealthy housing by requiring good construction, light, space, ventilation, freedom from damp. The regulations go into great detail on construction of buildings, including various services and fittings. Regulations may control services, fittings and equipment as well as the design and construction of the building. They apply to alterations and extensions, to a change of use, and to installation of new services, as well as to the original construction. The regulation-making power in s. 1 of the Act refers specifically to the health and safety of persons in or about buildings, and others who may be affected by them. Also s. 38 specifically allows an action for breach of statutory duty except where expressly excluded by the regulations.

In Scotland there is different legislation, the Building (Scotland) Act 1970 as amended by s. 75 and Sch. 7 of the Health and Safety at Work Act 1974. This also authorises an action for damages for breach of building standards regulations.

The liability of an *occupier* of premises of any kind to persons visiting them is a long-established head of liability in both English and Scottish law. In England and Wales the law is now contained in the Occupiers' Liability Act 1957, which sets out common law principles in a revised form and is extended to trespassers by the Occupiers' Liability Act

10 This section is of little importance now that the House of Lords have decided that builders are under a general duty of care.
11 Gas supply installations are regulated by the Gas Safety (Installation and Use) Regulations SI 1984 No. 1358; electricity by the 'supply' regulations noted in Chapter 16.

1984. There is a similar Act in Northern Ireland. The Scottish counterpart—the Occupiers' Liability (Scotland) Act 1960—is different in some respects, and where it differs it is superior to the English Act: Scottish lawyers have always thought that the English law was too narrow, especially on liability for independent contractors and liability for trespassers.

Before summarising these two statutes, it is convenient to set out the old law as a background to them; some decisions are still in point under the new law[12].

(1) Summary of the old law

Lord Wright explained in *Glasgow Corpn v Muir* [1943] AC 448 at 461, [1943] 2 All ER 44 at 50 that this branch of the law is 'a special subhead of the general doctrine of negligence'. The term 'premises' includes 'places and structures of all sorts upon which persons may be invited to come': ibid. at 461, 50.

The person responsible for dangerous premises was normally the occupier, i.e. the person who is in possession and control. A landlord or owner was not liable, even if, as between himself and the occupier, he was responsible for repairs: *Cavalier v Pope* [1906] AC 428. The strictness of the duty varied according to the relationship between the occupier and the person who entered and sustained injury. The case of visitors who enter under the terms of a special contract is irrelevant for present purposes; usually it arose in connection with sports grounds and theatres rather than places of work; if, in the case of an injured workman, there was a special contract, it would be between the third party and the employer and would not affect the workman's rights.

Apart from contract, then, the law used to recognise three types of visitors: the *trespasser*, who enters without permission at all; the *licensee*, who is allowed to enter as a matter of grace for his own purposes, which are of no concern to the occupier; and finally the *invitee*, who enters for purposes which concern both himself and the occupier: *R. Addie & Sons*

---

12 Another reason for retaining a summary of the old law is that this book is relied on in other English-speaking jurisdictions outside the United Kingdom (roughly one copy in three goes overseas, and the author takes a keen interest in the needs of overseas users).

(Collieries) v Dumbreck [1929] AC 358. The duties of the occupier were these:

To the invitee:	To take reasonable care to protect him against *unusual* dangers of which he knows *or ought to know*.
To the licensee:	To warn him against *concealed* dangers of which he *actually knows*.
To the trespasser:	*No duty at all*, as regards the condition of the premises: but the occupier must not intentionally injure the trespasser; and if he starts some dangerous activity *with actual knowledge* that the trespasser is in the way, he must take care for his safety.

The following sections contain some authorities on liability to invitees, licensees and trepassers under the old law.

(i) Liability to an invitee

The leading case on liability to an invitee was *Indermaur v Dames* (1866) LR 1 CP 274, where a workman employed by gas-fitters went to a sugar-refinery to test some gas-burners, and fell into an unfenced shaft. The occupiers of the factory were held liable for the accident, and Willes J said:

> 'And, with respect to such a visitor at least, we consider it settled law, that he, using reasonable care on his part for his own safety, is entitled to expect that the occupier shall on his part use reasonable care to prevent damage from unusual danger, which he knows or ought to know; and that, where there is evidence of neglect, the question whether such reasonable care has been taken, by notice, lighting, guarding, or otherwise, and whether there was contributory negligence in the sufferer, must be determined by a jury as a matter of fact.'

What is an invitee? In *Addie (R.) & Sons (Collieries) v Dumbreck*, p. 180, *ante*, Lord Dunedin, following Lord Kinnear in *Devlin v Jeffray's Trustees* (1902) 5 F 130, said that the invitee is a person who is present for some purpose in which he and the occupier have a joint interest. Some English cases added the gloss that a 'material' interest was necessary; this unreasonable limitation was the main reason why reform of the law became necessary.

When is a workman an invitee? It is clear from *Indermaur v Dames* that a workman who goes to do work, or to inspect installations, for the benefit of the occupier, ranks as an invitee; and that a workman visiting a shop, or warehouse, or other premises, to deliver or take delivery of goods, or take a message, falls into the same category: *Smith v London and St. Katharine Docks Co* (1868) LR 3 CP 326. Similarly a workman employed by contractors or sub-contractors for the ultimate benefit of the occupier is an invitee, as in the common case of repairs to ships: *Wilkinson v Rea Ltd* [1941] 1 KB 688, [1941] 2 All ER 50; *London Graving Dock Ltd v Horton* [1951] AC 737, [1951] 2 All ER 1.

The extent of the invitation   The House of Lords held in *Walker v Midland Rail Co* (1886) 55 LT 489 that the occupier of a building was not responsible for the safety of an invitee in every part of the building, but only in those parts where he might be expected to go in the belief that he was entitled or invited to go there; thus, a guest in an hotel could not recover damages for an accident he sustained through straying down a dark corridor to an unknown part of the hotel. When an invitee moves outside the scope of his invitation he becomes a trespasser, or at most a licensee.

'Unusual' dangers   The invitor's duty was confined to protection against 'unusual' dangers. The House of Lords held in *London Graving Dock Co Ltd v Horton* [1951] AC 737, [1951] 2 All ER 1 that a danger is unusual if an invitee of the particular class concerned would not usually encounter it on premises of that type. Thus, a staging which includes a slippery angle-iron is an unusual danger to a welder on board a ship, and does not cease to be 'unusual' because he knows it is there: 'a tall chimney is not an unusual danger for a steeplejack, though it would be for a motor mechanic, but I do not think that a lofty chimney presents a danger less unusual for the last named because he is particularly active or untroubled by dizziness': per Lord Porter, ibid. at pp. 745, 5. Similarly a loose window sash is not an unusual danger to a window-cleaner, since such risks are frequently encountered in his type of work: *Christmas v General Cleaning Contractors Ltd* [1952] 1 KB 141, [1952] 1 All ER 39.

While the invitor's liability was normally founded on such static defects as unfenced holes, uneven floors and unsafe steps or ladders, an 'unusual' danger might also arise from active use of the premises by the invitor or a third party; but in the case of the activities of a third party, the invitor was not liable for dangers which he could not reasonably foresee: *Glasgow Corporation v Muir* [1943] AC 448, at 462, [1943] 2 All ER 44 at 51.

Where the defendant himself was conducting some activity on the land, such as running trains, he had a duty to exercise reasonable care for the safety of persons present; this was distinct from his duty as occupier, and does not turn on the distinction between invitee and licensee: *Slater v Clay Cross Co Ltd* [1956] 2 QB 264, [1956] 2 All ER 625. In Prof. F. H. Newark's words, this is 'Activity Duty' as distinguished from 'Occupancy Duty'[13].

Where a contractor such as a window-cleaner or repairer goes on to premises, the occupier cannot be expected to know what methods he will use, and accordingly, if an unusual danger arises owing to the contractor's special method of work, the occupier is not liable: *Bates v Parker* [1953] 2 QB 231, [1953] 1 All ER 768 (window-cleaner was in the habit of holding on to a piece of ply-wood in a window-pane: occupier, not knowing of this habit, loosened the ply-wood); *Heggie v Edinburgh and Leith Window Cleaning, Glazing and Chimney Sweeping Co Ltd* 1959 SLT 30 (window-cleaner rested ladder against balcony which collapsed: no liability).

The extent of the duty   If the matter rested solely on *Indermaur v Dames*, the duty of the invitor would simply be to take reasonable care for the safety of the invitee, and in some cases a warning might be sufficient, while in other cases something more might be necessary. In principle, indeed, this was the law: the invitor was not bound to make the premises safe, but to take reasonable care for the invitee's safety. However, *Indermaur v Dames* was qualified by *London Graving Dock Co Ltd v Horton* [1951] AC 737, [1951] 2 All ER 1, where the House of Lords held that, once the invitee has full knowledge and appreciation of the risk, the duty of the invitor is at an end[14]. The High Court of Australia has declined to follow this decision: *Australian Safeway Stores Pty Ltd v Zalwzna* (1987) 69 ALR 615. In Canada the duty has been described as

13 17 Mod. L.R. 102.
14 The decision (by a majority of three to two) was criticised by professional opinion, headed by the great authority of Lord Wright (67 LQR 532). Two objections to the decision may be mentioned: (i) the case decides as a matter of law what is really a question of fact dependent on the circumstances—viz., that a full warning is *always* a sufficient discharge of the duty of care; (ii) it is unreal to say that the invitor can ignore the workman's obligation to do his work, when this is the very purpose for which he has been invited to the premises.

For a Scots criticism, see 1952 SLT (News) 95.

The Third Report of the Law Reform Committee accepted these criticisms as valid, and the decision in *Horton's* case was overruled by the Occupiers' Liability Act 1957, and by the similar Scottish Act of 1960.

a duty to make the premises safe for the invitee: *Oulette v Daon Development Corpn* [1988] 4 WWR 366 (a child fell from the top of an escalator).

Liability for negligence of independent contractors   There were conflicting opinions on whether the occupier's duty is of such a fundamental character that, like an employer, he remained liable although performance was delegated, as Viscount Simon and Lord Wright said (*obiter*) in *Thomson v Cremin* [1953] 2 All ER 1185, or whether he fulfilled his duty by choosing a competent contractor[15]. The English and Scottish Acts have also adopted different views. In general a person is not liable at common law for the acts of an independent contractor where a duty of care does not arise from the very nature of the work delegated but from the method the contractor chooses: *Salsbury v Woodland* [1970] 1 QB 324, [1969] 3 All ER 863 (felling of tree involved no danger to highway except from the way it was done).

(ii) Liability to a licensee

A licensee is, or was, a person who is allowed to enter premises for purposes of his own, which are of no benefit, or at any rate of no material benefit, to the occupier. He may have received express permission to enter: alternatively, permission may be implied if he is known to visit or pass through the premises, and the occupier makes no objection: *Lowery v Walker* [1911] AC 10. 'But repeated trespass of itself confers no licence': *Edwards v Railway Executive* [1952] AC 737, [1952] 2 All ER 430 per Lord Goddard. A workman was ordinarily an invitee, but could be a licensee, as where he used a short cut over dock sidings or other adjoining property (*Bolch v Smith* (1862) 7 H & N 736; *Ashdown v Samuel Williams & Sons Ltd* [1957] 1 QB 409, [1957] 1 All ER 35), or was doing work at premises occupied by a tenant, and had to pass over a forecourt or passage, or use a lift or a staircase, which was retained in the possession of the landlord: *Jacobs v London County Council* [1950] AC 361, [1950] 1 All ER 737. A person who entered premises to seek orders, or ask for work, was usually a licensee: *Dunster v Abbott* [1953] 2 All ER 1572.

---

15 See Lord Reid's criticisms in *Davie v New Merton Board Mills Ltd* [1959] AC 604, [1959] 1 All ER 346 at 365–7. With respect, Lord Wright's dictum seems entirely convincing. The slurs on *Thomson v Cremin* because it was reported so late are irrelevant.

The status of the licensee hinged entirely on the fact that he was given the gratuitous use of the premises, and that his presence was a matter of indifference to the occupier. 'The principle of law as to gifts', said Willes J in *Gautret v Egerton* (1867) LR 2 CP 371 at 375, 'is that the giver is not responsible for damage resulting from the insecurity of the thing, unless he knew of its evil character at the time and omitted to caution the donee'. 'If I dedicate a way to the public, which is full of ruts and holes, the public must take it as it is': ibid. at 373.

The law was elaborated further in Lord Sumner's speech in *Mersey Docks and Harbour Board v Procter* [1923] AC 253 at 274:

> 'A licensee takes premises . . . just as he finds them. The one exception to this is that, as it is put shortly, the occupier must not lay a trap for him or expose him to a danger not obvious nor to be expected there in the circumstances. If the danger is obvious, the licensee must look out for himself. . . . *The licensor must act with reasonable diligence to prevent his premises from misleading or entrapping a licensee . . .*'

The words italicised in this extract show that there was a *limited* duty of care to a licensee, not indeed to protect him from dangers on the premises, but to prevent him from being misled by a deceptive appearance of safety: and it follows that—except for children—the occupier's duty of care was fully discharged by giving a warning. Hence, it was often said that the duty of the occupier was simply to warn the licensee of concealed dangers.

The occupier could reduce his liability still further by limiting the scope of the licence, for example, by displaying a notice that there is danger from shunting trains and persons enter at their own risk: such a notice was binding on a licensee who saw that it was a warning notice but did not trouble to read it: *Ashdown v Samuel Williams & Sons Ltd* [1957] 1 QB 409, [1957] 1 All ER 35.

The occupier was liable only for concealed or hidden dangers: *Fairman v Perpetual Investment Building Society* [1923] AC 74 at 96. Common examples are: a floorboard which appears to be strong, but is rotten and suddenly gives way; a ladder in which one of the rungs is loose; or a door opening on to a sudden steep drop. There was no absolute rule, at all events in built-up areas, that a danger which is obvious by day cannot become a concealed danger by night: *Hawkins v Coulsdon and Purley Urban District Council* [1954] 1 QB 319, [1954] 1 All ER 97. A concealed danger is sometimes described as a 'trap'.

Further, the occupier was liable only for concealed dangers of which he actually knew: *Pearson v Lambeth Borough Council* [1950] 2 KB 353, [1950] 1 All ER 682. 'Actual knowledge' was, however, given a broad interpretation. 'Provided that actual knowledge of the source of a danger is brought home to a licensor, it is sufficient ... to show that a reasonable man would have appreciated the dangerous quality of the source, whether or not the licensor appreciated it himself': per Romer LJ in *Hawkins v Coulsdon and Purley Urban District Council* [1954] 1 QB 319, [1954] 1 All ER 97 (defendants knew step was in defective condition and lighting poor, but had not appreciated danger during hours of darkness).

Finally, 'when current operations are being carried out on the land' by the occupier, such as running trains, he has a duty of care towards invitees and licensees alike, which is independent of the duties he owes as occupier: *Slater v Clay Cross Co Ltd* [1956] 2 QB 264, [1956] 2 All ER 625 (train did not whistle when entering tunnel where public allowed to walk).

(iii) Liability to a trespasser

A workman may become a trespasser if, as in *Hillen and Pettigrew v I.C.I. (Alkali) Ltd* [1936] AC 65 he moves outside the limits of the invitation. Such cases often occur when workmen on board a ship stray away from the hold or other place where they are working: see *Henaghan v Rederiet Forangirene* [1936] 2 All ER 1426 where, however, on the facts the workman had not ceased to be an invitee. A slight deviation will not turn a workman into a trespasser, for example, where the plaintiff, being a licensee authorised to walk beside a railway track, unintentionally stepped a few inches on to the sleepers: *Braithwaite v South Durham Steel Co Ltd* [1958] 3 All ER 161. The duty towards a trespasser was, and still is, the lowest of all: indeed, there was no duty to a trespasser in connection with the state of the premises, and this position was not changed by the Occupiers' Liability Act 1957. (But in Scotland, under the Occupiers' Liability (Scotland) Act 1960, the position of the trespasser was improved and in English law a trespasser is now covered by the Occupiers' Liability Act 1984.) Formerly the occupier had *no duty at all in his capacity as occupier*, but might be liable for dangerous activities which he intentionally carried out on the premises with knowledge of the trespasser's presence. 'There must be some act done with the deliberate intention of doing harm to the trespasser, or at least some act done with reckless disregard of the presence of the trespasser': per Viscount Hailsham LC in *Addie (R.) & Sons (Collieries) v Dumbreck* [1929] AC 358 at 365.

It was clear from the Scottish case of *Haughton v North British Rail Co* (1892) 20 R 113 (approved in *Addie (R.) & Sons (Collieries) v Dumbreck, supra,* at p. 367) that when the occupier carried out a dangerous operation, such as the shunting of trucks, with the knowledge that a trespasser was in the vicinity, he had to take reasonable care for his safety. The same principle was applied in *Excelsior Wire Rope Co Ltd v Callan* [1930] AC 404, where a haulage machine was started with the knowledge that children had been 'swarming' over it a few moments before, and in *Mourton v Poulter* [1930] 2 KB 183 where a tree was felled when children were known to be in the vicinity[16]. The occupier was not liable if he did not know that trespassers were in the vicinity *at that particular time,* even if he knew that trespassers were quite likely to be there: *Addie (R.) & Sons (Collieries) v Dumbreck, supra.*

It will be clear, then, that (except in Scotland at any rate) even if there was a source of grave danger on the land, the occupier was not bound to fence it, and to warn trespassers away: and trespassers failed to recover damages for coming into contact with such unknown perils as moving machinery and high voltage electrical installations: *Hardy v Central London Rail Co* [1920] 3 KB 459; *McLaughlin v Antrim Electricity Supply Co* [1941] NI 23.

The Court of Appeal expressed the view that an occupier of premises, while under no liability in his capacity as occupier, may owe a duty of care to trespassers where he is carrying out activities likely to endanger them, but this would not extend to a trespasser whose presence was unforeseen: *Videan v British Transport Commission* [1963] 2 QB 650, [1963] 2 All ER 860. *Contra,* the Judicial Committee reaffirmed the strict old rule that there was no liability except for wilful or reckless harm to a known trespasser: *Railways Commissioner v Quinlon* [1964] 1 All ER 897. The point was made that it is an unreasonable restriction of the use

16 In these two cases the defendants were not the occupiers, but that seems to make no difference to the principle which is clearly established by *Haughton's* case. In *Hillen and Pettigrew v I.C.I. (Alkali) Ltd, supra,* Lord Atkin clearly recognises that there is a duty of care—as distinguished from a duty not to inflict intentional injury—to a 'known' trespasser. *Grand Trunk Rail Co of Canada v Barnett* [1911] AC 361 is at first sight an authority to the contrary, but in reality does no more than decide that where a trespasser steals a ride on a train, the railway do not owe to him the same positive duty (to carry safely) as they do to ordinary passengers.

of premises if an occupier has always to take account of trespassers.

All these cases are now superseded in English law because, although trespassers were not at first protected by the Occupiers' Liability Act, the House of Lords subsequently defined the duty to a trespasser in new terms and this in turn has been replaced by the Occupiers' Liability Act 1984.

(2) The Occupiers' Liability Act 1957[17]

The Occupiers' Liability Act 1957 replaced most of the old law set out in the preceding pages. It applies to England and Wales, and there is a similar Act in Northern Ireland.

The Act abolished the distinction between invitees and licensees, and defined the duty which the occupier owes to all visitors who are on the premises by his invitation or permission. Trespassers, who enter without any permission, express or implied, did not come within the Act, but are now protected by the Occupiers' Liability Act 1984.

In the words of the Act, it regulates 'the duty which an occupier of premises owes to his visitors in respect of dangers due to the state of the premises or to things done or omitted to be done on them' (s. 1(1)). This means 'the duty imposed by law in consequence of a person's occupation or control of premises and of any invitation or permission he gives (or is to be treated as giving) to another to enter or use the premises' and it is owed to the persons who would, at common law, be invitees or licensees: they are now combined in a single class (s. 1(2)).

Occupation or control is a question of fact, and does not depend on having a legal interest: thus brewers were the occupiers of the private part of an inn occupied by their manager who sometimes took in lodgers, the manager also being occupier: *Wheat v E. Lacon & Co Ltd* [1966] AC 552, [1966] 1 All ER 582 (in such a case, the care to be expected from the two occupiers may cover different matters, e.g. structure for one, day-to-day matters such as lighting for the other); where a club included a restaurant run by a licensee, he and the club were both occupiers: *Fisher v C.H.T. Ltd* (No 2) [1966] 2 QB 475, [1966] 1 All ER 88. The main contractors of a London underground tunnel under construction, who retained general control although at the weekend sub-contractors

17 23 Halsbury's Statutes, 3rd Edn., 792.

came in to overhaul plant, were held to be the occupiers: *Bunker v Charles Brand & Son Ltd* [1969] 2 QB 480, [1969] 2 All ER 59. But in some circumstances a sub-contractor may be sole occupier e.g. of a scaffolding: *Kearney v Eric Waller Ltd* [1967] 1 QB 29, [1965] 3 All ER 352; more dubiously, a self-employed man alone on a building site was said to be the occupier of the relevant part of it (ladder propped against scaffold) under the Scottish Act: *Poliskie v Lane* 1981 SLT 282.

By s. 2, the occupier owes to all visitors a 'common duty of care', which is a duty to take reasonable care 'to see that the visitor will be reasonably safe in using the premises for the purposes for which he is invited or permitted by the occupier to be there'. This is not a statutory duty in the technical sense, but sets out a revised principle of the common law: *Roles v Nathan* [1963] 2 All ER 908 per Lord Denning MR. The duty extends to visitors who enter in the exercise of a right conferred by law (s. 2 (6)) and the purpose for which the right is given is treated as a purpose for which permission is given. However, a person who uses a right of way to reach a place where he is a lawful visitor is *not* a visitor to the land which he crosses and is not protected by the 1957 Act: *Holden v White* [1982] QB 679 [1982] 2 All ER 328. He will be protected by the more limited duty under the 1984 Act. The old law about 'unusual' or 'concealed' dangers or 'traps' has completely gone: there is a general duty to protect the visitor from any danger which he may encounter within the scope of his invitation or permission, including dangers (e.g. to a visiting workman) from the work being carried on: *Savory v Holland Hannen and Cubitts (Southern) Ltd* [1964] 3 All ER 18[18]. This does not mean every imaginable danger, and no precautions may be required where a careful visitor should run no risk: *Wheat v E. Lacon & Co Ltd, supra* (back stair where hand-rail stopped before foot; even when unlit, stair was safe if not used imprudently).

But by s. 2 (3), a person who is present in the exercise of his calling may be expected to 'appreciate and guard against any special risks ordinarily incident to it, so far as the occupier leaves him free to do so': e.g. a window-cleaner may be expected to look out for defective sashes and rotten wood-work, but a plumber would not expect the stairs to collapse. Thus under the Scottish Act the occupier was not liable when a

---

18 *Sed quaere* whether, as this case suggested, the duty extends to telling a visiting workman how to carry out his *own* work. But it has been held to require provision of boards to cover a staircase well for self-employed men working above it: *Sole v W. J. Hallt Ltd* [1973] QB 574, [1973] 1 All ER 1032.

bar on a window came out when grasped by the window-cleaner: he had no duty to inspect: *Kilbride v Scottish and Newcastle Breweries Ltd* 1986 SLT 642. Fumes are a special risk of a chimney-sweep's calling: *Roles v Nathan, supra.* Lord Denning MR said in *Woollins v British Celanese Ltd* (1966) 1 KIR 438 that s. 2(3) means

> 'special risks incident to the work, such as live wires to an electrician . . . [Not] an ordinary risk incident to the premises themselves.'

So the risk of putting a foot through a fragile roof was not a special risk of this kind to a Post Office engineer. Where demolition contractors were employed on the premises, and one of their men was injured because of an unsafe method of work, his employers alone were liable: the occupier had no responsibility for supervising the work: *Ferguson v Welsh* [1987] 3 All ER 777, [1987] 1 WLR 1553.

Under the Scottish Act the House of Lords has held that there is no duty to foresee and provide against the risks to firemen in case of fire, e.g. as to dangers in gaining access: *Bermingham v Sher Bros* 1980 SLT 122 (it was alleged there should have been a fire screen protecting the stairway of a warehouse). But if the occupier is in breach of his duty to other visitors, for example by negligently starting the fire, he will also be liable to a fireman: *Salmon v Seafarer Restaurants Ltd* [1983] 3 All ER 729, [1983] 1 WLR 1264.

It is expressly declared—s. 2 (4)—that warning or notice does not, in itself, absolve the occupier from liability, unless in all the circumstances it was sufficient to enable the visitor to be reasonably safe: this overrules *London Graving Dock Co Ltd v Horton* [1951] AC 737, [1951] 2 All ER 1. In *Roles v Nathan, supra*, the occupier was exonerated by a warning given by his expert to chimney-sweeps on the danger from fumes. But in *Bunker v Charles Brand & Son Ltd* [1969] 2 QB 480, [1969] 2 All ER 59 knowledge or warning that the means of access to a machine was over precarious rollers did not exonerate the occupiers as there was no other way and something safer could have been provided. Failure to warn may be negligent although no other action is called for, e.g. *McDowell v F.M.C. (Meat) Ltd* (1968) 3 KIR 595 (high voltage line crossing showground). These provisions, however, deal with the question whether a warning is sufficient performance of the duty, assuming it to exist. In some cases, a prominent notice or other warning may exclude the duty. Section 2 (5) preserves the defence of *volenti non fit injuria*, if it would have been available at common law. For this purpose it has to be shown that the visitor knew of the risk, and consented to it in circumstances where he was free to decide. It does not apply to a workman who, being required to enter a place in the course of his work, is not free to refuse: *Burnett v British Waterways Board* [1973] 2 All ER 631 (man on barge entering dock injured by breaking rope: notice excluding dock's liability ineffective). In other cases a warning notice, if read, may be enough to establish voluntary acceptance of risk (e.g. 'cliff paths subject to landslips—visitors use at own risk'). Apart from this, s. 2 (1) says that the occupier owes the duty 'except in so far as he is free to and does extend, restrict, modify or exclude his duty . . . by contract or otherwise'.

This leaves in Delphic obscurity the question of how far the occupier *is* free to limit his duty. By contract he can clearly limit or exclude it: a common example is the purchase of a ticket with conditions printed on it. But where an occupier is not obliged to admit a visitor—where admission is gratuitous—it would seem that he can admit him on conditions such as 'admittance at own risk', and these will effectively limit the duty if prominently displayed or, presumably, printed conspicuously on a permit: *White v Blackmore* [1972] 2 QB 651, [1972] 3 All ER 158[19].

The position is now further complicated by the Unfair Contract Terms Act 1977, s. 2, under which it is not permissible to exclude liability for death or injury due to negligence by either a contract or a notice—and 'negligence' is defined by s. 1(1)(c) to include liability under the Occupiers' Liability Act. By s. 1(3), this restriction applies only to a 'business' liability—something which arises either from a 'business' activity or the occupation of 'business' premises. Under an amendment in s. 2 of the Occupiers' Liability Act 1984 this does not include liability to a person obtaining access 'for recreational or educational purposes' by reason of the 'dangerous state of the premises' unless access is given as part of a business. So if a person makes a charge to see a waterfall or enjoy a woodland walk, he cannot restrict his liability—unless he can prove that the charge is not intended to make a profit and so does not amount to carrying on a business. At any rate, there seems no reason why a private owner who allows free public access for enjoyment should not limit his duty by a public notice.

19 Where invitation subject to time limit, this should be made plain: *Stone v Taffe* [1974] 3 All ER 1016.

Section 2 (4)(b) of the 1957 Act sets up an involved and uncertain rule where a danger was due to faulty work by an independent contractor: the occupier is not vicariously liable for the faulty work if he acted reasonably in entrusting the work to an independent contractor and took such steps (if any) as were reasonable to satisfy himself that the contractor was competent and the work was properly done. He may, however, be liable on other grounds, for example, if he became aware of the danger after the contractor had finished, and failed to have it put right.

The common duty of care is also owed to persons who enter under the terms of a contract, unless the contract contains express terms on the subject (s. 5). But where persons enter under the terms of a contract made by another person—e.g. when workmen enter premises under a contract made by the occupier with their employer—the occupier's duty cannot be restricted or excluded: on the other hand, such a contract may extend the occupier's duty, for under s. 3(1), if he has undertaken additional obligations, for instance to make scaffolds safe, the duty of care is enlarged to incorporate those obligations. This innovation may enable a workman to sue, in substance, upon the terms of a contract made with his employer (but in such a case the occupier's vicarious liability for independent contractors cannot be enlarged except by express words (s. 3(2)). Subject to any lawful limitation of duty under the contract, a person entering under a contract who sustains injury does not need to sue for breach of contract: he can sue in tort under s. 2, so that contributory negligence will reduce the damages instead of being a complete defence: *Sole v W. J. Hallt Ltd* [1973] QB 574, [1973] 1 All ER 1032.

Under s. 4 of the Defective Premises Act 1972 (which replaces in wider terms s. 4 of the 1957 Act) a landlord who is responsible for repairs under the tenancy may be liable to a visitor endangered by defects for which the landlord is responsible, provided that the landlord knows or ought to know of the defect. There need not be a tenancy in the strict sense: occupation under a contract or a statutory right is sufficient. By s. 4(4), a landlord who is entitled to enter the premises to do maintenance or repair is treated for the purpose of the section (but not as between himself and the tenant where the duty to repair is expressly imposed on the latter) as if he were responsible for repairs within the scope of his right of entry. A landlord who retained possession of common parts was liable for an accident to a meter inspector, though (following disconnection of the electricity) the local authority had taken over payment for electricity and were collecting rents to reimburse themselves: *Jordan v Achara* (1988) 20 HLR 607, CA. Under the Scottish Act it has been held that a landlord is under no duty to inspect and is not liable unless he has notice of the defect, and the position is clearly the same in England: *Murray v Edinburgh DC* 1981 SLT 253. Under this section, a workman may sometimes be in a position to sue the landlord of his own employer.

There is no definition of 'premises' in the Act, but the duties declared by it extend to persons 'occupying or having control over any fixed or movable structure, including any vessel, vehicle or aircraft' (s. 2(3)).

Trespassers and other uninvited visitors
The old law on trespassers was, as explained above, that an occupier was not liable unless he injured them wilfully or recklessly. This might make sense in the 18th century when intruders were mainly burglars or poachers. It does not make sense when trespassers are straying children or even adults taking unauthorised short cuts or policemen or firemen trying to safeguard the premises: so many attempts were made by the courts to distinguish the old law out of existence, and a very confusing situation resulted (pp. 186–188, *ante*).

Finally, in *British Railways Board v Herrington* [1972] AC 877, [1972] 1 All ER 749 the House of Lords decided that the old law should no longer be followed. While in general an intruder on another person's land is there at his own risk—having forced his presence uninvited—an occupier must act according to standards of 'common humanity'. This involves a limited duty of care, where the occupier knows that trespassers are present or likely to be present, to take reasonable steps to protect them from serious dangers on his land whether due to the state of the land or to some activity carried on there. The duty is more likely to apply to young children than to adults: in *Herrington's* case the railway were held liable for failing to repair a gap in a fence near an electrified line. But there are two big limits to any duty. There is no general duty to fence a railway: *Proffitt v British Railways Board* [1985] CLY 2302; and in any case an occupier cannot be expected to maintain a perfect burglarproof or 'boyproof' fence: *Edwards v Railway Executive* [1952] AC 737, [1952] 2 All ER 430; and he is entitled to make full use of his land, he is not required to desist from dangerous activities because they may injure uninvited intruders. In the case of adults liability is unlikely to arise unless there is a hidden danger: yet even for adults a fence may be necessary to prevent *accidental* straying into an area of unknown danger such as invisible radiation.[20]

In *Southern Portland Cement Ltd v Cooper* [1974] AC 623, [1974] 1 All ER 87 liability was established—again to a child—because a mound of rubble had piled up so as to bring within reach an overhead electric cable. This created a danger which could have been avoided without expense or trouble. Lord Reid said that where an occupier himself created a new source of danger he might well be expected to incur expense on safeguards: but he is under no duty to investigate whether any danger has arisen without his knowledge, or to incur expense in safeguards against things for which he is not responsible. In *Pannett v P. McGuiness & Co Ltd* [1972] 2 QB 599, [1972] 3 All ER 137 demolition contractors were negligent for failing to keep children away from bonfires of debris.

While these decisions will still be helpful as a guide to the standard of care, they have been superseded by the Occupiers' Liability Act 1984. By s. 1, this defines the duty of an occupier to a person other than 'his visitors', that is to persons who do not enter by his permission or invitation and are not within the 1957 Act. Therefore it includes not only trespassers but borderline cases such as persons using a right of way who were held to be outside the 1957 Act. The duty covers dangers due either to the state of the premises or activities (or omissions) on them: s. 1(1)(a).

Three conditions must be satisfied before a duty arises: s. 1(3).

(a) The occupier must know of the risk, or have reasonable grounds to believe that it exists;

(b) He must also know, or have reasonable grounds to believe, that the person concerned is already in, or may come within, the vicinity of the danger—whether lawfully or not; and finally

(c) 'the risk is one against which . . . he may reasonably be expected to offer the other some protection'.

The third condition, cl. (c), is the critical one, and though it is expressed as a factual test it is of course completely a matter of opinion[1].

---

20 And if land is fenced off, an occupier may reasonably believe that entry is unlikely: *White v St. Albans City* (1990) Times, 12 March.
1 It may seem unkind to describe a piece of law reform as pointless or even fatuous: but we are unfortunately seeing only too many elaborate verbalisations like s. 1 (3) (c), which may roll off the tongue impressively but are quite meaningless. This subsection, which purports to define the scope of the duty, is the *centre piece* of the Act. Everything else merely leads up to it. It should be something solid and real, but it is not. So the two House of Lords' decisions will continue to be important as they do indicate what degree of care is appropriate.

When the duty exists, it is to protect the person concerned against injury from the perceived danger: s. 1(4); and in appropriate cases it may be discharged by giving a warning or deterring entry: s. 1(5). No duty is owed to a person who willingly accepted the risk: s. 1(6). (This merely re-enacts the principle *volenti non fit injuria*.)

No duty is owed under the Act to persons using the highway: s. 1(7); and there is no liability for loss of or damage to property, which would of course include clothing, vehicles and anything carried in the pockets: s. 1(8).

(3) The Occupiers' Liability (Scotland) Act 1960

The Act of 1960 was moulded by Scottish lawyers in accordance with the distinctive rules of Scottish law, which had been misinterpreted in decisions of the House of Lords so as to conform to the rigid rules of English law.

The Act regulates the duty of the person 'occupying or having control of land or other premises' (the 'occupier') 'towards persons entering on the premises in respect of dangers due to the state of the premises or to anything done or omitted to be done on them and for which he is in law responsible' (s. 1(1)). The common law rules still decide who is 'the occupier' (s. 1(2)). To remove previous doubts in Scottish law, premises include both fixed and movable structures, in particular 'any vessel, vehicle or aircraft' (s. 1(3)(a))[2].

An examination of s. 1(1) shows that it is limited to the duty arising 'by reason of such occupation or control'—*occupancy* as distinct from *activity* duty, to use Prof. F. H. Newark's terms—and that it applies without reservation to the *state* of the premises, but that as regards the conduct of third parties on the premises it is restricted to things 'for which he is in law *responsible*'. This cannot be a reference to vicarious liability for agents and servants: it must mean that liability depends on the degree of *control*.

The duty is—s. 2(1)—to take reasonable care 'to see that that person' [i.e. any person 'entering on the premises': s. 1(1)] 'will not suffer injury or damage by reason of any such danger'[3]. The occupier is not required to

2 A scaffold may be included and be in separate occupation. *Poliskie v Lane* 1981 SLT 282.
3 The Scottish Act therefore avoids the woolly phrase of the English Act—*reasonable care* that 'the visitor will be *reasonably* safe'.

foresee and take measures against risks to a fireman in the event of a fire: *Bermingham v Sher Bros* 1980 SLT 122. But it is thought that in Scotland, as in England, if the occupier is negligent in breach of his duty to other persons, for example by causing a fire, he is equally liable to a fireman: *Salmon v Seafarer Restaurants Ltd* [1983] 3 All ER 729, [1983] 1 WLR 1264.

But this duty is without prejudice to (i) the defence of *volenti non fit injuria* where available under the *general* law of negligence (s. 2(3)); (ii) any higher standard of care under any other rule of law (s. 2(2)); and (iii) cases where the occupier 'is *entitled* to and *does* extend, restrict, modify or exclude by *agreement* his obligations' (s. 2(1)). The effect of any agreement excluding or limiting liability must, of course, be judged by the pre-existing law. The Unfair Contract Terms Act 1977, s. 16 and s. 15(2)(d) prohibit the exclusion of liability for 'breach of duty' causing injury or death, but of course if the duty itself is lawfully restricted there will be no breach of it.

By s. 3 of the Act of 1960, a landlord (including the landlord of a subtenancy) who is responsible (either by agreement or by a statute such as the Housing Acts) for 'maintenance or repair' has the same liabilities as the occupier for dangers arising from his default. This applies to existing as well as future tenancies. But a landlord is under no duty to inspect the premises and is liable only for defects of which he has had notice: *Murray v Edinburgh District Council* 1981 SLT 253.

Unlike the English Act, the Scottish Act contains no special provision relieving the occupier of his vicarious liability for independent contractors, under such authorities as *Thomson v Cremin* [1953] 2 All ER 1185; *sub nom, Cremin v Thomson* 1956 SLT 357.

Again unlike the English Act, the duty is not confined to persons entering 'by invitation or permission', so trespassers are not as a matter of law excluded. It would, of course, be a question of fact in any particular case whether any and if so what degree of care should be exercised for the safety of a trespasser. The fact that the visitor is a trespasser is one of the circumstances determining the degree of care: *McGlone v British Railways Board* 1966 SLT (Notes) 72 (boy injured climbing transformer); a trespasser takes the risk of a railway being operated in the normal and usual way if he chooses to go through a fence to cross it, though the fence has gaps—in other words the railway is under no duty to repair a fence to keep out trespassers, at any rate if old enough to know what they are doing: *Titchener v British Railways Board* [1983] 3 All ER 770, [1983] 1 WLR 1427.

(4) Duties of contractors and other persons using premises

Persons using the same premises—principal contractors, sub-contractors and the like—are naturally responsible to one another for damage caused by the negligent conduct of their activities: but they may in addition be responsible for dangers arising from the static condition of the premises, if due to their acts or omissions. In *Grant v Sun Shipping Co Ltd* [1948] AC 549, [1948] 2 All ER 238, ship-repairers' men went away leaving a hatch uncovered and in darkness, and a stevedore, without any negligence on his part, fell into the hatch. The House of Lords held that the ship-repairers, having worked at the hatch and left it in an unsafe condition, were liable for the accident at common law quite apart from their duties under the Docks Regulations[4].

In the same way contractors working on premises may be liable to casual visitors. In *Kimber v Gas Light and Coke Co* [1918] 1 KB 439, the gas company's workmen had removed floorboards to alter the gas fittings in an unoccupied house: the plaintiff, a prospective tenant with an order to view, was admitted by the workmen, who saw her go upstairs where the boards had been removed, but gave no warning. The court held the company liable, and expressly rejected the argument that in such a case the contractors are not liable unless they commit a negligent act, such as dropping a hammer on somebody's head.

The House of Lords has now held, in general terms:

> 'that a person executing works on premises . . . is under a general duty to use reasonable care for the safety of those whom he knows or ought reasonably to know may be affected by or lawfully in the vicinity of his work': *A. C. Billings & Sons v Riden* [1958] AC 240, [1957] 3 All ER 1 (per Lord Somervell)[5].

Anyone who starts a fire negligently on any premises is liable to those who are endangered, and this includes professional firemen who are at risk in spite of their skill: *Ogwo v Taylor* [1988] AC 431, [1987] 3 All ER 961: but in Scotland it has been held that where a building worker

---

4   Cf. *Baron v B. French Ltd* [1971] 3 All ER 1111 (electrician sub-contractor's employee tripped over rubble heap left by head contractors in badly-lit corridor).
5   Overruling *Malone v Laskey* [1907] 2 KB 141 and *Ball v L.C.C.* [1949] 1 All ER 1056. See also *Christie v James Scott & Co Ltd* 1961 SLT (Notes) 5; *Johnson v Rea Ltd* [1962] 1 QB 373, [1961] 3 All ER 816.

entered premises to investigate after a fire had been started by a sub-contractor, a fall into an unguarded drop was not within the scope of the fire risk: *Reid v Sir Robert McAlpine & Co* 1986 SLT 108.

5 Dangerous activities

Persons who, in the course of industrial undertakings, carry on activities which are likely to endanger other persons, owe a duty to those other persons to exercise reasonable care. This proposition is founded directly on the general principles of negligence, and does not need so much elaboration as the liability for dangerous plant and premises; it will be enough to mention a few characteristic examples. It need hardly be said that there is no duty when the defendants have no reason to expect that anyone is in the vicinity: *Batchelor v Fortescue* (1883) 11 QBD 474.

(i) Handling objects liable to fall from a height
Illustrations are:
   Barrels rolled along the upper floor of a warehouse: *Byrne v Boadle* (1863) 2 H & C 722.
   Loads swung overhead on cranes: *Scott v London Dock Co* (1865) 3 H & C 596.
   The felling of trees: *Mourton v Poulter* [1930] 2 KB 183.
These cases are examples *par excellence* of the maxim *res ipsa loquitur*, and, assuming that the operation was under the sole management of the defendant, there will be a presumption of negligence: see Chapter 2, section 5.

(ii) Control or operation of dangerous machinery
See *Excelsior Wire Rope Co Ltd v Callan*, p. 187, *ante*.
   In *Field v E. E. Jeavons & Co Ltd* [1965] 2 All ER 162 occupiers of a factory who left a circular saw in a position where it would move forward if switched on were held liable to an electrician who wired it and switched it on for testing, although he should first have asked the foreman's permission.

(iii) Manoeuvring or driving railway engines, trucks, cranes and other vehicles

This is not the place to enter into a lengthy explanation of the duties of a careful driver, which are, in essence, to keep his vehicle under control and at a controllable speed, to keep a look-out, not to alter his course or speed without warning, and to avoid collision with other persons.

On or near a highway, an injured workman has the same rights as any other member of the public. On private property a driver must exercise the same reasonable care as he should on the highway: *Bowie v Shenkin*, 1934 SC 459; but this is subject to the proviso that he must know, or have reason to suppose, that other persons may be in the vicinity: *Johnson v Elder Dempster Lines Ltd* (1948) 81 L1 LRep 335 (a case of a crane on a dockside). A crane-driver may be held negligent for lifting his load without a preliminary test lift to check that it is correctly centred: *Staveley Iron and Chemical Co Ltd v Jones* [1956] AC 627, [1956] 1 All ER 403. Whether such a check is necessary must depend, of course, on the nature of the load. In general, a crane-driver is in much the same position as a motor-driver, and cannot be held negligent if, while he is keeping a good look-out and has his crane well under control, someone moves without warning into the track of the load: *Smith v Port Line Ltd* [1955] 2 All ER 297.

(iv) Negligent instructions

Such a person as an architect may be liable if he intervenes personally in an operation and gives instruction for work to be done in an unsafe way: see p. 92, *ante*.

A firm selling a machine owe a duty, in demonstrating it, to give clear instructions to the customer's workmen as to safe operation: *William v Trim Rock Quarries Ltd* (1965) 109 Sol Jo 454, Times, 25 May, CA (machine toppling during demonstration in quarry).

Chapter 6

Breach of statutory duty: general principles

1 When action available

Where duties are imposed on any person by an Act of Parliament, and are not carried out, it is a question of 'construction' or interpretation—that is, of the true intention of the Act—whether a private person injured by this breach of statutory duty can bring an action for damages or not. If no special remedy is provided, then the rule is that an indictment lies in the criminal courts for breach of the Act, and a private individual may bring an action for damages if he has been injured. But most modern statutes are enforced at any rate by penalties, and it is then necessary to consider the whole purview of the Act to see whether the common law right of action is intended to be taken away.

In *Cutler v Wandsworth Stadium Ltd* [1949] AC 398, [1949] 1 All ER 544 Lord Simonds said:

> 'The only rule which in all circumstances is valid is that the answer must depend on a consideration of the whole Act and the circumstances, including the pre-existing law, in which it was enacted. But that there are indications which point with more or less force to the one answer or the other is clear from authorities which, even where they do not bind, will have great weight . . . For instance, if a statutory duty is prescribed, but no remedy by way of penalty or otherwise for its breach is imposed, it can be assumed that a right of civil action accrues to a person who is damnified by the breach. For, if it were not so, that statute would be but a pious aspiration. But, as Lord Tenterden CJ said (1 B & Ad 859) in *Doe d. Rochester (Bishop v Bridges)*:
>> ". . . where an Act creates an obligation, and enforces the performance in a specified manner, we take it to be a general rule that performance cannot be enforced in any other manner."

'. . . But this general rule is subject to exceptions. It may be that, though a specific remedy is provided by the Act, yet the person injured has a personal right of action in addition.'

It will be sufficient for present purposes to give one example where the court held that the right of action arose, and another example where the court held that it did not.

In *Atkinson v Newcastle Waterworks Co* (1877) 2 Ex D 441 the defendant company were required by statute to maintain a certain pressure of water in their pipes for extinguishing fires. The court held that this was a purely public duty which was sufficiently enforced by a penalty, and that a person whose house had been burnt down due to a breach of the duty could not bring an action for damages.

In *Monk v Warbey* [1935] 1 KB 75 the Road Traffic Act 1930, s. 35 imposed heavy penalties on persons who allowed motor cars to be used on the highway without being insured against third party risks. The Court of Appeal held, in spite of the penalties, that a person injured by breach of this duty had a right of action: for the whole purview of the Act showed that it was passed for the benefit and protection of persons injured in road accidents, and the mere imposition of penalties would not compensate such persons for their injuries.

It will be seen that the fact that a statute is passed for the benefit of a class of persons may be a decisive factor. On this principle, it has long been established that an action lies for the breach of the general statutes passed for the protection and safety of workers. The particular cases are discussed in the next section. But the principles outlined above must be kept in mind, as there may be some statutes, even for the benefit of workers, where the right of action is not clear. For example, the Court of Appeal was divided upon the question whether an action lies for failure to maintain fire escapes in accordance with the London Building Acts: *Solomons v R. Gertzenstein Ltd* [1954] 2 QB 243, [1954] 2 All ER 625[1]. Moreover, under the Factories Act itself, there are some sections which

---

1 Romer LJ said in this case that it is 'of cardinal importance, in considering whether a civil suit lies . . . to see whether . . . [the] duty has been imposed for the general welfare . . . or in the interests of individuals or of a defined or definable class of the public'. Perhaps the ultimate question is whether the statute is not only passed for the benefit of a class of persons, but is intended to create a legal duty towards each member of the class as an individual. Thus the Factories Act, in general, is for the benefit of 'persons employed' as individuals: but statutes like Public Health Acts are usually for the benefit of the public as a whole, not as individuals.

do not give rise to an action for damages. Under s. 17(1) of the Act, certain parts of machines must be encased so as to prevent danger: if this is not done, the occupier will be liable to a penalty and to an action for damages. By s. 17(2) it is further provided that a person who supplies such a machine not in accordance with s. 17(1) shall be liable to a penalty: but it has been held that, on the true meaning of the Act, it is not intended that the supplier should be liable to an action for damages: *Biddle v Truvox Engineering Co Ltd, Greenwood and Batley Ltd (Third Party)* [1952] 1 KB 101, [1951] 2 All ER 835.

2 The Factories and Mines Acts and other safety legislation

While it is now clear that an action lies for breach of the Factories and Mines Acts, this was established only by degrees (Chapter 1, section 7).

In *Groves v Wimborne (Lord)* [1898] 2 QB 402 the question was fully argued before the Court of Appeal whether an action lay against the occupier of a factory for failing to fence dangerous machinery as required by the Factory and Workshop Act 1878. The Court of Appeal decided than an action did lie, and their decision has been accepted as good law ever since and approved by the House of Lords in many subsequent cases. Vaughan Williams LJ made the following general observations at p. 415:

'It cannot be doubted that where a statute provides for the performance by certain persons of a particular duty, and some one belonging to a class of persons for whose benefit and protection the statute imposes the duty is injured by failure to perform it, *prima facie* and if there be nothing to the contrary, an action by the person so injured will lie against the person who has so failed to perform the duty.'

A. L. Smith LJ said with regard to the Factory and Workshop Act 1878 (at p. 406):

'The Act in question, which followed numerous other Acts *in pari materia*, is not in the nature of a private legislative bargain between employers and workmen . . . but is a public Act passed in favour of workers in factories and workshops to compel their employers to do certain things for their protection and benefit.'

This decision related to the section requiring dangerous machinery to be fenced: but it applies in principle to every obligation under the Factories Act which is intended to protect workers from personal injury. Thus, without doubt, actions can be brought under all the provisions of Part II of the Factories Act 1961, which deals expressly with the safety of workers[2]. But it must not be assumed that an action lies for every breach of the Factories Act: it seems improbable, for instance, that the courts would allow a workman to claim damages because he had worked longer hours than are allowed by the Act[3]. Again, caution must be exercised in approaching the portions of the Act which are designed to protect the health of the workmen as distinct from their safety. An action can hardly lie for failing to keep the factory floors clean. However, pollution of the atmosphere may well be sufficient to found an action, and many actions have succeeded where diseases have been caused by abrasive dust or other unhealthy conditions. In general, the courts are now willing to admit claims based on disease as well as on personal injuries: this attitude of mind has been conditioned by a whole series of cases under the Workmen's Compensation Acts (now repealed) under which the onset of a disease was held to be a 'personal injury by accident'.

As regards the Coal Mines Acts, an action based on these had been allowed before 1898 in a number of cases, including *Baddeley v Granville (Earl)* (1887) 19 QBD 423. In *David v Britannic Merthyr Coal Co* [1909] 2 KB 146 Fletcher Moulton LJ said:

'By embodying in the provisions of an Act, such as the one now under consideration, those precautions which it is advised should be observed in the management of these dangerous undertakings the Legislature erects a standard of carefulness and requires all who carry them on to come up to that standard. It no longer is left to the chance opinion of a jury to decide whether these precautions may properly be omitted. The Legislature decides the question for them, and accordingly non-compliance with the provisions of the statute carries

2   It does not follow that an action can be brought against every person liable to a penalty. Under s. 17 of the Act, both the occupier and the supplier of machinery are liable to a penalty if certain parts of it are not safely encased: an action lies against the occupier for a breach of the section, but not against the supplier: *Biddle v Truvox Engineering Co Ltd, Greenwood and Batley Ltd (Third Party)* [1952] 1 KB 101, [1951] 2 All ER 835.

3   *Aliter*, perhaps, if long hours caused tiredness which occasioned an accident.

with it the same civil consequences as a verdict of negligence would
do.'

These remarks were approved by the House of Lords in *Butler (or Black)
v Fife Coal Co Ltd* [1912] AC 149; and in that case Lord Kinnear further
said with reference to the Coal Mines Regulation Act then in force:

'If the duty be established, I do not think there is any serious question
as to the civil liability. There is no reasonable ground for maintaining
that a proceeding by way of penalty is the only remedy allowed by the
statute. . . . We are to consider the scope and purpose of the statute
and in particular for whose benefit it is intended. Now the object of
the present statute is plain. It was intended to compel mine-owners to
make due provision for the safety of the men working in their mines,
and the persons for whose benefit all these rules are to be enforced are
the persons exposed to danger. But when a duty of this kind is
imposed for the benefit of particular persons, there arises at common
law a correlative right in those persons who may be injured by its
contravention.'

Here again, as under the Factories Act, the right to bring an action
clearly applies to every breach of the *safety* provisions of the Act: thus
Lord Atkin said in *Lochgelly Iron and Coal Co v M'Mullan* [1934] AC 1 at
8, referring to the duty under the Coal Mines Act 1911, ss. 49 and 52[4] to
support the roof of the working-place:

'. . . if it were necessary to show that they are designed to secure the
safety of persons employed in the mine, it is only necessary to refer to
the terms of the sections themselves and to the fact that they are
contained in Part II of the Act which is entitled "Provisions for
Safety".'

It does not necessarily follow, however, that an action can be brought on
sections of the Act which lie outside these safety provisions.

Recent legislation has set a new pattern by stating expressly whether
there is to be an action for breach of statutory duty. Thus, by the Mineral
Workings (Offshore Installations) Act 1971, s. 11 there is an action for
injuries due to breach of a duty under the Act, and also for breach of
regulations if the regulations say that s. 11 applies.

This method has been adopted by the Health and Safety at Work Act
1974, and will therefore become universal as regulations under the Act
supersede the existing safety legislation. Section 47 says that no action

4   16 Halsbury's Statutes, 2nd Edn., 133, 136.

will lie for a breach of the very general safety duties under ss. 2 to 7, but it will lie for a breach of health and safety regulations under s. 15 unless the regulations exclude it. The incidence of civil liability under existing legislation is left undisturbed: s. 47(1)(b).

3 The nature of the action for breach of statutory duty: its resemblance to negligence

The nature of the action for breach of statutory duty was considered by the House of Lords in a case which turned on s. 29 of the Workmen's Compensation Act 1925. This section provided that a workman could elect between his right to weekly payments of compensation and his right to damages at common law: but that the employer should not be liable (apart from the Act) except for his own 'personal negligence or wilful act', or that of some person for whom he was responsible. Throughout the history of the Workmen's Compensation Act, it was assumed that these words were inserted only to emphasise the fact that the common law doctrine of common employment remained unaltered, and no one had imagined that they took away the right of action for breach of statutory duty. Nevertheless, it was argued before the House of Lords in *Lochgelly Iron and Coal Co v M'Mullan* [1934] AC 1 that breach of statutory duty was not 'personal negligence' and that s. 29 operated to bar an action by a workman for breach of statutory duty unless in the circumstances the breach was negligent or wilful. The House of Lords rejected this contention. The *Lochgelly* case is no longer of importance, except in so far as it gave an opportunity to the House to discuss the nature of the action for breach of statutory duty. In substance, their conclusions came to this, that breach of statutory duty is closely analogous to negligence. Just as, in common law negligence, there is a duty to take care, followed by breach of the duty, and damage, so also in breach of statutory duty there is the duty imposed by statute, the breach, and the resulting injury. The House was not, of course, dealing with *all* cases of statutory duty, but only with those which impose requirements for the safety of a class of persons. Lord Wright said, however (at p. 23):

> 'In such a case as the present [where it was alleged that mine-owners had failed to support the roof of the mine] the liability is something

which goes beyond and is on a different plane from the liability for breach of a duty under the ordinary law, apart from the statute, because not only is the duty one which cannot be delegated but, whereas at the ordinary law the standard of duty must be fixed by the verdict of a jury, the statutory duty is conclusively fixed by the statute. But the duty is the same in kind in this respect, that it is a duty to take precautions and care for the safety of the workmen; it is a duty to take care which is owed to the workman, and which if broken constitutes negligent conduct, for which, if damage ensues to the workman affected, damages are recoverable. Hence the breach of such a duty as that in question has been, I think, correctly described as statutory negligence.'

In spite of the close analogy, however, it is not correct to say that negligence and breach of statutory duty are one and the same thing[5]. Thus Lord Wright himself later said, in *Caswell v Powell Duffryn Associated Collieries Ltd* [1940] AC 152 at 178, [1939] 3 All ER 722 at 739:

'I do not think that an action for breach of a statutory duty such as that in question is completely or accurately described as an action in negligence. It is a common law action based on the purpose of the statute to protect the workman, and belonging to the category often described as that of cases of strict or absolute liability. At the same time it resembles actions in negligence in that the claim is based on a breach of a duty to take care for the safety of the workman.'

The same learned Lord added in *London Passenger Transport Board v Upson* [1949] AC 155 at 168, [1949] 1 All ER 60 at 67:

'I think that the authorities . . . show clearly that a claim for damages for breach of a statutory duty intended to protect a person in the position of the particular plaintiff is a specific common law right which is not to be confused in essence with a claim for negligence. The statutory right has its origin in the statute, but the particular remedy of an action for damages is given by the common law in order to make effective for the benefit of the injured plaintiff his right to the performance by the defendant of the defendant's statutory duty. It is an effective sanction. It is not a claim in negligence in the strict or ordinary sense . . . whatever the resemblances, it is essential to keep in mind the fundamental differences of the two classes of claim.'

5   In Scots law, negligence and breach of statutory duty alike fall under the generic concept of 'fault'; and both alike are 'claims at common law' within the meaning of an indemnity contract: *Hamilton (William) & Co Ltd v Anderson (W. G.) & Co Ltd* 1953 SC 129.

For example, it is essential to set out a breach of statutory duty clearly in the pleadings in an action: and the defences are not quite the same as in a claim based on negligence.

4 The conditions of liability

The plaintiff in an action for breach of statutory duty must prove three things:

(a) that the statute imposes upon the defendant a duty, which is intended to protect the plaintiff against harm of some kind;

(b) that the defendant has failed to perform his duty; and

(c) that this breach of duty has resulted in harm to the plaintiff, which is of the kind contemplated by the statute.

Under the first of these conditions of liability, it is not enough to show that a duty is imposed upon the defendant: it must also be shown that this duty is owed to the plaintiff, or rather to a class of persons (such as 'persons employed' in factories) to which he belongs.

Under the third condition, it is important to note that the harm which the plaintiff sustains must be harm of a type which is within the scope of the statute: for example, where pens have to be provided for animals on board ship to prevent the spread of disease, no action will lie if they are swept overboard owing to the absence of pens. The authorities on this subject—which have often been misunderstood—are summarised later in this chapter.

Causation in cases of breach of statutory duty

The most important requirement, however, is that the breach of statutory duty should have caused the injury complained of. Lord Macmillan said in *Caswell v Powell Duffryn Associated Collieries Ltd* [1940] AC 152 at 168, [1939] 3 All ER 722 at 732:

> 'The mere fact that at the time of an accident to a miner his employers can be shown to have been in breach of a statutory duty is clearly not enough in itself to impose liability on the employers. It must be shown that the accident was causally associated with the breach of statutory duty.'

The plaintiff must, therefore, satisfy the court that his injuries were caused by the breach of statutory duty. This question is decided according to the principles already explained (pp. 53–72, *ante*) in connection with negligence at common law; and the plaintiff will succeed on this issue (as on all issues in civil actions) if he establishes a balance of probability in his favour: *Dawson v Murex Ltd* [1942] 1 All ER 483.

It was formerly held that where a statute requires safety measures to be taken for avoiding a particular type of accident (such as injury from a circular saw) or a particular disease (such as silicosis from dust), and a breach of the statute is followed by an accident or disease of that particular kind, there is a *presumption* that the breach of statutory duty has caused the injury[6]. The House of Lords overruled these authorities in *Bonnington Castings Ltd v Wardlaw* [1956] AC 613, [1956] 1 All ER 615 and held that there is no such presumption. It is, however, sufficient evidence of causation to show that there has been exposure or increased exposure to conditions giving rise to a disease, and it is not necessary that the increased exposure should be the *sole* cause of the disease provided that it has made a material contribution. The pursuer in the *Bonnington* case sustained silicosis after exposure to separate sources of noxious dust, only one of which was in breach of statute (because the dust should have been extracted at the point of origin). His claim succeeded on the ground of increased exposure making a material contribution though there was no presumption of law in his favour.

Lord Reid said:

> 'The employee must in all cases prove his case by the ordinary standard of proof in civil actions: he must make it appear at least that on a balance of probabilities the breach of duty caused or materially contributed to his injury.'

Lord Keith said that the pursuer would have failed if the dust in question had been released so infrequently, or in such an insignificant quantity, that even over a long period it could not be regarded as a material factor.

Most of the decisions on this subject are illustrations of the working of

---

6 *Lee v Nursery Furnishings Ltd* [1945] 1 All ER 387 (gap between fence and circular saw rather wider than it should have been); *Hughes v McGoff & Vickers Ltd* [1955] 2 All ER 291 (fall of object from scaffold without toe-boards); *Vyner v Waldenberg Bros Ltd* [1946] KB 50, [1945] 2 All ER 547 (fencing of saw); *Cork v Kirby Maclean Ltd* [1952] 2 All ER 402 (absence of rail on scaffold). Most (if not all) of these cases can be justified on normal rules of evidence without applying any presumption: per Lord Keith in the *Bonnington* case [1956] 1 All ER 615 at 621.

the rules of circumstantial evidence, and particularly of the legitimate inference that an injury or disease would probably not have been sustained if exposure to the risk had been limited by safety measures: the court is not bound to make such an inference where the facts as a whole do not justify it: *Qualcast (Wolverhampton) Ltd v Haynes* [1959] AC 743, [1959] 2 All ER 38 (per Lord Denning at 762, 46) (workman would not have worn protective clothing even if urged to do so)[7]. The following are examples.

(i) Exposure or increased exposure to disease-producing conditions
Prolonged exposure to fractured silica dust was sufficient evidence that it caused silicosis in *Quinn v Cameron & Roberton Ltd* [1958] AC 9, [1957] 1 All ER 760. In *Nicholson v Atlas Steel Foundry & Engineering Co Ltd* [1957] 1 All ER 776 where the breach of statutory duty consisted of insufficient ventilation to remove the dust, Lord Simonds said (p. 779):

> 'I do not think it can be wrong to approach this question from the angle that, if the statute prescribes a proper system of ventilation by the circulation of fresh air so as to render harmless . . . all fumes, dust and other impurities that may be injurious to health . . . and if it is proved that there is no system, or only an inadequate system, of ventilation, it requires little further to establish a causal link between that default and the illness due to noxious dust of a person employed in the shop.'

Something more was required, he continued: but that little extra was supplied by the fact that the sooner the cloud of dust dissipated, the shorter the exposure and the less the risk. In *Gardiner v Motherwell Machinery and Scrap Co Ltd* [1961] 3 All ER 831 a man had been exposed to conditions liable to produce dermatitis, and (as it turned out) sustained dermatitis of the type which might be expected. Lord Reid said:

> 'When a man who has not previously suffered from a disease contracts that disease after being subjected to conditions likely to cause it, and when he shows that it starts in a way typical of disease caused by such

7 It is said that there must be *positive* proof of causation in Scottish law. Thus Lord President Clyde said in *McWilliams v Sir William Arrol & Co Ltd* 1961 SLT 265 at 270: 'In almost all reparation cases evidence is led as to what the consequences would have been if something other than what was done had been done.' *Quaere* whether such evidence is of more than *formal* value: e.g. if a witness says 'The pursuer would probably not have fallen off the scaffold if there had been a guard rail', it is not true evidence of *fact* but of opinion and inference which the court is equally able to make. And see Lord Donovan's remark at p. 35, *ante.*

conditions, he establishes a *prima facie* presumption that his disease
was caused by those conditions.'

'Presumption' must here be read to mean a legitimate inference—the
Bonnington case having shown that there is no presumption of law.

In *McGhee v National Coal Board* [1972] 3 All ER 1008 a man was
necessarily and unavoidably exposed to abrasive dust through working
in brick kilns, but the exposure was greater because there were no
washing facilities and he had to cycle home caked with dust. He
contracted dermatitis. The House of Lords held that the absence of
facilities materially increased the risk, and neglect to provide them was a
cause of the disease. (The House of Lords, however, has since
disapproved of passages in Lord Wilberforce's speech which seem to
suggest that, where there is a breach of statutory duty which *may* have
contributed to the disease, there is a presumption that this rather than
other possible causes is responsible: *Wilsher v Essex Area Health
Authority* [1988] AC 1074, [1988] 1 All ER 871, HL.) Similarly in
Ransom v Sir Robert McAlpine & Sons Ltd (1971) 11 KIR 141, increased
risk of 'compression sickness' due to carelessness in operating the
de-compression chambers was sufficient to establish a causal
connection.

(ii) Increased exposure to accident
Where, for example, regulations allow a gap between a fence and a
circular saw, and the gap is rather greater than it should be, it is
legitimate to infer that the increased exposure has contributed to the
accident, as in *Lee v Nursery Furnishings Ltd* [1945] 1 All ER 387. So,
too, with the absence of a guard rail on a scaffold: *Cork v Kirby Maclean
Ltd* [1952] 2 All ER 402; or a rail on a working platform below which
there is a space where a man working in a squatting position may fall
through: *McClymont v Glasgow Corpn* 1971 SLT 45; or with the absence
of a fence on a machine, though it is possible that the workman might
have removed it, for the presence of a fence would at least be a 'warning
or deterrent': *Hodkinson v Henry Wallwork & Co Ltd* [1955] 3 All ER
236; *Allen v Aeroplane and Motor Aluminium Castings Ltd* [1965] 3 All
ER 377. It is not necessary to prove exactly how a man's hands got into
an unfenced machine, when they could not have got in if it were fenced:
Johnson v F. E. Callow (Engineers) Ltd [1970] 1 All ER 129; *sub nom.
Callow (F.E.) Engineers Ltd v Johnson* approved on appeal [1970] 3 All

ER 639 at 645. In general, if there is a reasonable probability that some safety measure would have given extra protection, and was not taken, the causal connection is sufficiently shown, as for example in *Clarke v E. R. Wright & Son* [1957] 3 All ER 486 where inquiries about a scaffold by the employers might have revealed a defect[8]. Where a safety regulation could have been carried out in alternative ways, only one of which would have prevented the accident, the court must decide on the facts which method would probably have been adopted: *Corn v Weir's Glass (Hanley) Ltd* [1960] 2 All ER 300 (a 'hand-rail' had to be provided: it need not necessarily have taken the form of a 'guard rail' which would be a barrier to a fall).

Where a safety device, if provided, would not have prevented the accident, there is of course no liability: *Curran v William Neill & Son (St. Helens) Ltd* [1961] 3 All ER 108 (no time to grip rail); *Corn v Weir's Glass (Hanley) Ltd* [1960] 2 All ER 300 (light hand-rail might not have withstood weight in fall); *Lancaster v Wigan Brick Co* (1960) (Court of Appeal, unreported) (workman removed fence from machine)[9].

(iii) Safety belts and other optional devices

It is no longer good law—as stated in *Roberts v Dorman Long & Co Ltd* [1953] 2 All ER 428—that where a safety belt or other optional device has not been provided, the defendant cannot set up the defence that in any event it would not have been used: *Qualcast (Wolverhampton) Ltd v*

---

8 In *Shepherd v J. and J. White Ltd*, noted in [1955] 105 L Jo 106, it was held by Lord Migdale in the Court of Session that a workman who slipped and fell into a vat, which was not fenced or covered as required by regulations, could not recover damages because there was no causal connection between the failure to fence and the slip. With respect, this cannot be right. An omission to interpose a safeguard against a specific danger is at least one cause of the continuance of that danger and therefore of accidents resulting from exposure to it. Otherwise no workman could ever recover damages for failure to fence machinery or scaffolding. *McClymont v Glasgow Corpn, supra*, shows that the Scottish courts no longer take such a narrow view.

9 In a case where the House of Lords divided on the facts, a workman fell over a piece of metal on a factory floor. There was no proof of how the obstruction had got there. *Held* by a majority, assuming it might be a breach of s. 28 of the Factories Act 1961 to fail to instruct employees to keep the floor clear, that there was no proof of causal connection in the absence of evidence that the metal had been put there by an employee. *Contra*, Lords Reid and Morris, on the ground that the employers had made no real efforts to keep the floor clear and any serious attempt on their part would probably have made a vast improvement: *Fairfield Shipbuilding and Engineering Co Ltd v Hall* [1964] 1 Lloyd's Rep 73.

Haynes [1959] AC 743 at 762, [1959] 2 All ER 38 at 46. The onus is always on the plaintiff to prove that the breach of statutory duty was a cause of the accident. Where a safety belt or other optional safeguard is not provided or available as required by statute, it may be legitimate in the first instance to infer that, since it is required by statute (per Lord Reid in the *McWilliams* case), 'it is of some use and that a reasonable man would use it'; but if the evidence shows that on the balance of probabilities the workman would not have used the device, there is no causal connection and the action must fail: *Cummings (or McWilliams) v Sir Wm. Arrol & Co Ltd* [1962] 1 All ER 623, *Wigley v British Vinegars Ltd* [1964] AC 307, [1962] 3 All ER 161; see also *Qualcast (Wolverhampton) Ltd v Haynes, supra,* and *James v Hepworth and Grandage Ltd* [1968] 1 QB 94, [1967] 2 All ER 829 (safety spats); *Nolan v Dental Manufacturing Co Ltd* [1958] 2 All ER 449 (goggles).

5 The construction of the Factories Act and similar statutes

From time to time it becomes necessary for the courts to decide the meaning of various statutes, or, as lawyers say, to determine their true construction or interpretation.

Technically speaking, the construction of a statute is a question of law: that is to say, it is always decided by the judge and never by a jury, and an appeal lies even in cases where there is no appeal on a question of fact. In reality, however, and from the point of view of strict logic, the construction of a statute is a question of fact, unless there are authorities on the meaning of the statute or of a statute worded in a similar way. The court has to decide as a fact what is meant by particular words or phrases used in a particular context—and, as everyone knows, the meaning of words and phrases differs vastly from one context to another. Once the court has arrived at its decision, the meaning given to the statute has the force of law. Moreover, the decision will be followed in interpreting the same words in the same sort of context: for example, a decision on the meaning of the expression 'reasonably practicable' as used in the Mines and Quarries Act will also apply to the Factories Act, and the word 'dangerous', as used in connection with machinery, has the same meaning in both Acts[10]. So, too, the words 'properly maintained', interpreted under the Factories Act as imposing a continuous obligation to keep in good order, as distinct from regular 'servicing', have been given the same meaning in the Mines and Quarries Act 1954: *Hamilton v National Coal Board* [1960] AC 633, [1960] 1 All ER 76.

The established principles or 'canons' of construction do not call for more than a brief mention here. In the main, they simply recognise the facts of the English language. *Ordinary words* are taken to be used in their ordinary sense, for which the standard dictionaries are a valuable guide, although they are not accepted as conclusive. *Technical words* are understood in their technical sense, which may have to be explained by expert witnesses, but it has first to be shown that the expression is used in a technical sense: *London and North Eastern Rail Co v Berriman* [1946] AC 278, [1946] 1 All ER 255 ('permanent way men'). Where a word has several possible meanings, the context will show which meaning is intended. *Sentences and phrases* are construed according to the ordinary rules of grammar, unless there is something in the context which necessitates a deviation from these rules. Weight must be given to the whole of the statute, so that an ambiguity in one section may vanish when other sections are taken into account. The meaning of words may be controlled by the context of many sections[11]. Lastly, the whole *scheme* of the statute is important—the purpose for which it was passed, and the manner in which it is drawn up to effectuate this purpose. Thus the Factories Act was passed for the protection of workmen, and Part II is expressly directed to their safety: and these facts control the interpretation of individual sections. If a section can be read in two alternative ways, one of which will carry out the object of the statute and one of which will not, the section should be interpreted in accordance with the maxim *ut res magis valeat*—so that the statute will work: *Potts (or Riddell) v Reid* [1943] AC 1 at 16, [1942] 2 All ER 161 at 168.

---

10 Whether a slight variation in wording makes any difference is a question of fact (in the sense explained above). The use of the expression 'exposed and dangerous' in the Mines and Quarries Act, for instance, does not limit the meaning of 'dangerous'.

11 E.g. 'machinery' was interpreted in the context of the Factories Act to mean machinery used in the factory, as distinct from machines made there: *Parvin v Morton Machine Co Ltd* [1952] AC 515, [1952] 1 All ER 670; and 'scaffold', in the Building Regulations, means a scaffold 'in use', as distinct from under construction: *Sexton v Scaffolding (Great Britain) Ltd* [1953] 1 QB 153, [1952] 2 All ER 1085.

There is a further rule which must be explained in rather greater detail, because it has often been invoked in cases under the Factories Act.

Strict construction of penal statutes

Breaches of the Factories Act and of the Coal Mines Act are criminal offences which render the offender liable to penalties. There is authority for saying that statutes creating penalties must be construed strictly, so that the benefit of any doubt must be given to the alleged wrongdoer: *Tuck & Sons v Priester* (1887) 19 QBD 629. But this does not mean that the plain meaning of the statute can be cut down by artificial doubts: *A-G v Lockwood* (1842) 9 M & W 378; *Dyke v Elliott* (1872) LR 4 PC 184. According to Denning LJ in *McCarthy v Coldair Ltd* [1951] 2 TLR 1226:

> 'So far as the Factories Act is concerned, the rule is only to be applied when other rules fail. It is a rule of last resort.'

In *Harrison v National Coal Board* [1951] AC 639 at 650, [1951] 1 All ER 1102 at 1107 Lord Porter said:

> 'It was suggested . . . that the Coal Mines Act 1911, is a measure imposing criminal liability, and, therefore, should be interpreted as throwing no greater burden on the employer than its words compel. It has, however, to be remembered that this Act is also a remedial measure passed for the protection of the workmen and must, therefore, be read so as to effect its object so far as the wording fairly and reasonably permits.'

The rule as to strict construction, therefore, has no great force in this particular context. In particular, it is 'an illegitimate method of interpretation of a statute, whose dominant purpose is to protect the workman, to introduce by implication words of which the effect must be to reduce that protection'; for example by reading into the words 'securely fenced' the qualification 'so far as practicable': per Viscount Simonds in *John Summers & Sons Ltd v Frost* [1955] AC 740 at 751, [1955] 1 All ER 870 at 872[12]. Likewise, Hodson LJ said in *Ebbs v James*

---

12 Evidently the earlier dictum of Lord Simonds in *Berriman's* case, that a penal statute, even for the benefit of workmen, must be construed where possible so as to avoid the penalty, does *not* mean that the full and fair meaning of the statute must

Whitson & Co Ltd [1952] 2 QB 877 at 886, [1952] 2 All ER 192 at 195:

> 'I do not think it is legitimate to import into the language of the statute words attributing knowledge, or a duty of knowledge, to the occupiers. The words *may be injurious* must be given their natural meaning, as opposed to *may possibly* or *may probably*[13].'

Similarly the court declined to restrict the full and fair meaning of the Act in *Thurogood v Van den Berghs and Jurgens Ltd* [1951] 2 KB 537, [1951] 1 All ER 682, and declined in *Norris v Syndic Manufacturing Co Ltd* [1952] 2 QB 135, [1952] 1 All ER 935 to give a lenient meaning to s. 119 of the 1937 Act, which imposed duties on the workman, the point being that 'the Act is intended to prevent accidents to workmen', and for that purpose imposes strict duties on workmen as well as on employers.

Nevertheless, there are two cases where the maxim as to strict construction of penal statutes has some force. First, there may be an *ambiguity*: but, said Denning LJ in *McCarthy's* case, *supra*, 'this . . . does not mean every ambiguity which the ingenuity of counsel may suggest, but only an ambiguity which the settled rules of construction fail to solve'. Such an ambiguity occurred in *London and North Eastern Rail Co v Berriman, supra*, where a doubt arose whether 'repairs' to a railway line included the oiling of signals. Another example was *Richard Thomas and Baldwins Ltd v Cummings* [1955] AC 321, [1955] 1 All ER 285, where the question was whether machinery is 'in motion' when the power is cut off and it is moved by hand. The second type of case is not really an application of the rule at all, although it has sometimes been treated as if it were. It arises where the court refuses to give an equitable or benevolent construction to a statute by stretching its meaning beyond what is fairly expressed. An example in point is *Beadsley v United Steel Companies Ltd* [1951] 1 KB 408, [1950] 2 All ER 872 where the Court

---

be cut down where possible. The dictum was, however, applied in this sense by a majority of the Court of Appeal in *Burns v Joseph Terry & Sons Ltd* [1951] 1 KB 454, [1950] 2 All ER 987, and consequently an unduly narrow construction has been given to the words 'securely fenced' in relation to machinery: see p. 335, *post*, and also a criticism by Prof. A. L. Goodhart in [1951] 67 LQR 7–10.

13 On the same principle, it appears to be equally illegitimate to introduce such words as 'foreseeable' or, *a fortiori*, 'reasonably foreseeable', into the Act. This is translating concepts from the law of negligence into a context to which they do not belong: yet this has happened in a number of cases, e.g. 'secure' fencing, 'safe' means of access. See an article by the present author on *Foreseeability and the Factories Act* in (1952) 102 L Jo 549. But to question this is now a lost cause, except for the purpose of amending legislation.

of Appeal held that the requirements (under s. 23 of the Factories Act, now s. 26 of 1961) that lifting tackle shall be of 'good construction' does not necessitate that it shall be of the right design and type for each particular occasion of use[14]. Another example is *Haigh v Charles W. Ireland Ltd* [1973] 3 All ER 1137 where 'plant' in s. 31 (4) of the Factories Act was held to mean 'plant installed in the factory', not articles brought there for treatment; it was said that the court should not put 'a strained meaning on the words' merely because the general intention of the Act is to protect the workman.

Problems of construction: some illustrations

In practice problems of construction reduce themselves to three main headings, which are much the same as the questions which have to be answered in actions for negligence.

(i) Upon whom is the statutory duty imposed?
Under the Factories Act, no difficulty arises, because the duty ordinarily rests on the occupier, and where this is not the case, under regulations for example, the person responsible is expressly designated.

Under the Coal Mines Act 1911 it was held that the owners were responsible when obligations were expressed impersonally, but not when they were imposed on a specified person such as the shotfirer: *Harrison v National Coal Board* [1951] AC 639, [1951] 1 All ER 1102. Under the Mines and Quarries Act 1954, s. 159 the owners have been made responsible for breaches of duty by persons such as shotfirers who are employed by them. Most duties under the 1954 Act are imposed on the manager or some other specific person.

(ii) To whom is the duty owed?
This is not always an easy question to answer. In *London and North Eastern Rly Co v Berriman, supra*, the duty to provide a look-out man was

14 See also *Rees v Bernard Hastie & Co Ltd* [1953] 1 QB 328, [1953] 1 All ER 375 (cutting by *electrical process* does not include cutting by shears worked by electrical power). This decision was followed in *Hunter v Singer Manufacturing Co Ltd* 1953 SLT (Notes) 84, 104 Sol Jo 58, but the dicta of Somervell LJ upon the strict interpretation of the statute were dissented from, as being in conflict with *Chalmers v Speedwell Wire Co* 1942 JC 42 at 47.

owed to men engaged in 'repairs' to the permanent way, and it was held that this did not include men engaged in oiling signals apparatus. Under the Factories Act, the duties are generally owed to persons working in the factory, even if they are outside contractors or temporary visitors (see pp. 277–279, *post*). Under regulations made under s. 76 of the Factories Act, they are owed to 'persons employed': *Hartley v Mayoh & Co* [1954] 1 QB 383, [1954] 1 All ER 375.

(iii) The extent of the duty

Illustrations may be found in *Beadsley v United Steel Companies Ltd, supra*, and the decisions, Chapter 11 section 2, that the duty to fence machinery does not extend to giving protection against breakage.

For some purposes it is necessary to add a fourth question:

(iv) What dangers does the duty guard against?

An action for breach of statutory duty will fail if the damage done is not the kind of harm which the statute is designed to give protection against. Thus in *Gorris v Scott* (1874) LR 9 Exch 125 where sheep were swept overboard from a ship owing to the absence of pens, the action failed because the pens were required by statute to prevent disease, and not to prevent accidents.

While, however, the damage sustained must be, in a broad sense, harm of the type visualised by the statute, it is not necessary that it should be sustained in the precise manner which the statute appears to contemplate[15]. For example, in *Grant v National Coal Board* [1956] AC 649, [1956] 1 All ER 682 the House of Lords held that the object of the Coal Mines Act 1911 was to safeguard the miners against accidents generally; and accordingly an action could be brought under s. 49 (duty to keep roof secure) not only in a case where the roof had fallen on the pursuer but also in a case where he was injured by the derailment of a bogie when it struck stone previously fallen from the roof. In *Donaghey v Boulton & Paul Ltd* [1968] AC 1, [1967] 2 All ER 1014 a regulation

---

15 The rule in *Gorris v Scott*. Few would contest the decision in this case, where the two types were *totally* different. Unfortunately, the existence of such a rule may lead to the purpose of a statute being interpreted narrowly, as in the parallel case of negligence and 'foreseeable' harm. That is why it has been held in at least one case in the U.S. Supreme Court—*Kernan v American Dredging Co* (1958) 78 S Crt 394—that the violation of a statute which in fact contributes to an injury creates liability, regardless of whether the injury was the type the statute sought to prevent.

requiring crawling boards above a fragile roof was held to give protection against any fall from the roof, although the fragile material was not broken. In *Millard v Serck Tubes Ltd* [1969] I All ER 598 it was irrelevant that a man's arm was drawn into a machine in an unexpected way, by loose strips of metal swarf. In *Rutherford v R. E. Glanville & Sons (Bovey Tracey) Ltd* [1958] 1 All ER 532 where a carborundum wheel was liable to disintegrate and the purpose of the hood or guard over it was to give protection against flying fragments, the claim succeeded although the plaintiff was struck by a piece of the guard itself and not by a fragment of the wheel[16]. A plaintiff who is attempting to remove a danger created by breach of regulations is within the scope of the duty under those regulations: *McGovern v British Steel Corpn* [1986] 1 CR 608; [1986] IRLR 411, CA.

In general, the obligation to fence dangerous machinery is to prevent the worker from coming into contact with the machine, not to protect him against materials such as pieces of wood thrown out of it: *Nicholls v Austin (Leyton) Ltd* [1946] AC 493, [1946] 2 All ER 92; and similarly the duty to fence transmission machinery is not intended to give protection against an accident such as the breaking of a belt: *Carroll v Andrew Barclay & Sons Ltd* [1948] AC 477, [1948] 2 All ER 386. However, both these cases seem to be decisions on the nature of the fence to be provided, i.e. on the extent of the duty, rather than applications of *Gorris v Scott*. A fence might comply with the statute and be sufficient to preclude contact, but (as was pointed out in the *Carroll* case) it might not be heavy or strong enough to contain bursting fragments of machinery such as a heavy flywheel; moreover a mesh guard may preclude contact but will not prevent the escape of pieces of wood or wire through the mesh. In both cases, in fact, the action failed because the fence complied with the statute and there was no breach of statutory duty. They illustrate the point that it is always relevant to look at the dangers contemplated by the statute with a view to determining the extent of the duty[17].

16 Overruled by the House of Lords on other grounds: *Close v Steel Co of Wales Ltd* [1961] 2 All ER 953.
17 In *Kilgollan v William Cooke & Co Ltd* [1956] 2 All ER 294 where a piece of wire flew out of a machine into the plaintiff's eye, the claim succeeded on the ground of negligence. There was a guard of wire mesh which did not comply with s. 14. Morris and Romer LJJ though that s. 14 could have been complied with by a mesh guard which might still have let fragments through, and therefore left open the question of statutory duty. Singleton LJ thought that, on the assumption that there

6 Statutory duty: how far absolute

It is often said that statutory duties are absolute. But the word 'absolute', in this sense, has no fewer than three different meanings, and in two of these meanings the general principle is subject to certain qualifications.

(1) Statutory duties may be absolute in the sense that they cannot be delegated.

(2) They may be absolute in the sense that the statute requires a certain result, and it is a breach of statutory duty if this result is not attained, though the person liable to perform the duty has done everything within his power.

(3) They are *always* absolute in the sense that whatever the statute prescribes must be strictly performed.

(1) Liability unaffected by delegation

If a statute places duties on a person, and he delegates them to a subordinate or to an independent contractor—however competent—he remains liable if the duties are not performed.

The Coal Mines Act 1911, s. 49 enacted that 'The roof and sides of every travelling road and working place shall be made secure...' This duty rested on the owners of a mine, and if they left it to subordinates to carry it out, they were personally responsible for default on the part of those subordinates. Thus Lord McLaren said in *Bett v Dalmeny Oil Co* (1905) 7 F 787 (cited with approval in *Butler (or Black) v Fife Coal Co Ltd* [1912] AC 149):

> 'The statutory duty of the mine-owner is to give the necessary support to the roof, and in my opinion it is not an answer to a case of neglect of that duty to say that the employer had delegated the performance of the duty to a competent manager.'

---

was a breach of statutory duty which caused the accident, the claim under this head would nevertheless fail because the injury was of a kind outside the scope of the section. This view is difficult to reconcile with the majority of the speeches in *Grant v National Coal Board, supra.* See also the speech of Lord Morris in *Close v Steel Co of Wales Ltd* [1961] 2 All ER 953 where he contemplates that absence of a fence to protect against contact, as the statute requires, might give a cause of action if it would also have stopped flying fragments.

In *Lochgelly Iron and Coal Co v M'Mullan* [1934] AC 1 (where the above passage was again approved) Lord Atkin said, at pp. 8–9:

> '. . . the duty is imposed upon the employer, and it is irrelevant whether his servants had disregarded his instructions or whether he knew or not of the breach.'

So far as delegation to servants is concerned, these decisions have lost some of their importance since the master became vicariously liable for the torts of his servants to one another. However, they have a wider scope, because the person upon whom a statutory duty is laid is responsible for the default of independent contractors and even third parties. In *Hosking v De Havilland Aircraft Co Ltd* [1949] 1 All ER 540 an independent building contractor dug a ditch in the grounds of a factory and used an unsound plank as a bridge over the ditch. The occupier of the factory was held liable, as it was his responsibility under s. 26(1) of the Factories Act 1937[18], to see that all 'means of access' to places of work within the factory were safe.

In some circumstances, however, where a breach of the employer's duty is brought about by the plaintiff himself, he may be held to be the sole cause of the accident: see Chapter 23, section 6.

There is another class of cases where, at first sight, delegation appears to be a defence. This is best illustrated by *Watkins v Naval Colliery Co* (1897) *Ltd* [1912] AC 693 where the law was explained, though the actual decision turned on another point. Section 49 of the Coal Mines Regulation Act 1887 contained general rules which imposed obligations on officials and other persons working in the pit. But, as Lord Atkinson explained (at p. 705):

> 'The 50th section goes further. It makes each of the following persons, the owner, agent and manager, *prima facie* guilty of an offence against the Act if any of the rules have been violated, or not observed, by a person or persons other than themselves. . . . The section, however, provides for the person or persons thus vicariously made liable for the acts of others a means of escape from all liability. It is only necessary for them to establish that they have taken all reasonable means, by publishing, and to the best of their power enforcing, the rules and regulations for the working of the mine, in order to protect themselves from this liability.'

---

18 Cf. now s. 29 (1) of the 1961 Act.

These cases do not depend on delegation. The statutory duty rests primarily on the subordinate, and the owner, agent or manager is liable, if at all, for his failure to supervise. This becomes clear when we consider, for instance, the rules for the conduct of shotfiring in a mine—rules which can be carried out only by the men engaged in the work—which were the subject of *Britannic Merthyr Coal Co Ltd v David* [1910] AC 74 and *Harrison v National Coal Board* [1951] AC 639, [1951] 1 All ER 1102.

This type of case does not arise under the Mines and Quarries Act 1954, which (by s. 159) makes the owners liable in a civil action for the statutory defaults of their subordinates: but it may arise under other statutes or regulations.

(2) Liability not generally dependent on negligence or practicability

Liability for breach of statutory duty is not, as a rule, dependent on proof of negligence: nor, in general, can it be avoided by proving that it was impracticable to comply with the statute. Statutes lay down positive obligations which have to be complied with, irrespective of practical difficulties. For instance, by s. 22 (1) of the Factories Act 1937 (read with s. 152 (1))[19], 'Every ... lift shall be properly maintained ... in efficient working order.' In *Galashiels Gas Co Ltd v O'Donnell (or Millar)* [1949] AC 275, [1949] 1 All ER 319 a workman was killed by the failure of the automatic braking mechanism in a lift, a failure which no one could account for and which could not have been detected beforehand. Nevertheless the occupiers of the factory were held liable. Lord MacDermott said, at pp. 286, 324, after quoting the section:

> 'My Lords, if this means that every lift shall be kept continuously—or at least while it is available for use as a lift—in efficient working order, the nature of the obligation is clear. It then falls into a category long recognised and firmly established by authority; it is a strict or absolute duty and neither intention nor lack of care need be shown in order to prove a breach of it. . . . There was abundant proof that the mechanism had failed and that that failure resulted in the death of the respondent's husband. Once the absolute nature of the duty imposed by the statute is established that is proof enough.'

19 Cf. now ss. 22 (1), 176 (1) of the 1961 Act.

Another example is the obligation to fence dangerous machinery. In this connection Lord Normand observed, in *Carroll v Barclay (Andrew) & Sons Ltd* [1948] AC 477 at 487, [1948] 2 All ER 386 at 391:

> 'The subsection imposes an absolute obligation in the sense that the obligation, whatever its meaning and effect, must be actually fulfilled and not merely that the occupier of the factory must do his best to fulfil it.'

It is no defence to say that the machine, if securely fenced, cannot be used: *John Summers & Sons Ltd v Frost* [1955] AC 740, [1955] 1 All ER 870. But a statute may, of course, say that reasonable care is all that is required. It is difficult to find an example which does precisely this, but a very near case is to be found in the Factories Act 1961, s. 63 which deals with processes in factories which give off dust or fumes. The section says that 'all practicable measures shall be taken' to protect work-people exposed to the dust or fumes. This calls for something more than reasonable care, but it is not, in the strict sense, an absolute obligation.

Again, there are a number of sections in the Factories Act 1961 which direct that certain things are to be done 'so far as it is reasonably practicable': see, for instance, s. 29 (1) with regard to safe means of access to a place of work. The Mines and Quarries Act 1954 goes further and erects the test of practicability into a general means of avoiding liability. Under s. 157 it is a defence to a civil action for any breach of the Act if it is proved 'that it was impracticable to avoid or prevent the breach'.

(3) Contravention of statute automatically establishes liability

Whether an Act requires something to be done without qualification, or allows exceptions for things which are not practicable, depends on the true construction of the Act. If the Act, according to its true construction, has not been complied with, liability is automatic. In this sense, every statutory duty, without exception, is absolute. This is the meaning of Lord Atkin's words in *Smith v Cammell Laird & Co Ltd* [1940] AC 242 at 258, [1939] 4 All ER 381 at 390:

> 'It is precisely in the absolute obligation imposed by statute to perform or forbear from performing a specified activity that a breach of

statutory duty differs from the obligation imposed by common law, which is to take reasonable care to avoid injuring another.'

In this sense, a statutory duty is absolute even though it is qualified by the words 'as far as is reasonably practicable': for it is a question of fact whether a thing is practicable or not, and unless, on the facts, it is impracticable, the requirement must be carried out: see *Marshall v Gotham Co Ltd* [1954] AC 360, [1954] 1 All ER 937.

7 Defences to an action for breach of statutory duty

Using the word 'defence' in its broadest sense, the defence to an action for breach of statutory duty may take the form of denying that the duty was imposed on the defendant, that it was as wide or absolute as alleged, or that it has been broken. Alternatively, the defendant may deny that the plaintiff was within the benefit of the statute, that his injuries have been caused by the breach, or that the accident was the sort of occurrence which the statute was designed to prevent. All these points are essential ingredients in the plaintiff's cause of action.

But there are other defences which set up exceptions—complete or partial—to a *prima facie* liability.

It is established law that the defence of *volenti non fit injuria* is not available in answer to a breach of the employer's statutory duty *(Baddeley v Granville (Earl)* (1887) 19 QBD 423; *Wheeler v New Merton Board Mills Ltd* [1933] 2 KB 669; but it may be a defence to a breach of statutory duty imposed on fellow-workmen, for which the employer would otherwise be vicariously liable: *Imperial Chemical Industries Ltd v Shatwell* [1965] AC 656, [1964] 2 All ER 999.

On the other hand, contributory negligence is always a good defence: *Caswell v Powell Duffryn Associated Collieries Ltd* [1940] AC 152, [1939] 3 All ER 722; and it was held by the House of Lords in *Harrison v National Coal Board* [1951] AC 639, [1951] 1 All ER 1102 that common employment (before its abolition) was a good defence, in the sense that employers were not liable for the breach of a statutory duty resting directly upon a fellow-servant.

In some cases a man who brings about breach of his employer's statutory duty may be totally precluded from recovering damages: see Chapter 23, section 6.

The defence of impracticability, which can be raised under some statutes, is considered in the next section.

8 'Practicable' and 'reasonably practicable'

The words 'practicable' and 'reasonably practicable' recur throughout the Factories Act 1961 as limitations on various statutory duties. Some of the duties in the Act are absolute, others are qualified by these words. Thus under s. 28 it is an imperative requirement that such things as floors, stairs and ladders shall be 'of sound construction': but as regards any 'means of access' not included in s. 28, the duty under s. 29 (1) is only to keep them safe 'so far as is reasonably practicable'.

The Mines and Quarries Act 1954 goes further. Under s. 157 it is a general defence, where any breach of the Act has been committed, to prove that 'it was impracticable to avoid or prevent the breach'.

To do what is practicable involves more than taking reasonable care. 'Practicable' means that which is feasible, that which can be done. Lord Goddard said in *Lee v Nursery Furnishings Ltd* [1945] 1 All ER 387:

> ' "Practicable" is defined in the *Oxford Dictionary* as "capable of being carried out in action" or "feasible".'

And Hallett J said in *Schwalb v Fass (H.) & Son Ltd* (1946) 175 LT 345:

> 'Clearly, the fact that the use of the appliances[20] would slow up production does not render their use impracticable; and I have no right to substitute for the word "impracticable" expressions such as "difficult", "not too easy" or "inconvenient" or any other word.'

If, for example, there is a large unfenced hole it will usually be 'practicable' to fence or cover it unless it is being used at the time, and even if it is in use a fence does not become impracticable merely because it is inconvenient: *Street v British Electricity Authority* [1952] 2 QB 399, [1952] 1 All ER 679; but a duty to take reasonable care might involve no more than lighting the place and warning workmen or visitors. The

---

20 I.e., a push-stick in wood-working operations.

standard of practicability is an entirely objective one: but naturally what is practicable when considered in isolation is not necessarily practicable when the work which has to be done is taken into account. A guard may have to be removed from a machine while it is being repaired, and this was a good defence under the Coal Mines Act 1911, s. 102 (8)[1], if the guard was not taken off for longer than necessary: *Coltness Iron Co Ltd v Sharp* [1938] AC 90, [1937] 3 All ER 593.

In considering what is practicable, account must be taken of the state of knowledge at the time. 'Practicable' is defined in *Webster's Dictionary* as 'possible to be accomplished with known means or resources', and defendants cannot be held liable for failing to use a method which, at the material time, had not been invented: *Adsett v K. and L. Steelfounders and Engineers Ltd* [1953] 2 All ER 320; or for not taking measures against a danger which was not known to exist: *Richards v Highway Ironfounders (West Bromwich) Ltd* [1955] 3 All ER 205; subsequent proceedings [1957] 2 All ER 162 (invisible dust not known at the time to be the cause of silicosis, therefore not practicable to insist on masks where only advantage over others was protection against invisible dust).

If, instead of saying that 'all practicable measures' are to be taken (as in the Factories Act 1961, s. 63)[2] the statute limits the obligation to what is *reasonably* practicable (as in s. 29(1) of the same Act), this introduces a qualification: nevertheless, something more than reasonable care is still required (see the remarks of Tucker LJ in *Edwards v National Coal Board* [1949] 1 KB 704 at 709, [1949] 1 All ER 743 at 746 and *Marshall v Gotham Co Ltd* [1954] AC 360, [1954] 1 All ER 937, *passim*). In *Wales v Thomas* (1885) 16 QBD 340 it was said that the effect on the earning of profits was not to be taken into consideration, and that only such matters as physical and engineering difficulties were to be brought into account. The courts will certainly not pay undue regard to expense where lives are at stake, but there is authority for saying that in determining what is reasonable, it is right to take into account, in addition to physical difficulties, such matters as expense and trouble, and whether they are disproportionate to the result to be attained. Thus in the *Coltness* case, *supra*, where machinery was left unfenced for repairs, Lord Atkin said:

1 This Act used the expression 'not *reasonably* practicable', as distinct from 'impracticable' in the present Act.
2 Now repealed.

'The time for non-protection is so short, and the time, trouble and expense of any other form of protection is so disproportionate, that I think the defence is proved.'

In *Edwards v National Coal Board, supra,* which concerned the duty of a mine-owner to support the roof, the guiding principle was stated as follows by Asquith LJ at pp. 712, 747:

> ' "Reasonably practicable" is a narrower term than "physically possible", and seems to me to imply that a computation must be made by the owner in which the *quantum* of risk is placed on one scale and the sacrifice involved in the measures necessary for averting the risk (whether in money, time or trouble) is placed in the other, and that, if it be shown that there is a gross disproportion between them—the risk being insignificant in relation to the sacrifice—the defendants discharge the onus on them. Moreover, this computation falls to be made by the owner at a point of time anterior to the accident. The questions he has to answer are: (a) What measures are necessary and sufficient to prevent any breach of s. 49[3]? (b) Are these measures reasonably practicable?'

This passage was referred to with approval in *Marshall v Gotham Co Ltd* [1954] AC 360, [1954] 1 All ER 937, a case decided under the Metalliferous Mines Regulation Act, which, as expanded by regulations, required the roof of a mine to be made secure so far as reasonably practicable. The usual practice in a gypsum mine is to test the roof with a hammer and bring down unsafe portions of the roof, as distinct from the practice in coal mines of having systematic support by means of props. The roof of a mine had been tested in this way, but collapsed owing to a rare geological fault which had not been known to occur in the mine for twenty years. Further, systematic support would not have prevented the fall though it might have minimised it. The House of Lords held that it was the known risk which had to be taken into account, and balanced against safety measures, and that in the circumstances the defence was established. Lord Reid said (at pp. 373, 942):

> '. . . if a precaution is practicable it must be taken unless in the whole circumstances that would be unreasonable. And as men's lives may be at stake it should not lightly be held that to take a practicable precaution is unreasonable. . . . The danger was a very rare one. The trouble and expense involved in the use of the precautions, while not

3 Now s. 48 of the 1954 (Mines) Act.

> prohibitive, would have been considerable. The precautions would not
> have afforded anything like complete protection against the danger,
> and their adoption would have had the disadvantage of giving a false
> sense of security.'

The last sentence is important. If the value of systematic support had not
been so much in doubt, the decision would clearly have gone against the
defendants, regardless of expense. Their Lordships discouraged
comparisons between what is 'reasonably practicable' and reasonable
care at common law, since such comparisons are not helpful and tend to
divert the attention of the court away from the language of the statute
which it has to apply.

In cases under the Mines and Quarries Act 1954 the onus of
establishing the defence under s. 157 evidently rests upon the
defendants.

The onus of proof under the Factories Act 1961 s. 29, and other
sections which require a duty to be performed so far as reasonably
practicable, is discussed with s. 29 itself in Chapter 10.

Chapter 7

The Health and Safety at Work
Act 1974

1 General

The Health and Safety at Work etc.[1] Act 1974 brought together under a single Act and a single safety authority all matters of safety, health and welfare in any form of employment: in other words it generalised the safety legislation which hitherto applied to factories, mines and other specific situations. Shipping (a specialist subject with an international character) does not come under the Act: but similar general duties have been imposed by statutory order under the Merchant Shipping Acts (see Chapter 20, section 3).

Agriculture and forestry were originally under the special jurisdiction of the Ministry of Agriculture, but the special arrangements were repealed by the Employment Protection Act 1975, s. 116 and Sch. 15.

Ultimately the Act will supersede all existing safety legislation and replace it by degrees with regulations and codes of practice. In the meantime the existing Acts and regulations continue in force within the general framework of the Act, and their effect in creating liability for damages for breach of statutory duty is also unchanged[2].

---

1 To repeat incessantly the 'etc.' in the title of the Act would be pedantic and in practice it will no doubt be dropped.
2 Numerous regulations have been made repealing and modifying existing legislation so far as it contains powers to appoint inspectors, hold inquiries, make regulations and prosecute: those relating to factories, mines and quarries, shops, offices and railway premises and agriculture are referred to in the chapters on these subjects. There are also an increasing number of safety codes which apply to all places of work: see Chapter 8.

There must continue to be differences between industries, mines requiring stricter control and inspection than most other industries, offices and schools having trivial dangers in comparison with most factories. But uniformity is gradually being established in such things as safety of structures and means of access, lifting apparatus, and fencing of machines; and there are a number of codes of regulations which apply to all places of work.

The Act has been applied to offshore installations and pipelines in territorial waters and in areas designated under the Continental Shelf Act 1964: also specifically to works of construction, loading and unloading of ships, shipbuilding and repair and diving operations, in territorial waters: Health and Safety at Work etc. Act 1974 (Application outside Great Britain) Order 1989 (S.I. 1989 No. 740).

The immediate effect of the Act on civil liability and on detailed safety obligations was small, for most forms of employment were already covered. Such things as schools, hospitals, theatres and road transport were outside previous cover, except that special legislation applied to radioactive substances used in hospitals and various dangerous substances carried by road. The Act is essentially a tidying-up operation. Its importance is in administration, by bringing safety matters under a unified authority with wider powers. In due course the detailed safety obligations under existing codes will be replaced by regulations under the Act. So far the most important cases where regulations have been made which apply to all places of work are those which relate to diving operations (Chapter 19), to lead, asbestos, hazardous substances generally, and radiation (Chapter 8); and to electricity (Chapter 16). There are also the Health and Safety (First-Aid) Regulations 1981 (S.I. No. 917).

The Act also made a big innovation by integrating in the same code, in addition to the safety laws for the protection of persons employed in industry, the laws for protecting the public against dangers created by industry, notably by harmful emissions from factories and by the use of dangerous substances. Thus its purpose is to integrate, in addition to the Factories and Mines Acts and similar legislation, numerous existing Acts such as the Petroleum Acts, the Alkali Works Regulation Acts, the Boiler Explosions Acts and the Explosives Acts. The inspectorates under all these Acts are absorbed into the new Health and Safety Executive. This aspect of the Act was accentuated by the coincidence, while it was passing through Parliament, of a catastrophic explosion at a chemical factory in Lincolnshire[3]. The responsibility for public safety has since been extended by the Gas Act 1986 (safety of gas in pipes) and the Consumer Protection Act 1987 (manufactured products).

Another innovation (s. 78) was to bring factories and other places of work within the Fire Precautions Act 1971, which has now been amended by the Fire Safety and Safety of Places of Sport Act 1987[4].

Finally, Part III of the Act enlarged the scope of the Building Regulations under the Public Health Act 1936. These regulations replaced the former building bye-laws made by local authorities for the sound construction of buildings with their fittings. One of their objects is now the safety of persons in or about the buildings or affected by them, and an action for damages will lie for breach of the regulations. This was an innovation under the 1974 Act. It has now been replaced by the Building Act 1984 and the Building Regulations 1985: see Chapter 5, section 3.

Part I of the Act is declared by s. 1(1) to have four purposes:

(a) the health, safety and welfare of persons at work;
(b) the protection of *other* persons against risk to health or safety arising from the activities of persons at work;
(c) the control of explosive, highly 'flammable' or other dangerous substances;
(d) the control of the emission of noxious or offensive substances[5] from premises of any class prescribed.

To these the Gas Act 1986 s. 18 added protecting the public from dangers arising from gas in pipes; and the Consumer Protection Act 1987 s. 36 and Sch. 3 added protection from dangers in articles supplied for use at work, and also specifically in 'fairground equipment'.

---

3 For regulations made for general public safety see the Health and Safety (Emissions into the Atmosphere) Regulations 1983, S.I. No. 943 amended by S.I. 1989 No. 319. Notification of Installations Handling Hazardous Substances Regulations 1982, S.I. No. 1357; Notification of New Substances Regulations 1982, S.I. No. 1496.
4 For a summary of fire safety requirements see Chapter 10, section 10.
5 These include gases and liquids: s. 53.

2 Administration

The Minister ultimately responsible under Part I is the Secretary of State for Employment, to whom is given the power to make 'health and safety regulations' under s. 15. Under his direction, the Health and Safety Commission are responsible for carrying Part I into effect, in particular by encouraging research, training and dissemination of information, and holding inquiries into accidents or other matters (ss. 10–14)[6].

Under the Commission is the Health and Safety Executive (s. 11), the enforcement authority which takes over the existing inspectorates. The Secretary of State may delegate powers to local authorities in specified matters, and has delegated enforcement powers to them for most offices, shops and warehouses: Health and Safety (Enforcing Authority) Regulations 1989 (S.I. 1989 No. 1903)[7]. Both the Executive and such authorities may appoint inspectors with powers of entry to premises (ss. 19, 20) and the power to issue 'improvement' notices[8] or 'prohibition' notices (s. 21, and s. 22 as amended by Sch. 3 of the Consumer Protection Act 1987) where the safety legislation is contravened or is likely to be contravened. There is also power to seize dangerous articles or substances in an emergency (s. 25).

Under Part II of the Act, the Employment Medical Advisory Service is continued.

Agriculture originally stood somewhat apart: under ss. 29 and 30 'the appropriate Agriculture Minister' (i.e. the Minister in England, the Secretary of State in Scotland) was responsible for safety in agriculture and for making safety regulations. These special arrangements were repealed by the Employment Protection Act 1975 (s. 116 and Sch. 15)

6 See Reporting of Injuries, Diseases and Dangerous Occurrences Regulations 1985 (S.I. No. 2023).
7 Also miscellaneous places such as zoos, saunas, recreational centres, but not large-scale storage as at airports and docks. If the character of premises changes, they automatically come under the control of the appropriate authority: *Hadley v Hancox* (1986) 151 JP 227.
8 An improvement notice could require an 'anti-bandit' screen to protect building society staff: *West Bromwich Building Society v Townsend* [1983] ICR 257.

but the Minister for Agriculture still has a concurrent power to make regulations[9].

Fire precautions (especially fire certificates, fire escapes) are mainly the responsibility of fire authorities (see Chapter 10, section 10).

3 The general safety duties

Sections 2 to 8 impose a series of general safety duties on various persons. These are largely modelled on the common law duties of care, but require a rather higher standard in that they have to be carried out 'so far as is reasonably practicable'. They do not give rise to civil liability (s. 47), but to criminal prosecution (s. 33): in such a prosecution the onus of proving that something was *not* reasonably practicable is placed on the defence (s. 40) and failure to comply with the 'codes of practice' issued for guidance under s. 16 raises a presumption that a related safety requirement was not complied with (s. 17).

The duties are as follows:

Employer (s. 2).   He must ensure 'the health, safety and welfare at work of all his employees', with particular regard to plant and system of work, handling of articles and substances, instruction, training and supervision, place of work and access (where under his control), safe and healthy working environment. By s. 52(1)(b), an *employee* is not 'at work' except 'during the course of his employment'.

This general duty for the safety of the employer's own workforce may involve giving information and instructions to persons *not* in his employment, and supervising their system of work, if it might otherwise endanger his own employees: *R v Swan Hunter Shipbuilders Ltd* [1982] 1 All ER 264, [1981] ICR 831 (shipbuilders gave instructions to own employees for safe use of oxygen equipment but gave no instructions to sub-contractors).

---

9   The Act, which followed a Royal Commission, was agreed policy for both the major parties. One introduced it, the other re-introduced and passed it. But agriculture was a major bone of contention, the Conservatives saying safety could not be separated from other agricultural matters, Labour contending that it should be unified like everything else.

An employer must put on record a statement of his policy and organisation for safety and welfare, and publicise it to employees[10]. There are arrangements for safety representatives to be nominated from among the employees, and where appropriate a safety committee: s. 2(4), (6), (7): Safety Representatives and Safety Committees Regulations 1977 (S.I. 1977 No. 500) and similar regulations for offshore installations (S.I. 1989 No. 971).

Conduct of undertaking by employer (s. 3).   This must be such that persons who are *not* employees are not exposed to risks to health and safety[11]. This duty extends not only to other workers but to the general public. A similar duty applies to self-employed workers, for their own safety and that of others. The general duty to ensure safety under s. 3(1) may require instructions and information to be given, to non-employees as well as employees, for instance about fire risks from the use of oxygen: it is irrelevant that s. 3(3) specifically provides for giving 'information' in circumstances which have not yet been prescribed by regulations: *R v Swan Hunter Shipbuilders Ltd, supra*; *Carmichael v Rosehall Engineering Works Ltd* [1983] IRLR 480.

Person in control of premises (s. 4).   Where these are *non-domestic* and are used as a place of work (or a place of resort to use plant or substances) by persons who are *not* employees of his, such a person has a duty to see that the premises, access to them, and plant and substances provided by him are safe for the persons using them. This has been held to include the lifts and other installations in private blocks of flats so as to require the protection of persons who came to repair or maintain them: *Westminster City Council v Select Management Ltd* [1985] 1 All ER 897, [1985] 1 WLR 576. The duty is to make the place safe for the purposes for which the visitors are expected to use them: *Mailer v Austin Rover Group PLC* [1989] 2 All ER 1087 (no liability for unexpected risk taken by cleaners).

10 A *written* statement is not required if there are no more than five workers: Employers' Health and Safety Policy Statement (Exceptions) Regulations 1975 (S.I. 1975 No. 1584).
11 There was a breach of this duty when a cleaning company left a machine with an electrical defect at the works of a customer who had permission to use it: *R v Mara* [1987] 1 All ER 478, [1987] 1 WLR 87, CA. The defect was a breach of the duty to their own employees under s. 2(2)(a), and leaving the machine was part of the conduct of their own undertaking which affected third parties.

Emissions from premises (s. 5).   The person in control must adopt 'the best practicable means' to prevent emission of noxious or offensive substances[12] into the atmosphere.

Designers, manufacturers, importers, suppliers, erectors and installers of articles and substances for use at work (s. 6, as extensively amended by Sch. 3 of the Consumer Protection Act 1987).   They are under very detailed duties for safety and health, including testing, inspection, research and passing on information required for safe use[13].

Employees at work (s. 7).   Must take reasonable care for the safety of themselves and all other persons affected by their acts and omissions at work; also 'co-operate' with their employers and other persons on whom duties are imposed under any relevant health and safety legislation, so far as necessary to enable the duties to be performed. Further (s. 8) *no* person must intentionally interfere with or misuse anything provided under relevant legislation.

Section 53 defines an 'employee' as a person who works under a contract of employment which in turn is defined to include apprenticeship. Under the Health and Safety (Training for Employment) Regulations 1988 (S.I. No. 1222 amended by S.I. 1989 No. 1039) trainees under various Government schemes are treated as employees at work, and 'the immediate provider . . . of the training' is treated as the employer. Training in schools and polytechnics is excluded: but not in Government training centres. 'Self-employed' persons are those who work for reward but not under a contract of employment (whether or not they employ others). In deciding what is a contract of employment in borderline cases, the courts will no doubt follow the decisions under the National Insurance Acts: the dominant test has been whether the person in question is part of the employer's organisation or is on his own, though the nature of payment (salary or otherwise), the provision of equipment and the extent of control have also been taken into account[14]. At common law, on the other hand, the test was the ultimate right of control.

---

12 Including liquids and gases: s. 53.
13 Under the Health and Safety (Leasing Arrangements) Regulations 1980 (S.I. 1980 No. 907), the duties of a supplier are in certain cases imposed on the person who provides finance for leasing.
14 See p. 88, note 8 for some typical cases.

'Premises' are defined by s. 53 to include, *inter alia*, ships, aircraft, hovercraft, vehicles, offshore installations, tents, moveable structures, but also mean any 'place': so that there need not be any installation or structure at all. (Safety in shipping and aircraft operation, however, is not subject to the Act but to the Merchant Shipping Acts and Air Navigation Acts which are the responsibility of the Department of Trade.)

The duty of persons in control of premises under s. 4 does not apply to 'domestic premises' (private residences and their appurtenances): (s. 53) and employment in a private household as a domestic servant is specifically excluded by s. 51. On the other hand, premises which are not in exclusive occupation as private residences, such as lifts and electrical installations in the common parts of a block of flats, are 'non-domestic' premises and the person in 'control' owes the duties under s. 4 of the Act to visiting workmen: *Westminster City Council v Select Management Ltd* [1985] 1 All ER 897, [1985] 1 WLR 576.

4 Health and safety regulations

Health and safety regulations (ss. 15, 50) provide the real teeth of the Act. They are made by the Secretary of State, either on the proposal of the Commission, or on his own initiative (after consulting the Commission) and in either case various Government departments and other interested bodies must be consulted (s. 50). Under amendments made by the Employment Protection Act 1975 (Sch. 15, paras. 6, 16) ss. 15 and 50 are amended to give a concurrent power to make regulations to the Minister responsible for agriculture, who under the 1974 Act had an exclusive jurisdiction in purely agricultural matters.

By s. 1(2), the power to make regulations is to be exercised to replace by degrees existing safety and health legislation (listed in Schedule 1 to the Act), which (with the 1974 Act and its regulations) is referred to in the Act as 'the relevant statutory provisions'[15].

Regulations may be general, or apply to particular circumstances or even a particular case. They may specify the persons who have to comply with requirements, the persons liable to prosecution for contravention

---

15 The Merchant Shipping Acts are not included.

and (to some extent) the limits of a prosecution (e.g. whether summary only, restriction of penalties, special defences). They may also grant exemptions, exclude general duties, and (of course) repeal existing legislation in Schedule 1.

The subject-matter for which regulations may be made—broadly covering every type of premises, plant, material, process and operation, also administrative matters such as registration, records, powers of search—is set out at length in Schedule 3:

SCHEDULE 3
Subject-matter of health and safety regulations

1.—(1) Regulating or prohibiting—
  (a) the manufacture, supply or use of any plant;
  (b) the manufacture, supply, keeping or use of any substance;
  (c) the carrying on of any process[16] or the carrying out of any operation

(2) Imposing requirements with respect to the design, construction, guarding, siting, installation, commissioning, examination, repair, maintenance, alteration, adjustment, dismantling, testing or inspection of any plant.

(3) Imposing requirements with respect to the marking of any plant or of any articles used or designed for use as components in any plant, and in that connection regulating or restricting the use of specified markings.

(4) Imposing requirements with respect to the testing, labelling or examination of any substance.

(5) Imposing requirements with respect to the carrying out of research in connection with any activity mentioned in sub-paragraphs (1) to (4) above.

2.—(1) Prohibiting the importation into the United Kingdom or the landing or unloading there of articles or substances of any specified description, whether absolutely or unless conditions imposed by or under the regulations are complied with.

(2) Specifying, in a case where an act or omission in relation to such an importation, landing or unloading as is mentioned in the preceding sub-paragraph constitutes an offence under a provision of this Act and of the Customs and Excise Act, 1952, the Act under which the offence is to be punished.

3.—(1) Prohibiting or regulating the transport of articles or substances of any specified description.

(2) Imposing requirements with respect to the manner and means of transporting articles or substances of any specified description, including requirements with respect to the construction, testing and

16 For the meaning of 'process' under this paragraph, see Chapter 10, section 2.

marking of containers and means of transport and the packaging and labelling of articles or substances in connection with their transport.

4.—(1) Prohibiting the carrying on of any specified activity or the doing of any specified thing except under the authority and in accordance with the terms and conditions of a licence, or except with the consent or approval of specified authority.

(2) Providing for the grant, renewal, variation, transfer and revocation of licences (including the variation and revocation of conditions attached to licences).

5.—Requiring any person, premises or thing to be registered in any specified circumstances or as a condition of the carrying on of any specified activity or the doing of any specified thing.

6.—(1) Requiring, in specified circumstances, the appointment (whether in a specified capacity or not) of persons (or persons with specified qualifications or experience, or both) to perform specified functions, and imposing duties or conferring powers on persons appointed (whether in pursuance of the regulations or not) to perform specified functions.

(2) Restricting the performance of specified functions to persons possessing specified qualifications or experience.

7.—Regulating or prohibiting the employment in specified circumstances of all persons or any class of persons.

8.—(1) Requiring the making of arrangements for securing the health of persons at work or other persons, including arrangements for medical examinations and health surveys.

(2) Requiring the making of arrangements for monitoring the atmospheric or other conditions in which persons work.

9.—Imposing requirements with respect to any matter affecting the conditions in which persons work, including in particular such matters as the structural condition and stability of premises, the means of access to and egress from premises, cleanliness, temperature, lighting, ventilation, overcrowding, noise, vibrations, ionising and other radiations, dust and fumes.

10.—Securing the provision of specified welfare facilities for persons at work, including in particular such things as an adequate water supply, sanitary conveniences, washing and bathing facilities, ambulance and first-aid arrangements, cloakroom accommodation, sitting facilities and refreshment facilities.

11.—Imposing requirements with respect to the provision and use in specified circumstances of protective clothing or equipment, including affording protection against the weather.

12.—Requiring in specified circumstances the taking of specified precautions in connection with the risk of fire.

13.—(1) Prohibiting or imposing requirements in connection with the emission into the atmosphere of any specified gas, smoke or dust or any other specified substance whatsoever.

(2) Prohibiting or imposing requirements in connection with the emission of noise, vibrations or any ionising or other radiations.

(3) Imposing requirements with respect to the monitoring of any such emission as is mentioned in the preceding sub-paragraphs.

14.—Imposing requirements with respect to the instruction, training and supervision of persons at work.

15.—(1) Requiring, in specified circumstances, specified matters to be notified in a specified manner to specified persons.

(2) Empowering inspectors in specified circumstances to require persons to submit written particulars of measures proposed to be taken to achieve compliance with any of the relevant statutory provisions.

16.—Imposing requirements with respect to the keeping and preservation of records and other documents, including plans and maps.

17.—Imposing requirements with respect to the management of animals.

18.—The following purposes as regards premises of any specified description where persons work, namely—

(a) requiring precautions to be taken against dangers to which the premises or persons therein are or may be exposed by reason of conditions (including natural conditions) existing in the vicinity;

(b) securing that persons in the premises leave them in specified circumstances.

19.—Conferring, in specified circumstances involving a risk of fire or explosion, power to search a person or any article which a person has with him for the purpose of ascertaining whether he has in his possession any article of a specified kind likely in those circumstances to cause a fire or explosion, and power to seize and dispose of any article of that kind found on such a search.

20.—Restricting, prohibiting or requiring the doing of any specified thing where any accident or other occurrence of a specified kind has occurred.

21.—As regards cases of any specified class, being a class such that the variety in the circumstances of particular cases within it calls for the making of special provision for particular cases, any of the following purposes, namely

(a) conferring on employers or other persons power to make rules or give directions with respect to matters affecting health or safety;

(b) requiring employers or other persons to make rules with respect to any such matters;

(c) empowering specified persons to require employers or other persons either to make rules with respect to any such matters or to modify any such rules previously made by virtue of this paragraph; and

(d) making admissible in evidence without further proof, in such circumstances and subject to such conditions as may be specified, documents which purport to be copies of rules or rules of any specified class made under this paragraph.

22.—Conferring on any local or public authority power to make bye-laws with respect to any specified matter, specifying the authority or person by whom any bye-laws made in the exercise of that power need to be confirmed, and generally providing for the procedure to be followed in connection with the making of any such bye-laws.

Interpretation

23.—(1) In this Schedule 'specified' means specified in health and safety regulations.

(2) It is hereby declared that the mention in this Schedule of a purpose that falls within any more general purpose mentioned therein is without prejudice to the generality of the more general purpose.

5 Codes of practice

On a more informal level, s. 16 enables the Commission itself to approve and issue 'Codes of Practice' for giving practical guidance on health and safety duties. These correspond to the useful booklets formerly issued by the Factories Department on such matters as lifting and handling loads and on removal of dust from workrooms, or by the Mines Department on roof support systems. They have the advantage of giving simple explanations (without the necessity for legal precision) of established safety methods, often with illustrations.

Although the Act does not say so, they will clearly be admissible in civil actions as evidence of good practice and what is 'practicable'[17]. By s. 17, failure to comply with them raises a *presumption* in criminal proceedings that the related safety requirement has been contravened: this may be displaced only by proof that the duty was carried out in some other way.

6 Civil and criminal liability

By s. 47(2), an action for damages lies for breach of health and safety regulations (s. 15) unless the regulations exclude it. Section 47(1)(a)

17 See p. 52, *ante*.

expressly excludes civil liability for breach of the general safety duties (ss. 2–8) and there is nothing else in the Act itself which could give rise to an action for breach of statutory duty.

By s. 47(1)(b), civil liability for breach of the existing safety codes (pending their replacement) is not affected in any way: nor is liability independently of the Act—i.e. common law liability for negligence is untouched: s. 47(4).

Any agreement excluding or limiting civil liability for contravention of health and safety regulations is void, unless allowed by the regulations: s. 47(5).

Where under the terms of any regulations a defence such as due diligence is available in a criminal prosecution for breach of regulations, it does not afford a defence in civil proceedings unless this is expressly provided by the regulations: s. 47(3). This follows the established law under the Mines and Factories Acts.

Prosecution, usually by summary proceedings, is the normal sanction for contravention of the general safety duties and of regulations, and there are some special rules and powers (e.g. time limits, place of hearing, bringing third parties before the court, responsibility of officers of bodies corporate, inspector's power to appear as prosecutor, evidence from registers, power to remedy or confiscate cause of offence) in ss. 33–42. Details are outside the scope of this book[18].

There is no time limit for prosecution for breach of the general duties under ss. 2–7; or, apparently, for any of the offences under s. 33: *Kemp v Liebherr-GB Ltd* [1987] 1 All ER 885, [1987] 1 WLR 607.

---

18 See however the comments on p. 272 and fn. 10 as to the position when an offence is alleged to be due to the default of a third party, which I have added at the request of Mr. H. R. Williams, H.M. Senior Principal Inspector of Factories, though I doubt whether it is important since s. 161 of the Factories Act was repealed in 1977.

Chapter 8

Safety regulations at all places of work: dangerous substances and radiation

1 General

The safety regulations in this Chapter are made under the Health and Safety Act, and, unlike previous regulations under the Factories and Mines legislation and other specific legislation, they apply to all places of work. In general, the duty to comply with the regulations is imposed on the employers (and also on the self-employed); and the regulations are intended to operate not only for the protection of workers but also for the protection of others who may be endangered by their activities.

The main effect of these codes of regulations is to require work with dangerous substances to be planned in advance and carried out in such a way as to minimise risk, where this cannot be eliminated completely except by closing down valuable and useful industries. The use of some substances has to be notified in advance to the Health and Safety Executive, to enable them to exercise oversight, and they also have to be informed of accidents and emergencies. However, when it comes to the details of safety measures, these are rather vague and often qualified by what is 'reasonably practicable'. Nothing in this Chapter therefore adds much to the employer's common law duty to establish and operate a safe method of work, except that an employer could not maintain that he was not aware of the risks involved by substances specifically mentioned in the regulations. Of course, breach of the regulations involves liability to prosecution and penalties.

2 Substances hazardous to health

The Control of Substances Hazardous to Health Regulations 1988 (S.I. 1988 No. 1657, in force 1 October 1989) establish a uniform code for the control of almost anything which may be harmful to health. They replace a large number of regulations under the Factories Act and other legislation which covered a wide range of particular substances as various as horse hair (which might carry anthrax germs), silica dust (causing silicosis), cyanide, chromium and agricultural pesticides. Specific mention of these is retained, to show they have not lost their importance; and some substances, such as yellow phosphorus and some cancer-producing chemicals and agricultural pesticides, whose use was totally prohibited by previous Acts or regulations, continue to be totally prohibited.

Apart from this, reg. 2(1) contains a wide definition of 'substances hazardous to health'. First it cross-refers to lists of particular substances which are poisonous, corrosive or otherwise harmful to health, or for which a maximum exposure has been fixed: it then adds 'micro-organisms' hazardous to health, dust *of any kind* in substantial concentration, and any substance which creates comparable hazards.

Regulations 6–12—the main part of the code—do not apply to lead and asbestos (which have their own separate codes), or underground in mines, or to substances which are dangerous only because radioactive, inflammable, explosive, or at a high or low temperature or under high pressure.

Since the regulations cover such a wide area—ranging for instance from farm workers spraying fields to dust in metal foundries, for both of which there used to be specific regulations—the requirements are rather general and do not add much to an employer's normal duty at common law: thus under regs. 6 and 7 he is required to plan and carry out the work so as to minimise any risk.

Certain things are prohibited altogether, or prohibited for certain purposes: reg. 4. Examples are sand or free silicon as a blasting abrasive, white or yellow phosphorus for matches and chemicals such as benzidine (prohibited for all purposes).

The exposure of employees to dangerous substances must be precluded altogether or kept to a minimum, and where there is a standard limit for exposure, the exposure of employees must be kept below that limit: reg. 7. There must be regular monitoring of the level of exposure, and medical surveillance of employees where appropriate: regs. 10, 11.

Exposure must be prevented where possible by a 'control measure'. This is a vague expression, which means such things as ventilation by an exhaust draught to draw away dust or fumes at source: regs. 7(2), 8. Protective clothing or equipment such as respirators may also be required: reg. 7(3), (6). All such 'controls' and 'equipment' must be kept in good order: reg. 9; and the employer must see that they are used: reg. 8(1). Workers are required to make full use of 'controls' and 'equipment' and report faults: reg. 8(2).

Any worker whose work may expose him to risk must be given full information, instruction and training so that he understands the risk and can protect himself: reg. 12.

Fumigation with hydrogen cyanide and certain other gases is not to be carried out without notification to specified authorities and display of warning notices: reg. 13.

3 Control of lead at work

The Control of Lead at Work Regulations 1980 (S.I. No. 1248) establish a uniform code for all places of work within the Health and Safety Act: painting and decorating, for example, and buildings as well as factories. They replace a number of old regulations which applied to particular types of work, such as manufacture of paint, enamelling, lead smelting, indiarubber and accumulators.

Under the regulations the employer's duties extend to all those affected by his activities—the self-employed and employees of other persons as well as his own workers. The main requirements are:

(a) the assessment in advance of the degree of exposure to lead involved in the work, warning of the risk and medical checks;
(b) control and limitation of exposure;
(c) respirators and protective clothing where necessary;
(d) complete isolation of areas for eating and drinking from any exposure to lead.

4 Control of asbestos at work

Asbestos is the generic name for various fibrous materials which are fire-resistant. These have been of enormous value in fire-proofing of clothing, also in buildings and ships. Unfortunately the fibrous dust gives rise to lung disease and also (as became known only in recent times) if swallowed it can cause cancer in the stomach.

The Asbestos (Prohibitions) Regulations 1985 (S.I. 1985 No. 910, amended by 1988 No. 711) totally forbid the importation, supply, or use at work, of two forms of asbestos—crocodilite and amosite, 'blue' and 'brown' asbestos—and products containing them. They also forbid (with minor exceptions) spraying with any asbestos composition: reg. 6; and the installation of asbestos insulation: reg. 7. The Health and Safety Executive may, however, grant exemptions subject to strict conditions: reg. 8.

These prohibitions are as much for the protection of the public as of the workers.

In all other respects, the use of asbestos is regulated by the Control of Asbestos at Work Regulations 1987 (S.I. No. 2115, in force 1 March 1988). These apply to all workplaces (including those such as oil rigs outside territorial waters) where there is exposure to asbestos, even if this is quite small and incidental to other work: reg. 21.

The employer must ascertain the type of asbestos, or assume it is the most dangerous type: reg. 4. (This affects permitted levels of exposure.) He must then make—and review from time to time—an assessment in advance of the risks involved in working with it and the measures required to reduce them: reg. 5. There is a general duty—reg. 8—to *prevent* exposure, or *reduce* it to the lowest practicable level: reg. 7. Obviously it may be possible to preclude the exposure of *some* workers altogether, but only to reduce it for others. For this purpose he may designate an area as an 'asbestos area'—where standards of exposure over a 12-week period would be exceeded—or a 'respirator zone'— where respirators must be worn because normal short-term 'control limits' would be exceeded—or may designate the area under both heads: reg. 14. The asbestos area is the more dangerous zone. Only workers who are specifically 'authorised workers' may enter these zones, and no one must eat, drink or smoke there. Employees must be given protective clothing where required: reg. 11; also full information about the risks and all necessary training: reg. 7. The health of employees exposed to risk must be checked periodically: reg. 17.

There are general duties to prevent the spread of asbestos, keep the place clean (using vacuum equipment) and check concentration in the air: regs. 12, 13, 15. But the main safety precaution is likely to be what are described as 'control measures': this probably means in practice a mechanical appliance which extracts harmful dust from the air at its point of origin: reg. 8(1)(b). Such appliances must be kept in good order: reg. 9. If such measures fail to bring exposure down to the official 'control limits', respirators must be provided: reg. 8(2).

Other regulations require washing and changing facilities: reg. 17; and the safe storage and distribution of raw asbestos and asbestos waste in sealed containers properly labelled: reg. 18.

5 Ionising radiation

'Ionising radiation' means radiation of such intensity that it can dislodge particles from atoms, and is therefore capable of damaging or distorting living cells. Alteration of a molecule in a cell, for instance, may result in disordered growth and therefore in cancer, or may damage the hereditary genes in the reproductive organs. Since, however, the spaces within atoms are vast, a stream of radiation may pass through with no impact at all: so the risk of damage is to some extent statistical, depending on the chance of impact, and increases with frequency of exposure. But even one short exposure, for instance an X-ray of a tooth, could cause damage. Also there is a natural level of radiation, varying from place to place, which cannot be avoided[1].

The Ionising Radiation Regulations 1985 (S.I. 1985 No. 1333, in force 1 January 1986) apply to 'work with ionising radiation' at all places of work subject to the Health and Safety Act 1974, including those outside territorial waters such as oil rigs: regs. 5(1), 17. However, various types of work with only mild exposure are excluded by Sch. 3 (e.g. keeping luminous watches and nursing patients receiving radiation for cancer) and so is work at licensed nuclear installations (which have their own strict safety requirements). Exemptions may be given for the armed forces, including visiting forces: reg. 40. The duty of complying

1 In fact radiation involves two components: the rays themselves (gamma rays and X-rays) and streams of α-particles (helium nuclei) and β-particles (electrons). The rays themselves are similar to ultra-violet and very penetrating: they cause direct damage and destruction of living cells by a process similar to invisible burning. The particles do not penetrate deeply but are liable to be absorbed by the skin or by breathing, and then may continue to radiate and cause damage to the organs. So the risk is partly cumulative and partly statistical.

with the regulations rests on the employer (or a self-employed person) undertaking 'work with ionising radiation', and he has to notify the Health and Safety Executive when he first starts to do so. He owes the duty not only to his own employees but also to others who may be affected by his activities, and employers whose workers may be affected are expressly required to co-operate, for instance in checks of the exposure to their workers: regs. 5, 4.

'Ionising radiation' is defined to include (a) gamma rays; (b) X-rays; and (c) streams of particles capable of producing ions (electrically charged sub-atomic particles): reg. 2.

'*Work* with ionising radiation'—which is the critical test for coming within the regulations—includes (a) production, use, transport or handling in any way of radioactive substances (including 'sealed sources'); (b) the operation or use of any 'radiation generator' except a cathode ray tube (as used for instance in a television set) or computer screen where radiation does not exceed the normal level; (c) work exposing anyone to more than a certain level of radon emanations in the atmosphere (i.e. work where the natural level of radiation is high, as may occur in caves or underground areas).

The first duty of the employer is to assess in advance the risks of his particular work and the means of reducing them, including plans for an emergency: regs. 25, 26. In some cases involving substantial risk, details of the assessment must be notified to the Health and Safety Executive.

The employer's main duty is then to restrict the exposure of employees and other persons to the fullest extent 'reasonably practicable': reg. 6.

This is to be done in two ways. First—reg. 6(2)—by 'engineering controls' and 'design features' (a term which must include the lay-out of the site, as well as the equipment). These newly invented and somewhat artificial expressions are intended by their civil service inventors to be very wide and open-ended, like the similar term 'control measure' in the Hazardous Substances regulations. Examples are shielding, ventilation, prevention of contamination and warning devices such as lights and notices.

The second main safety measure—reg. 6(3)—is to restrict the exposure of particular persons, for instance by limiting entry into risk areas, and providing protective equipment when necessary.

Dose limits

An important feature of the regulation is the specified 'dose' limits to which employees and other persons may be subjected. These dose limits are set out in Sch. 1 to the regulations, and there are separate limits for the whole body and for particular organs such as the eye or the feminine reproductive organs.

The employer is under an important duty to 'ensure' that this limit is not exceeded for any person: reg. 6. For this purpose regular checks and medical supervision are required: regs. 13 to 17.

Danger areas

Any area where exposure is likely to exceed *three-tenths* of the dose limits—and more particularly the limits in Sch. 6—must be set aside as a *controlled area*: reg. 8. In general only 'classified persons' specially authorised (and not under 18) are allowed in these areas, but there are exceptions if exposure is limited to a low dosage: regs. 8(6), (7).

A less dangerous area—where exposure would exceed one-third of the dose limit for a controlled area—must be designated as a *supervised area*: reg. 8(2). There is no specific restriction in such an area, but the general duty to limit exposure requires persons to be kept out unless their presence is necessary.

The radiation in both types of area must be checked regularly: reg. 24.

Handling radioactive substances

If used as a source of radiation, they must when 'reasonably practicable' be held in a 'sealed source' adequately shielded and constructed and regularly tested: reg. 18. Whether sealed or not, they must be stored in safe receptacles, and records kept: reg. 20. 19. If transported, they must be in safe receptacles, labelled and with full information for the carrier: reg. 21.

Miscellaneous

Washing and changing facilities must be provided: reg. 22. Respirators and other protective equipment must comply with official standards and be properly maintained: reg. 23. Employees must be given full information and training (including in the case of women warning of the risks in pregnancy): reg. 12. Manufacturers, suppliers and installers of equipment for use with ionising radiation are under specific duties to ensure that it is safe, and, in the case of those who install it, to make full tests after installation: reg. 32. There is a similar duty for medical equipment: reg. 33.

The Ionising Radiation Regulations apply, of course, to hospital equipment and staff just as they do to any other place of work: but there are separate regulations for the protection of patients, the Ionising Radiation (Protection of Persons undergoing Medical Examination and Treatment) Regulations 1988 (S.I. No. 778).

For the Nuclear Installations Act and civil liability under it, see p. 81.

6 Noise at work

The Noise at Work Regulations 1989 (S.I. No. 1790, in force 1 January 1990) require workers to be protected from the risks of exposure to noise above specified levels.

All employers must reduce risk to hearing from noise to the minimum practicable, inform employees who are at risk, and in particular make an assessment of any whose exposure may exceed 85 dB(A): regs. 6. 11, 4. Ear protectors may have to be provided and worn in danger zones: regs. 8, 9. Exposure must not exceed a 'peak level' of 90 dB(A): reg. 7.

Chapter 9

The Factories Act 1961: the factory and the occupier

1 The general scope of the Factories Act 1961

Factories are regulated by the Factories Act 1961[1]. This now takes effect within the framework of the Health and Safety at Work Act 1974 and is liable to be superseded by regulations under that Act. The legislation on this subject is concerned with many other things besides the safety of factory workers. It controls, for example, the employment of women and young persons and their hours of work, and has many provisions which relate to welfare (such as canteens and washing facilities) as distinct from safety. There are also a number of administrative provisions, as to the keeping of records, giving notice of accidents, and similar matters. Many of the administrative provisions (e.g. power to make regulations, powers of inspectors, inquiries, prosecutions) have been repealed by regulations under the 1974 Act because they are no longer required in view of the wider powers given by that Act[2]. The Health and Safety Executive appointed under the 1974 Act are responsible for the administration of the Factories Act and inspectors of factories are now part of their organisation.

1 The Act of 1961 is substantially the same as the 1937 Act which it consolidated with minor intervening amendments. But the Factory and Workshop Act 1901, which the 1937 Act replaced, was on a completely different plan. The modern code therefore dates from 1937.
2 Factories Act 1961 (Repeals and Modifications) Regulations, S.I. 1974 No. 1941; also Factories Act 1961 (Repeals) Regulations, S.I. 1975 No. 1012 and 1976 No. 2004.

The requirements of the Factories Act 1961 must be complied with inside the boundaries of every place defined as a factory by the Act (s. 172)[3]. If there is any contravention of the Act, the occupier of the factory is in general responsible (s. 155(1)); he is liable to criminal proceedings, and also to an action for breach of statutory duty. In certain special cases the owner of the factory, or of machinery installed there, may be liable instead of the occupier.

The Factories Act does not apply to premises which form part of a mine or quarry: Mines and Quarries Act 1954, s. 184(1): except that, by s. 184(5), s. 127 of the Factories Act, and therefore the Construction Regulations made under it, apply to building operations on the surface.

In its application to docks (s. 125), ships in wet docks (s. 126), building operations and engineering operations (s. 127) and electrical stations (s. 123), the Act is subject to special modifications: and it is broadly true to say that these places and operations are governed by special codes of regulations of their own rather than by the Act (Docks Regulations 1988; Electricity at Work Regulations 1989; Shipbuilding and Ship-repairing Regulations 1960; Construction Regulations 1961 and 1966).

These special cases are therefore treated separately.

The administration of the Factories Act 1961 is the responsibility of the Secretary of State for Employment acting, under the Health and Safety at Work Act 1974, through the Health and Safety Commission, the Executive and their inspectors[4].

2 The definition of a factory

The Factory and Workshop Act 1901 made a distinction between factories and workshops, and also a further distinction between textile factories (which are often known as 'mills') and non-textile factories.

---

3   The territorial operation of the Act is neatly illustrated by *Hunter v Glenfield and Kennedy* 1947 SC 536 where a workman, who was erecting a staging *outside* a factory, put his arm through a gap in the factory wall, where he was injured by a passing overhead crane, in breach of s. 24(7) of the 1937 Act (now s. 27(7) of the 1961 Act). His arm being inside the factory, where the breach was committed, the action succeeded.

4   The Secretary of State replaces the Minister of Labour, defined as 'the Minister' in s. 176. References to the Minister must be understood accordingly.

These distinctions were abandoned by the Act of 1937, which contained an entirely new definition of a factory, now reproduced in s. 175 of the Factories Act 1961. It is, however, useful to remember that the former Acts contained an express reference to workshops. Many small premises which fall within the new definition of a factory would not usually be described as factories, but could certainly be described as workshops.

Section 175 starts with a general definition of a factory, according to which it includes every place where manual labour is used in the manufacture of goods or certain analogous processes, for trade or for profit. It then goes on to deal with a number of special cases, in some cases to put the matter beyond doubt, and in other cases to include premises which would otherwise be outside the definition.

It is not in general necessary that machines or mechanical power should be in use; there is no criterion depending on the size of an establishment (except in the one case of gasholders); and though in general the undertaking must be carried on for profit, this requirement is waived in the case of premises occupied by the Crown or some other public authority, which would in other respects qualify as factories.

A factory need not be, or include, a building: it may be carried on entirely in the open air.

Under s. 137 of the Act the occupier of a factory must give notice of his occupation of the premises as a factory to the Health and Safety Executive: in practice, however, many owners of small workshops do not realise that they are 'factories', and consequently there are many cases where this notice has never been given.

The text of the definition is as follows[5]:

'**175. Interpretation of expression "factory".** (1) Subject to the provisions of this section, the expression "factory" means any premises in which, or within the close or curtilage or precincts of which, persons are employed in manual labour in any process for or incidental to any of the following purposes, namely:–
    (a) the making of any article or of part of any article; or
    (b) the altering, repairing, ornamenting, finishing, cleaning, or washing, or the breaking up or demolition of any article; or
    (c) the adapting for sale of any article; or

---

5   This definition is quoted in full for easy reference; but anyone who is reading through the text should pass straight on to the end of the quotation, where the definition is broken up into simpler terms.

(d) the slaughtering of cattle, sheep, swine, goats, horses, asses or mules; or

(e) the confinement of such animals as aforesaid while awaiting slaughter at other premises, in a case where the place of confinement is available in connection with those other premises, is not maintained primarily for agricultural purposes within the meaning of the Agriculture Act 1947 or, as the case may be, the Agriculture (Scotland) Act 1948, and does not form part of premises used for the holding of a market in respect of such animals[6];

being premises in which, or within the close or curtilage or precincts of which, the work is carried on by way of trade or for purposes of gain and to or over which the employer of the persons employed therein has the right of access or control.

(2) The expression "factory" also includes the following premises in which persons are employed in manual labour (whether or not they are factories by virtue of subsection (1) of this section), that is to say:–

(a) any yard or dry dock (including the precincts thereof) in which ships or vessels are constructed, reconstructed, repaired, refitted, finished or broken up;

(b) any premises in which the business of sorting[7] any articles is carried on as a preliminary to the work carried on in any factory or incidentally to the purposes of any factory;

(c) any premises in which the business of washing[8] or filling bottles or containers or packing articles is carried on incidentally to the purposes of any factory;

(d) any premises in which the business of hooking, plaiting, lapping, making-up or packing of yarn or cloth is carried on;

(e) any laundry carried on as ancillary[9] to another business, or incidentally to the purposes of any public institution;

(f) except as provided in subsection (10) of this section, any premises in which the construction, reconstruction or repair of locomotives, vehicles, or other plant for use for transport purposes is carried on as ancillary to a transport undertaking or other industrial or commercial undertaking[10];

6   Paras. (d) and (e) were first introduced into the definition by s. 7 of the Slaughterhouses Act 1958. Previously it had been held that a live animal was not 'an article' and therefore slaughtering in itself was not an 'adaptation for sale': but premises would rank as a factory, even before 1958, where (as normally happens) work was done on the *carcases* after slaughter to adapt them for sale; for carcases are articles: *Fatstock Marketing Corpn Ltd v Morgan* [1958] 1 All ER 646.

7   This overrules *Paterson v Hunt* (1909) 101 LT 571.

8   This overrules *Kavanagh v Caledonian Rail Co* (1903) 5 F 1128 and *Keith Ltd v Kirkwood* 1914 SC(J) 150.

9   This overrules *Caledonian Rail Co v Paterson* (1898) 1 F 24.

10 Para. (f) must be read with sub-s. (10). They incorporate an amendment made by the Factories Act 1959, which brought all railway running sheds under the Factories Act. See further Chapter 20 on 'Railways'.

(g) any premises in which printing by letterpress, lithography, photogravure, or other similar process, or bookbinding is carried on by way of trade or for purposes of gain or incidentally to another business so carried on;

(h) any premises in which the making, adaptation or repair of dresses, scenery or properties is carried on incidentally to the production, exhibition or presentation by way of trade or for purposes of gain of cinematograph films or theatrical performances, not being a stage or dressing-room of a theatre in which only occasional adaptations or repairs are made;

(j) any premises in which the business of making or mending nets[11] is carried on incidentally to the fishing industry;

(k) any premises in which mechanical power is used in connection with the making or repair of articles of metal or wood incidentally to any business carried on by way of trade or for purposes of gain;

(l) any premises in which the production of cinematograph films is carried on by way of trade or for purposes of gain, so, however, that the employment at any such premises of theatrical performers within the meaning of the Theatrical Employers Registration Act, 1925[12], and of attendants on such theatrical performers shall not be deemed to be employment in a factory;

(m) any premises in which articles are made or prepared incidentally to the carrying on of building operations or works of engineering construction, not being premises in which such operations or works are being carried on;

(n) any premises used for the storage of gas in a gasholder having a storage capacity of not less than five thousand cubic feet. (*Metric measurement of 140 cubic metres now substituted by S.I. 1983 No. 978.*)

(3) Any line or siding (not being part of a railway or tramway) which is used in connection with and for the purposes of a factory, shall be deemed to be part of the factory; if any such line or siding is used in connection with more than one factory belonging to different occupiers, the line or siding shall be deemed to be a separate factory.

(4) A part of a factory may, with the approval in writing of the chief inspector, be taken to be a separate factory and two or more factories may, with the like approval, be taken to be a single factory.

(5) Any workplace in which, with the permission of or under agreement with the owner or occupier, two or more persons carry on any work which would constitute the workplace a factory if the persons working therein were in the employment of the owner or occupier, shall be deemed to be a factory for the purposes of this Act, and, in the case of any such workplace not being a tenement factory or part of a

11 This overrules *Curtis v Shinner* (1906) 95 LT 31.
12 35 Halsbury's Statutes, 3rd Edn., 306.

tenement factory, the provisions of this Act shall apply as if the owner or occupier of the workplace were the owner of the factory and the persons working therein were persons employed in the factory.

(6) Where a place situated within the close, curtilage, or precincts forming a factory is solely used for some purpose other than the processes carried on in the factory, that place shall not be deemed to form part of the factory for the purposes of this Act, but shall, if otherwise it would be a factory, be deemed to be a separate factory.

(7) Premises shall not be excluded from the definition of a factory by reason only that they are open air premises.

(8) [*Power for the Minister to make regulations under which branches or departments in a factory are treated as separate factories: this does not affect safety measures, but only such matters as hours of work.*]

(9) Any premises belonging to or in the occupation of the Crown or any municipal or other public authority shall not be deemed not to be a factory, and building operations or works of engineering construction undertaken by or on behalf of the Crown or any such authority shall not be excluded from the operation of this Act, by reason only that the work carried on thereat is not carried on by way of trade or for purposes of gain.

(10) Premises used for the purpose of housing locomotives or vehicles where only cleaning, washing, running repairs or minor adjustments are carried out shall not be deemed to be a factory by reason only of paragraph (f) of subsection (2) of this section, unless they are premises used for the purposes of a railway undertaking where running repairs to locomotives are carried out.'

Now the kernel of this complex definition, the prototype factory as one might say, is plainly a building where articles are manufactured for sale: but the definition has been extended to include all kinds of other undertakings, carrying out repairs, for example, or other processes, and presenting a more or less close analogy to this prototype factory. Almost every aspect of this definition requires further explanation. The essential elements are (1) the factory premises; (2) the processes which constitute a factory; (3) the fact that they are carried on for trade or gain; (4) the use of manual labour; and (5) the employer's right of access.

(1) Manual labour

'Manual labour' includes work done with the hands, although highly skilled and technical: *J. and F. Stone Lighting and Radio Ltd v Haygarth* [1968] AC 157, [1966] 3 All ER 539 (radio mechanic). Under the present definition a place may be a factory though no machines or mechanical power are used, except in the special case of workshops under s. 175 (2) (k)[13]. Manual labour is used in many types of premises, but does not, without more, convert them into factories. Thus a porter in a chemist's shop is engaged in manual labour, but this does not make the shop a factory, because his work is not incidental to a factory process: *Joyce v Boots Cash Chemists (Southern) Ltd* [1950] 2 All ER 719, affirmed [1951] 1 All ER 682. On the other hand, the employment of *one man* in a factory process—e.g. to chop firewood in a shed—is enough to turn the premises into a factory: *Griffith v Ferrier* 1952 JC 56, 1952 SLT 248. A photographic agency, which made and loaned photographic prints for reproduction at a fee, was held to be a factory as a whole by reason of the use of manual labour in making prints in two rooms on the premises: *Paul Popper Ltd v Grimsey* [1963] 1 QB 44, [1962] 1 All ER 864. That case suggests that where manual labour is purely incidental to a shop, e.g. unpacking goods or making some adjustment in a back room, the Act does not apply: but it certainly applies where regular maintenance work is done, even on articles previously sold by the shop.

(2) The factory premises

The premises may be a building, or part of a building, with or without outside precincts: or they may be entirely in the open air (s. 175 (7))[14] as in the case of a brickfield. In *Back v Dick Kerr & Co Ltd* [1906] AC 325 at 334, Lord Atkinson said that

> '. . . the walls or fences built around the factory or dock, as the case may be, fix the boundaries and determine the area.'

A factory, therefore, is a place with definite boundaries, and outside those boundaries the Act does not apply.

The question has sometimes arisen whether detached premises form part of a factory. In *Rimmer v Premier Gas Engine Co Ltd* (1907) 97 LT 226, for instance, an electrical station at some distance from a dock was

---

13 Under the 1901 Act premises where mechanical power was not used were 'workshops'.

14 This section overrules cases decided in the 19th century, e.g. *Kent v Astley* (1869) LR 5 QB 19 (slate quarry—which, however, is not within the present Act); *Redgrave v Lee* (1874) LR 9 QB 363 (cement works).

held by the Court of Appeal to be outside the dock boundaries, though established purely for dock purposes[15]. Similarly, in *Spacey v Dowlais Gas and Coke Co* [1905] 2 KB 879, the argument that the gas mains connected with a gasworks formed part of the factory was rejected.

On the other hand, in *Re London County Council and Tubbs* (1903) 68 JP 29 an arbitrator was held to be right in finding that two buildings connected by a bridge and used in conjunction were a single factory; and the opinion was expressed by the Court of Appeal in *Cox v S. Cutler & Sons Ltd and Hampton Court Gas Co* [1948] 2 All ER 665 that two or more pieces of land, with the buildings on them, may constitute one factory[16]. Two adjacent open areas, bounded by a quay, warehouses and access roads, and used for storing and assembling steel components to construct a floating dock, were held to be a factory: *Barry v Cleveland Bridge and Engineering Co Ltd* [1963] 1 All ER 192.

When it is found that premises with defined boundaries are occupied as a single unit, and that manual labour is employed at any point within the precincts on manufacture or on the other processes specified in the Act, the place becomes a factory, and the Act must be complied with at all points within the boundaries. Thus in *Hosking v De Havilland Aircraft Co Ltd* [1949] 1 All ER 540 the occupiers of a factory were held liable for an unsafe plank laid by contractors over a ditch in the factory grounds. Furthermore, if a man has only part of his body over the boundary, and that part is injured by a breach of the Act within the boundary, he is entitled to succeed: *Hunter v Glenfield and Kennedy* 1947 SC 536.

Excluded parts of factories
This rule that the factory precincts constitute a single entity is subject to one important exception under s. 175 (6). Where there is a clearly demarcated area within the factory precincts, which is not being used for the purposes of the factory processes, but is being put to some distinct use, then it falls outside the factory area. Such an excluded area may, nevertheless, be a factory on its own account, if processes are being carried on which bring it within the general definition; or it may be subject to some other Act, such as the Offices, Shops and Railway Premises Act 1963.

---

15 Such a station would now usually be within the Act as a separate factory under
    s. 123.
16 See also *Hoyle v Oram* (1862) 12 CB NS 124.

An obvious example of excluded premises would be a dwelling-house (or a shop) adjoining the factory. Offices are also excluded, according to a decision in a de-rating case, *Cardiff Revenue Officer v Cardiff Assessment Committee and Western Mail Ltd* [1931] 1 KB 47[17]; so was a three-storey block consisting only of a dining-room for administrative staff, an office and a games room for apprentices: *Thomas v British Thomson-Houston Co Ltd* [1953] 1 All ER 29, [1953] 1 WLR 67. But an administration block approached by a separate entrance was held not to be excluded from the factory, inasmuch as design and draughtsmanship were done there for the factory: *Powley v Bristol Siddeley Engines Ltd* [1965] 3 All ER 612. (Where an office is excluded by s. 175 (6), the Offices, Shops and Railway Premises Act 1963 will apply to it.) The exclusion need not be permanent: it has been held that a workshop in a factory, which had been cleared of machines and was being decorated for a Christmas party, was temporarily excluded from the factory: *King v Magnatex Ltd* (1951) 101 L Jo 650. The following cases deserve special mention:

(a) Premises under construction or repair. A gasholder, which had been damaged by enemy action and was wholly in the hands of contractors for reconstruction, was held to be excluded from the gasworks: *Cox v S. Cutler & Sons Ltd and Hampton Court Gas Co, supra.* A similar conclusion was reached in *Lewis v Gilbertson & Co Ltd* (1904) 91 LT 377 (where a new building was under construction on a defined site in the factory grounds). Section 175 (6) will also apply where part of the main building is in the hands of contractors: it is not restricted to places which are in the factory grounds, but outside the main factory. In *Street v British Electricity Authority* [1952] 2 QB 399, [1952] 1 All ER 679 a power station was under construction: certain bays on a floor were complete and already in operation, while other bays, where boilers were still being installed, were screened off by a tarpaulin. The bays under construction were held to be excluded by s. 175 (6). So too a furnace floor under construction: *Johnston v Colvilles Ltd* 1966 SLT 30. Similarly where a hangar was occupied as a factory together with an adjacent concrete apron forming part of the precincts, the apron was excluded by s. 175 (6) when contractors took it over in successive strips

17 *De-rating.* When industrial property was granted partial remission of local rates in 1929, the definition of a factory (under the Act of 1901) was used, with modifications, as the test for reduction of liability. Thus many decisions on the old definition were given in rating cases.

to break up the concrete: *Walsh v Allweather Mechanical Grouting Co Ltd* [1959] 2 QB 300, [1959] 2 All ER 588, CA.

(b) Canteens. Under the Factory and Workshop Act 1901—as applied to de-rating—it has been held that a canteen within the curtilage of the factory and used by the workers is a part of the factory, to which its use is incidental: *London Co-operative Society Ltd v Southern Essex Assessment Commmittee* [1942] 1 KB 53, [1941] 3 All ER 252. In *Luttman v I.C.I. Ltd* [1955] 3 All ER 481 it was held, following this decision, that a canteen for work-people is not excluded by what is now s. 175 (6), because the feeding of work-people is a purpose incidental to the factory processes. On the other hand, a building which was mainly used as a restaurant for administrative staff, as distinct from industrial workers, was held to be excluded from the factory: *Thomas v British Thomson-Houston Co Ltd* [1953] 1 All ER 29.

(c) Maintenance workshops. A workshop within the factory precincts, where the factory machinery is repaired, is part of the main factory, to which the repairs are incidental: *Thurogood v Van den Berghs and Jurgens Ltd* [1951] 2 KB 537, [1951] 1 All ER 682.

(d) Water pumping stations. Although water is an 'article' and a filter station which 'alters' it is a factory, it has nevertheless been held that a pumping house within the precincts is not used for the factory purposes and is excluded by s. 175 (6): *Longhurst v Guildford, Godalming and District Water Board* [1963] AC 265, [1961] 3 All ER 545. But a pump house in a separate locked building, used for pumping water into a bleaching works, could not be treated as an excluded part of the works, since the pumping was incidental to the factory processes: *Newton v John Stanning & Son Ltd* [1962] 1 All ER 78.

A railway line or siding used in connection with a factory is part of it, and it does not seem to be necessary that it should be adjacent to the factory (s. 175 (3)). Where a line or siding is shared, it becomes a separate factory.

The regulations in s. 175 (4), (8), as to dividing factories, or treating several factories as one, need not be considered here as they do not affect safety obligations, but only such matters as hours of employment.

(3) Processes which constitute a factory

(i) The making of an article or part of an article

This is the prototype case, a place where the manufacture of commodities is carried on. The word 'article' is quite general and includes, for instance, coal gas: *Cox v Cutler (S.) & Sons Ltd and Hampton Court Gas Co* [1948] 2 All ER 665. So a gasworks is a factory within the definition; but a gasholder is not necessarily included unless it is laid out and occupied as a single unit with the gasworks. It was expressly declared in s. 103 (5) of the 1937 Act that electricity is not deemed to be an 'article', but this subsection has been omitted in s. 123 of the 1961 Act which in other respects re-enacts s. 103 and makes special provisions for electrical stations. Water handled in bulk at a waterworks is an 'article', and so, generally, is any commodity in bulk, whether in solid, liquid or gaseous form: *Longhurst v Guildford, Godalming and District Water Board* [1963] AC 265, [1961] 3 All ER 545; but a part of a waterworks such as a pumping station where water is not treated but just passed on is not a factory. It does not matter how large the 'article' is. A shipyard is expressly included in the definition, but the ship is an 'article' under manufacture there: *Gardiner v Admiralty Comrs* [1964] 2 All ER 93, [1964] 1 WLR 590. Similarly an oil rig is an 'article' and the yard where it is built is a factory: *Faith v C.B.I. Constructors Ltd* 1987 SLT 248.

(ii) The altering, repairing, ornamenting, finishing, cleaning, or washing, or the breaking up or demolition of any article

Repairing brings in such places as garages. But there is no 'breaking-up' at a sewage pumping station where solid sediment is simply allowed to accumulate at the bottom of a tank and is then removed: *McIlhagger v Belfast Corpn* [1944] NI 37.

Cleaning brings in, for example, laundries and dry cleaning works.

(iii) Adapting for sale

There is a fair amount of case-law on this subject.

'Adapting for sale' includes packing chocolates in boxes: *Fullers Ltd v Squire* [1901] 2 KB 209; arranging flowers into wreaths: *Hoare v Green (Robert) Ltd* [1907] 2 KB 315; unpacking and cutting bacon and cheese for sale in a grocer's shop in a room behind the shop: *McLeavy v Lipton's* (1959) 228 LT Jo 195; bottling beer: *Hoare v Truman, Hanbury, Buxton*

& Co (1902) 71 LJ KB 380[18]; preparation and packaging of parts of motor vehicles to preserve them against tropical or frigid conditions in transit: *Cockram (Valuation Officer) v Tropical Preservation Co Ltd* [1951] 2 KB 827, [1951] 2 All ER 520; and compression of paper into bales: *Kinder v Camberwell Borough Council* [1944] 2 All ER 315; but not the cooling and cleaning of milk at a special station: *Wiltshire County Valuation Committee v London Co-operative Society Ltd* [1950] 1 All ER 937.

Whether sorting amounts to adapting for sale was a question of degree under the old law, which is still in force in places where nothing but sorting is done. Scrutton LJ said in *Bailey (Stoke-on-Trent Revenue Officer) v Potteries Electric Traction Co Ltd* [1931] 1 KB 385 at 494:

> 'The process of sorting may be so complicated and mechanical as to deserve the name of a manufacturing process.'

The question whether sorting is an adaptation for sale depends on whether it converts articles in an unsaleable form into articles which are saleable. In *Richardson (A.) & Son v Middlesbrough Borough Assessment Committee* [1947] KB 958, [1947] 1 All ER 884 a Divisional Court held on this ground that an egg-packing station, where eggs were sorted and graded, was a factory. A similar conclusion was reached where the work consisted of separating out the saleable parts of the town refuse: *Henderson v Glasgow Corpn.* (1900) 2 F 1127[19].

Where sorting is a preliminary to work in any factory, or incidental to such work, s. 175 (2) (b) now puts it beyond doubt that it is a factory process.

Packing, bottling and cleaning bottles are also expressly made factory processes when carried on incidentally to the work of any factory—not necessarily, it seems, the same factory: see s. 175 (2) (c). Thus, a packing station may be some distance from the factory or factories which it serves, but is nevertheless a factory on its own account.

How far *testing* can be treated as an adaptation for sale is not clear. In

---

18 The earlier case of *Law v Graham* [1901] 2 KB 327 turned on the fact that the bottling was not done by mechanical means, as was necessary under the old law.
19 For the approach to this question, see further *Davis Cohen & Sons Ltd v Hall* [1952] 1 All ER 157 (sorting of Government surplus stores for re-sale not an 'adaptation'); also *Wilson Bros Ltd v Edwards* [1958] 3 All ER 243 (arranging of Christmas cards in groups not adaptation for sale: part of normal handling in wholesale trade); *Hudson's Bay Co v Thompson* [1959] 3 All ER 150 (sorting and grading of skins from bales of skins held to be adapting for sale).

Grove (Dudley Revenue Officer) v Lloyd's British Testing Co Ltd [1931] AC 450 an establishment existed solely for the purpose of testing cables and anchors, and giving certificates of soundness. The occupiers claimed that it was a factory and should be de-rated as an 'industrial hereditament'. The House of Lords decided that it was not a factory, and Viscount Dunedin said, at p. 467:

> 'I think adapting for sale points clearly to something being done to the article in question which, in some ways, makes it in itself a little different from what it was before. Now, testing does not in any way make the article different as an article from what it was before. It only proclaims its character.'

Therefore, an establishment which exists only to test the products of other firms is not a factory. On the other hand, in *Acton Borough Corpn v West Middlesex Assessment Committee* [1949] 2 KB 10, [1949] 1 All ER 409 an aircraft company maintained an establishment to test its own propellers, and the Divisional Court held that this was *incidental* to the 'making' of a propeller, and that the establishment was a factory.

Under the wording of the section, as the above decision shows, a place may be a factory though none of the specified processes is carried on there, so long as the work done is *incidental* to those processes. This is an important point, which seems to have escaped notice before the *Acton* case.

(4) Carrying on for trade or gain

In the prototype case of a factory engaged in manufacture, articles are made for direct sale to wholesalers or to the public. That is, the manufacturing process is carried on for the *direct* purpose of trade or gain. But is it necessary that the trade or gain should be directly connected with the process? In *Nash v Hollinshead* [1901] 1 KB 700 the Court of Appeal thought that it was, and A. L. Smith MR said, at p. 704:

> 'I think that the "gain" intended by this section is a direct gain.'

However, the case really turned on another point, and in *Bailey (Stoke-on-Trent Revenue Officer) v Potteries Electric Traction Co Ltd* [1931] 1 KB 385 Scrutton LJ took the opposite view. He said, at p. 492:

> 'I cannot think, however, that when there is a manufacture of articles to be employed in carrying on a trade, though that trade is one of supplying services for reward, as carriage by land or water, and not of supplying goods, the manufacture is not for purposes of trade.'

And further, at p. 496:

> '[A process] will be carried on "for trade or gain" if its products are to be sold in trade, or used directly in carrying on a trade.'

These remarks seem to be an accurate statement of the law. On this view, the general definition will, of its own force, include such things as the printing of tramway tickets, which, however, are now specially referred to in s. 175(2)(g). Further examples are:

Grinding coffee for sale in the company's own shops: *Barton (Stepney Revenue Officer) v Twining (R.) & Co Ltd* [1931] 1 KB 385.

Repair of barges by a lighterage company: *Barton (Poplar Revenue Officer) v Union Lighterage Co Ltd* [1931] 1 KB 385.

The matter was carried further in *Stanger v Hendon Borough Council* [1948] 1 KB 571, [1948] 1 All ER 377, where a consulting engineer made concrete out of materials supplied to him, in order to test the soundness of the materials. The Court of Appeal accepted the views of Scrutton LJ (quoted above), as sound. They held that it is not necessary that articles should be manufactured for direct gain in the sense of sale, but that an indirect gain is sufficient; and, therefore, the premises were a factory.

Work is not done 'by way of trade' when it is carried out by an incorporated club, for the benefit of members, and there is no intention to make any profit: *Automobile Proprietary Ltd v Brown (Valuation Officer)* [1955] 2 All ER 214. (This case concerned the rating of the workshops of the Royal Automobile Club.)

Under s. 175(9), premises belonging to or occupied by the Crown, or by a municipal or public authority, do not need to satisfy the test that they are carried on for 'trade or gain': but they must fall fairly within the scope of the definition as a whole, i.e. they must be establishments which would be factories if they were carried on for profit[20]. Thus in *Weston v*

20 There is no doubt that electricity stations and other places carried on by nationalised industries are within the Act. Nationalised boards are, it is thought, 'public authorities', but even if this were wrong, the work is carried out for trade or gain: how the profits are limited, or what is done with them, is an irrelevant question.

London County Council [1941] 1 KB 608, [1941] 1 All ER 555 it was held
that a technical institute where wood-working was taught did not fall
within the Factories Act. Similarly, a prison workshop is not within the
Act: *Pullen v Prison Commissioners* [1957] 3 All ER 470; *Macdonald v
Secretary of State for Scotland* 1979 SLT (Sh Ct) 8. The reasoning in the
Weston case seems to suggest that only large establishments can be
described as factories, but of course small 'workshops' have always been
within the Act. A better reason for excluding schools is that they are
places for learning, not workplaces. At any rate, a hospital workshop
with grinding and other machines used for repairs to hospital equipment
was held to be fairly and squarely within the definition of a factory except
that it was run by a public authority and not for profit, and it was
therefore subject to the Act: *Bromwich v National Ear, Nose and Throat
Hospital* [1980] 2 All ER 663, [1980] ICR 450.

Apart from s. 175(9), the Act is expressly applied by s. 173 to factories
owned or occupied by the Crown. But in case of public emergency the
Minister has power to make an order exempting not only Crown
factories, but also other factories where work is done for the Crown,
from such parts of the Act as are specified in the order. It may safely be
assumed that any special order would relate to such matters as hours of
work, and would not waive the fundamental safety requirements such as
the fencing of machinery.

(5) Employer's right of access

The employer may not be the occupier of the premises, but under
s. 175(1) they are not a factory unless he has the right of access or
control. However, under s. 175(5) a place is a factory (if otherwise
within the definition) if the owner or occupier lets out working-space to
at least two other persons, though he is not their employer, and even if
they have no employer. In these exceptional cases the owner or occupier
(whichever lets out the space) is responsible for carrying out the Act.

(6) General scope of the definition

The wide definition in s. 175 must be read from a common-sense point
of view, and as a whole. Thus in *Nash v Hollinshead* [1901] 1 KB 700 the

Court of Appeal refused to hold that a part of a farm, where a steam engine was being used to crush meal, was a 'factory'. At that time mechanical power was necessary to constitute a factory: under the present definition, read literally, it might be argued that the whole farm was within the Act, as the use of mechanical power is no longer the test. Collins LJ said in the above case, at p. 706:

> 'The context of the Act must be regarded. Its context shows that the Act was intended to apply to places in the nature of manufactories, for it contains a series of elaborate provisions appropriate to such places.'

Nevertheless, a workshop or similar place on a farm, as distinct from the whole farm, might well be a factory[1]. On similar grounds the Court of Appeal held in *Wood v London County Council* [1941] 2 KB 232, [1941] 2 All ER 230 that a kitchen attached to a mental hospital was outside the Act, and Mackinnon LJ indicated that he would take the same view of a kitchen attached to a large trading establishment such as a hotel[2].

(7) Establishments specially mentioned

After giving the general definition, s. 175 goes on to list a whole series of establishments which are to be regarded as factories, whether strictly within the definition or not.

Some of these places do fall fairly within the definition, but the matter has been put beyond doubt, either to overcome doubts expressed in the courts or to overrule old decisions. Other places would perhaps fall outside the Act, apart from this special mention. They are listed below with the letter of the relevant paragraph in s. 175 (2).

(i) Processes incidental to any factory
Premises in which the following processes are carried on for the purpose of some factory—not necessarily the same one—are themselves factories

---

1   See further as to farms Chapter 21.
2   Somewhat surprisingly, a Divisional Court held in *Simmonds Aerocessories (Western) Ltd v Pontypridd Area Assessment Committee* [1944] KB 231, [1944] 1 All ER 264 that a factory canteen, not within the precincts of the factory, was a factory in its own right, being a place where articles (viz. food) were made or adapted for sale. If this reasoning is correct it would apply to any hotel kitchen, and would be in

(b) Sorting of articles;

(c) Washing bottles; filling bottles; filling containers; packing articles.

(ii) Processes incidental to special trades

(e) Laundries ancillary to some business (e.g. a hotel) or to a public institution.

(f) Locomotive works, garages, barge depots and the like, ancillary to a transport or other undertaking, except—see s. 175 (10)—places used for housing transport where only cleaning and running repairs and adjustments are done[3], but including railway running sheds where running repairs are carried out.

(h) Workshops ancillary to the cinema and theatre industries.

(k) Workshops handling wood or metal articles incidentally to *any* business, provided that mechanical power is in use[4].

(m) Workshops, etc. incidental to building and engineering operations.

(n) Gasholders with a storage capacity of five thousand cubic feet (now altered to 140 cubic metres) or more (but gasholders with smaller capacity might come within the general definition, if forming part of the gasworks).

(iii) Particular undertakings

(a) Shipbuilding or ship-repairing yards and dry docks[5].

(d) Hooking, plaiting, lapping, making-up or packing of yarn or cloth.

---

conflict with *Wood v LCC* (which was not cited to the court). See also *Thomas v British Thomson-Houston Co Ltd* [1953] 1 All ER 29 at 34–35 where the *Simmonds* case was not followed in the case of a restaurant for administrative staff, and the comment was made that *Wood v LCC* had not been cited. For factory canteens generally, see p. 258, *ante*.

3   Where substantial repairs were done at a tramshed, such as the fitting of new parts after a collision, it was held to be a factory within this clause: *Griffin v London Transport Executive* [1950] 1 All ER 716. A place which is excluded from para. (f) because only cleaning or running repairs are done, is excluded from the definition of a factory although it would otherwise come within the general words of the definition such as 'cleaning or washing any article': *Jones v Crosville Motor Services Ltd* [1956] 3 All ER 417.

4   This is probably intended to bring in workshops attached to shops.

5   Where a ship-repairing yard had a frontage to the Manchester Ship Canal, it was held that a ship moored for repairs at a jetty belonging to the yard was not within the factory precincts: *Chatburn v Manchester Dry Dock Co Ltd* (1950) 83 Ll L Rep 1, CA.

(g) Printing and binding works.

(l) Cinema studios. (Theatrical performers, as defined in the Theatrical Employers Registration Act 1925[6], are not deemed to be employed in a factory: this seems to affect such matters as hours of employment, but not to exclude these persons from the benefit of the safety provisions of the Act[7].)

Public institutions. In this long list the only matter which calls for special notice is the term 'public institution'. It has been decided that this includes public charities such as a boys' school (*Royal Masonic Institution for Boys' Trustees v Parkes* [1912] 3 KB 212), or an orphans' home (*Seal v British Orphan Asylum Trustees* (1911) 104 LT 424) and a laundry run by such a charity to wash its own linen and clothing is a factory. The institution itself will in some cases be within the Act under s. 124 *(infra)*.

The Factories Act does not normally apply to premises which form part of a mine or quarry: Mines and Quarries Act 1954, s. 184 (1). But by s. 184 (5), s. 127 of the Factories Act applies to building operations if carried out on the surface and not underground.

(8) Newly constructed premises

The question has been raised, when do newly constructed premises become a factory? In *Barrington v Kent Rivers Catchment Board* [1947] 2 All ER 782 the defendant Board had a building constructed as a workshop for their mechanical department, but no power supply had been introduced into the building, nor was any of the machinery capable of being worked. However, a lorry had been brought in to be painted, and was standing beside an open inspection pit when the plaintiff fell into the pit. 'Altering' of articles under s. 175 (1) includes painting, and thus, though in a very slight way, one of the processes for which the premises were to be occupied had commenced. This was held sufficient to bring the building within the Factories Act.

> 'If in one corner of it somebody has begun to do one of the things which it is intended shall be done there when it is a completed factory,

6 35 Halsbury's Statutes, 3rd Edn., 204.
7 A film studio has been held to be within the primary definition in s. 175 (1) (a): *Dunsby v BBC* (1983) Times, 25 July but this is of little significance in view of the express provision in s. 175 (2) (1).

and if that thing comes within the definition in s. 151[8] . . . then the building is a factory.'

The same view was taken in Scotland in *Ward v Coltness Iron Co Ltd* 1944 SC 318 where the factory was still under construction, but its furnace had been kindled, and a crane was in operation which injured a workman employed by the building contractors.

(9) Institutions

By s. 175(2)(e) a laundry ancillary to a public institution is within the definition of a factory for all purposes.

However, an institution—public or private—may itself be subject to the Act under s. 124.

Section 124(1) applies to premises forming part of an institution which is carried on for charitable or reformatory purposes, and where manual labour is used, in one or other of the recognised factory processes, to produce articles not intended for the use of the institution. For instance, an institute for the blind would fall, *prima facie*, within the subsection; and so, perhaps, would a prison.

Sections 124(2)–(3) have been repealed.

(10) Slaughterhouses

Slaughterhouses are now normally within the definition of a factory: see s. 175(1)(d) and (e) and relative footnote, p. 252, *ante*. S.I. 1962 Nos. 2345 to 2347 apply to these a number of existing regulations.

(11) Warehouses

Some of these are subject to the Factories Act, others to the Offices, Shops and Railway Premises Act 1963: see Chapter 14, section 4, and Chapter 22.

8 Now s. 175 of the 1961 Act.

3 The occupier

It is the occupier of the factory, with certain exceptions, who is responsible for ensuring that the Act is complied with (s. 155). He is liable to penalties if any of the requirements of the Act are contravened, and he is the person who is liable to an action for breach of statutory duty. He may or may not be the employer of the persons working in the factory: more often than not, he will be.

There is no definition of 'the occupier' in the Act. Normally it will be the person who is in legal possession of the premises, as tenant or owner, but a licensee may well be the occupier if, *de facto*, he has exclusive possession. In *Cox v Cutler (S.) & Sons Ltd and Hampton Court Gas Co* [1948] 2 All ER 665, for example, a ruined gasholder was being re-constructed, and the contract provided that the site should be 'handed over' to the contractors. It was held by the Court of Appeal that the contractors were the occupiers. The following remarks of Lord MacLaren in the Scottish case of *Ramsay v Mackie* (1904) 7 F 106 are generally taken as a guide:

> 'While the language is wide in order to prevent evasion yet "occupier" plainly means the person who runs the factory . . . who regulates and controls the work which is done there and who is responsible for the fulfilment of the provisions of the Factory Act within it.'

In one word, that is, the test is *control*—control, of course, of the premises (not of the work). In *Meigh v Wickenden* [1942] 2 KB 160, [1942] 2 All ER 68, a receiver for debenture-holders was held liable, on the ground that 'he was complete master of the affairs of the company'. For instance, he alone could have sanctioned expenditure in carrying out safety requirements.

Apart from the exceptional cases where, with the sanction of the chief inspector, a factory is divided into two, or where an area within factory grounds is used as a separate factory altogether, a factory has only one occupier: *Smith v Cammell Laird & Co Ltd* [1940] AC 242, [1939] 4 All ER 381. Lord Atkin said in that case, after rejecting the contention that there might be separate occupiers of separate parts of a shipyard:

> 'Nor is "occupier" the right word to describe the person controlling the work in doing which the accident happened, or the person using the machinery which gives rise to an accident.'

In *Turner v Courtaulds Ltd* [1937] 1 All ER 467 the respondents were the occupiers of the factory at large, but the complaint was based on a breach of regulations at an electrical switchboard which was being installed by contractors and had not yet been handed over. The respondents were held liable as occupiers of the factory. Similarly occupiers of a shipyard were liable for the failure of contractors erecting a crane to provide safety belts for workmen at a height: *McWilliams v Sir Wm. Arrol & Co Ltd* 1961 SLT 265. Lack of knowledge of the circumstances was no defence.

In *Meigh v Wickenden (supra)* Viscount Caldecote LCJ said:

> 'The occupier's responsibility under the Act does not depend on proof of personal blame or even upon knowledge of the contravention.'

Lord Wright, in *Smith v Cammell Laird & Co Ltd (supra)*, gave the following reasons for this onerous liability:

> 'This may appear somewhat out of the course of the common law, but the statute is remedial. It is for the protection of work-people, and that object can best—perhaps can only—be secured by fixing liability on a single person, and by defining the obligation in absolute and mandatory terms.'

And in the same case Lord Atkin shows, with reference to a shipyard, why the Act selects the occupier as the person liable:

> 'The occupiers of a shipbuilding yard . . . have complete control over their yard, and can impose their own conditions upon those who enter the yard, and use either their own plant or that of the occupiers of the yard. They can insist upon the plant being constantly maintained in a safe condition, can terminate the licence to enter the premises or use the plant in case of breach, and can take any indemnities they think fit.'

Within the confines of the factory, the occupier is liable for any contravention of the Act. The case of *Turner v Courtaulds Ltd*, where contractors were installing electrical machinery, has already been quoted. In *Whitby v Burt, Boulton and Hayward Ltd* [1947] KB 918, [1947] 2 All ER 324, contractors were repairing the roof of a factory and failed to provide safe means of access for their workmen, as required by s. 26(1) of the 1937 Act (s. 29(1) of the Act of 1961). The occupiers of the factory were held liable. Denning J said:

> 'I hold . . . that for the safeguarding of people in factories s. 26 applies and puts the responsibility on the occupier even though the building operations are being carried out by a contractor.'

Likewise in *Hoskins v De Havilland Aircraft Co Ltd* [1949] 1 All ER 540 occupiers were liable for an unsound plank put over a ditch in the factory grounds by contractors.

The occupier's remedy, is, as suggested by Lord Atkin, to take an express indemnity from contractors entering the premises against breaches of the Factories Act: for an example, see *Hosking v De Havilland Aircraft Co Ltd* (*supra*).

4 Special cases where owner of premises or machinery, or contractor or employer, liable instead of occupier

Nevertheless, there are certain cases where the owner is liable instead of the occupier.

First, there is the case of the *tenement factory*, defined in s. 176(1) as premises including two or more separate factories occupied by different persons, which, however, receive mechanical power from a prime mover located on the premises[9]. Here the essence of the situation is that the owner farms out mechanical power to tenants in different parts of the factory. Therefore, the owner is made responsible by s. 121 for matters which fall within his control, and in particular, as regards the safety requirements, for the following:

(1) Under Part II, the provision and maintenance of fencing and safety appliances, construction and maintenance of machinery and plant (such as lifts, hoists, boilers) and of floors, passages and stairs.

(2) Under Parts I and III, such matters as lighting, ventilation, washing facilities.

But the owner is not responsible for contraventions in the *use* of fencing, plant, etc. where the use is outside his control (s. 121(2)); nor for ventilation, lighting, etc., in a room occupied by one tenant only unless there is a defect in the structure or in plant belonging to the owner (s. 121(3)).

---

9   The requirement that the prime mover shall be on the premises overrules *Mumby v Volp* [1930] 1 KB 460.

Moreover, any part of the building which is not comprised in one of the separate factories is nevertheless treated as a factory, and the owner is treated as the occupier (s. 121(6)).

In case of doubt as to who is responsible in particular cases, reference should be made to the section (s. 121).

A similar case arises when part of a building is let off as a separate factory, though the building is not a tenement factory. Under s. 122, if any part of the building, though not comprised in the factory, is used for factory purposes—e.g. as a means of access or for power supply—the owner is responsible for complying with most of the safety requirements of Part II of the Act (e.g. such things as boilers, hoists, floors, fencing of transmission machinery and other machinery) and for cleanliness and lighting under Part I.

The owner is defined by s. 176(1) (as respects England and Wales) as the person who receives the rackrent of the premises, whether on his own account or as a trustee, or would receive it if the premises were let at a rackrent: that is, it means the *immediate landlord*, whether or not he is the absolute owner. There is a similar definition for Scotland.

Where a third party—as distinct from the occupier—is the owner or hirer of machinery or a mechanical implement in a factory, he is deemed to be the occupier, so far as concerns persons working in connection with the machine, who are in his own employment or pay (s. 163). That is, the third party, and not the general occupier of the factory, is liable for injuries caused by the machine to his own employees or to contractors paid by him, if their work brings them into contact with the machine. The occupier of a factory was held to be exonerated from liability by this section where a workman employed by a contractor, using a mechanical pick belonging to the contractor to break up concrete, was struck in the eye by a fragment, no goggles having been provided as required by s. 49 of the 1937 Act (s. 65 of the 1961 Act): *Whalley v Briggs Motor Bodies Ltd* [1954] 2 All ER 193.

Under ss. 123 and 125–127 of the Act, the Act itself or regulations may apply to premises of a special kind, or sites where operations are going on, 'as if' they were factories. These sections generally make some other person liable rather than the occupier, so if the Act does not apply to the premises at large for some other reason, the occupier will be exonerated. In *Fisher v C.H.T. Ltd (No 2)* [1966] 2 QB 475, [1966] 1 All ER 88 electrical repairs were being done at a restaurant: under s. 127 (building and engineering operations) the person undertaking the operations was 'deemed' to be the occupier and liable accordingly. Similarly for shipbuilding and repair (s. 126) the person undertaking the work is responsible, for electricity stations (s. 123) the employer, for docks etc. (s. 125) the person carrying out 'processes' such as loading.

5 Defences to criminal proceedings: whether they affect civil liability

The effect, if any, on civil liability, of defences to criminal proceedings under the Factories Act will be of diminishing importance as regulations under the Health and Safety at Work Act 1974 take its place. The infringement of requirements under the 1974 Act, or regulations made under it, is an offence under s. 33(1) of that Act. However, offences under pre-existing safety legislation and regulations are still charged under that legislation.

Section 155 of the Factories Act provided for two distinct cases. Under s. 155(1) the occupier (or in some cases the owner) was guilty of an offence for *any* contravention of the Act. Under s. 155(2), where a duty was expressly imposed on some person other than the occupier— either by the Act, or, more usually, by regulations—*that* person was guilty of an offence and the occupier was liable if (but only if) he had 'failed to take all reasonable steps to prevent the contravention'.

These provisions were supplemented by s. 161, by which, if a person was charged with an offence under either s. 155(1) or (2)—i.e. not just the occupier but others as well—he could bring before the court a third party who was alleged to be the real offender[10]; section 161 has been

---

10 There is no longer a procedure by which the person charged can bring a third party before the court. Under that procedure an employer was not necessarily responsible for the acts of his own employees and could bring an employee in as third party: a company is for this purpose identified only with its governing body: *Tesco Supermarkets Ltd v Nattrass* [1972] AC 153, [1971] 2 All ER 127. However, there was a heavy onus of proof on the governing body to show that they had done everything in their power to ensure compliance with the law, and it was no defence then, and is not now, merely to say they had appointed competent persons to supervise. However, if in other respects the system set up to ensure compliance with the law was satisfactory, they would not be responsible for the default of a subordinate manager who failed to supervise properly, and could bring him in as a third party. That is what the *Nattrass* case decided.

superseded by s. 36 of the 1974 Act, but s. 155 is still in force, and the question has arisen in the past whether it had any effect on civil liability. Section 47 (1)(a) of the 1974 Act declares that the extent of liability under existing legislation is not affected. So the case-law summarised below, although reflecting long-dead controversies, cannot yet be ignored.

(1) Duty imposed on the occupier

Under the old s. 161(1), where an occupier (or owner) was charged with an offence, there was a procedure by which he could bring the actual offender before the court: he himself would not be guilty of an offence if he proved that he 'used all due diligence to enforce' the Act and regulations, and that the offence was committed 'without his consent, connivance or wilful default'. Under s. 161(4), the factory inspector could short-circuit this procedure by prosecuting the actual offender in a case where the occupier was evidently not to blame. In Scotland under s. 161(3) the procedure was simplified, in that an occupier could set up this defence without bringing the actual offender before the court.

The House of Lords expressed the strong opinion that this section did *not* afford a defence in a civil action, and for practical purposes (though not actually decided)[11] this has settled the matter: *Potts (or Riddell) v Reid* [1943] AC 1, [1942] 2 All ER 161. Lord Thankerton said, for example, at pp. 11, 165:

> '. . . These sections, which relate solely to criminal prosecutions and contain no reference to civil liability, do not affect the existence of a contravention of the Act or the Regulations. . . . It would need some provision in the Act as to civil liability in order to relieve the employer of his absolute obligation towards the workmen.'

(2) Duties not directly imposed on the occupier

Section 155 (2) is completely different. It relates to contravention of the Act by some person other than the occupier, upon whom a duty is

---

11 In *Harrison v National Coal Board* [1951] AC 639 at 657, [1951] 1 All ER 1102 at 1111 Lord Porter thought that the House decided that s. 137 affords no defence to a civil action. See also *Gallagher v Dorman Long & Co Ltd* [1947] 2 All ER 38.

expressly imposed. It enables the occupier to be prosecuted for such a contravention if, but only if, he failed to take reasonable steps to prevent it. There is no contravention by him, and no failure to comply with the Act unless it is proved that he failed to take such steps. There is no civil liability without such proof: *Butler (or Black) v Fife Coal Co Ltd* [1912] AC 149; *Harrison v National Coal Board* [1951] AC 639, [1951] 1 All ER 1102 (Mines Act cases).

Where the occupier is also under a direct duty to comply with the Act or regulations in a distinct capacity, e.g. as the person 'carrying on operations' on a building site, s. 155(2) affords no defence to liability for contravention in the latter capacity, although the actual breach was by workmen: *Wagon Repairs Ltd v Vosper* (1968) 3 KIR 605. In such a case the occupier can and should be prosecuted under s. 155(2) for breach of his own absolute duty, not as occupier but in his other relevant capacity as contractor or employer: *Davies v Camerons Industrial Services Ltd* [1980] 2 All ER 680. *A fortiori* s. 155(2) gives no defence to a claim for damages.

6 Regulations for dangerous trades

In addition to the statutory duties laid down by the Factories Act, safety regulations could be made for particular processes, trades, machines and other things under s. 76 of the Act, and breach of these regulations is equally a breach of statutory duty. It is superfluous now to set out full details of s. 76, as it is superseded by the power to make safety regulations under s. 15 of the Health and Safety at Work Act 1974.

However, under s. 76[12] numerous existing regulations have been made, for instance, the Woodworking Machines Regulations 1974, the Shipbuilding and Ship-repairing Regulations 1960, and the Construction Regulations 1961 and 1966.

The case-law on the effect of regulations under s. 76 will gradually become obsolete, but cannot yet be ignored.

Regulations could impose duties on other persons besides the occupier. This practice was upheld by the House of Lords in *Mackey v Monks (Preston)* [1918] AC 59 as being *intra vires* of the Act of 1901, and

12 Or s. 79 of the Act of 1901 or s. 60 of the 1937 Act.

was expressly sanctioned by s. 76(2). On the other hand, regulations under s. 76 do not create duties towards any persons except 'the persons employed': consequently other persons, although lawful visitors to the premises, cannot claim damages for a breach of the regulations: *Hartley v Mayoh & Co* [1954] 1 QB 383, [1954] 1 All ER 375 (member of fire brigade called to fire). It has been decided by the House of Lords that regulations under either s. 79 of the Act of 1901, or s. 76 in its present form, may be made for the protection of all persons employed in the factory, or 'notional' factory, whether or not they are employed by the occupiers: *Canadian Pacific Steamships Ltd v Bryers* [1958] AC 485, approving *Massey-Harris-Ferguson (Manufacturing) Ltd v Piper* [1956] 2 QB 396, [1956] 2 All ER 722 and disapproving a dictum to the contrary in *Stanton Ironworks Ltd v Skipper* [1956] 1 QB 255, [1955] 3 All ER 544. Any man 'who is ordinarily and regularly employed' in the premises is certainly within the protection of the sections: how far they extend to persons who attend to do work on the premises, but not 'ordinarily and regularly' has been left uncertain. The large number of floating workers on a building site must surely be within s. 76, even if their employment on the site is not 'ordinary and regular'. A *self-employed* independent contractor is not protected by regulations under s. 76: *Herbert v Harold Shaw Ltd* [1959] 2 QB 138, [1959] 2 All ER 189; although regulations may impose *duties* on him for his own safety: *Smith v George Wimpey & Co Ltd* [1972] 2 QB 329, [1972] 2 All ER 723; nor is a workman who stays at the premises after working hours to help another man with a private piece of work: *Napieralski v Curtis (Contractors) Ltd* [1959] 2 All ER 426. But a man is still 'employed' and protected by the Act and regulations although he has gone for reasons of his own to a place where he is not authorised to be: *Uddin v Associated Portland Cement Manufacturers Ltd* [1965] 2 QB 582, [1965] 2 All ER 213 (trying to catch pigeon above machine); *Westwood v Post Office* [1974] AC 1, [1973] 3 All ER 184 (man going through motor room of lift, though entry forbidden, for air and relaxation on roof of telephone exchange, injured when trap-door gave way). Some recent codes of regulations specifically exclude such cases from protection.

Although s. 76 (and the old s. 79) give power to make regulations for the benefit of all 'persons employed', it does not follow that this power is exercised in full every time. A code of regulations, or even a particular regulation, may be made for the benefit of a more restricted class of persons; it is always necessary to examine the regulations and to see exactly whom they were intended to benefit. Thus it was held in the *Bryers* case that the Shipbuilding Regulations are for the benefit of all 'persons employed', but no view was expressed on the Docks Regulations, which have given rise to a number of conflicting decisions. Viscount Kilmuir LC thought that express words would be required to limit the scope of regulations.

It is now accepted that regulations under s. 76 may modify the general requirements of the Act, for example, by allowing a limited type of fence to be used on machinery instead of the absolutely 'secure' fencing required by the Act: *John Summers & Sons Ltd v Frost* [1955] AC 740, [1955] 1 All ER 870. Whether regulations actually supersede sections of the Act where it is permissible to do so is a question of interpretation: *Benn v Kamm & Co Ltd* [1952] 2 QB 127, [1952] 1 All ER 833. Contemporary practice, e.g. in the Woodworking Machines Regulations 1974, is to include an express statement on the point.

Regulations made under s. 79 of the Act of 1901 were continued in force by s. 159 of the Factories Act 1937, as if made under s. 60 of that Act, now s. 76 of the 1961 Act; but this did not enlarge their original scope, which must be determined as at the date when they were made: *Canadian Pacific Steamships Ltd v Bryers* [1957] 3 All ER 572. This is why, when railway running sheds and slaughterhouses were brought within the definition of 'factory', existing regulations were expressly applied to them, a somewhat cumbersome procedure.

Regulations made under the Factories Act continue in force in spite of the repeal of the regulation-making power by the Health and Safety at Work Act 1974. However, they are not continued as if made under the 1974 Act and their validity, if brought into question, has still to be tested by seeing whether they were within the powers given by s. 76.

The powers given by the 1974 Act, though modelled on s. 76, are much wider: they allow, for example, regulations to be made for the protection of self-employed persons and of anyone else affected by work activities.

Chapter 10

The Factories Act 1961: general safety requirements

1 General

The requirements as to safety—i.e. safety from personal injuries—are contained in Part II of the Act (ss. 12–56). Part IV contains some further safety requirements for special cases such as injury to the eyes, but was mainly concerned with possible damage to health, such as the effect of dust and harmful substances, and is now replaced by regulations for all places of work (see Chapter 8).

While the safety requirements are imposed primarily for the benefit of the persons normally employed in the factory—ordinarily the employees of the occupier—it has for many years been held that other persons working in the factory from time to time may be within the protection of the Act. In *Lavender v Diamints Ltd* [1949] 1 KB 585, [1949] 1 All ER 532 occupiers were liable to a window-cleaner for failing to provide safe means of access, and in *Whitby v Burt, Boulton and Hayward Ltd* [1947] KB 918, [1947] 2 All ER 324 they were similarly liable to a builder's labourer. In *Ward v Coltness Iron Co Ltd* 1944 SC 318 a workman employed by contractors was injured by the movement of a crane, contrary to s. 24(7) of the Act of 1937 (now s. 27(7)). The occupiers were held liable on the ground that the Act was for the protection of 'all persons ... legitimately present', in addition to the occupiers' own employees. This, however, is too widely stated.

In fact there is some variation from one section of the Act to another: in s. 14 (fencing machinery) it is 'any person employed *or working* on the premises'; in s. 76 (regulations) 'persons employed' only; in s. 29 (safe access) it is 'any person', but the limitation to a place where he 'has to work' makes this also equivalent to 'persons working'.

The House of Lords has held that in s. 29 'any person' means a person working for the purposes of the factory but, within these limits, includes even a person who is self-employed, such as a window-cleaner (for his work is part of the maintenance work in the factory): *Wigley v British Vinegars Ltd* [1964] AC 307, [1962] 3 All ER 161. Such visitors as film actors, police and firemen entering to do their own work (no doubt also factory inspectors, lawyers and technical witnesses) were said to be excluded[1].

'Persons employed', for instance under s. 76 of the Act (authorising regulations) is in one respect narrower (it cannot include a 'self-employed' person), in another wider (it includes employees who are not for the moment actually doing work). In *Canadian Pacific Steamships Ltd v Bryers* [1958] AC 485, [1957] 3 All ER 572 the House of Lords held that the term includes persons employed in a factory, whether or not employed by the occupiers; at least every man 'who is ordinarily and regularly employed' in the premises. But a legitimate visitor to the premises, such as a fireman, who is not a 'person employed', cannot claim damages for breach of the regulations: *Hartley v Mayoh & Co* [1954] 1 QB 383, [1954] 1 All ER 375. Similarly a self-employed contractor is not a 'person employed': *Herbert v Harold Shaw Ltd* [1959] 2 QB 138, [1959] 2 All ER 189; nor is a man who stays late at the factory to help a workmate with a private job: *Napieralski v Curtis (Contractors) Ltd* [1959] 2 All ER 426. While these decisions were given under regulations, they depend on the term 'person employed' in what is now s. 76 of the Act, and therefore would apply to all sections of the Factories Act which, expressly or by implication, are for the benefit of 'persons employed' only. 'Persons employed' includes apprentices (s. 176(7)).

In general 'persons employed' are protected even when they are not actually 'working', and have gone to a place in the factory where they are not authorised to be: *Uddin v Associated Portland Cement Manufacturers*

---

1   Following this a fireman was held not to be protected by s. 29 when injured by an explosion while actually fighting a fire in circumstances outside the occupier's control: *Flannigan v British Dyewood Co Ltd* 1970 SLT 285; but there was some divergence of reasoning, Lord Milligan for instance suggesting that a fireman may be protected when using a means of access to get to a fire, or visiting to check fire precautions.

Ltd [1965] 2 QB 582, [1965] 2 All ER 213 (man chasing pigeon behind machinery). This was approved by the House of Lords in the similar context of the Offices, Shops and Railway Premises Act 1963: *Westwood v Post Office* [1974] AC 1, [1973] 3 All ER 184. But it is subject to the terms of the sections, e.g. safe means of access (s. 29) is required only for a place where a man *has* to work: *Davies v John G. Stein & Co Ltd* 1965 SLT 169[2]. The Shipbuilding Regulations expressly exclude any duty in most cases to persons not doing work and at an unauthorised place: reg. 4(9). So to some extent do the Construction Regulations (reg. 3(1)(a) in both 1961 codes) and the Construction (Working Places) Regulations 1966 (reg. 3(1)(a)).

It is convenient to deal with Part II in the following order:

The static condition of the premises (ss. 28, 29); lifting apparatus (ss. 22–27); vessels containing dangerous liquids (s. 18); fumes in confined spaces (s. 30); explosive and inflammable vapours (s. 31); steam and compressed air apparatus (ss. 32–38); gasholders (s. 39). Fire precautions now fall under special legislation.

The fencing of machinery (ss. 12–17 and 19–21) is so large and important a subject that it requires a chapter to itself.

In general, all obligations under the Factories Act are absolute, unless some such words as 'so far as is reasonably practicable' are used: see, e.g. *Galashiels Gas Co Ltd v O'Donnell (or Millar)* [1949] AC 275, [1949] 1 All ER 319; *John Summers & Sons Ltd v Frost* [1955] AC 740, [1955] 1 All ER 870.

2 Expressions commonly used in the Act: 'of sound construction', 'properly maintained', 'safe', 'secure', etc.

The expression 'sound construction' is used, for example, in s. 28(1) with regard to floors. It implies that the floor shall not only be properly put together but also constructed from 'sound material'. On the other hand, 'good mechanical construction' in s. 22 (hoists and lifts), or 'good construction' in s. 26 (lifting tackle), refers only to the way in which the

---

2   This decision, however, may have taken too narrow a view: see p. 291.

apparatus is pieced together, and therefore these sections add as a further requirement that the lift or hoist must also be of 'sound material'. Apparatus is not of 'good construction' if the design is bad: *Smith v A. Davies & Co (Shopfitters) Ltd* (1968) 5 KIR 320 (horizontal scaffold pole projecting between rungs of ladder).

Material or apparatus may be of 'sound construction' though it breaks down under some exceptional strain: for no material can withstand every possible stress. Things are therefore accepted as 'sound' if they are solid enough to stand the strains capable of arising from normal use at a factory: *Mayne v Johnstone and Cumbers Ltd* [1947] 2 All ER 159. However, it is not enough that material should *appear* to be sound even on the most careful inspection. In deciding this point in *Whitehead v James Stott & Co* [1949] 1 KB 358, [1949] 1 All ER 245, Lord Green MR said:

> 'I cannot read the subsection as referring to anything but an absolute test of soundness.'

A requirement that tackle shall be of sound or good construction, or of adequate strength, or properly maintained, does not mean that it must be of the right design or type for a particular task: *Beadsley v United Steel Companies Ltd* [1951] 1 KB 408, [1950] 2 All ER 872; *Gledhill v Liverpool Abattoir Utility Co Ltd* [1957] 3 All ER 117. The word 'suitable' would have to be used if this meaning were intended.

When the Act uses the expression 'properly maintained', it might be thought that this refers to maintenance in the accepted engineering sense, i.e. inspection and overhaul according to a recognised schedule. This construction, however, was rejected by the House of Lords in *Galashiels Gas Co Ltd v O'Donnell (or Millar)* [1949] AC 275, [1949] 1 All ER 319. S. 176(1) defines 'maintained' to mean 'maintained in an efficient state, in efficient working order, and in good repair'; and the House of Lords decided that as soon as a thing breaks down, it ceases to be 'maintained in efficient working order', and *ipso facto* the statutory duty is broken[3]. The definition must be applied of course according to

---

3   Followed in *Hamilton v National Coal Board* [1960] AC 633, [1960] 1 All ER 76 (under Mines and Quarries Act). Lord Keith reserved the question of breakdown through a 'latent defect' if—which seems improbable—such a latent defect could be present in the first instance consistently with 'good construction, suitable material, adequate strength', etc. as required by the Mines and Quarries Act 1954, s. 81.

the context. Where a *floor* has to be 'of sound construction and properly maintained'—s. 25(1) of the Act of 1937, now the first clause of s. 28(1)—obviously the words 'in efficient working order' have no application at all; and the words 'in an efficient state' are limited to keeping the permanent structure and surface of the floor in a good condition, so that this part of the subsection has nothing to do with articles or liquids lying on the floor: *Latimer v AEC Ltd* [1953] AC 643, [1953] 2 All ER 449. (Words have since been added to meet the latter case.)

The Act frequently uses the expression 'provide and maintain'. Here 'provide' refers to the initial supply, and 'maintain' to keeping the thing supplied in continuous good condition[4]. In general, where a safety appliance is in question, it is not 'provided' unless it is available and ready to hand: *Norris v Syndic Manufacturing Co Ltd* [1952] 2 QB 135, [1952] 1 All ER 935. If, unknown to the workman, it is available in the stores, that does not comply with the statutory requirement: *Finch v Telegraph Construction and Maintenance Co Ltd* [1949] 1 All ER 452. 'Providing' equipment such as goggles does not involve giving orders that they must be used: *Bux v Slough Metals Ltd* [1974] 1 All ER 262. Where authorised equipment or facilities have been 'provided' by the employer and are available, equipment substituted by an employee on his own initiative has not been 'provided' by the employer so as to make him responsible for any deficiency in it: *Smith v British Aerospace* [1982] ICR 98.

All general expressions relating to good construction and maintenance are concerned with the safety aspect, so that a floor which has a shallow depression but is not unsafe does not contravene the Act: *Payne v Weldless Steel Tube Co Ltd* [1956] 1 QB 196, [1955] 3 All ER 612.

In a number of sections it is provided that inspection or testing must be carried out by a 'competent person'. There is no definition of this term: but on the analogy of *Butler (or Black) v Fife Coal Co Ltd* [1912] AC 149, a case decided under the Coal Mines Act, it would seem that a competent person must have, in addition to any necessary technical knowledge, the practical experience required to recognise the dangers likely to arise[5]. Under the regulations for work in compressed air, a man was not 'competent' to be in charge of a decompression chamber when he did not

4   As to 'provide' and 'maintain', see also the cases cited at pp. 296–297, *post*.
5   This paragraph is inserted in response to an inquiry from the Royal Society for the Prevention of Accidents. For details of the case cited, see p. 132, *ante*.

appreciate the importance of his duties and of strict compliance with the regulations: *Ransom v Sir Robert McAlpine & Sons Ltd* (1971) 11 KIR 141.

'Plant' is a word with a wide *potential* meaning which takes its colour from the context: thus in *Haigh v Charles W Ireland Ltd* [1973] 3 All ER 1137 it meant the factory's own installations, not articles brought in for processing.

'Process' is a word whose meaning may vary according to the context. If the context is limited to a manufacturing establishment which carries on the same activities continuously, it may mean an operation which is continuously repeated and exclude a single operation such as dismantling a structure. But in the context of regulations limiting exposure to asbestos dust, which applies not only to factories but to building operations, 'process' includes a single operation such as demolition of a structure if it has some degree of continuity or repetition: *Nurse v Morganite Crucible Ltd* [1989] AC 692, [1989] 1 All ER 113, HL, overruling *R. v AI Industrial Products PLC* [1987] 2 All ER 368.

The expressions 'practicable' and 'reasonably practicable' are explained in Chapter 6, section 8.

The words 'safe', 'secure' and 'dangerous' recur again and again throughout the Factories Act, and, indeed, throughout all safety legislation. So far as any general meaning can be given to these words, 'secure' and 'safe' appear to mean the same thing, while 'dangerous' has exactly the opposite meaning. Thus machinery is 'securely' fenced if the 'danger' contemplated by the statute is removed: *John Summers & Sons Ltd v Frost* [1955] AC 740, [1955] 1 All ER 870. In earlier cases the point was emphasised that 'safe' means absolutely safe, in others it was said that it is in some way relative. The opinion of Lord Reid in *Summers v Frost* throws new light on this problem. The proper approach in each case is: what is the danger contemplated by the statute? A thing will then be 'safe' if the danger in contemplation is removed, but not otherwise. Thus the working face is intended to be 'secure' against accidental fall, but not against deliberate operations to bring down the coal: *Gough v National Coal Board* [1959] AC 698, [1959] 2 All ER 164. In one sense, therefore, 'safety' is relative, as it is related to some specific danger: in another sense it is absolute, as the specific danger must be completely eliminated. Modern authorities, including *Summers v Frost*, have adopted as a test for 'danger', at any rate as regards fencing of machinery, that injury from the machine must be 'reasonably foreseeable', and this interpretation has spread to 'safety' in other connections such as means of access or electrical safety. This is an unfortunate gloss on the statute, which has led to great and unnecessary uncertainty, as defendants constantly argue that a particular accident is 'unforeseeable', and when it is a matter of looking into the future, instead of looking at the machinery or other thing in itself, everyone has different ideas. At first sight this appears to discard the older case-law which required 'absolute safety', but such an impression may be misleading. It has long been established that in deciding on danger or safety, the careless or inadvertent worker as well as the prudent must be taken into account: e.g. *Keenan v Rolls-Royce Ltd* 1970 SLT 90. In fact the 'foreseeability' test was originally introduced to widen rather than restrict the safety legislation, because it was argued that machinery or access, as the case may be, need only be safe for persons using it correctly. The foreseeability test emphasises that careless or even wilful misuse may have to be allowed for.

But 'safe' and 'dangerous' are ordinary English words, which can in most cases be applied in a common sense way without further elaboration.

3 The condition of the factory premises

(1) Floors, steps, stairs, passages and gangways

By s. 28(1):

> 'All floors, steps, stairs, passages and gangways shall be of sound construction and properly maintained. . . .'

This requirement may extend to places outside the factory as well as inside, such as a plank over a ditch in the factory grounds: *Hosking v De Havilland Aircraft Co Ltd* [1949] 1 All ER 540.

The requirement that the floors and other places mentioned shall be of sound construction was considered in *Mayne v Johnstone and Cumbers Ltd* [1947] 2 All ER 159 where the floor of a factory gave way when a heavy machine fell on to it in the course of installation. On the facts, the court decided that the floor was not sound, but did not think it necessary that, to comply with the statute, a floor should be capable of withstanding every strain, however great. It must be 'sound' in the sense that it is 'fit for the work which it is anticipated is to be done on it'—i.e. fit for use as the floor of a factory. Within these limits, the obligation to keep the floor sound is an absolute one, and it is no defence to show that the defect could not have been discovered by reasonable inspection: *Whitehead v Stott (James) & Co* [1949] 1 KB 358, [1949] 1 All ER 245 (a decision on similar words in s. 22). Thus, under s. 28, the occupier is liable for undiscoverable latent defects in the structure: *Latimer v AEC Ltd* [1952] 2 QB 701 at 711, [1952] 1 All ER 1302 at 1306. A minor defect such as a shallow depression in a floor does not contravene the section unless it makes the floor unsafe: *Payne v Weldless Steel Tube Co Ltd* [1956] 1 QB 196, [1955] 3 All ER 612; and the words 'sound construction' (which mean 'well built', 'well made'), are not infringed by a small defect in design, such as a small difference in level between a grating and a manhole, if indeed the section contemplates faulty design at all: *Hawkins v Westinghouse Brake and Signal Co* (1958) 109 L Jo 89[6]. But wearing and chipping of stone steps which creates risk of tripping is a breach of s. 28(1): *Fisher v Port of London Authority* [1962] 1 All ER 458.

The term 'floor' includes the raised platform of a gantry: *Morris v Port of London Authority* (1950) 84 L1 LRep 564; and also, it seems, a raised sill running round the side of a dry dock: *Taylor v Green (R and H) and Silley Weir Ltd* [1951] 1 Lloyd's Rep 345. It does not include planks laid in an irregular way across the open steelwork of a gantry: *Tate v Swan Hunter and Wigham Richardson Ltd* [1958] 1 All ER 150; nor the earth surface of an open woodyard: *Sullivan v Hall Russell & Co Ltd* 1964 SLT 192; nor (for the purpose of 'obstruction') a part of the floor set aside for storage: *Pengelley v Bell Punch Co Ltd* [1964] 2 All ER 945; nor the floor of a furnace under construction: *Johnston v Colvilles Ltd* 1966 SLT 30. But it was held to include the bottom of a concrete duct on which employees were, from time to time, required to stand and walk: *Devine v Costain Concrete Co Ltd* 1979 SLT (Notes) 97.

A roadway 30 feet wide outside the factory buildings is neither a 'gangway' nor a 'passage': *Thornton v Fisher and Ludlow Ltd* [1968] 2 All ER 241.

---

6   *Good* construction covers design: *Smith v A. Davies & Co (Shopfitters) Ltd* (1968) 5 KIR 320.

The duty to 'maintain' (i.e. as defined in s. 176, 'in an efficient state . . . and in good repair') was limited, as the section originally stood in the 1937 Act, to the structure of the floor and its permanent surface and fitments: it did not apply to 'a transient and exceptional condition' such as a pool of slippery liquid or an obstruction: *Latimer v AEC Ltd* [1953] AC 643 at 654, 656, [1953] 2 All ER 449 at 452, 453, approving *Davies v De Havilland Aircraft Co Ltd* [1951] 1 KB 50, [1950] 2 All ER 582[7]. But the following words have now been added at the end of s. 28(1) in the 1961 Act:

> '. . . and shall, so far as is reasonably practicable, be kept free from any obstruction and from any substance likely to cause persons to slip.'

Obstructions and slipperiness may now, therefore, give rise to liability under the section, but this is not, as will be seen, an absolute liability like those arising from structural defects. *Obstruction* is a vague and troublesome word which is always giving rise to litigation. It means, broadly, something which is in the way and has no business to be there. So it does not include projecting parts of fixed machinery: *Drummond v Harland Engineering Co Ltd* 1963 SC 162; or materials stored regularly adjacent to storage racks: *Pengelly v Bell Punch Co Ltd, supra*; or a cable, unless it had ceased to be in use and should have been removed: *Lynch v Babcock Power Ltd* 1988 SLT 307n; or a trolley delivering material to machines: *Marshall v Ericsson Telephones Ltd* [1964] 3 All ER 609. If the trolley had been left unnecessarily long it would have become an obstruction, like the heavy metal plates covering pits which had been removed and had not been replaced when work in the pits was finished (or suspended): these were held by the House of Lords to be obstructions: *Dorman Long (Steel) Ltd v Bell* [1964] 1 All ER 617. It was also held in this case that 'slipperiness' on the obstructing plates, as

---

7   Under the Woodworking Machines Regulations 1974, reg. 11, the floor surrounding such a machine must be kept in good and level condition, and free (as far as practicable) from chips and other loose material, and must not be allowed to become slippery; under the Horizontal Milling Machines Regulations reg. 1, the floor 'immediately surrounding' these machines must be kept in good and even condition and free from loose material, and 'effective' measures must be taken to prevent it from becoming slippery. Regulation 17 of the Abrasive Wheels Regulations 1970 is similar. See the appropriate sections of Chapter 11.

The opinions in *Latimer v A.E.C.* do not entirely coincide. Lords Reid and Asquith limit the duty to the structure of the floor, while apparently Lords Porter and Oaksey consider that a general dangerous condition of the floor, not merely temporary, would be a breach of the section.

distinct from the floor, is a breach of the section. The high-water mark on obstructions is *Jenkins v Allied Ironfounders Ltd* [1969] 3 All ER 1609 where castings were put in a pile on the foundry floor, and as soon as part of the pile had been cleared, metal scraps left behind were held to become obstructions: but on the facts (as usually happens in such extreme cases) it was not reasonably practicable either to prevent the scraps breaking off, or to clear them away at once. A screw which caused a wheelbarrow to swerve was held to be an obstruction, but here too it was not practicable to do more than the employers were doing to keep the floor clear: *Gillies v Glynwed Foundries* 1977 SLT 97.

Even water (wet patches left after cleaning), where lying on a metal grating, has been held to be a 'substance likely to cause persons to slip': *Taylor v Gestetner Ltd* (1967) 2 KIR 133. However, where the tiled floor of a dairy was kept constantly wet for hygienic reasons, there was no infringement of s. 28(1), presumably because no other course was practicable: *Gay v St Cuthbert's Co-operative Association* 1977 SC 212 (the claim succeeded on the ground that taking bottles across the floor by hand was an unsafe system).

'Reasonably practicable' is a matter of fact, and may require the bringing of a crane, though inconvenient, to replace heavy metal covers: *Dorman Long (Steel) Ltd v Bell, supra*; and keeping a bus depot floor free of oil patches: *Fern v Dundee Corpn* 1964 SLT 294; where the obstruction or slippery substance has properly arisen in the first place, it is sufficient to prove a regular system for clearing up: *Braham v J. Lyons & Co Ltd* [1962] 3 All ER 281. But it may also be reasonably practicable to prevent the danger arising at all, for example by instructions against littering the floor: *Hall v Fairfield Shipbuilding & Engineering Co Ltd* 1964 SC (HL) 72; or by stopping excessive use of grease on an overhead crane: *Williams v Painter Bros Ltd* (1968) 5 KIR 487. The duty under s. 28(1) is not only to clean the floor but to prevent substances from getting there: *Johnston or Caddies Wainwright* [1983] ICR 407. Nevertheless where the pursuer slipped on a patch of water no bigger than a 10p coin (3cm. diameter) the defenders were not required to prove that this did not come from any source for which they were responsible in order to establish the defence: *Brown v Rowntree Mackintosh* 1983 SLT (Sh Ct) 47.

The decisions on 'obstructions' summarised above also turn on what is reasonably practicable, in so far as they relate to things 'in the way' for the purpose of work being done, but not left for longer than necessary.

Other cases on 'reasonably practicable' and in particular the onus of proof are discussed under s. 29 (means of access).

(2) Rails for staircases

By s. 28(2):

> 'For every staircase in a building or affording a means of exit from a building, a substantial handrail shall be provided and maintained, which, if the staircase has an open side, shall be on that side.'

The subsection goes on:

> 'In the case of a staircase having two open sides, or in the case of a staircase which, owing to the nature of its construction or the condition of the surface of the steps or other special circumstances, is specially liable to cause accidents, such a handrail shall be provided and maintained on both sides[8].'

In this section, apparently, in view of the word 'substantial', a handrail is intended to serve the purpose of a guard-rail as well as a handhold: *Corn v Weir's Glass (Hanley) Ltd* [1960] 2 All ER 300. Finally, there is this further requirement in s. 28(3):

> 'Any open side of a staircase shall also be guarded by the provision and maintenance of a lower rail or other effective means.'

Here 'effective means' must be taken to be something which in fact accomplishes the purpose of protection, at any rate to the same extent as a lower rail: see *Lotinga v North Eastern Marine Engineering Co (1938) Ltd* [1941] 2 KB 399, [1941] 3 All ER 1.

Sections 28 (2) and (3) use the term 'staircase', as distinct from 'steps' and 'stairs' in s. 28(1). It has been held that 'staircase', in the everyday use of the word, does not include a set of three steel steps leading to a platform: *Kimpton v Steel Co of Wales Ltd* [1960] 2 All ER 274.

---

8 'Special' liability for accidents can hardly be inferred when no accident has occurred for many years; and neither the occasional presence of a little grease, nor the presence of a highly polished strip of metal, can be treated as a 'special circumstance' necessitating a second handrail: *Harris v Rugby Portland Cement Co Ltd* [1955] 2 All ER 500.

(3) Openings in floors[9]

By s. 28(4):

> 'All openings in floors shall be securely fenced, except in so far as the nature of the work renders such fencing impracticable.'

A dry dock is not an 'opening in a floor' within this subsection: *Bath v British Transport Commission* [1954] 2 All ER 542. But a surface of sand in a foundry is a 'floor' and a hole cut out to form the bed of a casting is an 'opening': *Harrison v Metropolitan-Vickers Electrical Co Ltd* [1954] 1 All ER 404. So is a shallow pit: *Sanders v F. H. Lloyd & Co* [1982] ICR 360. A furnace floor under construction, with an open flue, is not within s. 28(4): *Johnston v Colvilles Ltd* 1966 SLT 30. The edge of a floor, for instance at a loading bay, is not an 'opening' in the floor: *Allen v Avon Rubber Co* (1986) Times, 20 May, CA. The point had been left open in earlier cases.

In *Barrington v Kent Rivers Catchment Board* [1947] 2 All ER 782 a plaintiff recovered damages when he fell into an open inspection pit at a garage, no work being done at the time which would render fencing impracticable. Even where work is in continual progress, it is not necessarily 'impracticable' to have fencing, e.g. it may be practicable, though inconvenient, to have a 'gate' to allow access: *Street v British Electricity Authority, supra.* On the other hand, the subsection does *not* say that openings are to be fenced *or covered over* unless the nature of the work renders this impracticable. They are to be fenced, but if this is impracticable there is no further obligation (at any rate under this subsection) to minimise the risk by covering the hole[10].

(4) Ladders

By s. 28(5):

> 'All ladders shall be soundly constructed and properly maintained.'

For the meaning of 'soundly constructed' and 'properly maintained', see

---

9   See also s. 22(4) and s. 24 as to lift and hoist shafts, pp. 302–304, *post.*

10 The burden of proving impracticability is on the defendant: *Buchan v Hutchison & Co Ltd* 1953 SLT 306.

section 2 of this Chapter, *ante*. 'Maintained' means maintained 'in an efficient state . . . and in good repair' (s. 176(1)). A step-ladder is a 'ladder' within the subsection: *Ross v British Steel Corpn (Colvilles) Ltd* 1973 SLT (Notes) 34.

In *Cole v Blackstone & Co Ltd* [1943] KB 615 the rung of a ladder gave way unexpectedly, though all reasonable care had been taken to inspect the ladder. Macnaghten J said:

> 'The fact that the rung gave way establishes . . . that the ladder was not in an efficient state and in good repair at that time.'

This decision was approved by the House of Lords in *Galashiels Gas Co Ltd v O'Donnell (or Millar)* [1949] AC 275, [1949] 1 All ER 319.

(5) Safe means of access and safe place of work

Section 28 deals with various parts of the factory which are usual means of access, such as floors, steps and passageways. Under s. 28 there is absolute liability for structural defects in those particular places. There is also—under words which were originally added by the Factories Act 1959—a qualified liability (limited to what is 'reasonably practicable') for slippery surfaces and obstructions.   s. 28

Section 29(1) is much more general. Originally (as s. 26(1) of the Factories Act 1937) it related only to 'means of access' to places of work. An amendment made by the Factories Act 1959 extended it to the place of work itself. Section 29(1) now reads as follows, the words in italics having been added in 1959:   History

> 'There shall, so far as is reasonably practicable, be provided and maintained safe means of access to every place at which any person has at any time to work, *and every such place shall, so far as reasonably practicable, be made and kept safe for any person working there.*'

Many cases were decided under the old s. 26(1). They were not always consistent, and most of them must now be considered out-dated. The subsection lost some of its importance when slipperiness and obstructions were brought within s. 28, but is widened by the extension to the place of work.

Section 29(1) is in three ways in marked contrast to s. 28:

(i)   it is quite general: it applies to all means of access and all places of work;

(ii) s. 28 was originally confined to structural safety, though later extended to slipperiness and obstructions; but s. 29(1) leaves the question of 'safety' completely at large—slipperiness and obstructions have always been accepted as grounds of liability, and so have incidental hazards such as furnaces, electrical apparatus and flying particles, especially in the Scottish cases;

(iii) liability for structural safety under s. 28 is absolute; but under s. 29(1) the occupier of the factory is not bound to do more than is 'reasonably practicable'.

These various aspects of s. 29(1) must now be examined in detail.

(i) What are means of access?

Section 29(1) applies to every means of access to every place of work without exception, even such unusual places as roofs and tall chimneys. The occupiers were held liable when a window-cleaner had to climb over an asbestos roof which gave way: *Lavender v Diamints Ltd* [1949] 1 KB 585, [1949] 1 All ER 532. The Court of Appeal rejected the argument that the section applied only to access inside the factory, and Tucker LJ said:

> 'Safe access must be provided to all places within the curtilage or precincts where any person has to work.'

A fortiori a ladder, and a plank across a ditch, are within the section: *McCarthy v Coldair Ltd* [1951] 2 TLR 1226; *Hosking v De Havilland Aircraft Co Ltd* [1949] 1 All ER 540. More generally, Lord Greene MR said in *Hopwood v Rolls-Royce Ltd* (1947) 176 LT 514:

> 'A workman is entitled to have a safe means of access to his work whatever other workmen may use that means of access, and even if it is not a recognised gangway, or something of that kind.'

So—as shown by *Hopwood*—a workman may use a 'means of access' simply by moving across the factory floor from one point to another in the course of his work. The House of Lords have similarly said that the section is wide enough to include all means of access within the factory perimeter, and in particular means of access over an article under manufacture or repair—in this case a ship in a shipyard: *Gardiner v Admiralty Comrs* [1964] 2 All ER 93, [1964] 1 WLR 590. That part of an outside car park over which workers had to walk to reach the pathway to the factory was within the section: *Woodward v Renold Ltd* [1980] ICR 387.

(ii) Place of work

'Place' itself is interpreted in a broad sense: the cabin of a fire engine was a place of work for an electrician carrying out maintenance: *Cox v HCB Angus Ltd* [1981] ICR 683.

(iii) Place where a person 'has to work'

In the older cases the words 'has to' work were interpreted very narrowly: for example claims failed in *Davies v J. G. Stein & Co Ltd* 1965 SLT 169 where a man worked on planks by a machine when he could have worked in a safer position, and in *Dryland v London Electrical Manufacturing Co Ltd* (1949) 99 L Jo 665, where a man supervising the erection of an aerial on a roof moved over to remove an old aerial as to which he had been given no instructions. Such cases must be considered obsolete in view of the decision of the House of Lords in *Smith (or Westwood) v National Coal Board* [1967] 2 All ER 593, [1967] 1 WLR 871 where, under similar words in Mines Regulations, it was held that 'required to go' did not mean instructed or ordered but included all places where a man reasonably went for the purposes of his work.

On the other hand a means of access is not protected unless it leads to a place where a man has to work. So there was no liability in *Rose v Colvilles Ltd* 1950 SLT (Notes) 72 where red-hot slag fell on a man as he was going to a toilet; or in *Davies v De Havilland Aircraft Co Ltd* [1951] 1 KB 50, [1950] 2 All ER 582 where the plaintiff was on the way to a canteen. However, it could be argued that this line of reasoning too is mistaken, because a 'means of access' leads both ways, to the toilet or canteen but also back to work: and if it must be safe in one direction, surely it should also be safe in the other direction and it does not matter which way a person is going.

(iv) Distinction between place of work and access to it

This is of diminished importance since the protection of the section was extended to the place of work, but may still perhaps arise. Under the old case-law in England, the place of work itself could not at the same time be a 'means of access', even when the plaintiff was working from a staging which would naturally fall within that description: *Lovell v Blundells and Crompton & Co Ltd* [1944] KB 502, [1944] 2 All ER 53; and continuous movements within a work area, doing work all the time, were not using means of access: *Dorman Long & Co Ltd v Hillier* [1951] 1 All ER 357 (removing sheets of corrugated iron from roof); *Australian Iron and Steel Pty v Luna* (1969) 44 ALJR 52 (moving along train applying fireclay from barrow). On the other hand, moving from one work point to another, though fairly close, was protected: *Hopwood v Rolls-Royce Ltd* (1947) 176 LT 514, CA (carrying cylinder across floor to inspection point, and then a short way beyond as directed); *Taylor v Coalite Oils and Chemicals Ltd* (1967) 3 KIR 315 (walking a short distance along railway track to pick up shovel). But the Scottish courts saw no reason why a man should not be at his place of work and yet using a means of access—as when a man was engaged in stacking rolls of paper in a passageway used for access: *Alison v Henry Bruce & Son Ltd* 1951 SLT 399.

Common sense suggests that under the present section, once a person has entered the perimeter of the factory or other workplace, he will either be at his place of work or using access to it unless he is carrying out unauthorised exploration of places where he is not supposed to be. Parliament must certainly have intended that the two alternatives should together give comprehensive cover. In a Scottish case, however, the appeal court took a narrow view. The pursuer was fixing a duct in the ceiling, working from a trestle, stepped down from the trestle, moved away a few paces and stepped on a sheet of cardboard covering the floor which slipped under him. It was held that, having moved away, he was neither at his place of work nor using access to it: *Morrow v Enterprise Sheet Metal Works (Aberdeen) Ltd* 1986 SLT 697.

(v) When is access—or place—unsafe?
The meaning of 'safe' and 'dangerous' under the Factories Act was discussed at p. 282, *ante.* 'Safe' is, however, a simple English word and there is no reason why it should not be decided as a pure question of fact whether a place is 'safe' or not. Unfortunately, the vague and uncertain notion of 'foreseeability' has been introduced as a test. So long as it is used as no more than a test, there is no great harm, but it would be unfortunate if it were used to limit and circumscribe the plain meaning of 'safe'. In *Robertson v R B Cowe & Co Ltd* 1970 SLT 122 the Court of Session said that 'foreseeability' does not have to be proved to establish that a thing was unsafe, but only at the later stage of deciding what was 'reasonably practicable'. In the later case of *Morrow v Enterprise Sheet Metal Works (Aberdeen) Ltd* 1986 SLT 697, on the other hand, they

applied the foreseeability test to decide that there was nothing 'unsafe' about cardboard sheets protecting the floor surface, which slid away when trodden on.

(a) Structural safety   A place or means of access may be unsafe because of a structural fault, as in *Lavender v Diamints, supra,* where a window-cleaner had to climb over an asbestos roof too weak to bear his weight; *Hosking v De Havilland, supra,* where a plank broke; *Whitby v Burt, Boulton and Hayward Ltd* [1947] KB 918, [1947] 2 All ER 324, where a roof of corrugated iron was supported by unsound timber which gave way. A trestle was *ipso facto* unsafe when it gave way under a painter working in a normal manner, the court having rejected the contention that he overreached to save the trouble of moving the trestle: *Robertson v R. B. Cowe & Co Ltd, supra.*

The failure to provide a structural aid which is necessary for safety may likewise be a breach of the statutory duty, as in *Bowen v Mills and Knight Ltd* [1973] 1 Lloyd's Rep 580 where cross beams in a dry dock gave inadequate access to staging and a ladder should have been provided; and in *Smith v British Railways Board* [1986] CLY unreported appeal No. 20, where, because a storage area was frequently used, the court held that a fixed ladder was necessary for safe access.

(b) Obstructions and slipperiness   The section has never been limited to structural faults. In several cases the means of access (usually the factory floor) has been rendered unsafe to workers by obstructions, especially when they were carrying loads or moving backwards: *Callaghan v Kidd (Fred) & Son (Engineers) Ltd* [1944] 1 KB 560, [1944] 1 All ER 525 (iron bars caused plaintiff to fall against grindstone); *Hopwood v Rolls-Royce, supra* (a man walking backwards carrying one end of heavy cylinder caught foot on obstruction). Loose piping in the cab of a fire engine, which could have been moved to one side, was in breach of the section: *Cox v HCB Angus Ltd* [1981] ICR 683; but rubber pipes one inch in diameter which crossed a gangway were not unsafe as workers could see them, though they had also to watch an adjacent crane: *Brown v Redpath Brown & Co Ltd* 1963 SLT 219.

Slipperiness and unevenness in the floor or other means of access may be a breach of the section, but the courts tend to disregard trivial faults. So slight unevenness between a piece of linoleum and the edge of a step did not make the place unsafe: *Joyce v Boots Cash Chemists (Southern) Ltd* [1951] 1 All ER 682n.; nor a small patch of oil or mud in a factory passage: *Davies v De Havilland Aircraft Co Ltd, supra*; nor a tile raised by ¼ inch: *Pickford v Control Data* [1985] CLY unreported appeal No. 40; nor a sheet of cardboard protecting a floor, which slid when stepped on: *Morrow v Enterprise Sheet Metal Works (Aberdeen), supra*. On the other hand a ladder was an unsafe means of access when it rested on a surface where it was liable to slip: *McCarthy v Coldair Ltd* [1951] 2 TLR 1226; and if a ladder has to be secured or held to prevent slipping, it is not safe until secured or held: *Geddes v United Wires Ltd* 1974 SLT 170. The mere fact that a ladder slipped is sufficient proof that it was unsafe if the defendants call no evidence: *Gardner v John Thompson (Wolverhampton) Ltd* (1969) 6 KIR 1. The iced-up surface of a car park which passengers had to walk across to reach the factory was unsafe as a means of access and ought to have been gritted: *Woodward v Renold Ltd* [1980] ICR 387; but failure to salt ice before 0745 a.m. was not necessarily a breach of the section: *Darby v G. K. N. Screws and Fasteners Ltd* [1986] ICR 1. Such cases depend on what is 'reasonably practicable'.

In England, in spite of all these authorities, it was suggested in one case that the section requires structural safety only and that all previous decisions should be reconsidered: *Levesley v Thomas Firth and John Brown Ltd* [1953] 2 All ER 866, [1953] 1 WLR 1206. Slipperiness or obstructions, it was said, cannot be a breach of the obligation to *provide* safe means of access but only of the obligation to *maintain*; and it was said that 'once a safe means of access is provided . . . the occupier is not responsible for every temporary obstruction' or transient condition, such as a patch of oil. These doubts were unquestionably misconceived and due to a misunderstanding of a House of Lords decision, as will be explained below under 'Provide and maintain', where there is an authoritative statement of the correct principle by both English and Scottish judges. The actual decision and others which followed it[11] can be justified on the ground that there was a reasonable system of clearing. Of course, if a condition is transient or temporary there may not have been time to rectify it and the defence that it was not reasonably practicable to do so may succeed.

(c) Other dangers The earlier English cases treated 'safety' as something quite general, the *Levesley* case being a transient aberration;

---

11 *Woods v W H Rhodes & Son Ltd* [1953] 2 All ER 658; *Taylor v Coalite Oils and Chemicals* (1967) 3 KIR 315; *Stanley v Concentric (Pressed Products) Ltd* (1971) 11 KIR 260.

and the Scottish authorities have consistently followed the same line. Thus safety might be affected by the location of the access or place of work in proximity to such dangers as unfenced drops, furnaces, machinery, flying particles and electrical apparatus: *Rose v Colvilles Ltd* 1950 SLT (Notes) 72 (red-hot slag); *Street v British Electricity Authority* [1952] 2 QB 399, [1952] 1 All ER 679 (unfenced drop). The edge of a loading bay was unsafe without a fence when it was practicable to fence it: *Allen v Avon Rubber Co Ltd* [1986] ICR 695. But in another case coloured tape was held sufficient protection round a hole in the floor: *Rigg v Central Electricity Generating Board* (1985) Times, 23 February. The absence of a guard rail may make the place of work unsafe under s. 29(1) although there is sufficient handhold and therefore no guard rail is required under s. 29(2): *Keenan v Rolls-Royce Ltd* 1970 SLT 90 (foreseeable that man might overbalance when unscrewing pipe with heavy wrench); so may an inadequate guard rail with only a top bar: *McClymont v Glasgow Corpn* 1971 SLT 45 (platform 4 ft. high for servicing buses, guard rail provided but man fell through gap below it while squatting to carry out work). Even excessive noise (drop hammers loud enough to cause pain and deafness) has been held to make the place unsafe: *Carragher v Singer Manufacturing Ltd* 1974 SLT (Notes) 28. Lord Maxwell saw no reason why the section should not cover 'safety from heat, light and noise' as well as tangible things. This was followed in *Canning v Kings & Co Ltd* 1986 SLT 107 where the place of work was rendered unsafe by dangerous fumes. Another example is contamination by liquid causing dermatitis: *Yates v Rockwell Graphic Systems* [1988] ICR 8. But an electric heater which, though turned on, was not visibly glowing, did not infringe the section when there was no foreseeable risk that someone would fall against it: *Hunter v British Steel Corpn* 1980 SLT 31[12].

It is to be noted that although there is no explicit decision in the House of Lords under s. 29(1) on this particular point, they have taken it for granted on no fewer than three occasions that in a similar context safety is quite general and certainly includes a fall from a height: *O'Donnell v Murdoch Mackenzie & Co Ltd* 1967 SC (HL) 63; *Gibson v British Insulated Callenders Construction Co Ltd* 1973 SLT 2; *Nimmo v Alexander Cowan & Sons Ltd* [1968] AC 107, [1967] 3 All ER 187. In

---

12 The pursuer said he had stumbled and fallen against it: the sheriff held that he had a blackout and sat on it.

Nimmo—the only case under s. 29—the risk was the collapse of a load from a railway wagon.

(d) No liability for use of access by others   Liability under s. 29 is limited to the *condition* of the access and does not extend to the use of it by others, though of course the employer or occupier may be liable for this on other grounds. So there was no liability for the negligent driving of a lorry in the factory yard: *Higgins v Lyons (J.) & Co Ltd* (1941) 85 Sol Jo 93; nor where an apprentice jumped up and collided with the pursuer: *Hawkins v McCluskey* 1987 SLT 289.

(vi) More than one means of access
It has been said that where there are two means of access or routes 'equally liable to attract a workman', both ought to be kept safe, but it is otherwise if one route is safe and the workman is unlikely to choose another: *Donovan v Cammell Laird & Co* [1949] 2 All ER 82. But in Scotland it has been held that if the access is unsafe because of obstructions, it is no excuse that another route was available: *Kirkpatrick v Scott Lithgow Ltd* 1987 SLT 654. It is thought that there is no absolute rule either way, and much depends on the lay-out. For example if the means of access are inside a building and are 'provided' there, such as two staircases, both must obviously be kept 'safe' unless one of them is officially 'closed'. The difficulties arise where the access is over outside areas or through plant and machinery, and there is no officially designated way, so that workers are left to make the choice. At any rate, where there is a good wide and safe route which can be followed, a court is entitled to find that the section has been complied with, although there is another narrow and dangerous route: *Street v British Electricity Authority, supra*. Where employers had provided a perfectly safe fixed flight of steps with a handrail for access to staging round an aircraft, they were not liable to a plaintiff who chose to use portable steps: they had not 'provided' them: *Smith v British Aerospace* [1982] ICR 98.

(vii) 'Provided and maintained'
These are now standard terms in the Factories Act and other safety legislation, and a general explanation was given in Chapter 10, section 2.

In general, equipment such as a ladder is 'provided' as a means of access when, although it is not in position, the workman knows where he can get it: *Farquhar v Chance Bros Ltd* [1951] 2 TLR 666. More generally a moveable appliance is provided if it is 'ready to hand in a proper place': *Norris v Syndic Manufacturing Co Ltd* [1952] 2 QB 135, [1952] 1 All ER 935.

'Maintain' is defined in s. 176(1) of the Factories Act as a requirement to maintain 'in an efficient state, in efficient working order and in good repair'. This definition has to be applied to a wide variety of things and must be interpreted according to the subject-matter, which can be anything from rough open ground to a floor or machinery. In *Latimer v A.E.C.*, which was fully considered at p. 285, *ante*, the House of Lords had to apply the definition to a floor under s. 28. Now s. 28 (at that time) was concerned solely with structure, so it is not surprising that the House of Lords held that 'maintain' was limited to maintaining the structure and had nothing to do with transient slipperiness on the surface, unless perhaps this was due to a material such as varnish incorporated in the structure. Unfortunately in the *Levesley* case (p. 294, *supra*) the Court of Appeal misunderstood this and suggested that it applied also to s. 29, so that the obligation to provide related only to the structure and there was no liability for transient conditions. This is clearly inconsistent with whole lines of authority. When the definition of 'maintain' is applied to 'safe means of access' the correct interpretation is plain enough. The duty to 'provide' is to provide (i) a means of access (ii) which is safe. So the duty to 'maintain' it is not only to maintain it as a means of access, but to maintain it in a safe condition—subject, of course, as both branches of the duty are, to what is 'reasonably practicable'. As Scott LJ said in *Callaghan v Kidd (Fred) & Son (Engineers) Ltd, supra*, 'those words are equivalent to maintain the safety of the access, and impose a positive and continuing duty'. Lord Robertson said in a valuable judgment in *Geddes v United Wires Ltd* 1974 SLT 170:

> 'It is certainly the *means* of access which has to be provided, but it has to be a "safe" means of access at the start, and . . . must be "maintained" . . . as a safe means of access, in its condition, location and structure.'

These words, 'condition, location and structure', admirably sum up the very general nature of the protection which the section gives.

(viii) 'So far as is reasonably practicable'
This is now a standard expression in the Factories Act and other safety legislation to indicate a rather less strict statutory duty, and there is a full

explanation in Chapter 6, section 8. 'Practicable' by itself means that which is feasible or possible. In considering what is 'reasonably practicable', however, the expense and other disadvantages of safety measures must be balanced against the magnitude of the risk. Thus, as was said in *McCarthy v Coldair Ltd* [1951] 2 TLR 1226, it would not be reasonably practicable to have a man at the foot of every ladder to prevent it from slipping, as this would involve an excessive requirement for manpower. Again, while such things as obstructions and ice and snow make the access 'unsafe', a temporary delay in removing them is not a breach of the section if a reasonable system is in operation: *Thomas v Bristol Aeroplane Co Ltd* [1954] 2 All ER 1; *Levesley v Thomas Firth and John Brown Ltd* [1953] 2 All ER 866, [1953] 1 WLR 1206. But the system of clearing away dangers after they have arisen is not the only thing which has to be examined: it is also necessary to consider whether the trouble could have been prevented from arising in the first place, for example by giving instructions not to clutter up floors: *Hall v Fairfield Shipbuilding and Engineering Co Ltd* 1964 SC 72, HL.

Although the standard of what is 'reasonably practicable' has some affinity with the standard of care for common law negligence, the House of Lords have said that comparison of the two is of no value and in a case under the statute the court is concerned only to apply the words of the statute.

The only question under this head is whether—by objective standards—it was 'reasonably practicable' for someone to provide (or maintain) whatever the section requires: whether it was reasonable that it should be provided by some other person, rather than the factory occupier who is liable under the section, is irrelevant: *McWilliams v Sir William Arrol & Co Ltd* 1961 SLT 265 (the Court of Session held the occupier of a shipyard liable as well as the contractor for failure to supply safety belts to the contractor's men who were setting up a crane). This point was not discussed when the case went to the House of Lords, no doubt because the decision was so clearly right. The policy of the Factories Act is to make the occupier responsible for compliance with the Act throughout the factory. It is therefore surprising that in England where contractors left a board with a nail projecting, the occupiers were held not liable as it was not reasonably practicable for them to prevent or remove the danger, and the fact that the contractors could have done so was said to be irrelevant: *Taylor v Coalite Oils and Chemicals Ltd* (1967) 3 KIR 315. This decision must be considered dubious.

The onus of calling evidence that no safety measures were reasonably practicable is on the defendants: *Nimmo v Alexander Cowan & Sons Ltd* [1968] AC 107, [1967] 3 All ER 187[13].

(6) Place of work more than 2 metres high

By s. 29(2):

> 'Where any person has to work at a place from which he will be liable to fall a distance more than 2 metres, then, unless the place is one which affords secure foothold and, where necessary, secure handhold, means shall be provided, so far as is reasonably practicable, by fencing or otherwise, for ensuring his safety.'

This subsection contemplates that in many cases secure foothold is sufficient, while in other cases—for instance, in climbing a tall iron ladder—a firm handhold is also necessary. A window-cleaner's ladder is sufficient handhold without anything further: *Wigley v British Vinegars* [1964] AC 307, [1962] 3 All ER 161.

The distance of 2 metres was substituted for 6½ feet by the Factories Act 1961 etc. (Metrication) Regulations 1983 (S.I. No. 978).

It is only if these requirements (foothold and handhold) cannot be satisfied that there is any further obligation. Fencing is the obvious method of protection, as on such places as a high tower or chimney: but other methods may be used, such as a safety belt (*McWilliams v Sir Wm. Arrol & Co Ltd* 1961 SLT 265) or safety net.

The observation under s. 29(1) as to the necessity that the place should be one where the plaintiff *has* to work (as distinct from going there of his own choice), as to the meaning of 'providing', and as to what is reasonably practicable, apply with equal force to this subsection. Duckboards were sufficiently 'provided' when placed in view of the plaintiff for his use: *Ginty v Belmont Building Supplies Ltd* [1959] 1 All ER 414.

---

13 This has consistently been held in England, also in New Zealand: *Cox v International Harvesters Co of New Zealand Ltd* [1964] NZLR 376. The decision put an end to persistent attempts on the procedure roll in Scotland to make the pursuer allege and prove what was practicable. Once the evidence is before the court, it will form its own opinion and which way the onus lies is rarely decisive: *Jenkins v Allied Ironfounders Ltd* [1969] 3 All ER 1609.

(7) Lighting

Section 5 (1) provides:

> 'Effective provision shall be made for securing and maintaining sufficient and suitable lighting, whether natural or artificial, in every part of a factory in which persons are working or passing.'

This is in Part I of the Act, but doubts expressed in *Gibby v East Grinstead Gas and Water Co* [1944] 1 All ER 358 about whether an action lies under Part I (headed 'Health' as distinct from 'Safety') were dispelled when the House of Lords allowed a claim under s. 4 (ventilation): *Nicholson v Atlas Steel Foundry and Engineering Co Ltd* [1957] 1 All ER 776. The duty under s. 5 extends to lighting the open parts of the factory such as roads where persons may be passing: *Thornton v Fisher and Ludlow Ltd* [1968] 2 All ER 241. If the general lighting is adequate, the fact that shadows are cast in places does not contravene the section: *Lane v Gloucester Engineering Co Ltd* [1967] 2 All ER 293[14]. But the section imposes an absolute duty, which is broken automatically even if a bulb has just failed: *Davies v Massey Ferguson Perkins Ltd* [1986] 1 CR 580.

4 Lifting tackle and lifting machines

Lifting tackle and lifting machines are dealt with by ss. 22–27. Sections 22–25 deal with lifts and hoists; s. 26 with chains, ropes and lifting tackle; and s. 27 with cranes and other lifting machines.

(1) Lifts and hoists

No definition of a lift or hoist is given, but under s. 25(1) 'no lifting machine or appliance shall be deemed to be a hoist or lift unless it has a platform or cage the direction of movement of which is restricted by a

---

14 This case also decided that the Factories (Standards of Lighting) Regulations 1941 (S.R. & O. No. 94) which require a specific intensity at a place where 'persons are regularly employed' (reg. 2 (a)) do not apply when a workman has arrived before hours, and that reg. 2 (b)—'other parts'—does not apply in such a case. Note that reg. 4 requires prevention of shadows 'so far as reasonably practicable' if they would cause eyestrain or risk of accident.

guide or guides'. That is, there must be a platform or cage, and the movement of this must be guided by a shaft, or rudimentary shaft, or perhaps something in the nature of a rope or cable. A forklift truck is *not* a lift or hoist: *Oldfield v Reed & Smith Ltd* [1972] 2 All ER 104.

Absolute duty to keep sound and in good order.   By s. 22(1):

> 'Every hoist or lift shall be of good mechanical construction, sound material and adequate strength, and be properly maintained'—

i.e. by s. 176 (1):

> '. . . maintained in an efficient state, in efficient working order, and in good repair.'

This obligation is so strict that the House of Lords held in *Galashiels Gas Co Ltd v O'Donnell (or Millar)* [1949] AC 275, [1949] 1 All ER 319 that a breach of statutory duty arises automatically as soon as a lift breaks down. In that case the workman had taken a load of materials up by the lift, and the lift had an automatic braking system, which should have kept it in position until he returned with his empty bogie. For some unexplained reason the braking system failed to work, and the lift rose to the top of the shaft. On his return the workman failed to notice this, and fell down the shaft and was killed. The case turned on the words 'maintain . . . in efficient working order'. The appellants argued that the word 'maintain' was used in its engineering sense, as meaning 'regular servicing'. The House of Lords rejected this argument, for reasons explained in the following extract from the speech of Lord MacDermott:

> 'The terms of the definition . . . indicate conclusively that in s. 22 (1) "maintained" is employed to denote the *continuance* of a state of working efficiency. . . . There was abundant proof that the mechanism had failed. . . . Once the absolute nature of the duty imposed by the statute is established that is proof enough.'

'Good mechanical construction' refers to the manner in which the mechanism is pieced together; 'sound material' implies that there must be no defect in the component materials; and 'adequate strength' suggests the ability of the whole system to withstand the strain to which it will be subjected in its intended use.

The words 'sound material' were considered by the Court of Appeal in *Whitehead v James Stott & Co* [1949] 1 KB 358, [1949] 1 All ER 245 where, owing to a latent defect, material at the top of a lift shaft broke and fell on to the head of the lift operator. The court held that the occupiers were liable, though they could not have discovered the defect by inspecting the shaft.

Testing   Every hoist or lift must be examined every six months by a competent person (s. 22(2))[15]. (Every 12 months—see s. 25(2), (3)—for continuous or hand-operated lifts.) In view of the absolute warranty of soundness under s. 22(1), it will be unnecessary to found an action on a breach of this requirement.

Maximum load   By s. 22(8):

'There shall be marked conspicuously on every hoist or lift the maximum working load which it can safely carry, and no load greater than that load shall be carried on any hoist or lift.'

As 'adequate strength' under s. 22(1) might be held to refer to adequate strength for the authorised load, it might be necessary to rely on this obligation.

Enclosure and gates   By s. 22(4):

'Every hoistway or liftway shall be efficiently protected by a substantial enclosure fitted with gates, being such an enclosure as to prevent, when the gates are shut, any person falling down the way or coming into contact with any moving part of the lift or hoist.'

This imposes an absolute duty to provide an enclosure and outer gates which will prevent contact with any part of a moving lift, and a claim succeeded where the plaintiff, under the mistaken impression that the inner gate was not closed, put his hand through to close it and was injured: *Blakeley v C. and H. Clothing Co* [1958] 1 All ER 297. Section 22(5), (6) goes on to provide that the gates shall be incapable of being opened unless the lift is opposite them, with certain qualifications where the lift was in existence when the Factories Act 1937, was passed.
By s. 22(5), (6):

'(5) Any such gate shall [*subject to ss.* 22(6) *and* 25] be fitted with efficient interlocking or other devices to secure that the gate cannot be opened except when the cage or platform is at the landing and that the

15 See p. 281. If the report shows that the lift cannot be safely used unless repairs are carried out at once or within a specified time, a copy must be sent to the Factory Inspector (s. 22(3)).

cage or platform cannot be moved away from the landing until the gate is closed.

(6) If, in the case of a hoist or lift constructed or reconstructed before [30 *July* 1937] it is not reasonably practicable to fit it with such devices as are mentioned in [*s.* 22(5)], it shall be sufficient if the gate (a) is provided with such arrangements as will secure the objects of that subsection so far as is reasonably practicable, and (b) is kept closed and fastened except when the cage or platform is at rest at the landing.'

These two subsections do not apply to a 'continuous' hoist or lift (s. 25(2)); or to one which is not connected with mechanical power (s. 25(3)). But in the latter case the gates must 'be kept closed and fastened except when the cage or platform is *at rest* at the landing'.

Protection against trapping against shaft or counterbalance   By s. 22(7):

'Every hoist or lift and every such enclosure as is mentioned in [*s.* 22(4)] shall be so constructed as to prevent any part of any person or any goods carried in the hoist or lift being trapped between any part of the hoist or lift and any fixed structure or between the counterbalance weight and any other moving part of the hoist or lift.'

Lifts used to carry persons; additional requirements   By s. 23:

'(1) The following additional requirements shall apply to hoists and lifts used for carrying persons, whether together with goods or otherwise:—

(a) efficient automatic devices shall be provided and maintained to prevent the cage or platform overrunning;

(b) every cage shall on each side from which access is afforded to a landing be fitted with a gate, and in connection with every such gate efficient devices shall be provided to secure that, when persons or goods are in the cage, the cage cannot be raised or lowered unless the gate is closed, and will come to rest when the gate is opened.

(2) In the case of a hoist or lift constructed or reconstructed before [30 *July* 1937] in connection with which it is not reasonably practicable to provide such devices as [*mentioned in s.* 23(1)(b)], it shall be sufficient if—(a) such arrangements are provided as will secure the aforesaid objects so far as is reasonably practicable; and (b) the gate is kept closed and fastened except when the cage is at rest or empty.

(3) In the case of a hoist or lift used as mentioned in [*s.* 23(1)] which was constructed or reconstructed after [29 *July* 1937], where the platform or cage is suspended by rope or chain, there shall be at least two ropes or chains separately connected with the platform or cage, each rope or chain and its attachments being capable of carrying the whole weight of the platform or cage and its maximum working load,

and efficient devices shall be provided and maintained which will support the platform or cage with its maximum working load in the event of a breakage of the ropes or chains or any of their attachments.'

This subsection does not apply to lifts or hoists 'not connected with mechanical power' (s. 25(3)).

Continuous lifts or hoists   The requirements as to gates and enclosures do not extend to 'continuous' hoists or lifts, nor do the requirements of s. 23 as to lifts carrying persons (s. 25(2)). 'Continuous' seems to mean those which may stop at any point, and not at definite landings, and would presumably include an oblique hoist.

Fencing of openings for hoisting or lowering goods   By s. 24:

'(1) Every teagle opening or similar doorway used for hoisting or lowering goods or materials, whether by mechanical power or otherwise, shall be securely fenced and shall be provided with a secure hand-hold on each side of the opening or doorway.
    (2) The fencing shall be properly maintained and shall, except when the hoisting or lowering of goods or materials is being carried on at the opening or doorway, be kept in position.'

Exemptions   The Minister has power, for special reasons, to grant exemptions by order from any of the requirements of ss. 22 to 24 and s. 25(3). The exemptions so far granted (Hoists Exemption Order, 1962)[16] relate to gates and enclosures (ss. 22(4) to (7) and s. 23). No exemptions have been granted under s. 22(1) (the absolute warranty of soundness), s. 22(8) (maximum load) (except in case 10, drop pit hoists for railway rolling-stock) or s. 24 (fencing of openings): nor in general are such exemptions likely. In effect ss. 22(4) to (7) and s. 23 represent a standard which the Act is aiming at, but which cannot be reached at once, or without exceptions for special cases.

(2) Chains, ropes and lifting tackle

Section 26, which deals with chains, ropes and lifting tackle, begins with an absolute obligation in s. 26(1)(a) that they shall not be used unless they conform to a certain standard of soundness.

16 S.I. 1962 No. 715, slightly amended by S.I. 1967 No. 759 and as to metrication by S.I. 1983 No. 1579.

The section applies to 'every chain, rope or lifting tackle used for raising or lowering persons, goods or materials'. Its chief object is not so much to protect persons being lifted (although no doubt it includes this case) as to protect all persons in the vicinity from being struck by falling objects. 'Lifting tackle' is defined as 'chain slings, rope slings, rings, hooks, shackles, and swivels' (s. 26(3)). There is a 'raising' operation when a crane is used to pull off a mass of metal scab stuck to the floor: *Ball v Richard Thomas and Baldwins Ltd* [1968] 1 All ER 389.

Tackle not to be used unless sound   By s. 26(1) (a):

> 'No chain, rope or lifting tackle shall be used unless it is of good construction, sound material, adequate strength and free from patent defect.'

The express mention of patent defects is not intended to free the occupier from liability for *latent* defects, because a latent defect must be either in the material or in the way it is put together: and therefore either the material is not 'sound' or the tackle is not of 'good construction', and in both cases there is an infringement of the section. It seems that the words 'free from patent defect' were inserted as a warning against taking into use tackle in which even a slight defect is visible; it is an additional requirement, and does not weaken the force of the earlier words. In *Reilly v William Beardmore & Co* 1947 SC 275 a cable on a crane parted, and a workman was injured. Previously it had been noticed that the cable was slightly frayed: but it was at a different point that it broke. The Court of Session held that there was a breach of statutory duty on the ground that the rope was not of adequate strength, and that the defenders were liable in the absence of evidence that the accident was due to some cause other than a breach of the subsection. The court was of the opinion that the strength of a rope must be 'adequate' for the load or stress which is in fact placed upon it (a conclusion also reached in *Milne v C. F. Wilson & Co* 1960 SLT 162). These decisions have been followed in England, where a hook which opened out in pulling metal scab stuck to the floor was held *ipso facto* not to be of 'adequate strength', although the strain could not be estimated in advance: *Ball v Richard Thomas and Baldwins Ltd* [1968] 1 All ER 389; and in Eire, where under the (Eire) Factories Act 1955, s. 34(1)(a) there was held to be an absolute duty to conform to the requirements of the section which was broken when a crane hook gave way: *Doherty v Bowaters Irish Wallboard Mills* (1968) IR 277.

In *Reilly v Beardmore, supra*, Lord Moncreiff was prepared to give judgment on the further ground that the cable was not 'free from patent defect'. He said, at p. 279:

> 'I find that the statute imposes an express obligation, which must be regarded as absolute, not to use tackle which is not free from patent defect . . . the factory owner who elects to employ material which shows signs, and visible signs, of a defect must do so at his peril.'

Lord Moncrieff's opinion was followed in *McNeill v Dickson & Mann Ltd* 1957 SLT 364 where it was held, on similar words in what is now s. 27(1), to be irrelevant (i.e. not a good defence in law) to plead that the defect was 'latent'[17].

In *Dawson v Murex Ltd* [1942] 1 All ER 483 a tray supported by chains, which was used for lifting metal, fell on the plaintiff. The Court of Appeal held that there was evidence of 'patent defects' in that the hooks supporting the tray were slightly opened out, and the chains were of unequal length.

In *Beadsley v United Steel Companies Ltd* [1951] 1 KB 408, [1950] 2 All ER 872 the selection of the wrong type of lifting tackle—in itself of good construction and adequate strength—resulted in an accident, in that a heavy mould came adrift from its fastenings and fell on to a workman. The Court of Appeal held that the section did not impose a requirement that tackle should not be used unless it was suitable for the particular task[18]. A similar decision was given in *Gledhill v Liverpool Abattoir Utility Co Ltd* [1957] 3 All ER 117 where a pig fell out of a chain sling which was too heavily constructed to be tightened properly. There was nothing wrong with the sling except that it was unsuitable.

A further question is whether s. 26(1)(a) imposes a *continuing* obligation. Unlike ss. 22 and 27, for example, it does not say that the equipment shall be 'properly maintained'. This, however, should not be

---

17 This construction is further supported by the fact that similar words occur in ss. 32 and 35, dealing with steam boilers and receivers, which may fairly be described as highly dangerous apparatus, so that even a small sign of a defect is a warning of danger. On similar words in s. 81 of the Mines and Quarries Act 1954, a defect was held to be 'patent' when it was in fact visible though no one actually saw it: *Sanderson v National Coal Board* [1961] 2 All ER 796. Note that in *Hamilton v National Coal Board* [1960] AC 633, [1960] 1 All ER 76, also a s. 81 case, Lord Keith, *obiter*, reserved his opinion on the effect of including the words 'free from patent defect', but (great and good judge though he was) no one has shared his doubt and it was not followed in *Davies v A.C.D. Bridge Co* 1966 SLT 339.

18 The decision, with respect, is clearly right. If the fastenings had *broken*, the position would have been quite different.

given too much weight, as the subsection is constructed on quite a different pattern: and it is suggested that the word 'used' does not refer to the first moment when the equipment is taken into use, but to its use at any point of time: see *Reilly v William Beardmore & Co, supra*. On this basis, s. 26(1)(a) clearly establishes a continuing obligation. It is noteworthy that in s. 26(1)(e)—referring to the initial test of tackle—the words chosen are, in contrast, 'taken into use'.

The subsection applies although tackle is used for a purpose not sanctioned by the employers; *Barry v Cleveland Bridge and Engineering Co Ltd* [1963] 1 All ER 192 (lifting men on rafts).

Safe working loads By s. 26(1)(b), the safe working load of every kind and size of chain, rope or lifting tackle is to be posted prominently in the store where the tackle is kept, and no tackle is to be used unless shown on the posted table. For multiple slings, the table must show the safe working load at different angles of the legs. In the case of 'lifting tackle' as distinct from chains and ropes, the safe load may be marked on the tackle instead of being shown on the table, provided that it is marked 'plainly': s. 26(2).

By s. 26(1)(c).

'No chain, rope or lifting tackle shall be used for any load exceeding its safe working load as shown by the table . . . or marked upon it . . .'

Inspection All chains, ropes and lifting tackle in use must be examined by a competent person every six months, unless the Minister allows a longer interval (s. 26(1)(d)). Furthermore, there must be an initial test and examination of all tackle, except fibre ropes and fibre rope slings, before it is taken into use: and the safe working load must be certified (s. 26(1)(e)).

Annealing of metallic tackle Metallic tackle must be annealed every fourteen months, or every six months in the case of small slings and chains, unless exempted by certificate of the chief factory inspector (s. 26(1)(f)).

(3) Cranes and other lifting machines

There is an exhaustive code on cranes and other lifting machines in s. 27. By s. 27(9), a 'lifting machine' is defined to be 'a crane, crab, winch, teagle, pulley block, gin wheel, transporter or runway'. A forklift truck is not a lifting machine, nor is it a 'transporter': *Walker v Andrew Mitchell & Co* 1982 SLT 266[19].

Sound construction   By s. 27(1):

> 'All parts and working gear, whether fixed or moveable, including the anchoring and fixing appliances, of every lifting machine shall be of good construction, sound material, adequate strength and free from patent defect, and shall be properly maintained.'

Here, as in s. 26, the words 'free from patent defect' do not qualify the other words in the section, but are a superadded requirement that apparatus must not be used if it shows visible signs of defect: it is therefore no defence to say that a breach of the section was due to a latent defect: *McNeil v Dickson and Mann Ltd* 1957 SLT 364 (gear wheel in crane broke and jib fell). Further, in view of the words 'properly maintained' and the decision in *Galashiels Gas Co Ltd v O'Donnell (or Millar)* [1949] AC 275, [1949] 1 All ER 319, any breakdown in the lifting machine is itself proof of a breach of statutory duty. 'Parts and working gear' include the electrical operating circuit and control button, and if the button is too stiff, so as to cause a finger injury, it is not 'properly maintained': *Evans v Sanderson Bros and Newbold Ltd* (1968) 4 KIR 115 (not following the dicta in *Gatehouse v John Summers & Sons Ltd* [1953] 2 All ER 117 that an electric cable to the magnet of an electro-magnetic crane was not part of it). It is doubtful whether a chain sling around a load is included in the 'parts and working gear': it is rather an attachment of the load and falls more properly under s. 26: *Gledhill v Liverpool Abattoir Utility Co Ltd* [1957] 3 All ER 117.

Safe working load   The provisions as to the safe working load are of the highest importance, as an overloaded crane may easily topple over: see, for instance, *Gallagher v Dorman, Long & Co Ltd* [1947] 2 All ER 38. Section 27 (4) therefore imposes the general requirement that:

> 'There shall be plainly marked on every lifting machine the safe working load or loads thereof—'

In the case of 'a jib crane so constructed that the safe working load

---

19 Overruling earlier Scottish decisions in *McKendrick v Mitchell Swire Ltd* 1976 SLT (Notes) 65 and *McDowell v British Leyland Motor Corpn Ltd* 1982 SLT 71.

may be varied by the raising or lowering of the jib', there must be attached to the crane *either*—

'an automatic indicator of safe working loads',
or
'a table indicating the safe working loads at corresponding inclinations of the jib or corresponding radii of the loads.'

By s. 27(5):

'No lifting machine shall, except for the purpose of a test, be loaded beyond the safe working load as marked or indicated under [s. 27(4)].'

Testing and examination A lifting machine must be thoroughly examined and tested, and its working load or loads certified, before it is taken into use in the factory for the first time (s. 27(6)). Afterwards, it must be thoroughly examined every fourteen months; if the examination shows that it cannot safely be used unless repairs are done—either at once or within a specified term—a copy of the report must be sent to the Factory Inspector (s. 27(2)).

Rails and track of travelling crane By s. 27(3):

'All rails on which a travelling crane moves and every track on which the carriage of a transporter or runway moves shall be of proper size and adequate strength and have an even running surface; and any rails or tracks shall be properly laid, adequately supported or suspended, and properly maintained.'

The main object here seems to be to prevent toppling or collapse.

Persons employed near overhead crane In *Fowler v Yorkshire Electric Power Co Ltd* [1939] 1 All ER 407 it was held that an overhead travelling crane was dangerous machinery within s. 10(1)(c) of the Act of 1901 (now s. 14 of the Act of 1961), and that it must either be fenced or in such a position that it was equally safe to all persons working in the factory. The Act of 1961, following the Act of 1937, meets the situation by the rather different method of insisting that a certain space around the machine must be kept clear (but this does not exclude s. 14 of the Act in a case where it can apply: *Carrington v John Summers & Sons Ltd* [1957] 1 All ER 457).

By s. 27(7):

'If any person is employed or working on or near the wheel-track of
an overhead travelling crane in any place where he would be liable
to be struck by the crane, effective measures shall be taken by
warning the driver of the crane or otherwise to ensure that the
crane does not approach within 6 metres[20] of that place.'

The words 'effective measures ... to ensure' impose an
unconditional obligation to keep the crane the specified distance
away from any place where a man is liable to be struck: *Lotinga v
North Eastern Marine Engineering Co* (1938) *Ltd* [1941] 2 KB 399,
1941 3 All ER 1; *Hunter v Glenfield and Kennedy Ltd* 1947 SC 536
(workman on scaffold outside put arm through wall).

'The place' where a man is liable to be struck is the broad area in
which he moves about, not the precise spot where he is standing:
Holmes v Hadfields Ltd [1944] 1 KB 275, [1944] 1 All ER 235 (man
using drill just beyond 20 feet, but crane knocked drill on top of him:
such an accident, though indirect, is within scope of section).

Section 27 (7), in its original form (which remains unchanged) was
confined to persons 'on or near the wheel-track' of an overhead
crane. Protection is extended to other persons working above floor
level by s. 27(8), which was introduced by the Factories Act 1959;
and reads as follows:

'If any person is employed or working otherwise than mentioned in
[s. 27(7)] but in a place above floor level where he would be liable
to be struck by an overhead travelling crane, or by any load carried
by such a crane, effective measures shall be taken to warn him of
the approach of the crane, unless his work is so connected with or
dependent on the movements of the crane as to make a warning
unnecessary.'

It will be seen that this subsection never requires more than a
warning, which must, however, be 'effective' i.e. it must *reach* the
person at risk, and reach him in time.

An 'overhead travelling crane' means one which travels above
ground: it does not include one which runs on wheels at ground level
though part of the structure (the 'crab') runs on an overhead girder:
Carrington v John Summers & Sons Ltd [1957] 1 All ER 457.

---

20 Substituted for 20 ft. by 1983 S.I. No. 978.

5 Fencing vats of dangerous liquids

Section 18 of the Factories Act 1961, which gives protection against tanks and other vessels containing dangerous liquids, replaced s. 18 of the Act of 1937 but with extensive amendments made by the Factories Act 1959.

Section 18 (1)—with 1959 amendments in italics—is as follows:

> 'Every fixed vessel, structure, sump or pit of which the edge is less than 920 mm. above the *highest* ground or platform *from which a person might fall into it*, shall, if it contains any scalding, corrosive or poisonous liquid, either be securely covered or be securely fenced to at least 920 mm. *above that ground or platform*, or where by reason of the nature of the work neither secure covering nor secure fencing to that height is practicable, all practicable steps shall be taken by covering, fencing or other means to prevent any person from falling into the vessel, structure, sump or pit.'

This obligation to give persons protection from falling into vats containing liquid is not, it will be seen, an absolute one: it is qualified by the nature of the work. It is not intended merely as a protection against drowning: the liquid must be dangerous in itself before the section will operate.

Section 18(2) and (3), added in 1959, require fencing and a minimum width for gangways, etc., over uncovered tanks or in between two such tanks:

> '18(2). Where any fixed vessel, structure, sump or pit contains any scalding, corrosive or poisonous liquid but is not securely covered, no ladder, stair or gangway shall be placed above, across or inside it which is not—
> (a) at least 460 mm. wide, and
> (b) securely fenced on both sides to a height of at least 920 mm. and securely fixed.
> (3) Where any [*vessels etc. mentioned in s.* 18(2)] adjoin, and the space between them, clear of any surrounding brick or other work, is less than 460 mm. wide or is not securely fenced on both sides to a height of at least 920 mm., secure barriers shall be so placed as to prevent passage between them.'

The duty to fence (and to provide a minimum width of 460 mm.) is not qualified in any way like the duty to cover or fence the tank itself under s. 18(1): it is an absolute duty, but is limited to any 'ladder, stair or gangway' located 'above, across or inside' the vat (i.e. vertically above the liquid). Where the space between two vats does not have the necessary width and fencing, entry must be barred.

By s. 18(4), fencing of a 'ladder, stair or gangway' is not sufficient unless there is either (i) sheet fencing or (ii) both an upper and lower rail and toe boards.

By s. 18(5), any part of the section may be extended to vessels which are not fixed, or to vessels containing substances which are not liquid.

By s. 18(6), the Minister may make exemption orders where the above requirements are 'unnecessary or inappropriate'.

6 Confined spaces: fumes, oxygen shortage and heat

Under s. 30(1), 'where work in any factory has to be done inside any chamber, tank, vat, pipe, flue or similar confined space in which dangerous fumes are liable to be present to such an extent as to involve risk of persons being overcome thereby', the following precautions must be observed:

(a) there must be a manhole of specified dimensions, unless there is other adequate means of escape (s. 30(2));

(b) no person is to enter or remain in the space except a duly authorised person who (i) is wearing suitable breathing apparatus and also (ii) where practicable, is wearing a belt attached to a rope held by a person outside: but these provisions do not apply where the tank has been certified free from fumes after cleaning, ventilation and testing (ss. 30(3), (4), (5));

(c) breathing and reviving apparatus must be accessible, properly maintained and periodically examined (s. 30(6));

(d) a sufficient number of the workmen must be trained in using such apparatus and in giving artificial respiration (s. 30(7)).

The chief inspector may give a certificate of exemption from any of these requirements if they are 'unnecessary or impracticable'.

Section 30 (9) contains an independent requirement for '*any* confined space' where the oxygen in the air is liable to have been reduced. No person is to enter or remain in such a space unless he is wearing breathing apparatus or the place has been tested and

otcenterned with dangerous fumes at all, but
simply with lack of oxygen.

Under s. 30(10):

> 'No work shall be permitted in any boiler-furnace or boiler-flue
> until it has been sufficiently cooled by ventilation or otherwise to
> make work safe for the persons employed.'

7 Explosive and inflammable dust, gas or substance

Section 31 contains a number of requirements which may be described
as precautions against explosions and fires.

(1) Explosive dust and inflammable liquids

Section 31(1) deals with grinding, sieving or other processes which give
rise to dust. Where dust may escape, and is of such a character and
present to such an extent as to be liable to explode on ignition, all
practicable steps are to be taken, by three different methods, to prevent
such an explosion.

The three methods laid down are these:
(a) enclosure of the plant or process;
(b) removal, or prevention of accumulation, of dust which escapes in
spite of the enclosure;
(c) exclusion or enclosure of possible sources of ignition[1].

Section 31(2) deals with the possibility of the explosion of dust within
the plant used in any of the above processes. Unless the plant is strong
enough to withstand the explosion, all practicable steps are to be taken
by means of chokes, baffles, vents or other effective appliances to restrict
the spreading of the explosion.

In the case of the grinding of magnesium, these requirements are

---

1 Formerly s. 31(1) did not apply unless dust was liable to escape 'into any
workroom'. These words were deleted by the 1959 Act.

reinforced by the Magnesium (Grinding of Castings and Other Articles) Special Regulations 1946 (S.R. & O. 1946 No. 2107), which provide for the following main objects:

(a) interception and removal of dust at the point of origin by an exhaust appliance;

(b) prevention of sparks;

(c) fire-resisting clothing;

(d) prohibition of smoking and exposed lights.

See also Chapter 12, section 6, for regulations on inflammable substances.

(2) Explosive and inflammable gas

Section 31(3) deals with any part of a plant containing explosive or inflammable gas at high pressure. Before the fastening of any part of the apparatus is loosened, the flow of gas into that part must be effectively stopped: and before the fastening is removed, the gas must as far as possible be reduced to atmospheric pressure. This is to prevent the gas from shooting out suddenly and catching fire.

(3) Containers of inflammable material: heat processes

By s. 31(4), where any plant, tank or vessel contains or has contained any explosive or inflammable substance, it is not to be subjected to any welding, brazing or soldering operation, or to any cutting operation which involves the application of heat, or to any operation involving the use of heat to take apart or remove the plant, or any part of it, until all practicable steps have been taken to remove the substance and any fumes from it or to render them safe. Moreover, after the completion of such an operation, no inflammable or explosive substance is to be allowed to enter the container until it has cooled.

In this context, 'plant, tank or vessel' means things which are part of the factory installation, and does not include, for instance, articles brought to the factory to be cut up which may (unknown to anyone) contain dangerous substances: *Haigh v Charles W. Ireland Ltd* [1973] 3 All ER 1137.

(4) Exemptions

The chief inspector has power to grant exemption by certificate from subsections (3) (gas at high pressure) and (4) (heat processes). Certain exemptions have been granted, under rigorous conditions, for gas mains and gasholders[2].

8 Steam and compressed air apparatus

Sections 32–38 contain a number of complex requirements to minimise the risk of explosions in steam boilers and other apparatus, and compressed air receivers. The main requirements centre round safety valves, safe working pressure and sound construction. A further object is the safety of persons who enter the apparatus.

(1) The definitions

Each type of apparatus is closely defined. Broadly speaking, a steam boiler is an apparatus in which steam is generated, and a steam receiver an apparatus where it is kept, in both cases at a high pressure. In a steam container, on the other hand, the steam is only at atmospheric pressure. An air receiver is a receptacle where compressed air is kept.

A *steam boiler* is 'any closed vessel in which for any purpose steam is generated under pressure greater than atmospheric pressure, and includes any economiser used to heat water being fed to any such vessel, and any superheater used for heating steam' (s. 38).

Sections 32–34 do not, however, extend to 'any boiler belonging to or exclusively used in the service of Her Majesty or belonging to or used by the United Kingdom Atomic Energy Authority, or to the boiler of any ship or of any locomotive which belongs to and is used by any railway company' (s. 37(1)).

Under the Boiler Explosions Act 1882[3], a boiler includes the steam

---

2   Certificates of exemption for gas and also for certain steam apparatus are quoted in *Redgrave: Health and Safety in Factories*. They are too detailed to be cited here.
3   13 Halsbury's Statutes, 3rd Edn., 311.

piping leading out as far as the stop valve: *R v Boiler Explosions Act 1882 Commissioners* [1891] 1 QB 703. No doubt a similar view would be taken under the Factories Act.

A *steam receiver* is 'any vessel or apparatus (other than a steam boiler, steam container, a steam pipe or coil, or a part of a prime mover) used for containing steam under pressure greater than atmospheric pressure' (s. 35(8)).

A *steam container* is 'any vessel (other than a steam pipe or coil) constructed with a permanent outlet into the atmosphere or into a space where the pressure does not exceed the atmospheric pressure, and through which steam is passed at atmospheric pressure or at approximately that pressure for the purpose of heating, boiling, drying, evaporating or other similar purpose' (s. 35(8)).

An *air receiver* is, under s. 36(6):

> '(a) any vessel (other than a pipe or coil, or an accessory, fitting or part of a compressor) for containing compressed air and connected with an air compressing plant; or
> (b) any fixed vessel for containing compressed air or compressed exhaust gases and used for the purpose of starting an internal combustion engine; or
> (c) any fixed or portable vessel (not being part of a spraying pistol) used for the purpose of spraying by means of compressed air any paint, varnish, lacquer or similar material; or
> (d) any vessel in which oil is stored and from which it is forced by compressed air.'

(2) Sound construction and maintenance

By s. 32(5):

> 'Every part of every steam boiler shall be of good construction, sound material, and adequate strength, and free from patent defect.'

Section 35(4) contains identical requirements for steam receivers.

There is no similar requirement for steam containers, where, of course, there is no similar danger of explosion, as the steam is at atmospheric pressure.

By s. 33(1).

> 'Every steam boiler and all its fittings and attachments shall be properly maintained.'

By s. 35(5):

> 'Every steam receiver and its fittings shall be properly maintained.'

By s. 36(3):

> 'Every air receiver and its fittings shall be of sound construction and properly maintained.'

On the meaning of 'sound construction' and 'properly maintained', see section 2 of this Chapter.

It will be seen that steam boilers and receivers—unlike air receivers—must be 'free from patent defect', as well as of sound construction. These words do not cut down the liability of the occupier, which would normally arise under the statutory warranty of 'sound construction', for latent as well as patent defects[4]. The words 'free from patent defect' seem to have been added to stress the fact that certain apparatus is not to be used even if there is a slight appearance of defect, although the apparatus as a whole is believed to be sound: and this view is supported by the present group of sections, where the highly dangerous steam apparatus must be 'free from patent defect', while for the less dangerous air receiver there is no such requirement.

As regards steam containers, s. 33(7) imposes the following limited obligation:

> 'Every steam container shall be so maintained as to secure that the outlet is at all times free from obstruction.'

There is no real danger from a steam container unless pressure is allowed to build up: and this could happen only if the outlet was blocked.

(3) Initial and periodic examination[5]

There are detailed instructions for the regular inspection of the apparatus, but it will not be necessary to rely on these as a cause of action, in view of the absolute obligation to keep the apparatus sound.

4 See p. 305.
5 These provisions were somewhat revised by the Factories Act 1959, s. 8. The Examination of Steam Boilers Regulations 1964 (S.I. No. 781)—now adapted to metrication by S.I. 1981 No. 687—came into force on 27 June 1964, and from the same day (by S.I. No. 782) the transitional provisions in Sch. 6, para 3, to the Act were terminated.

The instructions are summarised below.

Steam boilers   (s. 33(2) to (10)). Before a new boiler is taken into use, a certificate must be obtained showing the nature of the tests to which it has been subjected, and the maximum permissible working pressure. A boiler which has been used before, but is taken into use for the first time at a particular factory, must be thoroughly examined in accordance with regulations, usually by an experienced boiler inspector. In both cases, further examinations must be made at regular intervals prescribed by regulations or after any extensive repairs. The report on every examination must state the maximum permissible working pressure.

The following provision may form the basis of an action (s. 33(5)):

> 'Where the report of any examination under this section specifies conditions for securing the safe working of a steam boiler, the boiler shall not be used except in accordance with those conditions.'

Steam receivers   (s. 35(5)). These must be examined by a competent person every 26 months. The report must show the safe working pressure (s. 35(6)).

Air receivers   (s. 35(4), (5)). These must be cleaned, and examined by a competent person, every 26 months, but the period may be extended in some cases. The safe working pressure must be shown in the report.

Steam boilers (s. 32(2)(e)), steam receivers (s. 35(1)(e)), and air receivers (s. 36(1)(g)) must each bear a distinctive number or mark, unless only one boiler or receiver is in use at the factory. The purpose of this is to enable the apparatus to be linked up with any reports on examination.

(4) Maximum working pressure: gauges

By s. 38, the 'maximum permissible working pressure' of a boiler is that which is specified in the report made after the last examination by a competent person under s. 33. The 'safe working pressure' of a steam receiver is similarly defined, but is the pressure specified by the maker in the case of new apparatus (s. 35 (8)). There is no similar definition in the case of an air receiver, but no doubt the same principle applies.

By s. 32(1)(a), (2) (c), (d) every *steam boiler*, whether separate or one of a range, shall have attached to it—

> (2) (c) a correct steam pressure gauge connected to the steam space and easily visible by the boiler attendant, which shall indicate the pressure of steam in the boiler and shall have marked upon it in a distinctive colour the maximum permissible working pressure;
>
>   (d) at least one water gauge of transparent material or other type approved by the chief inspector to show the water level in the boiler, together, if the gauge is of the glass tubular type and the working pressure in the boiler normally exceeds 2.75 bars, with an efficient guard provided so as not to obstruct the reading of the gauge. . . .'

By s. 32(1)(b) and (c), every steam boiler, whether separate or one of a range—

> '(b) shall be provided with means for attaching a test pressure gauge; and
>
>   (c) shall, unless externally fired, be provided with a suitable fusible plug or an efficient low-water alarm device.'

These requirements do not extend to either economisers or superheaters, but only to boilers strictly so called.

All these fittings must, of course, be 'of sound construction' and 'properly maintained' (ss. 32(5), 33(1)).

A *steam receiver* may be 'so constructed and maintained as to withstand with safety the maximum permissible working pressure of the boiler or the maximum pressure which can be obtained in the pipe connecting the receiver with any other source of supply' (s. 35(1)). If the receiver is up to this standard of strength, there is no further obligation as to gauges or valves of any kind. Otherwise, the receiver must be fitted with:

> 'a correct steam pressure gauge, which must indicate the steam in the receiver' (s. 35(1)(c)).

This is to be fitted either on the receiver or on the supply pipe between the receiver and any valve or appliance which reduces the pressure (s. 35(2)).

A set of receivers supplied by a single pipe needs only one gauge, provided that the pressure-reducing appliance is on the supply pipe (s. 35(3)).

By s. 36(1):

'Every *air receiver:*—
   (a) shall have marked on it so as to be plainly visible the safe working pressure, and . . .
   (d) shall be fitted with a correct pressure gauge indicating the pressure in the receiver.'

Here, too, a set of receivers supplied by a single pipe needs only one gauge: but if a pressure reduction device is required in such a case, it must be located on the supply pipe, otherwise each receiver must have a separate gauge (s. 36(2)).

The sections do not lay down, in the case of any steam or air apparatus, an express obligation not to exceed the safe working pressure, except in so far as this follows (in the case of boilers) from the duty to comply with the conditions of the last inspection report (s. 33(6)); or from the duty to provided safety valves.

(5) Stop-valves

Stop-valves are required, to shut off the outflow of steam, in the case of every boiler except an economiser (s. 32(2)(b), (3)) and also in the case of every steam receiver which is not constructed so as to withstand the maximum possible inward pressure from the boiler and inlet pipe (s. 35(1)(d)).

(6) Safety valves

Safety valves are most important. While, if a boiler explodes at a safe working pressure, an action is likely to be founded on the unsoundness of the boiler, it is doubtful whether an action on this ground would be successful where the safe working pressure has been exceeded, and in such a case it will be necessary to rely on an allegation that the safety valve was unsound, or not in efficient working order or correctly adjusted.

By s. 32(1), (2):

'(i) . . . every *steam boiler*, whether separate or one of a range
   (a) shall have attached to it . . .
   (2) (a) a suitable safety-valve, separate from any stop valve, which shall be so adjusted as to prevent the boiler being worked at a pressure

greater than the maximum permissible working pressure and shall be fitted directly to, or as close as practicable to, the boiler.'

This subsection makes the occupier liable not only for a defect in the valve itself (which, under ss. 32(5), 33(1), must be of sound construction and properly maintained) but also for a faulty adjustment.

By s. 32(4):

'. . . a lever-valve shall not be deemed a suitable safety valve unless the weight is secured on the lever in the correct position.'

By s. 35(1), unless a *steam receiver* is able to withstand the maximum pressure from the boiler and intake pipe, it must be fitted with

'(b) a suitable safety valve so adjusted as to permit the steam to escape as soon as the safe working pressure is exceeded, or a suitable appliance for cutting off automatically the supply of steam as soon as the safe working pressure is exceeded.'

By s. 36(1), every *air receiver* must:

'(c) be fitted with a suitable safety valve so adjusted as to permit the air to escape as soon as the safe working pressure is exceeded.'

(7) Reduction valves

By s. 35(1)(a), a steam receiver, unless able to withstand the maximum intake pressure, must be fitted with a reducing valve or other automatic device to ensure that the safe working pressure is not exceeded. There is a similar requirement for air receivers (s. 36(1)(b)), if connected to an air compressing plant.

(8) Sets of air or steam receivers

A set of steam receivers supplied by a single pipe may be treated as one entity for the purpose of safety and reduction valves and gauges, on condition that the reducing valve is on the supply pipe: the gauge and safety valve, it seems, may be either on any one of the receivers, or on the pipe between the receivers and the reducing valve (s. 35(1) and (2)).

A set of air receivers may be treated on the same lines (s. 36(2)).

In contradistinction, where there is a set of boilers, each of them separately must comply with all requirements (s. 32(1)).

(9) Entry into one of a set of boilers

By s. 34, no person is to enter a steam boiler which forms one of a range of boilers, unless either (i) all inlets are disconnected or (ii) they are effectively sealed as indicated in s. 34(b).

(10) Entry into an air receiver

An air receiver must be fitted with a suitable appliance for draining it, and a manhole, 'handhole', or other means to allow the interior to be cleaned (s. 36(1)(e) and (f)).

(11) Exemptions

The chief inspector may, by certificate, grant exemptions from any of the requirements relating to air and steam apparatus (s. 37(2)).

A number of exemptions have been granted, but in all cases sound construction and proper maintenance are insisted upon, though in some cases safety valves are not required, if there is an equivalent safeguard[6].

(12) Boiler Explosions Acts 1882 and 1890

These Acts do not impose any special statutory duties, but simply authorise the holding of official inquiries. They now take effect under the Health and Safety at Work Act 1974[7].

---

6   For details, see *Redgrave's Health and Safety in Factories.*
7   Boiler Explosions Acts (Repeals and Modifications) Regulations 1974, S.I. 1974 No. 1886.

9 Water-sealed gasholders

Section 39 applies to water-sealed gasholders having a storage capacity of at least 140 cubic metres (s. 39(7)).

These gasholders must by s. 39(1) be 'of sound construction' and 'properly maintained': see p. 280, *ante*. There are requirements in s. 39(2) to (4) as to periodical examinations, especially of the internal condition of the sheeting where a lift has been in use for 20 years.

By s. 39(6), no gasholder is to be repaired or demolished except under the direct supervision of a competent person, who has knowledge of the precautions to be taken against the risks of explosion and of persons being overcome by gas.

10 Fire precautions

The Factories Act 1961 originally contained its own detailed code for safety in case of fire (ss. 40–52: fire escapes, doors opening easily outwards to give quick exit, fire prevention, fire fighting, fire alarms). The Offices, Shops and Railway Premises Act 1963 followed similar lines, and the Mines and Quarries Act 1954 also had its own self-contained code.

The position was changed by the Health and Safety at Work Act 1974, which brought all these different places of work under the Fire Precautions Act 1971. The result is a complicated network of legislation which is easier to understand if taken in stages.

The Fire Precautions Act 1971 was passed after a series of fire disasters which showed that in many buildings fire precautions were non-existent[8]. The scheme of the Act (s. 1) was that premises could not be *used* for certain purposes unless a fire certificate was issued by the fire authority. These purposes were to be designated by the Secretary of State and are referred to as 'designated purposes': s. 1(2) gave a list of uses which could be designated—mainly relating to such places as hotels, hostels, institutions, schools, places of entertainment, and places

8   These were not confined to any one type of premises. A big store in Liverpool, old-fashioned factories in Glasgow and Keighley, an old hotel in Oban, and (since the Act) a brand-new holiday complex on the Isle of Man were all major disasters.

such as shops and offices open to the public. Under this scheme the fire authority had to carry out a thorough inspection of fire escapes, fire alarms, and fire precautions generally, before granting a certificate, and could insist on improvements to the premises: s. 5. Under s. 5(5), inserted by s. 4 of the Fire Safety and Safety of Places of Sport Act 1987, 'means of escape' includes the safety of the areas to or through which escape has to be made—if it is an enclosed yard, for instance, quick means of exit may be required. They could also carry out inspections while the certificate was in force, and any material change in the premises (or the use of them) had to be notified: ss. 8, 19. Since this involved a great deal of work by the fire authorities, the intention was that the Act should be extended to various classes of premises by degrees. However, by s. 2 premises subject to the Factories Act 1961, the Offices, Shops and Railway Premises Act 1963 and the Mines and Quarries Act 1954 were excluded at that time and left subject to their own separate codes.

Under s. 6(1), the fire certificate has to specify the authorised use of the premises and set out in detail the fire precautions which have been provided: fire escapes, means of access to them, fire fighting appliances, fire alarms. By s. 6(2) it may impose *requirements* for proper maintenance of these facilities (free from obstruction), for fire drills and training, for limiting the numbers allowed in the premises and other fire precautions. Responsibility for carrying out these requirements rests primarily on the *occupier*—s. 6(5)—but may be imposed on the owner or some other person by the terms of the particular certificate, especially where there is multiple use of the premises: s. 6(6).

The Act also contained general powers to make regulations for fire precautions—including internal construction and lay-out and materials to be used: s. 12. It could be applied to vessels at moorings or on dry land, and to tents (no doubt this contemplates large marquees and circus tents) and to other moveable structures: s. 35.

The next stage was s. 78 of the Health and Safety at Work Act 1974, which added a new category to the uses which can be designed under the 1971 Act:

'(f) use as a place of work'.

So all places of work may now be brought within the 1971 Act, and the exception in s. 2 for premises subject to the Factories Act, the Offices, Shops and Railway Premises Act and the Mines and Quarries Act is repealed.

The Fire Safety and Safety of Places of Sport Act 1987 made a number of amendments to the Act of 1971 which is still the principal Act. Under s. 17 of the 1987 Act, the principal Act may be applied to another new category:

'(c) places of work in the open air of any prescribed description.'

Fire safety comes under the local fire authority and the Department of the Environment, but by s. 78(7)(c) powers may be delegated to the Health and Safety Executive for specified places of work.

By the Fire Precautions (Factories, Offices, Shops and Railway Premises) Order 1989 (S.I. No. 76), factory premises within the Factories Act 1961 (including electrical stations and institutions under s. 123(1) and s. 124—but *not* 'notional' factories), and office, shop and railway premises within the Act of 1963, are all formally 'designated' under reg. 4 as premises which require a fire certificate under the 1971 Act[9]. However, by reg. 5 premises are in general exempted from this requirement if not more than 20 persons are employed to work there at any one time, or not more than 10 elsewhere than on the ground floor, and if (on factory premises) there are no explosive or highly 'flammable' substances, or such as the fire authority does not regard as a serious additional risk. (Where several establishments are in one building, the total numbers of employees at all of them are aggregated to see whether the maximum of 20—or 10 away from the ground floor—is exceeded.)

This Order covers the normal case of factory, shop, office or railway premises where a certificate has to be obtained from the fire authority. But it excludes a special category of premises where, because of specially high risks, the application for a fire certificate has to be made to the Health and Safety Executive. These are listed in the Fire Certificates (Special Premises) Regulations 1976 (S.I. No. 2003) and are mostly factories or stores with explosive or inflammable materials or such other special hazards as radioactive substances. However, the list also includes—Sch. 1, para. 11—all buildings on the surface at a mine, and—Sch. 1, para. 15—buildings (whether temporary or existing buildings) on a building or engineering construction site, if used for the purpose of the operations.

These regulations too allow an exception where not more than 20 at a time are employed (or 10 away from the ground floor) provided that no

9   This replaced an earlier Order of 1976.

explosive or inflammable materials are stored and that there are sufficient fire escapes and unobstructed exits: Sch. 1, Part II.

In all the cases where a certificate is required, the approved precautions and requirements will be set out in the certificate.

Under a complicated series of amendments made by s. 16 of the 1987 Act introducing a new s. 28A and Sch. 2 into the 1971 Act, modifications are made where the place of work forms part of a larger building so as to make the owner responsible for fire safety and the fire certificate.

There remain a large number of small establishments—especially offices, shops and small workshops—where because of the numbers employed no certificate is required. In the case of these premises, a new s. 9A of the Act of 1971—inserted by s. 5 of 1987—simply requires 'such means of escape in case of fire, and such means for fighting fire, as may reasonably be required'. Earlier detailed regulations have been revoked, but a 'Code of Practice' may be issued under s. 9B with detailed guidance on carrying out these duties.

Before 1987 it might have been thought that failure to comply with the conditions of a fire certificate would give rise to an action for breach of statutory duty. But a new s. 27A (inserted in the 1971 Act by s. 12 of 1987) expressly excludes civil liability. However, failure to comply with the conditions will be exceedingly strong evidence of negligence, and in non-certificated cases the Code under s. 9B can be used as a guide to the standard of care.

Chapter 11

The fencing of machinery in factories

1 The duty to fence: an absolute obligation

The fencing of dangerous machinery is now regulated by ss. 12 to 16 of the Factories Act 1961[1].

The Act divides machinery into three classes:

(a) prime movers (s. 12), i.e. engines and other sources of mechanical power;

(b) transmission machinery (s. 13), which transmits the power;

(c) other 'dangerous parts' of any machinery (s. 14).

All these parts of the machinery must be 'securely fenced', except that in certain cases fencing may be dispensed with if the position or construction of the machine gives the same degree of safety as fencing would give.

'Secure' fencing. There has been extensive case-law upon the meaning of the words 'securely fenced'. The word 'securely' does not mean, as might at first sight appear, that the fence must be fixed firmly to the machine: it refers to the degree of protection which the fencing must give.

Earlier authorities are now superseded by the decision of the House of Lords in *John Summers & Sons Ltd v Frost* [1955] AC 740, [1955] 1 All ER 870. In this case the House reached the following conclusions:

(1) The duty to fence machinery is a strict or absolute obligation.

---

1 Machinery must also be fenced in mines and quarries, on docks, in shipbuilding and repairs, on construction sites, in offices, shops and railway premises, and on farms: see the appropriate chapters and index.

(2) It is no defence to say that it is impracticable to fence the machinery, or that the machinery, if securely fenced, will become useless.

(3) Fencing is not secure unless it gives complete protection against the danger contemplated by the sections, which is in general the danger from contact with machinery: *Close v Steel Co of Wales Ltd* [1962] AC 367, [1961] 2 All ER 953.

The House also expressed the opinion that, where a machine cannot be used if 'securely fenced', regulations under s. 76 of the Act could authorise a limited form of fencing instead of the complete fencing contemplated by ss. 12–14. (The regulation-making power is now contained in the Health and Safety at Work Act 1974 and is in much wider terms: see p. 236.)

It will be apparent that, in deciding whether machinery is securely fenced, it is essential to know what 'danger' it is for which fencing is required by the Act. As will appear more fully in the next section, it has been decided under ss. 12 and 13 (prime movers and transmission machinery) that fencing is intended to provide a safeguard against persons coming into contact with the machinery, and not against the risk that parts of the machinery, such as a transmission belt or flywheel, may break and fly out: after some doubt, it has been held that s. 14 is similarly intended to give protection against contact only, not against materials or machinery flying out. But, with this limitation, fencing is not secure until the danger is completely removed. Thus, where there is a danger of injury by contact, the fence is not secure unless it precludes contact: accordingly in *John Summers & Sons Ltd v Frost* a revolving grindstone was held not to be securely fenced when there was a space between an upper and a lower guard so that the hands of the operator could reach the revolving wheel. Complete protection against contact does not mean, however, that 'the fence must be so constructed that it cannot be climbed over, or broken down, by an employee who is determined to get at the machinery': per Lord Morton, ibid. at pp. 758 and 876 respectively.

The protection of the fencing sections, and of special regulations for particular types of machine, extends only 'to every person employed or working on the premises' (cf. ss. 12 (3), 13 (1), 14 (1)); not, for example, to a man staying late and using a machine for work of his own: *Napieralski v Curtis (Contractors) Ltd* [1959] 2 All ER 426. 'Employed' cannot be taken to mean 'engaged in work'. But a man 'employed' in the factory is still within the protection of the sections (subject to his own contributory negligence) even when he has gone for purposes of his own to a place in the factory where he has no right to be: for the words are 'employed *or* working': *Uddin v Associated Portland Cement Manufacturers Ltd* [1965] 2 QB 582, [1965] 2 All ER 213 (Pakistani trying to catch pigeon near shaft: four-fifths to blame); *Allen v Aeroplane and Motor Aluminium Castings Ltd* [1965] 3 All ER 377 (boy injured in circumstances for which his explanation was not accepted, perhaps playing about); *Smith v Supreme Wood Pulp Co Ltd* [1968] 3 All ER 753 (driver allowed to take surplus wood at timber depot, used saw without authority)[2]. The principle of these cases was approved by the House of Lords in the similar context of the Offices, Shops and Railway Premises Act 1963: *Westwood v Post Office* [1974] AC 1, [1973] 3 All ER 184.

2 The limits of the duty to fence

(1) Duty to fence against contact only: not against materials or machinery flying out

Does the word 'fence', as used in the Act, mean a barrier to keep the workmen away from the machine, or does it mean something which, in addition, will protect them from objects flying out?

Lord Simmonds said in *Nicholls v Austin (F.) (Leyton) Ltd* [1946] AC 493, 505, [1946] 2 All ER 92, 98:

> 'The fence is intended to keep the worker out, not to keep the machine or its product in.'

It is now established that this is in all cases the meaning of the sections.

(i) Materials flying out of machinery, or source of danger when moving within it

The position where materials are thrown out of a machine in motion was considered by the House of Lords in *Nicholls v Austin (F.) (Leyton) Ltd*,

---

2 It is not clear how this case is distinguished from *Napieralski v Curtis, supra*: presumably on the basis that a man ceases to be 'employed' if he stays late for his own purposes, but not if he carries them out in working time.

supra, where a circular saw, which was correctly fenced against contact with its operator, threw out a piece of wood and injured the operator's hand. The House held that the statute was not intended to give protection against this sort of accident. Lord Macmillan said, at pp. 501 and 96:

> '. . . the fencing did not prevent a fragment of wood flying off while the saw was working. Was it the statutory duty of the respondents so to fence the saw as to prevent this possibility? In my opinion, the statute imposes no such duty. The obligation under s. 14 to fence the dangerous part of a machine, as I read it, is an obligation so to screen or shield the dangerous part as to prevent the body of the operator from coming into contact with it.'

Accordingly there is no duty to provide a fence which will give protection against fragments of wire from being thrown out of a machine which is winding strands on bobbins: *Kilgollan v Wm. Cooke & Co Ltd* [1956] 2 All ER 294; or sharp metal cuttings emerging from a cutting tool: *Walker v Dick Engineering Co (Coalbridge) Ltd* 1985 SLT 465; or to provide a fence to prevent the lashing out of the end of a long wire which is being pulled through a hole (to reduce its thickness) by a revolving drum: *Bullock v G. John Power (Agencies) Ltd* [1956] 1 All ER 498. Such a wire cannot be treated as a temporary part of the machinery (as distinct from material in the machine) merely because it helps to pull the rest of the wire through.

S. 14(6) gave power to make special regulations for fencing materials or articles in a machine; it has now been superseded by the general regulation-making power in the Health and Safety at Work Act 1974, but some special regulations of this kind are in force[3].

It has been held, having regard to this express power, that there is no duty to fence against even the danger of contact where this is due *solely* to the material in motion in the machine: *Eaves v Morris Motors Ltd* [1961] 2 QB 385, [1961] 3 All ER 233 (hand cut on sharp edge of component held in machine). There is a duty to fence where danger arises from a moving part of machinery *in conjunction with* material fed in as part of the normal course of working: *Midland and Low Moor Iron and Steel Co Ltd v Cross* [1965] AC 343, [1964] 3 All ER 752 (nip between bar fed in and

---

3 See the Manufacture of Aerated Water Regulations 1921 (made under the Act of 1901), for the fencing of the filling apparatus to keep in fragments of bursting bottles; also the Woodworking Machines Regulations 1974 and Abrasive Wheels Regulations 1970, later in this Chapter. S. 14 (3), (4), (6) were repealed by S.I. 1974 No. 1941.

roller) and similarly where a moving part holding material (a 'workpiece') brings it against a stationary part of the machine: *F. E. Callow (Engineers) Ltd v Johnson* [1971] AC 335, [1970] 3 All ER 639. Also there is a duty to fence where it is part of the machinery which is dangerous by reason of its movement, although that part is covered with material and the operator is brought into contact only with the material: *Wearing v Pirelli Ltd* [1977] 1 All ER 339 (rubber stretched on revolving drum to form tyre).

(ii) Parts of machinery flying out

The principle that the intention of the fence is 'to keep the worker out, not the machine or its product in' was extended from materials to a broken part of the machinery itself in *Carroll v Andrew Barclay & Sons Ltd* [1948] AC 477, [1948] 2 All ER 386 where a driving belt, part of the 'transmission machinery', broke in the course of working, and struck a workman nearby. The House of Lords held that the occupiers were not liable, because, as Lord Porter said, at pp. 486 and 390:

> 'Fencing . . . means the erection of a barricade to prevent any employee from making contact with the machine, not an enclosure to prevent broken machinery from flying out.'

The case was decided under s. 13 (transmission machinery). *Prima facie*, it also applied to the other cases, certainly to 'prime movers' under s. 12, for, as Lord Normand said, at pp. 489 and 392:

> 'The word "fence" does not suggest to my mind the massive kind of structure which might be necessary to contain the parts of a large flywheel breaking apart while rotating at high speed.'

What, then, of the machinery governed by s. 14, which is neither transmission machinery nor a prime mover? It was for some time in doubt whether there was a duty to fence in the case of a machine which might be expected, in the course of working, to throw out flying pieces. But in *Close v Steel Co of Wales Ltd* [1962] AC 367, [1961] 2 All ER 953 where a shattered bit flew out from an electric drill, it was held by the House of Lords that machinery under s. 14, like other machinery, need only be fenced to prevent contact[4].

---

4   The decisions in *Dickson v Flack* [1953] 2 QB 464, [1953] 2 All ER 840 and *Rutherford v Glanville & Sons (Bovey Tracey) Ltd* [1958] 1 All ER 532—following a dictum of Lord du Parcq in the *Carroll* case—were overruled on this point.

These decisions may not apply where a part comes out of its normal position while remaining attached to the machine. In *Hindle v Birtwhistle* [1897] 1 QB 192 a shuttle flew out of a loom in the course of working: since such an occurrence might be expected as a result either of careless handling or impurity in the material, it was held that the machine ought to have been fenced. Lord Porter, in *Carroll's* case, referred to *Hindle v Birtwhistle* without disapproval, and said, [1948] AC 477 at 485, [1948] 2 All ER 386 at 390:

> '. . . in the case of the flying spindle[5] it was not a breaking of a part of the machine but an accident which might have been anticipated from its ordinary working which had to be guarded against. The machine was found to be a dangerous one because of the liability of spindles to fly out, and it was that danger which was liable to occur in the course of its ordinary working, not its abnormal action in breaking, for which a fence had to be provided.'

The case was also mentioned without disapproval in *Close v Steel Co of Wales, supra*. Similarly in *Kinder v Camberwell Borough Council* [1944] 2 All ER 315 a machine had a heavy handle which was liable to fly up, and the court held that it ought to be fenced[6].

Protection against contact with the machine means that the body of the worker must be precluded from coming into contact. It is possible, of course, that machinery may catch the clothing of the worker or some object he is holding and draw the worker himself into the machinery. Historically, these are just the type of accidents which the fencing requirements of the Factories Acts were intended to prevent; and there is no doubt that, if the fencing does not prevent the worker being drawn into contact with the machine, he is protected by the statute. This is so even though he is drawn into contact in an unexpected way: *Millard v Serck Tubes Ltd* [1969] 1 All ER 598 (arm caught by 'swarf' or metal strips from material being drilled). There is, on the other hand, *no* duty to fence machinery so as to prevent a hand tool or other object from coming into contact with the indirect result of injuring the plaintiff:

---

5   'Spindle' is a slip by Lord Porter. The object was a 'shuttle' which came out of a loom.

6   Perhaps this machine ought not, as a matter of *fact*, have been held to be dangerous: see Lord Normand's speech in the *Carroll* case.

Sparrow v Fairey Aviation Co Ltd [1964] AC 1019, [1962] 3 All ER 706
(tool threw plaintiff's hand violently against outer part of machine[7]).

(2) No duty to fence machinery produced in the factory, or otherwise not properly described as factory machinery

Another question which has arisen is the meaning of the term
'machinery' as used in the fencing sections. In *Parvin v Morton Machine
Co Ltd* [1952] AC 515, [1952] 1 All ER 670 the House of Lords held
that it does not include machinery which is a product of the factory, as
distinct from being used in the course of the factory processes. In this
case a machine known as a dough-brake had been made, assembled
(with a guard) and tested in the factory: and while the guard was
removed for an adjustment, a young person was allowed to clean the
machine, with the result that his hand was drawn into the rollers. It was
held that there was no breach of duty: and the decision extends to s. 20
(cleaning of machine by young persons) as well as to the more familiar
sections. Similarly a machine under repair would be excluded unless
part of the factory's own installation: *Thurogood v Van den Berghs and
Jurgens Ltd* [1951] 2 KB 537, [1951] 1 All ER 682. A fan fixed to a motor
engine under test in a workshop was held not to have become part of the
factory's installation although the fan had been fitted in reverse to heat
the workshop during a power cut: *Ballard v Ministry of Defence* [1977]
ICR 513.

When new machinery is being installed, the fencing requirements
apply as soon as a unit is complete, so the contractors' men installing it in
a factory may be protected when working on or near such a unit. A hoist
is a complete unit for this purpose although it is to be used in
conjunction with a conveyor belt still under construction: *Irwin v White
Tomkins and Courage Ltd* [1964] 1 All ER 545. Similarly, fencing was
required where a machine had been installed but was under test for an
experimental period to see whether modifications were necessary:
T.B.A. Industrial Products Ltd v Lainè [1987] ICR 75.

The fencing requirements extend to all machinery forming part of the

---

7   This seems to overrule *Johnson v J. Stone & Co. (Charlton) Ltd* [1961] 1 All ER 869
     (claim succeeded where workpiece came in contact with heavy pulley causing it to
     drop).

equipment of a factory, whether in a fixed position or capable of moving from place to place: thus they apply to a portable fire pump: *McNeill v Roche Products Ltd* 1988 SLT 704; and to a mobile crane and also vehicles used in a factory and a bucket on a ropeway, but not *visiting* vehicles such as lorries and cars: *British Railways Board v Liptrot* [1969] 1 AC 136, [1967] 2 All ER 1072[8]. What parts of a vehicle can be described as 'parts of the machinery' remains open to argument, and it seems that they do not include the wheels and bodywork which become dangerous only when the whole vehicle is in motion and are for this purpose just a platform on which machinery is mounted. The fencing requirements are not excluded for cranes and similar machinery by the fact that they are subject to detailed requirements under s. 27. A hook on the hoist of a crane, fitted with a safety-clip which trapped the plaintiff's hand, was however held not to be 'part of the machinery': *Mirza v Ford Motor Co* [1981] ICR 757.

A portable grinding tool is part of the machinery, although it can be plugged in anywhere: *Lovelidge v Anselm Odling & Sons Ltd* [1967] 2 QB 351, [1967] 1 All ER 459 (a building site case).

(3) Meaning of 'secure' fencing: perhaps no duty to fence against unforeseeable line of approach to machinery

In *John Summers & Sons Ltd v Frost* [1955] AC 740, [1955] 1 All ER 870, the House of Lords decided that machinery is 'securely fenced' if the fence gives protection against the danger which the statute contemplates. In the cases cited in section 2(1) of this chapter, they decided that under ss. 12 and 13 (prime movers and transmission machinery) the danger contemplated is the risk of injury through coming into contact with the machinery; and that under s. 14 too (other dangerous parts of machinery) the danger contemplated is *normally* the risk of contact, though it may be, exceptionally, that protection is also required against parts of the machinery coming out, if they are liable to do so in the ordinary course of working.

It follows that 'secure fencing' is that which gives complete protection against contact, and foreseeability of exactly how contact may be made

---

8   Overruling *Cherry v International Alloys Ltd* [1961] 1 QB 136, [1960] 3 All ER 264 and (by implication) *Quintas v National Smelting Co Ltd* [1961] 1 All ER 630.

does not come into it, except of course when the court is deciding whether machinery is 'dangerous' under s. 14. (Under ss. 12 and 13 prime movers and transmission machinery have to be fenced whether dangerous or not, which indicates that in the case of such machinery the legislation itself has exercised all the foresight that is necessary.) Viscount Simonds (with whom Lord Oaksey concurred) said, at p. 753 and p. 873:

> 'Since the danger to be guarded against is contact with the exposed part of the grindstone while it is in motion, that fencing is secure which effectively protects the workman from that danger.'

He also said (at pp. 752, 872) that the duty is 'absolutely to prevent the operator from coming into contact'. Lord Morton said at pp. 875 F, 876 H:

> 'the natural meaning of the word "securely" . . . is that the part must be so fenced that no part of the person or clothing of any person working the machine or passing near it can come into contact with it . . . What is contemplated . . . is that there shall be complete protection against contact. . . .'

A majority of the House therefore clearly expressed themselves in favour of complete prevention of contact, and a similar view was taken by the House as a whole in *Close v Steel Co of Wales Ltd* [1962] AC 367, [1961] 2 All ER 953. It would seem that if there are exceptional cases under s. 14 where protection is required against part of the machinery emerging, the fence would be 'secure' if it prevented the emerging part from making contact: see *Close v Steel Co of Wales Ltd* at 969 E.

Difficulty arises, however, from the earlier case of *Burns v Joseph Terry & Sons Ltd* [1951] 1 KB 454, [1950] 2 All ER 987, where a majority of the Court of Appeal apparently took the view that fencing is not required for a side of the machine where approach or contact is 'not reasonably foreseeable'. This case concerned a machine for cleaning cocoa beans. Some distance above the ground there was a shelf, upon which beans sometimes fell, and below the shelf there were cog wheels (part of the transmission machinery under s. 13) covered in front (but not at the sides) with a circular mesh guard. A boy, on his own initiative, propped a ladder against a revolving shaft and climbed up to retrieve fallen beans: the ladder slipped sideways, and the boy's hand somehow went into the cogs from below the shelf and behind the guard. The court held (Denning LJ dissenting) that the fencing need only give security against such dangers as could reasonably be foreseen; that an approach to the cogs from this angle could not be foreseen; and that the guard was not inadequate by reason of its failure to cover the cogs. In *John Summers v Frost* Lord Reid agreed with this line of reasoning but in this respect he was in a minority as shown by the extracts from the speeches of the other Lords quoted above. In this and other cases there seems to be a fallacious approach. The machine is looked at with the fence actually on it. The court decides that there was only a small risk (with that fence in position) that someone would come into contact; that since there was only a small risk, injury was not 'reasonably foreseeable'; and that therefore *in that condition*, as fenced, the machinery was not 'dangerous'. The correct approach, surely, in considering whether fencing is required, is to look at the machinery *without any fence at all*: per Lord Keith of Avonholm in *Summers v Frost* at 888 C to D; per Denning LJ in *Burns v Terry* at 992 D. In that unfenced and exposed condition, as both those judges said, there is nothing 'unforeseeable' about approach from any direction. 'Secure' fencing is therefore required, and the only question is whether it precludes contact. The fence in *Burns v Terry* did not, because it was open at the sides.

The balance of authority indicates that the majority decision in *Burns v Terry* was wrong, and the dissenting judgment of Denning LJ correct. The decision has not been followed in Scotland. In *Simpson v Hardie & Smith Ltd* 1968 SLT 261 the High Court of Justiciary held that on a charge of failing to fence transmission machinery securely under s. 13 it was 'irrelevant' (the technical Scottish term for 'no defence') to say that an accident was not reasonably foreseeable.

But if (contrary to these views) it is necessary for the precise angle or method of approach to the machine to be foreseeable, account must be taken of the remarks of Lord Normand in *Lyon v Don Brothers, Buist & Co Ltd* [1944] JC 1:

> 'Occupiers of factories . . . are bound to take into account the
> possibility of negligent, ill-advised or indolent conduct on the part of
> their employees, and even of frivolous conduct, especially where young
> workers are employed.'

The fence must give protection against all foreseeable conduct, even wilful acts in disobedience to instructions, as in *Smith v Chesterfield and District Co-operative Society Ltd* [1953] 1 All ER 447 where a girl put her hand underneath the guard to press pastry against the rollers of a machine. If the inner parts of a machine are easily accessible by removal of an inspection hatch, they should be fenced: *Clews v B.A. Chemicals Ltd* 1988 SLT 29. In other words, the hatch alone is not sufficient.

3 The alternatives to fencing: safety by position or construction

Prime movers (other than the electrical apparatus mentioned in s. 12(3)) must be securely fenced, and no alternative is allowed; but other machinery need not be fenced if it is safe by position or construction.

To satisfy these alternatives the machine must, by its position or construction, be 'actually safe', i.e. as safe as it would be if securely fenced[9]. As regards *position*, therefore, if a workman has to go near the machinery in the ordinary course of his work, and is then injured, it cannot be said that the requirements of the section have been fulfilled. Thus in *Atkinson v London and North-Eastern Rail Co* [1926] 1 KB 313 a workman was instructed to move a belt from a shaft to a pulley while the shaft was revolving. The place was not accessible in the normal way and the workman had to climb up a ladder and stand on a beam. It was held that, as the shaft was unsafe to this workman in the ordinary course of his work—though inaccessible to others—the Act had been contravened[10].

It is not in itself a sufficient defence, therefore, to say that on account of the height of a shaft or belt, fencing is unnecessary. Indeed, it seems debatable whether mere height above ground is ever sufficient to excuse

9 I.e. whatever meaning is ultimately given to 'securely fenced', the safety given by position or construction must be equivalent. It has been said that safety by position or construction involves 'foreseeability': *sed quaere*. It is, surely, a simple question of fact whether there is equivalent protection. If 'secure fencing' would preclude contact altogether, or preclude contact from a certain angle, the position or construction is 'safe' if it precludes contact to the same extent. Obvious examples would be a machine whose moving parts are encased—safety by construction—or a machine whose moving parts are against a wall or another machine so that they cannot be reached—safety by position.
10 Approved in *Carroll's* case [1948] AC 477 at 485, [1948] 2 All ER 386 at 390. Similar decisions were given in *Findlay v Newman, Hender & Co Ltd* [1937] 4 All ER 58, *Fowler v Yorkshire Electric Power Co Ltd* [1939] 1 All ER 407, *Dunn v Bird's Eye Foods Ltd* [1959] 2 QB 265, [1959] 2 All ER 403, and *Hodkinson v Henry Wallwork Ltd* [1955] 3 All ER 236 where it was held that ropes and pulleys nine feet above the ground should be fenced.

lack of fencing, since it is always foreseeable that maintenance men, cleaners or decoraters will be above floor level. A good example of safety by position is machinery with unfenced inner workings against a wall.

As to the safety afforded by the *construction* of a machine, the same principles apply. It is not enough to say that the machine was safe if the workman had obeyed instructions: *Sutherland v James Mills Ltd, Executors,* [1938] 1 All ER 283. The machine itself must be as safe by construction as if it were securely fenced—for instance, if the dangerous parts are enclosed in a case, which cannot be removed more easily than a fence. The onus of establishing safety by position or construction, as an excuse for failure to fence, rests on the occupier: *Chalmers v Speedwell Wire Co* 1942 JC 42.

4 Prime movers

By s. 176(1), 'prime mover' means—

> 'Every engine, motor or other appliance which provides mechanical energy derived from steam, water, wind, electricity, the combustion of fuel or other source.'

That is, a prime mover is a source of mechanical power. It is not necessarily the main source of power, and there may be a number of prime movers in a factory.

By s. 12(1):

> 'Every flywheel directly connected to any prime mover and every moving part of any prime mover, except such prime movers as are mentioned in [s. 12(3)], shall be securely fenced, whether the flywheel or prime mover is situated in an enginehouse or not.'

The subsection, it will be noted, does not require the prime mover *as a whole* to be fenced or encased: it identifies the particular parts which are dangerous, the flywheel and any moving parts, and requires those parts to be fenced. In this case, safety by position or construction is not allowed as an alternative. Thus there must be fencing even on the inner side of a flywheel, for some person may have to go on that side to oil or clean the machinery: *Britton v Great Western Cotton Co* (1872) LR 7 Exch 130.

By s. 12(2):

'The head and tail race of every water wheel and of every water-turbine shall be securely fenced.'

These places probably received special mention because they cannot be described as 'moving parts' of a prime mover.

By s. 12(3):

'Every part of electric generators, motors and rotary converters, and every flywheel directly connected thereto, shall be securely fenced unless it is in such a position or of such construction as to be as safe to every person employed or working on the premises as it would be if securely fenced.'

In the case of electrical apparatus, the choice of fencing or safety by position or construction is given: but in this case the obligation extends to every part, and not merely to every moving part, because even the static part of such apparatus may be electrically dangerous. 'Every part' would not, it is thought, include outer casing, at any rate if properly insulated and earthed.

5 Transmission machinery

'Transmission machinery' is defined by s. 176(1) to be:

'Every shaft, wheel, drum, pulley, system of fast and loose pulleys, coupling, clutch, driving-belt or other device by which the motion of a prime mover is transmitted to or received by any machine or appliance.'

In *Deane v Edwards (H. F.) & Co Ltd* [1941] 2 All ER 274 a rope by which power from an electric motor was transmitted to a lift was held to be 'transmission machinery' within the definition. Some of the dangers attendant on the movement of lift machinery are now regulated by s. 22. Apparently machinery does not cease to be 'transmission machinery' because the power is temporarily cut off.

By s. 13(1);

'Every part of the transmission machinery shall be securely fenced unless it is in such a position or of such construction as to be as safe to every person employed or working on the premises as it would be if securely fenced.'

This subsection is followed by some further detailed requirements, set out below, which are subject to this qualification, that the Health and Safety Executive may grant exemption in particular cases where compliance is 'unnecessary or impracticable' (s. 13(5) as modified by S.I. 1974 No. 1941).

Disconnecting mechanism

By s. 13(2):

> 'Efficient devices or appliances shall be provided and maintained in every room or place where work is carried on by which the power can promptly be cut off from the transmission machinery in that room or place.'

That is, in case anyone is caught in a machine, there must be some means of switching off the power supply without going outside the room or other place, a procedure which would involve delay.

Driving belts

By s. 13(3):

> 'No driving belt when not in use shall be allowed to rest or ride upon a revolving shaft which forms part of the transmission machinery.'

A driving belt which for the time being is out of use must, therefore, be kept away by some device from the revolving shaft at the transmission end: and under the next subsection, precautions are to be taken against a driving belt creeping on to a fast pulley so that it changes speed without warning.

By s. 13(4):

> 'Suitable striking gear or other efficient mechanical appliances shall be provided and maintained and used to move driving belts to and from fast and loose pulleys which form part of the transmission machinery, and any such gear or appliances shall be so constructed, placed and maintained as to prevent the driving belt from creeping back to the fast pulley.'

6 Other machinery which is 'dangerous'

The parts of prime movers and transmission machinery which have been mentioned above are treated as dangerous *per se*. They must be fenced, whether or not they are dangerous in fact.

On the other hand, the remaining machinery, i.e. the machines actually used in the factory processes, must be proved to be 'dangerous' before it can be held that there is an obligation to fence: for, under s. 14(1), the duty to fence applies to 'every dangerous part of any machinery'. A distinction is therefore drawn between 'parts' of machinery which are 'dangerous' and 'parts' which are not. There is no statutory definition of 'dangerous', and *prima facie* it would carry its everyday meaning of something which involves risk of injury[11]. There is, however, extensive case-law on the subject, which has not always coincided with the everyday understanding of the word.

What is a 'dangerous part' of machinery?

The House of Lords considered the question of what is meant by 'dangerous' machinery in *John Summers & Sons Ltd v Frost* [1955] AC 740, [1955] 1 All ER 870 and gave general approval to the test of 'reasonable foreseeability' of injury and other tests suggested in the decided cases, provided that they are read together[12]. However, the whole tenor of the speeches indicates that in the opinion of the House the question whether a part of machinery is dangerous ought not to be approached in an elaborate and artificial way, but simply by an examination of the machinery and its working. Thus a grindstone

---

11 It is important to note that the distinction is not between safe and dangerous machines, but between safe and dangerous *parts*. It is therefore consistent with the view that most machines driven by mechanical power are in some way dangerous, and also many hand-operated machines. Parts will ordinarily be dangerous if they move fast, or if, though moving quite slowly, they are capable of crushing or cutting the limbs of the operator. As a matter of history, it is probable that the fencing requirements visualised the exposed inner mechanism of a machine, rather than such things as knives, rollers and presses which had to be exposed for actual use: and this was in fact held in the old Canadian case of *Hamilton v Groesbeck* (1891) 18 AR 437. Such a construction cannot now be supported.

12 See in particular Viscount Simonds at p. 873 where he makes it clear that these are only 'tests', and adds 'whatever test is adopted, there will be borderline cases'. Also Lord Reid at pp. 882–3.

moving at 1,450 revolutions per minute was held to be dangerous and Lord Keith said (at p. 777 and p. 890):

> 'The experience of the workman operating the machine, the infrequency of accidents, and the views of factory inspectors or other interested authority on the working of grinding machines are not here relevant considerations . . . unless possibly in a marginal case, such matters . . . can carry no weight[13].'

In the subsequent case of *Close v Steel Co of Wales Ltd* [1962] AC 367, [1961] 2 All ER 953 the House treated the 'foreseeability' test as the usual approach. It is not, however, the only approach. The word 'dangerous' is an ordinary, simple English word, and the court usually has little difficulty in deciding as a fact whether a part of machinery is dangerous or not. The elaborate reasoning in the decided cases has mostly arisen to rebut artificial arguments for the defence. In particular the 'foreseeability' test, of which perhaps too much has been made, was introduced to counter the argument that machinery needs fencing only if it is dangerous in the normal course of working: the 'foreseeability' test allows also for carelessness.

A common fallacy in considering whether machinery is dangerous is to look at it as actually fitted with a guard though this may be incomplete. The tendency is then to say there is little risk of anyone getting through the gap accidentally; that therefore an accident is not 'reasonably foreseeable' (though this step is logically incorrect—a *little* risk is not *no* risk); and therefore there is no danger. The correct approach is to look at the machinery in a completely exposed state, without any fence at all: per Lord Keith of Avonholm in *Summers v Frost* at 888 C to D; per Denning LJ in *Burns v Joseph Terry & Sons Ltd* [1950] 2 All ER 987 at 992 D.

(i) The words of the Act are paramount

Various tests have been formulated in the decided cases to meet different circumstances, but it is well to remember that no test can be a complete substitute for the words of the statute, which remain paramount. This principle was frequently affirmed by the House of

---

13 In *Carr v Mercantile Produce Co Ltd* [1949] 2 KB 601, [1949] 2 All ER 531 Lord Goddard CJ attached importance to the factory inspector's failure to require a fence: but this is, after all, only hearsay evidence of expert opinion, and therefore dubious in more than one respect.

Lords under the Workmen's Compensation Acts, where thousands of decisions were given on the meaning of the words 'accident arising out of and in the course of the employment', and such judicial tests as 'added perils' and 'locality risks' were formulated to meet recurring situations, but were held not to be conclusive. In *Blair & Co Ltd v Chilton* (1915) 84 LJ KB 1147 at 1148, for example, Earl Loreburn said:

> 'The words of the Act itself rule in every case. Previous decisions are illustrations of the way in which judges look at cases, and in that sense are useful and suggestive; but I think that we ought to beware of allowing tests or guides . . . suggested by the court in one state of circumstances . . . to be applied to other surroundings, and thus by degrees to substitute themselves for the words of the Act itself.'

Likewise, in *Harris v Associated Portland Cement Manufacturers Ltd* [1939] AC 71 at 89, [1938] 4 All ER 831 at 842, Lord Wright referred to 'the salutary rule that a test convenient in a particular case must not be allowed to dislodge the original words of the Act'. This salutary rule surely applies with equal force to s. 14 of the Factories Act.

(ii) Danger is a question of fact and degree

The Scots cases contain an illuminating approach. In *Mackay v Ailsa Shipbuilding Co Ltd* 1945 SC 414 at 418 Lord Jamieson said:

> 'The question whether or not danger exists is primarily one of fact and to a large extent one of degree, and in some cases it may be difficult to determine whether a given machine, or part of a machine, does or does not fall within the definition of "dangerous" . . .'

In *Mitchell v North British Rubber Co* 1945 JC 69 rollers were held to be dangerous when rubber had to be put between them and the forearm of the operator was caught in the 'nip'. Lord Cooper LJ-C said at p. 73:

> 'The question is not whether the occupiers of the factory knew that it was dangerous; nor whether the factory inspector had so reported; nor whether previous accidents had occurred; nor whether the victims of these accidents had, or had not, been contributorily negligent. The test is objective and impersonal. Is the part such in its character, and so circumstanced in its position, exposure, method of operation and the like, that in the ordinary course of human affairs danger may reasonably be anticipated from its use unfenced, not only to the prudent, alert and skilled operative intent upon his task, but also to the careless and inattentive worker whose inadvertent or indolent conduct may expose him to risk of injury or death from the unguarded part?'

Lord Cooper went on to say that immunity from accident and the non-intervention of the factory inspector are both relevant in evidence, although neither carries great weight and such evidence is frequently disregarded. This passage was expressly approved by the House of Lords in *John Summers & Sons Ltd v Frost* [1955] AC 740, [1955] 1 All ER 870. Lord Cooper's test, it may be noted, has the great merit of focusing attention upon the machine itself and its propensities rather than upon the probable behaviour of the operator.

(iii) The contingency of carelessness and other foreseeable conduct
The Scottish cases quoted in the foregoing section show that it is not enough to say that the part of the machine in question was safe in the ordinary course of working. The contingency of negligence and other foreseeable conduct in the vicinity of the machinery must be taken into account. This principle has been applied in a long series of cases in England, which were approved by the House of Lords in *John Summers & Sons v Frost* [1955] 1 All ER 870 at pp. 873, 882–883, provided that they are read in conjunction with the words of Lord Cooper which have already been quoted.

In *Hindle v Birtwistle* [1897] 1 QB 192 (a case where a shuttle was liable to fly out of a loom) Wills J said, at p. 195:

> 'Machinery or parts of machinery is and are dangerous if in the ordinary course of human affairs danger may be reasonably anticipated from the use of them without protection . . . it is . . . out of the question to say that machinery cannot be dangerous unless it is so in the course of careful working[14].'

This latter point, that account must be taken of possible carelessness, was again stressed by the Divisional Court in *Blenkinsop v Ogden* [1898] 1 QB 783.

In *Walker v Bletchley Flettons Ltd* [1937] 1 All ER 170 the plaintiff was employed by brickmakers and was learning to drive a mechanical excavator. In going to the tool-box he slipped, and caught his hand in a cog wheel which was neither fenced nor cased. Du Parcq J gave the following explanation of what is meant by 'dangerous':

> 'A part of machinery is dangerous if it is a possible cause of injury to anybody acting in a way in which a human being may be reasonably

---

14 *Hindle v Birtwistle* was followed in Scotland in *Lauder v Barr and Stroud* 1927 JC 21 and subsequent cases.

expected to act in circumstances which may reasonably be expected to occur.'

For 'possible cause' of injury, Lord Reid in *John Summers & Sons Ltd v Frost* [1955] AC 740, [1955] 1 All ER 870 substituted 'a reasonably foreseeable' cause and his amendment was adopted by the House of Lords in *Close v Steel Co of Wales Ltd* [1962] AC 367, [1961] 2 All ER 953. It must, however, be read in the light of Lord Reid's repeated statements that a reasonable man will not disregard any risk unless it is very small, and, even then, cannot be eliminated without disproportionate effort: see Chapter 2 section 2. This test (which should not be treated as a definition replacing the words of the statute) takes into account the possibility of carelessness and even wilful misuse of such a character that it can be foreseen. Thus deliberate acts which can be foreseen, such as putting a hand into the machine contrary to express orders, must be taken into account: *Smith v Chesterfield and District Co-operative Society Ltd* [1953] 1 All ER 447. In *Chasteney v Michael Nairn & Co Ltd* [1937] 1 All ER 376 some pinion wheels were safe unless a man put his hand inside to grease them while in motion. It was held, in view of this possible carelessness, that the wheels were dangerous and must be fenced. In *Wood v London County Council* [1940] 2 KB 642, [1940] 4 All ER 149, reversed on appeal on other grounds at [1941] 2 KB 232, [1941] 2 All ER 230, an electric mincing machine was held to be dangerous when a young girl could push her hand through a narrow aperture which would not admit the hand of a man. Again, in *Smithwick v National Coal Board* [1950] 2 KB 335 there was a narrow aperture leading to a belt and rollers, which were held to be 'exposed and dangerous' because a conscientious workman might carelessly put his head or part of his body inside to see what was wrong[15]. On the other hand, it was held by the Court of Appeal in *Higgins v Harrison* (1932) 25 BWCC 113 that a machine did not need to be fenced when danger arose only because the operator deliberately went round to the back and put her hand inside; and in *Carr v Mercantile Produce Co Ltd* [1949] 2 KB 601, [1949] 2 All ER 531 the Divisional Court, following *Higgins v Harrison*, upheld a finding by a magistrate that the revolving worm of a macaroni extruding machine was not dangerous, when it could be

15 *Rushton v Turner Bros Asbestos Ltd* [1959] 3 All ER 517 is out of line with these cases.

reached only by putting the fingers through a narrow opening[16]. It is doubtful whether these two cases would now be decided in the same way.

The foreseeability test as formulated by Du Parcq J turns on human behaviour rather than, like the Scottish tests, the propensities of the machine itself. Can conduct of the workman be foreseen which will bring him into contact with the machine? If he is brought into contact, can it be foreseen that he will be injured? In *Smithwick v National Coal Board* [1950] 2 KB 335, a case under s. 55 of the Coal Mines Act 1911, Denning LJ said:

> '. . . it is not only the likely but also the unlikely accident that the occupier must guard against. He must guard against all conduct which he might reasonably foresee. The limit of his responsibility is only reached when the machinery is safe for all except the incalculable individual against whom no reasonable foresight can provide—the individual who does not merely do what is unlikely but what is unforeseeable . . .'

The weakness of the 'foreseeability' test is that opinions differ so much as to what can be foreseen[17]. Its importance is to show that careless as well as careful conduct should be kept in contemplation.

(iv) Some examples

The following are common examples of parts of machinery which have been held to be dangerous: revolving rollers, cog wheels, knives, cutting machines and presses. In *Kinder v Camberwell Borough Council* [1944] 2 All ER 315 even the handle of a machine, which was liable to fly up, was held to be dangerous. A hot drum with rollers, for reproducing blue prints, was held dangerous in *Stimson v Standard Telephones and Cables Ltd* [1940] 1 KB 342, [1939] 4 All ER 225. Points where conveyor belts pass over rollers have frequently been held to be dangerous, although

---

16 This type of machine is now expressly listed as a dangerous machine on which young persons must not be employed without proper training: see p. 358, note 1, item (7), *post*.

17 Especially when qualified by 'reasonableness'. In the test as now adopted, 'reasonably' occurs no fewer than three times. The principal result is—cynics may think—that, so long as the right formula is used, it can be used to justify a decision either way. How much easier to say that 'danger' is a question of fact and degree, depending on the known propensities of the machine!

not moving fast: *Williams v Sykes & Harrison Ltd* [1955] 3 All ER 225[18]. Where scrap was fed into revolving cutters, sometimes stuck and had to be pushed down, the employer had warned workmen, and there had previously been a guard, no other conclusion was held possible than that the machine was foreseeably dangerous: *Woodley v Meason Freer & Co Ltd* [1963] 3 All ER 636.

In deciding whether any parts of machinery are dangerous, the correct approach must surely be to disregard any *partial* fence or casing which protects them. If, without that cover, they would be dangerous, there must be 'secure' fencing which precludes contact. If the machinery is looked at *with* the partial fence and the question is asked whether in that condition it is dangerous there is a tendency to say there is not much risk, and that it is 'reasonably' safe, though no one could possibly reach that conclusion by viewing the machinery as exposed.

(v) Inadmissible defences
Once a part of a machine is found to be dangerous, it is no defence to say that (1) it was safe if the workman had been careful, and obeyed instructions, or (2) the machine had been passed by the factory inspector, or (3) it had been in use for a long period without accident: *Sutherland v Jas. Mills Ltd, Executors* [1938] 1 All ER 283; *Mitchell v North British Rubber Co* 1945 JC 69.

(vi) Machinery which is not dangerous in the absence of materials, or tools left in the machine
Difficulty has arisen where machinery becomes dangerous only when materials are present. This is especially liable to happen with machine tools, where there may be a wide gap between the components of the machine when it is empty, but the gap becomes narrow and dangerous when the metal workpiece is inserted.

Since there is no duty to fence dangerous material in a machine, no

18 Machinery may be dangerous if likely to knock someone down, though moving quite slowly (bucket on aerial ropeway): Willmer LJ, in a dissenting judgment in *Quintas v National Smelting Co Ltd* [1961] 1 All ER 630. *Quaere* however whether a 'traffic' danger is within the fencing requirements: *British Railways Board v Liptrot* [1969] 1 AC 136, [1967] 2 All ER 1072. A small nip between the centre of a horizontal bar mounted on a tractor and the edge of the cylinder into which its shaft retracted quite slowly was not dangerous, though a freak accident occurred when a man slipped in clay and his foot was thrown up into this small area just as it closed: *Rodgers v London Brick* Co Ltd (1970) 8 KIR 843.

duty arises when the danger is due to the material itself: *Bullock v G. John Power (Agencies) Ltd* [1956] 1 All ER 498 (lashing end of wire drawn through hole by drum); *Eaves v Morris Motors Ltd* [1961] 2 QB 385, [1961] 3 All ER 233 (sharp bolt mounted on moving machine tool caught plaintiff's hand). There was formerly a conflict of opinion, where danger is due to the machinery and the workpiece in conjunction. When a workpiece was moved by a revolving plate against a vertical borer, producing a dangerous 'nip' between borer and workpiece, it was held that the machinery should be fenced: *Hoare v M. & W. Grazebrook Ltd* [1957] 1 All ER 470. *Contra*, it was held that no fence was required when a moving table carried a metal block beneath a stationary plane or shaver: *Lewis v High Duty Alloys Ltd* [1957] 1 All ER 740. These decisions could not be reconciled except on the artificial ground that in the second case the component of the machine which caused the danger was not moving. In *Midland and Low Moor Iron and Steel Co Ltd v Cross* [1965] AC 343, [1964] 3 All ER 752 the House of Lords held that machinery must be fenced where, in the course of working, material is brought up against a moving part and danger arises from the juxtaposition (bar fed between grooved wheels): and subsequently generalised this to all danger arising from the interaction of two parts, with a 'workpiece' or other material between them, whichever part is stationary: *F. E. Callow (Engineers) Ltd v Johnson* [1971] AC 335, [1970] 3 All ER 639 (overruling *Lewis v High Duty Alloys*). Further, if injury is caused by part of a machine, it is irrelevant that the part is covered with material when it causes the injury: *Wearing v Pirelli Ltd* [1977] 1 All ER 339 (rubber stretched on revolving drum).

The right approach is to remember that the Act is concerned with the safety of machinery in actual use in factories, not merely when revolving *in vacuo*. If the components of the machine come together in a dangerous way when one of them is carrying a workpiece, they are dangerous machinery which ought to be fenced. The danger where a moving part carries material against a fixed part springs from the machinery carrying the workpiece, or rather from the way the moving and fixed part are brought together when the machine is doing its work, not from the workpiece itself. But in *Hindle v Joseph Porritt & Sons Ltd* [1970] 1 All ER 1142 where the movement of felt, pulled forward by rollers, threw the operator's arm against the frame of the machine, it was held that s. 14 did not apply. This seems absolutely right, the accident not being due to movement of one part of a machine in relation to another, but only to movement of material.

A hexagonal tool with the function of a screwdriver, used intermittently to fix the article to be worked on to a machine, was held not to be a 'part' of the machinery, so the fencing requirements did not apply to danger from the tool when the machine was set in motion accidentally with the tool attached: *Sarwar v Simmons and Hawker Ltd* (1971) 11 KIR 300.

(vii) Danger arising from abnormal behaviour of machine
In *Eaves v Morris Motors Ltd, supra,* Willmer LJ expressed the opinion that s. 14 does not apply to danger 'from a machine going wrong or operating in a way that it was never designed to do'. There is no other authority for this view. Certainly if parts of the machinery are dangerous and ought to be fenced, it cannot be an excuse that an accident occurs because of some unexpected malfunction.

(viii) Danger in conjunction with adjoining machinery
Danger caused by a moving part (safe in itself) travelling towards adjoining machinery is not within the protection of s. 14: *Pearce v Stanley-Bridges Ltd* [1965] 2 All ER 594.

Obligation to fence

By s. 14(1):

> 'Every dangerous part of any machinery, other than prime movers and transmission machinery, shall be securely fenced unless it is in such a position or of such construction as to be as safe to every person employed or working on the premises as it would be if securely fenced.'

Special exception: automatic safety device

Then there follows this special exception:

> '(2) In so far as the safety of a dangerous part of any machinery cannot by reason of the nature of the operation be secured by means of a fixed guard, the requirements of [s. 14(1)] shall be deemed to have been

complied with if a device is provided which automatically prevents the operator from coming into contact with that part.'

The obligation to fence by means of a fixed guard is normally imperative: and the proviso quoted above only operates *when a fixed guard will not make the machine safe.* The point is an important one, because, while any person working in the factory may sue on a breach of the general fencing obligation, only the operator of the machine is protected by the proviso: *Associated Motor Cycles Ltd v Bramley Harker* 18 November 1942 (unreported) KBD and dictum of Lord Normand in *Carroll v Barclay (Andrew) & Sons Ltd* [1948] AC 477 at 491, [1948] 2 All ER 386 at 393.

Stock-bar in lathe

By s. 14(5):

'Any part of a stock-bar which projects beyond the headstock of a lathe shall be securely fenced'

unless it is safe by position or construction.

Special types of guards

The Minister had power under s. 76, by safety regulations, to order special types of guards. Special regulations for woodworking and horizontal milling machines, power presses and abrasive wheels are summarised at the end of this chapter. A further example is the Jute (Safety, Health and Welfare) Regulations 1948 (S.I. 1948 No. 1696, slightly amended by S.I. 1987 No. 1141), which, in Part VI, regulate the type of guards required on newly constructed machines, but make it clear that this does not weaken the general obligations under s. 14(1) and s. 17(1). In future, special regulations will be made under the Health and Safety at Work Act 1974.

7 Duty to fence is a continuing obligation during 'motion or use'

In *Thomas v Thomas Bolton & Sons Ltd* (1928) 139 LT 397 workmen had removed certain guards from rollers, and an accident happened before they were replaced. The occupiers were held responsible, and Shearman J said that the Act imposes an obligation:

'Not only to provide adequate fencing, but to keep it in position during the whole of the time when the machine is working.'

Similarly where the guard consisted of a loose lid, the machinery ceased to be fenced as soon as the lid was lifted: *Charles v S. Smith & Sons Ltd* [1954] 1 All ER 499; and the occupier is automatically in breach of s. 14 if an inadequately fenced machine is started, although by an unauthorised operator: *Leach v Standard Telephones and Cables Ltd* [1966] 2 All ER 523; or if no guard is required for normal working of a machine tool and the operator fails to put on a special guard to be used while re-setting: *Foster v Flexible Metal Co Ltd* (1967) 4 KIR 49.

This obligation now depends on s. 16, the first part of which reads as follows:

'All fencing and other safeguards provided in pursuance of the foregoing provisions of this Part of this Act shall be of substantial construction, and constantly maintained and kept in position while the parts required to be fenced or safeguarded are in motion or in use . . .'

except in certain special conditions.

In *Smith v Morris Motors Ltd and Harris* [1950] 1 KB 194, [1949] 2 All ER 715 it was held that the substantive duty to fence arises under ss. 12–14, of which s. 16 is in effect an explanation. Accordingly, where there was a failure to comply with s. 16, a summons could properly be taken out for an offence against s. 14.

Section 16 does not require the fencing to be kept in position unless the parts to be fenced are 'in motion or in use'. It has been held by the House of Lords that this expression refers to the normal running of a machine, and does not apply when the power has been cut off and the machinery is turned over by hand in the course of repairs: *Richard Thomas and Baldwins Ltd v Cummings* [1955] AC 321, [1955] 1 All ER 285. Similarly a machine is not 'in motion or in use' when, in the course of repairs or cleaning, it is moved slowly by an inching device: *Knight v*

Leamington Spa Courier Ltd [1961] 2 QB 253, [1961] 2 All ER 666; *Finnie v John Laird & Son Ltd* 1967 SLT 243. More dubiously, as an extension of this, it has been held that it is not in motion when switched on and off rapidly to move it a few inches in the course of repairs, provided it has only moved a short distance and slowly: *Mitchell v W. S. Westin Ltd* [1965] 1 All ER 657, [1965] 1 WLR 297; and even (purporting to follow this case) where the operator intended to switch on a machine tool in slow gear during re-setting but inadvertently switched on fast: *Foster v Flexible Metal Co Ltd* (1968) 4 KIR 49. But a printing machine was 'in motion' when switched on and off quickly during setting up to turn a cylinder, as it had picked up some speed: *Stanbrook v Waterlow & Sons Ltd* [1964] 2 All ER 506; and if the power is switched on normally but by accident, the sections apply and there is an automatic breach of duty: *Horne v Lec Refrigeration Ltd* [1965] 2 All ER 898. So too a machine continues 'in motion' when it is still running after being switched off: *McLean v Glenrobert Wood Wool Industries Ltd* 1969 SLT (Notes) 29; *Campbell v John A. Best & Co* [1969] NI 123 (guillotine reached a momentary point of balance when switched off, then fell under its own weight); and it is in motion although the movement is slow, provided always that there is some danger which brings the fencing requirements into operation: *Joy v News of the World* (1972) 13 KIR 57 (printer caught hand in 'nip' of cylinder trying to prevent torn paper from clogging it).

The term 'in use' does not include cleaning: *Finnie v John Laird & Son Ltd* 1967 SLT 243; or altering the setting of a machine tool: *Foster v Flexible Metal Co Ltd, supra.* It is difficult to visualise a case where machinery 'in use' has caused an accident without being 'in motion'. The fencing requirements apply once the machine is in motion (e.g. run on completion of installation) although not yet taken into commercial use: *Irwin v White Tomkins and Courage Ltd* [1964] 1 All ER 545.

8 Examination, lubrication and adjustments, exceptions to duty to fence, or give safety by position or construction

There are certain special cases where the fencing may be removed although the machinery is 'in motion or use'.

In these cases, two considerations must be kept in mind. First, the occupier cannot claim the benefit of these special exceptions unless he has fulfilled his primary duty to fence or to make safe. If he has never fenced the machine or made it safe at all, he cannot rely on a special exception: *Atkinson v Baldwins Ltd* (1938) 158 LT 279.

Secondly, the exceptions are granted only upon certain rigorous conditions: and if the conditions are not fulfilled, the exception cannot be pleaded as a defence (s. 155(3), and see *Nash v High Duty Alloys Ltd* [1947] KB 377, [1947] 1 All ER 363).

When fence may be removed

Section 16, after saying that the fence must be kept in position while the parts safeguarded are 'in motion or in use', continues:

> '. . . except when such parts are necessarily exposed for examination and for any lubrication or adjustment shown by such examination to be immediately necessary, and all such conditions as may be specified in regulations made by the Minister are complied with.'

Section 15 is constructed on rather a different pattern. The effect is that, in deciding whether a machine is safe by construction or position,

> '(a) no account shall be taken of any person carrying out, while the part of the machinery is in motion, an examination thereof, or any lubrication or adjustment shown by such examination to be immediately necessary, if the examination, lubrication or adjustment can only be carried out while the part of the machinery is in motion; and
> (b) in the case of any part of transmission machinery used in any such process as may be specified in regulations made by the Minister, being a process where owing to the continuous nature thereof the stopping of that part would seriously interfere with the carrying on of the process, no account shall be taken of any person carrying out, by such methods and in such circumstances as may be specified in the regulations, any lubrication or any mounting or shipping of belts.'

By a proviso the exemption applies only when the operation is performed by a person of or over eighteen[19] and strictly in accordance with the regulations.

These complex requirements need careful dissection.

First, it is clearly envisaged that as a general rule all examination,

19 But see p. 256, n. 21.

lubrication and adjustments will be carried out when the machine is stopped and out of use. Only in exceptional cases will these exemptions apply.

Secondly—leaving aside transmission machinery—it must be shown that the operation can be carried out only while the machine is in motion. It must also be shown that the parts of the machinery have to be exposed: *Nash v High Duty Alloys Ltd, supra.*

Thirdly, the exemption only applies to—

(a) examination;

(b) lubrication;

(c) adjustment[20].

Cleaning does not fall within any of these heads.

Fourthly, in the special case of transmission machinery, there is a separate exemption which extends to—

(a) examination;

(b) mounting or shipping of belts.

This exemption applies only to certain specified processes, and even then only if, on the particular occasion, to stop the machinery would cause serious interference.

Fifthly, the benefit of the exemption is lost at once if there is a deviation from the regulations.

Operations at unfenced machinery regulations

The conditions imposed under these sections are contained in the Operations at Unfenced Machinery Regulations, 1938 (S.R. & O. 1938 No. 641, as amended by S.R. & O. 1946 No. 156 and S.I. 1976 No. 955).

The substance of these regulations is that in general operations can be carried out only by qualified 'machine attendants' who have been properly instructed and issued with a certificate and the official leaflet on precautions; that machine attendants shall be persons aged eighteen[21]

---

20 This does not include a test made after adjustment: *Nash v High Duty Alloys Ltd, supra.* The occupier is therefore in breach of duty if a workman makes an adjustment and does not replace the fence for the test: but the workman too is in breach of duty for failing to use the 'appliance'—the fence—provided: s. 119 of the Act of 1937, now s. 143 and *Norris v Syndic Manufacturing Co Ltd* [1952] 2 QB 135, [1952] 1 All ER 935.

21 But see p. 356, n. 23.

or over; that another person shall stand by in case of emergency; that a barrier shall be interposed to keep unauthorised persons away from the machinery; and that overalls shall be worn which cannot easily catch in the machinery. The former requirement that a machine attendant must be 'male' was removed by the Sex Discrimination Act 1975.

The processes in which transmission machinery may be attended to while in motion are listed in the Schedule to the Regulations of 1946 and include certain chemical and electrolytical processes, as well as processes in making beet sugar, linoleum, paper and film, in milling cereals and in extracting oil from cereals or seeds.

9 Machines constructed after the Factories Act 1937: additional requirements

Section 17 (1), which applies to machinery constructed after 29 July 1937, provides as follows:

> 'In the case of any machine in a factory being a machine intended to be driven by mechanical power—
> (a) every set-screw, bolt or key on any revolving shaft, spindle, wheel or pinion shall be so sunk, encased or otherwise effectively guarded as to prevent danger; and
> (b) all spur and other toothed or friction gearing, which does not require frequent adjustment while in motion, shall be completely encased unless it is so situated as to be as safe as it would be if completely encased.'

This, in effect, imposes safety by construction in a limited class of mechanical parts.

By s. 17(2), a seller or hirer may be liable if he supplies, for use in a factory, a machine which does not comply with the section[22]. It has been held that the purpose of the subsection is to impose a penalty on the seller or hirer, but not to render him liable to an action for damages: *Biddle v Truvox Engineering Co Ltd, Greenwood and Batley Ltd (Third Party)* [1952] 1 KB 101, [1951] 2 All ER 835: so an action for breach of

---

22 This is applied by the Construction (General Provisions) Regulations 1961, reg. 57, to machinery on building and engineering sites.

statutory duty may be brought against the occupier of the factory under
s. 17(1), but not against the supplier under s. 17(2).

Under s. 17(3), the Minister has power to impose additional
requirements for any class of new machinery. He has exercised this
power in Part VI of the Jute (Safety, Health and Welfare) Regulations
1948 (S.I. 1948 No. 1696), reg. 43 of the Construction (General)
Regulations 1961 (S.I. 1961 No. 1580), the Abrasive Wheels Regulations
1970 and the Woodworking Machines Regulations 1974 (sections 13 and
16 of this chapter).

10 Cleaning machinery: women and young persons

By s. 20:

> 'A woman or young person shall not clean any part of a prime mover
> or of any transmission machinery while [it] is in motion.'[23]

This prohibition is absolute, and forbids the cleaning even of stationary
parts while other parts are in motion: *Pearson v Belgian Mills Co* [1896] 1
QB 244. Under this section any kind of movement is sufficient, even
with an inching button, and the decisions on 'motion' under s. 16 do not
apply: *Kelly v John Dale Ltd* [1965] 1 QB 185, [1964] 2 All ER 497;
Denyer v Charles Skipper and East Ltd [1970] 2 All ER 382.

The section continues:

> '—and shall not clean any part of any machine if the cleaning thereof
> would expose the woman or young person to risk of injury from any
> moving part either of that machine of any adjacent machinery.'

A 'young person' is one who has not attained the age of eighteen.

The removal of fluff counts as 'cleaning': *Taylor v Dawson (Mark) &
Son Ltd* [1911] 1 KB 145.

In this section, as in ss. 12 to 14, 'machine' means a machine used as part
of the factory installation, and does not include the products of the factory:
Parvin v Morton Machine Co Ltd [1952] AC 515, [1952] 1 All ER 670.

The fact that this express prohibition of cleaning machinery in motion
does not apply to men may have some relevance to the application of the

23 Employment Act 1989, ss. 9, 10, now delete 'woman' and redefine 'young person'.

general fencing requirements to cleaning: *Finnie v John Laird & Co Ltd* 1967 SLT 243; but is not relevant in deciding whether cleaning machines in motion is a safe system: *Murray v Donald MacDonald (Antartex) Ltd* 1968 SLT 10.

It is thought, however, that the cleaning of machinery in motion is *prima facie* both contrary to the fencing sections and a dangerous system, and little weight should be given to the fact that a specially strong prohibition applies to women and young persons who, at one time, would have been the obvious choice for such tasks.

11 Training and supervision of young persons working at dangerous machines

By s. 21(1):

> 'No young person shall work at any machine to which this section applies, unless he has been fully instructed as to the dangers arising in connection with it and the precautions to be observed, and—
> (a) has received a sufficient training to work at the machine; or
> (b) is under adequate supervision by a person who has a thorough knowledge and experience of the machine.'

The section imposes, therefore, three conditions:
(i) instruction in dangers and precautions; and *either*
(ii) training in the work; *or*
(iii) experienced supervision.

There is an absolute prohibition against employing a person under eighteen unless these conditions are satisfied ((ii) and (iii) being alternative), and an action will lie if injuries result from a breach of the section: *Shearer v Harland and Wolff Ltd* [1947] NI 102; *M'Cafferty v Brown* 1950 SC 300. These cases establish that while the section imposes an absolute duty on the occupier, it does not impose any duty on the young worker.

A list of the machines to which the section applies is given in the Schedule to the Dangerous Machines (Training of Young Persons) Order 1954 (S.I. 1954 No. 921)[1].

12 Self-acting machines

Section 19 deals with 'self-acting' machines, i.e. those which have a fixed part and also a traversing part which moves backwards and forwards. The danger here is that someone may be trapped between the traversing part and fixed structure.

The section applies to factories erected after 1895, or reconstructed after 30 July 1937; and to extensions to factories constructed after the latter date (s. 19(2)).

Section 19(1), amended to metric measurements by S.I. 1983 No. 978, applies where the traversing part of the machine runs over a space 'over which any person is liable to pass whether in the course of his employment or otherwise'. In such a case there is an absolute prohibition against the traversing part, or material carried on it, going

1 *Machines worked with mechanical power:*
    (1) Brick and tile presses.
    (2) Machines for opening or teasing in upholstery or bedding works.
    (3) Carding machines in wool textile trade.
    (4) Corner staying machines.
    (5) Dough brakes.
    (6) Dough mixers.
    (7) Worm pressure extruding machines.
    (8) Gill boxes in wool textile trade.
    (9) Following in laundries:
        (a) hydro-extractors;
        (b) calenders;
        (c) washing machines;
        (d) garment presses.
    (10) Meat mincing machines.
    (11) Milling machines in metal trades.
    (12) Pie and tart making machinery.
    (13) Power presses, including hydraulic and pneumatic presses.
    (14) Loose knife punching machines.
    (15) Wire stitching machines.
    (16) Semi-automatic wood turning lathes.
    Machines worked with or without mechanical power:
    (17) Guillotine machines.
    (18) Platen printing machines.

within 500 mm of any fixed structure (not being part of the machine) in either direction.

By a proviso, the carriage of a self-acting spinning mule may run to a point 310 mm. from the headstock of a similar machine.

Section 19(3) contains this further requirement, which, it will be noted, is not absolute[2]:

> 'All practicable steps shall be taken by instructions to the person in charge of the machine and otherwise to ensure that no person employed shall be in the space between any traversing part of a self-acting spinning mule and any fixed part of the machine towards which the traversing part moves on the inward run, except when the machine is stopped with the traversing part on the outward run.'

The Regulations for Spinning by Self-Acting Mules 1905 (S.R. & O. 1905 No. 1103), impose stricter requirements, and in particular the minder of the machine must not start it without ascertaining that the space between the fixed and traversing part is clear.

13 Woodworking machines

The Woodworking Machines Regulations 1974 (S.I. 1974 No. 903) replace the old regulations made in 1922. Most of the case-law which grew up round the old regulations is superseded.

The new regulations are exceedingly detailed, and can only be summarised in a general way. For complete precision—exact definitions, exceptions, qualifications—the regulations themselves must be checked.

In general they operate *in addition* to the requirements of the Factories Act. However, where dangerous parts of machinery come within the regulations, the 'guards or other safeguards' required by the regulations take the place of s. 14(1) of the Factories Act, and of the similar requirements in the Shipbuilding and Ship-repairing Regulations 1960, reg. 67(2), and the Construction (General

---

2   Under the present wording *Crabtree v Fern Spinning Co Ltd* (1901) 85 LT 549 is obsolete: it does not apply to s. 19(1), or to s. 19(3). The decision was that 'shall not allow' is not equivalent to 'shall prevent'. That is true enough where it is a question of allowing a person into a space, but not in reference to allowing a machine to pass a defined limit.

Provisions) Regulations 1961, reg. 42, that 'dangerous parts' of machinery shall be fenced: regs. 1(3), 3(2) and (4). Section 14(1) or its counterpart will of course apply to any dangerous part for which the regulations do not provide. Section 3(1) of the Factories Act (temperature of workrooms) is excluded where reg. 12 applies.

The regulations apply—reg. 3(1)—not only to factories in the strict sense, but to all premises to which the Factories Act applies under ss. 123–127. Thus they apply, for example, to building sites. The Chief Inspector may grant exemptions: reg. 4.

The field of operation is widened further by the definition of a woodworking machine—reg. 2(2)—to include any of the 12 types of machine listed in Schedule 1 if used on wood, cork, or fibre board, or any combination of these materials. The 12 types are:

1. Sawing machine with circular blades.
2. Grooving machine.
3. Sawing machine with continuous band or strip.
4. Chain sawing machine.
5. Mortising machine.
6. Planing machine.
7. Vertical spindle moulding machine (including high speed routing machine).
8. Multi-cutter moulding machine (having two or more spindles).
9. Tenoning machines.
10. Trenching machines.
11. Automatic and semi-automatic lathes.
12. Boring machines.

General conditions of work

Space (reg. 10)   There must be 'sufficient clear and unobstructed space' round every woodworking machine to enable work to be done, so far as reasonably practicable, without risk to 'persons employed'—a term which includes *all* workers, not just those working at the machine.

State of floor, or surface of ground (reg. 11)   Around a woodworking machine, this must be maintained in good and level condition, and (as far as reasonably practicable) free from chips and other loose material, and must not be allowed to become slippery. Persons employed are under a specific duty (reg. 14) to report if the floor or ground is *not* good and level, or is slippery. It will be appreciated that the regulations apply to many outdoor sites, e.g. at saw-mills and construction sites.

Temperature (reg. 12)   There must be a reasonable temperature in every workroom, usually not below 13°C. Any heating appliance should be enclosed to prevent material catching fire, and fumes should not enter the work room.

Light (reg. 43)   This must be 'sufficient and suitable' at every machine: artificial light should not shine directly into an operator's eyes and glare should be kept down.

Noise (reg. 44)   'Ear protectors' must be provided and used if exposure reaches a certain level (90 decibels for an eight hour shift) in a factory mainly devoted to woodworking, and noise must be reduced as far as practicable (now replaced by the Noise at Work Regulations 1989: see p. 248).

Woodworking machines generally

The machine itself (reg. 42(1))   There is a provision, unusual under the Factories Act, that the machine itself and every part of it, including cutters and cutter-blocks, shall be of good construction, sound material and properly maintained.

Stability of machine (reg. 42(2))   It must be securely fixed to the floor or other structure (unless it is a hand-held machine). Where this is impracticable (for example at an outdoor site) other arrangements must be made 'to ensure' stability.

Stopping and starting devices (reg. 9)   These must be such that they can be operated 'readily and conveniently' by the operator.

Guards for cutters, and alternative safeguards   There is a general requirement in reg. 5(1) for *all* woodworking machines that the cutters (defined to include every kind of cutting edge) shall be enclosed to the greatest extent practicable having regard to the work being done, *unless* the cutters are in such a position as to be as safe as if enclosed: in view of this general rule for all cutters, s. 14(1) can *never* apply to the cutters in any woodworking machine, and the regulation imposes a less strict standard ('reasonably practicable'). Guards must be of 'substantial construction': reg. 5(2). By reg. 8, neither this general requirement for guards, nor specific requirements for machines within regs. 16, 21, 22, 26, 28, 30, 31 and 36, shall apply to a machine which has other 'safeguards' making it as safe as if these requirements were satisfied. At all times when the cutters are in motion, the guards (or equivalent devices or safeguards) shall be kept in position and properly secured and adjusted: except *when*, and *so far as*, because of the nature of the work being done, the use of the guard, device or safeguard is rendered impracticable: reg. 7(1). (This exception, which in some cases allows guards to be dispensed with altogether, does *not* apply in the cases covered by regs. 18(1), 21(1) (2), 22(1), 23, 28, 30, 31—which either forbid certain work with particular machines or require indispensable guards.) Guards, devices and safeguards must be properly maintained: reg. 7(2). It seems clear that where the regulations allow guards to be dispensed with altogether, s. 14(1) is still excluded. Even under the former regulations, which did not specifically exclude s. 14(1), compliance with the regulations was held to satisfy the Act: *Automatic Woodcutting Co Ltd v Stringer* [1957] AC 544, [1957] 1 All ER 90.

Adjustment (reg. 6)   No part of a machine may be adjusted while the cutters are in motion unless there is a 'means'—a control of some kind—for doing this safely—and the guard must not be adjusted unless it can be done safely. This is an obligation resting on the employer, though phrased 'No person shall . . .' (see p. 357, *ante*).

Training, and instruction on dangers (reg. 13)   No person is to be employed at a machine unless trained to work at that particular machine *and* instructed about the risks, precautions and uses of guards. If under 18, he is not allowed to work on certain machines—circular saws, planing machines, vertical spindle moulders—without first completing an officially 'approved' course.

Cleaning   The blade of a sawing machine must not be cleaned by hand while in motion: reg. 40. Certain planing and moulding machines must have exhaust appliances to remove chips and particles: reg. 41.

Sale and hire of machines (reg. 15)   This is forbidden unless they comply with the regulations as to guards and other devices.

Duties of persons employed (reg. 14)

While operating a machine they must use and keep in proper adjustment the guards or other devices and safeguards provided, and use the push-sticks, jigs and other appliances provided. They must also report defects in machines or guards, and (as already noted) in floor condition. It is particularly to be noted that the statutory duty of the operator is only to *keep* the guards in proper adjustment. The duty to ensure that the guards *are* properly adjusted (which usually means so as to leave as small a gap as the size of the wood permits) rests fairly and squarely on the occupier under regs. 7 and 6, although he may well entrust the execution of the duty to the operator or the foreman. The point is that if the duty is placed on the occupier he cannot excuse a breach by saying that he left it to the operator. The same position was established by case-law under the old regulations: *Lay v D. & L. Studios Ltd* [1944] 1 All ER 322; *Cakebread v Hopping Bros (Whetstone) Ltd* [1947] KB 641, [1947] 1 All ER 389. It is perhaps superfluous to mention the obvious point that the operator has on any view no duty until guards (or other appliances) are 'provided', which is not the case if, though available within the factory, their use is forbidden: *Murray v Schwachman Ltd* [1938] 1 KB 130, [1937] 2 All ER 68.

Circular sawing machines (part III, regs. 16–20)

These are defined—reg. 2(2)—as a sawing machine comprising a saw bench (including a roller table, or bench incorporating a travelling table) with a spindle below the machine table to which a circular saw blade can be fitted for the purpose of dividing material into separate parts: but excluding a mutiple rip sawing machine, a straight line edging machine and *any* machine in which the blade moves towards the material to be cut.

Thus the ordinary circular saw has the upper part of the saw rising vertically above the table through a slot, and the wood is moved towards the teeth and out at the back of the saw. Three distinct guards are required to cover the full circle of the saw:

(1) Below the table the blade must be guarded to the fullest extent practicable, which must normally mean completely covered: reg. 16(1).

(2) Behind the saw and in direct line with it, a riving knife. This serves the dual purpose of keeping open the cut in the wood as it passes the back of the saw, and of guarding the back. It is fixed at a point below the table, and must be adjustable and in fact adjusted as close as possible to the saw—maximum 12 mm. at table level. It must form an arc of a circle with radius no greater than the largest saw for which the saw is designed: reg. 16(2).

(3) Over the top of the saw, from the top of the riving knife to the top of the material fed to the saw, there must be a strong, easily adjustable guard—with flanges on each side deep enough to cover the teeth of the saw to their roots: reg. 16(3) (4). The gap where the wood is fed being the chief danger, the gap must be adjusted 'as close as practicable'. The gap must not exceed 12 mm. when 'squared stock' (anything with uniform rectangular cross-section) is fed by hand[3].

Other regulations on circular saws are:

(1) The smallest saw used on a machine must not be smaller in diameter than ⁶⁄₁₀ of the largest for which that machine is designed: reg. 17.

(2) Use of a circular saw is prohibited for: (i) tenoning, recessing, moulding—unless the part of the blade or cutter above the table is effectively guarded;[4] (ii) ripping—unless the teeth of the saw show above the top of the wood throughout the operation; and (iii) cross-cutting logs or branches, unless firmly held in a gripping device fixed to the table: reg. 18.

(3) Push-sticks must be used when feeding by hand to maintain pressure on the last 300 mm. (or on any item not over that size): reg. 19.

(4) Where a second man besides the operator is employed to take delivery of the cut material, he must be at the back of the table—at least 1200 mm. (just under 4ft.) from the blade: reg. 20.

---

3 Under the old regulations a half-inch gap was held excessive: *Lee v Nursery Furnishings Ltd* [1945] 1 All ER 387.

4 I am indebted to R. Evans of Ashford Kent—who obviously knows far more about woodworking than I do—for drawing my attention to an error in summarising this regulation in previous editions—the saw *can* be used for tenoning etc. if *effectively guarded*.

Vertical spindle moulding machines (regs. 32–39)

These consist of a spindle or shaft rising vertically above the table armed with revolving cutters which can shape the wood. The fence mentioned in these regulations is not a guard, but a raised fence normally on the operator's left which serves to guide material to the cutters. Cutters—or material—are liable to be thrown out by centrifugal force, and this risk is covered by the regulations. The guard must be capable of 'containing' cutters or material ejected: reg. 35. Detachable cutters must be fixed safely: reg. 32. The workpiece must be held in a jig or holder where it is not practicable to enclose the cutters: reg. 34. Spikes and push-sticks must be used where they will reduce risk: reg. 38. A 'false' fence must be used to reduce the gap between cutters and workpiece: reg. 33. (This is a thickness of wood between the true fence and the material, with a hole cut through it to enable the cutters to reach the material.) If work does not start at the end of a surface—i.e. moulding has to be started away from the edges, there must be a 'back stop' to prevent it being thrown back if a jig or holder is not practicable: a jig or holder must be used unless the material is moving the same way as the cutters: regs. 36, 37. If the machine has two speeds, it must not be capable of starting at the higher speed: reg. 39.

These machines are defined to include high speed routing machines: reg. 2(2).

Other machines

Planing machines (for smoothing surfaces) and thicknessing machines (for reducing to a specified thickness) are similar in principle, and often combined. The simplest form is a feed table in front; then a gap with a revolving block armed with cutters, over which the material passes, then a delivery table. There is a 'fence' as guide on the left. The substance of regs. 24–28 (planing machines for surfacing not mechanically fed) is that the cutter block must be cylindrical—this means cutters are recessed into a revolving cylinder and projecting to the minimum extent—there must be a bridge guard over it, a guard over the end of the cylinder on the far side of the fence, the bridge guard must be adjusted to the minimum gap, and there must be a minimum gap between the delivery table and the back of the cylinder. Push blocks are required for material too short to adjust bridge guard: reg. 29. The cutter block of a combined thicknessing machine must be guarded where exposed by the table: reg. 30. There must be a device to protect the operator of a thicknessing machine against material thrown back—except for existing machines to which only one piece is fed: reg. 31. The use of planing machines for work such as recessing or moulding is forbidden unless effectively guarded: reg. 23.

Narrow band saws   move in a continuous band from a pulley above through the bench to a lower pulley and are used for shaping. The upper and lower pulleys must be enclosed, with a flanged plate guarding the band from the top down to the part at bench level which is necessarily exposed: reg. 22.

The only other machines specially mentioned are multiple rip sawing machines and straight line edging machines, which must have a device to prevent ejection of material: reg. 21.

General   Woodworking machines nearly always involve a gap between the guards where the wood is fed in or taken out. The regulations meet this by saying that the guards must be adjusted as close as practicable. In many cases, therefore, the result of an action for damages will turn on the question of fact whether the gap was too wide.

14 Horizontal milling machines

There are special regulations for the fencing and use of horizontal milling machines: S.R. & O. 1928 No. 548 and 1934 No. 207. These require (*inter alia*) that the floor round the machine shall be kept in a safe condition, free from loose materials and from slippery suds (reg. 1), that there shall be suitable lighting (reg. 2), and a starting and stopping device within easy reach (reg. 4). The cutters must have strong guards, properly adjusted to the work, which must enclose the whole cutting surface except that part which is necessarily exposed for the milling operation; and the protection must extend over the sides, except in the case of cutters used for face milling (reg. 3)[5]. The guard need not be kept in position when the

---

5   In *Lineker v Raleigh Industries* [1980] ICR 83 there was a breach of reg. 3 because the edges of the guard had worn away leaving too wide an opening. But the accident happened because the operator changed the cutter (which he knew he was not supposed to do) and replaced the guard loosely; so it would have happened even with an adequate fence, and the breach of reg. 3 had no causal effect on the accident.

machine is not in motion: reg. 6; *Morris Motors v Hopgood* [1957] 1 QB 30, [1956] 3 All ER 467 (in this case the machine could not start unless the guard was in position: the workpiece slipped forward, started the cutters and closed the guard, apparently over the injured man's hand. No breach of the regulations.)

The relationship between these regulations and the duty to fence under ss. 12–14 of the Act is somewhat complex. Where the cutters of a machine are subject to reg. 3 and have guards complying with that regulation, there is no further scope for the operation of s. 14. Certain processes, however, are exempted from the regulations, and in this case it is expressly declared that the operation of the fencing sections is not prejudiced. Thus when the plaintiff came into contact with a revolving cutter while doing 'automatic profiling' (exemption (vii)), there was a breach of s. 14: *Quinn v Horsfall and Bickham Ltd* [1956] 2 All ER 467. Lastly, reg. 3 does not deal with any part of a machine except the cutters; and if *other* parts of the machinery are dangerous, there is the usual duty to fence under ss. 12 to 14: *Benn v Kamm & Co Ltd* [1952] 2 QB 127, [1952] 1 All ER 833. But if a part of a machine is correctly fenced in accordance with the regulations, it is correctly fenced for all purposes: *Automatic Woodturning Co Ltd v Stringer* [1957] AC 544, [1957] 1 All ER 90.

15 Power presses

The Power Presses Regulations 1965 (S.I. No. 1441), slightly amended in 1972 (S.I. 1972 No. 1512) regulate the use of power presses and press brakes (provided that, as is usually the case, they are power-driven and embody a flywheel and clutch mechanism) when used either for working metal by tools, or for die proving: reg 2(2). But machines in actual use or being prepared for use in working *hot* metal are excluded: reg. 3(2). The regulations are restricted to factories in the narrow sense and electrical stations within s. 123(1): reg. 3(1). They are in addition to and not in substitution for other statutory requirements under the Act: reg. 3(3).

The important requirement is that the setting up or preparation of these machine tools and their fences or other safety devices may now be done only by properly authorised and competent persons: reg. 4. These persons must be at least 18, appointed in writing in a special register, and trained in a number of matters which are precisely set out in a Schedule. Trainee-workers are allowed, but must be specially entered on the register and work under the immediate supervision of an authorised person. A loose system of allowing anyone to do these tasks merely because he has watched for a while and picked up some working knowledge will render the use of the machine unlawful.

Inspection and testing of the machines and their safety devices on installation and at specified intervals is required, and the use of the machine is forbidden where this has not been done within the specified period: reg. 5. If the authorised person finds a defect when inspecting, he may put the machine out of use either at once (if there is immediate danger) or after the lapse of a stated period, and the Factory Inspector must be informed: reg. 6. After each setting or adjustment of the machine, its use is forbidden until the authorised person has certified in writing that the safety devices are in 'efficient working order': reg. 7. (Safety devices include both fencing and automatic devices for keeping the operator away.) Flywheels must be marked with the maximum speed and the direction of rotation: the speed must not be exceeded or (except in emergency) the rotation reversed: reg. 10.

The Chief Inspector has power by reg. 12 to grant exemptions.

16 Abrasive wheels

The Abrasive Wheels Regulations 1970 (S.I. No. 535) establish a self-contained safety code for the use of abrasive wheels (a term which covers a wide range of abrasive tools, or components in machine tools, as well as grinding wheels of the common sort). They apply to all factories and other places subject to the Factories Act: reg. 3(1)—and supersede s. 14 of the Factories Act and the similar requirements in the Construction and Shipbuilding Regulations—reg. 3(2) and (4)—so that an abrasive wheel which complies with the regulations needs no other fencing.

What is an abrasive wheel?

The definition (reg. 2) is complex. It must, in the first place, be power-driven (not e.g. worked only by hand or foot) and used for grinding or cutting. Four types are then defined (as will be seen, some types are exempted from various requirements).

(a) A wheel, cylinder, disc or cone which consists of abrasive particles (with or without other material) held together by mineral, metallic or organic bonds, natural or artificial.

(b) A '*mounted* wheel or point' (defined as fixed permanently to a 'mandrel or quill', i.e. its own solid or hollow shaft) and a wheel or disc having separate segments of abrasive material. (Such segments, each in its own 'chuck' or holder, radiate from a common centre to form a wheel.)

(c) A wheel or disc of metal, wood, cloth, felt, rubber or paper having a surface wholly or partly of abrasive material.

(d) A wheel, disc or saw to any surface of which there is attached a rim or segment consisting of diamond abrasive material.

For simplicity let us call the items under (b), (c) and (d) 'mounted and segmented wheels', 'coated wheels' and 'diamond tools'. Some of these items—perhaps points and discs more than wheels—may be components in larger machine tools.

Exceptions (reg. 4)

Some of the regulations do not apply to certain types of wheel, as indicated below.

Coated wheels	Regulations 6 and 7 (speeds), 11(a) and (b) and 12 (fence to protect against bursting), 19
Wheels with purely natural bonds, e.g. made of abrasive stone in its solid state, not broken up and compounded with another substance	Regulations 11(a) and (b), 12
Segmented wheel	Regulation 6 (maximum speed of wheel—but reg. 7 applies as to speed of *spindle*).

Wheel in portable *machine* if (i) not over 235 mm. diameter and (ii) coated with abrasive material on cloth, felt, rubber, paper	Regulations 6, 7, 10(1), 11, 12, 18, 19 (these wheels are therefore totally exempt from all speed control and fencing requirements)
Wheel for grinding glass	Regulations 7, 10(1), 11, 12
Diamond tools	Regulations 6, 7, 12, 19 (speed restrictions do not apply, but fencing requirements do)

Speed of wheel and spindle: marking

By reg. 6, a wheel is not to be taken into use unless the maximum speed (in revolutions per minute) is marked on it, if over 55 mm. diameter, otherwise posted prominently nearby. It is not to be worked in excess of that speed (with adjustment as the diameter is reduced). By reg. 7, every spindle on which a wheel may be mounted must have fixed to it a notice of the maximum speed or range of speeds: that speed must not be exceeded and if the spindle is air-driven there must be a governor or other device (properly maintained) to hold it within the limit.

Guards

By reg. 10(1), a guard must be provided and kept in position at every wheel in motion unless—reg. 10(2)—'the use of a guard is impracticable' because of the nature of the work, or of the wheel. The guard must—'so far as reasonably practicable'—be designed and constructed to hold the fragments if the wheel or part of it breaks when in motion: reg. 11(a); also maintained and secured so that the guard itself is not displaced in that event: reg. 11(b). Lastly—this covers the s. 14 risk of injury by contact, as well as by bursting—it must enclose the whole wheel except the sector exposed for the work being done (the work usually done if the guard is not adjustable): reg. 11(c). Where the work usually done involves an exposed arc of more than 180°, it is compulsory to use a 'tapered' wheel—thick at the centre, thin at the rim—mounted between two protective flanges of rather smaller diameter: reg. 12 (this is another precaution to hold at least the larger fragments if it breaks). Where a rest is used to support a workpiece, it must be 'secure', and adjusted as close as possible to the exposed arc: reg. 15.

Maintenance and general

Wheels (other than mounted wheels) are to be mounted only by qualified persons who have received full instruction in both the risks and technical skills (set out in the Schedule) and are duly authorised by an entry in an official register: reg. 9. All wheels are to be properly maintained: reg. 8. Warning of risks must be displayed: reg. 16. Controls to switch off power must be efficient and within easy reach of the operator: reg. 14. All practicable steps shall be taken to select the right wheel from the point of view of safety: reg. 13. Round a fixed machine, the floor must be good and even, and so far as practicable free from loose material and slipperiness: but round a portable machine, it is sufficient if all 'reasonably practicable' steps are taken: reg. 17. Employed persons must make full and proper use of guards and other things provided: reg. 18. By reg. 19, sale or hire of wheels and spindles without the markings under regs. 6 and 7 is forbidden.

Chapter 12

The Factories Act 1961: dust, fumes and humidity; harmful substances and processes; protection of eyes

1 General: actions founded on disease

Part IV of the Act contains a number of requirements under the heading of 'Health, Safety and Welfare (Special Provisions and Regulations)', and Part I contains requirements relating to 'Health (General Provisions)'; these sections may or may not, upon their true construction, confer a right of action in the event of breach. A few of them are intended to give protection against actual injury. Many are intended as a safeguard against disease. Others, it seems, are intended only to create conditions of reasonable comfort in a factory, and it cannot be supposed that an action would lie for a breach of these requirements: for example, an action could hardly be brought for failing to keep the factory floor clean or to whitewash the walls, yet it has been held in Scotland that an action will lie for a breach of what is now s. 58 (washing facilities) when the absence of these facilities has resulted in dermatitis: *Reid v Westfield Paper Co* 1957 SC 218.

Accordingly, in some cases the preliminary question arises whether a breach of the statute gives rise to an action for damages at all: but, once it is held that the breach of duty is actionable, no distinction can be made between cases where the resulting harm is a disease, and cases where it is a physical injury[1]. An action will lie, in a proper case, for a breach of statutory duty causing a disease although this is due to continual exposure over a long period: see, for example, *Bonnington Castings Ltd v Wardlaw* [1956] AC 613, [1956] 1 All ER 615. It was held in a series of

1 Similarly an action may lie where negligence at common law has caused a disease.

decisions under the repealed Workmen's Compensation Acts that a disease may be a 'personal injury by accident': see *Roberts v Dorothea Slate Quarries Co Ltd* [1948] 2 All ER 201. In view of the words 'by accident', those decisions excluded cases where a disease was contracted over a period, as distinct from being contracted on a single occasion. That limitation does not apply to an action at common law.

The position of a plaintiff has been made a great deal easier by the *Bonnington* case, and the authorities which have followed it. In these cases the House of Lords held that the plaintiff discharges the burden of proof if he shows that the breach of the statute has made 'a material contribution' to the disease, although other factors, which would not give a right of action, have operated simultaneously or in succession[2].

So much of this field of law is covered by regulations of a detailed nature and subject to many qualifications, that it is impossible to do more than give a bird's-eye view.

2 General ventilation; humidity

By s. 4(1):

> 'Effective and suitable provision shall be made for securing and maintaining by the circulation of fresh air in each workroom the adequate ventilation of the room . . . '

The latter part of this subsection, relating to dust and fumes, has been repealed by the Hazardous Substances Regulations which now control all risks of this kind: see Chapter 8.

Section 68 controls artificial humidity in factories and s. 6 the drainage of wet floors. It is unlikely but not perhaps impossible that an action could be founded on humidity or wet alone.

3 Dust and fumes

Section 63 of the Factories Act, and numerous special regulations giving protection against dust and fumes have been repealed and

2 For a full account of these authorities, see Chapter 6, section 4.

replaced by the Control of Substances Hazardous to Health Regulations 1988, which apply to all places of work. Under these regulations, dust of any kind is 'hazardous' if present in substantial quantity: smaller quantities will be hazardous if they come within the definition in the Regulations. See Chapter 8. The case law under s. 63 is all obsolete.

However, some special codes remain in force. These vary greatly in their strictness, and reference must be made to the actual regulations for details. The type of measures ordered are in the main as follows:

(a) Materials such as coal dust and refractory materials are to be broken up in the open, and to be enclosed when moved about inside a factory.

(b) Where processes in a workroom give rise to dust or fumes, these are to be kept out of other workrooms.

(c) Inside the workroom, there is to be ample inlet ventilation, and an exhaust draught or other appliance near the point of origin of the dust or fumes. Damping or spraying is sometimes necessary.

(d) Respirators and protective clothing are sometimes necessary. The regulations fall conveniently under the following headings:

Asbestos

The Control of Asbestos at Work Regulations 1987 apply to all places of work and replace those under the Factories Act: see Chapter 8.

Pottery

The following regulations remain in force to some extent, though modified and largely superseded by the Control of Substances Hazardous to Health Regulations 1988 and the Control of Lead at Work Regulations 1990:

Pottery (Health and Welfare) Special Regulations 1950 (S.I. 1950 No. 65) (ventilation, exhaust draught, suppression of dust, protective clothing, washing facilities, handling of clay dust and raw lead, employment of women and young persons restricted).

Pottery (Health) Special Regulations 1947 (S.R. & O. 1947 No. 2161) (restrict use of glazes containing lead, and of powdered flint or quartz). (Both adapted to metrication by S.I. 1982 No. 877.)

Textile dust

The following regulations also remain modified by the Hazardous Substances Regulations (Chapter 8):

Regulations for Spinning and Weaving Flax and Tow 1906 (S.R. & O. 1906 No. 177) (regs. 1, 2 and 12 revoked: what remains is about temperature and humidity).

Regulations for Spinning and Weaving Hemp 1907 (S.R. & O. 1907 No. 660) (regs. 1, 2 and 7 revoked: what remains is about temperature and humidity).

Jute (Safety, Health and Welfare) Special Regulations 1948 (S.I. 1948 No. 1696), Part III. (All Part III revoked except reg. 11, removal of steam or vapour.)

For full details of all these regulations, as amended from time to time, reference should be made to Redgrave's *Safety and Health in Factories.*

4 Poisonous and harmful processes

Sections 67 and 74 of the Factories Act, and various regulations concerning lead, are repealed and replaced by the Hazardous Substances Regulations and the Control of Lead at Work Regulations which apply to all places of work: see Chapter 8.

Cotton processes
The Factories (Cotton Shuttles) Special Regulations 1952 (S.I. 1952 No. 1495) apply to cotton cloth factories. They prohibit the use of shuttles which can be threaded by mouth suction.

The Mule Spinning (Health) Special Regulations 1953 (S.I. 1953, No. 1545), which applied to the spinning of cotton and other staple fibre on self-acting mules, are replaced by the Hazardous Substances Regulations (Chapter 8) which continue the prohibition on the use of oil other than refined white oil of mineral origin, or oils of animal or vegetable origin.

5 Infectious materials

(i) Anthrax
Regulations relating to materials liable to carry anthrax germs are all replaced by the Hazardous Substances Regulations (Chapter 8).

(ii) Dangerous pathogens
The Health and Safety (Dangerous Pathogens) Regulations 1981 (S.I. No. 1011) forbid the keeping, handling or transport of certain listed pathogens unless 30 days' advance notice has been given to the Health and Safety Executive.

6 Inflammable substances

The Highly Flammable Liquids and Liquefied Petroleum Gases Regulations 1972 (S.I. 1972 No. 917) apply to all places subject to the Factories Act where highly flammable liquids or (as the case may be) liquefied petroleum gas are present for the purposes of any undertaking (which includes the Crown and any municipal or public authority— reg. 2(2) at end) or any trade or business[3].

There are three general exceptions:
(a) places subject to the Explosives Act 1875;
(b) places where the special regulations for testing aircraft engines, mentioned below, apply;
(c) the ordinary storage tanks (including cargo tanks) of ships: reg. 3 (4), (5), (6).

The requirements are *in addition* to anything in the Factories Act: reg. 3 (7). The Chief Inspector may grant exemptions: reg. 4.

Highly flammable liquid   means a liquid, liquid solution, emulsion or suspension with a flashpoint below 32°C, but excluding 'liquefied petroleum gas' as defined and also other liquefied gases which would normally vaporise at 20°C but are kept under pressure or refrigeration. Ammonia too is excepted.

The regulations provide for storage in fixed tanks in a safe position and other forms of closed storage, for the closing of all openings and precautions against leaks, spills and other escapes: reg. 5; for marking tanks and containers 'Highly Inflammable' or actual flashpoint: reg. 6. Movement within the premises should be by an enclosed system, with minimum quantities in any workplace and systematic removal of empty containers: reg. 8. Where a 'dangerous concentration' of vapours may

---

3   According to the O.E.D. 'flammable' = 'inflammable', a word which expresses more naturally a propensity to burst 'into flames'.

be expected, there must be no source of ignition, and smoking is forbidden where any highly inflammable liquid is present: regs. 9, 14; contaminated cotton waste or other material must be cleared away at once, and deposits of cellulose nitrate removed from any hot surface: reg. 9. There is also a general requirement to prevent or remove solid deposits: reg. 13. Measures must be taken to prevent the escape of inflammable vapour into the general atmosphere of any workplace; in some cases processes giving off vapour may have to be restricted to enclosed places with a mechanical exhaust draught of which the ducting must be fire-resistant; from 21 June 1974, such an enclosure must be a fire-resistant structure: reg. 10. Fire-resistant structures must have provision for 'pressure relief' in case of explosion—in other words a kind of safety valve—venting to a safe place: reg. 11.

There are requirements for fire escapes and fire fighting—regs. 12, 17—which, however, apply only to docks, warehouses and construction sites subject to the Factories Act 1961, ss. 125 and 127 (other cases presumably are sufficiently provided for). The burning of inflammable liquid is permitted only in suitable plant or apparatus, but waste may, in the alternative, be burnt by a competent person in a safe place: reg 15.

Persons employed must *comply* with regulations which require them to (a) do an act (b) refrain from an act or (c) use equipment. They must also 'co-operate', and report any defect: reg. 18.

Liquefied petroleum gas   defined as commercial butane or propane or a mixture of them, is treated separately: apart from the formal parts and the duties of persons employed, only reg. 7 applies to it. This imposes strict requirements for storage and marking and forbids the presence of liquefied petroleum gas in a workplace except in cylinders or pipelines and then to the minimum extent practicable. Empty cylinders must be removed promptly.

These new regulations are far from giving a comprehensive coverage of inflammable substances, and there are other special codes. In general, like the regulations summarised above, they cover the following points:

(a) Storage in a safe place, which is sometimes required to be fireproof.

(b) Use of the minimum quantity in a workroom, which in some cases must also be fireproof.

   (c) Prohibition of naked lights, and of electrical apparatus capable of sparking.

   (d) Prohibition of smoking.

For further details see:—

The Explosives Act 1875.

The Petroleum (Consolidation) Act 1928.

Celluloid Regulations 1921 (S.R. & O. 1921 No. 1825).

Cinematograph Film Manufacture Regulations 1928 (S.R. & O. 1928 No. 82). (Regulation 12 revoked by the Electricity at Work Regulations.)

Stripping of Cinematograph Film Regulations 1939 (S.R. & O. 1939 No. 571). (Regulation 14 revoked by the same regulations.)

The Factories (Testing of Aircraft Engines and Accessories) Special Regulations 1952, S.I. 1952 No. 1689. (These apply to all factories where testing of aircraft engines, carburettors and fuel pumps is carried out; require testing to be carried out separately from other work, in fireproof test rooms, where the quantity of petroleum spirit is kept to a minimum; contain safeguards against electrical sparking and prohibit naked flames; require provision of fire escapes and fire-extinguishers; and instruct persons engaged on testing to report defects. They were amended by S.I. 1983 No. 979 to substitute metric measurements, and by the Electricity at Work Regulations to revoke regs. 14–18 and associated definitions.)

7 Other dangerous substances

Special regulations for chemical works concerning acids and other dangerous chemicals, also regulations about cancer-producing substances (carcinogenous substances) were revoked and replaced by the Hazardous Substances Regulations (Chapter 8).

8 Radioactive substances

Regulations under the Factories Act have been replaced by the Ionising Radiation Regulations 1985 which apply to all places of work except licensed nuclear installations (see Chapter 8, section 5).

The Nuclear Installations Act 1965 and 1969, as amended by Part II
of the Energy Act 1983, control the use of sites for nuclear installations
(e.g. nuclear reactors or processing or storage of nuclear material in
bulk) and require operators to be licensed[4]. They create absolute
liability for nuclear risks emanating from these sites, from their waste, or
from their materials in transit[5]. A similar liability applies to the Atomic
Energy Authority in respect of its own operations and also to
government departments which operate without a licence.

9 Protection of the eyes in certain processes

By s. 65:

> 'In the case of any [process specified in regulations] which involves a
> special risk of injury to the eyes from particles or fragments thrown
> off in the course of the process, suitable goggles or effective screens
> shall, in accordance with . . . the regulations, be provided to protect
> the eyes of persons employed in the process.'

The Protection of Eyes Regulations 1974 (S.I. 1974 No. 1681,
amended by S.I. 1975 No. 303) have been made under this power. They
apply not only to factories in the narrow sense, but also to all places and
operations made subject to the Factories Act 1961 by ss. 123–127 of the
Act, if certain specified processes are carried out there: reg. 3(1)(a), (b).
A long list of processes which may throw out sparks or fragments or
acids or involve other dangers is set out in two Schedules (1 and 2) which
are reproduced at the end of this section. The regulations replace the
Protection of Eyes Regulations 1938 (which applied only to factories) as
well as similar provisions in regulations for foundries, construction,
shipbuilding and chemical works. The requirements are in addition to
anything else in the Factories Act (e.g. safe place of work and safe
access): reg. 3(2).

For most of these processes the regulations require what are called
'eye protectors', which means something worn by a person
individually—goggles, visors, spectacles and face shields. (The old

---

4 See also Nuclear Installations Regulations 1971 (S.I. 1971 No. 381).
5 Liability under these Acts is not affected by the Health and Safety at Work Act
   1974 (see s. 47).

regulations only referred to 'goggles'.) In other cases they require a 'shield', or 'fixed shield', or allow these as an alternative to 'eye protectors'. A 'shield' means a helmet or handshield, designed to be worn or held by a person. A 'fixed shield' is a screen which stands free, or is attached to machinery, plant or equipment, or to a building or structure. In general the protectors or shields must be of a type 'approved' for the particular process by certificate of the Chief Inspector (the only exception is Part IV of Schedule I where *fixed* shields do not need to be approved). All these definitions are in reg. 2 (2).

There are two distinct categories of persons for whom protection is required; those who are actually working in the processes, and those who, although not working in them, are at risk from the processes. Presumably a worker on his way to and from his own work could be a person 'at risk'.

Persons employed in Schedule 1 processes (reg. 5)

The employer of every person who is employed in a process in part I of Schedule 1 must provide[6] him with individual 'eye protectors'. For processes in Parts III and IV a 'shield' (helmet, or hand-held, it will be remembered) or fixed shield is a permissible alternative: for processes in Part II (exposed electric arc or arc plasma) a 'shield' or fixed shield is obligatory. It was decided under the old regulations that protection ceases to be obligatory after the 'process' is completed—if, for instance, a fragment flies out when the article is removed from the machine: *Hay v Dowty Mining Equipment Co Ltd* [1971] 3 All ER 1136.

Adjacent places of work (reg. 5(2)). Fixed shields must be provided between adjacent positions in which persons are working on processes 6, 7 or 32 of Schedule 1 (various processes of chipping, knocking out and fettling).

Persons at risk, but not employed in process (reg. 6)

There is an entirely separate list of processes for this purpose (Schedule 2). For most of the processes—if there is a foreseeable risk of eye injury—sufficient fixed shields must be provided. For process 3 (drop

---

6   Goggles were not 'provided' under the old regulations merely by being available in the foreman's office or elsewhere; the workman had to be told where to get them: *Finch v Telegraph Construction and Maintenance Co Ltd* [1949] 1 All ER 452; *McFarlane v Williamson* 1971 SLT (Notes) 72. Where the present regulations require an individual issue, actual delivery seems necessary.

hammers etc.) eye protectors or shields are an alternative. The duty under process 3 falls on the employer of the persons at risk; in other cases it falls on the employer of those carrying out the processes.

General requirements for equipment
Eye protectors must be issued individually except for those 'occasionally employed' (defined roughly—reg. 2 (2)—as not more than two days a week or 15 minutes on one day) when a supply must be 'readily available': reg. 7. If eye protectors are issued to an employee for his use when required, it is not necessary to tell him what specific process they are provided for: *Lees v Grahamston Iron Co* 1984 SLT 184. Replacements must be issued when necessary and a supply kept in reserve: reg. 8. Eye protectors and shields must be 'suitable for the person' who is to use them, conform to the approved specification for the particular process, and be marked to show the purpose for which they are designed: reg. 9. Fixed shields must be of approved specification for Part II and III processes, be properly maintained and (if transparency is necessary) kept clean, and be so constructed and kept in position as to give the required protection 'so far as practicable': reg. 10. Under the old regulations goggles were not suitable if fragments could get round the sides or through the ventilation holes: *Lloyd v F. Evans & Sons Ltd* [1951] WN 306; *Rodgers v George Blair & Co Ltd* (1971) 11 KIR 391: but 'suitable' does not mean 'perfect', and goggles are not unsuitable because they have a tendency to mist over with the result that the wearer lifts them to clear and is then exposed to fragments: *Daniels v Ford Motor Co Ltd* [1955] 1 All ER 218; *Bux v Slough Metals Ltd* [1974] 1 All ER 262; *Marshall v Babcock and Willcox Ltd* 1961 SLT 259.

Duties of persons employed (reg. 11)
Briefly, the duties of employed persons are to *use* eye protectors or shields provided except where the regulations allow a fixed shield as sufficient, to take care of them and not misuse them, and to report loss, deterioration or any defect: it is only if such a report is made that the employer has to provide a replacement under reg. 8.

Exemptions (reg. 4)
Exemptions may be given by the Chief Inspector.
Schedules 1 and 2 are as follows:

'SCHEDULE 1

Specified Processes

Part I

Processes in which approved eye protectors are required
1. The blasting or erosion of concrete by means of shot or other abrasive materials propelled by compressed air.
2. The cleaning of buildings or structures by means of shot or other abrasive materials propelled by compressed air.
3. Cleaning by means of high-pressure water jets.
4. The striking of masonry nails by means of a hammer or other hand tool or by means of a power driven portable tool.
5. Any work carried out with a hand-held cartridge operated tool, including the operation of loading and unloading live cartridges into such a tool, and the handling of such a tool for the purpose of maintenance repair or examination when the tool is loaded with a live cartridge.
6. The chipping of metal, and the chipping, knocking out, cutting out or cutting off of cold rivets, bolts, nuts, lugs, pins, collars, or similar articles from any structure or plant, or from part of any structure or plant, by means of a hammer, chisel, punch, or similar hand tool, or by means of a power driven portable tool.
7. The chipping or scurfing of paint, scale, slag, rust or other corrosion from the surface of metal and other hard materials by means of a hand tool or by means of a power driven portable tool or by applying articles of metal or such materials to a power driven tool.
8. The use of a high-speed metal cutting saw or an abrasive cutting-off wheel or disc, which in either case is power driven.
9. The pouring[7] or skimming of molten metal in foundries.
10. Work at a molten salt bath when the molten salt surface is exposed.
11. The operation, maintenance, dismantling or demolition of plant or any part of plant, being plant or part of plant which contains or has contained acids, alkalis, dangerous corrosive substances, whether liquid or solid, or other substances which are similarly injurious to the eyes, and which has not been so prepared (by isolation, reduction of pressure, emptying or otherwise), treated or designed and constructed as to prevent any reasonably foreseeable risk of injury to the eyes of any person engaged in any such work for any of the said contents.
12. The handling in open vessels or manipulation of acids, alkalis, dangerous corrosive materials, whether liquid or solid, and other substances which are similarly injurious to the eyes, where in any of

7   See note [8] to item 18.

the foregoing cases there is a reasonably foreseeable risk of injury to the eyes of any person engaged in any such work from drops splashed or particles thrown off.

13. The driving in or on of bolts, pins, collars or similar articles to any structure or plant or to part of any structure or plant by means of a hammer, chisel, punch or similar hand tool or by means of a power driven tool, where in any of the foregoing cases there is a reasonably foreseeable risk of injury to the eyes of any person engaged in the work from particles or fragments thrown off.

14. Injection by pressure of liquids or solutions into buildings or structures or parts thereof where in the course of any such work there is a reasonably foreseeable risk of injury to the eyes of any person engaged in the work from any such liquids or solutions.

15. The breaking up of metal by means of a hammer, whether power driven or not, or by means of a tup, where in either of the foregoing cases there is a reasonably foreseeable risk of injury to the eyes of the person engaged in the work from particles or fragments thrown off.

16. The breaking, cutting, cutting into, dressing, carving or drilling by means of a power driven portable tool or by means of a hammer, chisel, pick or similar hand tool other than a trowel, of any of the following, that is to say—

(a) glass, hard plastics, concrete, fired clay, plaster, slag or stone (whether natural or artificial);
(b) materials similar to any of the foregoing;
(c) articles consisting wholly or partly of any of the foregoing;
(d) stonework, brickwork or blockwork;
(e) bricks, tiles or blocks (except blocks made of wood),

where in any of the foregoing cases there is a reasonably foreseeable risk of injury to the eyes of any person engaged in the work from particles or fragments thrown off.

17. The use of compressed air for removing swarf, dust, dirt or other particles, where in the course of any such work there is a reasonably foreseeable risk of injury to the eyes of any person engaged in the work from particles or fragments thrown off.

18. Work at a furnace containing molten metal, and the pouring or skimming of molten metal in places other than foundries, where there is a reasonably foreseeable risk of injury to the eyes of any person engaged in such work from molten metal[8].

19. Processes in foundries where there is a reasonably foreseeable risk of injury to the eyes of any person engaged in any such work from hot sand thrown off.

20. Work in the manufacture of wire and wire rope where there is a

8 'Pouring' includes incidental matters such as putting on a lid or handling a ladle in preparation for pouring: *Smith v James Dickie & Co Ltd* 1961 SLT (Notes) 32.

reasonably foreseeable risk of injury to the eyes of any person engaged in the work from particles or fragments thrown off or from flying ends of wire.

21. The operation of coiling wire, and operations connected therewith, where there is a reasonably foreseeable risk of injury to the eyes of any person engaged in any such work from particles or fragments thrown off or from flying ends of wire.

22. The cutting of wire or metal strapping under tension, where there is a reasonably foreseeable risk of injury to the eyes of any person engaged in any such work from flying ends of wire or flying ends of metal strapping.

23. Work in the manufacture of glass and in the processing of glass and the handling of cullet, where in any of the foregoing cases there is a reasonably foreseeable risk of injury to the eyes of any person engaged in the work from particles or fragments thrown off.

Part II

Processes in which approved shields or approved fixed shields are required

24. Any process involving the use of an exposed electric arc or an exposed stream of arc plasma.

Part III

Processes in which approved eye protectors or approved shields or approved fixed shields are required

25. The welding of metals by means of apparatus to which oxygen or any flammable gas or vapour is supplied under pressure.

26. The hot fettling of steel castings by means of a flux-injected burner or air carbon torch, and the de-seaming of metal.

27. The cutting, boring, cleaning, surface conditioning or spraying of material by means of apparatus (not being apparatus mechanically driven by compressed air) to which air, oxygen or any flammable gas or vapour is supplied under pressure excluding any such process elsewhere specified, where in any of the foregoing cases there is a reasonably foreseeable risk of injury to the eyes of any person engaged in the work from particles or fragments thrown off or from intense light or other radiation.

28. Any process involving the use of an instrument which produces light amplification by the stimulated emission of radiation, being a process in which there is a reasonably foreseeable risk of injury to the eyes of any person engaged in the process from radiation.

Part IV

Processes in which approved eye protectors or approved shields or fixed shields are required

29. Truing or dressing of an abrasive wheel where in either of the foregoing cases there is a reasonably foreseeable risk of injury to the eyes of any person engaged in the work from particles or fragments thrown off.

30. Work with drop hammers, power hammers, horizontal forging machines, and forging presses, other than hydraulic presses, used in any case for the manufacture of forgings.

31. The dry grinding of materials or articles by applying them by hand to a wheel, disc or band which in any such case is power driven or by means of a power driven portable tool, where in any of the foregoing cases there is a reasonably foreseeable risk of injury to the eyes of any person engaged in the work from particles or fragments thrown off.

32. The fettling of metal castings, involving the removal of metal, including runners, gates and risers, and the removal of any other material during the course of such fettling, where in any of the foregoing cases there is a reasonably foreseeable risk of injury to the eyes of any person engaged in the work from particles or fragments thrown off[9].

33. The production of metal castings at pressure die casting machines where there is a reasonably foreseeable risk of injury to the eyes of any person engaged in such work from molten metal thrown off.

34. The machining of metals, including any dry grinding processes not elsewhere specified, where there is a reasonably foreseeable risk of injury to the eyes of any person engaged in any such work from particles or fragments thrown off.

35. The welding of metals by an electric resistance process or a submerged electric arc, where there is a reasonably foreseeable risk of injury to the eyes of any person engaged in any such work from particles or fragments thrown off.

SCHEDULE 2

Cases in which protection is required for persons at risk from, but not employed in the specified processes.

---

9 'Fettling' does not include trimming of a mould by a fitter to fit a machine: *Prophet v Platt Bros & Co Ltd* [1961] 2 All ER 644.

1. The chipping of metal, and the chipping, knocking out, cutting out or cutting off of cold rivets, bolts, nuts, lugs, pins, collars, or similar articles from any structure or plant[10], or from any part of any structure or plant, by means of a hammer, chisel, punch or similar hand tool, or by means of a power driven portable tool where in any of the foregoing cases there is a reasonably foreseeable risk of injury to the eyes of any person not engaged in any such work from particles or fragments thrown off.

2. Any process involving the use of an exposed electric arc or an exposed stream of arc plasma.

3. Work with drop hammers, power hammers, horizontal forging machines and forging presses other than hydraulic presses used in any case for the manufacture of forgings.

4. The fettling of metal castings, involving the removal of metal, including runners, gates and risers, and the removal of any other material during the course of such fettling, where in any of the foregoing cases there is a reasonably foreseeable risk of injury to the eyes of any person not engaged in any such work from particles or fragments thrown off.

5. Any process involving the use of an instrument which produces light amplification by the stimulated emission of radiation, where in any such process there is a reasonably foreseeable risk of injury to the eyes of any person not engaged in the process from radiation.'

10 Lifting excessive weights

Requiring a workman to lift an excessive weight, by reason of which he is injured, might be actionable at common law. It is now generally enacted by s. 72(1)[11] that:

'A person shall not be employed to lift, carry, or move any load so heavy as to be likely to cause injury to him.'

It is not necessary to show that the load was likely to injure the particular employee by its weight alone: the other circumstances in which it is handled must also be taken into account: *Black v Carricks* (*Caterers*) [1980] IRLR 448 (where the Court of Appeal said that any statement to the contrary in *Kinsella v Harris Lebus Ltd* (1963) 108 Sol Jo 14 was

10 'Plant' includes aircraft sent to the factory for dismantling: *Watts v Enfield Rolling Mills* (*Aluminium*) *Ltd* [1952] 1 All ER 1013.
11 Formerly this applied only to young persons, but was made a rule of universal application by the Act of 1959.

confined to the facts of that case, which should no longer be cited as authority)[12]. But the question of whether a load is likely to cause injury is related to the particular employee, and where the employers had no reason to think that an employee was susceptible to a heart attack there was no liability for injury due to such an attack: *Power v Greater Glasgow Health Board* 1987 SLT 567.[13]

It has however to be shown that the workman was 'employed' to handle the excessive load, in the sense that the task was given to him. This gives rise to troublesome questions of fact, which were examined by the House of Lords in *Brown v Allied Ironfounders Ltd* [1974] 2 All ER 135. It is, of course, a clear case if a man is expressly told to lift objects too heavy for him, either as a regular job or on a particular occasion. But the House held that there was a breach where a woman was told to paint heavy articles, a task which involved turning them over although they were too heavy for one woman to handle. It was held to be immaterial that she could have asked for help, and the opinion to the contrary in *Peat v N. J. Muschamp & Co Ltd* [1970] 7 KIR 469 was disapproved: since she had not been *told* to ask for help, she was 'employed' to do the task single-handed (Viscount Dilhorne [1974] 2 All ER at p. 139b). It was, however, said that where work is given to a gang to carry out which is within their collective capabilities, there is no breach of the section if a man by his own choice lifts more than he should (ibid. at p. 141a-b).

Apart from this general prohibition, by s. 72(2), the Minister could regulate the maximum weights to be carried by any workman[14]. The following regulations are in force on the subject:

> Pottery (Health and Welfare) Special Regulations 1950 (S.I. 1950 No. 65) adapted to metrication by S.I. 1982 No. 877.
> Woollen and Worsted Textiles (Lifting of Heavy Weights) Regulations 1926 (S.R. & O. 1926 No. 1463).
> Jute (Safety, Health and Welfare) Regulations 1948 (S.I. 1948 No. 1696), Part II.

---

12 In *Kinsella*, the man was injured lifting 145 lbs. He succeeded at common law because it was not sufficient in the circumstances to leave a man to ask for help on his own initiative. In *Peat v Muschamp*, it was pointed out that help was not readily available and men were discouraged from asking for it: a system whereby they are left to ask for help is not necessarily wrong at common law.

13 The English Court of Appeal gave a similar decision in *Whitfield v Johnson* (1990) Times, 6 March (unknown spinal weakness).

14 Section 72(2) was revoked by S.I. 1974 No. 1941 as regulations would now be made under the Health and Safety at Work Act 1974.

11 Washing and drinking facilities

Washing facilities including, in general, clean running hot and cold or warm water are required by s. 58: see also Washing Facilities (Running Water) Exemption Regulations 1960 (S.I. 1960 No. 1029) and Washing Facilities (Miscellaneous Industries) Regulations 1960 (S.I. 1960 No. 1214). Drinking water is required by s. 57. These are primarily welfare facilities, but may be relevant in dermatitis or poisoning cases: see *McGhee v National Coal Board* [1972] 3 All ER 1008.

12 Other special regulations

The Kiers Regulations 1938 (S.R. & O. 1938 No. 106, adapted to metrication by S.I. 1981 No. 1152) control the use of the kier process by which boiling liquid is circulated in printing, dyeing and bleaching works.

The Manufacture of Aerated Water Regulations 1921 (S.R. & O. 1921 No. 1932, adapted to metrication by S.I. 1981 No. 686) contain precautions against the explosion of bottles. The filling apparatus is to be constructed or fenced so as to keep in fragments of bursting bottles, and in certain cases face guards and gauntlets must be provided.

Protection against dermatitis and corrosive or irritating substances
There is a large group of 'welfare' orders which also appertain to 'safety', as they are designed to give protection against dermatitis, corrosive liquids and even (in the case of cement) dust-irritation of the eyes. The regulations vary in detail, but characteristic requirements are (i) protective clothing, sometimes including water-tight boots and goggles; (ii) display of notices concerning dermatitis; (iii) washing facilities. Processes and industries affected are: tinplate manufacture (1035/17), glass processes (558/18 and 288/21), laundries (654/20), gut and tripe preparation (1437/20), cleaning sacks (860/27), cement works (94/30) and clay works (1547/48).

Chapter 13

Metal foundries

1 Iron and steel foundries

Iron and steel foundries are factories in the full sense of the word, and all
the requirements of the Factories Act 1961 apply to them. Further safety
requirements are imposed by the Iron and Steel Foundries Regulations
1953 (S.I. 1953 No. 1464), amended by the Health and Safety
(Foundries etc.) (Metrication) Regulations S.I. 1981 No. 1332[1].

Definitions

'Iron foundry' and *'steel foundry'* are defined by reg. 2(2) to mean 'those
parts of a factory in which the production of iron castings or . . . steel
castings (not being the production of pig-iron or . . . of steel in the form of
ingots and not including die-castings) is carried on by casting in moulds
made of sand, loam, moulding composition or other mixture of materials,
or by shell moulding, or by centrifugal casting in metal moulds lined with
sand'. They also include 'any part of the factory in which any of the
following processes are carried on as incidental processes in connection
with, and in the course of, such production, namely,

1 The report of a Standing Committee on Steel Foundries shows that many
  accidents still occur from poor floors and gangways, and obstructions on them, and
  from lack of instruction in safe methods of handling heavy loads, whether by hand
  or by crane. The minimising of dust (liable to cause silicosis) is also a serious
  problem: *Times* 14 August 1961. This is now governed by the Hazardous
  Substances Regulations (Chapter 8).

the preparation and mixing of materials used in the foundry
process,
the preparation of moulds and cores,
knock-out operations and dressing or fettling operations'.
These definitions may be paraphrased broadly by saying that the
regulations apply to three types of workshop, namely:
moulding shops;
places where 'knock-out' operations are performed (this may be
done in the moulding shop, or it may be done elsewhere);
fettling-shops, where the castings are cleaned up after they have
been 'knocked-out'.
It is important to note that the regulations do not apply to shops which
simply produce pig-iron or steel ingots: nor to die-casting, where
molten metal, at a lower temperature than in other forms of casting, is
injected into a hollow metal mould or die and instantly compressed and
ejected.

General tidiness and safety

By reg. 4, moulding-boxes and other heavy objects are to be 'so
arranged and placed as to enable work to be carried on without
unnecessary risk'; suitable and accessible racks or receptacles are to be
provided and used for storage of gear and tools; and where there is bulk
storage of sand or other materials, suitable receptacles are to be
provided.

The object of this regulation, apparently, is to minimise the risk of
dangerous obstruction, which is, of course, particularly serious in a
place where molten metal and heavy castings have to be moved.

Work near cupolas and furnaces: prohibition of work in danger area

Regulation 5 (as amended to metric measurement by S.I. 1981 No.
1332) defines a danger area within the vicinity of cupolas and
furnaces—which, by reg. 2(2), include 'a receiver associated therewith'.
With certain exceptions, 'No person shall carry out any work within' the
danger area defined.

The area includes all places which are *either*—

(a) within 4 metres 'from a vertical line passing through the delivery end of any spout of a cupola or furnace, being a spout used for delivering molten metal'; *or*

(b) within 2.4 metres 'from a vertical line passing through the nearest part of any ladle which is in position at the end of such a spout'.

This prohibition applies at all times unless the exceptions contained in the regulation can be invoked.

There are two exceptions.

The first case is 'where it is *necessary* for the proper *use or maintenance* of a cupola or furnace that that work should be carried out within' the danger area. Under this heading, therefore, 'necessity' must be proved: it is not enough to prove convenience or conformity with trade practice. It must be strictly necessary for that particular piece of work to be done within the danger area if 'proper use' is to be made of the plant, or proper 'maintenance' is to be carried out.

The second exception is where the 'work is being carried out at such a time and under such conditions that there is no danger to the person carrying it out from molten metal which is being obtained from the cupola or furnace or is in a ladle in position at the end of the spout'. Two conclusions may be drawn from the wording of this exception. First, the prohibition against work in the danger area does not apply at all unless molten metal is actually being poured, or has just been poured into a ladle which is still in position at the delivery point. In other words, reg. 5 gives protection against accidents during the pouring operation, but not against accidents due to the escape of molten metal from the furnace in any other way, e.g. by bursting. Secondly, the wording of the exception requires the employer to prove that there is '*no danger*'. If there is the slightest danger to a worker during a pouring operation, his presence within the danger area cannot be brought within the second exception, but must be justified by proof of strict necessity under the previous exception.

Regulation 5 may therefore be paraphrased broadly as follows: no person is to be allowed to work within the danger area during a pouring operation except in case of (a) strict necessity or (b) total absence of danger to him. The regulation is strict and applies to persons pouring metal as well as to others. There was a breach where a man holding a ladle from 40 inches away was splashed, since clearly there was danger, and the operation was not proved to be impossible from over 8 feet (now 2.4 metres) away: *Lewis v Matthew Swain Ltd* (1969) 6 KIR 481.

Gangways and pouring aisles where molten metal is handled

The requirement in the Factories Act 1961, s. 29—that safe means of access shall be provided—failed to give reasonable protection to workers in foundries, where the movement of hot metal and of heavy loads, combined with uneven floors, narrow gangways and heavy obstructions, may create substantial dangers. Regulation 6 makes a determined effort to overcome these difficulties.

First of all, reg. 6 does not apply to every part of an iron or steel foundry, but only to those parts where 'molten metal is transported or used'. Those parts are described as 'workrooms' to which the regulation applies, but they need not be rooms in the strict sense of the word, e.g. an open yard would be within reg. 6 if molten metal were taken through it.

Next, a distinction is made between *new* workrooms and *old* workrooms. (Regulation 6 does not use the terms 'new' and 'old', but they conveniently express the effect of longer expressions.) A *new* workroom is one which has been 'constructed, re-constructed or converted for use' as a workroom to which reg. 6 applies—i.e. as a place where molten metal is transported or used—after the making of the regulations. The regulations were *made* on 1 October 1953 although they did not come into force until later. Therefore, every workroom within reg. 6 is a new workroom if the construction, re-construction or conversion 'was begun'—reg. 6(3)—after 1 October 1953. Otherwise, it is an old workroom, for which the requirements are less strict.

Also, where the premises or plant existed or were under construction before December 1981, it is sufficient if the old measurements in the 1953 regulations are satisfied, as distinct from the new metric measurements.

(i) Main gangways

Main gangways are governed by reg. 6(1). This must be strictly complied with in new workrooms, and in old workrooms must be complied with 'so far as reasonably practicable'.

The regulation starts by saying that 'sufficient and clearly defined main gangways shall be provided and properly maintained'. Thus the gangways must be sufficient in number; they must be clearly marked out; they must not only be provided but kept, in all material respects, in continuous good order.

By reg. 6(1)(a), they 'shall have *an even surface of hard material* and shall, in particular, not be of sand or have on them more sand than is necessary to avoid risk of flying metal from accidental spillage'.

By reg. 6(1)(b), they 'shall be kept so far as reasonably practicable *free from obstruction*'.

There are also varying requirements for the width of a main gangway, depending upon the purpose for which it is used. If it is not used for carrying molten metal, the minimum width is 920 mm. (formerly 3 ft.): reg. 6(1)(c). Otherwise, the minimum width varies, under reg. 2(1)(d), according to the manner in which the metal is carried, as shown in the following table:

   (i) truck ladles exclusively—600 mm. (formerly 2 ft.)
  (ii) hand shanks carried by not more than two men—920 mm. (formerly 3 ft.)
 (iii) hand shanks carried by more than two men—1.2 metres (formerly 4 ft.)
 (iv) travel in both directions by men with hand shanks—1.8 metres (formerly 6 ft.)

(ii) Pouring aisles

Regulation 6(2) relates to pouring aisles. Regulation 2 defines these as aisles which lead—either 'from a main gangway or directly from a cupola or furnace'—to a point 'where metal is poured into moulds'.

The operation of reg. 6(2) is somewhat limited. By sub-para. (c), it does not apply at all to a workroom or part of a workroom if, 'by reason of the nature of the work done therein', the floor has to be of sand.

In the case of a new workroom—reg. 6(2)(a)—'sufficient and clearly defined pouring aisles shall be provided and properly maintained'. In the case of an old workroom—reg. 6(2)(b)—the only difference is that the aisles need not be 'clearly defined'. Aisles are not 'clearly defined' if several founders adjacent to one another are left to their own devices in marking off their areas in a large bay of a workshop and leave only vague passages between them for metal to be carried: *Hawkins v Ian Ross (Castings) Ltd* [1970] 1 All ER 180.

In new workrooms, the aisles 'shall have an *even surface of hard material* and shall, in particular, not be of sand or have on them more sand than is necessary to avoid risk of flying metal from accidental spillage'. In old workrooms, the only requirement is that the surface shall be 'firm and even'.

In both old and new workrooms, pouring aisles are to be kept 'so far as reasonably practicable *free from obstruction*'. In both cases, too, the aisles must 'be wide enough not to imperil the safety of persons carrying or pouring molten metal', and in any case must not be less than 920 mm. (formerly 18 inches) wide. Under this regulation the aisle may have to be wider than the minimum 920 mm. (18 inches), depending on the size of the ladle which has to be carried through and how far moulding boxes or other objects are piled up: projecting handles of moulding boxes may amount to 'obstructions': *Hawkins v Ian Ross (Castings) Ltd* [1970] 1 All ER 180.

Protection against dust and fumes

This is now governed by the Hazardous Substances Regulations (Chapter 8).

Protection of eyes

This is now governed by the Protection of Eyes Regulations 1974 which apply to all places subject to the Factories Act and replace previous special regulations: see Chapter 12, section 9.

Protection of hands

By reg. 8(1)(1), the occupier must also provide and maintain 'suitable gloves or other protection for the hands' for workers engaged in either—
  (a) 'handling any hot material likely to cause damage to the hands by burn, scald or sear', or
  (b) 'handling pig-iron, rough castings or other articles likely to cause damage to the hands by cut or abrasion'[2].

---

2   In process (b), 'handling' must clearly mean handling by direct contact. *Quaere*, whether its meaning is equally limited under process (a). 'Hot material' would, *prima facie*, include molten metal, which is certainly not 'handled' by hand, but is 'handled', in a broad sense, when it is poured out or moved in a ladle, just as a load is 'handled' by a crane. Also, if direct manual contact alone were contemplated, the word 'burn' would have been sufficient and it would not have been necessary to

Protective equipment: duty of employed persons

No express duties are imposed upon employed persons except with regard to equipment provided for their protection under reg. 8(1), i.e. gloves and goggles. By reg. 8(2), they must 'make full and proper use' of such equipment and report to the occupier or other responsible person, without delay, any loss or defect.

Exemptions

Under reg. 10, the Chief Inspector has power to suspend or relax any requirement of regs. 5, 6, 7 and 9, either in particular foundries or in a specified class of foundries. Conditions may be attached to such exemptions.

Regulation 9—baths and lockers for clothing—is a welfare regulation which does not affect safety requirements.

2 Other foundries

These, like iron and steel foundries, are factories subject to all the normal requirements of the Act.

In addition, the Non-ferrous Metals (Melting and Founding) Regulations 1962 (S.I. 1962 No. 1667) (amended for metrication purposes by S.I. 1981 No. 1332) contain a new code of regulations, similar in general scheme to the Iron and Steel Foundries Regulations, but applying to non-ferrous metals. They revoke the Casting of Brass Regulations 1908 (which were limited to the control of fumes, ventilation and washing facilities). The regulations are in addition to and not in substitution for any other requirements under the Factories Act, except that reg. 15 (washing facilities) takes the place of s. 58(1) of the Act.

---

add the words 'scald'—which involves molten metal in this context—and 'sear', which, like scorching, implies burning by radiation rather than contact. It is, therefore, submitted that this regulation applies to the handling of molten metal and is intended to give protection against splashes of such metal, as well as against such injuries as burns from handling hot castings.

Broadly, by reg. 3(1), the whole of the regulations apply to parts of factories where the casting (in moulds or by other methods) of non-ferrous metals is carried on, or preparation of materials or moulds, or knock-out or dressing operations, incidental to casting; they do not apply to the making of patterns or dies in a separate workshop.

By reg. 3(2), Part I only (regs. 1 to 16) applies to parts of factories where casting as above described is not carried on, but non-ferrous metals are melted and cast for ingots and like purposes.

Regulation 3(3) excludes a number of processes: those subject to the Lead Smelting Regulations 1911 or the Electric Accumulator Regulations 1925; those carried out for printing purposes; smelting by reducing (i.e. getting the metal from its oxide); manufacture of solder; melting of lead and its alloys. Further exemptions, general or limited, may be given under reg. 4.

By reg. 6, workshop floors must not be of sand except where the work makes this necessary. They must have an even hard surface or, if of sand, be kept as even and firm as practicable. By reg. 5, daily cleaning of floors is required, or in the case of sand keeping it 'in good order'.

By reg. 7, persons handling molten metal liable to splash must be given a safe and adequate working space, as free from obstructions as practicable, and the carrying of metal containers must be over a floor at the same level, unless a working space at a different level is required for safety reasons. Regulations 8 and 9 provide for orderly storage and for disposal of waste, obviously with a view to keeping the workshop free from obstructions.

Regulation 10 lays down requirements for the width and condition of gangways and pouring aisles used for carrying molten metal. These vary according to whether they were constructed or converted after the regulations were made (30 July 1962) or before; for new gangways and aisles greater width is required. Metric measurements were introduced in 1981 but the old measurements are sufficient where the premises, or plant, existed or were under construction before December 1961.

Other requirements are for protection in certain cases by gloves against burns or rough material (reg. 13); and for temperature control and facilities for washing, clothing accommodation and meals (regs. 14 to 16). For protection of eyes, see the regulations in Chapter 12, section 9, which apply to all places subject to the Factories Act.

The additional requirements of Part II, applicable where casting as distinct from mere melting down into ingots is carried on, cover cleaning of workshop walls (reg. 17), a weather-proof building for dressing operations (reg. 18) and safe arrangement of material out of doors, leaving safe means of access with firm and even surface free from obstructions (reg. 20). 'Dressing' operations include (reg. 2(2)) all kinds of fettling, stripping and cleaning.

3 All types of foundry: footwear and gaiters

The Foundries (Protective Footwear and Gaiters) Regulations 1971 (S.I. 1971 No. 476) apply both to iron and steel foundries and to other (non-ferrous) foundries: these are defined in detail in reg. 3 in much the same way as in the two general codes (pp. 389, 395, *ante*) and with similar exceptions such as lead smelting, accumulator manufacture, printing foundries, smelting processes, production of steel ingots and lead ingots. By reg. 4, the Chief Inspector may grant exemptions.

The protection of the regulations extends—reg. 5(1)—to employees engaged, in the authorised course of their work, in four types of task:

(a) working at a spout of a cupola or furnace, or attending to the cupola or furnace, where material hot enough to burn may come in contact with them;

(b) pouring molten metal (or assisting);

(c) moving by hand a ladle or mould containing molten metal;

(d) knocking-out operations while the material is hot enough to burn.

By reg. 5(2), the employer must issue to each of these employees personally 'suitable' footwear and gaiters, conforming—reg. 2(3)—to an approved specification, sufficient when worn to prevent (so far as reasonably practicable) burns to feet and ankles. Gaiters must be issued *at once* to every person within these categories, footwear as soon as practicable with a maximum delay of 28 days. Footwear is normally boots, but an employee may ask for clogs instead. By reg. 5(6), the employer must issue replacements when necessary, and, by reg. 6, provide personal lockers for the equipment. By reg. 7, it is a positive duty for the employee to wear the equipment when working at any of the processes, to look after it, put it in the locker at the end of work and report loss or defects.

4 Miscellaneous

For regulations intended to keep down harmful dust in grinding and other processes, and to give protection against lead fumes and lead poisoning in smelting processes, see the Hazardous Substances Regulations (Chapter 8). Schedule 2 to the regulations (replacing earlier specific regulations for foundries) expressly forbids the use of sand or other substances containing free silica for blasting purposes, and the use as a parting material in making metal castings of substances containing more than 3 per cent silica, or dust or other material deposited from fettling or blasting.

Chapter 14

Shipbuilding yards and docks

1 General remarks

The older case-law on shipbuilding yards and docks is confusing unless it is realised that these have been brought within the Factories Acts by successive stages—sometimes completely, sometimes to a limited extent.

Shipbuilding yards as a whole, including any fitting basins and dry docks, have always been factories in the strict sense, even under the Act of 1901. 'Public dry docks' were brought clearly within the definition only by the Act of 1937.

The ordinary docks and harbours of commerce were within the Act of 1901 for certain purposes only, to enable regulations to be made for the safety of the dockside and for the safe conduct of loading and unloading ships.

The repair and construction of ships in ordinary docks was not brought within the Acts until 1937, again for the limited purpose of enabling regulations to be made.

Now, broadly, the comprehensive new code of Shipbuilding Regulations, made in 1960 under the Act of 1937, more or less applies to all shipbuilding and ship-repairs wherever carried on; and in the case of docks, in practice all safety requirements are contained in the Docks Regulations 1988 made under the Health and Safety at Work Act 1974.

It is possible—in the ordinary docks—to have both the Shipbuilding Regulations and the Docks Regulations applying to a ship at the same time, if, for example, repair or painting is going on at the same time as a cargo is discharged. In such cases there may be overlapping of duties, such as the duty to fence open hatchways.

2 Shipbuilding yards

In order to understand how the Factories Act 1961 applies to shipbuilding, it is necessary to distinguish three different cases:

    (i) a shipbuilding yard (including any wet or dry dock which forms part of it);

    (ii) a public dry dock;

    (iii) a public wet dock where ships are built or repaired.

A *shipbuilding yard* is a factory (in the strict sense of the term) by the express terms of s. 175(2)(a), and the whole of the safety requirements of the Factories Act 1961 automatically apply to it. It is unnecessary, therefore, in connection with shipbuilding yards, to rely on ss. 125 and 126 (as they now are in the 1961 Act) which bring docks within the Act to a limited extent and for limited purposes: per Lord Atkin in *Smith v Cammell Laird & Co Ltd* [1940] AC 242, [1939] 4 All ER 381. This automatic application of the Act—all of it—to shipbuilding yards as a whole is in no way affected by the special provisions (s. 126) as to ships in wet docks, or by the existence of requirements, differing from the Act, in the Shipbuilding Regulations: so, for example, s. 29 (safe means of access) applies to access throughout a shipbuilding yard, including access over the deck of a ship under repair: *Gardiner v Admiralty Commissioners* [1964] 2 All ER 93.

Shipbuilding yards were described in the Act of 1901—Sixth Schedule, Part II, para. 25—as 'any premises in which any ships, boats or vessels used in navigation are made, finished or repaired'. The Act of 1901 did not apply unless mechanical power was used: but there is no such restriction in the Act of 1961.

Under the old definition the House of Lords held in *Smith v Cammell Laird & Co Ltd, supra,* that if a wet dock is included in a shipbuilding yard, it forms part of the yard, and the occupier of the yard is responsible for complying with the Act on vessels lying in the dock, though such a vessel is not in itself a factory, but simply an article under construction or repair inside the factory. Lord Wright said ([1940] AC at 267, [1939] 4 All ER at 396):

> 'The respondents' yard included all the premises within its perimeter, including the fitting-out basin, or wet dock, in which the vessel was lying for the purpose of being completed. The work of fitting out a vessel after she is launched is often more lengthy and elaborate than the actual construction of the hull. In practice, it can only be done at a

wet basin or fitting-out quay after the vessel is afloat, and hence such a basin or wharf is an essential and integral part of the shipbuilding yard.'

The description given in the present Act is as follows (s. 175(2)(a)):

'Any yard or dry dock (including the precincts thereof) in which ships or vessels are constructed, repaired, refitted, finished or broken up.'

Undoubtedly the word 'yard' continues to include a private wet dock or basin within the precincts. But in *Chatburn v Manchester Dry Dock Co Ltd* (1950) 83 LI LRep 1 where a ship-repairing yard fronted on to the Manchester Ship Canal and comprised a wharf on the canal, the Court of Appeal held that a trawler moored at the wharf for repairs was not within the 'precincts' of the factory, and it must always be a question of fact how far the precincts extend.

'Repair' includes painting with anti-fouling composition: *Day v Harland and Wolff Ltd* [1953] 2 All ER 387; *Hurley v J. Sanders & Co Ltd* [1955] 1 All ER 833; but does not include ordinary internal painting in a ship's hold: *Taylor v Ellerman's Wilson Line Ltd and Amos and Smith Ltd* [1952] 1 Lloyd's Rep 144.

The words 'dry dock' were probably added to the definition in the Act of 1937 (and now of 1961) in order to include *public dry docks*, i.e. those which do not form part of a shipbuilder's yard, but are hired out as required. Under the Act of 1901 a public dry dock, unlike a shipbuilding yard, was not *per se* a factory, but became a 'notional' factory for limited purposes under the section relating to docks: *Raine v Jobson & Co* [1901] AC 404. The consequence was that the person having the 'actual use and occupation' (usually the hirer of the dock) was treated as the occupier. Under the present law, a 'dry dock' of any kind is *ipso facto* a factory for which the occupier is responsible.

As to *wet* docks, it was held under the Act of 1901 that they are not turned into a shipbuilding yard by the mere fact that repairs to ships are carried out while they are lying in the dock: *Spencer v Livett (Frank) & Son* [1900] 1 QB 498. Otherwise, as the Court of Appeal said in that case, the odd result would follow that the docks at a place like Southampton would be turned into a factory as soon as one ship began to undergo repairs[1].

---

1 *Spencer v Livette* was followed in Scotland: *Bowman v Ellerman Lines Ltd* 1953 SLT 271.

Section 126 of the Act of 1961 (replacing s. 106 of the Act of 1937 as slightly amended in 1948) deals with this situation by turning the ship itself (when under repair in an *ordinary* dock) into a 'notional factory', as it is convenient to call it, for certain limited purposes.

Section 126(1) provides as follows:

> '. . . the provisions of this Act specified in subsection (2) of this section shall apply to any work carried out in a harbour or wet dock in constructing, reconstructing, repairing, refitting, painting, finishing or breaking up a ship or in scaling, scurfing or cleaning boilers (including combustion chambers or smoke boxes) in a ship, or in cleaning oil-fuels tanks or bilges in a ship or any tank in a ship last used for oil of any description carried as cargo or any tank or hold last used for any substances so carried of a description specified in regulations of the Minister as being of a dangerous or injurious nature.'

Then follows a long list of the portions of the Act which apply. But, from the point of view of safety requirements, the only things made applicable were the power to make special safety regulations (s. 76), the duties of persons employed (s. 143), liability for offences (Part XII), and the interpretation sections (Part XIV). Part II as a whole is *not* applied. The powers to make regulations and the duties of persons employed are now superseded by the wider powers and duties in the Health and Safety at Work Act 1974, and s. 126 has been modified in accordance with that Act: S.I. 1974 No. 1941. The practical result is that the Shipbuilding Regulations contain all the safety requirements for ships under repair or maintenance work (as described in the section) in an open dock.

The master and crew of the ship, whose rights and duties between themselves are controlled by the Merchant Shipping Acts, are excluded from the section. This does not mean that the master or crew cannot be made liable to persons working on the ship, if, for instance, the master is required by regulations to provide lighting during repairs; it only excludes them from the *benefit* of the Factories Act, for example, if seamen paint the ship's sides in dock.

Furthermore, the section does not apply to *anyone* while the ship is out on a trial run, though the ship-repairer's men may remain on board.

These qualifications are contained in s. 126(3), which is as follows:

> 'Nothing in this Act shall apply to any such work as is mentioned in subsection (1) of this section which is done by the master or crew of a ship or done on board a ship during a trial run.'

A yard where an oil rig is under construction is within the definition of a factory, the oil rig being an 'article' under manufacture: so such a yard, like a shipyard, is subject to all the requirements of the Factories Act including safe access over the rig itself: *Faith v C B I Constuctors Ltd* 1987 SLT 248.

3 The Shipbuilding Regulations

The old Shipbuilding Regulations were made in 1931 under the Factory and Workshop Act 1901, and applied to both shipbuilding yards and public dry docks. Though continued in force by s. 159 of the Factories Act 1937, they had to be interpreted in the light of the power under which they were made, i.e. s. 79 of the Act of 1901: *Canadian Pacific Steamships Ltd v Bryers* [1958] AC 485, [1957] 3 All ER 572. Consequently they did not apply (as they could have been made to do under s. 106 of the 1937 Act) to ships in public wet docks, and were never extended to them: *Garcia v Harland and Wolff Ltd* [1943] 1 KB 731, [1943] 2 All ER 477; *Lovell v Blundells and Crompton & Co Ltd* [1944] KB 502, [1943] 2 All ER 53.

The 1931 regulations were replaced by the Shipbuilding and Ship-repairing Regulations 1960 (S.I. 1960 No. 1932), amended, for metrication purposes, by the Docks, Shipbuilding etc. (Metrication) Regulations 1983 (S.I. No 644). These have a wider application and include ships under repair or maintenance work within s. 126.

The scope of the regulations

The regulations apply:
  first, by reg. 2(1)(a) to work on 'operations' in 'shipyards' properly
    so-called;
  secondly, by reg. 2(1)(b), to work on 'operations in a harbour or wet
    dock', with important exceptions.
The second heading, therefore, gave effect for the first time to the change made by the Act of 1937 which brought work in docks and harbours, though not comprised in any shipyard, within the scope of the legislation. A number of important points have to be noticed under both headings.

(i) Work in shipyards

'Shipyard' is defined much as in the Act of 1937 (now the consolidating Act of 1961) to mean 'any yard or dry dock (including the precincts thereof) in which ships or vessels are constructed, reconstructed, repaired, refitted or finished' (reg. 3 (2)). But (unlike the Act) it does not include a yard or dock where they are broken up. 'Dry dock' evidently includes a 'public dry dock', defined by reg. 3 as one 'available for hire'.

(ii) Ships in docks and harbours

It is necessary to distinguish here between 'ship' and 'vessel' as defined in the Merchant Shipping Acts. 'Vessel' includes any ship or boat used in navigation; 'ship' includes only any vessel used in navigation not propelled by oars—i.e. it is a powered sea-going (at any rate water-going) craft or sailing ship. In shipyards, work on all ships or vessels is subject to the regulations—in docks and harbours only work on 'ships'. Work is excluded if done (i) by the master or crew of a ship or (ii) by anyone on board during a trial run—these are the same exclusions as in s. 126 of the Act of 1961—or (iii) to raise or remove a sunk or stranded ship or (iv) on board a ship not 'under command' (i.e. not under control) to bring it 'under command': see reg. 2(1)(b) for exact details. Broadly speaking, (iii) and (iv) exclude salvage operations, but it may be noted that the Diving Operations at Work Regulations 1981 (S.I. No. 399) apply in these cases as they apply to all places of work.

(iii) Exclusions: small vessels, etc.

Many of the regulations are excluded in the case of small vessels.

(a) Shipyards   By reg. 2(2)(a), all but the regulations mentioned below are excluded for work on vessels unless both (i) the overall length exceeds 30 metres and (ii) the overall depth exceeds 2.9 metres.

But reg. 6 (safe access), regs. 31 to 67 (lifting appliances, dangerous fumes, fencing machinery) and regs. 73–4 (protective wear for cutting, welding, riveting, handling plates) apply even to work on small vessels. So did regs. 75, 78 (asbestos, lead paint) and reg. 76 (dust) but these are now superseded by wider regulations, also including control of dust and fumes which apply to places of work in general: see Chapter 8.

(b) Ships in harbours and docks (reg. 2(2)(b))   The same limits of size apply, but, as in shipyards, regs. 6, 31 to 67 and 73 to 78 apply even to small ships. ('Vessels other than ships' are not within the regulations at

all when in harbours or docks not part of a shipyard.) In addition reg. 80 (young persons) applies.

(c) Public dry docks (reg. 2 (2) (c))   Where a vessel does not exceed the limits of size stated above for shipyards, regs. 7 (access to vessels), 12 to 24 (access and staging) and 26 to 30 (openings, fall of objects) are excluded. It follows that all the other regulations apply in a public dry dock even to small vessels and that, although strictly a public dry dock is only one kind of 'shipyard', for this purpose reg. 2(2)(c) is an exhaustive statement of the position in such docks and reg. 2(2)(a)—heading *Shipyards* above—does not apply.

(iv) Operations to which the regulations apply

The conditions which bring work within the regulations are somewhat involved. There must be (a) work (b) either in a shipyard or on a ship in wet dock and (c) it must be work 'carried out' in specified '*operations*'. These are defined by reg. 3(2) to mean, in relation to a ship or vessel:

   (1) construction and reconstruction;
   (2) repairing and refitting;
   (3) painting and finishing;
   (4) scaling, scurfing or cleaning of boilers (including combustion chambers or smoke boxes);
   (5) cleaning of bilges, oil-fuel tanks last used for carrying oil of any kind.

(v) General

The Chief Inspector has a sweeping power to grant exemptions: reg. 2(3). By reg. 2(4), the requirements of the regulations are in addition to the requirements of the Factories Acts (which, of course, apply in full to shipyards, though not to ships in wet docks) except under regs. 32, 52, 53, 67 and 68 where there are special provisions.

Persons owing duties under the regulations

Under the 1931 regulations, the occupier was responsible in a shipyard, the head contractor in a public dry dock, and the shipowner in certain cases for lighting and hatchways. There is now a more detailed division of duties.

(i) Employers undertaking operations (reg. 4(1))

They are responsible to their *own* employees, broadly, for such things as means of access, safe staging, protective wear; they are responsible for complying with regs. 6, 8(2), 11(1), 13, 14(1) to (3) and (5), 15, 17(1) to (4) and (6), 18, 19(1), 20 to 24, 25(2), 28(1), 48 to 51, 56(2), 60(1) and (2), 70(1) and (4), 73 and 74, 80 and 81; also for regs. 11(2), 16, 69(1), 26 and 70(2) and (3), except so far as these duties devolve on persons in control of docks and ships.

Employers are responsible to *all* persons for protection against the fall or throwing down of loose articles—regs. 27, 29(1), 30(1), fire and other dangers on oil tankers—regs. 59, 62 to 66, and insecure hatch beams and bolts for plates—regs. 71, 72. In these matters they are responsible only for things arising out of their own operations: and are not responsible under regs. 59 and 62 in cases where the duty falls under reg. 4(7)(a) on those in control of the ship.

In a *public dry dock* an employer is, in addition, responsible to his own employees for complying with regs. 7, 9, 10 and 12 (access to and between vessels) except where the duty devolves on the dock management or the ship: reg. 4(5)(b).

Further, although an employer as such is not responsible for safety of plant and machinery, by reg. 4 (2) he must not *use* plant which does not comply with regs. 33 to 39 (lifting appliances and gear) or regs. 67 and 68 (fencing of machinery, air receivers).

Lastly, by reg. 4(9), an employer does not owe a duty to an employee who is not present in the place in the course of doing his employer's work, or with the express or implied permission of the employer. A provision in this form is fairly new in regulations under the Factories Act, but there are similar provisions in the Construction Regulations and also in the regulations for safety in agriculture. There is, no doubt, scope for permission to be 'implied' by the court when a man strays in ignorance, e.g. looking for materials or a lavatory: see *Henaghan v Rederiet Forangirene* [1936] 2 All ER 1426 on rather different words in the Docks Regulations. Regulation 4(9) does *not* apply to regs. 48 to 51, 59, 60, 65 and 70, so in these cases the duty is unqualified.

(ii) Machinery, plant and equipment

(a) Owners They are responsible under reg. 4(2) for complying with regs. 33 to 39 (lifting appliances and gear), also 67 and 68 (fencing of

machinery, air receivers). Where such plant is carried on a ship, the ship is also responsible. The word 'owners' is not defined: it is thought that it does not necessarily mean absolute ownership in the sense of property law, but includes persons who are for the time being entitled to possession of the plant, as distinct from those who use it by permission. The duties must, for example, be performed by contractors who hold plant on hire-purchase or even on straight hire, though in both cases the true owners may also be responsible.

(b) Installers and erectors   They are responsible under reg. 4(3)(a) for complying with regs. 42, 55(1) and (2), 56(1)(a) and 57—lifting appliances, gas cylinders, acetylene and welding plant, etc.

(c) Users   They must, by reg. 4(3)(b), work or use the plant in compliance with regs. 40 to 47, 55(1) and (2), 56, 57(1) to (4), 58, 69(4) and (5) (safety of loads and use of lifting gear, gas, acetylene, welding plant, oil lamps).

(iii) General management of shipyards, etc.
The persons having 'general management and control' of these places have duties under the following regulations (see reg. 4(4) to (6)), except in certain cases where responsibility rests on the ship under reg. 4 (7):

(a) Shipyards   Regulations 7, 8, 9, 10, 12, 17(5), 25(1), 59, 62, 79—which relate to safe access, safety and fencing of dry docks, lights on tankers, and first aid.

(b) Public dry docks   Regulations 7, 9, 11(2), 12, 16, 17(5), 25(1), 69(1), 79(1) and (2): broadly, safety of means of access, floating platforms and staging materials actually provided by the dock, safety and fencing of dry docks, lighting the approaches to the dock, and first aid arrangements.

(c) Dock, wharf or quay where ship is lying   Regulation 69(1), lighting of approaches.

(iv) Responsibilities of ship
The ship—i.e. the owners and the master or officer in charge—have under reg. 4(7) the following duties:
   (a) to comply with regs. 9(1), 10 and 12 as to means of access provided by them, reg. 59 as to naked lights on tankers as regards

acts done by the ship, reg. 62 as to posting up certificates obtained by the ship;

(b) where they retain general control of the ship, to protect under reg. 26 hatches not in use for the 'operations', and to comply with regs. 69(2) and 70(2) and (3)—lighting, and work on boilers;

(c) not to remove fencing from hatches and openings except as allowed by reg. 26.

There is a proviso that where a stevedore or other person is responsible under the Docks Regulations for the protection of a hatch, that person is *solely* responsible for maintaining in position the fencing, cover or other protection required by reg. 26.

(v) Persons employed

They must, by reg. 4(8), carry out the requirements of those regulations—listed in reg. 4(8)—which impose an express duty on them, and report defects in plant and machinery promptly.

To whom duties are owed   Like all duties imposed by regulations under s. 76 of the Factories Act 1961 these duties are for the benefit of 'persons employed' only, and do not, for example, include a subcontractor working personally on his own account: *Herbert v Harold Shaw Ltd* [1959] 2 QB 138, [1959] 2 All ER 189. However, the regulations are for the protection of all 'persons employed', whether or not employed in shipbuilding processes; the expression 'persons employed', whatever its precise ambit, certainly includes 'a man who is ordinarily and regularly employed' in the area covered by the regulations, and therefore a member of the ship's crew may recover for damages for breach of the regulations, e.g. an unguarded opening or hatchway: *Canadian Pacific Steamships Ltd v Bryers* [1958] AC 485, [1957] 3 All ER 572. There may be liability for breach of the regulations in parts of the ship where a man is not normally employed if it is foreseeable that he should go there: *Mullard v Ben Line Steamers Ltd* [1970] 2 Lloyds Rep 121 (open unlighted hatch where man might go back to recover his tools: breach reg. 6, 26, 69—safe access, hatch covers, lighting) (appeal as to contributory negligence only [1971] 2 All ER 424).

The content of the regulations

The regulations enter into great detail, and it is only possible to give a brief résumé, concentrating on the important points. The re-drafting of the regulations has taken full account of difficulties which arose under the 1931 regulations, and most of the case-law under those regulations is obsolete.

The regulations consist of nine parts: Part I, which contains regs. 1 to 5, deals with interpretation and general matters.

Part II. Means of access

There is first of all a comprehensive requirement for safe means of access in reg. 6. This is 'without prejudice' to the other regulations. It is split up below into portions to show the different requirements.

> 'There shall, so far as is reasonably practicable, be provided and maintained safe means of access to every place at which any person has at any time to work in connection with the operations, which means of access shall be sufficient having regard to the number of persons employed and shall, so far as is reasonably practicable, be kept clear of substances likely to make foothold or handhold insecure and of any obstruction.'

All the old case-law under s. 26(1) of the Factories Act 1937, as to whether 'safe means of access' extended to slipperiness or obstructions is rendered superfluous by the express words at the end. But it remains true under reg. 6 that it is the access to work, not the place of work itself, which is to be safe: cf. *Lovell v Blundells and Crompton & Co Ltd* [1944] KB 502, [1943] 2 All ER 53.

This is followed by precise requirements for particular means of access: safe construction (including guard rails and toe-boards) and safe placing of gangways from shore to vessel (reg. 7)[2], handrails or fencing on steps leading down into a dry dock (reg. 8), access by accommodation ladder or gangway to vessels at wharf or quay or dry dock (reg. 9), access between vessels (reg. 10), safe transport over water (reg. 11), sound construction and proper maintenance of floating platforms (also reg. 11), and means of access to ship's deck where gangway rests on bulwark (reg. 12).

The next regulations link up with 'staging'.

---

2 Regulation 7 does not apply to a 3-foot extension joining the main gangway to the jetty, and no handrail is required except for the main gangway: *Williams v Swan Hunter Shipbuilders Ltd* (1988) Times, 24 March, CA.

Staging

'Staging' is the term used in shipbuilding for what would be called scaffolding in building on land. 'Stage' means—under reg. 3—a 'temporary platform' from which work is done but does not include a boatswain's chair. 'Staging' includes any stage and the uprights and other components (not being part of the structure of the vessel) used in supporting it, also guard rails connected with a stage.

By reg. 16, 'sound and substantial material and appliances' must be available for staging, and must be examined by a competent person before being taken into use (or re-use).

By reg.17(1):

> 'All staging and every part thereof shall be of good construction, of suitable and sound material and of adequate strength for the purpose for which it is used and shall be properly maintained, and every upright and thwart shall be kept so fixed, secured or placed in position as to prevent, so far as is reasonably practicable, accidental displacements.'

This is a key regulation, which imposes strict or absolute liability for non-compliance, and is in no way cut down by subsequent words requiring inspection to be carried out: so the House of Lords held on similar wording in *Smith v Cammell Laird & Co Ltd* [1940] AC 242, [1939] 4 All ER 381. It applies for the protection of the stagers themselves when dismantling the staging: *Graham v Greenock Dockyard Co* 1965 SLT 61 (lack of rigidity in iron support). Under the old regulations ('securely constructed of sound and substantial material') neither overlapping planks nor the existence of a gap was a contravention: *Slayford v Harland and Wolff Ltd* (1949) 82 Ll L Rep 160; *Revie v Fairfield Shipbuilding and Engineering Co Ltd* (1955) 105 L Jo 123. But the new wording requires 'good construction' which may make a difference[3]. Planks forming stages must in general be fastened to prevent them slipping (reg. 17 (2)). Planks supported on ladder rungs must not be used to support stages (reg. 19). Stages suspended by ropes and chains must be secured to prevent swinging, the chains, ropes and other gear used for suspension must be sound and kept from contact with sharp edges (fibre ropes are in general forbidden) (reg. 20).

---

3   See *Smith v A. Davies & Co (Shopfitters) Ltd* (1968) 5 KIR 320 (projection of scaffold pole between rungs of ladder not 'good construction' under Construction Regulations).

Boatswain's chairs and the gear used for their suspension must be sound and strong and securely attached, with protection against spinning which might tip out the occupant (reg. 21). Stages must be of sufficient width (reg. 23); and planks in a rising stage—i.e. with an upward tilt—at the bow of a vessel must be fastened to prevent slipping (reg. 22).

Where a person is liable to fall from a stage either more than 2 metres—or into water—there are stricter requirements in reg. 24. There must in general be close boarding to avoid gaps, and guard rails or ropes at the sides.

At outside staging in a shipyard, there must be ladders giving direct access to the stages, and where workers have to pass over or along a ship under construction, sufficient planks and ladders must be provided to give access (reg. 13). This requirement is imperative; if there are not ladders giving direct access, there is a breach of the regulation: *Bowen v Mills and Knights Ltd* [1973] 1 Lloyd's Rep 580. Plankways must be at least 430 mm. wide (reg. 13(3)). Ladders used for access, communication or support must be of sound construction, adequate strength and securely fixed (reg. 14). There are exceptions for portable ladders and rope ladders, but the latter must have adequate footholds.

Dry dock altars and shoring sills—i.e. the steps leading down inside a dry dock—from which work is done must be of sound construction and properly maintained (reg. 17(5)); and these places, together with stages and footways, must as far as reasonably practicable be kept clear of slippery substances (reg. 17(6)).

Uprights used for hoisting blocks must be kept secure from displacement (which might endanger the staging) (reg. 18).

Part III. Precautions against fall of persons and materials

By reg. 25 fencing must be provided at the edges of dry docks (including edges over steps and chutes) and kept continuously in position except when it has to be removed to allow movement of persons and things. By reg. 26, openings in a deck or tank top of a vessel have in general to be fenced at every side or edge which may be a source of danger, and the fencing must be kept in position except when removed to allow access of persons or materials: but fencing is not required for openings which are securely covered, or at the head of stairways in use for 'the operations': nor does the regulation apply to the open parts of a deck or tank top, which have yet to be plated, except where an opening is deliberately left for the purpose of the shipbuilding or repairing operations. (As to plankways over open decks, see reg. 13.)

There are a number of regulations to minimise the risk of articles being dropped from a height: planks on outside stages must be so placed that articles cannot fall on to persons at work underneath (reg. 27), boxes must be provided and used for rivets, nuts, bolts, etc. (reg. 28), parts of staging, tools, etc., must be lowered, not thrown down, where they would cause danger (reg. 29) and loose articles must not be left lying about (reg. 30).

Part IV. Lifting gear

Regulations 31 to 47 contain detailed requirements for chains, ropes, lifting gear and lifting appliances, of which there is a definition (reg. 3) wide enough to include cranes, transporters, derricks and all associated tackle. (It is the tackle which is called 'lifting gear'.)

By reg. 32, in the case of a 'shipyard' (which is a factory proper), these requirements are *in substitution* for s. 23 and parts of s. 24 of the Factories Act 1937 (now ss. 26 and 27 of the Act of 1961).

In general, by reg. 33, all lifting appliances, and gear for anchoring or fixing them, must be

'of good construction, sound material, adequate strength and free from patent defect, and shall be properly maintained.'

Such appliances must also be tested, examined and (with certain exceptions for dock and ship gear) marked with the safe working load (or loads for different positions of the jib) (reg. 34).

In the case of chains, ropes and lifting gear, reg. 35 imposes the same requirements as reg. 33 except that it does not add 'shall be properly maintained'. Instead regs. 36, 37, 39 and 43 provide for periodic testing and examination, the correct splicing of wire ropes and discarding of frayed or worn ropes. A table of safe working loads must be posted near ropes, chains and other gear (reg. 38).

Lifting appliances and gear must be adequately supported or suspended (reg. 42). This applies although no load is being carried, so the fall of an empty sling from a hook was a breach of the regulation: *Forsyth's Curator Bonis v Govan Shipbuilders Ltd* 1988 SLT 321. Safe working loads must not be exceeded, loads must be securely attached or supported, and special precautions must be taken if the moving load is liable to displace some other object nearby (regs. 40, 41). Chains and ropes must be kept from sharp edges, and chains or wire ropes joined together by knotting or similar improvisation must not be used (regs. 45, 44).

In general loads must not be left hanging from any unattended appliance (reg. 46).

Part V. Ventilation, fumes and explosives

Much of Part V is concerned with work on oil-tanks, but its provisions are of general application to work in confined spaces where there may be fumes or insufficient air—e.g. cleaning boiler spaces, or painting below deck.

There are general requirements for good ventilation and precautions against inflammable vapours in regs. 48 and 49. Under regs. 50–52, where there is a confined place likely to be short of oxygen or subject to dangerous fumes, entry is forbidden without breathing apparatus unless the place is tested and certified safe, and stand-by apparatus for rescue must be available; and an 'appropriate' safety lamp must be used. (This is *in substitution* for s. 27 of the Factories Act 1937, now s. 30 of the Act of 1961.) By reg. 53 (which was in substitution for s. 63 of the Act of 1961) there had to be protection against inhaling injurious dust or fumes, including where practicable an exhaust appliance to draw them off at source. (This is now replaced by general regulations for the control of hazardous substances at all places of work: see Chapter 8.) Rivet fires are forbidden in confined spaces not adequately ventilated (reg. 54). Gas (including oxygen) cylinders must be kept away from sources of heat and unventilated places (reg. 55). This also applies to acetylene generators, for which there are further requirements in reg. 56 (in particular prohibition of naked lights and smoking). Under regs. 57 and 58, pipes or hoses for supplying gas to apparatus for cutting, welding or heating metal must be of good construction, securely attached to the apparatus and other connections (e.g. the gas cylinders), and there must be efficient reducing and regulating valves; the apparatus must (apart from meal intervals, when only the supply valves need be closed) be disconnected or brought to the open deck when not in use. Regulations 59–66 control entry into oil-tanks: they restrict work involving naked light, fire or lamp (except an 'appropriate' safety lamp) unless a special certificate of safety has been obtained, also entry into tanks without breathing apparatus unless certified safe, and lay down a method of cleaning and ventilation to be carried out before testing for a naked light certificate. Some minor repairs to the outside can be done (reg. 66(1), (2)), without obtaining such a certificate.

Parts VI to IX. Miscellaneous and general

Fencing of machinery

Motors, gearing and shafting on a vessel, which are used for 'the operations', must be fenced so far as reasonably practicable unless safe by position or construction (reg. 67(1)). In the case of a shipyard this is in substitution for s. 14 of the Factories Act (but only, of course, as regards machinery 'on a vessel'). By reg. 67(2), there is a general requirement for fencing 'dangerous parts' of machinery in a place or part of a vessel to which Part II of the Factories Act does not apply, if used for 'the operations', unless safe by position or construction. Reg. 67(3) allows lubrication, adjustment or repair where the fence has to be removed, upon certain conditions.

Regulation 67 is somewhat obscure, but it seems that reg. 67(1) applies in all cases, to the exclusion of every other duty, to the motors, gearing and shafting on a vessel: and the standard of duty is what is reasonably practicable. Any other dangerous machinery is either directly subject to Part II of the Factories Act (which includes s. 14), or if not is subjected to a similar provision by reg. 67(2).

Air receivers

Section 31 of the Act of 1937, now s. 36 of the Act of 1961, is applied by reg. 68, except to the permanent installation in a ship.

Lighting (reg. 69)

Parts of a vessel and other places where operations are carried on, together with all the approaches, must be sufficiently lighted. In a wet dock or harbour where the shipowner retains control, the permanent lighting of the ship must be kept going to light the ship and access to it: but by reg. 69(3) a failure of electric lighting is not a breach of the regulations if other lighting is provided as soon as practicable. This overrules *Wilkinson v Rea Ltd* [1941] 1 KB 688, [1941] 2 All ER 50. Petrol or other spirit with a high flash point is forbidden in portable lamps.

Miscellaneous

Work is not allowed in a boiler or associated furnace or flue until it is cool and entry into a steam boiler forming part of a range is forbidden unless steam and hot water are disconnected or sealed off (reg. 70). Hatch beams taken off a hatch in use must be secured to prevent displacement (reg. 71). Jumped-up bolts are not to be used for securing plates on the sides of vessels (reg. 72). Hand protection is required in certain processes such as using welding apparatus with gas under pressure or handling plates (reg. 73); also breathing apparatus in processes involving dust from boilers or combustion chambers (reg. 76, which is now replaced by general regulations for hazardous substances and also for asbestos: see Chapter 8; reg. 77, concerning the employment of young persons in dust processes, was also revoked). Young persons must not be employed where they may fall from a stage more than 2 metres, or into water, unless they have been in shipyards for at least six months, and persons under 16 must be in the charge of an experienced workman (reg. 80). Stretchers and ambulances must be provided in case of accident (reg. 79) and in large shipyards there has to be a full-time safety officer (reg. 81). Protection of eyes (formerly required by regs. 74, 75) is now governed by the Protection of Eyes Regulations 1974: see Chapter 12, section 9.

4 Docks and associated premises, and warehouses

Safety legislation in docks is a tangled story. It now consists mainly of the Docks Regulations 1988, but first it is necessary to say something about the direct application of the Factories Act to docks (chiefly the sections about fencing of machinery and about hoists and lifts).

As explained earlier in this Chapter, a 'dry dock' is expressly included in the definition of a factory by s. 175(2)(a) of the Factories Act 1961 and the whole Act applies to it; a 'wet dock' is not within the definition except in the special case where it is part of a shipbuilding yard.

However, the ordinary docks of commerce where ships load and unload were brought within the Act to a limited extent by a special section, s. 125, which has been amended and extended by reg. 23 of the Docks Regulations 1988 (S.I. No. 1655), made under the overriding powers in the Health and Safety at Work Act 1974.

Section 125 applies the Act to docks in two separate ways:
(i) under s. 125(1) and (2), and again under s. 125(7) as added in 1988, it applies certain sections of the Act to the dock premises themselves;
(ii) under s. 125(3), it applies it to the *processes* of loading and unloading as if they were carried on in a factory and the person carrying them on were the occupier.

The section also applies the Act to 'warehouses', both on a dock and off it, but this requires separate treatment.

Application of the Factories Act to dock premises

Under s. 125(1) and (2), very limited provisions of the Act were applied to 'every dock, wharf or quay': only those relating to steam boilers (with the modification that the owner was responsible instead of the occupier) and the power to make regulations (now exercised under the 1974 Act). A dock includes lines and sidings which do not form part of a railway or tramway undertaking. But under this subsection—as distinct from the subsection about loading 'processes'—'dock' means 'the solid structure and body of the dock and not the water space within its limits': *Houlder Line Ltd v Griffin* [1905] AC 220; nor, therefore, does it include the ships. 'Wharf' means a place contiguous to water and does not include a timber yard some distance away: *Haddock v Humphrey* [1900] 1 QB 609; but it is a matter of degree, and land 40 yards away from the water, connected to the wharf by rail, was held to be part of it: *Kenny v Harrison* [1902] 2 KB 168. A structure moored in mid-river was held to be a wharf: *Ellis v Cory & Son Ltd* [1902] 1 KB 38.

The person responsible under these subsections was not the 'occupier' of the dock as a whole, but the person having the 'use and occupation' of dock premises. This could be something less than a full occupier: thus contractors altering upper floors of a warehouse had 'use and occupation': *Weavings v Kirk and Randall* [1904] 1 KB 213; occupiers of a dockside hut who let out horses and gear had 'use and occupation' of an adjacent area of dock: *Pacific Steam Navigation Co v Pugh & Son* (1907) 23 TLR 622; stevedores may have 'use and occupation' of the area where they are operating: *Merrill v Wilson, Sons & Co Ltd* [1901] 1 KB 35. But these old cases are of little importance now as duties are defined by the regulations.

Much more important is the further application of the Factories Act which was made by the 1988 Regulations, adding new subsections (7), (8) and (9). These introduce a different definition. 'Dock premises'—s. 125(9)—now means

> 'any dock, wharf, quay, jetty or other place at which ships load or unload goods or embark or disembark passengers, together with neighbouring land or water which is used or occupied, or intended to be used or occupied, for those or incidental activities, and any part of a ship when used for those or incidental activities.'

So 'dock premises' is wider than 'dock', as defined by the case-law above. It includes the water, and ships in the dock.

To 'dock premises' as so defined, s. 125(7) applies all the sections of the Factories Act which relate to the fencing of machinery and to hoists and lifts (ss. 12–16 and 22–23); the person 'having the control' of the machinery is responsible instead of the occupier.

However, nothing in the section—and therefore nothing in the Docks Regulations made under it—applies to machinery or plant on board a ship which is owned by the shipowner or charterer (or held by him on hire, hire purchase or conditional sale): s. 125(4) as substituted in 1988. This is governed by Merchant Shipping Regulations: see Chapter 20.

Application of the Act to 'loading and unloading' processes

There is, however, a separate and independent provision in s. 125(3) which singles out the important *processes* of loading and unloading and treats them as if they were carried on in a factory.

Section 125(3) applies on the process 'of loading, unloading or coaling of any ship in any dock, harbour[4] or canal'. Certain provisions of the Act apply to all these processes 'as if' they were carried on in a factory, 'as if' the machinery or plant used in the processes were in the factory, and 'as if' the person carrying on the processes were the occupier. The provisions of the Act applied are:

Sections 32 to 35 as to steam boilers, for which the owner of the boiler is liable (but the sections do not apply to the ship's boilers);

Section 76, giving power to make regulations (now superseded by the wider powers in the Health and Safety at Work Act 1974: S.I. 1974 No. 1941).

Eliminating legal fictions, therefore, the substance of the subsection is that the person carrying on any of the above processes is responsible for carrying out duties which, by regulations, are imposed on him; and the regulations may extend to the condition and use of plant and machinery, which by the express terms of subsection (5), includes 'any gangway or ladder'.

The process of 'loading' continues until the hatch covers are replaced, though the stevedores may have left the ship: *Stuart v Nixon and Bruce* [1901] AC 79; *Hawkins v Thames Stevedore Co Ltd and Union Cold Storage Co Ltd* [1936] 2 All ER 472. This is so, although, without replacing the hatch covers, the stevedores have put fencing round the hatches: *Coggins and Griffith (Liverpool) Ltd v Peacock* (1933) 46 Ll LRep 113.

The same principle applies to 'unloading', i.e the process is not complete until the hatch covers are put back, and until that moment the regulations continue to apply: *Manchester Ship Canal Co v Director of Public Prosecutions* [1930] 1 KB 547.

Apart from this, 'unloading' of a cargo in bags is not complete on the removal of the bags from the hold if spillage still has to be cleared: *Mace v R. and H. Green and Silley Weir Ltd* [1959] 2 QB 14, [1959] 1 All ER 655.

Warehouses

Large portions of the Act are applied by s. 125(1) and (6) to certain warehouses.

The old cases on the meaning of the word 'warehouses' are now of little

---

4   Defined in Merchant Shipping Act 1894, s. 742, 31 Halsbury's Statutes, 3rd Edn., 407.

importance, since if they do not come within the Factories Act they come within other safety legislation, such as the Offices, Shops and Railway Premises Act 1963. In general, storerooms attached to retail shops do not qualify as warehouses: *Burr v W. Whiteley Ltd* (1902) 19 TLR 117; *Colvine v Anderson and Gibb* (1902) 5 F 225. On the other hand, a place which is a warehouse in the ordinary sense is not disqualified because it is occupied in conjunction with a shop: *Green v Britten and Gilson* [1904] 1 KB 350. Open air storage yards are not warehouses: *Buckingham v Fulham Corpn* (1905) 69 JP 297; *M'Ewan v Perth Magistrates* (1905) 7 F 714.

Section 125 applies to two classes of warehouses:

(i) those belonging to dock authorities;
(ii) those where mechanical power is used—unless they are within the Act as a whole, as being part of a factory.

To these warehouses s. 125(1) applies the sections relating to steam boilers—with the proviso that in this case the owner of the boiler is alone responsible—and the sections giving power to make regulations (now superseded by the Health and Safety at Work Act 1974).

In addition, s. 125(6) applies large portions of Part II of the Act, namely, everything relating to machinery (ss. 12–17 and 20–21), everything relating to lifting machines and lifting tackle (ss. 22–27), also s. 28 regarding floors, passages and stairs. However, under an amendment made by the Docks Regulations 1988 reg. 23, ss. 22–27 relating to lifting machines and tackle do not apply to warehouses on docks; the safety requirements under regs. 13–16 of the Docks Regulations apply to them instead.

A warehouse may, of course, be part of a factory, in which case every section of the Act applies. But if a warehouse does not belong to a dock authority, nor form part of a factory, and no mechanical power is used, it falls outside the Factories Act 1961. Wholesale warehouses are now subject to the Offices, Shops and Railway Premises Act 1963—ss. 1(3)(a)(ii), and 85(1) and (2)—if they are neither factories within the strict definition, nor dock warehouses brought in by s. 125(1): by s. 75(3) of the 1963 Act, the Factories Act is excluded for such wholesale warehouses even where mechanical power is used. It seems unlikely therefore that s. 125 can apply to a warehouse away from a dock.

In the case of warehouses subject to s. 125, as in the case of docks, liability falls on the 'notional' occupier who has the 'actual use and occupation'. It seems that the occupier in the strict sense of the word will always be liable: but in addition, liability may extend to a contractor who is carrying on work in the warehouse (*Weavings v Kirk and Randall* [1904] 1 KB 213) or to a third party carrying out loading or unloading operations on the premises (on the analogy of *Merrill v Wilson, Sons & Co Ltd* [1901] 1 KB 35). Where a transit shed belonged to and was partly used by the dock authority, but space was let to a shipping company as licensees, both were held liable as occupiers: *Fisher v Port of London Authority* [1962] 1 All ER 458.

5 The Docks Regulations 1988

The Docks Regulations 1988 (S.I. No. 1655) came into force (with minor exceptions) on 1 January 1989. They were made under the Health and Safety at Work Act 1974 and have a wider scope than the former regulations of 1934 made under the Factories Act. All the case-law under those regulations is obsolete. The new regulations enter into great detail, especially in the definitions (reg. 2) and can only be summarised in a general way, with particular attention to requirements likely to apply in injury cases. The regulations are accompanied by an approved Code of Practice, which is mainly an explanation of the regulations but goes into detail on practical application such as the standard of lighting.

The regulations apply to 'dock operations' in Great Britain and within the 12 miles territorial limit: reg. 3. These operations mean (a) loading and unloading of goods, (b) embarkation and disembarkation of both passengers and crew—which was not within the old regulations—and (c) incidental activities such as supplies to a ship, transport on the dockside and preliminary handling of goods and passengers: provided that these various activities are carried on at 'dock premises', which means any dock, wharf or other place where ships land or take on goods or passengers, together with adjacent land and those parts of the ship involved in the operation: reg. 2(1). But the definition excludes landing of fish, services to pleasure boats which do not carry fare-paying passengers—as in a yacht marina—also military beach landing operations (but not ordinary dock operations by the armed forces, for instance at a naval dockyard). Working from lighters in territorial waters is obviously included by reg. 3.

There is a general requirement to plan and execute operations safely: reg. 5. The duty to comply with the regulations is normally imposed on employers, on self-employed persons, and on those in control of premises where others work, to the extent of their control: reg. 4(1). Employees must comply with regulations which apply to their own behaviour: reg. 4(2). Employees (and self-employed) must also report faults in plant they are 'required to use': reg. 20. But the master and crew of a ship, and their employers, are excluded from the regulations so far as regards the ship's own plant, and activities on the ship which involve only the master and crew: reg.4(4).

These general rules as to duties do not apply to regs. 8(4), 11(5), 17, 19(2) to (5) and 20 which impose duties on specific persons: these are mainly about keeping records.

The duties are not owed to employed persons only, as they were under the Factories Act regulations of 1934: the Act of 1974, under which they are now made, is for the protection of all persons at work and it seems that they also extend to the protection of other persons such as passengers who may be endangered by working activities at the dock: see s. 1(1)(b) and (3) of the Act.

A Access and general safety on dockside and ships

(i) Access
Safe means of access must be provided and maintained to 'every part of dock premises which any person has to visit for the purpose of dock operations': reg. 7(1). 'Has to visit' does not necessarily mean that he has been ordered to go there: it is sufficient that his work takes him to the place: *Westwood v National Coal Board* [1967] 2 All ER 593, [1967] 1 WLR 871. The regulation goes on to forbid the *use* of various particular means of access—steps, stairs, floors, passages—unless of adequate strength, sound construction and properly maintained. In other words, if they are not in that condition, they must be put out of use.

Regulation 7(2) requires floors, steps and other means of access to be kept free of slippery substances and 'obstacles'—but this applies only so far as 'reasonably practicable'. (As to which see Chapter 6, section 8; Chapter 9, section 3(6)(vi)).

All this applies to access and other facilities on the ship, as well as on land.

(ii) Ladders
Portable ladders are forbidden as a means of access to ships, or to holds and container stacks on ships: also to stacks of three or more on land: reg. 7(3); there is an exception if 'no other safer means of access' is reasonably practicable. All ladders must be of 'good construction, sound material, adequate strength, free from patent defect and properly maintained': reg. 7(4) (for similar words see Chapter 10, section 3(4), 4(1) and (2)).

A ladder must not be used unless effective measures are taken to prevent it slipping or falling—e.g. by fastening both ends—and the top must extend at least 1 metre above the landing place unless there is other adequate handhold: reg. 7(5).

(iii) Fencing open places
Fencing is required at breaks, corners and other danger points on the dockside, also on open sides of gangways and bridges and any other place (except the dockside) where there is a drop of over 2 metres: reg. 7(6). There are exceptions where fencing is impracticable because of work actually going on.

(iv) Lighting
All parts of the premises used for dock operations must be adequately lit, with 'obstacles or hazards' highlighted by colouring or otherwise: reg. 6. A temporary interruption of lighting was, under the former regulation, an automatic breach of the requirement: *Wilkinson v Rea Ltd* [1941] 1 KB 688, [1941] 2 All ER 50; *Grant v Sun Shipping Co Ltd* [1948] AC 549, [1948] 2 All ER 238.

B Safety crossing water and on ships

Vessels used to transport dock workers must be safe, properly constructed and maintained, not overloaded or overcrowded, and under the charge of a competent person; they must also have a current safety certificate: reg. 8.

By reg. 10, hatch covers and beams are not to be used unless of sound construction and material, adequate strength, free from patent defect and properly maintained: they must be capable of removal and replacement without danger, and must be replaced in the correct position as shown by permanent marks. The hatch itself is not to be used unless the cover is completely off or securely replaced. Loads are not to be placed on hatch covers if this is likely to make them unsafe or endanger any person. Except in emergency, any power-operated hatch cover, car-deck ramp (including one on the dockside) is to be operated only by an operator specifically authorised.

C Lifting plant and lifting operations

'Lifting plant' includes both lifting 'appliances' and lifting 'gear'. Lifting *appliances* means such things as cranes and other apparatus for raising or lowering loads or moving them, and includes 'lift trucks' such as the common forklift, which have been held to be outside the definition in the Factories Act and existing regulations; but does not include such things as conveyors, pipes and moving walkways and escalators: reg. 2(1). Lifting *gear* means the device attaching the load to the lifting appliance but not forming part of it, with some exceptions such as 'one-way' slings which make one journey only and slings already on the load when it entered the dock.

Lifting plant (of both kinds) must not be used unless of 'good design and construction', 'adequate strength', 'sound material', 'free from patent defect', 'properly maintained' and 'properly installed': reg. 13(2). For case-law under the Factories Act see Chapter 10, sections 2 and 4 but this regulation is more extensive than the Act and revised to override some of the case-law.

The excepted types of sling, also pallets and attachments integrated with the load, must be of 'good construction', 'adequate strength' for the purpose for which they are actually used, and 'free from patent defect': reg. 13(2).

There is a general duty to operate lifting plant safely, and in particular not to exceed the safe working load which must be marked on or near it: regs. 13(3) and (4), 16. Periodic testing and examination are required: regs. 14 to 16 (reg. 14(2), on the testing of ships' appliances, is not in force until 1993).

Lifting appliances are to be operated only by competent persons who are specifically authorised, and records of names and training must be kept: reg. 11.

Hoists and lifts are not within these regulations, but under s. 125(7) of the Factories Act—as amended by reg. 23(c)—the sections in the Act on hoists and lifts are applied to all 'dock premises', and also (by s. 125(6) as amended) specifically to warehouses.

D Vehicles

These must be properly maintained, and driven only by authorised and competent persons: reg. 11 and 12.

There must be arrangements for road and rail safety throughout the docks, including safety of re-fuelling facilities, security of loads (e.g. on cranes and lorries) and safe handling of containers: reg. 11(2). With giant cranes operating and heavy traffic on the move, docks are much more dangerous than the highway but the Road Traffic Acts do not necessarily apply, so the dock authority is responsible for safe control of traffic.

E Miscellaneous

Miscellaneous requirements include safety measures in confined spaces where there may be fumes or lack of oxygen: reg. 18; welfare facilities, safety helmets, and high visibility clothing in some situations: reg. 19; equipment for rescue, fire-fighting and life-saving must be available round the docks: reg. 9.

There is power to grant exemptions from the regulations, normally on conditions setting out alternative safety arrangements.

6 Other regulations in docks

The Loading and Unloading of Fishing Vessels Regulations 1988 (S.I. No. 1656, in force 1 January 1989) are a parallel code to the Docks Regulations but much shorter.

They require a safe place of work and safe access to that and other places which any person has to visit for the purpose of loading or unloading processes or incidental activities such as mooring and supplying ships: reg. 5(1). But so far as safety depends on keeping surfaces free from slippery substances, this applies only so far as reasonably practicable: reg. 5(2). Danger spots have to be fenced as under the Docks Regulations: reg. 5(3). Lighting must be adequate: reg. 5(4). Rescue, life-saving and fire-fighting equipment must be provided: reg. 5(5). Safe plant and equipment must (so far as reasonably practicable) be provided and maintained: reg. 6(2). A further duty under reg. 6(1) to plan and execute operations safely adds nothing to an employer's common law duty.

The duty to comply with the regulations is imposed (reg. 4) on employers and the self-employed, on those who provide places of work and on skippers of fishing vessels, but in each case so far only as they have control. Exemptions may be granted: reg. 7.

The regulations extend to the 'handling' of wet fish at the dockside, including gutting, but not freezing or other processes: premises where these are carried on will be subject to the Factories Act.

The regulations do not apply to fishing vessels used only for sport or recreation, or to cargo and passenger vessels which carry fish only as an incidental activity: reg. 2.

The Dangerous Substances in Harbour Areas Regulations 1987 (S.I. No. 37, in force 1 June 1987) are for the protection of the public in general rather than dock workers as such. 'Dangerous substances' are defined very widely (reg. 3) to include anything which creates a risk to health or safety when in a harbour; they include automatically anything listed in the Merchant Shipping (Dangerous Goods) Regulations 1981: but do not include food, feeding stuffs, cosmetics, medicines or drugs. Tanks which have contained a dangerous substance are within the regulations until fumes and residues are cleared.

Vessels carrying such substances must give notice before entering the harbour and comply with the harbour master's directions. Warning flags and lights have to be displayed. The ship must be anchored or moored at a safe place and be ready to move at short notice (regs. 6–15).

In the handling of dangerous substances, employers and others in control must plan the operations safely (reg. 16), and ensure that workers have sufficient information and training, also safety equipment and protective clothing (reg. 17). Where there is a risk of fire or explosion, preparations must be made in advance to prevent or minimise this if necessary: reg. 18.

There is an elaborate code (regs. 19–22) for liquid substances in bulk, such as petrol or liquefied gas, including control of cleaning operations. Other regulations deal with the marking of containers or tanks holding dangerous substances (regs. 23–25), emergency plans (regs. 26–27), storage on the docks (regs. 29–32) and explosives (regs. 33–42).

Under the Dangerous Vessels Act 1985, a harbour master may prohibit the entry into harbour of a ship if the ship or its cargo is a source of imminent danger, and may likewise require such a ship to leave the harbour area.

Chapter 15
Building and engineering operations

1 Building and engineering operations

Certain provisions of the Factories Act 1961 were applied by s. 127 to 'building operations' and to 'works of engineering construction', provided that they were undertaken (i) 'by way of trade or business' or (ii) 'for the purpose of any industrial or commercial undertaking' or (iii)—see s. 175(9)—'by or on behalf of the Crown or any [municipal or other public] authority'.

While a large number of sections of the Act were applied to these operations, the only ones which concern the safety of the workmen, and on which an action of breach of statutory duty can be founded, were as follows:

    (a) ss. 32 to 38 (steam boilers and air receivers),

    (b) s. 76 (power to make special regulations) and ss. 50 and 51 (fire regulations).

The main result of s. 127, therefore, was that the Minister had power to make detailed regulations for the safety of workmen in building and engineering operations: it is the regulations which are really important. The power to make regulations is now superseded by the wider powers in the Health and Safety at Work Act 1974.

For the purpose of enforcing the Act and regulations, 'any place where such operations or works are carried on' is treated 'as if' it were a factory (the term *notional* factory is often used); and 'any person undertaking any such operations or works' is treated as the occupier of the factory (s. 127(4)).

By the Factories Act (Docks, Building and Engineering Construction etc.) Modification Regulations 1938 (S.R. & O. 1938 No. 610), the requirements of the Act of 1937 (now replaced by the Act of 1961) as to steam boilers and air receivers were slightly modified in their application to building and engineering operations. A steam boiler need not be examined before it is first taken into use on a site, as usually required by s. 29(9), but it must have been examined within the preceding fourteen months. An air receiver must have been examined within the preceding twenty-six months, with certain exceptions.

The Building (Safety, Health and Welfare) Regulations 1948 (S.I. No. 1145), made under the Act of 1937, replaced regulations of 1926. They were in turn largely replaced by the Construction (General Provisions) Regulations 1961 (S.I. No. 1580) and the Construction (Lifting Operations) Regulations 1961 (S.I. No. 1581) which apply not only to building but also to engineering construction. The last remaining section of the Building Regulations which dealt with scaffolding, and some other miscellaneous provisions, was replaced by the Construction (Working Places) Regulations 1966 (S.I. No. 94), also applying to both types of operation. In addition there are the Work in Compressed Air Special Regulations 1958 (S.I. No. 61), as amended in 1960 (S.I. No. 1307)[1]. In general the regulations create absolute and continuing duties: *Potts (or Riddell) v Reid* [1943] AC 1, [1942] 2 All ER 161.

There is one important difference between the Act of 1961 (replacing in this respect the Act of 1937) and its predecessors. It is now unnecessary that mechanical power should be used on the site. Before the 1937 Act, unless mechanical power was used, a site could not qualify as a 'notional' factory, nor could the regulations apply to it: see, for instance, *Kearns v Gee, Walker and Slater Ltd* [1937] 1 KB 187, [1936] 3 All ER 151 where the question arose whether electricity counted as mechanical power.

The 'notional' factories created by s. 127 are definite sites, with

---

1 The Woodworking Machines Regulations 1974 (S.I. No. 903) and Protection of Eyes Regulations 1974 (S.I. No. 1681) also apply to building and engineering sites; so do the Electricity at Work Regulations 1989 (Chapter 16). There are also the Construction (Health and Welfare) Regulations 1966 (S.I. No. 95), amended slightly by S.I. 1974 No. 209, as to first aid, canteens, etc. Many special regulations, e.g. for abrasive wheels, asbestos, ionising radiation, also apply to every place subject to the Factories Act. The Diving Operations Special Regulations 1960 (S.I. No. 688) made under the Factories Act have been replaced by a uniform code which applies to all places of work: see Chapter 19, section 2.

ascertainable boundaries. Inside those boundaries the Act applies, but outside them it does not. Thus Lord Robertson said in *Back v Dick Kerr & Co., Ltd,* [1906] AC 325:

> 'I hold that when the statute[2] uses the words "on or in or about" an "engineering work", the "work" spoken of is something having geographical boundaries.'

Those boundaries, however, are naturally more difficult to ascertain then they are for an ordinary factory: and a building or engineering operation may comprise several different sites, all of which become 'notional' factories under the sections.

As regards building operations, it seems that when a number of buildings are being constructed on a large site, the whole of the site is a single 'notional' factory: so that under pre-1937 law, the use of mechanical power on any part of the site brought in the code of building regulations: *Potts (or Riddell) v Reid* [1943] AC 1, [1942] 2 All ER 161. But once a building is fully constructed—though not sold or occupied—it ceases to be part of the site: *Pease v W. J. Simms Sons and Cooke Ltd* [1932] 1 KB 723.

By s. 127(1), a building or engineering site includes 'any line or siding which is used in connection therewith and for the purposes thereof', provided that it is not part of a railway or tramway. This brings in the special regulations on factory sidings (S.R. & O. 1906 No. 679)[3]. Workshops ancillary to building or engineering operations are factories *per se*, under s. 175(2)(m) of the Act.

Both building and engineering operations are defined in s. 176(1).

'Building operation' means 'the construction, structural alteration, repair or maintenance of a building (including re-pointing, re-decoration and external cleaning of the structure), the demolition of a building, and the preparation for, and laying the foundation of, an intended building, but does not include any operation which is a work of engineering construction within the meaning' of the Act[4].

A 'work of engineering construction' means 'the construction of any

2   The statute referred to was the Workmen's Compensation Act 1897 which used some of the definitions in the Factories Acts to define employments in which compensation was payable.
3   Chapter 20, *post*.
4   This definition is further explained in connection with the regulations later in this chapter.

railway line or siding otherwise than upon an existing railway, and the construction, structural alteration or repair (including re-pointing and re-painting) or the demolition of any dock, harbour, inland navigation, tunnel, bridge, viaduct, waterworks, reservoir, pipe-line, aqueduct, sewer, sewage works, or gasholder, except where carried on upon a railway or tramway': it also includes such other works as may be specified by regulations. The list has been extended to include 'the construction, structural alteration or repair (including re-pointing and re-painting) or the demolition of *any* steel or reinforced concrete structure[5] other than a building, any road, airfield, sea defence works or river works, and any other civil or constructional engineering works of a similar nature to any of the foregoing works': see the Engineering Construction (Extension of Definition) Regulations 1960 (S.I. No. 421). This extended list, however, specifically excepts works carried on in a factory as defined by s. 151 of the 1937 Act (i.e. a factory proper), or in electrical stations within s. 103(1) of that Act (now s. 123 of the Act of 1961) or on a railway or tramway. 'Pipe-line' originally meant water-pipe and did not include a gas main: *Griffith v Scottish Gas Board* 1963 SLT 286; by the Engineering Construction (Extension of Definition) (No. 2) Regulations 1968 (S.I. No. 1530) the definition now covers work on a pipe-line for the conveyance of things other than water, except work carried on upon a railway or tramway. A ship is not a 'structure' within the extended definition: *Shepherd v Pearson Engineering Services (Dundee)* 1980 SC 269, 1981 SLT 197.

Before the Factories Act 1948 it was held that when building operations are carried out in a factory, the entire Act applies for the benefit of the building workers, and accordingly the occupiers are liable for failure to provide safe means of access: *Whitby v Burt, Boulton and Hayward Ltd* [1947] KB 918, [1947] 2 All ER 324; see also *Lavender v Diamints Ltd* [1949] 1 KB 585, [1949] 1 All ER 532.

S. 14(4) of the Act of 1948 (now replaced by s. 127(8) of the 1961 Act) dealt expressly with the position where premises are subject to the Act both because they are the site of a building or engineering operation, and also independently of this. Section 127 (8) has the following effect—

5 'Steel structure' may include a crane: *British Transport Docks Board v Williams* [1970] 1 All ER 1135 (crane mounted on platform and whole structure moved on rails: supporting structure and platform held within definition, question of crane itself left open).

   (i) building and engineering works are brought within the Act by
      s. 127—and therefore any special regulations apply—
      notwithstanding that the Act already applies for some other
      reason to the premises affected;

  (ii) nevertheless, the Act continues to apply to the premises
      independently in their capacity as a factory proper, or a dock,
      or whatever it may be.

In *Whincup v Woodhead & Sons (Engineers) Ltd* [1951] 1 All ER 387,
McNair J followed *Whitby v Burt, Boulton and Hayward Ltd* and held
that the decision was not affected by the Act of 1948. Thus in many
cases the workman has a dual remedy: first against the actual occupier of
the factory for breach of the Act, and secondly against the 'notional'
occupier of the building or construction site under the Construction
Regulations. The point to be stressed is that premises may be subject to
the Act in two capacities, which are not mutually exclusive. In such a
case the premises need not be a factory proper. For example a dock may
be the site of an engineering work. In that case the Act applies to the
premises:

  (a) as a dock, to the extent set out in s. 125; and

  (b) as an engineering work, under s. 127.

Furthermore, both the Docks Regulations and the Construction
Regulations will apply.

    Where, however, a part of a factory is handed over to contractors and
is not in use for factory purposes, the part handed over will be excluded
from the factory by s. 175(6) of the Act[6].

2 The Construction (Working Places) Regulations 1966

The Building Regulations 1948 were largely replaced by the two new
Construction Codes issued in 1961, one General, the other for Lifting
Operations, which are summarised in the next section. The
Construction (Working Places) Regulations 1966 replaced the rest of
the 1948 regulations, and are concerned mainly with scaffolds, safe

6 See Chapter 9.

means of access, and roof work. They also replaced part of the General Regulations of 1961 (regs. 7 and 54 as to safe access and safety belts). The Chief Inspector has power to grant exemption certificates (reg. 5), usually subject to conditions[7].

The 1966 regulations apply (by reg. 2, which follows the words of s. 127 of the Act) to both building operations and works of engineering construction, including associated lines or sidings (not being part of a railway or tramway). Thus the case-law on the scope of the 1948 regulations, which were limited to building operations, is of diminishing importance, but some of it is still relevant to show the extent of both types of operation as defined in the Act, and is therefore summarised for convenience.

Building   The meaning of the word 'building' varies according to the context. It may for some purposes include an artificial erection such as a railway viaduct, but 'an ordinary building is an enclosure of brick or stonework covered in by a roof': *Moir v Williams* [1892] 1 QB 264. In statutes for the protection of workmen it has been given a wide meaning and may include a temporary wooden structure for the support of a crane: *Aylward v Matthews* [1905] 1 KB 343; and disused gas retorts enclosed in brick arches: *Knight v Demolition and Construction Co Ltd* [1953] 2 All ER 508; affirmed [1954] 1 All ER 711 n, but not a concrete foundation supporting a crane: *M'Callum v Butters Brothers & Co Ltd* 1954 SLT (Notes) 45.

A building does not cease to be a building because—like a power station, for example—it is not intended to be anything more than an outer shell containing plant and machinery: *Elms v Foster Wheeler Ltd* [1954] 2 All ER 714. Thus a nuclear reactor may be a building: *Byers v Head Wrightson & Co Ltd* [1961] 2 All ER 538; and an oil-tank: *Boyle v Kodak Ltd* [1969] 2 All ER 439.

The extended definition of engineering works now includes work on 'any steel or reinforced concrete structure': p. 430, *ante*.

---

7   For example, by a certificate of the Chief Inspector dated 7 April 1976 steeplejacks were exempted from regs. 13(5), 25(3), 26(1) and 28 of the Construction (Working Places) Regulations subject to conforming to strict alternative requirements: for details of this and other exemptions, see *Redgrave's Health and Safety in Factories*.

The scope of building and engineering operations

The definition of building operation includes preparation of the site, construction, repair, alteration and demolition. It is evidently intended to cover every phase in the life of a building, as Lord Macnaghten said of a much less comprehensive definition in an earlier Act: *Hoddinott v Newton, Chambers & Co* [1901] AC 49. 'Repair' would, of its own force, include painting and whitewashing: *Dredge v Conway, Jones & Co* [1901] 2 KB 42; but the definition expressly declares that it includes 're-decoration' of all kinds. It is a reasonable inference that 'construction' includes the original decoration. 'External cleaning of the structure' does not include window-cleaning: *Lavender v Diamints Ltd* [1949] 1 KB 585, [1949] 1 All ER 532; but it does include cleaning a glass roof which forms a large part of the roof area: *Bowie v Great International Plate Glass Insurance Cleaning Co* (1981) Times, 14 May, CA. Internal cleaning of soot and oil after a fire is not a 'building operation': *Tucker v Hampshire County Council* [1986] CLY unreported appeal No. 18 (it was argued that this qualified as 'maintenance' work). Making the 'profile' of a gutter (i.e. a wire pattern) is not part of the work of 'repair', but only preparatory work not covered by the regulations: *Sumner v Robert L. Priestley Ltd* [1955] 3 All ER 445. But where joiners came to repair a leak in a roof, repair had started when they were trying to find the leak: *O'Donnell v Cochran & Co (Annam) Ltd* 1968 SLT (Notes) 76; and painters doing preliminary dusting of the roof trusses had started on 're-decoration': *O'Brien v U.D.E.C. Ltd* (1968) 5 KIR 449. In *Vineer v C. Doidge & Sons Ltd* [1972] 2 All ER 794 the measuring of windows by a glazier in houses under construction was held to be part of the work of 'construction'. *Sumner v Priestley* was distinguished as turning on special facts[8]. In *Drysdale v Kelsey Roofing Industries* 1981 SLT (Notes) 118 an employee doing a preliminary survey of a roof for the purpose of repairs was held to be engaged in a building operation.

It has been contended that the installation of plant in a building under construction is not part of a building operation. Of course, if machinery is merely *put into* a building, even if it is a large machine which has to be erected and attached in some way to the structure, there is no building

---

8 It is difficult to see the difference between measuring windows and measuring a gutter, or why preliminary measurement should be part of 'construction' but not of 'repair'. It would seem that the court thought the earlier decision was unsatisfactory.

operation: *Hutchinson v Cocksedge & Co Ltd* [1952] 1 All ER 696 n. On the other hand, plant and machinery is in many cases so closely connected with the structure of the building that the work of installing the plant is at one and the same time part of the work of constructing the building, as in *Elms v Foster Wheeler Ltd* [1954] 2 All ER 714 (steam generating plant in a power station), *Baxter v Central Electricity Generating Board* [1964] 2 All ER 815 (pulverising machine at power station) and *Hughes v McGoff and Vickers Ltd* [1955] 2 All ER 291 (electric lighting system in large building). The preliminary examination of a shaft where a lift has to be installed is part of the work of construction of the building: *Simmons v Bovis Ltd* [1956] 1 All ER 736. No clear principle has yet emerged for distinguishing the two types of case, and each case must be decided upon its own facts. Similarly the question whether an installation on the outside of a building is part of it or not is a question of fact: neon lighting signs outside a cinema are not part of the building: *Price v Claudgen Ltd* [1967] 1 All ER 695. The installation of a new lighting system by fluorescent tubes at a dock shed has, however, been held to be within the definition of building or construction: *Morter v Electrical Installations Ltd* (1969) 6 KIR 130.

The erection of scaffolding was an operation within the 1948 regulations, either as a necessary incident of the building operations specified, or because it related to plant used in the operations: but it did not follow that all the regulations applied, e.g. reg. 24 as to guard rails, because it might appear from the context that the regulation applied only to scaffolds 'in use', as distinct from those being erected or dismantled: *Sexton v Scaffolding (Great Britain) Ltd* [1953] 1 QB 153, [1952] 2 All ER 1085. Under the Construction (Working Places) Regulations, the erection of scaffolding has simply been treated as part of the building or engineering operation in which it is used: *Smith v Vange Scaffolding and Engineering Co Ltd* [1970] 1 All ER 249; *Singh v Vange Scaffolding and Engineering Co Ltd* (1969) 7 KIR 101[9].

Preparation for an intended building includes the removal of heavy tanks from a factory site by means of an excavator: *Beech v Costain & John*

---

9   In *Ritchie v James H. Russell & Co Ltd* 1966 SLT 244 it was held that the erection of a scaffold to repair a building did not come within the definition of 'building operation' so that reg. 7 (safe access) of the Construction (General Provisions) Regulations did not apply. Yet the court accepted that the scaffolding part of the 1948 regulations (which was then still in force) would apply, and so presumably would the Construction (Working Places) Regulations which have replaced them.

Brown Ltd (Lord Blades, Ct of Sess 30 June 1950, noted in 100 L Jo 455); also laying effluent pipes on the intended site of a sewage pumping station: *Horsley v Collier and Catley Ltd* [1965] 2 All ER 423.

Some of these cases (e.g. as to installing plant) may apply to 'engineering construction' but the definition of this makes no *express* reference to preparing the site or foundations.

Persons on whom duties are imposed

Regulation 3 allocates responsibility among various persons (being 'contractors or employees of workmen') for complying with the regulations. Four cases must be distinguished.

In particular the first two cases—employers under 3(1)(a), contractors under 3(1)(b)—must be kept clearly apart. Under head (a), 'employers' are responsible for one block of regulations to their own employees only; under head (b) 'contractors' are responsible to *all* persons employed on the site for another block of regulations but only so far as their own operations are concerned. An unfortunate confusion arose because the wording of head (a) required an employer to observe such regulations '*as affect him* or any workman employed by him' and the words italicised were at one time held to make an employer responsible to all persons for his own operations even under (a). The Court of Appeal has decided that this is wrong: the words mean only that an employer working personally must comply with regulations affecting his own safety: *Smith v George Wimpey & Co Ltd* [1972] 2 QB 329, [1972] 2 All ER 723[10].

Employers

They are responsible under reg. 3(1)(a) to their own men—provided that the men are present in the course of their employment or with the employer's permission—for any breach of most of regs. 6–36 and 38 (means of access and scaffolds), but in the case of regs. 24, 26–29 and 33–35 so far only as they relate to persons falling or slipping. So long as a man is genuinely going to a place in the course of his work, although he gets into the wrong place in a way which the employer did not foresee,

---

10 Disapproving *Upton v Hipgrave Bros* [1965] 1 All ER 6; *Baron v B. French Ltd* [1971] 3 All ER 1111.

the proviso does not take him outside the protection of the regulations: *Moir-Young v Dorman Long Bridge and Engineering Ltd* (1969) 7 KIR 86. A person who is not an employee cannot sue under this head: *Claydon v Lindsay Parkinson Ltd* [1939] 2 KB 385, [1939] 2 All ER 1, *Wingrove v Prestige & Co Ltd* [1954] 1 All ER 576.

Contractors undertaking operations
Under reg. 3(1)(b), contractors who undertake the actual performance of any work, act or operation are responsible to all persons for breach of certain regulations connected with the safety of their operations; but they are *not* responsible for breaches by sub-contractors except where they themselves are actually controlling operations, as where several 'labour only' gangs are supervised: *Donaghey v Boulton and Paul Ltd* [1968] AC 1, [1967] 2 All ER 1014[11]. An owner of property who, instead of engaging a main contractor, employs various specialists, does not thereby become a 'contractor undertaking operations': *Kealey v Heard* [1983] 1 All ER 973, [1983] 1 WLR 573. The regulations under this heading are 37 (shock to or overloading of scaffolds) and (as to falling materials or articles, but not the fall of persons) 24, 26–29 and 33–35 (scaffolds and roof work) so far as their requirements 'relate to any work, act or operation performed or about to be performed' by the contractor in question.

Erectors of scaffolding
This includes, in addition to ordinary builders and contractors who erect their own scaffolding, contractors who specialise in the erection of scaffolding and nothing else: *Sexton v Scaffolding (Great Britain) Ltd, supra*. It is a separate and additional duty and does not exonerate scaffolding contractors from their duties under the other heads, e.g. to their employees: *Smith v Vange Scaffolding and Engineering Co Ltd* [1970] 1 All ER 249. The duty of every person who erects or alters any scaffold is to comply with the regulations as to erection or alteration 'having regard to the purpose or purposes for which the scaffold is designed at the time of erection or alteration'. Thus if a scaffold erected by one contractor is also intended to be used by others, such use must be taken into account: *Pratt v Richards* [1951] 2 KB 208, [1951] 1 All ER 90 n.;

11 Overruling in this respect *Mulready v J. H. & W. Bell Ltd* [1953] 2 QB 117, [1953] 2 All ER 215.

and when a scaffold is altered, regard must be had to all the purposes it is at that time designed to serve, not merely the purpose for which it is altered: *Martin v Claude Hamilton (Aberdeen) Ltd* 1952 SLT (Notes) 14. Sub-contractors who erected temporary planking to examine a lift shaft were held liable under this heading to a foreman of the main contractors who accompanied them on their inspection: *Simmons v Bovis Ltd* [1956] 1 All ER 736.

Users of plant and equipment

Every contractor or employer who 'erects, installs, works or uses any other plant or equipment to which any of the regulations apply, must comply with them'. A contractor who hires a machine with a driver is 'using' it within the meaning of reg. 3: *Gallagher v Wimpey & Co Ltd* 1951 SC 515; but the plant hire company itself is a contractor 'undertaking operations' so far as the machine is involved, and is apparently also 'using' the plant through its driver: *Williams v West Wales Plant Hire Co Ltd* [1984] 3 All ER 397, [1984] 1 WLR 1311. More dubiously owners who hired out a crane *without* driver were held to be 'users' because they alone had power to adjust it and were 'using' it to earn money: *Teague v Wm Baxter & Son* 1982 SLT (Sh Ct) 28.

Machinery is worked or used if it is activated for any purpose, whether or not an industrial or commercial purpose, for instance cleaning or maintenance: *Smith v W. & J. R. Watson Ltd* 1977 JC 52; *Johns v Martin Simms (Cheltenham) Ltd* [1983] 1 All ER 127, [1983] ICR 305.

Finally, reg. 3(2) requires *persons employed* to comply with the regulations so far as their own acts are concerned, to co-operate in all other cases, and to report defects: a breach of this duty ranks as contributory negligence. The case-law on the extent of duties expressed in this way is summarised in Chapter 23, section 5.

The fact that several classes of persons have duties under the regulations, which sometimes overlap, may mean that an injured person has a remedy against more than one person: e.g. against his own employer as well as against a scaffolding contractor.

On the other hand, no duty is owed under the regulations to anybody who is not an employed person: *Hartley v Mayoh & Co* [1954] 1 QB 383, [1954] 1 All ER 375. A self-employed man, who hired himself out as an independent contractor to do skilled roofing work, was therefore unable to sue for a breach of the old reg. 31 (safety on sloping roof), though this was one of the regulations which the person undertaking the work as main contractor must comply with for the benefit of sub-contractors' workmen: a self-employed man is not 'a person employed': *Herbert v Harold Shaw Ltd* [1959] 2 QB 138, [1959] 2 All ER 189; *Poliskie v Lane* 1981 SLT 28. A working director may however be 'a person employed': *Aitken v John R. Bryson Ltd* 1966 SLT 234 (joiner)[12].

Part III. Working places, access and egress

Part III, which contains the bulk of the regulations (regs. 6–38), deals with working places and access, and chiefly with scaffolds. A reference is added ('B.R.' or 'C.G.R.') after each regulation to the part of the Building Regulations or in some cases the Construction (General) Regulations 1961, which it replaces. Some of the case-law quoted may be effected by changes in wording.

Working places and access

Regulations 6(1), access, 6(2), place of work, and 7, scaffolds to be provided where necessary, take the place of C.G.R. 7. They are requirements of a general nature and are expressly *without prejudice* to other requirements of the regulations (which go into more detail).

Regulation 6 directs that, so far as reasonably practicable, there shall be:

> 'suitable and sufficient safe access to and egress from every place at which any person at any time works, which access and egress shall be properly maintained',

and further that every such place shall itself:

> 'be made and kept safe for any person working there.'

This is worded so as to eliminate most of the doubts which have arisen under s. 29 of the Factories Act. The place need not be one where a person 'has to' work[13] and, provided it is a place where work is done,

---

12 For the distinction between employed persons and self-employed see pp. 88–89, *ante*; and *Maurice Graham Ltd v Brunswick* (1974) 16 KIR 158 where the tests used in cases under the National Insurance Acts were assumed to apply.

13 So the strict interpretation of this to mean 'must' in *Kendrick v Cozens and Sutcliffe Ltd* (1968) 4 KIR 469 is obsolete; it was probably inconsistent with *Smith (or Westwood) v National Coal Board* [1967] 2 All ER 593 where the House of Lords gave a broad interpretation to the word 'required' and said it was enough that a man's work reasonably took him to the place.

there seems no reason to restrict it to any type of place[14]. It included a public street adjacent to a demolition site, rendered unsafe by an unstable chimney: *Glasgow v City of Glasgow District Council* 1983 SLT 65.

The wording of the regulations avoids the ambiguity of s. 29 of the Factories Act by saying that it is the *access* which has to be safe, not just the *means* of access. Also it is a distinct and separate requirement that the 'place at which any person at any time works . . . shall be made and kept safe'. However this too has its limits: a man moving along the top of a wall with a pneumatic drill was held not to be 'working' there: *Brady v Dundee District Council* 1980 SLT (Notes) 60. In a Scottish case, a man was installing a duct in a roof, working from a trestle; he stepped down, walked away a few paces, and stepped on sheets of cardboard, placed there to protect the floor, which slid under him. The Inner House took a somewhat narrow view and held that he was neither at his place of work nor using access to it; they also held that the place was 'safe' as it was not reasonably foreseeable that the cardboard could be a source of danger: *Morrow v Enterprise Sheet Metal Works (Aberdeen) Ltd* 1986 SLT 697.

There is a similar requirement in reg. 16 of the Construction (Health and Welfare Regulations 1966 (S.I. No. 95) as to the safety of wash-places, lavatories, first-aid rooms, canteens etc and the access to them.

The access may be safe for a building operative where it would not be safe for the general public: *Sheppey v Matthew T. Shaw & Co Ltd* [1952] 1 TLR 1272; thus, an obvious hole in a floor which can easily be avoided does not make the access unsafe: *Martin v Holland and Hannen & Cubitts (Scotland) Ltd* 1967 SLT (Notes) 117; but it is no defence to say that, although the access is unsafe, steel erectors are used to unsafe places: thus a high girder, 10 feet long, 3 inches wide and without a handhold is unsafe even for a steel erector, because a man, however skilled, may slip: *Trott v W. E. Smith (Erectors) Ltd* [1957] 3 All ER 500. In *Gibson v B.I.C.C.* 1973 SLT 2 a man standing on a narrow beam at the top of an electricity pylon which he had just helped to erect had to use both hands to dismantle a derrick fixed at the top: the House of

14 Even the top of a lorry may be a place: *H.M. Inspector of Factories v Cementation Co Ltd* 1968 SLT (Sh Ct) 75, following *Nimmo v Alexander Cowan and Sons Ltd* [1968] AC 107, [1967] 3 All ER 187 (rail wagon); *Ritchie v James H. Russell & Co Ltd* 1966 SLT 244 can hardly be right in excluding work on an unfinished scaffold. Under reg. 28, the position is different, as 'working place' is bracketed with 'working platform' and means something analogous.

Lords held there was a breach of the regulation; the place was unsafe and the defenders had failed to establish that it was not reasonably practicable to make it safe.

It has been said that the lack of safety must arise from the place of work and not from temporary activities carried on there: *Evans v Sant* [1975] QB 626 ('test head' laid in a trench to test water pressure blew off pipe-line)[15]. But in Scotland fumes have been held sufficient to make the place of work unsafe: *Canning v Kings & Co* 1986 SLT 107.

Holes in a road or cables over which people may trip may be sufficient to render access unsafe: it is a matter of degree—*Singh v Vange Scaffolding and Engineering Co Ltd* (1969) 7 KIR 101; *Smith v Vange Scaffolding and Engineering Co Ltd* [1970] 1 All ER 249. A platform was unsafe as a place for work which involved swinging pig-iron when the footing was rendered treacherous by furnace ashes: *Busby v Robert Watson & Co (Constructional Engineers) Ltd* (1972) 13 KIR 498.

Weather conditions such as heavy rain making part of a roof slippery may be taken into account as making access unsafe: *Byrne v E. H. Smith (Roofing) Ltd* [1973] 1 All ER 490. The words of the regulation are 'at any time'.

The duty to provide safe access and place of work under reg. 6 rests on a man's own employer: *Wingrove v Prestige & Co Ltd* (1954) 1 All ER 576; *Smith v A. Davies & Co (Shopfitters) Ltd* (1968) 5 KIR 320; and this is so (as these two cases show) although the danger arises from, for example, an unsafe scaffold erected by another person. A scaffolding contractor may be responsible for breaches of other regulations—but not in any case for dangers unconnected with its use as scaffolding: *Wingrove v Prestige, supra* (clerk of works injured by striking pole when passing through opening). 'Access' is not, of course, restricted to scaffolds: *Brown v Troy & Co Ltd* [1954] 3 All ER 19. Under s. 29 of the Factories Act 1961 it has been given a wide meaning: Chapter 10, section 3(i): and this regulation has been applied to a narrow gutter along a roof where a workman followed the lead of a chargehand, although it was an

---

15 If this means that lack of safety must arise from the structure and not from other environmental factors, it is flatly inconsistent with a compelling line of authorities in Scotland and several decisions in the House of Lords: see pp. 292–296, *ante*. Those decisions were not quoted to the Divisional Court, which had before it only some unsatisfactory and (one hopes) outmoded dicta in the English Court of Appeal. A better line of distinction would be to say that a regulation requiring a safe place of work is not infringed by the choice of a wrong method of work for the particular task on which a person is engaged.

unusual means of access: *Byrne v E. H. Smith Ltd* [1973] 1 All ER 490.
It was held in Scotland that C.G.R. reg. 7 did not apply to scaffolders
putting up the structure: *Ritchie v James H. Russell & Co Ltd* 1966 SLT
244. It is difficult to see why scaffolders should not be given safe access
and place of work so far as is reasonably practicable. *Barclay v J. & W.
Henderson* 1980 SLT (Notes) 71 (scaffolding being dismantled) has
taken the same lines as the English cases, that the regulations apply to
scaffolders as far as they are capable of doing so.

Regulation 17 of the Construction (Lifting Operations) Regulations
1961 specifically requires safe means of access for any person engaged
in maintenance work on a lifting appliance. The contractor responsible
for the appliance itself must comply with this regulation.

By reg. 7 (formerly C.G.R. 7(2)):

> 'Where work cannot safely be done on or from ground or from part of
> a building or other permanent structure, there shall be provided,
> placed and kept in position for use and properly maintained, either
> scaffolds or where appropriate ladders or other means of support, all
> of which shall be suitable and sufficient for the purpose.'

Work 'cannot safely be done' kneeling on the edge of a roof
overlooking a fragile roof, and a scaffold of some kind should be
provided: *Harris v Bright's Asphalt Contractors Ltd* [1953] 1 QB 617,
[1953] 1 All ER 395[16]. The test of 'safety' is whether danger can
reasonably be foreseen: *Curran v Wm. Neil & Son (St Helens) Ltd* [1961]
3 All ER 108, or whether the work is shown by experience to be safe
without a scaffold: *Connolly v McGee* [1961] 2 All ER 111. At any rate,
where a man can in the ordinary way carry out the work from a particular

---

16 The decision of a divided House of Lords in *O'Donnell v Murdoch McKenzie & Co
Ltd* 1967 SC 63, 3 KIR 299 (HL) turned essentially on fact. Two men had to work
on a deep sill in a foundry wall—with drops both inside and outside—where a hole
had to be made in concrete with a jack-hammer. They obtained access by
makeshift trestle and planks. The hammer got stuck, and the pursuer overbalanced
on the inside pulling it out. *Held*—(i) the work could not be safely done from the
sill alone, (2) the makeshift scaffold was not 'suitable and sufficient', (3) although
the man fell inside, a proper platform outside would have given more room for
manoeuvre, though work had to be done on the sill; so the breach of reg. 7 (of
1961) was causally connected with the accident.

The suggestion of Winn LJ in *Woods v Power Gas Corpn, infra,* that 'safe' refers
only to the soundness of the *structure* against collapse, is not compatible with the
reasoning of the House in this case as they were plainly considering whether the
work could be safely performed without a scaffold. The key word, surely, is *cannot.*
Work *can* be done safely even if there is appreciable danger.

position, the fact that something unexpected may dislodge him does not make it 'unsafe': *Woods v Power Gas Corpn Ltd* (1970) 8 KIR 834 (man astride a girder overbalanced tightening nut). There was no breach of reg. 7 (then B.R. 5) when a ladder was sufficient and a man was stationed at the foot and could have held it: *Neeson v William Denny and Bros Ltd* 1963 SC 152. *Aliter* where a step-ladder was insecure by itself and the man holding it moved away: *Harkness v Oxy-Acetylene Welding Co Ltd* 1963 SC 642. A ladder is 'appropriate' if work can safely and conveniently be done from it, and not inappropriate just because a spanner may come off and cause loss of balance: *Wilkinson v Morrison Steel Erectors Ltd* 1969 SLT (Notes) 69.

When the regulation requires a scaffold to *work* from, it is not sufficient compliance to provide a scaffold giving *access*, e.g. to a fragile roof: *Connolly v McGee* [1961] 2 All ER 111, [1961] 1 WLR 811.

Scaffolds

Responsibility for complying with the scaffolding regulations rests both on the employers (whether they have erected the scaffolding or not) and on the contractors (whether the plaintiff's employers or not) who have erected or altered the scaffolding: reg. 3. But head contractors were not liable to a sub-contractor's man when they had the staging erected by a competent firm of scaffolders and it was afterwards altered by the sub-contractors, for the head contractors neither erected nor altered it: *Kearney v Eric Waller Ltd* [1967] 1 QB 29, [1965] 3 All ER 352; in addition, every contractor who takes over a scaffold which he has not erected is required—without prejudice to his other duties—to check the stability of the scaffold and the soundness of the material before using it: see reg. 23 (B.R. 21). Sub-contractors who sent a glazier to use a scaffold, but neither examined it nor made inquiries about its safety, were held liable under B.R. 21: *Clarke v E. R. Wright & Sons* [1957] 3 All ER 486; in a similar case where sub-contractors for glazing had sent a man to a building site to measure for windows, the fact that he was a competent and experienced man was not sufficient compliance with reg. 23 in the absence of instructions to him to inspect the scaffold first: *Vineer v C. Doidge & Sons Ltd* [1972] 2 All ER 794[17].

---

17 The sub-contractors were held liable to indemnify the main contractors for 20 per cent of the damages only, the latter having the primary responsibility for the scaffold.

Scaffold is defined by reg. 4 to mean:

> 'any temporarily provided structure on or from which persons perform work in connection with [a building or engineering operation], and any temporarily provided structure which enables persons to obtain access to or which enables materials to be taken to any place at which such work is performed.'

The definition entails that it is used by persons—or perhaps in some cases for moving materials unattended—and does not include a temporary scaffold to hold permanent guard rails in position on the edge of a jetty until the cement sets: *Singh v Vange Scaffolding and Engineering Co Ltd* (1969) 7 KIR 101.

The term includes:

> 'any working platform, gangway, run, ladder or step-ladder (other than an independent ladder or step-ladder which does not form part of such a structure) together with any guard rail, toe-board or other safeguards and all fixings'—

but does not include

> 'a lifting appliance or a structure used merely to support such an appliance or to support other plant or equipment.'

This is an exceedingly wide definition, and may include, for example, loose planks laid over a fragile roof: *Harris v Bright's Asphalt Contractors Ltd* [1953] 1 QB 617, [1953] 1 All ER 395; temporary planking to inspect a lift shaft: *Simmons v Bovis Ltd* [1956] 1 All ER 736; a single plank laid from ground to concrete step as gangway or for access to a scaffold: *Conlan v Glasgow Corpn* 1964 SLT 134; *Taylor v Sayers* [1971] 1 All ER 934; temporary planking to bridge a trench: *Byers v Head Wrightson & Co Ltd* [1961] 2 All ER 538. Further it seems that the *extension* of the definition—'working platform, gangway', etc.—may include something which is (or is intended to be) a permanent part of the structure; but a gutter under construction is not a 'gangway' or 'platform' merely because workmen pass over or stand on it: *Curran v William Neill & Son (St. Helens) Ltd* [1961] 3 All ER 108; nor is a passage in a half-constructed building, at any rate if access is across it and not along it: *Jennings v Norman Collison (Contractors) Ltd* [1970] 1 All ER 1121[18].

---

18 Under the Workmen's Compensation Act 1897 scaffolding included internal as well as external scaffolding: it included planks placed across trestles without any poles (*Hoddinott v Newton, Chambers & Co* [1901] AC 49), a crawling board hooked

In some regulations the term 'scaffold' has been taken to mean a scaffold 'in use', as distinct from one which is being erected or dismantled: *Sexton v Scaffolding (Great Britain) Ltd* [1953] 1 QB 153, [1952] 2 All ER 1085, but the applicability of the regulations depends on the stage which has been reached, e.g. 'maintaining' under what is now reg. 11 may not arise until the relevant part of a scaffold is complete—and does not apply during dismantling: *Barclay v J. & W. Henderson* 1980 SLT (Notes) 71—but it may be necessary to have 'proper strutting' for framework under reg. 15 though the planks have not been put on: *Moloney v A. Cameron Ltd* [1961] 2 All ER 934. But by reg. 12—B.R. 9 (2)—a scaffold must not be left partly erected or dismantled unless it complies with the regulations or is barred, either physically or by a notice[19]; this does not apply unless it is 'left' in that condition: *Barclay v J. & W. Henderson* 1980 SLT (Notes) 71.

The instructions for the safety of scaffolding (regs. 8–37) are long and detailed, so that it is only possible to select points of conspicuous importance.

The general obligation to provide scaffolds where necessary (reg. 7) has already been discussed.

Regulation 8 (B.R. 6) requires all scaffolding work (erecting, altering, dismantling) to be under the 'immediate supervision' of a competent person: the amount of supervision required is a question of degree: *Moloney v A. Cameron & Co Ltd* [1961] 2 All ER 934.

By Regulation 9(1)—B.R. 7(1):

> 'Every scaffold and every part thereof shall be of good construction, of suitable and sound material and of adequate strength for the purposes for which it is used.'

'Good construction' includes good design, and where the end of a horizontal scaffold pole protruded between two rungs of a ladder the regulation was infringed: *Smith v A. Davies & Co (Shopfitters) Ltd* (1968) 5 KIR 320; there is apparently at least a technical breach as soon as a

---

on to the ridge of a roof (*Veszey v Chattle* [1902] 1 KB 494), painter's steps (*Elvin v Woodward & Co* [1903] 1 KB 838) and even a ladder from which work was done (*O'Brien v Dobbie & Son* [1905] 1 KB 346). The present definition covers at least as wide a ground, except that ladders and step-ladders standing on their own are expressly excluded (but fall within regs. 31–2).

19 This includes a pole framework though the planks have been removed: *Skelton v APV Developments Ltd* (1970) 8 KIR 927.

part of a scaffold ceases to be of 'good construction' e.g. if accidentally loosened: *Barclay v J. & W. Henderson* 1980 SLT (Notes) 71.

The quality of timber and metal parts is specified in reg. 9(3)–(5), and the use of defective material is forbidden by reg. 10.

By reg. 11—formerly B.R. 9(1):

> 'Every scaffold shall be properly maintained, and every part shall be kept so fixed, secured or placed in position as to prevent so far as is practicable accidental displacement.'

There are detailed provisions in reg. 13 with regard to the fixing of the uprights, the ledgers and supports, and reg. 14 controls the use of ladders as uprights[20] (B.R. 10, 11).

By reg. 15 scaffolds must be fixed or suspended securely, and in some cases rigidly connected to the binding. Where a scaffold is slung from above, reg. 16 requires chains, ropes or lifting gear used for this purpose to be of 'sound material, adequate strength and suitable quality, and in good condition'. Suspended scaffolds must be anchored to give stability (B.R. 12, 13).

These regulations (at any rate regs. 11 and 15(3)(b)) are intended to protect persons below from falling objects, as well as those on the platform: *Paterson v Lothian Regional Council* 1979 SLT (Sh Ct) 7.

Regulations 16–21 (B.R. 14–19) enter into detail on various types of scaffold, reg. 20 restricts the use of equipment such as a boatswain's chair, and reg. 22 provides for regular inspection.

Regulations 24–30 (B.R. 22–28) deal with working platforms and places of work, also gangways and runs. They must be of a certain width, the planks must be of a certain thickness, and a plank must not project beyond its end support so that it is liable to tip. With certain exceptions, 'every working platform, gangway or run from any part of which a person is liable to fall . . . more than 6 feet 6 inches shall be closely boarded, planked or plated': reg. 24(1); this is intended to prevent persons or materials falling through—with possible damage to those falling or persons below; but not to prevent such minor gaps as may cause a fall or trip on the scaffold: *Black v Duncan Logan (Contractors) Ltd* 1969 SLT (Notes) 19.

---

20 The fact that an upright is out of the vertical is not a cause of an accident to a man who tries to put it right by an unsafe method: *Norris v (William) Moss & Sons Ltd* [1954] 1 All ER 324.

Regulation 28 (B.R. 24) is particularly important. Subject to a number of detailed exceptions:

> 'Every side of a working platform or working place, being a side thereof
> from which a person is liable to fall . . . more than 6 feet 6 inches, shall
> . . . be provided with a suitable guard rail or guard rail of adequate
> strength, to a height of between 3 feet and 3 feet 9 inches above the
> platform or place and above any raised standing place on the platform,
> and with toe-boards or other barriers up to a sufficient height [not]
> less than 6 inches so placed as to prevent so far as possible the fall of
> persons, materials and articles, from such platform or place.'

As the closing words show, this regulation too is designed to prevent the fall of objects as well as persons, and for this purpose toe-boards may be required on the inner side of a scaffold: *Hughes v McGoff and Vickers Ltd* [1955] 2 All ER 291. It is intended to protect the workmen against falls of any kind, and the absence of a guard rail was held to be a cause of the accident when a workman, in a fit, lost consciousness and fell: *Cork v Kirby MacLean Ltd* [1952] 2 All ER 402.

The expression 'working place' may include any part of a building from which persons are working: it is not restricted to places on a scaffold: *George Ball & Sons Ltd v Sill* (1954) 52 LGR 508; *Curran v William Neill & Sons (St. Helens) Ltd* [1961] 3 All ER 108; but it means something analogous to a working platform and does not include a working position from a ladder resting on a sloping roof: *Gill v Donald Humberstone & Co Ltd* [1963] 3 All ER 180; or from beams used temporarily for forming concrete components in buildings: *Buist v Dundee Corpn*, 1971 SLT (Notes) 76. Apparently it does not apply to sloping roofs at all, but can apply to a flat roof or part of one: *Kelly v Pierhead Ltd* [1967] 1 All ER 657[1]. Where, in the course of demolition, a 4 foot width of floorboards was left from which bricks and rubble were thrown to ground level, it was held to be a 'working place': it was a flat area comparable in size to a platform and affording facilities for work for an appreciable time: *Boyton v Willment Bros Ltd* [1971] 3 All ER 624. Similarly a flat roof was a 'working place' although the only work to be done was throwing down scaffold boards which would take 10 to 15 minutes: *Ferguson v Dawson & Partners (Contractors) Ltd* [1976] 3 All ER 817, [1976] 1 WLR 1213.

---

1 Where a man worked on a duck-board at the foot of a curved roof, with a short flat
  roof adjoining, the flat roof was not his 'working place': *Regan v G. & F. Asphalt*
  (1967) 2 KIR 666.

The old reg. 24 did not apply to a working platform which is being dismantled or erected, as distinct from a platform which is 'in use': *Sexton v Scaffolding (Great Britain) Ltd* [1953] 1 QB 153, [1952] 2 All ER 1085. This may be affected by the new wording in reg. 28(4), which allows rails or toe-boards to be left off or removed for access 'or other purposes of the work', but requires their erection or replacement 'as soon as practicable'[2].

There are similar provisions for gangways, runs and stairs (reg. 29, B.R. 27)[3]. Regulation 29(1) requires stairs to be provided with 'handrails or other efficient means to prevent the fall of persons'. 'Handrails' mean something which can be gripped (not a barrier to a fall) and 'other efficient means' must be understood in the same way: *Corn v Weir's Glass (Hanley) Ltd* [1960] 2 All ER 300. The requirement is quite distinct from 'guard rails' which are required (reg. 29(2)) only for a drop of more than 6 feet 6 inches. The above case also decides that reg. 29 includes stairs under construction in a building. 'Guard rails' means an effective barrier against falling over the side, and one rail will not be sufficient where, in the absence of a lower rail, a workman may fall through the gap, e.g. if he slips while carrying a burden: *Astell v London Transport Board* [1966] 2 All ER 748.

Platforms, gangways, runs and stairs are to be kept free from obstruction, and slipperiness is to be cut down to a minimum (reg. 30, B.R. 28). There was a breach of this regulation where a man stepped off a scaffold on to a tarpaulin under which a piece of wood was hidden: this counted as an 'obstruction': *Woodcock v Gilbert Ash (General Works) Ltd* 1987 SLT 678. Regulation 37 (B.R. 32–3) guards against overloading of scaffolds and sudden shocks[4].

---

2 Under B.R. reg. 24(5)(d) guard rails could sometimes be dispensed with on a 'temporary platform': but this means a *structure* which is temporary, and does not extend to exempting a fixed part of a building, such as a concrete roof, which is in temporary use as a 'working place': *Westcott v Structural and Marine Engineers Ltd* [1960] 1 All ER 775. The decision applies to the new reg. 28(6).
3 'Gangway' does not include part of a roof, or a single duck-board laid on it: *Regan v G. & F. Asphalt* (1967) 2 KIR 666; nor boards laid to support equipment, not to be walked on: *Howitt v Alfred Bagnall & Sons* [1967] 2 Lloyd's Rep 370.
4 Under these two regulations it is the contractor who does the dangerous act—not the employer—who is liable: reg. 3.

Ladders
By reg. 31(1)—B.R. 29(1):

> 'Every ladder and folding step-ladder shall be of good construction, sound material, and adequate strength for the purpose for which it is used.'

This is amplified at great length by the rest of the regulation, which expressly forbids the use of ladders with certain defects, and by reg. 32, which provides for stability and in some cases for handholds. Regulation 32 applies to any ladder actually *used* for access, though not placed there for the purpose, and such a ladder must be 'secured': *Lanigan v Derek Crouch Construction Ltd* 1985 SLT 346 (however, the pursuer was held to be the sole cause of the breach of statutory duty). By reg. 32(3), a second man may have to be stationed at the foot of a ladder not otherwise secure. This does not apply to a step-ladder: *McChlery v J. W. Haran Ltd* 1987 SLT 662.

Openings, etc. in roofs, floors and walls
With certain exceptions under reg. 34 (e.g. when openings are being permanently filled in, or during demolition operations) reg. 33 (B.R. 30) requires a guard rail or covering for every 'opening, corner, break or edge' where persons are liable to approach or pass and may fall more than 6 feet 6 inches (or into liquid or material which could drown or injure). This is much wider than the old regulation, and old decisions on what amounts to an opening are obsolete. Regulation 33(4) requires boarding over or other protection where work is done on or immediately above 'open joisting'. This expression does not include beams placed temporarily to form concrete elements in a building: *Buist v Dundee Corpn* 1971 SLT (Notes) 76.

Regulation 33 applies to floors, walls, roofs, similar parts, and to working platforms, gangways and runs.

Roof work[5]
Regulation 35 (a greatly revised version of B.R. 31) relates to work on or access over sloping roofs. These are defined in reg. 35(1) as roofs with a

---

5 See Health and Safety Executive booklet, *Safety in Construction Work: Roofing*; there are also booklets in other aspects of construction work such as scaffolding.

pitch over 10 degrees, but it seems (apart from reg. 35(8)) that duties arise only where such roofs also come within 35(2), either as having a slope over 30 degrees, or having a surface of such nature or in such condition that a man is liable to slip over the edge. In such cases, only 'suitable' men may be employed to work there. Further, both for work on the roof and access over it, crawling ladders or boards, of adequate strength and fixed to prevent slipping, must be provided unless the battens or other roof members give equally good foot- and handholds: reg. 35(3), (4), (5), (6). (Note that it is not enough to say that the sloping roof *surface* gave sufficient hold. Similarly, crawling boards must have proper battens, plain boards will not do: *Jenner v Allen West & Co Ltd* [1959] 2 All ER 115.) When work is done—unless it is 'not extensive'—there must in addition be a barrier at the roof edge or a proper working platform where the drop is over 6 feet 6 inches. The former regulation—B.R. 31 (1)—which showed by its wording that it was designed to prevent falls from a roof edge did not apply where there was no 'edge' because the roof sloped to a gutter or 'valley' between two adjoining roofs: *Donaghey v Boulton and Paul Ltd* [1968] A.C. 1, [1967] 2 All ER 1014; this seems to apply to the present regulations where the word 'edge' is used: but if the regulation does apply and the breach causes an accident, liability is not restricted to falls over the edge: *McInally v Frank A. Price & Co (Roofings)* 1971 SLT (Notes) 43.

Regulation 35(8) requires suitable means to prevent objects falling from a sloping roof (i.e. over 10 degrees); this imposes a strict duty to find suitable means, and the impracticability of some precautions is no excuse: *Todd v John Moulds (Kilmarnock) Ltd* 1968 SLT (Notes) 56.

Regulation 36—B.R. 31(3)—applies where persons 'pass across, or work on or from' fragile material such as a glass or asbestos roof; but not to someone who is not engaged in roof work but only making a preliminary survey of repairs: *Drysdale v Kelsey Roofing Industries* 1981 SLT (Notes) 118. Briefly, there must be crawling boards or ladders with sufficient spread and security to take a man's weight if the material gives way. Where anyone passes 'near' such material, a guard rail (or equivalent) is required. There must be a warning notice, except for glass where the danger is obvious. Although these precautions visualise a fall *through* fragile material, if there is a breach of the regulation and, in consequence, a man falls through an open space, the accident is within the scope of the regulation: *Donaghey v Boulton and Paul Ltd, supra.*

The wording is so much changed that case-law under B.R. 31 is largely obsolete[6].

Impracticability of preventing falls: Safety belts, nets, etc. Regulation 38 (C.G.R. 54) provides a limited dispensation from strict compliance with regulations (6–7, 24–30, 33, 35–6) concerning fall from a height if this is impracticable due to the special nature or circumstances of some part of the work, or access to or egress from it. But one or other of the special matters has to be proved, as well as impracticability; and a precaution such as a guard-rail is not 'impracticable' simply because it is inconvenient or unusual: *Boyton v Willment Bros Ltd* [1971] 3 All ER 624. If strict compliance is indeed impracticable, the regulations must still be followed so far as practicable, and in addition safety nets or sheets must be erected in positions where they will be effective. In some cases safety belts are an alternative, if not only provided but also 'used'. This is stricter than the previous regulation and the case-law is obsolete. However, reg. 38 is not an independent duty, but simply a reserve or 'fall-back' duty instead of the regulations specified, and one or other of these must be shown to be applicable before safety nets, sheets or belts are required: *Montgomery v A. Monk & Co Ltd* [1954] 1 All ER 252. Thus if the specific regulations do not apply because of inherent exceptions or limitations, neither will reg. 38. Somewhat surprisingly this has been held to be the case even where the only inherent limitations—as in reg. 6 (safe access and place of work)—is 'so far as reasonably practicable'. although impracticability is the precise circumstance which brings reg. 38 into operation: *Gardiner v Thames Water Authority* (1984) Times, 8 June.

Lead compounds   The Control of Lead at Work Regulations 1980 (Chapter 8) now apply where these are handled.

6   E.g. *Harris v Bright's Asphalt Contractors Ltd* [1953] 1 QB 617, [1953] 1 All ER 395 (worker on adjacent higher roof not protected). It is the duty of both employer and workman to 'use' the boards: *Ginty v Belmont Ltd* [1959] 1 All ER 414. This is in addition to the employer's duty to 'provide' the boards, which may be performed by showing the workman where they are available to hand on the premises of a third party where he is working. See generally *Jenner v Allen West & Co Ltd* [1959] 2 All ER 115. In *Regan v G. & F. Asphalt* (1967) 2 KIR 666, a duck-board on a slight slope, though wet with rain, was 'adequate foothold'. In *Byrne v E. H. Smith (Roofing) Ltd* [1973] 1 All ER 490, men passed 'over' fragile material though there was a possible way of walking safely with one foot in a gutter and the other on an underlying purlin: the court was divided on whether it was 'near' to the place of work, but under the present regulation it is enough if the fragile roof is near to the access.

3 The Construction (General and Lifting) Regulations

There are other codes of regulations applying to all forms of construction work:

the Construction (General Provisions) Regulations 1961 (S.I. 1961 No. 1580);

the Construction (Lifting Operations) Regulations 1961 (S.I. 1961 No. 1581).

Both of them apply (reg. 2 in each case) to (a) building operations and (b) works of engineering construction and to lines and sidings used in connection with them (not being part of a railway or tramway). The lay-out of both these codes is similar to the Working Places Regulations—persons owing duties, etc.—and reference should be made to section 2 of this Chapter for the case-law. The definition of 'scaffold'—also discussed in that section—is similar (reg. 4 of both Construction Codes). Exemptions may be granted under both codes: General, reg. 2(2); lifting, reg. 5.

The Construction (General Provisions) Regulations

Duties

Under reg. 3, duties are allocated between the various contractors as follows:

Employers (3(1)(a))   Responsible to their own workmen (while present at a place in the course of work or with the employer's permission) for complying with regs. 8 to 11, 13 (timbering and fencing of excavations), 15 to 17 (cofferdams and caissons), 21 (ventilation), 23–25 (safety near water, rails), 35, 36 (safety on vehicles), 45, 46(1), 47 to 49 (steam and vapour, protection from falling articles, lighting, projecting nails and loose material, danger of collapse, wet steelwork) and 55 (excessive loads). The words of para. (a)—'such as affect *him* or any workman employed by him'—do not make an employer liable to anyone except his own men: they were apparently introduced to indicate that an employer working personally is responsible for rules affecting his own safety:

Smith v George Wimpey & Co Ltd [1972] 2 QB 329, [1972] 2 All ER 723[7].

Contractors generally (3(1)(b))   Responsible, so far as their operations are concerned, to everyone on the site for complying with regs. 12, 14 (unsafe excavations), 18, 19 (cofferdams, explosives), 30 (derailed locomotives), 38 to 41 (demolition), 44, 46(2), 50, 51 (electricity, falling articles, collapsing structures, wet steelwork, etc.).

Installers and users of plant and equipment   Responsible for complying with regs. 26 to 29 (locomotives and gantries), 31 to 34 (use of locomotives and vehicles), 37, 42, 43 and 53 (vehicles near edges, fencing machinery, helmets for pile-driving).

Persons employed   They must comply with the regulations so far as their own acts are concerned, 'co-operate' in carrying them out, and report defects promptly (reg. 3(2)).

No duty is owed under these regulations to self-employed persons except by themselves, so where a self-employed bricklayer borrowed a cement mixer with a defective guard it was his own responsibility under reg. 42 to put it right: *Jones v Minton Construction Ltd* (1973) 15 KIR 309.

For other cases on the duties and the various persons responsible, see the case-law under the Working Places Regulations pp. 435–438, particularly as to 'users' of plant.

Part II. Supervision of safety
A special safety officer must be appointed where more than twenty persons are normally employed (not necessarily at the same site or time of day) (regs. 5, 6).

Part III. Working places, scaffolds, access
Now replaced by the Working Places Regulations 1966: see section 2 of this Chapter.

Part IV. Excavations, shafts and tunnels
The main danger in excavations, shafts and tunnels is the risk of collapse. Regulations 8 and 9 therefore impose on the employer the duty

---

7   See further p. 435, *ante.*

of daily inspection by a competent person, of providing timber or other material for support, and of using this to prevent danger so far as practicable. All timbering or other work for support must be under competent supervision (reg. 10(1)). Timbering or other support must be of good construction, adequate strength and properly maintained and struts and braces properly secured (reg. 10(2)).

Under reg. 11 there must be means of escape where there is risk of flooding.

A further duty imposed on employers for the protection of their own workmen is the duty under reg. 13 to fence shafts, openings and excavations, with certain qualifications, where there is a drop of 6 feet 6 inches or more. This duty is limited to excavations arising in the course of operations, and does not apply to a disused tank covered with slates and soil, whose existence is unknown to the contractor: *Knight v Lambrick Contractors Ltd* [1957] 1 QB 562, [1956] 3 All ER 746. A well may be a 'shaft' for this purpose though the removal of the lid is not the 'formation' of a shaft: but fencing may properly be dispensed with to allow access, and this includes not only going down the well but work on its edge: *Gardiner v Thames Water Authority* (1984) Times, 8 June.

Regulations 12 and 14 have to be carried out by the person undertaking the excavation, shaft or tunnel, and are for the benefit of all persons working in the vicinity, not merely their own workmen.

Under reg. 12, if the excavation is likely to affect the stability of any structure, 'adequate steps' must be taken to prevent danger to any person employed from the collapse of the structure or the fall of any part of it.

By reg. 14(1), material is not to be placed near the edge of a pit so as to endanger workmen employed below: and by reg. 14(2) loads are not to be placed near the edge of an excavation so as to cause risk of collapse.

Regulations 8 (support of sides or roof), 12 (collapse of structures) and 11 (escape in case of flooding) do not apply to tunnelling in an engineering operation where non-compliance is due to something outside the operator's control which it was not reasonably practicable to guard against.

Part V. Cofferdams and caissons

These are water-tight structures used for working on the foundations of bridges and other underwater constructions. They must be of good construction, adequate strength and properly maintained (reg. 15).

Strict supervision of work in erecting, altering and dismantling these structures is required, also strict and regular inspection of them (regs. 17, 18). So far as practicable, there must be means of escape in the event of flooding (reg. 16).

Part VI. Explosives

By reg. 19, these must be handled and used under the immediate control of a competent person, and persons employed are to be in a position of safety before a charge is fired.

Part VII. Dangerous or unhealthy atmosphere

Excavations, and confined spaces generally, must be ventilated, and entry restricted if the air is poisonous or asphyxiating (reg. 21). Regulations 20 and 22 (dust and fumes) are superseded by the general regulations for control of hazardous substances in Chapter 8.

Part VIII. Work on or near water

Where the place of work is approached by water, there must be safe transport free from overcrowding (reg. 23). Where there is liability to fall into water, fencing may be necessary, also rescue equipment (reg. 24).

Part IX. Transport

There are extensive requirements for good construction and lay-out of rails and locomotives, trucks and wagons, also of every power-driven capstan or winch for moving trucks (regs. 25, 26). Good clearance and adequate warning are required near rail tracks (reg. 27). Gantries with rails must have a footway, with guard-rails when at a height over 6 feet 6 inches (reg. 28). Locomotives and trucks must have adequate brakes (reg. 29); there must be means of replacing derailed vehicles (reg. 30). Locomotives must have warning devices and be driven by competent persons (regs. 31, 32). Power capstans or winches must also be operated by competent persons and not set in motion without warning (regs. 32, 33).

Mechanically-propelled vehicles and trailers These are governed by reg. 34. Broadly speaking, it applies to vehicles and trailers used for carrying men or loads for the purpose of construction operations (whether carrying anything at the time or not) and requires such vehicles to be 'in an efficient state, in efficient working order and in good repair'; not to be loaded so as to endanger the safe operation of the vehicle; not to be used in an improper manner; and to be operated (reg. 31) by a competent driver or operator over 18. Vehicles which have broken down or become damaged on the site may be moved subject to strict conditions, of which the most important is that no workmen must be carried. Regulation 34 does not apply to locomotives.

Part X. Demolition

The duties under regs. 38 to 41 are to be carried out by the person undertaking the operations, who is made responsible for the safety of all concerned, whether his own employees or not.

'Demolition' does not include removal of an asbestos roof to enable a tank to be taken out: *Fleming v Clarmac Engineering Co Ltd* 1969 SLT (Notes) 96.

Before demolition is commenced, and during its progress, any electricity which is a potential source of danger must be cut off (reg. 44); precautions must also be taken to prevent the risk of fire or explosion from gas or vapour, and the risk of flooding (reg. 40).

Floors, roofs and other parts of a structure are not to be overloaded with debris so as to be unsafe (reg. 41(1)).

All practicable precautions must be taken to avoid collapse when part of the frame of the building is removed (reg. 41(3)). During the progress of the work parts of the building may have to be shored up to guard against accidental collapse (reg. 41(4)). Shoring or equivalent precautions must be taken whenever a reasonable person who considered the situation would regard precautions as necessary, e.g. where workmen were set to clear rubble under a remaining wall of a partly demolished building: *Knight v Demolition and Construction Co Ltd* [1953] 2 All ER 508; affirmed [1954] 1 All ER 711 on other grounds. The purpose of reg. 41(4) is to require protection by shoring up or other support so as to prevent the collapse of a whole structure; it is intended to prevent *collapse*, and does not require precautions against the *breaking off* of planks at the edge of a floor or hole: *Mortimer v Samuel B. Allison Ltd* [1959] 1 All ER 567, [1959] 1 WLR 330. Further, it applies only while demolition is continuing and gives no protection if a wall has been left standing and collapses later; nor is any duty placed by reg. 50(2) on a contractor carrying out other operations at the time when the wall collapses unless his own operations were likely to affect the wall: *Clay v*

A. J. Crump & Sons Ltd [1964] 1 QB 533, [1963] 3 All ER 687. It did not apply where an unstable chimney was blown over by the wind, and not as a result of the demolition operations: *Glasgow v City of Glasgow District Council* 1983 SLT 65.

In general, all work must be carried out under experienced supervision, and in some cases immediate supervision by an experienced man is required (regs. 39, 41(2)). It cannot be said that there is no risk of collapse under reg. 41(2) if this risk may arise under some foreseeable method, although not the method intended by the employers; but the 'immediate supervision' required by the regulation is a question of fact and degree, not necessarily broken by a temporary absence of the foreman during which the men adopt a wrong method: *Owen v Evans and Owen (Builders) Ltd* [1962] 3 All ER 128.

Part XI. Miscellaneous
Machinery Regulation 42, which requires machinery to be fenced unless safe by position or construction, is on the same general lines as ss. 12–14 of the Factories Act 1961[8]. It is amplified by reg. 43, which requires fencing or safety by construction for certain parts of new machinery[9]. Liability under regs. 42–43 rests upon the person who 'erects, installs, works or uses' the machine. A machine is 'worked' if it is in motion, though only for cleaning or maintenance: *Smith v W. & J. R. Watson Ltd* 1977 SLT 204; *Johns v Martin Simms (Cheltenham) Ltd* [1983] 1 All ER 127, [1983] ICR 305. There is a breach of the regulation if it is not fenced when set in motion, whether or not for a commercial or industrial purpose. 'Use' includes the hiring out of a machine complete with operator: *Gallagher v Wimpey & Co Ltd* 1951 SC 515: that is to say, the owner is 'using' it so as to be responsible under the 'Duties' clause, but so also is the contractor who has hired it and is working it through the hired operator: *Williams v West Wales Plant Hire Co Ltd* [1984] 3 All ER 397, [1984] 1 WLR 1311. An electric heater for drying out a machine installed in a building was held not to be machinery, nor to be 'in use' when run for examination only: *Baxter v Central Electricity Generating Board* [1964] 2 All ER 815. A portable grinding tool which can be plugged in anywhere is machinery: *Lovelidge v Anselm Odling & Sons Ltd* [1967] 2 QB 351, [1967] 1 All ER 459.

8   See Chapter 11.
9   And reg. 57 forbids the sale or hire of new machinery which does not comply.

Electricity   The Electricity at Work Regulations (Chapter 16) apply to construction sites. Regulation 44 is revoked.

Lights and visibility   Working places and their approaches, also places where a lifting appliance is being used or where there are dangerous openings, are to be 'adequately and suitably lighted' (reg. 47). 'So far as practicable', steam, smoke and vapour must not be allowed to impair visibility (reg. 45).

These duties rest on the employer, and he is liable only to his own workmen.

Where a night-watchman sustained an injury during his rounds, it was held under the corresponding provision in the former regulations that such a watchman was a 'workman' to whom the employer owed a duty under the regulations, so far as applicable, but that a place on the watchman's rounds was not 'a working place'; and further, that if it had been a working place, it would have been necessary to light the place itself, as distinct from giving the watchman a lantern: *Field v Perrys (Ealing) Ltd* [1950] 2 All ER 521.

Falling materials   By reg. 46(1):

> 'At any place on the site of the operation or works where any person is habitually employed steps shall be taken to prevent any person who is working in that place from being struck by any falling material or article.'

This applies not only to places where someone is engaged in stationary work, but also to places where persons are habitually moving about: *Kearns v Gee, Walker and Slater Ltd* [1937] 1 KB 187, [1936] 3 All ER 151. It is not necessary that any particular person should be there continuously, for 'habitually' describes the place itself, and it is enough if 'habitually' workmen may be expected to work there: *Byrne v Truscon Ltd* 1967 SLT 159 (temporary floor in lift shaft under construction 'frequently used' for storing tools and materials); *McFadden v Crudens Ltd* 1967 SLT (Notes) 90 (road outside site of electrical station where men regularly worked). It does not apply to places which persons pass on their way: *Horsley v Collier and Catley Ltd* [1965] 2 All ER 423, [1965] 1 WLR 1359. Rather surprisingly, it has been held that a piece of masonry broken off from a building is not within the words 'falling material or article': *Bailey v Ayr Engineering and Construction Co Ltd* [1959] 1 QB 183, [1958] 2 All ER 222. Where reg. 46(1) applies, it imposes an absolute requirement and foreseeability or practicability are irrelevant: *McFadden v Crudens Ltd* 1967 SLT (Notes) 90.

Objects must not be thrown down from scaffolds, but lowered properly, unless persons below are adequately protected from falling debris: see reg. 46(2), which must be complied with by the contractor responsible for the operation. This regulation does not require that persons should be habitually below, and was broken when a foreman lobbed a hammer into an excavation: *Horsley v Collier, supra.*

Protection of eyes   The Protection of Eyes Regulations 1974 (Chapter 12, section 9) now apply to *all* places subject to the Factories Act and supersede the former reg. 52.

Temporary structures   By reg. 49, temporary structures which are not scaffolds (and are not supports for lifting apparatus) must be of good construction, sound material and adequate strength and stability, having regard to the purpose for which they are used. This regulation applies, for example, to wooden shuttering used as a mould for a concrete wall, and requires it to be safe while it is in use as a mould: but the regulation does not apply to the shuttering while it is being erected or taken down: *Grant v George Wimpey & Co Ltd* [1956] 3 All ER 470. It also applied to a safety net structure used on the Forth Road Bridge, and was not excluded while the structure was being moved along the bridge: there was absolute liability for a defective screw in a strut, although the defect was latent: *Davies v A.C.D. Bridge Co* 1966 SLT 339.

Other requirements   Other regulations require the avoidance of danger from projecting nails (reg. 48(1)), loose materials[10] (reg. 48(2)), collapse of structures[11] (reg. 50), the movement of ironwork or steelwork on which there is wet paint (reg. 51), strength and adequacy of

10 This requires proper storage or stacking of materials (e.g. timber, scaffold-poles) in stock to be used; it does not apply to an odd wire rope which has been used on a dock as a cargo sling: *Morter v Electrical Installation Ltd* (1969) 6 KIR 130. There is no breach of the regulation if the materials do not cause undue obstruction: *Reader v British Steel Corpn* [1986] CLY unreported appeal No. 19.

11 Regulation 50 does not apply to demolition, but to weakness in buildings under construction (or, presumably, alteration or repair): *Knight v Demolition and Construction Co Ltd* [1953] 2 All ER 508; affirmed [1954] 1 All ER 711; reg. 50 (2) however brings in work (such as repair) likely to affect stability, so it is not limited to new construction. Regulation 50 applied to a stanchion which gave way when a ladder was rested against it: *McMullen v Alexander Findlay and Co Ltd* 1966 SLT 146.

helmets or crowns for pile-driving (reg. 53) and a general prohibition against lifting excessive weights (reg. 55).

Miscellaneous   Riding on running-boards and other insecure positions is forbidden (reg. 35); also being on a vehicle when loose material is being loaded, e.g. by a grab (reg. 36). Vehicles used for tipping must be protected against running over the edge of the tip (reg. 37).

The Construction (Lifting Operations) Regulations 1961

These regulations (S.I. 1961 No. 1581) replaced Part III (regs. 34–74) of the Building Regulations 1948. They apply to building operations and works of engineering construction (reg. 2) and exemptions may be granted (reg. 5). Duties are allocated as follows (reg. 3):

Contractors who erect, install, work or use plant or equipment: to comply with regs. 8–46, 48 and 49(7)—most of the regulations in fact.

Employers   as regards their own men when present in the course of work or otherwise with the employers' permission, regs. 42(1) (hoistways), 47 (carrying persons).

Contractors carrying out operations: regs. 49(1) to (6) (security of loads) and 50 (reports, etc.).

Persons employed: to comply as regards their own acts, 'co-operate' generally and report defects.

For the case-law on duties and the various persons responsible, especially as 'users', see the Working Places Regulations, pp. 435–438, *ante.*

General exceptions
For details of the following exceptions, reference should be made to the exact words of regs. 6 to 9.

Lifting machinery and gear in factories, docks, etc. (reg. 6)   Where this is in 'incidental or occasional use' only, certain regulations set out in the First Schedule do not apply.

Lifting gear attached to loads when delivered (reg. 7)   Regulations 34, 35, 40, 41 (testing, safe load, etc.) do not apply to such things as ropes, chains, etc., intended to be used for removal from the delivery point to the site so long as they remain attached to the load, *unless* there is a patent defect *or* the gear is owned or hired by a contractor operating on the site.

Hoists in permanent structure or underground shaft (reg. 8)   Regulations 10, 15, 42 to 46 and 48 are excluded if certain conditions are observed in carrying passengers and loads and closing gates.

Hoists manufactured before the regulations commenced (reg. 9) Regulations 42(2) (3), 44 and 48 need not be fully complied with if not reasonably practicable, but a certificate of reasonable conformity must be obtained.

Lifting appliances
The word 'lifting appliance' (reg. 4(2)) means 'a crab, winch, pulley block or gin wheel used for raising or lowering, and a hoist, crane, sheer legs, excavator, drag line, piling frame, aerial cableway, aerial ropeway or overhead runway'. It means, therefore, the lifting mechanism as distinguished from slings or other tackle attached to it.
  By reg. 10(1):

> 'Every lifting appliance and every part thereof including all working gear and all other plant or equipment used for anchoring or fixing such appliances shall—
> (a) be of good mechanical construction, sound material, adequate strength and free from patent defect,
> (b) be properly maintained.'

It must also be inspected regularly. Lifting appliances are to be properly secured or anchored, and any supporting beam or structure must be sound and of adequate strength (regs. 11, 18).
  By reg. 16(1):

> 'Every crane, crab and winch (other than a jack roll) shall be provided with an efficient brake or brakes or other safety device. . . .'

By reg. 16(2), every lever or other control on a lifting appliance must in general be fitted with a locking device to prevent accidental displacement.

Stability By reg. 19(1):

'Appropriate precautions shall be taken to ensure the stability of lifting appliances used on a soft or uneven surface or on a slope.'

Cranes must be securely anchored or weighted down to ensure stability (reg. 9(2)) and the anchoring or weighting arrangements must be inspected and tested at the time of each erection and removal and also when weather conditions may have endangered their stability: reg. 19(3) to (7). Further, reg. 23 prohibits the use of a crane, except for vertical raising and lowering, if there will be any risk to its stability, and also forbids the use of a crane with a derricking jib to move a load beyond the maximum authorised radius of the jib.

Rail-mounted cranes By reg. 20, rails on which a crane moves must be securely constructed on an even running surface, and must not have curves which involve danger of derailment. There must be stops or buffers at the end of the track, brakes or chocks must be provided, and the crane must have guards to remove dangerous loose material from the rails.

Safe working load The safe working load must be marked on all apparatus (regs. 29 and 30)[12]. There is an absolute prohibition against exceeding the safe load except for testing purposes (reg. 31) and when lifting a load at or near the safe limit, the load must be halted, as a check on safety, after it has been lifted slightly (reg. 32(1)). Where two or more lifting appliances are used in conjunction, there must be special precautions under competent supervision (reg. 32(2)).

Operator A lifting appliance must not be operated by anyone but a person trained and competent on that appliance: reg. 26(1). But this was held not to apply when a lifting appliance was used to help an employee of an outside contractor who came on a steel site to repair site vehicles, on the ground that this employer was not engaged on 'engineering construction': *Park v Tractor Shovels* 1980 SLT 94. But it is difficult to see why anyone who comes on a construction site for purposes incidental to the construction work should not be protected by the regulations.

---

12 Where a crane has a variable operating radius, the safe load at various radii must be shown, and an automatic indicator is required (with certain exceptions) for a jib crane.

Signallers A competent signaller must be employed in certain cases unless the person in control of the lifting appliance has a clear view (reg. 26(3)–(5)); signals must be clear and distinctive (reg. 27(1)) and any signalling apparatus properly maintained[13].

Inspection, testing and examination These matters are governed by regs. 10, 19 and 28.

Chains, ropes and lifting gear
'Lifting gear' means 'a chain sling, rope sling, or similar gear, and a ring, link, hook, plate, clamp, shackle, swivel or eyebolt' (reg. 4(2)). Broadly, then, it includes all tackle attached to a lifting appliance as distinct from the appliance itself.

Under reg. 7, regs. 34, 35, 40 and 41 do not apply where a load is delivered to the site and is lifted from the delivery point with the lifting gear still attached, provided that there is no patent defect and the gear does not belong to any contractor on the site.

By reg. 34(1)(a):

'. . . no chain, rope or lifting gear shall be used in raising or lowering or as a means of suspension unless (a) it is of good construction, sound material, adequate strength, suitable quality and free from patent defect[14].'

Subsidiary provisions require inspection and testing (regs. 34, 35 and 40), also annealing where appropriate at certain intervals (reg. 41). Furthermore, the safe working load is to be certified, and must not be exceeded (reg. 34(4)).

Chains and wire ropes used in handling loads must not have knots tied in them, nor may chains be used when joined together by nuts and bolts (reg. 39).

Slings are to be 'securely attached' to the lifting appliance, and the risk of fraying against the edge of the load is to be avoided (regs. 37, 38).

Hooks must be shaped to minimise the risk that the load will slip off, or there must be some special safety device (reg. 36).

---

13 For case-law under the Docks Regulations, see Chapter 14.
14 On the meaning of these words, see Chapter 10 for similar provisions in the Factories Act.

Hoists

Hoists are included under the head of lifting appliances, but there are also some further requirements on the lines of ss. 22–25 of the Factories Act, for instance, as regards an enclosure and gates, an automatic safeguard against over-running, and an emergency support in case the rope breaks (reg. 42).

Where a hoist carries persons, there must be safety devices for opening and locking the gates, and the hoist must be constructed so that no one can be trapped between the moving parts and the shaft (reg. 48): furthermore, the hoist must be operated from one position only, not inside the cage unless reg. 48 is complied with (reg. 43).

The safe working load must not be exceeded (reg. 45), and periodical tests and examination are necessary (reg. 46).

There are special provisions where a hoist is part of the permanent equipment of a structure or underground shaft (reg. 8): in general the regulations do not apply but maximum loads must be fixed and not exceeded.

General

No person is to be 'raised, lowered or carried' by a power-driven lifting appliance except on the driver's platform of a crane, on a hoist, on a suspended scaffold, or in other cases under strict conditions (reg. 47[15]) which include safe control of the operation and a proper cage, chair or receptacle. The employer is the person responsible for a breach of this regulation.

Security of Loads   Loads are to be supported securely while being raised or lowered, and the risk of accidental slipping is to be reduced to a minimum (reg. 49). There is an absolute duty to fasten securely: *Kirk v Scaffolding (G.B.) Ltd* 1969 SLT (Notes) 64 (action failed because pursuer himself should have fastened). Loads are not to be left hanging from a crane which is not attended by a competent person (reg. 49 (7)). Containers of loads such as bricks are to be enclosed or designed to prevent accidental fall: reg. 49(3); trucks and wheelbarrows on hoists

15 Slightly amended by S.I. 1989 No. 114 which requires a suspended scaffold to be of good construction, sound material, adequate strength and properly maintained—formerly it had to be 'approved'.

are to be secure; reg. 49(5); and see *Upton v Hipgrave Bros* [1965] 1 All ER 6, [1965] 1 WLR 208 (wheelbarrow tipped by ledge). In general the contractor undertaking the operation is responsible for a breach of reg. 49, but under reg. 49(7) the contractor responsible for the crane is the person liable: see reg. 3.

4 Work in compressed air

The Work in Compressed Air Special Regulations 1958 (S.I. No. 61), largely reiterate rules established in practice for many years. The regulations originally applied (reg. 2(1)) to work in compressed air on any of the various types of 'works of engineering construction' mentioned in the Factories Act. By the Compressed Air (Amendment) Special Regulations 1960 (S.I. No. 1307) they were extended to all factories and to all other premises, places, processes and works for which special regulations could be made under ss. 103 to 108 of the Act of 1937 (now ss. 123 to 127 of 1961). It seems unlikely that they will have much application where no engineering operation is in progress—work at an existing dock or hydro-electric station, if it involved work in compressed air, would almost certainly be within the definition of engineering operations. The duty of complying with the regulations is imposed on every contractor as regards workmen employed by him, but no duty is owed to a workman present at a place where he is not authorised to be (reg. 4(1)). Further, an employer is not liable for matters beyond his control which he could not provide against or foresee (reg. 4(3)).

All work in compressed air must be under the supervision of a competent person (reg. 5). Bulkheads, air-locks and other structures used in connection with work in compressed air must be of good construction, sound material, and adequate strength and properly maintained (reg. 6). The air supply plant must be of suitable design and under the immediate charge of a competent person in constant attendance while any person is in compressed air (reg. 7).

Passage to and from the working chamber is by means of air-locks, where compression is applied gradually (on the way in) or removed gradually (decompression) (on the way out). Air-locks used for the passage of men ('man-locks') must be of adequate size, with clocks, pressure gauges, valves, taps and other necessary means of control over the compressed air (reg. 8). Normally man-locks must not be used for the passage of plant or material: they must be under the control of a competent lock attendant, who is in touch with the persons in the working chamber and the lock, can operate the controls from outside the lock, must comply with the rules for gradual compression and decompression, and must keep a register of times for each person (regs. 8–10). When a man-lock is not is use, the door from the working chamber should be kept open as a means of egress (reg. 11). The wet-bulb temperature in a working chamber must not, if possible, be allowed to exceed 80°F. (reg. 12). Men without previous experience must be given proper supervision at work, and advice during compression (reg. 13).

Persons employed on work in compressed air must be kept under close medical supervision (regs. 14, 15) and if the working pressure exceeds 18 lbs/sq. inch a special air-lock for medical treatment must be provided (reg. 18).

Changing and washing facilities and a place of rest must be provided for persons who have been working in compressed air (reg. 17), and special labels must be supplied for wear after leaving work, so that in case of illness members of the public may know the possibility of trouble and where the man should be taken for treatment (reg. 19).

In *Ransom v Sir Robert McAlpine & Sons Ltd* (1971) 11 KIR 141, liability was established for numerous breaches of regs. 4(1), 6, 8(1) and 10 (1) and (3) in that decompression chambers had ill-fitting doors, were over-crowded, were not properly supervised by a competent person, and in particular decompression times were not adhered to.

5 Diving operations

These are now subject to a comprehensive code which applies to all places of work: see Chapter 19, section 2.

6 Safety of buildings

The Building Act 1984 and the Building Regulations 1985 (S.I. No. 1065) made under it contain elaborate requirements for the safe construction and maintenance of buildings but are not concerned with the safety of building workers: see Chapter 5, section 4.

Chapter 16

Electricity stations and electricity regulations under the Factories Act[1]

1 Generating stations and other electrical stations

It was expressly declared in s. 103(5) of the Factories Act 1937 that electricity is not an article: consequently the generation of electricity was not the 'making of an article' so as to bring a generating station within

---

1 *Explanation of technical terms.* When electricity flows through a circuit, the volume or size of the current is measured in *amperes*, which correspond to gallons of water running down a river. The voltage or electrical pressure is the intensity of the force which drives the current through the circuit, like the head of water on top of a dam or waterfall or series of rapids. The resistance of the circuit may also be compared to a river: the narrower the wire, the greater the resistance, as in a gorge on a river, and the resistant wire (e.g. on a lamp or radiator) becomes heated just as water boils in fury through a narrow gorge. A *conductor*, generally copper wire, has negligible resistance and lets current through easily. The *apparatus* is the main resistance in the circuit, and the current does its work in overcoming the resistance (so giving light, or heat, or magnetic power to turn a motor). In normal supply systems, electricity is in the form of *alternating* current, the form in which it leaves the generator. This means that the voltage is constantly shifting from one end of the circuit to the other (i.e. each end in turn changes rapidly, through all stages from say, 250 volts plus to 250 volts minus and back again). In practice several alternating currents with successive peaks are combined (3-phase supply). Direct current is unusual in supply systems, but is familiar from batteries where one pole is always positive and the other negative. Alternating current is easy to transform from one voltage to another, either to facilitate its transmission over power lines or to make it suitable for some special use. In a *transformer*, there should be no connection between the circuits at different voltage: the two circuits have 'coils' in proximity and the voltage in one of these 'induces' a voltage in the other by magnetic force, the size of the voltage depending on the size of the conductors in the new circuit.

the ordinary definition of a factory. For some reason s. 103(5) is not repeated in the 1961 Act: however, the matter is of no great importance since s. 123 of the Factories Act 1961 (re-enacting s. 103 of the Act of 1937) expressly brings generating stations and many other electrical stations within the Act. Technically they are not factories, but the Act applies 'as if' they were factories.

By s. 123(1), the whole Act applies to any premises where persons are regularly employed in (a) generating, (b) transforming or converting, or (c) switching, controlling or otherwise regulating, electrical energy. However, to enable the premises to qualify under s. 123(1), the electricity must be supplied either:

(i) by way of trade; or
(ii) for a transport or other industrial or commercial undertaking; or
(iii) for a public building or public institution; or
(iv) for streets or public places.

Premises which satisfy these tests (and which may be described as electrical stations *proper*) are deemed to be factories, and the employer is deemed to be the occupier.

Premises may fall outside the definition because, though electricity is generated, transformed or controlled there for one of the purposes mentioned, persons are not regularly employed there. These places, if large enough to admit a person, fall within s. 123(2): the Act as a whole does not apply, but the places are subject to special regulations (now made under the Health and Safety at Work Act 1974)[2].

By s. 123(3), the Minister may apply special regulations to plant and machinery used for electrical processes, though it is not located on an electrical station either in the narrow sense indicated in s. 123(1), or in the broader sense indicated in s. 123(2).

Finally, by s. 123(4) (and subject to any contrary direction in special regulations) neither s. 123(1) nor s. 123(2) applies to premises where electricity is generated, transformed or controlled, for the *immediate* purpose of driving an electric motor, or providing light or heat, or transmitting or receiving messages, or for other purposes. For instance,

---

2 Thus a small transformer kiosk where no one works is an electrical station within s. 123(2): *Paine v Colne Valley Electricity Supply Co Ltd and British Insulated Cables Ltd* [1938] 4 All ER 803. Another example would be a generating shed attached to a private house or estate, which, however, is excluded by s. 123(4). It is thought that a case would fall within s. 123(2) if substantially the whole of a man's body could get in, as distinct from arms or head only.

the section would not apply to an outbuilding where electricity is generated for use in a large mansion house. Broadly speaking, s. 123(4) excludes small private generating stations from the operation of the Act, also wireless stations with their own generators.

Thus there are three distinct cases:

(a) Generating, transforming and other stations where men work regularly: subject to both Act and regulations.
(b) Places where no one works, but a man can get in: regulations only.
(c) Electrical plant and machinery generally: regulations so far as expressly applied.

2 The Electricity at Work Regulations

The Electricity at Work Regulations 1989 (S.I. No. 635), in force from 1 April 1990, apply to all places of work within the Health and Safety at Work Act 1974, including offshore installations (reg. 31) and mines and quarries which formerly had special regulations. They do not apply to the seaboard activities of the master and crew of a seagoing ship, or to aircraft and hovercraft moving under their own power.

Duties (reg. 3)

Employers and self-employed are required to comply with the regulations in all matters within their control, and so are the managers of mines and quarries. Employees are required to co-operate in the performance of these duties by employers, and to comply personally with the regulations on matters within their control.

General safety (reg. 4)

There are rather vague injunctions that electrical systems shall be so constructed and maintained, and work activities so carried out, as to avoid danger as 'far as reasonably practicable'. Protective equipment is to be 'suitable', and maintained in that state.

Specific safety requirements

(i) Insulation All conductors must be insulated or have equivalent protection: reg. 7.

(ii) Earthing Components which are potential conductors, though not part of the circuit, and may become live accidentally, must be earthed, and there must be no impediment in the earth connection: regs. 8, 9[3].

(iii) Connections Joints and connections forming part of an electrical circuit must be suitable both *electrically* and *mechanically*: reg. 10. Under the former regulation on this point, an action succeeded where a joint on a cable broke when pulled by an electrician and he lost his balance and fell to the ground: *Gatehouse v John Summers & Son Ltd* [1953] 2 All ER 117, [1953] 1 WLR 742.

(iv) Capacity of components The use of components in excess of their 'strength and capability' is prohibited: reg. 5. (The old regulation put it the other way round—components must be sufficient in power and size for their purpose.)

(v) Excess current There must be devices such as fuses and cut-outs to cut off the power if the current becomes excessive: reg. 11.

(vi) Cutting off electricity (reg.12) There must be means of cutting off the electricity to any piece of equipment and isolating it, such as switches and switchboards, with identifying signs or marks where necessary. This does not apply to a source of energy such as a generator, for which other 'reasonably practicable' precautions should be taken to prevent danger: reg. 12(3).

---

3   I have found that the necessity for earthing is often misunderstood. Briefly, in a piece of apparatus such as a domestic radiator, the electric current itself flows through the heating element and not through the metal casing, but by accidental contact of a loose wire somewhere the current may get into the case and so cause electric shock to anyone who touches it (because the voltage discharges through the body to the ground). The general mass of the earth is electrically neutral (its voltage is zero), so a wire from the metal to 'earth' gets rid of any accidental charges. In an alternating system with three-core cables (the normal supply system, having a positive, negative and neutral wire) metal is earthed to the neutral wire which itself is well-earthed.

Safety during work on or near installation

Where equipment is made dead to enable work to be done on or near it, precautions must be taken to prevent it becoming alive accidentally: reg. 13. Work is prohibited on or near a live conductor which is not completely insulated unless (a) it is positively 'unreasonable' to make it dead at the time, (b) it is nevertheless reasonable for the work to be done while it is live and (c) suitable safety measures are taken: reg. 14. There must be adequate means of access, working space and lighting for work at or near any electrical equipment which is a source of danger: reg. 15. Finally, no one is to be allowed to do any work unless he has all necessary technical knowledge and experience, or is working under adequate supervision: reg. 16.

3 The Electricity (Supply) Regulations

The Electricity (Supply) Regulations 1988 are a separate code for the construction, maintenance and operation of supply lines and installations from the generating station to the consumer, including overhead lines and underground cables, transformers and sub-stations. They are for the protection of the public rather than employees.

The dominant requirement is in reg. 17, under which all suppliers' works have to be 'sufficient' for the purposes for which they are used, and 'so constructed, installed, protected (both electrically and mechanically), used and maintained as to prevent danger', as far as reasonably practicable. There must be protective devices to cut off excessive current and prevent leakage from high voltage lines; the maximum permitted voltage is 440,000: regs. 2, 22, 18.

Sub-stations in the open air must be fenced off and overhead lines made inaccessible: in both cases warning notices are required. Under previous regulations, it was held that 'efficient' fencing of a pylon did not require absolute exclusion of access. The fence was 'efficient' if it was carried up to a reasonable height and prevented access up to that height: *Craigie v North of Scotland Hydro Electricity Board* 1987 SLT 178.

Suppliers may refuse to give a supply to a consumer whose installation is unsafe: but under earlier regulations electricity suppliers were held to be under no duty to make inspections and tests: *Sellars v Best* [1954] 2 All ER 389.

Chapter 17

Coal mines

Including mines of stratified ironstone, shale and fireclay

1 The Mines and Quarries Act 1954

All the legislation concerning safety in mines and quarries was brought up to date and replaced by the Mines and Quarries Act 1954.

Previously, safety in coal mines depended upon the Coal Mines Act 1911: in other mines, and in quarries, it depended upon the Metalliferous Mines Act and the Quarries Act. Although all mines and quarries are now governed by a single Act, the safety requirements are in many respects far more strict in the case of coal mines than they are in other cases. Accordingly, this chapter is primarily concerned with coal mines, and the application of the Act to other types of mines, and to quarries, is left over to a separate chapter.

Mines of stratified ironstone, shale and fireclay were, however, included with coal mines in the Act of 1911 and for the most part the same requirements apply to them. These classes of mines, therefore, are treated as coal mines in this chapter, and not as 'miscellaneous mines' in the next chapter[1].

The Act of 1954 now takes effect with the general framework of the Health and Safety at Work Act 1974, and like other existing legislation is gradually being replaced by regulations under that Act. However, mines are so different from anything else, and safety underground is so

---

1 The various codes of regulations are conveniently collected in a publication of H.M. Stationery Office entitled *The Law Relating to Safety and Health*: Vol. I, Mines of Coal; Vol II, Mines of Stratified Ironstone, Shale and Fireclay; Vol. III, Miscellaneous Mines; Vol. IV, Quarries.

paramount, that it is unlikely that the legislation built up over the years will be changed in anything but form.

Most of the administrative provisions of the Act—the powers to make regulations and grant exemptions, appointment of inspectors, conduct of inquiries and prosecutions—have been repealed or modified by regulations under the 1974 Act[2]. The Health and Safety Executive is now the authority responsible for enforcing the Mines and Quarries Act.

General scope of the Act

By far the most important part of the Act for present purposes is Part III (ss. 22–97) which is headed 'Safety, Health and Welfare (Mines)'[3]. Management and control of mines depends upon Parts I and II. (The corresponding provisions for safety and management in quarries are in Parts IV and V.) Notification of accidents and other dangerous occurrences is regulated by Part VI, and the inspection of mines on behalf of the workmen by Part VII.

The only other main subject dealt with by the Act is the employment of women and young persons (Part VIII)[4]. The remainder of the Act is taken up with administrative matters, i.e. records (Part IX), certificates of mining qualifications (Part XII), offences and legal proceedings (Part XIV) and miscellaneous matters such as definitions (Part XV). Most of Parts X and XI (regulations and inspectors) and much of Part XIV (as to prosecutions) are repealed and their place is taken by the Health and Safety at Work Act 1974 or regulations under it.

2 Mines and Quarries Acts 1954 to 1971 (Repeals and Modifications) Regulations, S.I. 1974 No. 2013 and 1975 No. 1102.
3 Most of these sections contain safety requirements of general application. Others, however, contained powers to require improvements in particular situations (e.g. roof support, roads, ventilation) or to make regulations; these have been repealed under the Health and Safety at Work Act 1974 on the basis that they are covered by the powers under that Act. Sections 22–25, 33–35 and 70 have been replaced by the Mines (Safety of Exit) Regulations 1988 (S.I. No. 1729).
4 *Women and young persons.* S. 124 (as amended by the Sex Discrimination Act 1975) restricts the employment of women below ground, and allows the employment of boys under 16 below ground only for the purpose of carefully regulated training. Sections 125–132 are mainly concerned with hours of work, and therefore with health and welfare rather than safety. In general work on night shifts is not allowed. As this book goes to press, most of the restrictions are removed by the Employment Act 1989, ss. 9, 10.

Part XIII (fencing of abandoned and disused mines and quarries) is intended for the protection of the public at large.

The Act is binding upon the Crown, and applies to mines and quarries belonging to the Crown or a Government department, or held in trust for the purpose of a Government department: see s. 179.

The Mines and Quarries (Tips) Act 1969 regulates the safety of tips, whether still in use or disused.

Administration of the Act

The administration of the Act was originally in the hands of the Minister of Fuel and Power (s. 182). References to 'the Minister' are now to be taken as references to the Health and Safety Executive[5].

The Health and Safety at Work Act 1974 now controls the making of regulations and the appointment and powers of inspectors. The Health and Safety Executive took over the former Mines Inspectorate, which continues as a specialist branch of the organisation.

Control and management of mines

Under s. 1 the ultimate responsibility for complying with all safety requirements under both the 1954 Act and the 1974 Act, and regulations under them, rests upon the *owners* of the mine. But the expression 'owner' is defined, by s. 181 (1), to mean 'the person entitled for the time being to work' the mine or quarry and therefore has much the same meaning as the occupier in the case of a factory. The National Coal Board—now renamed the British Coal Corporation: Coal Industry Act 1987—is the owner of most coal mines; but some small mines are still worked by private owners by licence of the Board under s. 36 of the Coal Industry Nationalisation Act 1946. Where (in the case of a mine or quarry under private ownership) a liquidator, receiver or manager is appointed, or some person is appointed having similar powers under an order of the court, he is treated as an additional owner: see s. 181(4).

5   Section 182 as amended by S.I. 1974 No. 2013. This is, of course, for the purpose of inspection and enforcement. Other functions of 'the Minister' such as the making of regulations are now exercised under the 1974 Act.

The owner of a mine may, by written instructions under s. 1, delegate his authority to a person appointed by him. Such persons were referred to in previous legislation as 'agents', and were often responsible for managing a group of mines. Private owners may still appoint an agent under s. 1; but the machinery of delegation may also be used by British Coal in decentralising their authority among regional officials.

At the mine itself complete powers of control are given by the Act to that very important official, the mine manager (ss. 2, 3), who in the case of a coal mine must hold a statutory qualification (s. 4) and may be assisted by under-managers (s. 6). The manager and under-managers must exercise personal supervision from day to day (s. 8). The Mines Management Act, 1971, authorises the appointment of 'manager's assistants' to whom statutory duties and powers of the manager may be delegated, provided that they hold the necessary qualifications. The Coal Mines (Mines Management) Regulations 1972 (S.I. No. 631) require such appointments to be made in coal mines with 750 or more employees, or with more than one shift in 24 hours at the coal face. Presumably they will be in charge of definite parts of a mine, or particular shifts.

A surveyor must be apppointed to be responsible for plans of the mine (s. 11)[6].

Below the manager, under-managers and manager's assistants, the most important officials are the *deputies*, who correspond to foremen in industry, and are each placed in charge of a specified district of the mine: see s. 12. The deputies are in immediate charge of the workmen, and have special responsibilities for carrying out inspections and ensuring safety[7]. In addition to the deputies, the manager must (by s. 13) appoint such

6 For further details see the Coal and other Mines (Surveyors and Plans) Order 1956 (S.I. No. 1760), the Coal and other Mines (Working Plans) Rules 1956 (S.I. No. 1782) and the Coal and other Mines (Abandonment) Plans 1956 (S.I. No. 1783); also ss. 17 to 20 of the Act (plans to be kept). Plans should show, *inter alia*, the workings, shafts and outlets in each seam, sections of the strata sunk or driven through, disused or abandoned workings in the vicinity, peaty or waterlogged strata, water dams, and geological faults; also details of the ventilation system.

7 For the qualifications and duties of the various officials and technicians, see the Coal and other Mines (Managers and Officials) Regulations 1956 (S.I. No. 1758), amended by S.I. 1961 No. 817, 1962 No. 594, 1963 No. 1617 and 1966 No. 882; also the Coal and other Mines (Mechanics and Electricians) Regulations 1965 (S.I. No. 1559 which, in addition to requiring regular maintenance schemes, contains some rules for electrical safety, notably requiring the power to be switched off during maintenance and forbidding flexible cables to be left live and unattended. Regulation 11(3) was revoked by the Electricity at Work Regulations which apply to mines.

other officials, engineers and technicians as are necessary. *Overmen* are an intermediate level of responsibility. The object of these detailed requirements is to allocate precisely between various persons the responsibility for complying with the safety requirements of the Act.

At *coal* mines in the strict sense, training officers may have to be appointed: Coal Mines (Training) Regulations 1967 (S.I. 1967 No. 82) Part VI.

Definition of 'mine'

Broadly speaking, the difference between a mine and a quarry is that a mine is approached by underground workings while a quarry consists of open excavations: *Sims v Evans* (1875) 40 JP 199. Thus open-cast coal workings are quarries.

'Mine' is defined more precisely by s. 180(1) of the Act to mean

> 'an excavation or system of excavations made for the purpose of, or in connection with, the getting, wholly or substantially by means involving the employment of persons below ground, of minerals (whether in their natural state or in solution or suspension) or products of minerals.'

Under s. 180(3)(a), the mine is taken to include the surface workings, i.e.:

> 'so much of the surface (including buildings, structures and works thereon) surrounding or adjacent to the shafts or outlets of the mine as is occupied together with the mine for the purpose of, or in connection with, the working of the mine, the treatment, preparation for sale, consumption or use, storage or removal from the mine of the minerals or products thereof gotten from the mine or the removal from the mine of the refuse thereof.'

By a proviso, however, premises on the surface do not form part of the mine if 'a manufacturing process is carried on otherwise than for the purpose of the working of the mine . . . or the preparation for sale of minerals gotten therefrom'.

By s. 180(4) and (5), a mine also includes refuse dumps and railway lines[8] serving it: if these serve more than one mine, the Health and

---

8   Railway lines are excluded if they belong to a 'railway company'—a curious expression which is defined to include British Rail and statutory undertakers.

Safety Executive has power to allocate them to one or other of the mines. Similarly, by s. 180(6), a conveyor or aerial ropeway provided for the removal of minerals or refuse is part of the mine.

There is a corresponding definition of a quarry and its associated workings. All that need be said at this stage is that a quarry is defined as a system of excavations for minerals which is *not* a mine. As the definition of a mine involves, 'wholly or substantially', 'means involving the employment of persons below ground', it appears that a *limited* degree of underground working will not convert a quarry into a mine.

The whole of these complex definitions may be summed up simply and broadly as follows: a 'mine' means underground excavations for obtaining minerals and includes the surface workings and associated railway lines, conveyors, ropeways and refuse or spoil dumps; but it does not include premises at the surface where minerals are subjected to a manufacturing process—such as the smelting of metals or the making of patent fuels from coal—as distinct from the mere preparation of the minerals for sale.

'Minerals' are defined by s. 182 to include 'stone, slate, clay, gravel, sand and other natural deposits except peat'. This is obviously not a comprehensive definition, since it does not mention the main minerals such as coal and metallic ores: it is merely inserted to put one or two borderline cases beyond doubt.

There is no definition of a 'coal mine': but a number of the stricter requirements of the Act (e.g. those relating to the necessity for two shafts) are limited to mines of 'coal, stratified ironstone, shale or fireclay'; and the term coal mine will be used in this chapter (as it was used in the Act of 1911) to include all these cases.

The working of a mine includes the driving of a shaft or outlet (s. 182(3)(a)); and the working of a mine continues—and therefore the Act applies—although the only operations in progress are being carried out with a view to abandonment, or to prevent the flow of water or fluid material into an adjacent mine or quarry (s. 182(3)(c)).

Excavations made for training purposes are deemed to be mines, but in this case the Minister (now the Secretary of State for Employment) may make an order applying the Act with modifications (s. 183)[9].

9 See also, on the subject of training, the Coal Mines (Training) Regulations 1967 (S.I. No. 82) which apply only to coal mines in the strict sense and restrict employment underground until proper instruction has been given.

Offices at mines and quarries are subject to the Offices, Shops and Railway Premises Act 1963 (see Chapter 22) unless underground (s. 85(3) of the Act).

Liability to actions for damages for breach of statutory duty[10]

Under the Coal Mines Act 1911 many sections of the Act, such as s. 49 with regard to the security of the roof, imposed a direct and personal duty upon the owners, who were therefore liable to an action for damages if the duty was not performed. Other duties under the Act and regulations, however, did not rest directly upon the owners, but were imposed specifically upon other persons: for example, the duties with regard to the use of explosives rested upon the shotfirer. In such cases the owners were not liable for the breach of duty, provided that they had taken all reasonable means to see that the Act and regulations were enforced: *Harrison v National Coal Board* [1951] AC 639, [1951] 1 All ER 1102. In the same case it was suggested that, even after the abolition of common employment, the owners would not become liable for the default of a shotfirer or other subordinate, because his statutory duty (it was said) was something independent of his employment. This point was left open by the House of Lords, and has now been met by s. 159 of the Mines and Quarries Act 1954, which provides as follows:

> 'For the removal of doubts it is hereby declared that the owner of a mine or quarry is not absolved from liability to pay damages in respect of a contravention . . . by a person employed by him of [a provision of the Act or of any order, regulation or notice under the Act] by reason only that the provision contravened was one which expressly imposed on that person or on persons of a class to which . . . he belonged, a duty or requirement, or expressly prohibited that person or persons of such a class, or all persons, from doing a specified act . . .'

The wording of this section is far from ideal: but it clearly is intended to make the owners liable for a breach of statutory duty by their

---

10 It is expressly declared by s. 193 that nothing in the Act (or orders or regulations made under it) is to derogate from the duties of the employer at common law—including in particular the duty to provide a safe system of working.

subordinates, provided that the breach arises in the course of the employment.

Accordingly, under the present Act it is possible to say in general terms that the owners are liable for all contraventions of the Act either by themselves or through the acts and omissions of their servants in the course of their employment: and the difficulties which arose under the previous law may now be regarded as obsolete.

However, under s. 157 of the Act it is a defence in an action for damages, based on a contravention of the Act, or of any order or regulations or other requirement under the Act, if the defendant is able to prove:

> 'that it was impracticable to avoid or prevent the contravention.'

The word 'impracticable' should be noted. The corresponding expression in s. 102(8) of the Act of 1911 was 'not *reasonably* practicable'. The change of wording implies that the standard of liability has been raised. The question now is whether it was 'practicable' or not to comply with the Act: and questions of reasonableness—which involved considerations of expense, and loss of productive effect—are no longer in issue[11]. The onus of establishing this special defence is clearly placed upon the defendant: *Gough v National Coal Board* [1959] AC 698, [1959] 2 All ER 164. Even under the wording of the old section, it was a heavy burden. Tucker LJ said in *Edwards v National Coal Board* [1949] 1 KB 704 at 710, [1949] 1 All ER 743 at 746:

> 'It was, I think, a heavy burden . . . [the owners] start as insurers and have by evidence to divest themselves of this status. . . .'

In effect, as the above case shows, the owners must explain in every detail what they have done, and must establish that they have left no stone unturned in trying to comply with the Act: it is not enough to show that the accident *might* have happened without their negligence, in spite of all practicable steps being taken: *Sanderson v National Coal Board* [1961] 2 QB 244, [1961] 2 All ER 796.

Comparisons with the law of negligence were discouraged even under the old wording by Lord Reid in *Marshall v Gotham Co Ltd* [1954] AC 360 at 373, [1954] 1 All ER 937 at 942. Under the stricter test of 'impracticability', it can hardly ever be right to say, as was

---

11 For a full discussion of practicability, see Chapter 6, section 8.

suggested *obiter* in *Jones v National Coal Board* [1957] 2 QB 55, [1957] 2 All ER 155, that if there was no negligence the defence will be established[12].

Where the duty of complying with the Act rests on a subordinate, the owners must show that it was not reasonably practicable (under the Act of 1954, 'impracticable') for the subordinate, their agent, to avoid or prevent the breach: *Yelland v Powell Duffryn Associated Collieries Ltd* [1941] 1 KB 154, [1941] 1 All ER 278; *Crane v William Baird & Co* 1935 SC 715; for he is the person who is complying with the Act on their behalf.

Under the Mines (Safety of Exit) Regulations 1988 (S.I. No. 1729) the defence under s. 157 is excluded: see reg. 11: this is because the individual regulations are restricted to what is 'reasonably practicable' where this is appropriate.

Relationship between the Factories Act and the Mines and Quarries Act

The interplay of the Factories Act and the Mines and Quarries Act was somewhat difficult under the original s. 184 of the Mines and Quarries Act, but has been greatly simplified by the repeal of most of the section under the Health and Safety at Work Act 1974.

By s. 184(1), the Factories Act does not apply to premises which (under the definitions discussed above) form part of a mine or quarry.

The exclusion of the Factories Act from mines and quarries is, however, subject to an exception under s. 184(5). The Mines and Quarries Act does not extend to works of building and engineering construction which are regulated by s. 127 of the Factories Act; but by s. 184(5), s. 127 is not to apply to *any* work of engineering construction at a mine or quarry, whether above or below ground, or to building operations below ground. This seems to be a roundabout way of saying that s. 127 of the Factories Act (and the Construction Regulations made

12 See also *Sanderson v National Coal Board* [1961] 2 All ER 796 and *Brown v National Coal Board* [1962] AC 574, [1962] 1 All ER 81 (per Lord Denning), which show that the test for 'impracticability' is not the same as for absence of negligence, and that it is a stricter requirement than 'not reasonably practicable' under the 1911 Act.

under the Act) applies to building operations on the surface, but otherwise has no application at a mine or quarry.

2 The security of the roof and sides

It has always been recognised that the security of the roof in a mine is a matter of great importance. Failure to make the roof safe might give rise to an action for negligence at common law, as in *Paterson v Wallace & Co* (1854) 1 Macq 748[13]. Section 49 of the Coal Mines Act 1911 (replacing a similar section under the Act of 1887) imposed a simple and unqualified duty in the following terms:

> 'The roof and sides of every travelling road and working place shall be made secure . . .'

This was held in the earlier cases to create an absolute duty to keep the roof secure, subject to the defence of impracticability: *Lochgelly Iron and Coal Co v M'Mullan* [1934] AC 1 approving *Bett v Dalmeny Oil Co* (1905) 7 F 787. But the old law has been changed.

Section 48 (1) of the Mines and Quarries Act 1954 provides as follows:

> 'It shall be the duty of the manager of every mine to take with respect to every road and working place in the mine, such steps by way of controlling movement of the strata in the mine and supporting the roof and sides of the road or working place as may be necessary for keeping the road or working place secure.'

By a proviso, this does not apply to parts of the mine which are fenced off under reg. 8 of the Mines (Safety of Exit) Regulations 1988 (formerly s. 33 of the Act) as not being fit for use or entry. By s. 48(2), the manager must ensure that he is in possession of all material information necessary for the discharge of his duty—for example, he must study the geological plans of the mine, and keep himself informed on the condition of peat or other water-logged strata on the surface whose weight may cause the workings to collapse.

13 See p. 9, *ante*.

The change in wording makes the duty more extensive and attaches responsibility more precisely. It is now expressly imposed upon the manager, and he is therefore, *prima facie*, the person liable to a criminal prosecution for a breach of the section; but in a civil action for damages, the owners are liable, under s. 159, for the manager's default. Further, the duty is not now limited to the security of working places and roads, taken piecemeal, but extends to watching and controlling the movements of the strata throughout the whole area of the mine workings. The duty is to be carried out not only by support measures but also by controlling the movement of the strata, which includes the bringing down of a dangerous mass of coal or other strata (*Robertson v William Crossen (Woodhall) Ltd* 1970 SLT 310) and bringing down stones in the roof such as balls of ironstone embedded in the strata, where the risk of falls is known to exist or ought to be known (*Davies v National Coal Board* (1974) 16 KIR 339).

On the other hand, the duty is no longer automatically broken by a fall of roof, and the onus is on the plaintiff to prove a breach of the section: *Aitken v National Coal Board* 1982 SLT 545. It is not broken unless the manager (or those delegated by him) has failed to take some step which was necessary in the light of the knowledge and information he has or ought to have: *Brown v National Coal Board* [1962] AC 574, [1962] 1 All ER 81 (roof secure until girder dislodged by a tub; electrician hit by stone while removing light from girder preparatory to replacement—no breach of manager's duty). There is no liability, therefore, for an unforeseeable geological fault: *Tomlinson v Beckermet Mining Co Ltd* [1964] 3 All ER 1; or where girders are fixed and boarded over to a width which leaves only a negligible risk of a fall: *Soar v National Coal Board* [1965] 2 All ER 318. But where shotfiring involved foreseeable risk that the sides of a clay mine would be weakened, liability was established for failure to take steps in advance to maintain security, although supports for sides are not customary in a clay mine: *John G. Stein Ltd v O'Hanlon* [1965] AC 890, [1965] 1 All ER 547.

The duty of the manager was described in one case as a 'general long-term obligation': it was held that while he must keep himself informed from day to day, there was no breach of duty merely because a subordinate official knew that a steel strut had been placed without a wooden lid so that it bit into the roof: *Robson v National Coal Board* [1968] 3 All ER 159.

This decision seems dubious[14]. No doubt there is a long-term obligation, but that does not mean there is no short-term obligation. The decision went on the basis that the section was broken only by the acts or omissions of the manager, and not by the acts of deputies or other officials. This is clearly wrong. In *Brown v National Coal Board, supra*, which the decision purported to follow, Lord Denning said (at pp. 597, 90) that the manager has to act through overmen and deputies and is responsible for them. In Scotland there is a consistent line of authorities that performance of the manager's duty must be judged *as if* he had inspected the place before the accident (even if he never went there). If, on such a visit, there would have been no indication of insecurity, there is no liability: *Aitken v National Coal Board* 1973 SLT (Notes) 48. But if danger was foreseeable by a skilled and competent manager, it would be his duty to give instructions (e.g. to bring down the roof or improve the support), not to leave this to the decision of the deputy or other men on the spot: *O'Hara v National Coal Board* 1973 SLT (Notes) 25 (a considered decision of the Inner House on appeal: it was held that a projecting nose of coal liable to collapse should have been brought down; the manager never inspected it and said in evidence that he would have thought it dangerous but left those on the spot to decide). In *Hill v National Coal Board* 1976 SLT 261 the roof was supported by girders and wooden cladding; shotfiring in the night shift might have weakened the roof; the following morning a stone fell on a miner clearing dust. The Inner House held that in the absence of evidence that the manager had actually made an inspection after the shotfiring, the claim succeeded; the pursuer did not have to prove that some fault would have been discovered. Although a roof fall does not automatically establish a breach of duty, once it is shown that the risk of fall should have been known to a competent manager, there is a duty to make the roof secure either by support or bringing dangerous parts down, and non-performance can be excused only by the defence of 'impracticability' under s. 157: *McFarlane v National Coal Board* 1974 SLT (Notes) 16 (the roof was brittle, there had been falls, the supports were too far apart: liability established); *Weir v National Coal Board* 1982

14 It cannot be right to reduce the manager's duty to long-term planning. It is worded as a continuous duty; as Lord Denning said in *Brown's* case, the manager has to carry it out through subordinate officials such as deputies, and there is a breach of his duty if they do not perform it.

SLT 529 (deputy knew of dangerous cavity though manager personally did not).

Although, as stated above, the onus of proof that there has been a breach of the section is in the final balance on the plaintiff, it has been held that a fall of roof raises a *prima facie* case, which requires to be answered by at least some evidence of what steps have been taken: *Sinclair v National Coal Board* 1963 SC 586; *Beiscak v National Coal Board* [1965] 1 All ER 895, [1965] 1 WLR 518. In *Stein v O'Hanlon, supra*, the House of Lords left the point open. But in *Hill v National Coal Board* 1976 SLT 261 the Court of Session made it clear that the *Sinclair* decision has not been overruled and will be followed in Scotland.

There is a further noteworthy change in the wording of the Act of 1954. Under s. 48 it is no longer the 'roof and sides' (as it was under the old Act) which have to be made 'secure'. It is the 'road or working place' itself which has to be secure, and not merely made secure but 'kept' secure, so that there is a continuing duty.

The expression 'working place' includes 'any place where a miner is set to work': *Lochgelly Iron and Coal Co v M'Mullan* [1934] AC 1 at 19. The area of a 'working place' varies according to the nature of the work, and includes all places where a man is properly working or may be expected to work, not necessarily excluding an area from which props are partly removed: *Venn v National Coal Board* [1967] 2 QB 557, [1967] 1 All ER 149; *Hammond v National Coal Board* [1984] 3 All ER 321. In *Shevchuk v National Coal Board* 1982 SLT 557 the Court of Session decided that the roof newly exposed behind a coal cutter was not a 'working place' (and in particular that the manager could not be expected to know that a miner would go under the exposed roof without extending the canopy from the mechanical chock for protection). In *Hammond v National Coal Board, supra*, the English Court of Appeal, by a majority, reluctantly followed this decision; accordingly there was no breach of s. 48, although this part of the roof was known to be brittle from previous falls after the cutter had passed the same point, and could have been made secure in advance. There is much to be said for the dissenting view of Parker LJ that 'working place' should be interpreted in a broad sense to include 'the whole of the roof from the waste behind the chocks to the face, wherever the face might from time to time be', because otherwise 'a mine manager could deliberately allow cavities to develop, the repair of which would necessarily expose miners to danger'. In both these cases the accident was to a miner engaged in repairing a cavity[15]. 'Road' does not—by s. 182(1)—include an 'unwalkable outlet', i.e. a vertical or steeply inclined shaft giving exit from the mine, but it appears to include every other track from one point to another in a mine[16].

The word 'secure' means the same thing as 'safe', i.e. free from danger: but the question has still to be asked. What dangers must it be free from[17]? The answer appears to be that the structure of the roof must be free from danger of collapse through its own inherent weakness, and perhaps also from the danger of collapse under the impact of some external forces. Lord Tucker said in *Marshall v Gotham Co Ltd* [1954] AC 360, [1954] 1 All ER 937 (a case decided under the Metalliferous Mines Regulations) at 374, 943:

> 'I agree that the word "secure" does not involve security from the effects of an earthquake or an atom bomb, but I think that it must include security from all the known geological hazards inherent in mining operations.'

On the other hand, it does not involve security from an abnormal explosion due to the fact that a large quantity of explosive is being carried in a manner prohibited by statute: *Jackson v National Coal Board* [1955] 1 All ER 145[18]; nor against the danger of a girder being knocked out by a moving tub: *Brown v National Coal Board*, p. 482, *ante*.

In *Gough v National Coal Board* [1959] AC 698, [1959] 2 All ER 164 where the question was whether the 'working face' is covered by the obligation to make secure, Lord Reid said:

15 An appeal to the House of Lords was settled, leaving the question open at that level. It is difficult for an outsider to understand what is the best mining technology for roof support, but it seems that the *Hammond* decision is contrary to the common sense view of experienced mine deputies. In the 1984 coal strike it was a source of friction between NACODS (the deputies' union) and the NCB.

16 In *Wraith v National Coal Board* [1954] 1 All ER 231 it was held that the term 'road' did not include a disused roadway which was under reconstruction: and that the work of repair did not make it a 'working place'. Under the present Act this would still be the position provided that the place is in a part of the mine fenced off under s. 33, but apparently not otherwise, as the wording of s. 48 does not follow the material part of s. 49 of the Act of 1911.

17 See p. 282, *ante*.

18 This case contains a reference to an unreported case of *Hayes v National Coal Board*, which decided that there was no breach of s. 49 of the Act of 1911 when a fall of roof occurred because a prop was accidentally knocked out. If this case is rightly decided, the protection of the section cannot extend to security against the shock of any external danger at all, and must be limited to collapse through inherent weakness.

'"Secure" here means in such a state that there will be no danger from accidental falls. . . . I can see nothing inconsistent in saying that a side or a roof shall be made secure against accidental falls at a time when steps are being taken to bring it down deliberately.'

It was held by the House of Lords under the old Act (*Grant v National Coal Board* [1956] AC 649) that the protection given by the section is not confined to persons liable to be struck by a fall of roof; it also extends to consequential risks arising after the fall, such as the derailment of a bogie which struck fallen debris, as in *Grant's* case, or the blockage of a means of egress from the workings.

Limits of the duty to keep secure

Notwithstanding the earlier authorities on the absolute character of the duty to make the roof and sides secure, later cases under the Act of 1911 reduced the scope of the duty. Some of these apply under the new Act.

(i) Applicability to the coal face
It was formerly held both in England and in Scotland under the 1911 Act that there was no duty to make the coal face itself secure, as distinct from the 'sides' and 'roof' adjacent to it: *Gough v National Coal Board* [1959] 1 QB 189, [1958] 1 All ER 754; *Elliot v National Coal Board* 1956 SC 484, 1957 SLT 193. These decisions were overruled in *Gough v National Coal Board* [1959] AC 698 [1959] 2 All ER 164 where the House of Lords held that the working face was a side, and has to be kept secure, subject to the paramount object of mining operations which is to bring down and remove the coal. In *Gough's* case, the accident took place on a shift when the coal was not being brought down, so the House had no difficulty in holding that support should have been provided, but accepted that there is no duty to keep the place secure when the coal is actually being brought down. This also applies under the 1954 Act. In *Anderson v National Coal Board*, 1970 SLT 214, for example, the coal face had been undercut and two men were approaching one another stripping the loose coal: a short length of face remained between them, which they expected to bring down by shotfiring, but in fact part came down prematurely. It was held that at this stage s. 48 did not apply. But where a projecting 'nose' of coal was left at the face by a machine, such a nose being liable to burst under pressure, proper 'control of the strata'

required its removal before the strippers came in: *Robertson v William Crossen (Woodhall) Ltd* 1970 SLT 310.

(ii) Formerly not applicable to persons engaged in 'repair' or making secure
The old s. 49, after stating the duty to make secure, went on to say that no person should enter a road or place not made secure, 'unless appointed for the purpose of exploring or repairing'. The courts held that the two parts of the section must be read together, and therefore it must be read as excluding from its protection persons engaged in exploration or repair. The new section does not include the relevant words, and, as was shown above, it is in wider terms than the old section. The cases on the subject are therefore thought to be obsolete; but some of them may still be followed on the broad ground that the duty to make secure cannot be owed to the persons who are actually making the place secure: *Stapley v Gypsum Mines Ltd* [1953] AC 663 at 686 (dictum of Lord Asquith).

In *Walsh v National Coal Board* [1956] 1 QB 511, [1955] 3 All ER 632 it was held, in general terms, that the old s. 49 did not apply to persons who were engaged in making the roof secure at a roadhead which was being enlarged. The court relied on the dictum of Lord Asquith in the *Stapley* case, and did not decide whether the plaintiff was engaged in 'repair' (he was removing debris to pack it under the adjacent sides). If he was, the old section expressly allowed him to be present. In *Mullen v National Coal Board* 1957 SLT 313 where the deceased was similarly engaged in building up 'packs' of debris to serve as support, he was held to be engaged in 'repair', and the fact that he had been detailed to do this work was sufficient to make him a person 'appointed' to repair. In *Burns v National Coal Board* 1958 SLT 34 it was held, perhaps more questionably, that a man at the face, who had removed coal and was about to put up supports for the first time, was engaged in 'repair' and not protected by the section. In *John G. Stein Ltd v O'Hanlon, ante,* the question whether this line of cases still applies under the 1954 Act was discussed but not decided. In Scotland the Court of Session has had no hesitation in deciding that a man engaged in repair is protected by the present s. 48: *Weir v National Coal Board* 1982 SLT 529.

(iii) Formerly excluded where 'not reasonably practicable' (now 'impracticable')
This was an application of the general defence under s. 102(8) of the

Act of 1911, that it was not 'reasonably practicable' to avoid or prevent a breach. Strictly speaking, the older cases are obsolete (for the purpose of the Mines and Quarries Act) now that defendants have the heavier burden of proving 'impracticability' under s. 157.

The defence of 'not reasonably practicable' failed in *Caulfield v P. W. Pickup Ltd* [1941] 2 All ER 510 where support by props and discs was inadequate, but props and bars could have been used; and in *Edwards v National Coal Board* [1949] 1 KB 704, [1949] 1 All ER 743 where the side of a road collapsed owing to a latent defect, no artificial support having been provided, and the defendants failed to prove that the cost of such support would be prohibitive. The defence succeeded in *Jackson v National Coal Board* [1955] 1 All ER 145, [1955] 1 WLR 132 (pit props dislodged by abnormal explosion) and in *Marshall v Gotham Co Ltd* [1954] AC 360, [1954] 1 All ER 937 (decided under the Metalliferous Mines Regulations). In the last-mentioned case, the roof of a gypsum mine collapsed owing to the presence of a rare geological fault, 'slicken-side'. There was no systematic support, the cost of providing it throughout the mine would have been considerable, and it was doubtful whether such support would have prevented the accident. The House of Lords considered that the case was near the border-line; but for the word 'reasonably' practicable, the decision would apparently have gone against the defendants. The defence also succeeded in *Walsh v National Coal Board* [1956] 1 QB 511, [1955] 3 All ER 632 where a stone had been spragged up by a chargehand after an unsuccessful attempt to dislodge it, on the ground that the spragging was done efficiently and the use of explosives would have involved greater danger.

Systematic support

In addition to the general duty to make the roof secure, ss. 49 to 54 of the Act contain provisions requiring 'systematic support' in certain cases, i.e. support by pit props set at regular intervals, or other artificial methods. Under the Act of 1911, the view was expressed in the House of Lords that corresponding sections in that Act did not detract from the absolute duty to make the roof secure, but were ancillary to it: *Lochgelly Iron and Coal Co v M'Mullan* [1934] AC 1 at 16, 18. As, however, a fall of roof no longer establishes liability—though it establishes a *prima facie* case—more attention must be given to the question of systematic support[19]. Section 49 itself is not automatically broken, any more than s. 48, by the fact that the roof collapses: *McDerment v National Coal Board* 1973 SLT (Notes) 60.

By s. 49(1) systematic support for the roof and sides must be provided

19 The rules as to systematic support become clearer if one forms a picture of a typical 'longwall' working in a coal mine. This consists of a long face of coal (part of a seam perhaps several feet thick lying between strata of rock) which has been exposed by previous working. The face is approached by roads at right angles to it, one at each end ('main gate' and 'tail gate'): i.e. there are two parallel roads—there must be two means of access to the workings—and the coal face runs across between the two roadheads. The roadheads move forward by degrees as the coal is removed and the coal face moves forward. We have, then, this method of working at the coal face though it has become more and more mechanised and the following description is now old-fashioned. The seam is undercut to a considerable depth by machinery: holing props or 'sprags' (wedges) are at once inserted to hold the coal up until it is about to be moved. A little way back from the face, just behind the miner, is the conveyor belt into which the coal is loaded, and which runs along the length of the face back to the roadhead. All this area (which may be only 3 feet or so high) is supported by props and bars at regular intervals. Immediately behind may be a row or rows of 'chocks' (square piles of flat timber) which give more solid support than props or bars but leave little space for movement. More commonly nowadays there are mechanical chocks with hydraulically-powered legs and rams. Behind these again (in the whole area between the roads from which the coal has been extracted and which is known as the 'waste') the roof is supported by 'packs' of rubble inside walls of stone or timber. As coal is worked the whole area with its supports advances. The movement has to take place systematically, i.e. props, chocks and packs have to be withdrawn in the correct order so that adjacent support remains. Withdrawal is therefore constantly taking place. Props are withdrawn from a safe distance by a device which includes a chain fixed at the end to the foot of an 'anchor' prop and at the other end to the top of the prop to be withdrawn. Sometimes the roof of the waste is allowed to 'cave' in or subside gently by removing the packs farthest back from the face. The practice is then to start with the inside packs and work back to the road. Care has to be taken that subsidence in the waste does not affect the security of the road, and the supports at the edge of the waste may have to be strengthened. As the roadhead itself is ripped, it has to be supported in three places. It has to be supported underneath, where it has been undercut (the edge or corner of this cutting is the 'ripping lip'); also at the face above the lip, which may be shored up by supports placed diagonally as on a shaky building; and at the newly exposed roof above. Further back, the roadway has strong permanent supports often including arched girders. This is broadly the traditional method, but the use of machinery has led to the adoption of 'powered' (i.e. hydraulic) supports with a special head which presses against the roof, and capable of being moved forward under hydraulic power. With a cantilever bar towards the face, the base of the prop can be farther back from the face and allow more room for the machinery. As the machinery progresses along the face, the conveyor and the rows of props are moved forward by degrees towards the face ready for the next journey. Under full mechanisation a rotating cutter directly fills the coal on to the conveyor.

and maintained at the following places in mines of coal, shale or fireclay[20].

(a) places where any mineral is worked (which has much the same meaning as 'working place', near the face at any rate, in s. 48: *Venn v National Coal Board* [1967] 2 QB 557, [1967] 1 All ER 149);

(b) roadheads;

(c) road junctions where vehicles or a conveyor run;

(d) lengths of road where persons work (unless the work is short or occasional).

The detailed method of support—i.e. the type of support used, distances apart, etc.—is prescribed by regulations; but it necessarily differs from mine to mine, according to the width of seam, fragility of the strata, extent of faulting, and method of work (especially where machines are used). So, subject to minimum general standards, it is prescribed by special 'Support Rules' in each mine: see ss. 49(5), 54. Under s. 49(5) the system must be 'consistent with the proper control of movement of the strata'. This means such control as will result in stability in the ordinary course: *Venn v National Coal Board* [1967] 2 QB 557, [1967] 1 All ER 149 (supports set irregularly and unevenly not sufficient). No materials are to be used for support except those provided by the owners, and 'a sufficient supply of suitable materials for support' must be 'at all times readily available' (s. 51(1), (3)). This does not mean that everything must be on the spot at the coal face: it is enough that there is a system for making things available when required: *Hills v National Coal Board* (1972) 13 KIR 486. A bent girder is not necessarily unsuitable material: *Grimstead v National Coal Board* [1965] 3 All ER 446, [1965] 1 WLR 1252.

The support regulations

Systematic support is now regulated by the Coal and Other Mines (Support) Regulations 1966 (S.I. No. 881, amended by S.I. 1974 No. 1075 to introduce the metric system), which differ from earlier regulations in providing for modern methods of support by hydraulic props with cantilever bars in fully mechanised mining, a matter formerly

20 None of the rules as to systematic support applies to stratified ironstone mines.

covered by conditions of exemption. The regulations apply to mines of coal, shale and fireclay (reg. 5)—but not ironstone. Exemptions may be granted.

Part III. Manner of setting supports
'Arch girders' (the strongest support, used on the more permanent parts of the mine, such as roads) must be set on a proper foundation, tight to roof and sides, and linked with their neighbours for stability (reg. 10). 'Props' (used at the coal face and roadheads) must be securely set on a proper foundation i.e. if the floor is not firm, they should be pushed through to solid rock, or rested on a lid; persons responsible for setting props must replace any which get broken or become unstable, or report to the person in charge if unable to do so[1]. The person in charge must take 'reasonable steps' to replace defective supports (reg. 6)[2]. For powered props—reg. 16(5), (6)—the position is a little different, as any defect has to be reported to the person in charge, who must arrange repair, replacement and substitute support. With certain exceptions (e.g. props under wooden bars, hydraulic props, spreading anti-friction heads), props require lids both for tight fit and to spread the stress (reg. 7). 'Chocks' (built foursquare out of pieces of wood behind the props) are to be built on a firm foundation out of flat timber and tight to the roof (reg. 8). 'Packs' (the last support left in the waste before it is left to cave in) are to be roof tight and (where built by hand or hand tools) with walls on a proper foundation and filled with debris (reg. 9).

Part IV. Systematic support at faces and roadheads
Where arch girders are used at roadheads, the intervals must not exceed 4 feet (reg. 15). Places at faces and roadheads which require systematic support are defined as follows (reg. 11, 2) viz. the roadhead within certain distances and the whole 'face working' roughly back to the front line of packs or last row of supports whichever is furthest (3.7 metres back from the face if support is not systematically withdrawn). By

1   A prop on a wooden block was held not to be on 'a proper foundation': *McDerment v National Coal Board* 1973 SLT (Notes) 60.
2   This does not impose a continuing absolute obligation to keep the prop secure, since the regulation itself provides for replacement of props broken or dislodged; *Mazs v National Coal Board* 1958 SLT 43. Under reg. 6 (2), any person responsible for setting props who actually sees the state of the prop must replace it forthwith; apart from this, the duty of the person in charge is limited to 'reasonable steps'.

regs. 12 and 13, rows of props have to be set at specified minimum intervals between rows and props in each row and at a minimum distance from the face. Where armoured conveyors are used (which normally means all-metal conveyors into which coal is loaded automatically, and which are moved forward without dismantling) only approved types of props can be used, presumably hydraulic ones, except where an irregular floor or roof makes them ineffective: reg. 12(4), (5). The intervals allowed where no one works in front of the conveyor (except briefly or occasionally) are set out in reg. 12(2), and there may be a gap of up to 2 m. between front prop and face (a 'prop-free' face allowing room for machinery), but when a person does go in front there must be a temporary support or cantilever bar within 0.9 m. (reg. 18). Where work in front is more than short or occasional, the minimum intervals are different, and the nearest prop must be 0.9 m. from the face (reg. 12(3)). Where an armoured conveyor is not used, the intervals are in reg. 13, again with a minimum of 0.9 m. from the face. By reg. 14, systematic support must include bars (or girders) at regular intervals, each supported by at least two props, but bars are not required at roadheads with arch girders, or at working faces where no machinery at all is used. Regulations 12–14 do not apply to 'powered supports' (those advanced and set under power, normally hydraulic) which are governed by regulation 16, but must be an 'approved' type where armoured conveyors are used, and are not to be used where persons work on the face side of the conveyor except briefly or occasionally. Under both reg. 16 and reg. 12, where a coal-cutting machine cuts to a depth over 0.4 m., supports must be set sufficient for the new exposure, before the machine approaches within 27 m.; and supports must be moved up behind a coal-cutting machine, except for 18 m. behind: regs. 12(6) and (7), 16(7) and (8). Where the roof of a roadhead or other advancing place is ripped, bars or other support must be provided as near as practicable to the ripping lip to support the adjacent roof, the newly exposed roof must be supported at once, as must the face of the ripping, and the length to be ripped at any stage must be limited to enable the roof behind to be secure: reg. 17. Temporary advance props are required for a newly exposed roof while filling or other work is done before the permanent supports are advanced: reg. 18. During holing at a working face—except where armoured conveyors are used and persons are only briefly or occasionally in front—holing-props, sprags or other supports must be set at maximum intervals of 1.8 m. until the mineral holed is about to be taken down (reg. 19)[3]. Holing supports may be impracticable under reg. 19 if the coal is too soft: *Morris v National Coal Board* [1963] 3 All ER 644, [1963] 1 WLR 1382. Supports and props may be moved temporarily (or setting postponed) to allow the movement or access of machinery (reg. 20) provided that continued support is provided, e.g. by the use of longer bars.

Part V. Miscellaneous

Where a fall of roof or side occurs and displaces supports at a place where any person has to work or pass, the exposed roof or side must be dressed and secured by supports before any debris is cleared, other than is necessary to set the supports (reg. 21). The setting of the system of packs to control caving-in of the waste is regulated by reg. 22. Where the system of work at the coal face involves withdrawing supports from the waste which is left behind as work progresses, supports must be set and maintained so that the caving in of the roof of the waste does not spread to the face working (this is a free rendering of reg. 23). Support rules at each mine must include diagrams to make the system clear (reg. 24).

Personal duties of miners themselves and of deputies in relation to support

Under reg. 5 of the Coal and other Mines (General Duties and Conduct) Regulations 1956 (S.I. No. 1762), every person engaged at a working face, or in ripping or repairing a road, or in setting or withdrawing supports, must make a careful examination of the place at the start of work and at suitable intervals, especially where any shot has been fired: where there are several men together and one of them is definitely in charge, it is sufficient for him to make the examination. Under the Support Regulations already summarised, it is the duty of the individual miner concerned to set props securely, replace any which are broken or unstable, and build chocks and packs properly and tightly

---

3   Under the 1956 regulations there was no 'holing' where the coal was cut by shearing machine, so as to require support. 'Holing' was said to refer to bringing down the face by shotfiring: *Hughes v National Coal Board* (1972) 12 KIR 419 (man stepped over conveyor to clear loose coal, unsupported roof in front of conveyor fell). The new regulation deals expressly with cases where there is an armoured conveyor.

(regs. 6 to 10). By s. 49(6) of the Act, a miner is also allowed to set additional supports if considered necessary. By s. 80, it is the duty of every miner to deal with or to report any danger which comes to his knowledge. By s. 51(3), he must withdraw if there is no material available for supports. Duties of this kind do not, of course, mean that the whole duty of support passes to the workman: *Caulfield v P. W. Pickup Ltd* [1941] 2 All ER 510; but a breach of duty by the workman may amount to contributory negligence which will reduce the damages.

Deputies, in carrying out inspections of their districts, are specially required to ensure that the Support Rules have been complied with and that all necessary additional supports are set (s. 53).

Method of withdrawing supports

Section 52(1) provides as follows:

> 'No person shall withdraw support from the roof or sides of any place in a mine otherwise than by a method or device by which he does so from a position of safety[4].'

Where the system in the mine is to withdraw supports (set up under 'Support Rules') from the waste or the wall adjoining the waste, s. 52(2) directs that no person is to withdraw the supports except in accordance with a system to be specified in the Rules[5].

The form of wording in this section—'No person shall'—is not to be read merely as a duty imposed upon the workmen: it is a duty resting upon the employers not to allow an unsafe method to be used; see *MacLaughlan v National Coal Board* 1953 SLT (Notes) 31 (decided under s. 49 of the Act of 1911). It has also been decided that the scope of the corresponding section previously in force was wide enough to give protection against the risk of a splinter flying from a metallic prop

---

4   I.e. 'A position where one is reasonably entitled to regard support as secure': *Venn v National Coal Board* [1967] 2 QB 557, [1967] 1 All ER 149 at 159.
5   Such a system may involve, for example, that when packs (built up out of rubble) are to be removed from the 'waste' where the coal has been worked, the packs must be removed in a definite order, e.g. the inside ones first, so that the workmen can work under a roof still supported by the outer packs. Props may be removed by a device which includes a chain operated from a short distance away, anchored at one end to the foot of an anchor prop and at the other end to the top of the prop to be withdrawn.

removed by an unsafe method—the use of a sledgehammer—as distinct from the risk of a fall of roof: *Paterson v National Coal Board* 1953 SLT (Notes) 57.

3 Shafts and entrances to workings

An unsafe shaft, like an unsafe roof, might give rise to an action at common law, subject to negligence being proved or inferred: *Brydon v Stewart* (1855) 2 Macq 30[6].

By s. 30(1) of the Mines and Quarries Act 1954:

'Every mine shaft and staple-pit shall, save in so far as the natural conditions of the strata through which it passes render it unnecessary . . . be made secure, and kept secure.'

It is a defence in a prosecution—but not, it seems, in a civil action—to show that the insecure place was not in use and was not the site of shaft-driving operations: s. 30(1), proviso. Security includes danger from things in the airspace of shafts, such as scaffolding and falling materials: *Coll v Cementation Co Ltd and National Coal Board* 1963 SLT 105. By s. 30(2), the same requirements extend to an 'unwalkable outlet' at a mine, i.e. an outlet from the mine which is too steep to 'walk up with reasonable convenience': see s. 182(1). A shaft is defined, by s. 182(1), as a shaft of which the top 'is, or is intended to be, at the surface'; and a staple-pit includes a 'winze' (a ventilating shaft between two levels)[7].

By s. 31, the surface entrance to a mine shaft and all other entrances to it, and all entrances to a staple-pit, must be provided with an enclosure or barrier to prevent persons from accidentally falling down the shaft or coming into contact with a moving part of the winding apparatus. This also applies to the superstructure of the shaft, and to disused shafts, except at a mine which has been abandoned or not worked for twelve months (such mines have to be fenced under s. 151). The enclosure or barrier is not to be removed or opened except as

6 See p. 9, *ante*.
7 A staple-pit is a shaft which does not come out on the surface, but at an underground level. The definition makes it clear that such shafts are included though not used for the movement of men or material. Of course a ventilating shaft may be an escape route.

necessary for the proper use of the shaft or for doing work upon it: see s. 31(2). The object of s. 31 is to protect against falls from the entrance down the shaft; it has no application where a person falls from the cage after entering it: *Rodgers v National Coal Board* [1966] 3 All ER 124, [1966] 1 WLR 1559.

By reg. 8 of the Mines (Safety of Exit) Regulations 1988—replacing s. 33 of the Mines and Quarries Act—there must be a barrier or enclosure to prevent access to any part of the mine where it is not for the time being safe to work, or pass through.

Second shaft in all mines

The Mines (Safety of Exit) Regulations 1988 (S.I. No. 1729) replaced various sections in the Mines and Quarries Act concerning safe exit from the mine and from the various underground workings. They came into force on 1 April 1989 for coal mines (including stratified ironstone, shale and fireclay) and for all *new* mines from that date; but do not apply to existing miscellaneous mines until 1 April 1994. Regulation 9 (which relates to ventilation) is also postponed to that date, even for coal mines.

Subject to these qualifications and exceptions—where existing rules will for the time being apply—the regulations apply underground at all types of mine: but the main requirements (regs. 3, 5, 7) that there shall be a minimum of two alternative shafts and two alternative ways of escape from every place of work do not apply to sinking a shaft or exploratory operations or the driving of an outlet other than a shaft if no more than 30 men are at risk: reg. 2. A shaft is defined to include a staple-pit, raise, winze or similar excavation sunk or in the course of being sunk: and the vertical continuation of the shaft above ground is deemed to be underground so as to bring it within the regulations: reg. 1(2).

By reg. 3(1), every mine must have at least two shafts, with two separate exits to the surface, and so situated that an accident to one shaft will not affect the other. If newly constructed after 1 April 1989, they must be at least 15 metres apart. By reg. 3(2) the manager must ensure that so far as reasonably practicable at least two exits are *kept available* when anyone is below ground. If, due to planned maintenance, one exit only is in use, only safety and maintenance staff are allowed below ground: reg. 3(6). There must also be a plan for emergencies when only one exit becomes available, and in that event no one must be underground except safety and maintenance men and workers staying to finish their shift; an emergency has to be notified to the mines inspector who may require even safety and maintenance men to be withdrawn: reg. 3(3) to (5).

Two separate exits from every workplace

By reg. 7 of the 1988 regulations, the manager has to ensure that from 'every place where any person works' there are two different ways, each entirely separate and leading to different exits from the mine. These ways must be marked to show which shaft they lead to, and workers must be made familiar with both ways. Regulation 7(4) allows exceptions:

(a) (i) at a heading or other place where not more than nine persons work (with up to three more temporarily); (a)(ii) at a heading where not more than 18 work, if the working face is not wider than the approach;

(b) if separate exits are 'not reasonably practicable';

(c) where there are 'special' and 'suitable' arrangements for safe exit without relying on two escape routes.

Cross access between shafts

By reg. 5, there must be access (by road, ladder or stairway) from every landing on a shaft or outlet to an alternative exit.

Provision of winding apparatus

By s. 28(1), every shaft and unwalkable outlet provided as a means of ingress or egress, at a mine of coal, stratified ironstone, shale or fireclay, must be provided with apparatus for carrying persons between the surface and the various entrances to the workings. The apparatus must comply with requirements laid down in regulations. The regulations now in force are the Coal and other Mines (Shafts, Outlets and Roads)

Regulations, 1960 (S.I. No. 69 amended by S.I. 1968 No. 1037), Part III, regs. 6–19, and part XI, regs. 65–70[8].

Section 28(2) similarly requires permanent apparatus to be provided in the shafts and unwalkable outlets at mines other than those mentioned above: but this does not apply unless the distance from the top of the shaft or outlet to the lowest entrance exceeds 150 feet (45 metres)[9] and in any case exemptions may be granted in the case of mines within this subsection.

By s. 28(3), apparatus provided under both these subsections must 'be properly maintained, and, when not in use, kept constantly available for use'. This does not mean that workmen may go up and down whenever they please; they must conform to the rules of the mine: *Herd v Weardale Steel, Coal and Coke Co Ltd* [1915] AC 67.

Under reg. 4 of the Mines (Safety of Exit) Regulations 1988, auxiliary apparatus and equipment must be provided and kept available to enable those below ground to reach the surface, and the miners must be trained to use such equipment. Auxiliary equipment, unlike the normal winding machinery, may be gravity-operated.

The manager is also under a specific duty to ensure the safety 'so far as reasonably practicable' of anyone who is endangered when the winding apparatus is put out of use or breaks down, particularly those travelling in a cage at the time of a breakdown.

These requirements replace s. 29 of the Act and the Mines (Emergency Egress) Regulations 1973[10].

Miscellaneous dangers in shaft

Under reg. 81 of the Coal and other Mines (Shafts, Outlets and Roads)

8 The regulations provide (*inter alia*) for mechanically-operated apparatus where the vertical depth exceeds 150 feet, automatic precautions against overwinding, adequate brakes, an automatic indicator showing the position of each cage in the shaft, guides for the cage, regular maintenance of winding ropes, and covering the top of the cage where used for carrying persons; also regular examination and maintenance of both shaft and apparatus. 'Overwinding' means raising or lowering the cage too fast so that, for instance, it overturns at the top or lands at the bottom violently. The regulations replace 1956 regulations of a similar character. See further p. 508, *post*.
9 Substituted by S.I. 1976 No. 2063 unless shaft sunk before 1 February 1977.
10 Except regs. 5 and 6 of 1973, which are re-worded by the 1988 regulations and allow the use of gravity-operated apparatus when authorised by reg. 4 of 1988.

Regulations 1960 (S.I. No. 69), reasonable protection must be provided in every shaft and staple-pit to prevent injury by articles falling down the pit to persons loading cages at entrances.

Under reg. 82(1), no one is allowed to go into or across an uncovered space at the bottom of a shaft or staple-pit except for the purpose of working there; under reg. 82(2), no work is to be carried on in such a space while any cage is in motion, except in a shaft in the course of being sunk.

Shafts in the course of being sunk

Part XII of the Coal and other Mines (Shafts, Outlets and Roads) Regulations 1960 (S.I. No. 69), contains a number of special requirements in the case of shafts and staple-pits which are being sunk. (These are in addition to the normal requirement that the place must be examined both before the work starts and subsequently at intervals by the deputy or person in charge, like any other part of the mine: Coal and other Mines (Managers and Officials) Regulations 1956 (S.I. No. 1758), reg. 32). Under Part XII, all gear by which any cradle, platform or other thing is suspended in a shaft must be thoroughly examined every 24 hours (reg. 71(1)). The shaft must be thoroughly examined before each shift in which 'walling or tubbing' is carried out, i.e. the work of lining the shaft (reg. 71(2)). Cradles and platforms must be securely fixed to prevent swinging, and fencing or other protection must be provided where there is a risk of falling off (reg. 72). The top of any shaft or staple-pit must be kept free of things which might fall into it (reg. 73). No engine which is not fixed must be used for raising and lowering (reg. 74). There is a special code of signals to control raising and lowering in shafts being sunk (reg. 75). When anything is to be raised or lowered in a kibble (which includes—by reg. 2—any form of bucket, basket or barrel), the deputy, banksman or other person authorised to transmit signals must ensure that it is properly loaded and in particular that it is free from dangerous projections: and objects lowered otherwise than in a kibble must be safely slung (reg. 76). Riding on the edge of a kibble is forbidden (reg. 77). The engineman when raising or lowering a kibble must stop it at a check point, short of the point it has to reach, until he receives a further signal (reg. 78). If a shaft is sunk through water-bearing strata, ladders must be provided as a means of escape in emergency (reg. 79).

The general effect of the amendments made by the 1960

regulations—replacing those of 1956—was to extend most of these requirements to staple-pits as well as to shafts opening on the surface.

4 Ventilation

By s. 55(1) it is the duty of the manager of every mine:

> 'to take such steps as are necessary for securing that there is constantly produced in all parts of the mine below ground ventilation adequate for the following purposes namely,—
> (a) diluting gases that are inflammable or noxious so as to render them harmless and removing them; and
> (b) providing air containing a sufficiency of oxygen.'

The words 'necessary' and 'securing' make it clear that this is an absolute obligation which applies to all mines: and although the duty is imposed on the manager, the owners are responsible in a civil action under s. 159.

Without prejudice to the generality of s. 55(1), there must not be a greater percentage of carbon dioxide in the air (by volume) than 1¼ per cent, and the air must contain at least 19 per cent of oxygen: see s. 55(2). By s. 55(3), the manager must aim, as far as possible, at reasonable working conditions as regards temperature, humidity and freedom from dust. By s. 55(4), ventilation is not required in a part of the mine which is stopped up, or in any waste: but by s. 56 precautions must be taken (by ventilation or other means) to prevent any dangerous emission of noxious or inflammable gas from any waste which has not been stopped off or stowed up[11].

The obligation under the section is to keep up a continuous flow of ventilation, even on Sundays or other days when no work is in progress: *Knowles v Dickinson* (1860) 2 E & E 705. The main purpose is to disperse 'inflammable' gases, such as firedamp, with the consequent risk of explosion. But a further object is to keep down other 'noxious' gases, i.e. poisonous ones such as carbon monoxide.

By s. 55(5), if the ventilation breaks down in any part of the mine,

---

11 Since there is no duty to ventilate the waste itself, there was no liability when miners went into the waste to smoke and caused an explosion of firedamp gas: *Kirby v National Coal Board* 1959 SLT 7.

access must be restricted, and no one may enter except for restoring the ventilation or in case of emergency.

Subsidiary sections enable an inspector to require improvement of the ventilation (s. 57) and require the provision of barometers and other instruments in coal mines (s. 60).

Section 58 requires mechanical apparatus to be maintained at the surface, capable of giving full ventilation to the mine, unless adequate ventilation is produced wholly by natural means, or unless the mine is exempted by regulations. The apparatus must be capable of reversing the direction of the air-flow. The use of a fire to assist ventilation in a mine is forbidden: so, too, is the use of compressed air to dilute gas, except with the consent of an inspector.

Where (in a mine of coal, stratified ironstone, shale or fireclay) there are two passages, of which one has been constructed after the commencement of the Act, it is not permissible to use one of the passages as an intake airway and the other as a return airway if there is any appreciable leakage of air between them: see s. 59. This does not apply to parts of passages within a reasonable distance (usually 150 metres)[12] from the working face served by the airway.

Under reg. 9 of the Mines (Safety of Exit) Regulations 1988—which does not come into force until 1 April 1994 and then applies to all mines—not more than 50 persons may be employed in any part of a mine (excluding those moving on a change of shift) unless there are *two* separate airways such that fire and smoke cannot pass from one to the other, or *one* fire-resistant intake free as far as reasonably practicable from fire risk.

In the meantime s. 70 of the Act remains in force. Under this section, where workings in a coal mine are served by only one intake airway and there might be difficulty in getting out in case of fire, not more than 100 men are to be employed below ground unless the airway is reasonably free from risk.

The Coal and other Mines (Ventilation) Regulations 1956 (S.I. No. 1764 as amended by S.I. 1960 No. 1116 and S.I. 1966 No. 1139) contain further detailed provisions with regard to keeping intake airways free from firedamp (inflammable gas), making regular checks of firedamp content in the air, and detection of firedamp by various means

12 Substituted by S.I. No. 2063 which also substitutes metric measurements in the Ventilation Regulations.

(including issue of safety lamps or other firedamp detectors to the miners), management of fans and other machinery for ventilation, and the prevention of air leakages by means of air-locks, ventilation doors and ventilation sheets. The ventilation doors and sheets are to prevent leakage of air between the intake and return airways which would short-circuit the ventilation flow.

The Coal Mines (Firedamp Drainage) Regulations 1960 (S.I. No. 1015), regulate the precautions to be taken when firedamp gas is collected in an undiluted state by means of boreholes and pipes to be removed from the mine. The precautions laid down are intended to prevent accidental ignition of the gas and also contamination of the ventilation system of the mine[13].

5 Lighting, safety lamps and contraband

Under s. 61, there is a general duty to provide 'suitable and sufficient lighting' in all parts of a mine (above or below ground) where 'persons work or normally pass', taking into account the lamps normally carried by those persons. This does not apply in places below ground where 'artificial lighting is inadvisable for reasons of safety'. All lighting installations must be 'properly maintained'. The use of electricity is now controlled by the Electricity at Work Regulations 1989 (section 13 of this Chapter).

There are certain mines (conveniently known as 'safety-lamp mines') where, under s. 62, no lamps or lights must be used except 'permitted lights', i.e. as defined in s. 182(1), locked safety lamps or other means of lighting which comply with reg. 19(2)(a) to (d) of the Electricity at Work Regulations 1989.

Section 62 applies to the following classes of mines:

(i) *coal* mines (in the strict sense) opened on or after the date of commencement of the Act;

(ii) mines of any kind which were 'safety-lamp' mines—i.e. where safety lamps were obligatory in the absence of a special exemption—under the previous Acts;

13 Amended by the Mines (Miscellaneous Amendments) Regulations 1983 (S.I. No. 1130) to allow the use of E.E.C. approved equipment.

(iii) mines of any kind where locked safety lamps were in fact in
use—except as a temporary precaution—immediately before
the commencement of the Act;

(iv) other mines opened before the Act and any mine opened after
it, where an explosion or fire has been caused by inflammable
gas naturally present, or locked safety lamps have been
introduced except as a temporary measure.

Once a mine has become a safety-lamp mine, it does not lose its
character unless special exemption is given by the inspector under
s. 62(5).

The construction and use of safety lamps is controlled by regulations
(s. 63) and safety lamps must not be used unless provided by the owner
and of a type which conforms to reg. 19 of the Electricity at Work
Regulations 1989 (s. 64)[14]. It is an offence under s. 65 for a person to
damage, destroy or lose a safety lamp issued to him, or to tamper with it.

It is also an offence to take or to have below ground, in a safety-lamp
mine or a safety-lamp part of a mine, matches, lighters or smoking
materials (s. 66) or any article capable of producing an unprotected
flame or spark (s. 67)[15]. In *Kirby v National Coal Board* 1959 SLT 7 the
employers were held not liable for an explosion caused by employees
who were smoking contrary to the Act of 1911. It is to be noted,
however, that the smoking took place in a part of the waste where the
men had gone for a quiet smoke, and the act was clearly outside the
course of their employment.

14 The Coal and other Mines (Safety Lamps and Lighting) Regulations 1956 (S.I.
No. 1765) regulate the inspection and maintenance of safety lamps and other
firedamp detectors (regs. 2 to 6); the careful handling of safety lamps by the
miners (regs. 7 to 11); method of re-lighting safety lamps underground (regs. 12 to
16); the lighting of entrances to shafts and other important points in the mine,
especially where vehicles are handled (reg. 17); the use of electricity for lighting,
subject to safeguards, in well-ventilated places at a safe distance from the
working face (regs. 18 to 20); the keeping of emergency lamps in places having
general lighting (regs. 21 and 22); and the whitening of the roof and sides at the
places where general lighting is required by reg. 17 (reg. 23). Regulations 4, 18,
18A and 19 were superseded and revoked by the Electricity at Work Regulations.
Section 63 is also repealed as being superseded by the general power to make
regulations under the Health and Safety at Work Act 1974.

15 See also the Mines (Manner of Search for Smoking Materials) Order 1956 (S.I.
No. 2016).

6 Protection against dust

By s. 74(1), it is the duty of the manager of every mine:

> 'to ensure that, in connection with the getting, dressing and
> transporting of minerals below ground in the mine, the giving off of—
> (a) any dust that is inflammable; and
> (b) dust of such character and in such quantity as to be likely to
>   be injurious to the persons employed;
> is minimised.'

This section is clearly directed against two distinct dangers: dust which
may catch fire or explode, and dust which may cause injury or disease
such as silicosis.

Section 74(2) deals with cases where an operation or process, either
below ground or on the surface, gives rise to inflammable or injurious
dust, and requires that measures shall be taken (a) to intercept the dust
as near as possible to its point of origin; (b) to trap or disperse dust which
is not intercepted; (c) to clean up or render harmless accumulations of
dust which cannot be prevented.

The Coal Mines (Precautions against Inflammable Dust) Order 1956
(S.I. No. 1769 as amended by S.I. 1960 No. 1738 and S.I. 1977 No.
913) contains a number of additional requirements which apply only to
coal mines in a strict sense. Coal dust from the screens on the surface
must be kept from entering downcast shafts (regs. 2 and 3) unless the
mine is naturally wet throughout (reg. 1). On underground roads,
except within 30 feet of the working face or in anthracite workings, a
proportion of incombustible matter, such as fine dust, must be added to
the coal dust (regs. 4–9). (There is an approved method of consolidating
dust on the floor of a road by adding stone dust and calcium chloride and
spraying the mixture.) Where a vehicle carries a load of coal dust along a
road where there is electrical apparatus, the material must be enclosed
to prevent the dust being thrown into the air if the vehicle is upset
(reg. 10). By reg. 10A (added by the amending regulations) barriers of
stone dust may have to be set up against the spread of fire in certain
areas. The areas in question are those which include a length of road
where coal conveyors are in use and which are exposed to the spread of
flame by ignition of gas or coal dust at the coal face or some other point
of danger.

The Coal Mines (Respirable Dust) Regulations 1975 (S.I. No.

1433), in force from 30 September 1975 (now amended by S.I. 1978 No. 807), require periodical samples to be taken in areas underground where harmful dust is likely to be present, also dust suppression schemes and medical checks of persons at risk. The risk visualised by these regulations is, of course, damage to the lungs resulting in silicosis.

7 Roads and transport

The main regulation on roads in a mine is now reg. 6 of the Mines (Safety of Exit) Regulations 1988. Under this, the manager must ensure that every road which persons walk along to or from a place of work must be (i) suitably constructed and maintained as a walkway, (ii) safe to walk along and normally not less than 1.7 metres high and (iii) kept free from obstructions. Exemptions may be granted under reg. 10, subject to conditions to ensure safety.

Under the previous legislation—s. 34 of the Act, repealed by the regulations—a damaged tram, which was being taken along a haulage road and was involved in a collision, was held not to be an 'obstruction' under similar wording of the Act of 1911, collisions being more properly a matter for traffic rules: *Alexander v Tredegar Iron and Coal Co Ltd* [1945] AC 286, [1945] 2 All ER 275. In general, things which form part of the equipment of the mine (and are in the place where they would normally be) are not 'obstructions' though out of use at the time: *Cook v National Coal Board* [1961] 3 All ER 220 (wire rope above rails, used for hauling tubs on other shifts); nor is material stacked in a reasonable position ready for use: *Jennings v National Coal Board* [1983] ICR 636. There is no 'obstruction' where a man is impeded in crossing from one side of a road to another as distinct from passing along: *Kerr v National Coal Board* 1968 SLT 49. As to the road itself, the essential requirement is a clear safe passage along some part of it. Given this, the old section was not contravened by unsatisfactory conditions in another part, such as uneven ballast between rails (*Wilson v National Coal Board* 1966 SLT 221) or a narrow and obstructed space on the opposite side of a conveyor (*Kerr v National Coal Board, supra*). Where a transformer in a temporary position partly blocked the way, it was not an obstruction, but because the narrow passage left was uneven, with rails, cross-pieces and a sharp drop at the side, it was 'unsafe to tread' in breach of the section: *Malone v National Coal Board* 1972 SLT (Notes) 55.

Like s. 48 (security of the roof), reg. 6 specifically makes the manager responsible and if he has taken all possible measures to inspect and clear the road there is no liability, for instance if there is a stone on the road within one hour after inspection: *Connolly v National Coal Board* 1979 SLT 51.

References to height in s. 34 were held to relate only to the structure of the road itself and had nothing to do with the lay-out of conveyors or other equipments which may reduce height at particular points: *Lister v National Coal Board* [1970] 1 QB 228, [1969] 3 All ER 1077.

Section 35 and the Coal and other Mines (Height of Travelling Roads) Regulations 1956, which formerly regulated height, were repealed by the 1988 regulations.

Regulation 6 also requires that all ladderways or stairways shall be so constructed, installed and maintained that they can be used safely.

Section 36(1) contains a general prohibition of the running of vehicles or conveyors in any length or road where they or their loads (or their haulage ropes, if any) may rub against the roof or sides or supports or anything else. Section 36(2) affords some special defences which apply only in a criminal prosecution.

In general, the safe operation of vehicles and conveyors in a mine is, under s. 37, to be governed by special 'Transport Rules' made by the manager of the mine. It is the duty of the manager to see that the rules are complied with. This means that the rules must not only be publicised but effectively enforced, by penalties where necessary: so where there were merely trivial and occasional fines for riding on conveyors, and the practice continued, there was a breach of the section: *Storey v National Coal Board* [1983] 1 All ER 375, [1983] ICR 156. The rules must, in particular, specify the standard height and width of roads used by vehicles and conveyors, specify maximum loads and speeds of vehicles, and restrict or control the carriage of persons on vehicles or conveyors.

Section 39 applies to every length of road used for the running of vehicles (unless moved by hand or by animals)[16]. The use of these roads by persons on foot is forbidden, except when the movement of the vehicles is 'specially stopped' to allow such use: and where the road is used by not fewer than ten persons at the beginning and end of their shift,

16 I.e. it applies—like s. 43 of the Act of 1911—where vehicles are moved by mechanical power or by gravity.

periods must be fixed when the traffic is stopped to allow them to move in safety. By s. 39(3), certain 'authorised persons' are allowed to enter roads when vehicles are running, e.g. officials of the mine and persons engaged in running the vehicles or in repair or inspections. But no person must accompany, on foot, a vehicle moved by rope haulage apparatus, unless authorised by regulations or by the manager (in writing): instructions by a subordinate official will not do: *Puller v National Coal Board* 1969 SLT (Notes) 62. A further requirement for roads where vehicles run is that (subject to exemptions) refuge holes shall be provided at intervals and places prescribed by regulations, and shall be kept free from obstruction: see s. 40.

By s. 41, automatic safety devices must be provided to prevent accidents caused by vehicles running away: and precautions must be taken to protect persons at work against such accidents. This means vehicles running away by accident, and does not include trams running free as intended: *Jones v National Coal Board* [1965] 1 All ER 221. The section does not impose an absolute duty to provide brakes which will never fail: *Brandreth v John G. Stein & Co Ltd* 1966 SLT (Notes) 87. (Faulty construction or maintenance may be a breach of s. 81.)

Further rules for safe movement in transport roads are contained in Part X (regs. 57–64) of the Coal and other Mines (Shafts, Outlets and Roads) Regulations 1960 (S.I. No. 69). Regulation 57 grants an exemption from s. 39(1)(a)—and therefore allows persons to move on foot along transport roads—in the following cases:

    (a) where there is a continuous clearance of 2 feet between vehicles and the road side and the maximum speed does not exceed 10 m.p.h.;

    (b) on certain roads of low gradient in mines opened before the Act of 1911 came into force (1 July 1912) where maximum speed does not exceed 3 m.p.h.

A clearance of 2 feet must be maintained between vehicles and road side at coupling places (reg. 58). Refuge holes must be at intervals varying from 30 feet to 60 feet (or, in the case of roads used by locomotives, 60 to 300 feet)[17] according to the gradient and curve of the road and the

17 Details of clearances required at the sides of roads where conveyors or rail vehicles run are set out in the Coal Mines (Clearances in Transport Roads) Regulations 1959 (S.I. No. 1217). As might be expected, they vary according to the type of traffic in use, are wider at boarding points and working places, and may be narrower in unsettled ground near the working face. Metric measurements are substituted by S.I. 1976 No. 2063 which does not, however, substitute new measurements in the Shafts Outlets and Roads Regulations 1960 (*supra*).

nature and speed of the traffic. By regs. 60–62, a train for carrying persons must be under the charge of a competent person; and no person is allowed to ride on a haulage rope, or to ride on vehicles moving faster than 3 m.p.h. for the purpose of attaching or detaching them from the rope. Except on a low gradient, a person moving a vehicle by hand down a slope is forbidden by reg. 63 to go in front; and movement by hand down a slope is forbidden unless the vehicle can be properly controlled from behind. By reg. 64, sprags, stop-blocks and similar contrivances must be provided to prevent accidents from runaway vehicles, especially on inclines, and means must be provided in certain cases to prevent accidental disconnection of vehicles from trains on which persons are carried. Regulation 64 does not affect the more general requirements of s. 41 of the Act.

8 Operation of winding and haulage apparatus[18]

Where winding or rope haulage apparatus is provided to carry persons, either through a mine shaft or elsewhere in a mine, and is operated by mechanical power or by gravity, it must be operated by a competent male person of at least 22 years of age (s. 42(1)). A person appointed under this section must be in constant attendance so long as persons are employed below ground at a mine where access is gained through a shaft or unwalkable outlet by means of winding or rope haulage apparatus; and in the case of a coal mine such a person is not to be on duty for more than eight hours in a day. Where persons are not carried in winding or haulage apparatus, the apparatus must still, under s. 43, be operated by

18 In the earlier days of mining there were many serious accidents involving pit cages: *Bartonshill Coal Co v Reid* (1858) 3 Macq 266 where the cage was upset at the top due to overwinding, is an example. The regulations are now strictly complied with, and accidents are rare. When they do occur, they are serious, and there is likely to be a public enquiry, after which liability may well be admitted. It is therefore unlikely that questions of liability in this type of case will come before the courts. In an accident in 1957, 28 men were injured when a cage landed too fast, and the Inspector drew attention to the increased risks with bigger mines and deeper shafts. Yet in 1973 at Markham Colliery, Derbyshire, 18 men were killed when the cage plunged to the pit bottom; and there have been disasters in the South African gold mines.

a competent male person not less than 21 (where the apparatus runs in a shaft or staple-pit) or 18 (in other cases): similarly, under s. 44, a conveyor operated along a working face in a mine must be worked by a competent male person of not less than 18.

There must be a proper signalling system in all shafts and unwalkable outlets (s. 45) extending to the surface exits and underground entrances at all stages, unless the maximum distance involved is 50 feet or less; and a signalling system is also required (s. 46) for lengths of road exceeding 90 feet where rope haulage apparatus or conveyors may be operated.

The Coal and other Mines (Shafts, Outlets and Roads) Regulations 1960 (S.I. No. 69, amended by S.I. 1968 No. 1037) contain extensive requirements for the construction, maintenance and operation of winding and rope haulage apparatus in shafts and unwalkable outlets. ('Winding apparatus' is used in shafts, 'rope haulage apparatus' in unwalkable outlets.) In general, where the depth exceeds 150 feet and more than 30 persons are employed underground, the apparatus must be mechanically operated (reg. 6) from a fixed engine (reg. 7) separated from any other engine or apparatus. Where the apparatus comprises a drum shaft, this must be bored longitudinally at the centre unless its diameter is less than 10 inches (reg. 8) and provided with flanges and other devices to prevent the rope slipping off (reg. 10). There must be brakes on the drum, an indicator showing the position of each cage, and a locking device on the drum capable of holding a loaded cage in position (reg. 9); and keps for supporting a cage must be provided and used at the top landing, are optional at the bottom landing but must not be used in between (reg. 15). There must be automatic protection against overwinding, i.e. against the cage descending too fast and striking the bottom violently or ascending too fast with the risk of overturning (reg. 11); the automatic contrivance must be engaged before anyone is permitted to enter the cage (reg. 53); and there must be gear to detach a cage and hold it stationary in case of too rapid ascent (reg. 16). Cages for carrying persons—except in the sinking, inspection or repair of a shaft or outlet—must be covered on top and at the two sides and have gates at the two ends (reg. 12). Winding ropes must not be spliced ropes, nor must they be used for more than three and a half years (reg. 17) and there are special provisions for capping and re-capping of winding ropes (Part XI, regs. 65–70). Fixed guides must be provided for the cage in a shaft where the depth exceeds 150 feet, and this applies also to the cage or kibble in a shaft being sunk, as soon as the depth exceeds 300 feet (reg. 14). All the apparatus must be inspected regularly (reg. 19).

The hours of employment of a winding engineman at a shaft are restricted by Part V (regs. 25–30). The operation of the cages in a shaft is in general under the control of a 'banksman' at the top (reg. 31 (1)) who is authorised to give signals to the engineman for movement of the cage in accordance with a signalling code in Part VI of the regulations (regs. 32–39). At underground entrances from which persons have to be raised, an 'onsetter' is in attendance who is authorised to give signals in co-operation with the banksman (reg. 31(2)).

Similar provisions applied from 1 February 1961 to staple-pits with winding apparatus (Part VII, regs. 40–45, and reg. 84). A 'travelling onsetter' may take the place of the normal 'banksman' and 'onsetter' in a staple-pit (reg. 42).

There is also a signalling code in Part VIII (regs. 46–50) for outlets and roads, which includes, in this context, unwalkable outlets.

In both shafts and unwalkable outlets, the engineman must remain at the controls when the apparatus is in motion or where anyone is believed to be in a cage, carriage or kibble (reg. 20). He must not act on indistinct or doubtful signals (reg. 24). He must inspect the apparatus, see that it is cleaned and oiled, carry out periodical checks by raising and lowering it without passengers (regs. 21, 22) and must not allow unauthorised persons to operate it (reg. 23).

Other miscellaneous rules are as follows: minerals and other loads must not, in general, be carried through a shaft or unwalkable outlet while persons are being carried through it, unless the shaft or outlet is divided by a substantial partition (reg. 51); the maximum number of persons to be carried in a cage or carriage (or kibble, where a shaft is being sunk) must be fixed, and displayed on a notice (reg. 52). A cage must not be signalled away till the gates are closed (reg. 54) and barriers at an entrance must not be removed until the cage is stationary opposite the entrance (reg. 55). Where a cage or carriage having more than one deck is to be raised, the top deck must be loaded first (reg. 56).

Most of these provisions are concerned with the safety of persons carried as passengers. Regulation 13 requires cages carrying vehicles to be provided with catches to prevent them falling out and reg. 81 requires protection for persons loading cages at underground entrances from articles falling down the shaft or staple-pit.

9 Use of engines and locomotives below ground

By s. 83, internal combustion engines, steam boilers or locomotives cannot be used below ground except as authorised by regulations or with the consent of an inspector.

Where such consent has been given (see reg. 34), the use of 'mechanically propelled vehicles running on rails and constructed or used for hauling other vehicles' is regulated by the Coal and other Mines (Locomotives) Regulations 1956 (S.I. No. 1771). They must be constructed as far as possible of non-inflammable material (inflammable components must have a metallic covering) and in such a manner that flames, sparks and hot exhaust gases are not emitted (reg. 3). They must have brakes, headlights, portable lamp, means of audible warning, speedometer and fire extinguisher (reg. 4). There are regulations for rails, track and clearances (regs. 6–8) and running is not allowed on a gradient exceeding 1:15 (reg. 9). In a safety-lamp mine or part of a mine, there must be special checks of firedamp content (regs. 11–16). Locomotives must be driven by authorised persons only (reg. 17) and not left unattended unless immobilised (reg. 18). A red light must be attached at the back of the locomotive or train (reg. 22). There are detailed provisions as to the filling of diesel engines, the handling of fuel oil and the control of exhaust gases (regs. 25–31) and as to charging the batteries of locomotives which run on storage batteries (regs. 32–33).

There are a number of variations in the regulations in their application to ironstone, shale and fireclay mines.

10 Construction and fencing of machinery and apparatus

Section 81 of the Mines and Quarries Act 1954 contains an important and sweeping requirement—more comprehensive than anything in the Factories Act—that all machinery and apparatus shall be of good construction. Section 81 (1) is as follows:

'All parts and working gear, whether fixed or moveable, including the anchoring or fixing appliances, of all machinery and apparatus used as, or forming, part of the equipment of a mine, and all foundations in or to which any such appliances are anchored or fixed shall be of good construction, suitable material, adequate strength and free from patent defect, and shall be properly maintained.'[19]

'Apparatus' is a wide expression: 'parts . . . of [the] apparatus' may include, e.g. a single rope or chain; the section was applied in Scotland to a foot-rail forming part of the installation in pit-head baths: *Sproat v National Coal Board* 1970 SLT (Notes) 31. But in other cases the line has been drawn, rightly or wrongly, at an ordinary timber pit prop or metal girder, as distinct from special types of supports with some mechanism: *Grimstead v National Coal Board* [1965] 3 All ER 446, [1965] 1 WLR 1252. A drill and mash used to break up a mine tunnel (*Samson v National Coal Board* 1980 SLT (Notes) 57) and a wooden trestle used as a working platform (*Harkin v National Coal Board* 1981 SLT 37) were likewise held to be outside the section. It is difficult to see why the section should be interpreted so restrictively: the wording is quite wide enough to cover any equipment in use in the mine. In *Brebner v British Coal Corpn* 1988 SLT 736, the Scottish appeal court emphatically took the view that the section is wide enough to include all equipment used for the purposes of the mine: the fact that it is fixed to the mine does not exclude it, and it does not need to be apparatus of a mechanical nature. Accordingly a broken rung in a fixed ladder contravened the section.

On the other hand, there was no breach of s. 81 when a man walked into a part of a gangway which was too low, presumably because there was nothing wrong with the gangway itself: *Taylor v National Coal Board* [1986] CLY 36.

The word 'maintained' in s. 81(1) is not limited to 'maintenance' in the sense of 'regular servicing'; it imposes an absolute obligation to keep the apparatus in the condition required by the subsection: *Hamilton v National Coal Board* [1960] AC 633, [1960] 1 All ER 76 (winch tilted owing to insecure anchorage); *Sanderson v National Coal Board* [1961] 2 QB 244 (hooks of conveyor belt came unfastened and caught plaintiff's leg: held to be a breach of s. 81(1) as soon as the hooks became

---

19 For a discussion of some of these expressions as used in the Factories Act, see Chapter 10.

fastened). Where a pump cover flew up as a man unfastened it for repair, it was held that the duty under s. 81 is owed to the repairer as well as anyone else, and the old decisions under s. 49 of 1911 (support of roof) excluding liability to repairers do not apply: *Chalmers v National Coal Board* 1963 SLT 358.

Sanderson v National Coal Board, supra, also decided that a 'patent defect' is one which can be seen, though nobody may be there to see it.

The Coal and other Mines (Mechanics and Electricians) Regulations 1965 (S.I. No. 1559) make the mechanical and the electrical engineer (or the mechanic and the electrician in charge) responsible for the installation, maintenance in safe condition, and systematic examination and testing of all the mechanical and electrical apparatus in the mine, and systematic maintenance schedules must be established: see regs. 5, 6, 9 and 10.

Fencing of machinery is regulated by s. 82, which is another new section in the sense that it is worded quite differently from its predecessor, s. 55 of the Act of 1911. Section 82 provides as follows:

'(1) Subject to the provisions of this section, every flywheel and every other dangerous exposed part of the machinery used as, or forming, part of the equipment of a mine shall be securely fenced; and where means of fencing are prescribed with regard to any such part of any such machinery as aforesaid, the fencing provided in pursuance of the foregoing provisions of this subsection for that part shall be provided by those means.

(2) It shall be the duty of the manager of every mine to ensure that fencing provided in pursuance of the foregoing subsection is properly maintained and is kept in position while the parts required to be fenced are in motion or in use, except where such parts are exposed for an examination or adjustment which it is necessary to carry out while they are in motion or use and all such conditions as may be prescribed are complied with.'

The case-law under ss. 12–14 of the Factories Act (see Chapter 11) will in many cases be relevant to this new section, which, however, expressly meets some of the difficulties which have arisen under the Factories Act. For instance, it is clear under s. 82 that if special fencing is prescribed, it is sufficient for all purposes.

Under the previous section, a barrier round the entire machine was not in itself sufficient fencing; there must be a fence precluding access to the dangerous parts: *Coltness Iron Co Ltd v Sharp* [1938] AC 90, [1937] 3 All ER 593, per Lords Thankerton and Macmillan. This still seems to be correct. However, where a mechanic entered a 'cage' guard round a conveyor drum and was trapped between the belt and drum, it was held that it is not necessary to fence each interior part separately: but the action succeeded (subject to 50 per cent contributory negligence) because the cage guard was not firmly fixed and could easily be moved aside: *Ewing v National Coal Board* 1987 SLT 414.

The removal of the fence for adjustments necessary while the machinery is in motion is expressly dealt with by s. 82(2), and such removal is permitted provided that all conditions prescribed are complied with[20].

The Act of 1911, like the present section, used the expression 'exposed and dangerous' in specifying the parts of machinery which must be fenced. It was nevertheless held that the test is the same as for deciding whether parts are dangerous under the Factories Act: carelessness and unwise actions must be taken into account, and it is enough if the parts will be 'exposed' to a workman acting carelessly: see *Carey v Ocean Coal Co Ltd* [1938] 1 KB 365, [1937] 4 All ER 219 and *Smithwick v National Coal Board* [1950] 2 KB 335, both cases where a workman gained access to rollers in haulage plant to find out what had gone wrong, in one case by crawling along a belt and in the other case by putting his head through a narrow aperture. In *Rodgers v London Brick Co Ltd* (1970) 8 KIR 843 where by a freak accident a man's foot got into a slowly-closing gap between the body of a tractor and a bar at the one spot where it could trap him, the parts were held not to be dangerous because they were slow-moving and in ordinary working no one would be near them. Danger arose only from an unexpected slip in hauling the tractor out of a clay-pit.

In *Boryk v National Coal Board* 1959 SLT (Notes) 3 it was held (on the old s. 55) that there might be liability under the fencing requirements where a piece of wood caught in a coal-cutting machine was thrown out and struck the pursuer. It has since been decided by the House of Lords that the fencing sections of the Factories Acts give no protection where objects are thrown out of a machine: *Close v Steel Co of Wales Ltd* [1962] AC 367. The decision turned largely, however, on words in the Factories Acts which indicated that they gave protection

20 Thus cases like *Coltness Iron Co Ltd v Sharp* [1938] AC 90, [1937] 3 All ER 593 (defence of 'not reasonably practicable' established where fence removed for temporary repairs) are now obsolete on this point.

against contact only, and not against materials in motion in the machine: so it may be that it does not apply to machinery subject to the Mines and Quarries Act.

It should be noted that ss. 81 and 82—like all sections of the Act, except where the contrary is stated, or some limitation is implied by the context—apply both above and below ground.

11 Cranes and other lifting machinery

By s. 85, every crane, crab or winch used as, or forming, part of the equipment of the mine must have its safe working load marked upon it: in the case of a jib crane so constructed that the safe working load may be varied by raising or lowering the jib, there must be an automatic indicator of the safe load, or a table showing the safe load at various positions of the jib.

The safe working load must not be exceeded, except for the purpose of a test.

Section 85 does not apply to winding or rope haulage apparatus, and may be excluded by regulations in other cases.

Cranes and similar apparatus are also, of course, within s. 81 (safe construction and maintenance).

12 Steam and compressed air apparatus

By s. 84(1):

'All apparatus used as, or forming, part of the equipment of a mine, being apparatus which contains or produces air, gas or steam at a pressure greater than atmospheric pressure shall be so constructed, installed, maintained and used as to obviate any risk from fire, bursting, explosion or collapse or the production of noxious gases.'

This, like s. 81—which must also apply to the air, gas and steam apparatus—is a remarkably wide and strict obligation. It includes, *inter alia*, steam boilers—the only apparatus of this kind mentioned in the Act of 1911—and compressed air apparatus.

Under s. 83, a steam boiler cannot be used below ground except with the consent of an inspector.

The Coal and other Mines (Steam Boilers) Regulations 1956 (S.I. No. 1772) require every steam boiler to have a suitable safety valve, steam gauge and water gauge (reg. 2). These gauges show the steam pressure and the height of the water in the boiler. The water gauge must have a protective covering or guard (reg. 3). The maximum permitted pressure is to be marked on the steam gauge (reg. 5) and must not be exceeded (reg. 7(d)). The safety-valve setting must not be altered without authority (reg. 4) and the boiler is under the charge of a specially appointed 'boiler-minder' (regs. 6, 7).

13 Electricity

The Electricity at Work Regulations 1989 apply to mines and quarries as well as to other places of work. The general part of these regulations is summarised in Chapter 16, section 2. But there are in addition some further regulations (17–28) which apply to mines alone. The defence under s. 157 (not reasonably practicable to avoid breach) is specifically excluded for these regulations, so there is an absolute duty to comply with them: reg. 28.

There are in the first place some regulations which apply to all mines. If electricity is supplied below ground from a power source at the surface, there must be switchgear at the surface to enable it to be cut off in case of danger, and adequate arrangements must be made to man and operate this, including means of communication from underground: reg. 22.

Equipment using oil for (i) cooling, (ii) insulation or (iii) arc suppression is prohibited underground: reg. 23. Where storage batteries are used underground they must 'so far as reasonably practicable' be 'used, stored, charged and transferred in a safe manner': reg. 27. In certain places where there is a risk of electric shock (notably near a generator, or arc welding) there must be a notice about first-aid treatment for shock: reg. 25. Plans of the electrical circuits must be kept in the mines office and at switchboards, except for low voltage systems such as signalling apparatus: reg. 24. There are special restrictions on filming underground, which involve giving prior notice to the Health and Safety Executive and avoidance of shotfiring, and of accumulations of dust which could be sparked off by the filming apparatus: reg. 17 and Sch.1.

In addition there are a number of regulations which apply only to firedamp mines where methane gas could be ignited by even a tiny spark from telephone apparatus. The mines inspector must be notified and given details before electricity is introduced underground at all: reg. 18. If firedamp concentration exceeds 1.25 per cent in any area, electricity must be cut off at once or equipment otherwise made safe: reg. 20. There must be plans of firedamp zones, and in those zones only officially approved types of apparatus (which are designed to be free from sparking risks) are to be used: reg. 19. In particular safety lamps, gas detectors, and telephone and other signalling apparatus must not be taken below ground unless it is of an approved type under the regulations (or was approved and taken into use under the previous regulations): reg. 21; and locomotives or vehicles using batteries as a power source are likewise forbidden unless they are of an approved type: reg. 26.

14 Water-logged strata and other external dangers to the workings

In addition to the risks of explosion and fire in a mine, there is also a serious danger of flooding: and, as was shown by the Knockshinnoch Castle Colliery disaster in 1951, there is sometimes a possibility that the working will collapse under the weight of water-logged peat or similar strata[1]. It is for this reason, among others, that the Act of 1954 attaches so much importance to plans of the workings, and to the duty of the manager to watch the movement of the strata.

The duties of the owner and manager are now set out in the Mines (Precautions against Inrushes) Regulations 1979 (S.I. No. 318), which replaced, as from 9 April 1979, ss. 75 to 77 of the 1954 Act and earlier regulations of 1956.

First of all, under reg. 3, the manager has a general duty to prevent any inrush into any working of the mine of either—

---

1   See *M'Fadyean v Stewart* 1951 JC 164.

(a) gas from disused workings (which includes abandoned shafts and boreholes) whether they are mine workings or not (they could, for instance, be old canal or waterworks tunnels); or

(b) water, or material that flows or is likely to flow when wet (whatever the source).

Next, under reg. 4, both the owner and manager are required to ensure that they have full information about disused workings in the vicinity, water-bearing strata and peat or other deposits liable to flow when wet.

In the particular case of workings carried on or proposed near the sea, a lake or river, or any other body of surface water, the owner and manager are both required by reg. 5 to 'ascertain'—which means find out for 'certain'—the total thickness of strata between the workings and the surface water, and satisfy themselves that the strata are sufficiently reliable to prevent an inrush of water.

Special precautions are required by reg. 6 before workings are carried out within 45 metres (measured in any direction) from the surface or water-bearing strata or peat or other substances likely to flow if wet, or disused workings (except mine workings). In the case of mine workings, the distance is reduced to 37 metres. In all these cases the manager must acquire sufficient information to form an opinion on whether an inrush may occur in the absence of precautionary measures. If he thinks it will not, he must notify the Mines Inspector 30 days in advance of working the place, but will still have to notify him again if there are signs of danger in the course of working. If he thinks special precautions are required, he must prepare a scheme for safe procedure to prevent inrushes, send a copy to the Inspector and workers' representatives 30 days in advance of working, and ensure that the scheme is complied with until working is completed.

15 The use of explosives: shotfiring

Section 69 (which has been repealed under the Health and Safety at Work Act 1974 as being no longer necessary) gave power to make regulations for the use of explosives, and the regulations made under the section continue in force. The main regulations for *coal* mines (in the strict sense) are now contained in the Coal Mines (Explosives) Regulations 1961 (S.I. No. 854).

This code of regulations has grown more and more detailed, and it is not possible here to do more than draw attention to salient points.

First of all, under Part III, there are certain mines and parts of mines where only certain 'permitted explosives' and 'permitted detonators' of a type and description approved by the Minister may be used[2]. This restriction applies, broadly, to every mine of which any part is a 'safety-lamp' mine, also to dry and dusty parts of mines; i.e. to places where firedamp gas or dry coal dust is likely to be present (reg. 7). More particularly it applies to roads which are main intake airways or used for transporting coal in conveyors or vehicles and places within 30 feet, except roadheads (reg. 7(3)).

Part V (regs. 13–20) regulates storage, issue and supply of explosives and detonators. All explosives taken below ground must be in cartridge form (reg. 18). Except where there is an approved scheme (under reg. 20) for conveyance in bulk, cartridges must be taken underground in closed canisters containing not more than 5 lbs. (reg. 19); explosives must be stored above ground in a special explosives store or issue station (reg. 13), except that under an approved scheme supplies for 24 hours may be kept at safe reserve points (reg. 20). The issue of detonators is under the personal control of the manager (reg. 15) and when taken underground these must be in a locked case where the leads are insulated safely from any external metal; delay detonators must be kept in a separate case from ordinary detonators and marked to show the period of delay (reg. 16). The shotfirer must keep personal control of his detonators, take one from the case only when required for immediate use, and return unused detonators (reg. 17).

By Part IV, shotfiring is to be done only by specially appointed persons[3], who must be given special authority if they are to use delay detonators or fire by the 'infusion method' or in a round of more than six shots (reg. 8). Shotfirers cannot be appointed to handle 'permitted explosives' unless they hold certain certificates of competence (reg. 10).

---

2 These are of a type which minimises the risk of combustion in the presence of firedamp or dry dust. They are made safe by adding to the explosive a chemical substance (an inert salt) which cools the flame without reducing the force of the blast. Some types are 'sheathed', i.e. completely surrounded by a sheath of the cooling agent. The most improved types incorporate the cooling agent with the explosives and are 'sheathed' in addition.

3 In the past deputies were generally the shotfirers, and often they still are. The present tendency is to separate the duties entirely, leaving the deputy free to concentrate on safety.

Under Part VI, equipment which must be provided (reg. 21) for each shotfirer includes a wooden tool for charging and stemming shot holes, a scraper for cleaning them out, and (in a 'safety-lamp' mine) a break detector (this is to detect breaks or cracks in the coal exceeding 1/8 inch, as shot holes having such breaks across them must not be charged or fired (reg. 52)). Where shotfiring is electrical, apparatus or cable not provided by the owner of the mine must not be used (reg. 22). Electrical firing (by means of approved apparatus) is compulsory in 'permitted explosives' mines (reg. 23). A shotfirer in charge of electrical apparatus must keep the detachable handle or key in his own possession and attach it to the apparatus only when about to fire (reg. 24). (In *Alford v National Coal Board* [1952] 1 All ER 754 there was held to be no breach of a somewhat similar regulation when an unauthorised person fired a shot by using a pair of pliers as an improvised handle.) Defective apparatus must be put out of use (reg. 25) and regular maintenance and testing is required for all electrical apparatus (reg. 26).

Part VII (regs. 28–43) controls shotfiring in all types of mines. While persons other than the shotfirer may drill holes, put in the shots (without over-charging or using force), and stem the hole with clay or other non-inflammable material, the shotfirer must personally supervise the charging and ensure that it is correctly done (reg. 30). Before firing the shot he must fix the danger zone likely to be created (reg. 41), and also give due warning (reg. 40) to persons in adjacent places to which the shot may blow through. He must clear the danger zone, post sentries and set up a danger sign, ensure that all persons have withdrawn from the place or taken shelter, and take shelter himself (reg. 41). Clearing the danger zone is an absolute duty and cannot be excused as impracticable if the shotfirer has failed to make a personal check: *Jayne v National Coal Board* [1963] 2 All ER 220. If the shotfirer is firing 'a round of shots'[4] electrically, he must first test the circuit for continuity, after everyone has withdrawn or taken shelter (regs. 37(7), 64). By reg. 42 all persons must keep out of the danger zone, even after the shot, until allowed to enter by the shotfirer or one of the sentries posted. The shotfirer must make a full examination for safety after each shot before allowing work to continue (reg. 43).

4   This means—reg. 2(1)—a number of shots fired in a single operation; the shots (when fired electrically) may go off simultaneously, or, with the aid of delay detonators, in succession.

Part IX contains further requirements where 'permitted explosives' are used. The shotfirer is not allowed to fire more than a certain number of shots in each hour and in each shift (regs. 45, 46): and the charging must be done by him personally or by a qualified shotfirer under his close supervision, and stemming must be done or supervised by the shotfirer (reg. 53). In 'safety-lamp' mines there must be a test for inflammable gas, and no firing is allowed if the percentage of this exceeds 1¼ per cent, or if gas shows up on a lowered safety lamp (regs. 47, 50); there is also a prohibition on firing in the 'waste' (i.e. where coal has been extracted) or in the roof between the waste and the face of a longwall working (reg. 49, new in 1961). The 1961 regulations—Part VIII, reg. 44—relax regs. 17(2) and 19(3) in the case of cross-measure drifts (which may be described, broadly, as ways driven through stone, as distinct from coal seams, for providing access between different seams or parts of the mine) so as to allow the shotfirer to prepare charges in advance at an authorised place before he is ready to fire them.

Part X (regs. 56–60) applies to the sinking of shafts. Explosives must not be taken into shafts or staple-pits until required for immediate use (reg. 56); but (notwithstanding the ordinary rules in regs. 16 and 19 as to closed canisters) a shotfirer may take a primer cartridge fitted with a detonator into a shaft or staple-pit provided that it is in a thick felt bag or other receptacle suitable for protecting it against shock (reg. 57). Shotfiring must be by means of an electric detonator (reg. 58). The firing cable must not be coupled to the detonator until all men are in a position to enter the kibble and the engineman is ready to raise it; and the firing apparatus must not be coupled to the cable until everyone is in a position of safety (reg. 59). No person may enter the shaft after a shot has been fired until the deputy has inspected it (reg. 60).

Part XI (regs. 61–72) deals with misfires and (*inter alia*) forbids any person to approach the shot until 30 minutes after the misfire (if a fuse was used) or five minutes (if the firing was electrical) (reg. 62). This regulation applies even if the shotfirer honestly believes that he did not ignite the fuse (or produce an electrical spark): *Costello v R. Addie & Sons Collieries Ltd* [1922] 1 AC 164.

Under the present regulations, the decision in *Coltness Iron Co Ltd v Baillie* [1922] 1 AC 170, that a workman other than a shotfirer who approaches within the forbidden time commits no breach of the regulations, is no longer applicable.

The remedial action to be taken in the event of a misfire is *not* to attempt to remove the explosive charge (reg. 69) but either (i) to remove the stemming from the hole with water and insert a new primer and fresh stemming or (ii) to dislodge the shot by firing another from an adjacent hole (reg. 63) in which case a search must be made for the dislodged shot (reg. 71).

Where there is multiple shotfiring, the precautions in case of a misfire are more elaborate (regs. 64–68).

The Coal Mines (Cardox and Hydrox) Regulations 1956 (S.I. No. 1942) regulate the use of cardox and hydrox shells for blasting[5]. These require special precautions in the filling of shells (normally above ground) and the provisions as to firing and taking shelter are broadly similar to those in the general regulations.

Similar regulations for blasting by compressed air (qualified persons only to fire, special key required for control valve, tests for firedamp, protection of persons in danger zone) are contained in the Coal Mines (Compressed Air Blasting Shells) Regulations 1960 (S.I. No. 1114).

Shotfiring in stratified ironstone, shale and fireclay mines is governed by the Stratified Ironstone, Shale and Fireclay Mines (Explosives) Regulations 1956 (S.I. No. 1943). In broad outline and in many details these regulations are similar to the coal mines regulations, but with less emphasis on 'permitted explosives'[6] and a less detailed procedure for misfires.

16 Structures and means of access on the surface

Section 86 of the Act contains the following wide and general direction:

> 'All buildings and structures on the surface of a mine shall be kept in safe condition.'

---

5 These are not strictly explosives but means of blasting by the expansion of gas from a liquid form. A cardox shell, for example, is a tube containing liquid carbon dioxide which, by an induced rise in temperature, is turned into gas of great expansive force.

6 Presumably because firedamp does not occur in most of these mines. The 'misfire' procedure is largely left to be regulated by local 'schemes'.

Section 87(1), which is evidently based on s. 26(1) of the Factories Act, 1937, provides as follows:

'There shall be provided and maintained safe means of access to every place in or on a building or structure on the surface of a mine, being a place at which any person has at any time to work.'

Section 87(2) similarly follows s. 26(2) of the Factories Act:

'Where a person is to work at any such place as aforesaid from which he will be liable to fall a distance of more than two metres[7], then, unless the place is one which affords secure foothold and, where necessary, secure handhold, means shall be provided by fencing or otherwise for ensuring his safety.'

Some of the decisions under the Factories Act (now s. 29 of 1961, see Chapter 10, section 3 (v)) may be material in applying these sections: but the wording of s. 87 is different in material respects. For instance, it does not apply to a place which is neither 'in' nor 'on' a building or structure; and it is an absolute obligation, breach of which cannot be excused in a civil action except upon proof of 'impracticability' under s. 157.

17 Inspections and the withdrawal of workmen

The provisions as to inspections of the mine are of fundamental importance, far more so than the requirements in the Factories Act for the inspection of machinery, because workmen must not be allowed in a part of the mine which has not been inspected for safety.

Section 12(1) of the Act of 1954 authorises the making of regulations for inspections by the deputies. The regulations now in force are the Coal and other Mines (Managers and Officials) Regulations 1956 (S.I. No. 1758) as varied slightly in 1961 (S.I. 1961 No. 817), Parts IV to VI, regs. 9–32.

Under Part IV of these regulations, each working district in the mine is in the charge of a deputy, who is responsible for all operations in the

---

7 Substituted by The Mines and Quarries (Metrication) Regulations 1976 (S.I. No. 2063).

district and for carrying out the statutory inspections; in general, he must not perform other duties, but is allowed to do shotfiring (reg. 9). Each district must be inspected by a deputy within two hours before the commencement of a shift, and particular attention must be paid to gas, ventilation, the roof and sides, and general safety: the workmen must not go beyond appointed 'meeting places' until the district has been pronounced safe (regs. 12–14). There must also be inspections during shifts, at intervals of not less than four hours (reg. 15). The deputy is also responsible for seeing that machinery, apparatus and other equipment are maintained in a safe condition (reg. 19).

Part V contains similar requirements for inspections of places such as roads and airways which are not in a deputy's district. (As to shafts and outlets, see reg. 18 of the Coal and other Mines (Shafts, Outlets and Roads) Regulations 1960, which require inspections at intervals of seven days, or of 24 hours if the shaft is in the course of being sunk; and reg. 20, as amended in 1988, which requires the deputy to familiarise himself with both escape routes from each working place and check their full length every two months.)

Part VI applies the provisions as to inspections by deputies to shafts in the course of being sunk: in particular the pre-shift inspection must be completed before the workmen are lowered—reg. 32(3)—there must be a fresh inspection after shotfiring—reg. 32(4)—and the deputy must not be raised to the surface until the last of the workmen on his shift leave and the deputy of the next shift (if any) has been lowered (reg. 32(6)).

Under s. 79 of the Act of 1954, if inflammable gas is excessive in any part of the mine, or any other danger is found to be present, the person in charge of the area must withdraw all persons employed there. Persons who have been withdrawn must not be allowed to return—except for restoring safety in the area or for saving life—until the area is free from excessive gas and every other danger. Gas is normally excessive if the percentage amounts to 2 per cent in a safety-lamp mine, or 1¼ per cent in other cases.

In *Sneddon v Summerlee Iron Co Ltd* 1947 SC 555 at 567 Lord President Cooper said:

> 'Danger for the purposes of this section must not be tested by the opinion of uninstructed laymen. . . . Mining is notoriously a dangerous trade . . . from which some element of danger is rarely absent. The matter must be judged with the aid of evidence based on skilled experience of the industry.'

Accordingly there was no duty to withdraw the men because of the presence of ice in the shaft, when there was no reason to expect a dangerous fall.

If men are withdrawn under s. 79 and re-admitted for fire-fighting, they must be withdrawn again if inflammable gas again reaches the dangerous percentage under s. 79(5): *Wing v Pickering* [1925] 2 KB 777.

Under reg. 11 of the Coal and other Mines (Fire and Rescue) Regulations 1956 (S.I. No. 1768), which applies only to safety-lamp mines, workmen may have to be withdrawn (from places which may be affected) if there is any smoke or other sign indicating that fire has broken out.

18 Miscellaneous: fire, rescue, medical examinations and training

Where workings in a coal mine are served by a single intake airway so that, if a fire occurred in that airway, the workmen might have difficulty in withdrawing, not more than 100 persons are to be employed below ground at any time (s. 70). This does not apply where the airway is reasonably free from fire risk. From 1 April 1994 this section is repealed and replaced by reg. 9 of the Mines (Safety of Exit) Regulations 1988 which will apply to every kind of mine. This prohibits the employment of more than 50 persons below ground unless there are *two* airways, or a single airway which is *fire resistant*: see section 4 of this Chapter.

Other sections provide for first aid (s. 91) and for means of escape (such as emergency exits) from places such as motor-rooms or other confined spaces where there is a special risk such as fire, steam or gas (s. 73)[8].

The Health and Safety at Work Act 1974, s. 78, extends the Fire Precautions Act 1971 to all places of work, which of course includes mines and quarries. Buildings on the surface of a mine, with certain exceptions, require a fire certificate from the Health and Safety

---

8 See also the Coal and other Mines (Fire and Rescue) Regulations 1956 (S.I. No. 1768) as amended by S.I. 1980 No. 942 and as to reg. 4 (portable apparatus) by the Electricity at Work Regulations; the Coal and other Mines (First Aid) Regulations 1962 (S.I. No. 1423) which, with s. 91(1), are now restricted to mines of coal, stratified ironstone, shale and fireclay; and the Health and Safety (First Aid) Regulations 1981 (S.I. No. 917) which apply to other mines and quarries (and places of work generally).

Executive. (For details of the Fire Precautions Act as applied, see Chapter 10, section 10.)

Medical examination of young persons entering the industry is compulsory[9]. No persons are to be employed in handling loads likely to cause injury to them (s. 93).[9a]

Section 88 restricts the employment of untrained persons until they are competent to work without supervision; this includes persons temporarily assigned to work which is different from their normal duties: *Thompson v National Coal Board* [1982] ICR 15: they must first be given adequate training and supervision. A breach of requirements under this section or associated regulations—e.g. by allowing a trainee to work at the coal face contrary to the directions of the training officer—will give rise to an action for damages; but the trainee himself, if knowingly disobedient, must share in the blame: *Laszczyk v National Coal Board* [1954] 3 All ER 205. The duty to train does not require instruction to be given on safety precautions in carrying out a practice which is itself forbidden: *England v Cleveland Potash Ltd* (1986) Times, 1 July (disposing of explosives by burning them). Under s. 124(2) of the Act and the Mines (Employment of Young Persons) (Appointed Day) Order 1957 (S.I. No. 1093) a young male person under 16 cannot be employed below ground except to receive instruction as authorised by regulations. The Coal Mines (Training) Regulations 1967 (S.I. No. 82) forbid, in general, the employment of any person below ground until he has received specified training in general safety and (if employed in coal production) on the working techniques. Persons under 16 are not allowed below ground at all except for training in a district set aside for that purpose. No one is allowed on the mechanical or electrical staff (except at a small mine with fewer than 30 persons) unless he has specified qualifications or training. A special training officer must be appointed.

19 Duties of workers

Statutory duties are imposed upon the workers by various sections. Breach of these duties may constitute contributory negligence or

---

9   See the Coal and other Mines (Medical Examinations) Regulations 1964 (S.I. No. 209) made under s. 92 of the Act which was repealed under the 1974 Act as no longer necessary.

9a As amended by the Employment Act 1989 which abolishes all restrictions on women and relaxes those on young persons.

(under s. 159) render the owners liable for injuries caused to other persons.

Thus (apart from the provisions mentioned at p. 502 with regard to safety lamps and contraband) it is an offence to tamper with a safety appliance (s. 90(2)) or, 'negligently or wilfully', either to do an act likely to endanger safety, or omit to do something necessary for safety (s. 90(1)). Under s. 89 it is an offence to disobey transport or support rules, or any order or direction[10] given with a view to safety: for example to jump off a man-rider: *McMullen v National Coal Board* [1982] ICR 148 (accident entirely own fault); or to ride on a conveyor: *Storey v National Coal Board* [1983] 1 All ER 375, [1983] ICR 156 (75 per cent contributory negligence). Also, under s. 80, where any danger comes to the knowledge of a person employed (other than an official) he must deal with it himself forthwith if it is within the scope of his normal duties, or, failing that, must make an immediate report to an official of the mine.

The Coal and other Mines (General Duties and Conduct) Regulations 1956 (S.I. No. 1762) contain a general code of behaviour for persons employed at a mine. They must obey safety instructions (reg. 2); enter the cage only when authorised, not interfere with the gates, and leave the cage only when it is stationary at a landing stage (reg. 3); travel only on authorised roads and keep out of unauthorised places, in particular engine houses (reg. 4); make a careful examination of the working place and leave it in safe condition (reg. 5)[11]; refrain from interfering with machinery (reg. 6) or wafting inflammable gas (reg. 7); and take their lamps with them when leaving their working place (reg. 8)[12]. Finally, by reg. 9, all persons at a mine (above or below ground) must behave in an orderly manner, must not be intoxicated and must not sleep below ground at all, or while in charge of any machinery or boiler at the surface[13].

---

10 Such a 'direction' may be quite informal, e.g. where the person in charge of a train said 'You had better come off': *Burns v M'Nicol* 1956 JC 47.
11 As to setting supports safely see the Coal and other Mines (Support) Regulations, pp. 493–494, *ante*.
12 Regulation 6(2) has been revoked—interfering with electrical apparatus now comes within the Electricity at Work Regulations.
13 Where a crowd of miners jumped off trams before they stopped and raced for the best place in the cage at the pit bottom, there was 'disorderly behaviour' in breach of reg. 9, but the employers were not liable because *volenti non fit injuria* applied; those who joined in accepted the risk: *Hugh v National Coal Board* 1972 SC 252.

20 Fencing of abandoned mines and quarries

If a mine has been abandoned, or has not been worked for a period of 12 months, it is the duty of the owner to erect fences or barriers, or block up the shafts or other entrances, for the protection of the public. If a quarry is near a highway or otherwise dangerous to the public, it must be fenced whether it is still being worked or not. Details of these requirements are given in s. 151. Under s. 20, plans of abandoned mines and mine workings must be preserved.

Under the old law the owner of a disused mine shaft ceased to be responsible when it was taken over for another purpose, such as a well: *Knuckey v Redruth Rural Council* [1904] 1 KB 382.

21 Safety of tips

The Mines and Quarries (Tips) Act 1969, like the provisions about abandoned mines and quarries, is intended to protect the public rather than the worker and was passed in consequence of the Aberfan disaster where a tip collapsed under the weight of rain and overwhelmed a school. There is a general duty under Part I to make and keep secure all tips at a mine or quarry still in operation, whether the tip itself is in active use or not (ss. 1, 2) and owners and manager must keep themselves informed (s. 3). Part II (ss. 11–36) contains provisions for making disused tips safe. The Mines and Quarries (Tips) Regulations 1971 (S.I. No. 1377) and the associated Mines and Quarries (Tipping Plans) Regulations 1971 (S.I. No. 1378) provide for drainage of tips, regular supervision by a competent person, notification and survey for suitability before a tip is taken into use (or fresh use after abandonment), plans showing underlying strata as well as surface features. Supervision and inspection are required for disused as well as active tips, and any abnormal or unusual feature must be reported.

22 Railway sidings at mines

See Chapter 20 for the regulations on this subject.

Chapter 18
Miscellaneous mines and quarries

1 Miscellaneous mines

Before the Mines and Quarries Act 1954 mines of coal, stratified ironstone, shale and fireclay were subject to the Coal Mines Act 1911 and all other mines were governed by the Metalliferous Mines Regulation Act 1872. The Metalliferous Mines Regulations 1938 were made under the authority of the Act of 1872, but in substance they replaced it and formed a complete and self-contained safety code, based in many respects upon the Coal Mines Act 1911.

The Mines and Quarries Act 1954 applies to all mines without exception. But there are many differences in practice between coal mines and other classes of mines. Other mines are usually on a smaller scale, less deep, and less dangerous. They may be approached by underground tunnels instead of by shafts, and will not require the same elaborate winding apparatus as a coal mine. They are less mechanized and have fewer officials: and the special dangers of coal mines—inflammable firedamp gas and coal dust and poisonous gases—are not usually encountered[1]. On the other hand, small mines have some special dangers of their own, such as the use of ladders or open skips to descend shafts[2].

---

1 Foul air, of course, occurs in all mines, so that a ventilation system is always necessary.
2 These remarks are, of course, limited to mines in the United Kingdom. Gold mines in South Africa are sometimes far deeper and are sunk through hard quartz rock so the technical problems are tremendous. Similar problems arise with large-scale open cast workings in Australia. In third world countries such things as copper and silver mines are appallingly dangerous.

In general, therefore, the requirements in coal mines and similar mines will continue, as they always have been, to be stricter than they are in other mines. The Act still puts mines of coal, stratified ironstone, shale and fireclay into a class of their own. Some sections of the Act are restricted to these mines, and so are most of the codes of regulations. The remaining mines are now grouped together (in the regulations which apply to them) as 'Miscellaneous Mines'.

Except where otherwise stated, however, all the safety requirements in the Act itself apply to mines of every class. In particular, all mines are subject to s. 48 (security of roof and sides), ss. 30–33 (shafts and entrances to workings), s. 28 (apparatus for shafts and unwalkable outlets)[3], ss. 55–58 (ventilation), ss. 61–65 (lighting, safety lamps and contraband), s. 74 (protection against dust), ss. 34–41 (roads and traffic), ss. 42–47 (operation of winding and rope haulage apparatus), s. 83 (engines and locomotives), ss. 81, 82 (construction and fencing of machinery), s. 85 (safe load of cranes), s. 84 (steam and compressed air apparatus), ss. 75–78 (water and other external dangers), s. 69 (explosives), ss. 86, 87 (structures on surface), s. 79 (inspections and withdrawal of workmen), and ss. 71–73, 91–93 and 88 (fire and rescue precautions, medical examinations, and training). Ss. 80, 89 and 90 (duties of workmen) and s. 151 (fencing of abandoned mines) also apply.

All these sections are summarised in the preceding chapter. (Some of them have been repealed in whole or part by regulations under the Health and Safety at Work Act 1974 as being no longer necessary in view of wider powers under that Act or new regulations.)

On the other hand, the following requirements are restricted to mines of coal, stratified ironstone, shale and fireclay, unless s. 49 and ss. 22–25 are expressly extended to other classes of mines by regulations:

Systematic support of roof and sides (s. 49). (This does not apply to ironstone mines.)

Provision of two shafts or outlets and two distinct exits from workings (ss. 22–25, 27).

Ventilation apparatus capable of reversing the direction of airflow (s. 58 (2)). (Restricted to coal mines.)

No communication allowed between intake and return airways (s. 59).

---

3 Winding or haulage apparatus is not required in miscellaneous mines unless the length of the shaft or outlet exceeds 45 metres and in any case exemptions may be granted (s. 28 (2)).

Fire precautions where there is only one intake airway (s. 70). (Restricted to coal mines.)

The Mines (Safety of Exit) Regulations 1988 (summarised in sections 2, 4 and 7 of Chapter 17) will in future require two separate shafts, two escape routes from every workplace, and (in some cases) two airways for ventilation. These will not come into force for existing 'miscellaneous' mines until 1 April 1994, but apply to new mines from 1 April 1989. The regulations will supersede ss. 22–25, 33–35 and 70 of the Act.

The Miscellaneous Mines Regulations

The Miscellaneous Mines Regulations 1956 (S.I. No. 1778), apply to all mines other than coal, stratified ironstone, shale and fireclay and came into force at the same time as the Act, i.e. 1 January 1957. These regulations, and also the Explosives Regulations which follow, have been amended by the Miscellaneous Mines (Metrication) Regulations 1983 (S.I. No. 994) to adapt them to the metric system.

Plans
Under Part II, plans must be kept of workings (reg. 2) and abandoned workings (reg. 3) where more than 12 persons are or have been employed below ground.

Inspections
Part III requires inspections of the ventilation, roof and sides and general safety of every working place and road in use by persons to be made during each mineral-getting shift (reg. 4(a)) and similar inspections of every walkable outlet and ladderway every day when mineral is got (reg. 4(b)); also inspections of shafts, staple-pits and unwalkable outlets every seven days (reg. 5), of means of ingress and egress not in ordinary use every three months and of airways every 30 days (reg. 6).

Shafts and outlets
Until 1994, when the Mines (Safety of Exit) Regulations 1988 come into force for existing mines as well as new ones, it is not obligatory under the Act to provide two shafts or outlets; but if there is only one shaft or outlet, in which winding or haulage apparatus is used, it must

have a special compartment provided with ladders or other means of egress, separated by a substantial partition from the part of the shaft where winding apparatus is used (reg. 7). A fixed ladder in use below ground must not be vertical or overhanging, but must be inclined at the most convenient angle in the space available (reg. 74(1)), there must be substantial platforms every ten metres and unless there are strong handholds the tops of the ladders must project at least 1 metre above each platform or landing (reg. 74(2)). The ladders in a shaft or outlet must be securely fastened to the lining or sides and each platform must be fenced (reg. 7(2)).

Disused shafts must not be entered until they have been tested for noxious gas (reg. 79).

Winding apparatus

Requirements for the construction and operation of winding apparatus in shafts (including staple-pits) and rope haulage apparatus in unwalkable outlets are similar to those in the coal mines regulations, but less strict. If the apparatus is mechanically operated—which does not appear to be obligatory in any case—there must be brakes, an indicator showing the position of cages, and devices to prevent the rope slipping off (reg. 8). Cages or carriages used for carrying persons must be covered at the top, closed at two sides and have gates at the ends (reg. 11), and the number of persons to be carried must be limited to a fixed maximum (reg. 12). In shafts over 45 metres deep (90 metres if being sunk) guides must be provided for the cage or kibble (reg. 9); keps are required to support cages at the top (reg. 10). There must be detaching gear in case of overwinding, but automatic protection against overwinding is not required unless the inspector gives special notice (reg. 14). In a cage or carriage used to carry vehicles, there must be means to prevent them falling out (reg. 13).

A banksman must be in attendance at a mine where persons are carried through a shaft whenever persons are about to be carried or more than 15 are below ground (reg. 15). Generally, movement through both shafts and outlets is controlled by signals (reg. 16) given by authorised persons only (reg. 17) who must not give the 'away' signal if more than the maximum number are carried or the gates are not shut (reg. 18). In general, loads are not allowed through a shaft or outlet while passengers are travelling through (reg. 19); and when a kibble is used where persons may be underneath, precautions are required against loose and projecting articles and against the kibble being unbalanced (reg. 20). The winding engineman must remain at the controls when the apparatus is in use or anyone is in a cage; he must examine the engine once every shift and must make a full test run of the empty cage before raising and lowering if winding has ceased for more than two hours before (reg. 21). Winding and haulage apparatus must be examined at regular intervals (regs. 39, 40) and there are special provisions as to ropes and cappings of ropes (regs. 41–50).

Haulage roads
Regulation 23 allows persons to travel on roads when vehicles are moving (notwithstanding s. 39 of the Act) if there is a 600 mm. clearance and speed is limited to 2.7 metres per second. Regulations 24–26 deal with the size and intervals of refuge holes, signals on roads, and the supply of sprags and other devices to hold vehicles on inclines.

Lighting, explosives, fire, floods etc.
General lighting must be provided at underground entrances to shafts and outlets and at adjacent sidings (reg. 27). Miners must carry their portable lamps with them (reg. 29) and in safety lamp mines the manager must ensure that safety lamps taken below are in safe working order and locked (reg. 28). Fire precautions (regs. 31–35) include restrictions on inflammable material and oil below ground. Precautions must be taken against inrushes of water, liquid matter or gas into the workings; these are now regulated by the Mines (Precautions against Inrushes) Regulations 1979 (S.I. No. 318) (Chapter 17, section 14), which replace the former reg. 36. Explosives were formerly (under reg. 30) left to be regulated by the local rules of the mine. There are now general rules with regard to the use of explosives, which are summarised at the end of this chapter along with the similar rules for quarries.

Other apparatus
Every crane, crab or winch used for lifting and operated by mechanical power must be examined at intervals (reg. 51) and provided with an efficient catch or brake (reg. 52).

Steam boilers must have a steam gauge and a water gauge (protected by a guard), also a low water alarm device and a safety valve whose setting must not be tampered with (regs. 53–55) and regular cleaning and examination are required (regs. 56–58). Air receivers must be marked with the maximum safe working pressure, have a pressure gauge and a safety valve, and be cleaned and examined at intervals (regs. 59–60).

Fencing of machinery
Section 82 of the Act is amplified by reg. 37, which forbids the cleaning of machinery, and, with certain exceptions, oiling and greasing as well, while the machine is in motion. By reg. 37(3) belts are not to be moved on and off, while machinery is in motion under mechanical power, except by means of a safety contrivance.

Fencing of certain places
By reg. 75, the top of every hopper and kiln is to be kept securely fenced. Gantries and platforms are also to be fenced on any open side where there is danger and to have skirting boards (reg. 76). Any underground road or way which passes or crosses a sink or stope must likewise be fenced on any dangerous open side (reg. 77). Ledges and landings must be kept clear of loose articles liable to fall (reg 78).

Personal duties of workman
Part X forbids intoxication (reg. 62), unauthorised travel on aerial ropeways (reg. 63) or underground roads, and entry into unauthorised parts of the mine (reg. 64) or beyond barriers and locked doors (reg. 66) and requires ventilation doors and screens to be kept shut (reg. 65). Persons at working faces (including places of ripping or repairs) or setting or withdrawing supports must examine their place of work (especially after shotfiring) and remove or secure loose parts of the roof, faces or sides (reg. 67). Work on an unfenced ledge or similar place without a rope or safety appliance is forbidden (reg. 68) and no person must be underneath anything suspended from winding or lifting apparatus except in a shaft being sunk (reg. 69).

Electricity
Electricity, both at the surface and below ground, is now governed by the Electricity at Work Regulations 1989. The regulations for all places of work are summarised in Chapter 16, section 2, and the additional requirements for mines in Chapter 17, section 13.

2 Quarries[4]

Before the Mines and Quarries Act 1954 quarries were not governed by a separate Act. Various sections of the Metalliferous Mines Acts, the Coal Mines Acts, the Quarries Act 1894 and the Factories Act applied to them, and the net result of a complex network of legislation was that regulations could be made. Quarries were in fact governed by two self-contained codes of regulations, the Quarries General Regulations 1938 and the Quarries General Regulations (Electricity) 1938, as amended.

The Mines and Quarries Act 1954 now governs all quarries. A 'quarry' is defined by s. 180(2) of the Act, as follows:

'an excavation or system of excavations made for the purpose of, or in connection with, the getting of minerals (whether in their natural state or in solution or suspension) or products of minerals, being neither a mine nor merely a well or bore-hole or a well or bore-hole combined.'

This definition must be read in conjunction with the definitions of 'mine' and 'minerals' (pp. 477, *ante*) and in particular it should be noted (a) that underground workings at a quarry, if of a subsidiary character, do not convert it into a mine and (b) that an open-cast coal site is a quarry[5]. Under s. 180(3)(b), a quarry, like a mine, includes the adjacent surface area and buildings if used for working the quarry or for handling and treatment of the minerals (except by a manufacturing process), or for disposing of refuse: similarly, too, refuse dumps and railway lines serving the quarry (though not in the immediate vicinity) are included. A quarry is governed by the same rules as a mine in determining whether the Factories Act applies or can be specially excluded. All these matters are fully discussed at pp. 477–481, *ante*.

So, too, under s. 181(1), the 'owner' is in general defined as the person for the time being entitled to work the quarry, and under s. 181(4) a liquidator, receiver or manager, or similar person is treated as an additional owner.

4 Section 151 of the Mines and Quarries Act 1954 replacing the Quarry (Fencing) Act 1887 requires certain quarries to be fenced, if dangerous. This is for the safety of the public at large, rather than of employees.
5 So, too, are sand and gravel pits. *Quaere* whether a disused mine or quarry tip, when combed over for useful material such as shale or floorspar, comes within the definition. The mineral is not a natural deposit, it is just a rubbish heap even if it becomes compacted, and digging or turning it over is not true 'excavation': see *Stow Bardolph Gravel Co Ltd v Poole* [1954] 3 All ER 637.

But in the case of a quarry where the working is 'wholly carried out by a contractor on behalf of the person entitled to work it', the contractor (to the exclusion of the other person) is taken as the owner (s. 181 (2)). And, where several persons are entitled to work a quarry independently, that one among them who is the licensor of the others is taken as the owner (s. 181(3))[6]. This presumably relates to such places as gravel-pits and chalk-pits where several persons, by arrangement with the owner, come and take what they need.

Quarries are regulated by Parts IV and V of the Act of 1954. Part IV (ss. 98–107) is mainly concerned with the appointment and duties of managers[7] and (where necessary) other officials. Section 103, which requires 'close and effective supervision over all operations in progress' by the manager, does not require him to be omnipresent but he is expected to know of all work in progress so as to deal with any dangers: the defence of impracticability is not established because work was going on unknown to him, if he ought to have known: *Sanderson v Millom Hematite Ore and Iron Co Ltd* [1967] 3 All ER 1050. Part V (ss. 108–115) contains the safety requirements. In all cases where actions are based on breach of these duties, the special defence may be raised under s. 157 that it was 'impracticable' to avoid or prevent the breach.

The main regulations under the Act are the Quarries (General) Regulations 1956 (S.I. No. 1780). There are others relating to ropeways, vehicles, tipping and explosives. All these have been adapted to metric measurements by the Quarries (Metrication) Regulations 1983 (S.I. No. 1026).

Safe means of access
By s. 109:

'there shall be provided and maintained safe means of access to every place at a quarry at which any person has at any time to work[8].'

This is wider than s. 87(1) of the Act, which does not require safe means

---

6   In Scotland, the person who has 'granted the right' to the others: s. 181(5).
7   It is possible to have two or more managers of a quarry, each having exclusive jurisdiction within his own area (s. 98(1)(b)). In quarries (unlike mines) an owner may appoint himself manager without having special qualifications (s. 98(3)); and where he does not do this, he may still reserve certain responsibilities to himself (s. 100).
8   For case-law under the corresponding section of the Factories Act, see Chapter 10, section 3, part (5).

of access at mine surfaces except to places 'in or on a building or structure'. Thus s. 109 applied where a man had to jump off a barge to the bank and fell into the water: *Collier v Hall and Ham River Co Ltd* (1968) 4 KIR 628. It has been held that s. 109 is restricted to the part of the quarry where quarrying work is being carried out, and does not apply to roadways outside this area: *English v Cory Sand and Ballast Co Ltd* (1985) Times, 2 April. This seems dubious. The approach roads to a factory have always been held to fall within s. 26 of the Factories Act (Chapter 9, section 3(5)(i)). By s. 115, ss. 86 and 87 of the Act (safety of buildings and structures, safe means of access and safe means of carrying out work—Chapter 17, section 16) which are in Part III of the Act, relating to mines, are also applied to quarries with the necessary modifications of wording.

In addition, by reg. 4 of the Quarries (General) Regulations, 1956, ladders used as access to or egress from a quarry must not be overhanging or at a steeper angle than 75°, and there must be a platform at least every 10 metres with a strong holdfast and having a portion of the ladder projecting at least 1 metre above platform level.

Safe working of quarry to avoid falls of rock, etc.

By s. 108(1) it is the duty of the manager 'to secure that any quarrying operations . . . are so carried on as to avoid danger from falls . . . whether of the minerals worked or of any other substance'[9]. In particular, subject to special exemption by regulations[10] or by the inspector, s. 108(2) requires him to secure that 'in no part of the quarry . . . shall the face or sides of the quarry or any gallery thereon be so worked as to cause any overhanging'. Under s. 108 it is an absolute duty not indeed to prevent

9 Just as the duty of a mine manager (s. 48) is to exercise general control over the strata of the mine so as to keep secure each particular working place and road, so too the quarry manager has a general duty to conduct operations throughout the quarry in such a way that danger from falls is avoided at any particular place: the duty will extend to underground workings at the quarry, if there are any.

10 The Gravel and Sand Quarries (Overhanging) (Exemption) Regulations 1958 (S.I. No. 1533) apply (reg. 3) to 'quarries of gravel or sand in which all or some of the mineral is normally got from under water' and exempt from s. 108(2) every part of the quarry where gravel or sand is normally got in this way (reg. 4). But safety rules must be made to ensure that no person employed is in danger from any fall from an overhanging face or side and in particular warning notices must be displayed at the approaches (reg. 5). There must also be precautions by fencing, notices or otherwise to prevent accidental access to ground which (being above or near an overhanging face or side) is liable to fall, i.e. to collapse under a person (reg. 6).

falls but to 'avoid danger' from them, subject to the defence of impracticability, which will not be established if the dangerous rock could have been removed before starting work: *Brazier v Skipton Rock Co Ltd* [1962] 1 All ER 955; or if a careful inspection before work might have revealed the risk: *Sanderson v Millom Hematite Ore and Iron Co Ltd* [1967] 3 All ER 1050. In this context, 'falls' is restricted to the fall of material from the quarry face and has no relevance to the fall of persons over the quarry edge: *English v Cory Sand and Ballast Co Ltd* (1985) Times, 2 April. (But see note 10, p. 537 for sand and gravel quarries.)

Furthermore, reg. 3 of the Quarries (General) Regulations requires the overburden[11] at or near the top of a face or side of a quarry to be cleared back to a sufficient distance and depth to avoid danger from falls, unless exemption is granted by the inspector.

Ropeways and vehicles
By s. 110(1), ropeways and vehicles were not to be used for carrying persons to their work after two years from the commencement of the Act, except as authorised by regulations[12]. By s. 110(2), so long as railed vehicles are in use, automatic safety devices must be provided to stop runaway vehicles, and under s. 110(3) precautions must be taken to protect persons at work from the danger of runaway vehicles.

Dust precautions
Precautions against dust in quarry processes are now determined by the Control of Substances Hazardous to Health Regulations 1988—Chapter

---

11 I.e. the earth or other unprofitable material overlying the mineral in the quarry.
12 The Quarries (Ropeways and Vehicles) Regulations 1958 (S.I. No. 2110). These regulations came into force on 1 January 1959 (reg. 1) and control the use of ropeways and of vehicles running on rails to carry persons employed at quarries to their working places. Such use is not allowed without the inspector's approval and is then subject to the regulations (reg. 3). A 'conveyance' (i.e. cage, carriage, etc.) on a ropeway must be fenced up to 1 metre on all sides to preclude projections and external contact, have a rigid handrail, and gates not opening outwards (reg. 4). There must be 'travelling rules' to control the number of passengers, and speed, signals and supervision (reg. 5). Spliced or knotted ropes are forbidden on ropeways or for hauling vehicles (reg. 6); ropes must not be in use for more than specified periods (reg. 7) and there are restrictions on the use of capped ropes and the method of capping and re-capping (regs. 8–11). Mechanical apparatus for moving a conveyance on a ropeway must have (a) brakes, (b) a device to hold the drum stationary when the clutch is out and (c) a safety device (presumably to detach the cage) in case of over-travelling or over-hoisting (reg. 12). The person in

8, section 2—which repealed s. 112 of the Mines and Quarries Act. Dust is a 'hazardous substance' if it is either present in quantity, or, though there is not a great quantity, it is of a kind which is likely to endanger health.

Machinery and other apparatus

Section 115 applies to quarries, the provisions of Part III of the Act relating to safe construction of machinery and apparatus (s. 81), fencing of machinery (s. 82), steam and compressed air apparatus (s. 84), and safe loading of cranes (s. 85).

In addition, the Quarries (General) Regulations contain some further requirements. Regulation 12 forbids the cleaning of machinery, and, with certain exceptions, oiling and greasing as well, while the machinery is in motion; and when machinery is in motion under mechanical power, belts must not be moved on and off pulleys except by means of a safety contrivance. Cranes, crabs and winches used as lifting machines must be examined at intervals and provided with efficient catches or brakes (regs. 13–14). Steam boilers must have a steam gauge and a water gauge (protected by a guard) also a low-water alarm device and a safety valve whose setting must not be tampered with (regs. 15–17); and regular cleaning and examination are required (regs. 18–20). Air receivers must be marked with the maximum safe working pressure, have a pressure gauge and a safety valve, and be cleaned and examined at intervals (regs. 21–22).

Fencing of platforms, shafts etc.

By reg. 5 of the Quarries (General) Regulations, 'the top of any shaft, hopper or kiln at a quarry shall be kept securely fenced'. Regulation 6 requires any gantry or platform (which presumably includes platforms on access ladders) to be fenced on any open side which would be dangerous to persons working on or passing along it, and there must also be a continuous skirting board. Regulation 6 does not apply to platforms for loading or unloading vehicles or to temporary wheeling planks.

---

charge of such apparatus (as also the driver of a locomotive) must be 21; he must stay at the controls when the apparatus is in motion or any person is believed to be in it (reg. 13). There must be a scheme for regular examination and testing of all apparatus, particularly ropes, safety devices, attachments of cages, and rail tracks (regs. 14 to 16). There is a general power to grant exemptions (reg. 18).

Explosives and fire-fighting
These are left to regulations (s. 114). Section 115 also applies s. 73 of the Act (exit from places such as engine-rooms exposed to special fire risk). For explosives regulations, see section 3 of this Chapter.

Personal duties of the quarrymen
These duties are defined by the Quarries (General) Regulations. Every person working or loading minerals must examine his working place at the start of and during each shift, especially after shotfiring, and remove dangerous loose material (reg. 7). Unauthorised travel on aerial ropeways is forbidden (reg. 9), likewise remaining underneath anything suspended from a lifting appliance or ropeway (reg. 10) and throwing down material in a manner likely to endanger others (reg. 8).

Miscellaneous
The Act requires 'suitable and sufficient' lighting where the natural light is insufficient (s. 111) and requires the workmen to be withdrawn in cases of danger (s. 113). Section 115 also applies to quarries the sections of Part III of the Act relating to training of inexperienced workers (s. 88), duties of workmen (ss. 80, 89 and 90) and first-aid, and lifting of heavy loads by women and young persons (ss. 91 and 93). Regulation 2 of the Quarries (General) Regulations provides for daily inspection by a competent person of working places and roads; of the top, faces, sides and overburden at the quarry; and of the external parts of machinery and appliances[13]. An experienced shotfirer may be a competent person, although his sight is impaired to some extent: *Brazier v Skipton Rock Co Ltd* [1962] 1 All ER 955, [1962] 1 WLR 471.
Quarry sidings (regs. 23–36) are discussed in Chapter 20.

Electricity
Electricity at quarries, as at other places of work, is now regulated by the Electricity at Work Regulations 1989 (Chapter 16, section 2).

Vehicles and trailers: safety in tipping
The Quarry Vehicles Regulations 1970 (S.I. No. 168) regulate the use at quarries of vehicles and trailers, which means (reg. 2) all vehicles and

---

13 For liability based on failure to inspect, see *Sanderson v Millom Hematite Ore and Iron Co Ltd* [1967] 3 All ER 1050.

mobile plant (unless running on rails or a ropeway, or controlled by a person on foot, and excepting motor-cycles). They must have means of audible warning of approach, and (except for mobile drilling machines) lights during hours of darkness: reg. 3. Drivers must have authorisation from the manager to drive the vehicle, or to receive instruction (under close supervision and with L-plates): reg. 9. Careless driving is an offence: reg. 7. Drivers are not to alight without securing the vehicle against movement: reg. 6. Notices must be posted to show the clearance of overhead structures and cables: reg. 10. A vehicle or trailer with a tipping body must have a safety device independent of the tipping mechanism to prevent collapse from the tipping position: reg. 4(1). As to the tipping operation itself, steps must be taken to prevent vehicles or trailers with tipping body or gear from 'running away, falling or overturning'—including where 'appropriate' such means as 'stop blocks, anchor chains or other suitable devices': reg. 4(2). Users of such vehicles must take precautions in tipping, including use of the safety devices provided: reg. 5. The manager may make rules for (in particular) tipping procedure and traffic control: reg. 8. Exemptions may be given: reg. 11.

3 Explosives in mines and quarries

Explosives in miscellaneous mines—all except coal, stratified ironstone, shale or fireclay—are now regulated by the Miscellaneous Mines (Explosives) Regulations 1959 (S.I. No. 2258), and explosives in quarries by the Quarries (Explosives) Regulations 1988 (S.I. No. 1930). The two codes are similar, and may conveniently be treated together. Exemptions may be granted (Miscellaneous Mines, reg. 3; Quarries, reg. 13).

There are strict requirements for the safe storage, handling and issue of explosives and detonators (M.M., Part IV, regs. 7 to 13; Q., regs. 3 to 11). In mines, supplies must generally be stored in an explosives store at the surface, but issue points may be authorised near the top of the shaft (M., reg. 7). Schemes may be authorised at mines for conveying explosives in bulk (in locked canisters) to reserve stations below ground (M., reg. 13). Issue of detonators is the personal responsibility of the manager, and they must be carried when underground in a locked detonator case (M., reg. 8, reg. 9). In general, explosives below ground must be in cartridge form and in a locked canister (M, reg. 11, reg. 12). Detonators and explosives must not be taken out until required for immediate use (M., reg. 10(1), reg. 12 (4)). The requirements at quarries are not quite so strict, but detonators and explosives have to be kept in a locked explosives store or under the constant supervision of a suitable person (Q., reg. 5(1), (2)(d) and (e)). They must not be handled by anyone except a shotfirer (including a trainee) or storekeeper or other person specifically authorised (Q., reg. 6). Smoking and naked flames—except for lighting a fuse—are forbidden within 10 metres of explosives (Q., reg. 12).

In a mine, shotfirers must be authorised persons not under 21, unless already appointed under previous regulations (M., reg. 6). Shotfiring must not be done by electrical apparatus, cable or fuse unless provided by the owner, and fuses must be safety fuses, detonating fuses or otherwise of an approved type (M., reg. 14). Detachable handles or keys for electrical firing must be held by the shotfirer and kept away from the apparatus except at the moment of firing (M., reg. 15). In a mine, electrical firing is only allowed by means of such a detachable handle, and shotfiring cable must not be used for any other purpose (M., regs. 14, 17). A defect in electrical apparatus must be reported at once and use of the apparatus suspended (M., reg. 16).

A regular procedure is laid down for general shotfiring in mines. The charging of shot-holes with cartridges and stemming must be done by the shotfirer or under his supervision: the jamming of explosives in too narrow a hole and the use of unauthorised tools are forbidden (M., regs. 18–24). Firing must not take place until surplus explosives have been cleared away (M., reg. 25). Warning must be given to neighbouring places where the shot may blow through, a danger zone fixed with sentries, and all persons required to withdraw or take proper shelter (M., regs. 28–30). The place must be examined for safety after firing (M., reg. 31). In shafts or similar places being sunk or deepened, there are further requirements. Electrical firing only is permitted (M., reg. 35); loose material must be cleared away in case there are old shot-holes (M., reg. 32). Explosives must not be taken in unless immediately required, and there is strict control of the taking in of a primer cartridge fitted with a detonator (M., regs. 33, 34). There is a procedure to be followed in case of misfires, involving a stated delay of 30 minutes after attempted firing (if by safety fuse) or five minutes after disconnecting the apparatus (if firing was electrical). The place may then be examined, and a further attempt made to fire: but a charge must not be removed unless it is a cartridge protruding from the hole (M., regs. 36–38).

In a safety-lamp mine, special regulations must be made for shotfiring (M., reg. 39) because of the risk from methane gas ('firedamp').

The Quarries (Explosives) Regulations 1988 do not enter into so much detail, but require the manager to make special rules regulating the procedure for shotfiring and for clearing misfires: reg. 5(2)(b). Shotfirers must be 21 and properly trained and competent: trainees must be under close supervision by a qualified shotfirer: reg. 7. Shots must be fired from a safe place, and only by means of an exploder—an electrical device—or a safety fuse: reg. 8. An exploder must have a removable handle or key, which must not be inserted until the shot is about to be fired, or the circuit tested (which is required as a preliminary to firing): reg. 9, reg. 8.

In case of a misfire, no one except the shotfirer or other authorised person may enter the danger area until 30 minutes have elapsed (if firing was by fuse) or five minutes (in other cases); reg. 10. Steps must be taken to investigate and deal with the misfire: reg. 10. Any attempt to remove the charge after the shot-hole has been charged and primed is expressly forbidden: reg. 11. The procedure is to explode a misfire by a fresh charge.

Shotfiring is forbidden in a tunnel or excavation (with some exceptions): reg. 11(1)(c). That means the shot-hole must be in the open face of the rock. Shotfiring is also forbidden during the hours of darkness: reg. 11(1)(a).

4 Safety of tips

The Mines and Quarries (Tips) Act 1969 (Chapter 17, section 21) applies to all mines and quarries.

Chapter 19

Mineral workings at sea and diving operations

1 Offshore installations and submarine pipe-lines

Under the Territorial Sea Act 1987 the territorial sea of the United Kingdom was extended to 12 nautical miles, measured from official base lines and subject to modification in narrow waters such as the straits of Dover. Within this area the United Kingdom and its courts exercise full sovereignty.

Extra-territorial jurisdiction had already been assumed over a much wider area. Under the Continental Shelf Act 1964 the United Kingdom assumed jurisdiction, in pursuance of international agreement, over the mineral resources of the continental shelf adjacent to British shores. Much of the 1964 Act has been replaced by ss. 22–23 of the Oil and Gas (Enterprise) Act 1982. Sections 21–24 of the Petroleum Act 1987 (replacing s. 21 of 1982) authorise the establishment of 500-metre safety zones round installations, to which entry is restricted, and numerous orders have been made for particular installations. The various areas of the continental shelf to which the 1964 Act (as amended) applies have been designated from time to time by Orders in Council under s. 1(7) of the Act[1]. Sections 22 and 23 of the 1982 Act

---

1 See S.I.s 1964 No. 697, 1968 No. 891, 1971 No. 594, 1974 No. 1489, 1976 No. 1153 (various areas adjacent to Scotland and England). Also S.I.s 1977 No. 1871 (further areas in English Channel and South Western approaches), 1979 No. 1447 (a northerly area of the North Sea) and 1982 No. 1672 (various areas off the Shetlands and in the southern North Sea and English Channel).

authorise the exercise of criminal and civil jurisdiction within the
'designated areas', and orders have been made dividing the continental
shelf for this purpose between the Scottish courts (which of course have
the major share) and the English courts[2]. These sections give
jurisdiction over delicts or torts on offshore installations though the
operator of the installation or other defendant is not resident in the
United Kingdom: *Johnston v Heerema Offshore Contractors Ltd* 1987
SLT 407; but this does not apply to fishing vessels moving within the
area: *Fraser v John N. Ward & Son* 1987 SLT 513. Under ss. 22(5) and
23(6)(c), jurisdiction may even be extended to the foreign side of the
international boundary where this intersects a field, but obviously no
such order would be made except by international agreement for mutual
convenience, e.g. between the United Kingdom and Norway.

The Mineral Workings (Offshore Installations) Act 1971 (now
extensively amended by the Petroleum and Submarine Pipe-lines Act
1975, the Oil and Gas (Enterprise) Act 1982 and the Petroleum Act
1987) exercises the legislative jurisdiction assumed by the United
Kingdom under the Act of 1964 to regulate various activities on the
continental shelf. The legislation was of course prompted by the
discovery of natural gas and oil in the North Sea, but it may apply in
future years to the recovery of solid minerals such as globules of
manganese from the sea bed. 'Mineral resources' are not defined, and
could include almost any valuable substance[3].

The safety requirements of the 1971 Act, and of the Petroleum and
Submarine Pipe-lines Act 1975 which amends it, take effect within the
general framework of the Health and Safety at Work Act 1974. Most of
the Act (ss. 1–59 and 80–82) was extended to offshore installations and
pipe-lines in territorial waters and areas designated under the
Continental Shelf Act by the Health and Safety at Work Act 1974
(Application outside Great Britain) Order 1989 (S.I. No. 840).

A number of definitions have to be considered to determine the

---

2 The Continental Shelf (Jurisdiction) Order 1980 S.I. No. 184, amended by Nos.
  559 of 1980 and 1523 of 1982.
3 Pending future developments, the Deep Sea Mining (Temporary Provisions) Act
  1981 requires a licence for the exploration or exploitation of 'the hard mineral
  resources of the deep sea bed' and a licence will normally be subject to conditions
  for the safety of persons employed. For the form of licence see the Deep Sea
  Mining (Exploration Licences) Regulations 1984 (S.I. No. 1230).

precise activities to which the 1971 Act applies. Under the original s. 1, the concept was fairly simple. It applied to 'exploitation' of minerals, and preliminary 'exploration' with a view to exploitation, if done from fixed or floating installations not permanently linked with dry land. The Oil and Gas (Enterprise) Act 1982 extended the Act to the storage of oil at sea and the operation of pipe-lines. For this purpose a new section 1 was substituted by s. 24 of the 1982 Act, and this contains a series of elaborate definitions. First of all 'controlled waters' are defined—s. 1(4)—to mean (i) tidal and other waters within the traditional 'territorial' seas; (ii) areas 'designated' under the Continental Shelf Act; and (iii) any inland waters that may be specified by Order in Council. An order may also be made—s.1(3)—applying the Act to foreign waters in an area specified under s. 22(5) of the 1982 Act where an oil field overlaps the international boundary.

Under the new s. 1, the 1971 Act applies to four specified activities if carried on in controlled waters:

from *or* by means of *or* on	an installation	fixed *or* floating	maintained	in the water *or* on the foreshore *or* on other land intermittently covered by water

provided that the installation is not connected with dry land by a permanent structure giving access at all times: s. 1(1). The four activities are: (i) exploitation of minerals or exploration with a view to exploitation (so a purely scientific investigation with no commercial purpose would be excluded); (ii) storage of gas in or under the shore, or the bed of the relevant waters, and subsequent recovery of gas so stored; (iii) the conveyance of things by means of a pipe or system of pipes in or under the shore or bed; (iv) accommodation for persons working on or from an installation for any of the above purposes.

Although at present offshore installations are generally well out in the open sea, they can be quite close to land or on a tidal foreshore provided that there is no permanent link with land above the tidemark (so a seaside pier adapted for the purpose would be excluded).

Section 1(5)(a) states that 'installation' *includes* a 'floating structure or device maintained on a station by whatever means'. This could include a ship (which may be kept in position by its anchors or indeed by its engines), not necessarily a vessel of specialised construction[4]. The definition is not, of course, an all-embracing one but is merely supplementary or explanatory and does not exclude the normal rig fixed to the sea bed or otherwise permanently anchored.

Section 1(5)(b) excludes pipe-lines. The line itself is not an installation in any circumstances: but s. 33 of the Petroleum and Submarine Pipe-lines Act 1975, as amended by s. 25 of the 1982 Act, defines a pipe-line to include its associated works such as pumping stations, valve chambers, power-transmission, signalling apparatus, cathodic protection and supporting structure, so that these are also excluded. Of course most of them will not be manned, or visited except on inspection. However, since running a pipe-line is one of the four activities mentioned in the definition of an installation, it is somewhat surprising to find apparently everything connected with the working of the line excluded, except that Orders may be made declaring that specified apparatus or works are installations. The Offshore Installations (Included Apparatus or Works) Order 1989 (S.I. No. 978) treats some apparatus connecting a pipe-line with an installation as part of the installation. Under the Offshore Installations (Emergency Pipe-line Valve) Order 1989 (S.I. No. 1029) an emergency shut-down valve must be incorporated in a pipe-line linked to an installation.

Some of the regulations made under the Act distinguish between 'fixed' and 'mobile' installations. A mobile installation is one which can be moved without major dismantling, though not necessarily under its own power (it may be towed)[5].

Installations are in some ways analogous to ships, in others to mines, in others (the superstructure) to factories, and the legislation is of a hybrid character, related to the law on all three.

Registration

Under s. 2 and the Offshore Installations (Registration) Regulations

---

4 Dredgers, if registered under the Merchant Shipping Acts, are excluded by the regulations for registration and for survey and certificates of fitness, and also by the general safety regulations.
5 Installations which move under their own power, strange though their shape may be, must also be registered as ships. This is certainly the case in Norway, or so I was told in Stavanger.

1972 (S.I. No. 702), no fixed installation is to be *established* in relevant waters, no mobile installation is to *enter* them with a view to being *stationed* there, no installation of either class is to be *maintained* there, unless registered with the Secretary of State for Energy. The application must show location, purpose, estimated length of stay: and subsequent changes must be notified.

Manager

Under ss. 4 and 5 and the Offshore Installations (Managers) Regulations 1972 (S.I. No. 703) the owner must appoint a competent person (with deputies where necessary) to take charge of the installation. The names and qualifications of the persons appointed must be notified to the Department of Energy and each of them while in charge is 'the manager'. There must be a manager on the installation at all times when it is manned (except for sudden sickness or other good reason). Like the master of a ship or the manager of a mine, he has full authority on the installation and full responsibility for safety, health and welfare.

Construction and survey: certificate of fitness

Under s. 3 and the Offshore Installations (Construction and Survey) Regulations 1974 (S.I. No. 289) a fixed installation established in the relevant waters and a mobile installation stationed there must, in addition to being registered, have a certificate of 'fitness' (which is analogous to a certificate of seaworthiness). This involves a preliminary survey of a great many matters set out in Schedule 2 to the Regulations, such as:

Fitness to withstand 'environmental conditions' (weather, sea, sea bed).
Foundations and their stability.
Secondary structures (watertight compartments etc.).
Superstructure (living quarters, lighting, means of access).
Helicopter landing.

These do not impose statutory duties, they are merely conditions for the issue of a certificate: but as an indication of safety matters affecting individuals (as distinct from dangers to the whole installation), Part V, para. 7 mentions non-slip surfaces on decks, walkways, stairways, ladders; fire protection and fireproof doors; para. 8 mentions escape routes (two from every manned position) and safe landing places.

A mobile station is not to be moved to a new station without a check on its fitness for 'environmental conditions' in the new position.

Safety

The manager has general responsibility for safety under s. 5(2), but the only specific statutory duty is under s. 5(4): he must not permit the installation to be used in any manner, or permit any operation to be carried out on or from it, if seaworthiness or stability is likely to be endangered. Under s. 6 and the Schedule to the Act, there is a wide power to make safety regulations for everything on or in the neighbourhood of the installation, including vessels, aircraft and hovercraft in the vicinity and work or operations in the sea or sea bed. The general code of safety regulations made under this power is summarised below. Regulations as respects offshore installations have also been made for inspectors and casualties (S.I. 1972 No. 1842) and for public inquiries (S.I. 1974 No. 338) and similar regulations have been made for pipe-lines (S.I. 1977 No. 835).

The main safety regulations

The main regulations for safety on oil rigs are the Offshore Installations (Operational Safety, Health and Welfare) Regulations 1976 (S.I. No. 1019) made under the 1971 Act as amended. They apply to all installations within the new definition in the Act of 1982: Offshore Installations (Application of Statutory Instruments) Regulations 1984 (S.I. No. 419). It is the duty of the installation manager, the owner and the concession owner to ensure that the regulations are complied with (reg. 32(1)); of an employer to ensure that each of his employees complies with regulations imposing a duty or prohibition on him (reg. 32(2)); and of all persons on or *near* the installation (a) not to endanger persons or render equipment unsafe; (b) to co-operate in carrying out the regulations; and (c) to report defects (regs. 32(3)). In general the manager, owner and concession owner are all guilty of an offence if the regulations are broken unless they can prove both due delegation and no default on their part: reg. 34. There is civil liability for damages for breach of the regulations: reg. 33.

I. General safety requirements

There are a large number of requirements which could apply to any place of work. Most of these are modelled on the Factories Act, but they have been simplified and improved.

Place of work and safe access   Regulation 14 says:

> 'At all times all reasonably practicable steps shall be taken to ensure the safety of persons at all places on the installation including the provision of safe means of access to and egress from any such place.'

It then continues with specific requirements: (a) Scaffolding to be secured to prevent accidental displacement. (b) Ladders to be fixed so that both sides are evenly supported or suspended, and secured to prevent slipping. (c) Working platforms to be at least 65 cm. wide (about 2 feet), securely fixed to supporting scaffolding or otherwise prevented from moving; also such platforms—and walkways—to have toe-boards and guard rails if there is a drop of over 2 metres or into the sea. If these safeguards are not practicable, (d), (e) and (f) give the alternative of safety nets and sheets, or where even that is not practicable of safety belts, or failing that life jackets.

Hazardous areas   (those where there is risk of fire or explosion) must have a 'Hazardous Area' notice in big letters on the door or other access: reg. 2.

Equipment   All necessary equipment must be provided on the installation (reg. 2). It must be of 'good construction, sound material, adequate strength and free from patent defect and suitable for *any* purpose for which it is used' (reg. 10). All parts of the installation itself as well as the equipment must be 'so maintained as to ensure the safety of the installation and . . . the persons thereon' (reg. 5(1)): and a scheme must be set up for regular examination and testing and for unsafe equipment to be put out of use (reg. 5(2) to (7) and Schedule 1).

Electrical equipment (reg. 11)   must be sufficient in size and power for its work and 'so constructed, installed, protected, worked and maintained as to prevent danger so far as practicable'. Private electrical equipment is not to be taken on the installation without the manager's permission (reg. 17(2)).

Fencing of machinery and apparatus (reg. 12) 'Every dangerous part of any machinery or apparatus shall so far as practicable be *effectively* guarded', which means in the case of a *moving* part either a fixed enclosure which prevents any person or his clothing from coming into contact, or a device which similarly encloses it while in motion. For a dangerous non-moving part, a fixed enclosure is required.

There are interesting differences here from the Factories Act; the regulation applies to *apparatus* as well as to machinery, and to fixed as well as moving parts.

Guards or other devices for a *moving* part must be kept in position while it is in motion unless *necessarily* exposed in motion for examination, adjustment or lubrication: in such a case the work must be done by a 'responsible person' (i.e. a competent man expressly and officially appointed) and another person with knowledge of emergency procedure must be standing by.

Lifting appliances and lifting gear (reg. 6) have to be tested by an independent person before being taken into use, or after alteration, and in any case at specified intervals: the safe working load must be marked on the equipment (reg. 13).

Dangerous substances (reg. 4), e.g. those which are radioactive, corrosive, toxic, explosive or kept above atmospheric pressure, must be kept in marked receptacles away from 'hazardous areas' and living accommodation, and the stores for inflammable substances must be away from any *other* hazardous area. Dangerous substances must not be used without 'all reasonably practicable precautions'.

Protective clothing etc. (reg. 16) There must be a safety helmet for every person on the installation: and protective equipment such as goggles, ear-muffs, breathing apparatus, gloves, safety boots must be provided for every person 'exposed to risk of injury or disease'.

Health and welfare There must be drinking water, wholesome food, a sick bay with medical orderlies capable in particular of giving artificial respiration: regs. 25 to 27, 31. No one under 18 is to be employed on an installation: reg. 28. An accurate record of hours worked by each man must be kept: reg. 29.

II. Systematic management and delegation of tasks
The regulations go to considerable trouble to ensure that there is a systematic delegation from the manager downwards, to 'responsible persons' appointed in writing who are 'competent' to carry out or closely supervise particular tasks: regs. 30, 32. For certain jobs—e.g. welding and other jobs involving fire risks, and work in confined spaces—a specific 'work permit' is required: reg. 3. There must be standing instructions on such matters as drilling procedure, operation of electrical and mechanical equipment and the safety of the installation: reg. 7 and Schedule 2.

III. Operational safety of the installation
Intelligence on weather etc. (reg. 20)   Instruments for measuring wind, temperature and atmospheric pressure must be kept on *all* installations, and a *mobile* installation must have means of checking the movement and heading of the installation and the sea state. Regular observations must be taken of these matters and of visibility and cloud cover.

Helicopters (regs. 21 to 23)   There must be a 'competent' Helicopter Landing Officer in immediate control. There must be continuous radio-telephone contact between pilot and installation (even for an unmanned installation the pilot must be in contact with the nearest manned installation). Equipment such as chocks, ropes and snow and ice clearing appliances must be available for safe landing as well as rescue equipment and fire appliances. The area must be cleared for take-off and landing, nearby cranes being stopped.

Vessels, aircraft and hovercraft (reg. 24)   are not to be moored at an installation or land anyone there without the manager's permission.

Radio-telephone (reg. 18)   R/T contact must be maintained with the shore, other installations, vessels and helicopters—it is required even on an unmanned installation if anyone is on it. There must be at least one qualified operator (reg. 19). The R/T cabin must not be in a 'hazardous area': it must have a full view of the helicopter landing area unless the operator can speak to the landing officer while *he* has a full view. An instruction card must be on display with distress and emergency signals.

Movement of installation (reg. 8)   When an installation is raised, lowered or dismantled, no person must be on board unless he is essential, and then only with the manager's written permission.

Safety during drilling (reg. 15 and Schedule 4 rules 1 to 7)   There must be equipment to give warning of loss of circulation or an incipient blow-out, and adequate hydraulic equipment for preventing blow-out, with dual controls—by the driller and also at a safe distance. When a stabbing board is used the fittings must be adequate to support the platform when manned. Any hook used to hoist this, or to hoist pipes or other equipment, must be safe against accidental detachment. Where sulphuretted hydrogen may be present, there must be detection equipment and breathing apparatus.

Safety during production (reg. 15 and Schedule 4, rules 8 to 11)   Completed wells must have control devices to a specified standard. Gas flare systems must be constructed and equipped to filter out inflammable solids and liquids. The same precautions are required for sulphuretted hydrogen as during drilling.

Drilling   The Offshore Installations (Well Control) Regulations 1980 (S.I. No. 1759) require all drilling operations, as well as operations over wells which are not under regular flow control, to be carried out under the immediate control of a qualified driller, who must in turn be under the supervision of a qualified supervisor.

Emergency requirements   There are three additional codes of regulations with requirements similar to those for ships at sea. All of these now apply to all installations within the extended definition introduced by the 1982 Act: Offshore Installations (Application of Statutory Instruments) Regulations 1984 (S.I. No. 419).

The Offshore Installations (Life-Saving Appliances) Regulations 1977 (S.I. No. 486) require life-boats, life rafts, life buoys and life jackets to be provided; also means of escape into the sea in emergency, and an alarm and loud-speaker system. The Offshore Installations (Fire Fighting Equipment) Regulations 1978 (S.I. No. 611) contain analogous requirements for fire-fighting[6].

The Offshore Installations (Emergency Procedures) Regulations 1976 (S.I. No. 1542) contain elaborate instructions for procedure not only in general emergencies (fire, explosion, blow-out, sea and weather conditions) but also particular ones such as a helicopter crash or diving accident. Among other things there are arrangements to muster

---

6   Frequent amendments applying to both these codes relate only to fees—e.g. S.I. 1987 No. 129.

personnel at 'emergency stations' allotted in advance where they have specific duties such as closing water-tight doors, stopping machinery, putting out fires, launching life-boats. These arrangements must be practised regularly. Under reg. 10, every installation which is manned must have a 'stand-by' vessel within 5 nautical miles in case of emergency: this must keep in R/T communication and be capable of taking the entire personnel on board if evacuated and of giving them first aid.

Diving operations   These are no longer controlled by a special set of regulations, but are subject to the general safety code for diving operations which applies to all places of work: see section 2 of this Chapter.

Submarine pipe-lines   It has already been noted that pipe-lines, as such, do not count as offshore installations, though apparatus and works connected with them may be brought within the definition by Order in Council. Pipe-lines have however their own statutory code, which is concerned with the safety of the pipe-line itself and ships and persons in the vicinity rather than with employees in particular.

The Petroleum and Submarine Pipe-lines Act 1975 (as amended by the Oil and Gas (Enterprise) Act 1982) applies to a pipe-line as defined by s. 33 of 1975 (as amended by s. 25 of 1982): a pipe or system of pipes for the conveyance of any thing, apparatus for treating or cooling anything which flows through the system, and ancillary apparatus and works such as pumping stations, valve chambers, power transmission, signalling apparatus, cathodic protection and supporting structures[7].

Under ss. 20–26 of the 1975 Act, pipe-lines cannot be laid, used or altered in, under or over 'controlled waters' unless authorised by the Secretary of State (Department of Energy) who may make safety regulations under s. 26. The Submarine Pipe-lines Safety Regulations 1982 (S.I. No. 1513 amended by S.I. 1985 No. 86) require (reg. 3) all parts of the pipe-line to be designed, constructed, operated and maintained 'to ensure, so far as . . . reasonably practicable' that: (a) every part is protected from damage; (b) no part is a danger to any person; (c) the position of the line does not change (except when operations are

---

7   Water pipes and chlorinating pipes at electrical power stations are exempted from control: Submarine Pipe-lines (Electricity Generating Stations) Regulations 1981 (S.I. No. 750).

carried out for the specific purpose of alteration). Regulation 4 requires systematic inspection at regular intervals by a competent person to check in particular for signs of damage, change in position, coverage of the line and marine growth and the state of the adjacent sea bed. Regulation 5 prohibits repair or alteration without notifying the Secretary of State. Regulation 6 requires means of control and cut-off, continuous monitoring of pressure and flow and stopping the flow if safe pressure is exceeded. Under reg. 7 there must be a 'manual' of standard procedure for emergencies such as fire, explosion or fracture. Regulations 8 and 9 regulate the movement and anchorage of vessels near the pipe-line, and the giving of information as to the position of the pipe-line to concession owners, ships and other persons in the vicinity of the line.

Action for breach of statutory duty

Section 11 of the 1971 Act expressly provides that breach of any statutory duty imposed on any person by the Act, or by regulations which apply s. 11, shall give rise to an action for damages for personal injuries (including disease or impairment) or death: but not for damage other than injuries or death. Defences available in criminal proceedings under s. 9(3) ('due diligence' etc.) or under regulations are not available in a civil action. The section binds the Crown in its official capacity. Section 30 of the 1975 Act (for pipe-lines) contains similar provisions. The general safety regulations all declare that there is civil liability for breach of these regulations.

2 Diving operations at work (everywhere)

Safety in diving operations was formerly regulated by three separate codes, depending on whether the diving took place from offshore installations, on submarine pipe-lines or in some other context such as engineering.

These codes have now been replaced by a single unified code, the Diving Operations at Work Regulations 1981 (S.I. No. 399); there is still a separate code for diving from ships, but this does not apply in United Kingdom waters (including the continental shelf) where the general code applies to ships as it does to any other 'installation'.

The summary which follows is of a general character, and is subject to many detailed qualifications. In addition, the Health and Safety Executive has power to grant exemptions (reg. 14) which are not likely to be given except in special situations and subject to strict conditions.

The regulations apply—reg. 3(1)—to all diving operations in which *any* diver taking part is 'at work as an employee or a self-employed person' as defined in the Health and Safety at Work etc. Act 1974, s. 53, provided that the operations are either in Great Britain or in places to which the Act is extended by the Health and Safety at Work etc. Act 1974 (Application outside Great Britain) Order 1989 (S.I. No. 840)—this means offshore installations and pipe-lines in designated waters of the continental shelf: see p. 545, *ante*.

However, by reg. 3(1) the Regulations do not apply unless at least one of the persons is a 'diver' *as defined in reg. 2(2)*: this excludes persons in a submersible chamber or craft or a pressure-resistant diving suit, if not normally exposed to more than 300 millibars above atmospheric pressure[8], and persons who use no underwater breathing apparatus except the snorkel type. It also excludes anyone who is not taking part either as an employee or as self-employed, and members of the British and visiting forces if on duty and engaged in operations or operational training.

On the other hand—reg. 3(3)—the regulations do apply (with certain exceptions) to cases where a person, though not going under water and therefore not technically 'diving', is exposed to more than 300 millibars above atmospheric pressure in a *surface compression chamber*, in connection with either (a) a diving operation or (b) testing or evaluation of plant or equipment for diving.

There are three levels of responsibility for safety: *owners* of offshore installations or pipe-lines, diving *contractors* (described in former regulations as 'employers of divers') and diving *supervisors*. Owners include the concession holder for a proposed installation and the intended owner of a proposed pipe-line.

Owners, as well as diving contractors, have a general duty to ensure

8 Normal atmospheric pressure varies around 1,000 millibars—a 30 per cent increase is therefore the critical limit.

that the regulations are complied with 'so far as is reasonably practicable': reg. 4(1). Among other things this gives both of them overall responsibility for at least the oversight of equipment and standard procedures. However, the key responsibility rests with the diving contractor (and where diving operations are not at an offshore installation or pipe-line he has sole responsibility as there are no owners). Under reg. 5(4), if there is a single employer he is automatically the diving contractor; if there are several, they must nominate one of their number by agreement; if all the divers are self-employed, the manager of an established installation is responsible for nominating a diving contractor, otherwise the concession owners for a projected installation and the owners for a pipe-line; where there is no installation or pipe-line, the 'self-employed' divers must nominate one of their own number.

Employers must not allow employees to take part in a diving operation, nor must 'self-employed' divers take part, until a diving contractor has been appointed *in writing*.

The diving contractor in turn must appoint a diving supervisor to be in immediate control: he must be a competent person with adequate knowledge and experience of the techniques to be used, and be a diver who has qualified in those techniques himself (or have had two years as diving supervisor, in the same techniques, before the 1981 regulations came into force): reg. 5(1)(a), (3). He must not take part in the diving himself: reg. 6(3).

Diving rules

The diving contractor must make 'diving rules'—these also to be in writing—for 'each diving operation': regs. 5 (1)(b), 9, Sch. 1. The expression 'rules' is misleading. The military analogy would not be 'Standing Orders', but an 'Operation Order' for the particular occasion. The purpose is to ensure that a safe method of work is thought out in detail in advance—as it must be since the 'rules' have to be in writing and copies have to be handed to each responsible person. In particular the 'rules' must cover planning (with due regard to weather, tide, shipping, underwater hazards, the equipment appropriate for the depth and type of operation, the persons available and their qualifications); preparations (including co-ordinating with shipping, checks of equipment and divers, signalling, underwater hazards); the actual diving procedure (including allocation of responsibilities, supply and pressure of breathing mixture, descent and return of divers or diving bell, limits on depth and time under water, the work to be done under water and the equipment to be used, decompression procedure) and finally emergency plans (including signalling, rescue, medical treatment). A log book has to be kept with full details of every dive: reg. 6, Sch. 2.

Diving base
The diving contractor has a special responsibility—reg. 5(2)—for arranging a 'suitable and safe place' from which diving can be carried out, including the availability of emergency services: these must include facilities for the transport and treatment of a diver while still under the proper pressure, if saturation techniques are in use. (This means procedures by which the diver avoids repeated decompression by being subject to a continuous pressure above that of the atmosphere so that all his tissues and blood are saturated with the inert gas such as nitrogen in the breathing mixture.) Where diving takes place from a ship or other mobile base, this must be held in position by anchor or otherwise; if the engines or other propulsion system are used to hold it in position, the diver must be protected from such dangers as the propellers or the currents set up: reg. 12(3).

Divers
They must hold valid certificates of training and qualification for the type of diving they are to undertake, and certificates of medical fitness (in force for a maximum of twelve months at a time): regs. 7, 10, 11. Each diver must keep a personal log book. There must be a sufficient team of divers (reg. 8) to carry out the operations safely, which generally means at least one 'standby diver' (on the watch in the diving bell if one is used, otherwise in immediate readiness or actually in the water and close enough to help the other diver). In some cases (e.g. diving to 30 metres or over, special hazards such as currents) there must be at least one more diver. The diving supervisor and persons working equipment must not be counted as part of the diving team, though a 'standby' designated as such may be given other duties if they will not prejudice the safety of anyone in the water. A solitary diver is permitted if the water is no deeper than 1.5 metres: reg. 8(5).

Equipment
(a) Specific requirements (reg. 12(1))   There must be plant to supply a

suitable breathing mixture, at the right rate and pressure, sufficient to sustain prolonged exertion at the pressure at which the diver is working. With certain exceptions, each diver must have a personal lifeline sufficient to lift him with his equipment. There must be means of communication from each diver to the supervisor, and from a diving bell to a diver outside it. There must be equipment to enable a diver to enter and leave the water safely, and means of keeping up the diver's temperature.

(b) Compression chamber A surface compression chamber is compulsory for all work in connection with an offshore installation or pipe-line, or when the depth is over 50 metres. It is also required in some cases if the depth is between 10 and 50 metres: reg. 12(1)(f)(ii). A diving bell—which is a submersible compression chamber in which the pressure may exceed 300 millibars above the atmosphere—is also compulsory for diving at a depth below 50 metres. Compression chambers and diving bells must comply with detailed requirements in Scheds. 5 and 6. In particular compression chambers are generally required to have two compartments adequately sealed—which means from one another as well as from the outside—and fitted with all facilities for a stay of some hours; a diving bell must be capable of returning to the surface in emergency without assistance, e.g. by releasing weights.

(c) General requirements Diving equipment must be of good design and construction, adequate strength, suitable for the operating conditions including the temperature: reg. 12(4). It is to be marked with the safe working depth and pressure where appropriate, and gas cylinders must show both the name and the chemical formula of the gas.

(d) Breathing mixture Compressed natural air is not permitted at a depth exceeding 50 metres: reg. 5(1)(e). 'Diving rules' must specify the breathing mixture to be used.

(e) Maintenance and testing (reg. 13) In addition to regular maintenance to 'ensure so far as practicable that it is safe while . . . being used', all the specialised equipment must be tested at frequent intervals by a competent person (especially for leaks). Use is prohibited unless there is in force a test certificate, which cannot last for more than six months and may be shorter. The equipment must also be checked within six hours before the operation begins.

(f) Responsibility for equipment   The diving contractor is the person primarily responsible for ensuring that all equipment is available for immediate use—reg. 5(1) (d)—and for ensuring that it has been tested and certified—reg. 6(2)(a)—but both he and the owner have a general responsibility under reg. 4(1) for providing and maintaining equipment which complies in all respects with the regulations.

Generally, it has to be remembered that the whole object of diving is to carry out various tasks under water, which are likely to be prolonged and technical, and may require more ingenuity and planning than the well-established techniques for the diving itself, in which the regulations are merely re-stating the rules of good practice as worked out over many years of experience. Therefore in preparing the diving rules—the 'operation order' for the particular occasion—great importance attaches to setting out in detail, as Sch. I requires, the work to be done under water and the equipment to be used.

As already stated, these regulations apply to ships as well as everything else in 'controlled' waters. The separate code for ships now therefore applies only outside these waters.

Part IV (ss. 16, 17) of the Merchant Shipping Act 1974 gave power to make regulations for the safety and safe operation of what is described as 'submersible or supporting apparatus' when used in United Kingdom waters (territorial or inland) or from ships registered in the United Kingdom. (The sections may also be applied to British ships registered elsewhere, presumably in dependent territories). 'Submersible apparatus' means apparatus for supporting human life on the sea bed (or lake or river bed) or otherwise under the surface of any water. In other words, it includes ordinary diving suits as well as elaborate equipment such as miniature submarines. 'Supporting apparatus' simply means apparatus used in support of diving operations.

The Merchant Shipping (Diving Operations) Regulations 1975 made under this power (S.I. No. 116 as amended by 1975 No. 2062) apply— reg. 2(1)—to all diving operations using 'submersible apparatus'. They are not limited to operations from a ship, and to emphasise this the word 'craft' is defined—reg. 1(2)—to include any 'vessel, vehicle, hovercraft or structure' which comprises, carries or is used with submersible apparatus. However, they apply only to operations carried on for trade or business or otherwise for hire or reward. The amendment regulations (1975 No. 2062) exclude operations at diving schools, also diving for archaeological or other non-commercial research.

There are several levels of responsibility. The *owner* of the craft—which, as stated above, may be a vehicle or structure—is responsible for effective organisation to ensure that the regulations are complied with, and for the safety of all equipment except the diving equipment itself: reg. 3. He has also to designate a 'competent person' for the key role of 'employer of divers'. The *master* of the craft (or other person in charge)—reg. 4—has to provide a safe base and equipment for diving operations (including protection from ships and other hazards in the vicinity), keep the supervisor informed about state of weather and sea, put out flags or other warnings while diving is in progress and ensure that no other activities go on which might endanger divers. The *employer of divers* must make diving rules (covering such things as weather, equipment, compression and decompression, signalling): regs. 5, 9, Sch. 1; he is also responsible for the safety of the diving equipment and for compliance with the regulations (reg. 5) and for appointing a *diving supervisor* who is in immediate control of the divers and personally present during operations: reg. 6.

There are general prohibitions of unsafe practices. By reg. 7, diving is forbidden (a) if the craft is 'under way'; (b) unless the diver is on a lifeline; (c) below 50 metres, except in a submersible compression chamber; (d) below 125 metres, or using 'saturation' techniques, except with prior official approval. By reg. 12, no person may be employed to dive, or actually dive, without a certificate of fitness (which lapses after seven days off for sickness or injury). By reg. 13, divers must be at least 18, fully instructed and trained, and *either* with experience of the particular depths, equipment and method to be used *or* under immediate supervision by a diver with such experience. A diver must not be under water more than three hours in 24 unless saturation techniques are used: reg. 8. For diving below 25 metres a deck compression chamber is required and for below 50 metres a submersible compression chamber: reg. 16.

The *employer of divers* must ensure that the diving equipment is in good order and examined and tested at intervals, all to be recorded in a register: regs. 5, 17. The *diving supervisor* must make a daily check of all equipment, especially of breathing apparatus for leaks: reg. 18. He must exercise close supervision of the diving base, diving equipment and diving procedure (regs. 6, 16) and both he and each diver must keep log books (regs. 10, 11). Breathing mixture is to be adequate, with a reserve on the craft and in any submersible chamber: compressed air must not be used in excess of the pressure of water at 50 metres: regs. 15, 14. Closed circuit apparatus is not allowed: reg. 16(2). A diver must not go under without means of communication, and (during darkness) lighting arrangements: reg. 19. Emergency services for rescue and medical help must be at hand during diving: reg. 25. Normally there must be two stand-by divers at the base, and one in any submersible compression chamber: reg. 6. A submersible compression chamber must be capable of returning to the surface unaided in emergency, e.g. by jettisoning weights: Sch. 2, para. 3 (b).

The Merchant Shipping (Submersible Craft) Operations Regulations 1987 (S.I. No. 311 amended by S.I. No. 1603) regulate the operation of submersible craft, mainly miniature submarines for underwater tasks in United Kingdom waters and from United Kingdom ships anywhere (or if the submarine itself is of United Kingdom registry). Procedure must be set out in an 'Operations Manual'. The master of the parent ship (if any) must ensure that the operation is carried out from a safe place and in a safe manner: in any case there must be an operations controller exercising direct supervision. The pilot must be trained and competent, and given full instructions about the procedure, the task to be carried out, and other relevant circumstances such as weather, currents and the configuration of the sea floor.

Chapter 20

Railways and rail sidings: shipping: aviation

1 Railways

There is no comprehensive Act providing for the safety of railway workers in all aspects of their work. The existing legislation which applies to various types of work and premises now takes effect under the Health and Safety at Work Act 1974, under which regulations can be made for any kind of work.

Railway workshops could be factories under s. 151(1) (vi) of the Factories Act 1937, which included workshops incidental to transport undertakings generally; but it excluded engine sheds where nothing was done to the locomotive except cleaning, running repairs and minor adjustments. This limitation was removed in 1959 as to sheds where running repairs are carried out. Now, under s. 175(2)(f) of the Factories Act 1961 the following premises are factories:

'(2) (f) except as provided in subsection (10) of this section, any premises in which the construction, reconstruction or repair of locomotives, vehicles or other plant for use for transport purposes is carried on as ancillary to a transport undertaking or other industrial or commercial undertaking.'

But by s. 175(10):

'(10) Premises used for the purpose of housing locomotives or vehicles where only cleaning, washing, running repairs or minor adjustments are carried out shall not be deemed to be a factory by reason only of [s. 175(2)(f)], unless they are premises used for the purposes of a railway undertaking where running repairs to locomotives are carried out[1].'

It is only sheds where *running repairs* are carried out that are brought within the Act: if nothing more than 'cleaning, washing or minor adjustments' is done, engine sheds are still not subject to the Factories Act.

Certain railway premises not within the Factories Act are now subject to the Offices, Shops and Railway Premises Act 1963, as to which see Chapter 22: its application seems rather limited.

As regards the risk of collisions between trains, or of being run down, railway employees have now, since the abolition of the defence of common employment, the same rights at common law as members of the public would have (if lawfully present) in respect of the negligence of engine-drivers, signalmen, shunters or other railway employees: in general they have no further rights. It is recognised that an engine-driver is in a difficult position, and cannot readily be found negligent, because he is on a fixed track, has to watch signals, cannot pull up quickly, and cannot lean out all the time: *Trznadel v British Transport Commission* [1957] 3 All ER 196. This does not mean, however, that drivers and guards are excused from the duty of keeping a look-out: *Braithwaite v South Durham Steel Co* [1958] 3 All ER 161. It may also be negligent to give no warning, or insufficient warning: *Geddes v British Railways Board* (1968) 4 KIR 373 (long sustained whistle, not short blast only, should have been given at spot known to be dangerous).

Further, the Railway Employment (Prevention of Accidents) Act 1900[2] gives power to make regulations in certain special cases set out in the Schedule to the Act (s. 1(1)), and also in any other case where there is avoidable danger (s. 1(2)). The most important of these special cases is item No. 12 in the Schedule: 'Protection to permanent way men when relaying or repairing permanent way'. Under this Act, the Prevention of

1 See also the Railway Running Sheds Order 1961, S.I. No. 1250; the Railway Running Sheds (No. 1) Regulations 1961, S.I. No. 1251, which extended to these sheds the Operations at Unfenced Machinery Regulations 1938 and 1946; the Hoists Exemption Orders 1938 and 1946; the Factories Act 1937 (Extension of s. 46) Regulations 1948, as to 'welfare'; and various orders requiring protection from lead compounds, etc.; and Railway Running Sheds (No. 2) Regulations 1961, S.I. No. 1768, which applied to railway sheds the electricity, woodworking, metal grinding and horizontal milling machine regulations.
2 26 Halsbury's Statutes, 3rd Edn., 860.

Accidents Rules 1902 (S.R. & O. 1902 No. 616) were made. The rules have been amended by S.R. & O. 1907 No. 696; 1911 No. 1058; 1926 No. 355 and 1931 No. 945.

The Act, by s. 16, applies to 'any railway used for the purposes of public traffic whether passenger, goods, or other traffic, and includes any works of the railway company connected with the railway'. The Act and the Rules would therefore apply not only to ordinary railway lines, but also to public lines and sidings on docks, which are not within the sidings regulations under the Factories Act.

Prevention of Accidents Rules 1902–31

(i) Safe running of trains

By reg. 3, all engines must be fitted with power brakes as well as hand brakes: but there is an exception where the engine is used exclusively for shunting, and the hand brakes are sufficiently powerful.

By reg. 8, all trains which are on running lines beyond the limits of stations must have brake vans or other suitable vehicles for the use of the men in charge of the train: and such vans must be attached so that they can be conveniently used, with due regard to the safety of the train. The regulations of 1907 grant an exemption from the requirement for certain trains on the Taff Vale railway.

Under the regulations of 1911, all wagons must have brake levers on both sides, complying with the conditions set out in the Schedule to the regulations. The Second Schedule contains a number of exemptions, in particular wagons used on railways with a gauge of less than 4 feet 8½ inches (i.e. less than the standard gauge).

By reg. 7, tool-boxes on running locomotives, where tools or other things are kept, are to be accessible without undue risk while the engine is in motion. Under the same regulation, there must be a water gauge or similar device on the engine or tender to show the level of the water in the tanks, and the gauge must be visible and accessible without undue risk.

(ii) Boiler gauges

By reg. 6:

'All boiler gauge glasses on locomotive engines or stationary steam boilers used in the working of railways must . . . be protected by a covering or guard sufficient to guard against accident to persons employed on the railway through the gauge glasses breaking.'

(iii) Point rods, signal wires and ground levers
By reg. 5, where point rods and signal wires are in such a position as to be a source of danger to railway workers, they must be sufficiently covered or otherwise guarded.

Ground levers working points must be so placed that the men working them are clear of the adjacent lines. In addition, the levers must either be parallel to the adjacent lines, or in such a position and of such form that they cause as little obstruction as possible. It has been held that if the lever (i.e. the direction of movement of the lever) is parallel to the adjacent line, the alternative requirement does not apply; and that it is sufficient for the lever to move parallel to the adjacent line which is 'relevant', i.e. apparently the one whose points it works, although there is a converging line with which it necessarily makes an angle: *Hicks v British Transport Commission* [1958] 2 All ER 39. The argument that the alternative, 'position' and 'form' involving the least obstruction, must necessarily apply where there are converging lines, was rejected.

(iv) Shunting
By reg. 4, all stations and sidings where shunting is frequently carried out after dark are to be sufficiently lighted.

By reg. 1, wagons must be labelled on both sides.

Regulation 2 forbids the moving of vehicles by means of a prop or pole, unless no other means of dealing with traffic is reasonably practicable. Towing with a rope or chain attached to a vehicle on an adjacent line is also forbidden, subject to the same exception.

(v) Look-out man to protect permanent way workers
Regulation 9, which requires a look-out man to be appointed where there is danger to workmen repairing or re-laying the lines, is the most important of the regulations, and reads as follows:

> 'With the object of protecting men working singly or in gangs on or near lines of railway in use for traffic for the purpose of re-laying or repairing the permanent way of such lines, the railway companies shall . . . in all cases where danger is likely to arise, provide persons or apparatus for the purpose of maintaining a good look-out or for giving warning against any train or engine approaching such men so working, and the persons employed for such purpose shall be expressly

instructed to act for such purpose, and shall be provided with all appliances necessary to give effect to such look-out.'

There is no automatic necessity to provide a look-out whenever men are working on the lines; the duty is imposed only 'where danger is likely to occur'. It was therefore argued in *Hutchinson v London and North Eastern Rail. Co* [1942] 1 KB 481, [1942] 1 All ER 330 that a look-out need not be provided on a fine day when there is good visibility for some distance along the lines, but only when there is some special danger such as bad visibility or a curve in the line. The Court of Appeal rejected this argument, but gave the following examples as cases where it might not be necessary to provide a look-out:

A branch line where trains only run occasionally.

A place where men are working 'near' the line, but not so near as to be in danger.

In *Cade v British Transport Commission* [1959] AC 256, [1958] 2 All ER 615 the House of Lords upheld a decision that no look-out need be provided where a single man was examining a track for defects and tightening bolts: a number of goods trains passed along the track, but not at high speed, and there was good visibility for quarter of a mile each way. Viscount Kilmuir LC said that it had to be shown in each case that danger was 'likely', as the rule requires, not merely 'possible'; and the estimate of danger must take into account 'the amount and speed of traffic on the line, the visibility allowed by gradients and bends and weather conditions, the nature of the work to be done, and also the skill and experience of the men or man about to do it'. In other words, the fact that a man working on his own may be absorbed in his work, at any rate if it is work of short duration, is not enough in itself to necessitate a look-out. But when three men were likely to be absorbed in a task which would take some time, near a live electric line where an unscheduled train or engine might appear unexpectedly, danger was held likely to arise: *Keaney v British Railways Board* [1968] 2 All ER 532, [1968] 1 WLR 879.

A workman is not within the scope of the rule unless three conditions are satisfied:

(i) He must be working on or near 'the permanent way'.

(ii) He must be a 'permanent way man'.

(iii) He must be 're-laying or repairing' the permanent way.

These conditions were considered by the House of Lords in *London and*

North Eastern Rail Co v Berriman [1946] AC 278, [1946] 1 All ER 255 where a workman was killed while oiling signals apparatus on the line. No look-out man had been appointed, and the railway company contended that they were under no duty to appoint one.

As regards the 'permanent way', it was argued that in railway vernacular this did not include signals apparatus, but only the line and track, and that it should be given the same meaning in the rules. A majority of the House thought that the words 'permanent way' retain their normal meaning and (per Lord Porter) included:

> 'Not only the track itself but also all the equipment of guiding a train on its proper course and on to its proper track as well as the metals on which it runs and the ground or structure supporting them.'

Similarly, it was argued that 'permanent way men' were a recognised category of railway employees to which persons attending to signals apparatus did not belong. Here, too, a majority of the House thought (per Lord Wright) that:

> 'No more is meant than "men whose work has to be done upon the permanent way".'

However, they decided that oiling of apparatus was not repair work, so the deceased workman was outside the scope of the rule. As was pointed out, the result is not as unreasonable as may at first sight appear. Men engaged in repair are likely to take some time and to become absorbed in their work; oiling, on the other hand, is a shorter process, and the workman may be expected to keep a look-out himself.

Repair work does include replacing of old wedges under the lines with new ones: *Ferguson v North British Rly Co* 1915 SC 566; it also includes the tightening of loose bolts: *Cade v British Transport Commission* [1959] AC 256, [1958] 2 All ER 615; *Reilly v British Transport Commission* [1956] 3 All ER 857; but it does not include carrying out an inspection of a stretch of line to see what repairs are required: *Judson v British Transport Commission* [1954] 1 All ER 624; *Douglas v British Railways Board* 1981 SLT (Notes) 50[3].

The nature of the duty to provide a look-out man was considered in *Vincent v Southern Rly Co* [1927] AC 430 where a foreman went off with another man to do repair work: apparently they stepped off one line to

---

3   In *Cade v British Transport Commission* [1959] AC 256, [1958] 2 All ER 615, however, the House of Lords doubted some of the reasoning in *Judson's* case.

avoid a train, but were killed by a train on the other line which they had not observed. There was nothing to show whether the foreman, Vincent, had appointed the other man as look-out, or had undertaken the duty himself. The company relied on a rule which said that it was for the foreman to decide whether a look-out was necessary, and to appoint one accordingly. The trial judge had expressed the opinion that the company had carried out their statutory duty merely by making the rule. Viscount Cave LC (with whom Lord Atkinson and Lord Shaw of Dunfermline concurred) said, at p. 437:

> 'The duty of a company in case of danger is an absolute duty to provide a look-out man and to see that he is instructed to act; and if in any case it were proved that the foreman . . . had not appointed a look-out man, the company might well be held liable for injury happening to any member of the gang other than the foreman himself.'

However, there was a two-fold difficulty in Vincent's way. First, there was no evidence that he had failed to appoint a look-out man. Secondly, if he had failed—

> 'In that case Vincent would have been in default for not complying with the company's regulations which bound him to appoint a proper look-out, and his representative could not recover for the consequences of his own default.'

The action, therefore, did not succeed.

The opinion was expressed that the look-out man could be a member of the gang; there was no need to appoint a completely separate person: but it has been held that in certain circumstances a look-out man may have to be free of all other duties, and that he must be instructed to ensure that his warning reaches each individual in the gang: *Redpath v London and North Eastern Rly Co* [1944] SC 154.

In some cases it may be necessary to appoint two look-out men. Thus in *Dyer v Southern Rly Co* [1948] 1 KB 608, [1948] 1 All ER 516 men were working in the outskirts of London, between a tunnel and a station, at a point where traffic was frequent in both directions, and it was held that, as one man could not keep an efficient watch on both the up line and the down line, the appointment of one look-out man was not sufficient to comply with the rule. Humphreys J held that:

> 'Compliance with the rule only takes place when apparatus reasonably effective or persons effective for the purpose required have been provided.'

The decision in *Redpath's* case, *supra*, implies that it may be necessary to have one look-out man at a distance, and another man, close to the gang, to receive and pass on his warning.

2 Private sidings attached to factories, mines and quarries

Factory sidings

Special regulations have been made under the Factories Acts for the use of locomotives and wagons on lines and sidings used in connection with premises subject to those Acts (S.R. & O. 1906 No. 679). These regulations apply mainly to sidings attached to factories in the strict sense of the term. They do not apply to sidings attached to mines and quarries. There are exemptions for lines of less than 3 feet gauge, lines where mechanical power is not used, and lines which lie outside the factory precincts and are used for running purposes only. Railway premises and tramsheds are excluded, also dock sidings and lines on building sites; but apparently the regulations do apply to engineering sites. Lastly, even if mechanical power is used on the sidings, the regulations do not apply when wagons are moved by hand. Apparently the regulations apply for the protection of all persons employed at the sidings, whether engaged in the movement of traffic or not: the dictum to the contrary in *Stanton Ironworks Co Ltd v Skipper* [1956] 1 QB 255, [1955] 3 All ER 544 was disapproved in *Massey-Harris-Ferguson (Manufacturing) Ltd v Piper* [1956] 2 QB 396, [1956] 2 All ER 722. The duty to comply with regs. 1 to 8 is imposed on the occupier: the person who 'carries on any . . . operations' is responsible for regs. 9 to 22, whether or not he is also the occupier: *Wagon Repairs Ltd v Vosper* (1968) 3 KIR 605.

As regards the protection of water gauges on boilers (reg. 22), the covering or guarding of point rods and signal wires (reg. 1) and the position and construction of ground levers (reg. 2), the requirements are the same as in the Prevention of Accidents Rules 1902, p. 565–566, *ante*. Lines of rails and points are to be examined regularly and kept in efficient order (reg. 3).

Coupling poles or similar mechanical appliances are to be provided (reg. 5) and in general only these appliances are to be used in coupling or uncoupling locomotives and wagons (reg. 11). Sprags and scotches are to be provided for holding wagons stationary (reg. 6) and used as and when necessary (reg. 12).

As under the Prevention of Accidents Rules 1902, wagons are not to be moved by means of a prop or pole, or towed by a chain or rope attached to a vehicle on an adjacent line, unless no other method is practicable; but there is an express exception where ladles containing hot material are moved near a furnace (reg. 13).

To avoid the danger of persons being crushed, when materials are placed within 3 feet of a line of rails at points where workmen have to pass, there must be recesses at 20-yard intervals (reg. 9). No person is to cross a line by crawling under wagons (reg. 10).

With certain exceptions, a warning must be given to persons in the vicinity before a locomotive or wagon is set in motion (reg. 16). Where a locomotive pushes more than one wagon, a man must usually be sent on ahead; but this does not apply to fly-shunting or to movements of wagons containing molten or other dangerous materials (reg. 14). A whistle or other warning must be given when a locomotive approaches a level crossing, or a dangerous curve, or other point of special danger (reg. 18). There are restrictions on riding on wagons and locomotives (reg. 15), and drivers and shunters must be at least 18 and 16 years old respectively (reg. 21). Where wagons are under repair, a danger signal must be displayed if there is any risk in the vicinity from moving locomotives or wagons (reg. 19).

During the hours of darkness (from one hour after sunset to one hour before sunrise), or in foggy weather, there must be efficient lighting while shunting or other operations are going on (reg. 7) and, unless the stationary lighting is sufficient, a moving locomotive or wagon must be preceded by a light (reg. 17).

A gantry must be provided with a footway, and also a fence, if necessary (reg. 4).

There are also regulations for the maintenance and use of capstans (regs. 8, 20).

Mine and quarry sidings

Sidings on or adjacent to the surface of a mine or quarry form part of the mine or quarry: Mines and Quarries Act 1954, s. 180(3). Railways *serving* a mine or quarry also fall within the Act, under s. 180(5), if they do not belong to the British Railways Board (or other statutory railway undertakers). Thus, traffic on these lines and sidings is subject to regulations made under the Act of 1954.

The regulations now in force are the Coal and other Mines (Sidings) Regulations 1956 (S.I. No. 1773), which apply to mines of coal, stratified ironstone, shale and fireclay, and the Quarries (General) Regulations 1956 (S.I. No. 1780), Part III, which apply to all quarries. There are no general regulations for miscellaneous mines: reg. 61 of the Miscellaneous Mines (General) Regulations 1956 (S.I. No. 1778) leaves the use of sidings to be regulated by the special rules of each mine.

The regulations for Coal and other Mines, and for Quarries, are almost word for word identical, and will be summarised together.

Application
They apply to all lines and sidings at the mine surface, or at the quarry, which form part of the mine or quarry under s. 180(3) or (5), except where the line is of less than 4 feet 8½ inches width (the standard gauge) (reg. 1 (mines), reg. 23 (quarries)).

Equipment, points etc.
Points rods and signal wires in a position causing danger must be covered or guarded (reg. 3(a), mines; reg. 24(a), quarries). A ground lever operating points on a line must be installed in such a way that the person operating it is clear of traffic on all lines, the direction of movement must be parallel to the nearest line, and the lever must cause the minimum of obstruction (reg. 3(b), mines; reg. 24(b), quarries): these requirements do not apply unless the line was constructed after 10 June 1911 (mines) or 29 June 1938 (quarries). Coupling poles or other appliances must be provided for coupling and uncoupling vehicles (reg. 4(a), mines; reg. 25(a), quarries) and where it is practicable to use such a pole or appliance, coupling or uncoupling a vehicle while in motion by any other method is forbidden (reg. 8, mines; reg. 27(3), quarries). There must be a supply of pointed wooden sprags and scotches (reg. 4(b), mines; reg. 25(b), quarries); and at a mine-surface where there is a 'self-acting incline' (i.e. an arrangement by which trucks running down one line by gravity pull trucks up another line) there must be safety devices to stop vehicles running away and also stop-blocks at

the top of each line (reg. 4(c): mines only). A vehicle must not be left on such an incline unless properly secured (reg. 15: mines only). Persons operating points must make sure they are left in the correct position (reg. 5, mines; reg. 26, quarries).

Movement of trucks and trains

No movement of any vehicle (which, of course, includes both trucks and locomotives) must take place unless 'under the charge of a competent person' (reg. 6, mines; reg. 27(1), quarries). A locomotive driver must be at least 18 and a shunter must be 16 (reg. 21, mines; reg. 36, quarries). At a *mine*, a train for the conveyance of workmen must be accompanied by a competent person in charge of both train and passengers, and persons are forbidden to get on or off such a train while it is moving or to ride on a footboard, buffer or coupling (reg. 2, mines only: this applies to lines of *any* gauge—see reg. 1). Where two or more vehicles are *pushed* by a locomotive, someone must in general go forward with or in front of the leading vehicle to keep a look-out and give warning (reg. 9, mines; reg. 27(4), quarries); and warning must be given when any vehicle is about to be moved (reg. 10, mines; reg. 27(5), quarries); but these rules as to look-out and warning do not apply if no person employed is exposed to danger. In the hours of darkness or in fog, a locomotive or train must not be moved in a part of the mine or quarry where persons pass on foot to work, unless there is sufficient fixed lighting or a warning light is fixed or carried at the leading end of the locomotive or train (reg. 11, mines; reg. 28, quarries). The driver of a locomotive or the person preceding it must give timely and audible warning at level crossings, curves which are not in full view, and other places of danger (reg. 12, mines; reg. 29, quarries). Vehicles must not be moved by means of a prop or pole if any other method is practicable (reg. 7, mines; reg. 27(2), quarries) nor must any attempt be made to move a vehicle by pushing a buffer (reg. 13, mines; reg. 30, quarries). Riding on a buffer is forbidden unless there is secure handhold, also standing on it unless there is a secure footplate: riding on a pole or prop drawn by a vehicle is also forbidden (reg. 14, mines; reg. 31, quarries).

Miscellaneous

Where a space is left between vehicles for passage across a line, the space must be at least 15 feet wide (reg. 16, mines; reg. 32, quarries). If a vehicle is under repair on a line, danger signs must be displayed at each end of the vehicle (or the train) to prevent it being struck or moved by another vehicle (reg. 17, mines; reg. 33, quarries). No person except the person in charge may pass in front of or between vehicles under screens (at a mine) or at a loading point (at a quarry) and crossing a line by passing underneath vehicles is also forbidden where there is any danger (regs. 18 and 19, mines; reg. 34, quarries). Finally, if material is placed within 3 feet of a line at a place where persons employed have to pass[4], it must be stacked in such a way that persons can pass safely, and if the distance involved exceeds 60 feet there must be recesses in the material every 60 feet (mines, reg. 20; quarries, reg. 35). At a mine this does not apply to a place ordinarily used for stocking material.

3 Shipping

Shipping law is a large subject, of which only a brief summary can be given. It is a maze of detailed legislation, much of it consisting of successive International Conventions which do not automatically apply to foreign ships in British waters unless their states of registration have acceded to them, though British safety legislation often applies to foreign ships in port. The monumental Merchant Shipping Act 1894 is still to some extent in force, like the trunk of an ancient banyan tree in the midst of a thicket of new shoots which have taken on independent life. The most important safety legislation is now contained in the Merchant Shipping (Safety Convention) Act 1977 which gave effect to the International Convention for the Safety of Life at Sea of 1974, and the Merchant Shipping Act 1979, which was legislation of domestic origin to modernise the position of seamen in matters of discipline at sea, and also included safety provisions. A further Convention—the Merchant Shipping (Minimum Standards) Convention 1976—was chiefly concerned with the safety of seamen in or about the ship, rather than the safety of the ship as a whole, and this has been brought into force by regulations under the 1979 Act. The Act of 1977 applies to

---

4   The words of reg. 20, 'required' to pass, do not mean ordered or instructed: it is sufficient if the route is a reasonable way to a place where a workman has to be: *Smith (or Westwood) v National Coal Board* [1967] 2 All ER 593, [1967] 1 WLR 871.

ships registered in the United Kingdom wherever they may be, and to ships of other countries which have acceded to the 1974 Convention while in United Kingdom ports. Previous legislation remains in force for other foreign ships in United Kingdom ports. (Earlier Acts of 1949 and 1964 had given effect to earlier Conventions.)

Sections 21–22 of the Act of 1979 give power to make regulations for the safety and health of persons on ships on similar lines to the power in the Health and Safety at Work Act 1974. Under this Act, the Merchant Shipping (Health and Safety: General Duties) Regulations 1984 (S.I. No. 408, amended by S.I. 1988 No. 1396) have been made. These impose a general duty on employers to ensure safety, particularly as regards equipment, place of work and system of work. This follows the lines of the similar duty under the 1974 Act, and failure to comply with it is a criminal offence: but from the point of view of civil liability for damages it adds nothing to the employer's common law duty from which it is of course derived.

There is also an official 'Code of Safe Working Practices for Merchant Seamen', which is intended as a guide for the seamen themselves, and every seaman is entitled to ask for a copy: S.I. 1980 No. 686; and the numerous safety regulations summarised later in this section have mostly been made under the Act of 1979.

The Merchant Shipping Act 1984 introduced a further innovation derived from the 1974 Act, by authorising the issue of improvement and prohibition notices in the interests of safety.

As regards collisions, members of a crew could not usually claim damages at common law for the negligence of their own ship, owing to the doctrine of common employment. Under the present law, as contained in the Law Reform (Personal Injuries) Act 1948, they have the same rights as members of the public.

Seaworthiness

The main statutory duty of a shipowner (and a master) to his crew is to see that the ship is seaworthy.

Under s. 30 of the Merchant Shipping Act 1988 (replacing s. 457 of the Act of 1894 which made it an offence to send an 'unseaworthy' ship to sea) it is an offence for any ship in a United Kingdom port, or a United Kingdom ship in a foreign port, to be in a state in which it would be dangerous to go to sea, whether due to the condition of the hull, equipment or machinery, or to undermanning, or to overloading or improper loading, or to anything else relevant to safety. It is a defence to prove that arrangements were in train to make the ship fit to go to sea. Under s. 31 of the Act of 1988, the owner may also be liable to prosecution for the unsafe *operation* of the ship. These sections are primarily concerned with creating criminal offences. Under s. 458 of the Act of 1894, which is still in force, it is an implied term in the contract of every seaman or apprentice that the owner, the master, and any agent in charge of loading

> 'shall use all reasonable means to ensure the seaworthiness of the ship for the voyage at the time when the voyage commences, and to keep her in a seaworthy condition for the voyage during the voyage.'

By a proviso to the section, default may be excused in special circumstances where it is 'reasonable and justifiable' to send a ship to sea when not completely seaworthy.

'Seaworthy' means 'fit to face the normal perils of the sea'. In *Hedley v Pinkney & Sons SS Co* [1894] AC 222 rails and stanchions had been provided on board the ship, but they had not been used to raise the bulwarks to a safe height at a certain point, and a sailor went overboard in a storm. The House of Lords held that the ship was not unseaworthy, as proper appliances had been provided, and the real cause of the accident was the master's failure to use them[5]. In *M'Leod v Hastie & Sons* 1936 SC 501 a windlass had been allowed to get rusty, and the pawl failed to operate as a brake, with the result that one of the ship's officers was injured. The Court of Session held that there was no breach of s. 458, as the defective condition of the windlass did not make the ship unfit to face the perils of the sea.

These very general duties are now less likely to be invoked to establish civil liability, because a large number of detailed regulations have been made under s. 21 of the Merchant Shipping Act 1979, and under the earlier Act of 1970 which gave power (ss. 19–21, 24–5) to make regulations about safe working and access, crew accommodation, provisions and water and medical stores and treatment.

These regulations fall into two main groups: those concerned with the

---

5   Under the doctrine of common employment, the owners were not at that date liable for the master's negligence.

safety of the ship as a whole, and those concerned with the safety of the seamen and others in and around the ship.

All of them apply in full to United Kingdom ships. For their application to other ships, it is necessary to look at the particular regulations. In general, safety regulations do apply to foreign ships in British ports and territorial waters (unless driven to take refuge by bad weather or other emergency) and there are sometimes powers to detain foreign ships which are in a dangerous state: but of course British regulations cannot apply to the permanent features of a foreign ship such as its structure and equipment, unless it belongs to a state which is a party to the corresponding International Convention. Some of the earlier regulations made around 1965 still apply to certain ships such as non-Convention ships and ships from British dependencies which are not within the later regulations: e.g. regulations on fire appliances, life-saving appliances and pilot ladders.

No ship may go to sea on an international voyage without a certificate of safety: Merchant Shipping (Safety Convention) Act 1949 s. 12 as amended by S.I. 1981 No. 573 and 1985 No. 211.

The safety of the ship as a whole

(i) Construction

Construction regulations—which vary according to the type and age of the ship—govern such matters as division into watertight compartments, bilge pumps, boilers, electrical installations, fire safety, machinery, anchors, guard rails, and roll-on roll-off ('RO/RO') arrangements for vehicle ferries. There are additional requirements for structural fire protection in more modern ships, and special regulations for submersible craft (submarines in civilian use) and tankers carrying liquid gas or chemicals. The current regulations (abbreviating 'Merchant Shipping' as 'M.S.') are as follows:

FOR SHIPS BUILT OR CONVERTED BEFORE I SEPTEMBER 1984
M.S. (Passenger Ship Construction and Survey) Regulations 1980: S.I. 1980 No. 535 amended by 1981 No. 580, 1986 No. 1070, 1987 No. 1886, 1987 No. 2238.
M.S. (Cargo Ship Construction and Survey) Regulations 1981: S.I. 1981 No. 572 amended by 1984 No. 1219 and 1985 No. 663.

FOR SHIPS CONSTRUCTED OR CONVERTED LATER

M.S. (Passenger Ship Construction and Survey) Regulation 1984: S.I. 1984 No. 1216 amended by 1985 No. 660, 1986 No. 1074, 1987 No. 1886, 1987 No. 2238.

M.S. (Cargo Ship Construction and Survey) Regulations 1984: S.I. 1984 No. 1217 amended by 1986 No. 1067.

OTHER REGULATIONS FOR SPECIAL MATTERS

M.S. (Gas Carriers) Regulations 1986: S.I. 1986 No. 1073.

M.S. (Chemical Tankers) Regulations 1986: S.I. 1986 No. 1068.

M.S. (Submersible Craft Construction and Survey) Regulations 1981: S.I. 1981 No. 1098 amended by 1987 No. 306.

M.S. (Fire Protection) Regulations 1984: S.I. 1984 No. 1218 amended by 1985 No. 1193 and 1986 No. 1070 (for ships constructed on or after 1 September 1984).

M.S. (Fire Protection) (Ships built before 25 May 1980) Regulations 1985: S.I. 1985 No. 1218 amended by 1986 No. 1070. (Ships built between 1980 and 1985 come within the general 'construction' regulations, above.)

(ii) Equipment and supplies

The titles of the regulations are self-explanatory. The requirements vary according to the size and type of ship.

M.S. (Navigational Equipment) Regulations S.I. 1984 No. 408 amended by 1985 No. 659 (compass, radar, echo-sounder, instruments to measure speed and distance).

M.S. (Carriage of Nautical Publications) Rules S.I. 1975 No. 700 (charts and other information relevant to the voyage).

M.S. (Automatic Pilot and Testing of Steering Gear) Regulations S.I. 1981 No. 571.

M.S. (Radio Installations) Regulations S.I. 1980 No. 529 amended by 1984 No. 346, 1984 No. 1223, 1985 No. 1216, 1986 No. 1075.

Anchors and Chain Cables Act 1967, and Rules, S.I. 1970, No. 1453. (Test and certification required.)

M.S. (Pilot Ladders and Hoists) Regulations S.I. 1987 No. 1961.

M.S. (Fire Appliances) Regulations S.I. 1980 No. 544 amended 1981 No. 574, 1985 No. 1194, 1986 No. 1070.

M.S. (Life-Saving Appliances) Regulations S.I. 1980 No. 538 amended

1981 No. 577, 1986 No. 1072. (Scales and types of life-boats and their equipment, rafts, life jackets, marker buoys, life lines.)
M.S. (Life-Saving Appliances) Regulations S.I. 1986 No. 1066 (new ships from 1 October 1987).
M.S. (Protective Clothing and Equipment) Regulations S.I. 1985 No. 1664 (for work on ships for which such protection is necessary, e.g. respirators for confined spaces with fumes).
M.S. (Provisions & Water) Regulations S.I. 1989 No. 102.
M.S. (Medical Stores) Regulations S.I. 1986 No. 144 amended by 1988 No. 1116.
M.S. (Crew Accommodation) Regulations S.I. 1978 No. 795 amended by 1979 No. 491, 1984 No. 41, 1989 No. 184 (cabins and their furniture and ancillary facilities: a seaman injured by a scalding shower recovered damages for a breach of the earlier regulations: *Foulder v Canadian Pacific Steamships Ltd* [1969] 1 All ER 283).

For gangways and accommodation ladders, see below ('Means of Access').

(iii) Cargo safety
Under a series of Acts it has become obligatory to paint load lines ('Plimsoll Lines') on a ship, and the ship must not be so loaded that at any time during the voyage it is submerged below these lines while on an even keel. The legislation now in force is contained in the Merchant Shipping (Load Lines) Act 1967 and the M.S. (Load Lines) Rules 1968 (S.I. 1968 No. 1053 amended by 1970 No. 1003, 1979 No. 1267 and 1980 No. 641). It does not apply to warships, fishing boats or private pleasure boats: other vessels may be exempted if very small or on sheltered voyages.

Under the same Act, deck cargo (particularly timber) is subject to strict regulations to ensure the stability of the ship: M.S. (Load Lines) (Deck Cargo) Regulations S.I. 1968 No. 1089.

The safe loading of grain—which may shift and endanger stability—is regulated by the M.S. (Grain) Regulations S.I. 1985 No. 1217.

Dangerous goods in general—of which chemicals, petrol and explosives are some examples—are controlled by the M.S. (Dangerous Goods) Regulations 1981 (S.I. 1981 No. 1747 amended by 1986 No. 1069), which require marking, labelling, specific notification to the master of the ship and safe stowage: see also the regulations under 'Docks' in Chapter 14 on dangerous substances in harbour areas.

The M.S. (Tankers) (E.E.C. Requirements) Regulations S.I. 1981 No. 1077 amended by 1982 No. 1637 require notification to the harbour master and safety precautions in the harbour area.

The Loading and Stability (RO/RO) Regulations—S.I. 1989 No. 100 for United Kingdom ships, 1989 No. 567 for others—relate to 'roll-on roll-off' ships carrying vehicles and require equipment to calculate stability. There are also the M.S. (Stability of Passenger Ships) Regulations S.I. 1988 No 1693.

(iv) Navigation and general safety
The M.S. (Distress Signals and Prevention of Collisions) Regulations 1989 (S.I. 1989 No. 1798) contain the full text of the International Regulations for the Prevention of Collisions at Sea, as well as the approved international distress signals. The occasions when such signals may be used are set out in the M.S. (Signals of Distress) Rules S.I. 1977 No. 1010.

The M.S. (Navigational Warnings) Rules S.I. 1980 No. 534 require warning to be given to the authorities, and to other ships, when dangers are encountered such as icebergs, derelicts and heavy storms.

The M.S. (Smooth and Partially Smooth Waters) Regulations S.I. 1987 No. 1591 define such areas for the purpose of navigational regulations.

The M.S. (Closing of Openings in Hulls and in Watertight Bulkheads) Regulations S.I. 1987 No. 1298 control the closing of watertight doors between compartments and require periodic testing at sea. The M.S. (Closing of Openings in Enclosed Superstructures and in Bulkheads above the Bulkhead Deck) Regulations S.I. 1988 No. 317 amended by 1988 No. 642 relate to watertight doors above deck level, such as vehicle doors on 'roll-on roll-off' ferries.

The M.S. (Certification and Watchkeeping) Regulations S.I. 1982 No. 1699 require continuous watches to be kept both at sea and when the ship is in port.

The M.S. (Musters and Training) Regulations S.I. 1986 No. 1071 require crew training for emergencies—some members of the crew may be sailing for the first time—and periodic assembly at emergency stations, commonly called 'life-boat drill'. (However, the practical exercises carried out by seamen are about fighting fires, the greatest danger at sea, even more than about preparations for 'abandoning ship'.

For diving and submarine operations from ships, see Chapter 19.

Safety of individuals on and about the ship

Several new codes of regulations, made in 1988 under the Merchant
Shipping Act 1979, have imposed for the first time safety requirements
on ships similar to those which apply to workplaces on shore. They are
in force from 1 January 1989. Many of these requirements, of course,
merely reflect the established practice of responsible shipowners.

They apply to United Kingdom registered ships, with the exception
of fishing vessels, private pleasure craft, offshore installations ('oil rigs')
if on or within 500 metres of their station, and unmanned ships if they do
not even have a watchman on board. In the case of foreign ships subject
to the 1976 Convention, infringements of safety rules may be reported
to their own state, and the ship itself may be detained if in a dangerous
condition. Although the regulations do not directly apply to foreign
ships, they set a standard of safety which has been internationally agreed
and infringement is therefore strong evidence of negligence, especially
in the case of ships of foreign registry owned by British shipowners.

(i) M.S. (Guarding of Machinery and Safety of Electrical Equipment)
Regulations S.I. 1988 No. 1636
Regulation 3(1) requires dangerous parts of the ship's machinery to be
securely guarded unless equally safe by position or construction.
Regulation 3(2) allows exceptions when the machinery *has* to be in
motion while *not* guarded, *either* to ensure the safety of the ship *or* for an
examination, adjustment, lubrication or test shown to be immediately
necessary: but this is subject to a number of conditions:
  (a) the exposure must be to the minimum extent necessary;
  (b) the operation must be authorised by a ship's officer;
  (c) it must be carried out by a competent person who has an adequate
       area to work in;
  (d) there must be a warning notice and persons nearby must be given
       safety instructions.
Under reg. 3(4) there must be a means of stopping machinery promptly
in emergency.

By reg. 4, the employers and the master must 'ensure' (a strong word)
that all electrical equipment and installations are 'so constructed,
installed, operated and maintained' that the ship and all persons are
protected against electrical hazards.

These requirements, both for machinery and electricity, are similar (with some variations) to those under the Factories Act, and much of the case law is relevant.

(ii) M.S. (Hatches & Lifting Plant) Regulations S.I. 1988 No. 1639

The requirements for hatches are the same as in the Docks Regulations, Chapter 14, section 5. In addition, power-operated hatch covers, and ramps on car decks, are not to be operated except on the authority of a ship's officer.

By reg. 6(1), 'lifting plant'—both the lifting 'appliance' such as a ship's derrick, and the lifting 'gear' attached to it such as a sling—must be of 'good design, sound construction and material, of adequate strength for the purpose for which it is used'—which must mean the *de facto* as distinct from intended use—also 'free from patent defect, and properly installed or assembled and maintained'. By reg. 6(2), pallets, slings and other lifting attachments must be of good construction, adequate strength for their actual use and free from patent defect. (For similar requirements under the Factories Act and Docks Regulations, and case-law, see Chapter 10, section 4 and Chapter 14, section 5.)

Regular tests and examinations are required: regs.7, 8. The safe working load is to be marked, and must not be exceeded: reg. 9.

(iii) M.S. (Means of Access) Regulations S.I. 1988 No. 1637

These replace, with improvements, earlier regulations of 1981.

By reg. 4, there must be safe means of access between the ship and the quay, pontoon or other ship alongside. However, where access is gained via another ship, the safety of the access from the other side of that ship is not the responsibility of the first ship: *Smith v Brown* 1988 SLT 151 (decided under the 1981 regulations).

In particular, such means of access must be properly constructed and maintained, put in position promptly, properly secured, adjusted for safety (e.g. for tide levels) and adequately lit.

Where access between ship and shore is 'necessary' but it is not alongside, access must be provided in a safe manner. This obviously involves both the use of boats and the means of embarking from the ship (accommodation ladder for example) and also of landing safely at the jetty.

Ships 120 metres long or over must carry an accommodation ladder (reg. 6) and those of 300 metres or over a gangway as well (reg. 5). Portable ladders and rope ladders must not be used for access if safer means are reasonably practicable (reg.7). A life buoy and safety line must be available at access points (reg. 8) also a safety net where there is a risk of falling (reg. 9). All persons must use the authorised access only (reg. 10).

(iv) M.S. (Safe Movement on Board Ship) Regulations S.I. 1988 No. 1641
The requirements are similar to those under the Factories Act, and the case-law is relevant: but the wording is improved to meet some of the difficulties which have arisen.

Safe means of access must be provided and maintained to 'any place on the ship to which a person may be expected to go': reg. 4.

The owners and master must 'ensure'—a strong word—that deck surfaces used for transit about the ship, and all passageways, walkways and stairs, are properly maintained 'and kept free from material or substances liable to cause a person to slip or fall': reg. 5.

All parts of the ship used for loading or unloading, or for other work, or for transit, must be adequately lit: reg. 6.

Guards or fencing must be maintained at any 'opening, open hatchway or dangerous edge' where a person is liable to fall, except where the opening is a means of transit, or where it is not practicable to maintain fencing because of work in progress: reg. 8.

Ladders must be of good construction, sound material, adequate strength for the purpose for which they are used, free from patent defect and properly maintained: reg. 9.

Vehicles and mobile lifting appliances on board must be properly maintained, and operated only by authorised and competent persons: reg. 10. Also, danger from their movement must be prevented as far as reasonably practicable: in other words there must be some sort of traffic control for movements on board ship.

In new ships, access ladders to the ship's holds must comply with official standards.

(v) M.S. (Entry into Dangerous Spaces) Regulations S.I. 1988 No. 1639
Standard procedures have to be established for entering dangerous spaces such as tanks where there may be fumes or foul air: reg. 5. Oxygen meters and other test devices must be kept: reg. 7. Rescue drills must be practised every two months, except for ships under 1,000 tons (or 500 if gas carriers): reg. 6.

Finally, entrances to unattended dangerous spaces must be kept closed except when entry is necessary: reg. 4.

Fishing vessels

These are in general excepted from the main regulations but have special codes of regulations of their own which apply to vessels of United Kingdom registry.

A series of disasters where fishing vessels capsized under a load of black ice, or vanished in severe gales or in unexplained circumstances, led to the Fishing Vessels (Safety Provisions) Act 1970 and the Fishing Vessels (Safety Provisions) Rules 1975 (S.I. 1975 No. 330 amended by 1975 No. 471, 1976 No. 432, 1977 Nos. 313 and 498, 1978 Nos. 1598 and 1873 and 1981 No. 567). These relate to construction and survey, equipment, life-saving and fire appliances, and navigational equipment including radio, D/F and radar. There are also the M.S. (Crew Accommodation) (Fishing Vessels) Regulations S.I. 1975 No. 2220; M.S. (Radio) (Fishing Vessels) Regulations S.I. 1974 No. 1919; M.S. (Medical Stores) (Fishing Vessels) Regulations S.I. 1988 No. 1547; M.S. (Provisions and Water) (Fishing Vessels) Regulations S.I. 1972 No. 1972; Fishing Vessels (Safety Training) Regulations S.I. 1989 No. 126.

The Safety at Sea Act 1986 required fishing vessels of a certain size (normally 12 metres or more) to carry radio beacons indicating their position, and life rafts automatically floating free on shipwreck; vessels under that size must carry life jackets for every person on board and some spares. More detailed requirements on these matters are now contained in the Fishing Vessels (Life-Saving Appliances) Regulations S.I. 1988 No. 38.

Special cases

(i) Hovercraft

The Merchant Shipping Acts, in particular the Collision Rules, are applied with modifications to hovercraft at sea: Hovercraft (Application of Enactments) Order 1972 (S.I. No. 971), as amended from time to time, made under the Hovercraft Act 1968. The Regulations for Prevention of Collisions at Sea and the Signals of Distress code were applied by S.I. 1977 No. 1257 and the Dangerous Goods Regulations by S.I. 1982 No. 715.

(ii) Seaplanes
These are brought within the collisions at sea regulations by the Collision Rules (Seaplanes) Order 1989 (S.I. 1989 No. 2005).

(iii) Diving operations
For regulations on diving operations from ships, see Chapter 19, section 2.

4 Aviation

Aviation law is now to be found in the Civil Aviation Act 1982 and the Air Navigation Order 1985 (S.I. No. 1643), the Air Navigation (General) Regulations 1981 (S.I. No. 57) and the Rules of the Air and Air Traffic Control Regulations 1985 (S.I. No. 1714) with their frequent small amendments. These codes contain many requirements for the safety of passengers, but nothing specifically directed to the safety of air crews and other employees.

Hangars and workshops on an airfield are factories under s. 175 (2) (*f*) of the Act of 1961, on the assumption that aircraft are 'vehicles', unless, indeed, nothing more is done on the premises than 'cleaning, washing, running repairs and minor adjustments'.

Under s. 76 (2) of the Act of 1982, there is absolute liability to an airfield employee (in common with other persons) who, through no fault of his own, is injured by an aircraft in flight, taking off or landing: but for this purpose 'take-off' does not commence until the pilot has taxi-ed to the duty runway, completed his cockpit drill, and started his take-off run: *Blankley v Godley* [1952] 1 All ER 436n.

Chapter 21

Agriculture and forestry

In safety standards, as in other aspects, agriculture has lagged a long way behind other industries. Towards the end of the nineteenth century, the Threshing Machines Act 1878 and the Chaff-cutting Machines (Accidents) Act 1897 required a certain amount of fencing for these particular machines. More recently, with the increase of chemical sprays, the Agriculture (Poisonous Substances) Act 1952 was passed to provide against this danger. Furthermore, it has always been possible for a workshop on a farm, e.g. where a circular saw is in use, to be a workshop subject to the Factories Acts[1].

The Agriculture (Safety, Health and Welfare Provisions) Act 1956

The Agriculture (Safety, Health and Welfare Provisions) Act 1956 was the first comprehensive Act for the protection of farm workers. It defines 'agriculture' at great length in s. 24(1) to include, in addition to farms in the ordinary sense, such things as orchards and nursery grounds; and farms are within the definition although they are run as ancillary to some other undertaking (whether profit-making or not) and

---

1 In *Longhurst v Guildford, Godalming and District Water Board* [1961] 1 QB 408 Devlin LJ raised the somewhat strange argument that premises on a farm cannot be within the definition of 'factory', because grain and similar things handled in bulk are not articles. If so, a flour mill cannot be a factory either. In any case, the Act of 1956 recognises that it is possible for parts of a farm to fall within the Factories Act, and gives power to exclude those Acts.

the crops are not for sale. Thus a seed-nursery is within the Act; and so is a kitchen-garden attached to a hospital. It also seems that the Act extends to forestry operations, because the definition includes 'the use of land as . . . woodland'. An 'agricultural unit' means land 'occupied as a unit for agricultural purposes'; this rather artificial term at least makes it plain that the Act applies to units which are not farms in the everyday sense. The Act now takes effect within the general framework of the Health and Safety at Work Act 1974, which contains wider powers to make safety regulations and other administrative powers: see Chapter 7, *ante*. Accordingly most of the Act has been repealed or modified: Agriculture (Safety, Health and Welfare Provisions Act 1956) (Repeals and Modifications) Regulations 1975 (S.I. No. 46). Regulations previously made under the Act, however, were continued in force by these regulations[2].

Section 1 of the Act authorised the making of regulations to protect 'workers employed in agriculture against risks of bodily injury or injury to health' arising out of the use of any machinery, plant, equipment or appliance, the carrying on of any operation or process, or the management of animals; the regulations could also require safe places of work and safe means of access, and protection from falls through apertures and from ladders, staircases and other places. They could impose duties on employers, on workers and on other persons. By s. 2, a young person under 18 was not to be employed 'to lift, carry or move a load so heavy as to be likely to cause injury to him', and regulations could prescribe maximum weights to be handled by adults. The Agriculture (Lifting of Heavy Weights) Regulations 1959 (S.I. 1959 No. 2120) fixed the maximum weight of any load consisting of a sack or bag (with contents) to be lifted or carried by one worker unaided at 180 lbs. This does not prejudice the statutory prohibition of too heavy loads for young persons, for whom 180 lbs. may, of course, be far too much. Section 6 of the Act requires a first-aid box or cupboard to be provided on every 'agricultural unit' where any worker is employed[3].

The Act expressly contemplates that an action for breach of statutory duty will lie under ss. 1, 2 and 6 and corresponding regulations, because

2 There have since been some further amendments to bring them into line with the 1974 Act, chiefly by transferring powers to the Health and Safety Executive: see Health and Safety (Agriculture) (Miscellaneous Repeals and Modifications) Regulations 1976 (S.I. No. 1247).

3 Amplified by the Agriculture (First Aid) Regulations 1957 (S.I. No. 940).

it provides in s. 22 that so far as liability in tort arises under those sections and regulations, they shall be binding on the Crown. Under s. 16, it is a defence for a person charged with a contravention of the Act or regulations to prove 'that he used all due diligence': this defence appears to apply only in criminal proceedings, and not to an action for damages[4].

Several codes of safety regulations were made under the Act, and as they are all rather detailed, they can only be summarised here. The Act and regulations apply to England and Wales and to Scotland. As stated above, the Health and Safety at Work Act 1974 is now the controlling legislation, and although the existing regulations are continued in force, future regulations will be made under s. 15 of that Act. The regulations were adapted to the metric system by the Agriculture (Metrication) Regulations 1981 (S.I. No. 1414).

Ladders

The Agriculture (Ladders) Regulations 1957 (S.I. No. 1385), go into great detail on the safe construction and condition of 'ladders', a term which excludes permanently fixed ladders and rope (or other non-rigid) ladders, but otherwise includes steps, trestle-ladders and every kind of ladder. The most important requirement is contained in reg. 3(1):

> 'The employer of a worker employed in agriculture shall not cause or permit to be used by any worker so employed, in the course of his employment, any ladder unless it is of good construction and sound material, and is properly maintained.'

Regulation 4 (which imposes an obligation on both the employer and the worker) forbids, among other things, the use of a ladder which is not strong enough for the purpose in hand, or has a rung missing, or is not securely placed or held. Regulation 5 requires a worker to report to his employer any defect such as a missing rung, but this does not in any way diminish the duties arising under regs. 3 and 4.

Power take-off of tractors

The Agriculture (Power Take-off) Regulations 1957 (S.I. No. 1386) require the 'power take-off', i.e. the primary transmission gear, of agricultural machinery to be guarded. They apply to all machinery, new

---

4 *Potts (or Riddell) v Reid* [1943] AC 1, [1942] 2 All ER 161, a case under the Factories Acts, is closely in point.

or old, subject (reg. 5) to certificates of exemption. A 'tractor' is defined to be any vehicle with a splined shaft for transmitting power to a machine; the splined shaft is the 'power take-off', and the shaft of the other machine which is coupled to this is described as the 'power take-off shaft'. By reg. 3 an employer must not cause or permit a tractor having a power take-off to be used while the engine is in motion, and a worker must not use such a tractor, unless either (i) the power take-off is shielded so as to preclude contact from above and from the sides or (ii) the power take-off is not in use and is completely enclosed by a cover. Regulation 4 contains, in similar terms, a prohibition on the use of a machine having a power take-off shaft unless, while it is in motion, the entire shaft is enclosed so as to preclude contact. In the case of certain old machines, partial enclosure of the shaft is permissible provided that the top is enclosed, and the sides as well to a depth of 50 mm. below the shaft, and provided also that the shaft is not more than 600 mm. above the ground at any point. The 'shaft' includes 'couplings and clutches up to the first fixed bearing of the machine' (reg. 2(1)).

Tractor Cabs

The Agriculture (Tractor Cabs) Regulations 1974[5] (S.I. No. 2034 amended by 1984 S.I. No. 605) require tractors to have a safety cab or frame of an approved pattern marked with an official sign (crown in triangle), with exceptions for use in hop gardens and orchards or inside farm buildings where use with the safety cab is not reasonably practicable. 'A safety cab' is one which is rigid enough to protect the driver if the tractor overturns. Workers must report overturning incidents or damage to the cab. The 1984 amendments require official approval to be given where cabs conform to E.E.C. standards for protection against noise and overturning.

Safeguarding of Workplaces

The Agriculture (Safeguarding of Workplaces) Regulations 1959 (S.I. No. 428) set out in Part II of the Schedule a series of detailed

---

5   Where a tractor was first supplied for use in agriculture before that date, the prohibition of hiring or use without a safety cab does not apply until 1 September 1977. The noise in these cabs is high, but there is a special mark with 'Q' for a quiet cab.

'requirements' to be complied with by the employer, or in certain cases, the occupier[6].

Stairways (including fixed ladders in or on buildings) and floors are to be as safe as reasonably practicable for the purpose for which they are used (Schedule, Part II, r. 1). Steps of a stairway must be secure, and none of them missing or defective (r. 2). Stairways must normally have handrails, especially on open sides (r. 3) and 'steep' stairways must have a handhold 920 mm. above the highest point (r. 4). Apertures in floors and walls, and open edges of floors, must be protected by covers, or fences, or guard rails, where there is a 1.5 metre drop (r. 5). Similar protection is required for grain pits, stokeholds and furnace pits (r. 6). The cover, fence or rail may be removed as 'necessary' for the access of persons or movement of materials.

Under reg. 3, the employer of an agricultural worker is responsible for these requirements on his own farm ('agricultural unit') and must not 'cause or permit' him to work at a place where they are not complied with. The 'occupier' of a farm has a similar responsibility where agricultural workers are employed on that farm by another employer. The regulations do not, however, apply even to an agricultural worker 'while working on the construction, alteration or maintenance of a building' (reg. 3(2))[7].

Regulation 4 of the Regulations and Part III of the Schedule impose corresponding duties on the workers: briefly, they must not remove or tamper with covers, rails or fences except as allowed by the regulations (Schedule, Part III, r. 7) and they must report defects such as missing steps (r. 8).

Circular saws

The Agriculture (Circular Saws) Regulations 1959 (S.I. No. 427) are drafted on a similar plan to the above regulations. An employer must not 'cause or permit' a worker to operate or assist at a circular saw where the requirements of Part I of the First Schedule are not complied with. Under Part I, circular saws must be 'substantially constructed and properly maintained' (r. 1) and the lighting must be adequate (r. 2). Saw blades with defects such as cracks, missing teeth or warped alignment

6 'Requirements' in the Schedule are abbreviated as 'r.' to distinguish them from the regulations ('reg.').
7 Construction regulations under the Factories Acts would normally apply.

must not be used 'knowingly' (r. 3). The protection required is similar to
the protection required under the Factories Act, i.e. enclosure by metal
plates below bench level (r. 6), riving knife behind the blade (r. 4) and a
top guard as close as practicable to the cutting edge (r. 5). There are
special requirements for saws with swinging tables designed for cross-
cutting only (r. 7). Workers are forbidden to interfere with safety devices
and required to keep them in position, except for adjustment when the
saw is not in motion (First Schedule, r. 8); they must also report defects
such as missing teeth or damaged guards (r. 9). Both employers and
workers are required to see that the floor is free from obstruction (r. 10),
that push sticks are used (r. 11) and that no adjustments are made while
the blade is in motion (r. 12).

Regulation 5 and the Second Schedule contain detailed rules to
ensure that no person shall work at a saw unless he has received full
instruction and demonstration of the working of the machine, and of the
safety rules, from an experienced person over 18 (Second Schedule,
rr. 1(1) and 3). A person under 16 is not allowed to operate or assist at a
saw at all (r. 2) and a person under 18 must not operate a saw unless
supervised by a thoroughly experienced person over 18 (r. 1(2)).

Fencing, etc., of stationary machinery
The Agriculture (Stationary Machinery) Regulations 1959 (S.I. No.
1216) are again built on a similar plan, with requirements (abbreviated
here as 'r.') set out in a Schedule.

By reg. 1, the employer of a worker 'employed in agriculture' is
forbidden to 'cause or permit' him in the course of his employment to
work at a stationary machine unless the requirements in Part II of the
Schedule are complied with. A broad distinction is made between the
feeding mouths and outlets of machinery, and the moving components.
Certain specified components—shafting, pulley, flywheel, gearing,
sprocket, chain, belt, wing or blade of a fan—must be so situated or
guarded as to preclude a worker or his clothing from contact (r. 2(3)).
(This does not apply to a tractor take-off, or to a primary driving belt
where the prime mover and machine driven by it are not both
permanently fixed.) Safety by situation is therefore always an alternative
to safety by fencing. But it is specifically declared that fencing is not
required for a component more than 2 metres from any place to which
the worker has access 'in the course of his employment' (r. 2(2)).
Fencing is not required for a belt or chain moving at less than 0.15

metres per second, or a conveyor belt or chain moving materials, *except* at the 'run-on point' where it goes on to the pulley or sprocket (r. 2(4)). All run-on points on a primary driving belt between a prime mover and a stationary machine must be similarly fenced or safe by situation, unless more than 2 metres from any place of access as above (r. 3). (This will apply where one or other of the machines is not *fixed*: if both are fixed, r. 2 normally requires the whole belt to be fenced or safe by situation.) The inlet and outlet of a stationary grain auger, and of every *power-driven* stationary machine for grinding, bruising or crushing grain must be guarded to preclude contact with the auger or any internal moving part; without prejudice to any obligation to fence the moving part itself under r. 2 (r. 4(1)). R. 4(2) contains a similar requirement for the feeding inlets and discharge outlets of machines used to cut or grind roots, hay and other feeding stuffs. There are requirements for accessible means of stopping a prime mover or disconnecting a machine from the power (r. 5). A disconnecting device must be safe from accidental reconnection by vibration (r. 5(6)). Belts must be properly maintained and not rest directly on revolving shafts (r. 6). Guards must be of adequate strength and properly maintained (r. 8). There must be adequate lighting (r. 7).

All this applies to every machine 'designed or adapted for stationary use only', including 'prime movers' which are internal combustion or electric motors (not, therefore, if such things are in use on farms, steam-engines, water-wheels or compressed air units). (But the fencing requirements for *components*—r. 2—apply to a stationary machine even if it is not power-driven at all)[8]. 'Stationary' does not necessarily mean 'fixed', but standing still when working, as distinguished from machines which work while on the move over the farm.

The regulations do not apply to any thresher, huller, baler or trusser: all these come under the next heading in the text. They apply to circular saws, in addition to the special regulations already mentioned.

Various duties are imposed on the worker, such as not interfering with or removing guards (except under specified conditions for cleaning, repair and adjustment) and reporting damaged guards (r. 9, r. 10).

Exemptions may be granted under reg. 5.

8 The requirements as to prime movers are somewhat confusing. The prime mover itself does not have to be fenced under r. 2 unless it is stationary. But the requirements as to guarding the transmission belt (r. 3) and stopping and disconnecting devices (r. 5) apply even if the prime mover is *not* stationary.

Threshers and balers

The Agriculture (Threshers and Balers) Regulations 1960 (S.I. No. 1199) also follow a similar plan, the requirements being set out in a Schedule, while the body of the regulations—regs. 3 and 4—forbid the employer to 'cause or permit' a 'worker employed in agriculture', 'in the course of his employment', to work at a thresher or baler unless the requirements are complied with. For this purpose, by reg. 2(2), a person assisting or doing incidental tasks is deemed to work 'at' the machine. Some duties are imposed on the worker, and there is also a concurrent list of requirements which both must comply with—i.e. the worker is in breach of duty if he disobeys these requirements, and the employer is in breach for allowing him to do so. There are special arrangements in reg. 6 under which contractors and farmers are made responsible for the safety of men, though not in their own employment. Where a 'worker employed in agriculture' works at a thresher or baler owned by an agricultural contractor (or hired or borrowed by him), the contractor alone has all the duties of an employer. Similarly where a man works away from his own employer's farm, the occupier of the farm ('agricultural unit') where the threshing or baling is carried out (or, if the machine belongs to a contractor, then the contractor) has the employer's duties.

Exemptions may be granted under reg. 7.

The regulations apply to threshers and balers only if they are stationary machines: Schedule, r. 1. This, however, does not mean 'fixed' but is contrasted with machines which work while on the move over the farm. Thresher includes 'a huller', but not a pea-viner; baler includes a 'trusser'. Therefore, with the exception of 'pea-viners', they include all machines which are excepted from the stationary machinery regulations[9].

The requirements as to fencing of belts, shafting and other components (r. 8), means of stopping or disconnecting the machine (r. 9), maintenance of belts and guards (r. 10 and r. 12) and adequate lighting (r. 11) are much the same as under the stationary machinery regulations. Balers must be guarded at both sides to preclude contact with the ram, and trussers must be guarded to preclude contact with the

9 'Pea-viners', it is believed, are not in any case 'threshers' or 'hullers', and the definition is just stating the obvious in excluding them. If this is right, they are subject to the Stationary Machinery Regulations.

discharge arms (r. 6). The drum feeding mouth of a thresher is to be guarded as far as practicable while produce is being fed in (r. 2) and covered when not being fed (r. 3). Guard rails are required for thresher decks if there is more than a 1.5 metre drop (r. 4). Pointed hooks and spikes are forbidden for attaching sacks or bags to a thresher (r. 5).

The requirements imposed on workers (not to remove or interfere with guards, to report damaged guards (r. 16, r. 17)) are similar to those under the stationary machinery regulations.

The middle group of requirements, however, which impose duties on both employer and worker, are something additional and important (Schedule, Part III, rr. 13–15). It is forbidden for a worker to stand on a surface which slopes down into the drum feeding mouth of a thresher while the drum is rotating (r. 13). The minimum age for a worker feeding produce into the drum feeding mouth of a thresher is 18 (r. 14). A worker is not to be on top of a baler while it is in operation (r. 15).

Field machinery

This is governed by the Agriculture (Field Machinery) Regulations 1962 (S.I. No. 1472). Field machinery is defined by Schedule 1, para. 1, to mean, broadly, all machines and tools which move under their own power, or are drawn, over the farm or woodlands, and to include load-carrying trailers; but not goods or passenger vehicles or aircraft, nor machinery for use in a stationary position. Regulation 3 imposes duties to comply with requirements set out in Schedule 1, which came into force on different dates. To take these somewhat out of order, Part V of the Schedule (r. 19) applies to employers, workers and others and forbids the starting of a machine except from the driving seat or other proper control position, and forbids leaving that seat or position except in an emergency. Part IV, duties of workers only (rr. 17 and 18), require damage or defects in safety devices to be reported, and forbid interference with or misuse of them; but a worker, not under 16, may remove the guard of a machine not in motion for cleaning, repair and adjustment, and may do an essential adjustment (if not otherwise possible) while it is in motion. Part III (r. 16) forbids riding on drawbars or linkages, or getting on and off machines while towing or propelling. Under Part II, towing devices must be secure (r. 14) and all field machines must be properly maintained for safety and their safety devices must be strong and securely fixed (r. 15).

Regulations 3 and Part II (rr. 2 to 15, including 14 and 15 above) are the obligations of the employer, analogous to the fencing requirements of the Factories Act, and he must not cause or permit a worker to work at a machine unless they are complied with. By regs. 3(3) and (4) an agricultural contractor who owns, hires or borrows a machine is deemed to be the employer of farm workers who work at the machine. By reg. 3(2) a man who works at a machine on another farm is deemed to be employed by the farmer or contractor on that farm.

Schedule 1, r. 2, deals with what may be called the inner workings of machines: gears, belts, chains, etc. If these are driven by the wheels on the ground, they must be 'so situated or so guarded' that the operator of the machine, in the normal operating position, is protected from contact. If they are *power-driven*, every worker at the machine must be protected from contact. There are some qualifications as to parts near the ground. Belts and chains are sufficiently protected by guards at run-on and run-off points and at other points of special risk of contact. Nothing in rr. 3 and 4 restricts the operation of r. 2. Rule 3 requires guards for the operating parts (knives, flails, etc.) of powered machines working near the ground, with certain exceptions. It visualises protection round the arc in which the blades, etc. operate, reaching as near to the ground as practicable. Rule 4 has special requirements for potato-spinners, chain-saws, rotary hedge cutters and pick-up balers. Other requirements deal with cutter bars (r. 5), stopping devices (r. 6), locking of differential gears (r. 7), valves and cocks on hydraulic or pneumatic systems (r. 8), provision of jacks for lifting or lowering drawbars (r. 9) and prohibition of pointed hooks or spikes for attaching containers (r. 10). There are also provisions about safe working platforms where workers have to stand on the machine when in operation (r. 11), about seats and footrests with guards for the operator (r. 12) and a safe step and handhold for getting on and off (r. 13).

Under reg. 4, the sale or letting on hire of machines which do not comply with Part II of Schedule 1 is forbidden.

Limits of liability

There are sharp limits to the civil liability of the employer under these regulations, which are framed in an entirely different manner from the Factories Act. Thus, in general the regulations only protect a worker who is engaged at the machine or place, and in the course of employment. They do not protect other persons, even if their work brings them into the vicinity, and they do not protect a worker who goes, however honestly, into a place where in fact he has no duties to perform—or so it seems. Furthermore, under these regulations, an employer is not in breach of duty unless he 'causes or permits' ladders or machinery or whatever it may be to be used contrary to the regulations. On similar language in the Road Traffic Acts it has been held that to 'cause or permit' involves knowledge in some sense of the contravention, or at least indifference to whether contravention takes place: *James & Son Ltd v Smee* [1955] 1 QB 78, [1954] 3 All ER 273.

Section 13 of the Act, under which workers were in breach of duty if they interfered with equipment or misused it, has been repealed, because ss. 7 and 8 of the Health and Safety at Work Act 1974 now set out the duties of employees in a comprehensive form.

Safety of children
In addition to providing for the safety of agricultural workers, the Act of 1956 is intended to prevent accidents to children, and under s. 7 of the Act and the Agriculture (Avoidance of Accidents to Children) Regulations 1958 (S.I. No. 366) children below the permitted age of employment (i.e. two years below school-leaving age, therefore at present 14) must not be allowed to ride on or drive certain vehicles, machines and implements.

Poisonous sprayings etc.
The Agriculture (Poisonous Substances) Regulations 1975, which regulated spraying and similar operations, have been replaced by the Control of Substances Hazardous to Health Regulations 1988 (as to which see Chapter 8). These prohibit or restrict the use of some substances and impose general requirements for safety and protective equipment.

Chapter 22

Offices, shops and railway premises

1 The Offices, Shops and Railway Premises Act 1963

This Act established a code of safety, health and welfare for most places of work not already covered by the Factories Act or other existing legislation. It now takes effect within the framework of the Health and Safety at Work Act 1974.

In comparison with factories and mines, offices and shops are hardly a serious safety problem, apart from the insistence on fire precautions and safe floors and staircases, which is everywhere necessary. Workshops attached to shops and large stores are already subject to the Factories Act. Thus the welfare, rather than the safety requirements (lighting, ventilation, washing facilities) are the important things in shops and offices. Liability for breach of the safety sections is likely to arise mainly from falls on unsafe floors or stairs.

The Health and Safety Executive is in general responsible for enforcing the Act: s. 52 as amended by S.I. 1976 No. 2005. However, powers of inspection have been delegated to local authorities for offices and shops but not railway premises: Health and Safety (Enforcing Authority) Regulations 1989 (S.I. 1989 No. 1903). Accidents must be notified to the appropriate inspecting authority: s. 48; the occupation of premises subject to the Act must also be notified under s. 49 ('registered' would have been a better description).

Most of the administrative provisions of the Act (regulations, prosecutions, exemptions) have been repealed or modified to conform to the Health and Safety at Work Act 1974, and future regulations will be made under that Act[1]. Minor amendments to conform to metrication were made by the Offices, Shops and Railway Premises Act 1963 etc. (Metrication) Regulations 1982 (S.I. No. 827). These amend requirements of ss. 5(2) and 6(2) and regulations under s. 10 relating to overcrowding, washing facilities and temperature.

2 Definition of premises subject to the Act

The Act, by s. 85(1), does not apply to premises forming part of a factory subject to the Factories Act 1961. Since the Factories Act is stricter, it continues to apply to such places as railway workshops, or workshops ancillary to shops, which are comprised in the existing definition of a factory. But the Act applies to *offices*—or, no doubt, shops—forming part of a factory, because these are 'excluded parts' under the Factories Act.

The Act is also excluded by s. 85(2) and (3) in the case of wholesale fish premises on docks and of premises underground in mines; and by s. 86 in the case of premises occupied for a temporary purpose, which means a purpose accomplished in six months, if the premises are movable, or in six weeks if not movable. (So if a temporary shop or office is set up in a permanent building, the Act must be complied with after six weeks; if it is set up in a movable building the Act must be complied with after six months, no matter how many moves have taken place.)

By s. 2, the Act does not apply to premises where only relatives of the employer work (this will exclude many family retail shops) nor, unlike the Factories Act, to the premises of outworkers. By s. 3, it is also excluded at premises (e.g. part-time charity offices) where work goes on for no more than 21 hours a week.

In general, under s. 83, the safety requirements of the Act apply to the Crown, and render it liable in tort (except to members of the armed forces, who are not to be treated as 'persons employed'); but there are some modifications of inspection arrangements. Section 84 excludes liability in tort towards members of certain visiting forces on the part of their own government.

With these exceptions and qualifications, the Act applies to the three distinct types of premises defined in s. 1:

1   S.I. 1974 No. 1943 and 1976 No. 2005.

(a) office premises;
(b) shop premises;
(c) railway premises;
provided that, in each case, persons are 'employed to work therein'.
The definitions of these three types of premises in s. 1 are
exceedingly detailed, and where doubtful border-line cases arise,
attention will have to be given to the exact wording. No more than a
broad summary of the definitions is given here.

Office premises (s. 1(2))
Briefly, this includes either an entire building or part of a building,
whose sole or principal use is for 'office purposes'. A single room may be
an office: *Oxfordshire County Council v Oxford University* (1980) Times,
10 December.

Office purposes has a wide definition to include clerical work,
administration, handling money and telecommunications.

Clerical work is again widely defined to include, apart from the obvious
things like writing, typing and filing, the use of computing machines,
draughtsman's work and editing.

Ancillary premises are included (e.g. strong rooms, filing cabinets,
washrooms). Thus the motor room at the top of the light shaft in a
telephone exchange is within the definition: *Westwood v Post Office*
[1974] AC 1, [1973] 3 All ER 184 (employees were in the habit of going
through it to the roof for fresh air, though forbidden to do so: a trap-door
gave way). Consulting rooms or conference rooms used primarily by an
employer personally seem to be border-line cases.

Office premises will, of course, include offices at factories, mines and
quarries, which are excluded from the scope of the Acts applying
generally to such places. Under ss. 74 and 75, the present Act also
applies, to the exclusion of the Factories Act, to offices at electrical
stations, institutions and docks.

Shop premises (s. 1(3))
This is also defined at great length to include, in addition to shops in the
ordinary way, all buildings or parts of them used for retail trade;
wholesale warehouses except at docks, wharves or quays; repair
premises; open-air fuel storage premises such as coal depots, except at
collieries or docks. It is to be noted that wholesale warehouses away

from docks are by s. 75(3) taken out of the Factories Act even when mechanical power is used. *Retail trade or business* includes sale of food or drink for immediate consumption, auction sales and lending of books or periodicals. Sale of food or drink for immediate consumption can hardly be limited to hot-dog and coffee stalls; it appears to include all kinds of catering establishments—cafes, restaurants and at any rate parts of hotels and inns—but the point is not free from doubt. By s. 51, regulations may be made adapting the Act to covered markets and may (it seems) allocate responsibility for the place as a whole: the section has never been brought into force.

Railway premises (s. 1(4))
This means a building or part of a building used for railway purposes *and* adjacent to the railway track, but excluding offices or shops, also excluding hostels for railway workers and hotels and electrical stations. Since most railway stations consist mainly of offices and shops, and hotels are excluded, and running sheds are within the Factories Act, the only obvious examples of railway premises are such places as signal boxes. The express exclusion of hotels (as well as shops) suggests that hotels as such are not within the 'shop' definition, but this does not necessarily exclude their restaurants and bars.

Canteens
By s. 1(5), if these are ancillary to office, shop or railway premises but do not form part of them, they are nevertheless to be premises of that class. This would include staff canteens at factories.

3 Safety, health and welfare requirements of the Act

The safety requirements follow similar provisions of the Factories Act 1961[2]. The protection of the Act does not extend to customers but only to persons employed: *Reid v Galbraiths Stores* 1970 SLT (Notes) 83. It does, however, protect employees in all parts of the premises, including

---

2   The explanations of similar sections in Chapters 10 to 12 are therefore in point.

(subject as always to questions of contributory negligence) places where they are not supposed to go: *Westwood v Post Office* [1974] AC 1, [1973] 3 All ER 184.

Section 16 requires floors, stairs, steps, passages and gangways to be in proper condition and free (so far as reasonably practicable) from obstruction and slipperiness; also protection on open staircases and from openings in floors. A hatchway in the serving area of a bar is an opening in the floor: *MacKay v Drybrough & Co* 1986 SLT 624. Section 16(5) adapts these requirements to open-air coal depots, etc. There is no counterpart to s. 29 of the Factories Act (means of access or place of work generally). The Offices, Shops and Railway Premises (Hoists and Lifts) Regulations 1968 (S.I. No. 849) introduce requirements similar to ss. 22 and 23 of the Factories Act 1961[3]. There are requirements for fencing dangerous parts of machinery (s.17), restricting cleaning of machinery by persons under 18 (s. 18), and prohibiting work at machines to be specified in regulations, except after full instruction or under supervision (s. 19)[4]. Sections 5 to 15 are predominantly of a welfare character and relate to cleanliness, overcrowding, temperature, ventilation, lighting, sanitary and washing facilities, drinking water, cloakrooms, seats for sedentary work or resting, and facilities for eating. However, s. 14(2), which requires a seat in use to be 'adequately supported', gives rise to absolute liability if a chair gives way though not known to be faulty: *Wray v Greater London Council* [1987] CLY 2560. By s. 23(1) no person is 'to be required to lift, carry or move a load so heavy as to be likely to cause injury to him'. In *Hamilton v Western S.M.T. Co.* 1977 SLT (Notes) 66, where two women were lifting between them boxes of coins weighing over 85 lbs. and one of them dropped her end, it was held that the court was entitled to decide as a fact that the weight was excessive. There was held to be a breach of the sections where a woman in her 40s strained her back in moving a crate of

3   Amended by S.I. 1974 No. 1943 to adapt them to the Health and Safety at Work Act, and by S.I. 1983 No. 1579 to substitute metric measurements.
4   For details see the Prescribed Dangerous Machines Order 1964 (S.I. No. 971). Mincers, guillotines, bacon slicers and garment presses are examples of the wide scope of the order. In *J. H. Dewhurst Ltd v Coventry Corpn* [1970] 1 QB 20, [1969] 3 All ER 1225 where a young person was left on his own to clean a bacon-slicing machine, with instructions not to clean it in motion but to move the blade to successive stationary positions and then clean, the employers failed to establish 'due diligence' which under s. 67 would exonerate them from criminal liability. This is, however, irrelevant to civil liability.

clothing weighing 80 lbs., though she did not have to lift it but only to pull it clear from the top of a pile of crates and let it fall: *Watson v Foster Menswear* 1982 SLT 448. But where the manageress of a baker's shop, left unexpectedly without any assistants, was told to 'do her best', and lifted a heavy tray to satisfy a shopful of customers, a majority of the Court of Appeal held that her claim failed because she had not been 'required' to do anything beyond her strength: *Black v Carricks (Caterers)* [1980] IRLR 448. (See also cases under the Factories Act, Chapter 12, section 10.)

Formerly fire precautions were covered in detail by ss. 28 to 41 of the Act. Now, however, these matters are regulated by the Fire Precautions Act 1971, which was extended to all places of work by s. 78 of the Health and Safety at Work Act 1974, and the old sections were repealed by S.I. 1976 No. 2005. (See Chapter 10, section 10, for a full explanation of the legislation.)

4 Responsibility for complying with the Act

This rests primarily on the occupier, who is by s. 63(1)(a) the person *prima facie* guilty of an offence if the Act is contravened. In some cases other persons are responsible in addition to the occupier or in substitution for him under s. 63(1)(b) or (c). Under ss. 42 and 43 owners of buildings may be responsible for such things as lighting, cleanliness, stairs, passages and fire precautions, but the sections are too complex to be summarised. Under s. 90, the 'owner' is (broadly) the person who receives the rent. Any person (including therefore persons employed) may commit an offence under s. 27 by doing an act which endangers safety, or by misusing or removing safety equipment. Thus for an employed person to remove a fence from a machine, or a barrier from an opening in the floor, would be a breach of his own statutory duty.

Chapter 23

Contributory negligence

1 Contributory negligence: general

The law of contributory negligence is explained at length in the standard textbooks on the law of tort. Here it is only necessary to sketch the main principles, and to stress those aspects of the matter which are of particular importance in employer's liability cases.

Hitherto it has been assumed[1], in explaining the *prima facie* liabilities of the employer, that his negligence or breach of statutory duty was the *sole* cause of the plaintiff's injuries. However, an accident may be due to *concurrent* causes. Leaving aside the case where two or more defendants are at fault—in which case they may claim contribution *inter se*—it may be caused both by the fault of the defendant and by the plaintiff's failure to take reasonable care for his own safety. As Lord Atkin said in *Caswell v Powell Duffryn Associated Collieries Ltd* [1940] AC 152, [1939] 3 All ER 722:

> 'The injury may . . . be the result of two causes operating at the same time, a breach of duty by the defendant and the omission on the part of the plaintiff to use the ordinary care for the protection of himself or his property that is used by the ordinary reasonable man in those circumstances. In that case the plaintiff cannot recover because the injury is partly caused by what is imputed to him as his own default.'

It is in such cases as this that the defence of contributory negligence is available. Under the old law, as indicated by the above quotation,

1 Apart from a discussion of 'sole cause' and 'concurrent causes' in Chapter 2, which must be read with this chapter.

contributory negligence was a complete defence, and if it was proved then the defendant was free of all liability. This rule was changed by the Law Reform (Contributory Negligence) Act 1945[2], under which the damages are now divided in proportion to the respective degrees of responsibility, and the plaintiff is entitled to recover damages reduced in amount according to the extent of his own negligence.

This change in the law brought about a certain shift in its practical application, as explained by Denning LJ in *Davies v Swan Motor Co (Swansea) Ltd* [1949] 2 KB 291, 322, [1949] 1 All ER 620, 630:

> 'The legal effect of the Act of 1945 is simple enough. If the plaintiff's negligence was one of the causes of his damage, he is no longer defeated altogether. He gets reduced damages. The practical effect of the Act is, however, wider than its legal effect. Previously, to mitigate the harshness of the doctrine of contributory negligence, the courts in practice sought to select, from a number of competing causes, which was *the* cause—the effective or predominant cause—of the damage and to reject the rest. Now the courts have regard to all the causes and apportion the damages accordingly.'

It is not necessary that the plaintiff should owe to the defendant any duty to take care: *Davies v Swan Motor Co (Swansea) Ltd, supra*; *Nance v British Columbia Electric Rail Co Ltd* [1951] AC 601, [1951] 2 All ER 448; but contributory negligence does involve 'the foreseeability of harm to oneself'.

> 'A person is guilty of contributory negligence if he ought reasonably to have foreseen that . . . he might be hurt himself; and . . . he must take into account the possibility of others being careless': per Denning LJ, *Jones v Livox Quarries Ltd* [1952] 2 QB 608 at 615.

Provided that the plaintiff can foresee that his conduct may expose him to injury it is not necessary that he should be able to foresee the precise manner in which the injury will occur: *Jones v Livox Quarries Ltd, supra*.

In all cases where contributory negligence is alleged, the question to be answered is: whose negligence (or breach of statutory duty) caused the accident? Was it that of the defendant alone, or of the plaintiff alone, or of both together? Lord Atkin said in *Caswell v Powell Duffryn Associated Collieries Ltd* [1940] AC 152 at 165, [1939] 3 All ER 722 at 730:

2   23 Halsbury's Statutes, 3rd Edn., 789; in Northern Ireland, the Law Reform (Miscellaneous Provisions) Act 1948 (N.I.).

'I find it impossible to divorce any theory of contributory negligence
from the concept of causation. . . . And whether you ask whose
negligence was responsible for the injury, or from whose negligence
did the injury result, or adopt any other phrase you please, you must in
the ultimate analysis be asking who "caused" the injury.'

If the plaintiff's conduct, although blameworthy, did not contribute to
cause the accident, it is irrelevant: thus the House of Lords held there was
not contributory negligence when a man fell through a door in a room
where entry was prohibited, since the notice contained no warning of
danger and disobedience to orders by entering the room was not in itself
negligence: *Westwood v Post Office* [1974] AC 1, [1973] 3 All ER 184.

The principles which guide the courts in deciding questions of
causation are explained at length in Chapter 2, section 4, where, in
particular, the distinction between concurrent causes and sole causes is
analysed.

2 The effect of contributory negligence: the Act of 1945

Section 1(1) of the Law Reform (Contributory Negligence) Act 1945
provides as follows:

'Where any person suffers damage as the result partly of his own fault
and partly of the fault of any other person or persons, a claim in
respect of that damage shall not be defeated by reason of the fault of
the person suffering the damage, but the damages recoverable in
respect thereof shall be reduced to such extent as the court thinks just
and equitable having regard to the claimant's share in the
responsibility for the damage.'

By s. 1(4):

'"fault" means negligence, breach of statutory duty or other act or
omission which gives rise to a liability in tort or would, apart from this
Act, give rise to the defence of contributory negligence[3].'

---

3 After a number of conflicting decisions, it is now clear that 'fault' will include a
   negligent breach of contract if, but only if, the negligence is concurrent with a
   liability in tort: *Forsikringsaktieselskapet Vesta v Butcher* [1989] AC 852, [1988] 2 All
   ER 43, CA.

This section enables the court to reduce the damages in proportion to the degree of responsibility for the accident; and the court may take into account not only the share of each party in causing the accident, but also the degree of blameworthiness. Denning LJ said in *Davies v Swan Motor Co (Swansea) Ltd* [1949] 2 KB 291 at 326, [1949] 1 All ER 620 at 632:

> 'While causation is the decisive factor in determining whether there should be a reduced amount payable to the plaintiff, nevertheless the amount of the reduction does not depend solely on the degree of causation. The amount of reduction is such an amount as may be found by the court to be "just and equitable", having regard to the claimant's share in the responsibility for the damage. This involves a consideration, not only of the causative potency of a particular factor, but also of its blameworthiness.'

Further, the question is how far each was responsible for the *damage*: so, in the case of a motor accident, even though the plaintiff was in no way responsible for the accident itself, there must be some apportionment of fault to him if failing to wear a safety helmet made his injuries worse, and this is so although it is impossible to say how far it made them worse: *Capps v Miller* [1989] 2 All ER 333, [1989] 1 WLR 839.

If there is found to be some degree of contributory negligence, though small, it cannot be ignored: there must be some reduction of damages: *Boothman v British Northrop Ltd* (1972) 13 KIR 112.

Where there are several defendants, the plaintiff's share of responsibility against all of them must first be assessed: then the balance divided between them: *Fitzgerald v Lane* [1989] AC 328, [1988] 2 All ER 961.

In looking at the apportionment of fault in particular cases, it must be remembered that this is always *comparative*: thus the fact that 75 per cent fault is attributed to a plaintiff does not necessarily mean that he was grossly negligent, it may only mean that the defendant's fault was slight and technical, or played a minor part in causation.

If there was 'fault' in the part of the defendant which contributed to cause the injury, there must be some apportionment of liability to him: see *Stocker v Norprint* and other cases at p. 71, *ante*; *Boyle v Kodak Ltd*, p. 626, *post*; *Gray v Camelot Hoods* [1983] CA Transcript 127. The suggestion in one case that there could be 100 per cent contributory negligence seems to have been made *per incuriam*[4].

---

4   *Jayes v IMI (Kynoch) Ltd* [1985] ICR 155 is an unfortunate decision which seems to have been made *per incuriam* as the House of Lords' decision in *Boyle v Kodak* was

3 Contributory negligence as a defence to breach of statutory duty

Formerly, it was uncertain whether contributory negligence was a valid defence to a breach of statutory duty.

In *Caswell v Worth* (1856) 5 E & B 849 a machine had been left unfenced, but the workman himself had set it in motion and thereby caused his accident. The court held that an action for breach of statutory duty was subject to the ordinary incidents of a common law action, and one of these incidents was that it might be met by the defence of contributory negligence. However, the action of the workman in that case was described as 'wilful misconduct': and for a long time it was doubtful whether anything less than misconduct could be a sufficient defence.

The law was finally settled in *Caswell v Powell Duffryn Associated Collieries Ltd* [1940] AC 152, [1939] 3 All ER 722 where the House of Lords held that contributory negligence is a defence to a breach of statutory duty just as it is a defence to an action founded on negligence. At that date the defence, if successful, had the effect of excluding liability altogether. Now, under the Act of 1945[5], the damages are reduced in proportion to the responsibility.

---

not cited. That case decided that employers cannot exonerate themselves from liability for a breach of statutory duty unless it was wholly brought about by the plaintiff. If it was, there is no liability, so the question of contributory negligence does not arise. If it was *not* wholly brought about by the plaintiff, there is automatically fault on the part of the employers whether they were negligent or not, from the mere fact of breach of the duty, and there must be an apportionment to them of some part of the damages. In *Jayes* there were breaches of the Unfenced Machinery Regulations (for which the plaintiff was not responsible) in that the mechanics attending the machine were not qualified 'machine attendants' and no barrier had been erected to keep other persons out. The plaintiff was a supervisor who had called in the fitters: he foolishly took a rag to stop oil running and his finger was caught. In *extempore* judgments the court upheld a finding by the judge that he was 100 per cent negligent for an 'act of folly'. The court purported to follow *Mitchell v Westin Ltd* [1965] 1 All ER 657, [1965] 1 WLR 297, the only case quoted: but the reasoning in that case is wholly discredited by *Boyle v Kodak*.

It is to be noted that the question of 100 per cent contributory negligence, which for these reasons is misconceived in a case of breach of statutory duty, could not arise at all where the claim is for negligence only: since if the plaintiff was 100 per cent negligent, the defendant was 0 per cent negligent, which means he did not begin to be liable at all.

5 23 Halsbury's Statutes, 3rd Edn., 789.

It was emphasised in *Caswell's* case, however, that the degree of care which a plaintiff is expected to take for his own safety must vary according to the circumstances, and allowance must be made for the conditions under which work is carried on in a factory or mine. This subject is considered at length in the next section.

4 What conduct by a workman amounts to contributory negligence?

There are two factors which are relevant in all cases of contributory negligence. The first is that all the circumstances must be considered, such as the fact that a man may have to give his attention to more than one thing. The second is that, just as a defendant is entitled to balance the disadvantages of safety measures against the risk involved, so too a plaintiff may expose himself to some degree of risk rather than submit to the curtailment of his activities. The question in every case is whether the plaintiff acted reasonably in taking a risk: *A. C. Billings & Sons Ltd v Riden* [1958] AC 240, [1957] 3 All ER 1[6]. The fact that there may be disadvantages as well as advantages is particularly important in connection with failure to use equipment. In *Gibson v British Insulated Callender's Construction Co Ltd* 1973 SLT 2 the House of Lords held that there was no contributory negligence in failing to wear a safety belt on the top of an electricity pylon: for though it could prevent a fall to the ground, it could in some circumstances cause a fall and would not prevent serious injuries.

Similarly, it may be legitimate to take a risk for the protection of other persons put in danger by the defendant's negligence: *Ward v T. E. Hopkins & Son Ltd, Baker v T. E. Hopkins & Son Ltd* [1959] 3 All ER 225; and the same principle may apply to a workman taking a risk for the protection of his employer's property, or otherwise in his employer's interests[7].

---

6 Examples are *Clayards v Dethick and Davis* (1848) 12 QB 439 (access to stable almost blocked by trench and rubble: owner justified in bringing horse out rather than stop business); *A. C. Billings & Sons Ltd v Riden, supra* (old lady justified in attempting to pass contractors' works to get home for the night); *Sayers v Harlow U.D.C.* [1958] 2 All ER 342 (attempt to escape from locked lavatory).

7 See the cases cited at pp. 610–611, *post.*

In addition, there are a number of authorities on the standard of care for his own safety which is expected from a worker in a factory or mine.

Lawrence J said in *Flower v Ebbw Vale Steel, Iron and Coal Co Ltd* [1936] AC 206 (quoted with approval by Lord Wright at 214):

'The tribunal of fact has to take into account all the circumstances of work in a factory and it is not for every risky thing which a workman in a factory may do in his familiarity with the machinery that a plaintiff ought to be held guilty of contributory negligence.'

And Lord Atkin said in *Caswell's* case, in agreeing with this statement:

'I am of opinion that the care to be expected of the plaintiff in the circumstances will vary with the circumstances; and that a different degree of care may well be expected from a workman in a factory or a mine from that which might be taken by an ordinary man not exposed continually to the noise, strain and manifold risks of factory or mine.'

Again, Lord Wright said in the same case ([1940] AC at 176–178, [1939] 3 All ER at 738–739):

'The jury have to draw the line where mere thoughtlessness or inadvertence ceases, and where negligence begins. . . . What is all important is to adapt the standard of what is negligence to the facts, and to give due regard to the actual conditions under which men work in a factory or mine, to the long hours and the fatigue, to the slackening of attention which naturally comes from constant repetition of the same operation, to the noise and confusion in which the man works, to his preoccupation in what he is actually doing at the cost perhaps of some inattention to his own safety.'

These authorities are to some extent an application of the ordinary rule that all the circumstances must be taken into account. However, so far as they excuse an injured workman for *inadvertence*, they establish a more lenient standard than the conduct of the reasonable man, which is the normal standard of comparison. Inadvertence is failing to give attention to what one is doing, and must imply some lack of due care[8]. The explanation of this lenient standard of care is that it was evolved in considering contributory negligence as a defence to breach of statutory duty, especially in cases of unfenced machinery. As the fencing of machinery is intended to protect the worker even when inadvertent or

---

8 Unless inadvertence means that a workman gives full attention to *his work*, and therefore neglects incidental danger to *himself*: but this is difficult to reconcile with the authorities in the House of Lords such as *John Summers & Sons Ltd v Frost* [1955] AC 740, [1955] 1 All ER 870.

inattentive, it would have been difficult to treat 'inadvertent' want of care as giving the employer a complete defence. But, once the lenient rule excusing inadvertence had been adopted in 'fencing' cases, it was applied in all actions by an injured workman based on breach of statutory duty. The point is that the employer's responsibility for statutory duties should not be reduced by throwing the blame on a man injured by a risk the duty was intended to prevent: and if the man's carelessness oversteps the boundary between inadvertence and negligence, the point is taken into account in *apportioning* the damages: *Mullard v Ben Line Steamers Ltd* [1971] 2 All ER 424, [1970] 1 WLR 1414 (contributory negligence reduced from half to a third).

But the lenient standard does not apply in other cases. Lord Tucker said in *Staveley Iron and Chemical Co Ltd v Jones* [1956] AC 627, [1956] 1 All ER 403, referring to the *dicta* in *Caswell's* case:

> 'While accepting without question this and other *dicta* to a similar effect ... in relation to cases under the Factories Acts and other statutes imposing absolute obligations ... I doubt very much whether they were ever intended or could properly be applied to a simple case of common law negligence ... where there is no evidence of workpeople performing repetitive work under strain or for long hours at dangerous machines[9].'

Conduct which is not contributory negligence: illustrations
Many of the cases are not anomalous at all, but simply recognise that the workman is not placed in the same circumstances as the employer: *General Cleaning Contractors Ltd v Christmas* [1953] AC 180 at 190, [1952] 2 All ER 1110 at 1114. Even a senior employee may not be wholly to blame though he has himself collaborated in devising an unsafe system of work: *Nicol v Allyacht Spars Pty* (1987) 163 CLR 611 (Australian High Court: director participated in 'Heath Robinson' contraption to take down flag—40 per cent blame).

It is not negligent for a workman to follow the method of work accepted by the employer, even if it involves some obvious risk. It is not the duty of a workman to break away from the employer's methods and devise a safer system, although he may have as much skill and

---

9   The true explanation of the 'inadvertence' cases appears to be that there is negligence, but it is 'excusable' negligence ('excusable lapses', Lord Reid said in the *Staveley* case) which is not allowed as a defence because the policy of the statute is to give protection against such lapses.

experience as the employer: *General Cleaning Contractors Ltd v Christmas, supra* (cleaning windows by holding on to sashes); *Harris v Bright's Asphalt Contractors Ltd* [1953] 1 QB 617 at 629, [1953] 1 All ER 395 at 399 (kneeling on edge of flat roof to chip away asphalt); *Barcock v Brighton Corpn* [1949] 1 KB 339, [1949] 1 All ER 251 (safety screen removed to test electrical apparatus); *McNeill v Roche Products Ltd*—1988 SCLR 629 (followed established practice of cutting off petrol supply to machine instead of switching off).

Similarly, it is not negligent to disregard personal danger because absorbed in work, or to take a deliberate risk in the employer's interests: *Hutchinson v London and North Eastern Rly Co* [1942] 1 KB 481, [1942] 1 All ER 330 (men working on railway line failed to keep sharp look-out for trains); *Neil v Harland and Wolff Ltd* (1949) 82 L1 L Rep 515, CA (man worked on cables without removing fuses, because removal of fuses would have stopped factory); *Norris v Syndic Manufacturing Co Ltd* [1952] 2 QB 135, [1952] 1 All ER 935 (machine tested without guard to avoid waste of time); *Machray v Stewarts and Lloyds Ltd* [1964] 3 All ER 716 (rigger used makeshift tackle for urgent job, proper tackle not available). But deliberate disobedience to regulations and the employer's own orders is not excused by impatience to get on with the work: *Imperial Chemical Industries Ltd v Shatwell* [1965] AC 656, [1964] 2 All ER 999.

Again, it is not necessarily negligent if a workman takes things for granted, where there is nothing to put him on inquiry. In *Grant v Sun Shipping Co Ltd* [1948] AC 549, [1948] 2 All ER 238 a workman went into an unlighted part of a ship, where repairers had been doing work, and stepped into an uncovered hatchway. The House of Lords held that, though this was not a case of inadvertence, the workman had acted 'without conscious thought', taking it for granted that the statutory duty to cover the hatchways had been complied with, and that in the circumstances this was not negligence. Lord du Parcq said, at pp. 567, 247:

> 'Almost every workman constantly, and justifiably, takes risks in the sense that he relies on others to do their duty, and trusts that they have done it. I am far from saying that everyone is entitled to assume, in all circumstances, that other persons will be careful. On the contrary, a prudent man will guard against the possible negligence of others, when experience shows such negligence to be common. Where, however, the negligence is a breach of regulations, made to secure the safety of workmen, which may be presumed to be strictly enforced in the

ordinary course of a ship's discipline, I am not prepared to say that a workman has been careless if he assumes that there has been compliance with the law.'

Other examples are *Wright v Richard Thomas & Baldwins Ltd* (1966) 1 KIR 327 (no reason to expect vehicle in steelworks to move without warning); *Kansara v Osram (G.E.C.) Ltd* [1967] 3 All ER 230 (mechanic adjusting machine, no reason to expect electrical danger); *Foulder v Canadian Pacific Steamships Ltd* [1969] 1 All ER 283 (seaman entered shower without testing—no reason to think it might be scalding); *Kealey v Heard* [1983] 1 All ER 973, [1983] 1 WLR 573 (planks on scaffold gave way: no sign of danger).

Inadvertence has been excused in many cases, e.g. *Pringle v Grosvenor* (1894) 21 R 532 (machine fenced on three sides only, woman cleaning inadvertently moved round to unfenced side); *Hunter v Glenfield and Kennedy* 1947 SC 536 (workman on scaffold put hand through factory wall and was injured by crane); *McArdle v Andmac Roofing Co* [1967] 1 All ER 583 (walked backwards pouring bitumen on roof—man behind had gone without warning and left hole); *Ryan v Manbre Sugars Ltd* (1970) 114 Sol Jo 492 (man knew of slippery step but forgot to put foot down carefully); *Stocker v Norprint Ltd* (1970) 10 KIR 10 (man collecting tags from guillotine machine put hand too far in inadequately guarded opening: preoccupied with clearing tags to find time to oil); *John v Martin Simms (Cheltenham) Ltd* [1983] 1 All ER 127 (excavator driver looking for leak in engine put hand near unfenced radiator fan).

Inadvertence has been excused even in the case of skilled men carrying out their skilled work without any special hurry or fatigue. In *Richard Thomas and Baldwins Ltd v Cummings* [1955] AC 321, [1955] 1 All ER 285 a skilled man trapped his fingers by pulling on a belt at a point too near to the pulley; in *John Summers & Sons Ltd v Frost* [1955] AC 740, [1955] 1 All ER 870 a skilled man held a piece of metal too near to a grinding wheel. Both men were exonerated from blame, and Lord Keith, in his speech in *Frost's* case, indicated that 'momentary inadvertence' is not enough, and something like 'disobedience to orders', or 'reckless disregard by a workman of his own safety', must be proved before he can be held negligent[10].

To this type of case we now turn.

---

10 *Thornton v Swan Hunter (Shipbuilders) Ltd* [1971] 3 All ER 1248n, [1971] 1 WLR 1759, CA seems at first sight out of line. Plaintiff repairing a paint-spraying

Disobedience of orders

In *Flower v Ebbw Vale Steel, Iron and Coal Co Ltd* [1936] AC 206 it was accepted by the House of Lords that disobedience of orders would, *prima facie*, be contributory negligence, but the defence failed on the facts. A case of long-standing authority on this point is *Senior v Ward* (1859) 1 E & E 385 where there had been a fire in a colliery, which might have affected the ropes suspending the cage. To the knowledge of the miners, there was an order in force requiring the ropes to be tested each day by raising and lowering the cage before passengers used it. The miners themselves disregarded this rule, by going down without any test being made: and it was held that their action failed. Other cases are *National Coal Board v England* [1954] AC 403, [1954] 1 All ER 546 (shotfiring rules in coal mine); *Smith v Chesterfield and District Co-operative Society Ltd* [1953] 1 All ER 447 (girl put hand under guard of pastry machine); *Stapley v Gypsum Mines Ltd* [1953] AC 663, [1953] 2 All ER 478 (miner disobeyed orders to make roof safe); *Tearle v Cheverton and Laidler Ltd* (1970) 7 KIR 364 (chief maintenance engineer, contrary to own instructions, switched off starter button only, not power switch, then accidentally caught button: two-thirds blame). In *Laszczyk v National Coal Board* [1954] 3 All ER 205 a trainee miner disobeyed statutory orders by working in a place where he ought not to have been, but as he had been told to go there by his superior, his fault was held to be slight (5 per cent reduction of damages). In *Storey v National Coal Board* [1983] 1 All ER 375, [1983] ICR 156 there was 75 per cent contributory negligence when an experienced miner rode on a conveyor belt though he knew this was prohibited and dangerous. In *Williams v Port of Liverpool Stevedoring Co Ltd* [1956] 2 All ER 69 a gang of six men disobeyed the foreman's orders as to the method of unloading bags from a hold: one of the men was injured by the fall of a bag and his damages were reduced by 50 per cent.

---

machine with a moving carriage removed the fence, completed repairs, switched on to test and caught a finger between the carriage and the rubber buffer: he was in a squatting position and had been distracted by the foreman who was discussing the job. This looks like inadvertence, yet the Court of Appeal approved an apportionment of 75 per cent against him because he was a skilled man and ought to have been on the alert. On the other hand apportionment is always *comparative*: the employer's breach of statutory duty was very technical, due to the fence not being put back in position during the test. Though there was no serious negligence by the plaintiff, the employer's responsibility was even slighter.

Disregard of obvious dangers

Disregard of obvious dangers was held to be negligent in *Ross v Railway Executive* 1948 SC, 58 (HL) (workman went between trucks during shunting); *Cork v Kirby MacLean Ltd* [1952] 2 All ER 402 (workman subject to epileptic fits took work at a height without informing his employers); *Kyle v Salvesen* 1980 SLT (Notes) 18 (drunken seaman fell off ship's gangway: 50 per cent deduction); *Jones v Livox Quarries Ltd* [1952] 2 QB 608 (riding in an exposed position on back of vehicle, crushed by another vehicle); *Storey v National Coal Board* [1983] 1 All ER 375, [1983] ICR 156 (riding on conveyor in coal mine contrary to orders and warning notices—75 per cent fault); *Hicks v British Transport Commission* [1958] 2 All ER 39 (guard riding on footboard of train and failing to see points lever); *Gatehouse v John Summers & Sons Ltd* [1953] 2 All ER 117 (man 20 feet high on crane used both hands to pull cable loose, and cable broke); *Quinn v Horsfall & Bickham Ltd* [1956] 2 All ER 467 (hand too near machine tool cutter not properly turned off); *Blakeley v C. & H. Clothing Co* [1958] 1 All ER 297 (hand through bars of lift gate); *Williams v Sykes & Harrison Ltd* [1955] 3 All ER 225 (cleaning conveyor belt in motion); *Hodkinson v Henry Wallwork & Co Ltd* [1955] 3 All ER 236 (climbed up to put rope back on pulleys while machinery in motion: knew it was not his job and he should have waited for mechanic); *Rushton v Turner Bros Asbestos Co Ltd* [1959] 3 All ER 517 (putting hand in moving machinery to clean); *Quintas v National Smelting Co Ltd* [1961] 1 All ER 630 (on roof in track of aerial ropeway with back turned); *Johnson v J. Stone & Co. (Charlton) Ltd* [1961] 1 All ER 869 (putting work-piece too near moving pulley); *Uddin v Associated Portland Cement Manufacturers Ltd* [1965] 2 All ER 213 (climbing on top of machine—where he had no right to be—to catch pigeon—80 per cent blame); *Upton v Hipgrave Bros* [1965] 1 All ER 6 (carelessly aligning wheelbarrow on hoist so that it was caught by a ledge and tipped); *Lovelidge v Anselm Odling & Sons* [1967] 2 QB 351, [1967] 1 All ER 459 (tie hanging over grinding tool with unfenced shaft, 50 per cent to blame); *Leach v Standard Telephones and Cables Ltd* [1966] 2 All ER 523 (using machine without authority and not adjusting fence—25 per cent); *Johnson v F. E. Callow (Engineers) Ltd* [1970] 2 QB 1, [1970] 1 All ER 129 (lubricated machine by hand to save trouble of automatic system—one-third); *Kerry v Carter* [1969] 3 All ER 723 (youth falsely told farmer he knew how to use circular saw—two-thirds); *Smith v Supreme Wood Pulp Co Ltd* [1968] 3 All ER 753 (driver used circular saw without experience—25 per cent); *Foster v Flexible Metal Co Ltd* (1967) 4 KIR 49 (did not ask for assistance—which was available—in re-setting machine tool); *Ball v Richard Thomas and Baldwins Ltd* [1968] 1 All ER 389 (too near crane when lifting—25 per cent); *Bunker v Charles Brand & Son Ltd* [1969] 2 QB 480, [1969] 2 All ER 59 (not keeping firm handhold when walking over rollers—50 per cent); *Mullard v Ben Line Steamers Ltd* [1971] 2 All ER 424, [1970] 1 WLR 1414 (walked several paces in pitch dark, fell down hatch—one-third); *Jennings v Norman Collison (Contractors) Ltd* [1970] 1 All ER 1121 (building foreman overbalanced pulling key out of door without handle near steep drop; could have fixed temporary handle to door, or safety rail: two-thirds blame); *Field v E. E. Jeavons & Co Ltd* [1965] 2 All ER 162 (electrician wiring electric saw not yet attached to bed: switched on to test without asking foreman's permission as was customary: 25 per cent); *Denyer v Charles Skipper and East Ltd* [1970] 2 All ER 382 (young man, properly instructed, supposed to clean rollers when stationary, put hand in before fully stopped: 50 per cent); *Callow v Johnson* [1971] AC 335, [1970] 3 All ER 639 (squeezed oil into machinery to avoid trouble of preparing for automatic system—one-third); *Rodway v P. D. Wharfage and Transport Ltd* [1973] 2 Lloyd's Rep 511 (guiding slow-moving crane where driver's view imperfect, too close in front—one-third); *Wheeler v Copas* [1981] 3 All ER 405 (builder used fruit-picking ladder for building work on farm though it was obviously too flimsy and both stiles gave way); *Allen v Avon Rubber Co Ltd* (1986) Times, 20 May: drove forklift over unfenced edge of loading bay—50 per cent; *Boyes v Carnation Foods Ltd* 1986 SLT 145 (mechanic cleaning hands with towel after adjusting machine, crouched too near and towel drawn in—50 per cent; *Anderson v Thames Case Ltd* 1987 SLT 564 (tried to remove rag from machine in motion—50 per cent).

Failure to be on the alert for dangers
Some of these cases are just over the border-line from 'excusable lapses': *Reilly v British Transport Commission* [1956] 3 All ER 857 (man tightening bolts on railway line failed to watch signals); *McDonald v British Transport Commission* [1955] 3 All ER 789 (foreman stepped on railway truck, failed to see large hole in floor); *Simmons v Bovis Ltd* [1956] 1 All ER 736 (foreman stepped on 'trap ends' on scaffold, i.e. planks overlapping supports and liable to tip up: slight blame—only 10 per cent). It is to be noted that in two of these cases the plaintiff was a

foreman, and the first case was a man working alone on a railway line. These might be expected to keep their eyes open. In *Smith (or Westwood) v National Coal Board* [1967] 2 All ER 593 a majority of the House of Lords assessed 25 per cent blame for scrambling up an awkward bank instead of stopping as a shunting train approached (Lords Hodson and Upjohn thought it was excusable misjudgment in emergency). Other examples are *Astell v London Transport Board* [1966] 2 All ER 748 (in manoeuvring long pipe round corner of stairs, crouched below level of safety rail—25 per cent); *Woollins v British Celanese Ltd* (1966) 1 KIR 438 (not testing fragility of flat roof before stepping on it—50 per cent); *Kendrick v Cozens and Sutcliffe Ltd* (1968) 4 KIR 469 (working from ladder, moved on to fragile roof to avoid sparks—75 per cent); *McDowell v F.M.C. (Meat) Ltd* (1968) 3 KIR 595 (experienced manager failed to spot overhead power line at showground—one-fifth blame); *Wheat v E. Lacon & Co Ltd* [1966] AC 552, [1966] 1 All ER 582 (overconfident that bottom of unlit staircase reached); *Baron v B. French Ltd* [1971] 3 All ER 1111 (tripped over rubble heap in poorly lit corridor, hospital under construction: 50 per cent); *Cox v Angus* [1981] ICR 683 (electrician working in cab of fire engine failed to see loose pipe lying there and tripped over it—50 per cent); *Sole v W. J. Hallt Ltd* [1973] QB 574, [1973] 1 All ER 1032 (stepped back near unfenced drop —one third); *Byrne v E. H. Smith, Ltd* [1973] 1 All ER 490 (walked along roof gutter, one foot on fragile asbestos—20 per cent); *Boothman v British Northrop Ltd* (1972) 13 KIR 112 (tripped over cable of own welding torch—25 per cent); *McClymont v Glasgow Corpn* 1971 SLT 45 (mechanic squatting by bus on 4 foot high servicing platform slipped under single-rail fence—75 per cent, perhaps not because mechanic was seriously negligent but because employer's default was small).

Failure to use equipment provided for safety or to follow standing instructions
In *Gibby v East Grinstead Gas and Water Co* [1944] 1 All ER 358 the workman had to go up on a dark night to a high gantry, which was not fenced. He did not take a lamp, and fell over the side. Scott LJ said, at p. 360: 'The omission to take a light . . . was an act of folly.'

Further illustrations are the failure to use a push-stick in woodworking operations (*Lewis v Denyé* [1940] AC 921, [1940] 3 All ER 299), an earthing rod when handling high voltage apparatus (*Proctor v Johnson and Phillips Ltd* [1943] KB 553, [1943] 1 All ER 565) and boards on an asbestos roof (*Jenner v Allen West & Co Ltd* [1959] 2 All ER

115). But in these cases the workman had failed to carry out an express statutory duty, and thus they verge on the subject treated in the next section. Failure by a workman in a foundry to wear protective boots or spats against splashes of metal, when he knew the boots were available at cost and spats free of charge, was held to be substantial contributory negligence (75 per cent) in *Haynes v Qualcast (Wolverhampton) Ltd* [1958] 1 All ER 441[11]; likewise failure to wear goggles which were available on request as a precaution against steel fragments: *Crouch v British Rail Engineering Ltd* [1988] IRLR 404, CA. A dustman was held 50 per cent to blame when he took off gloves provided and was cut by glass sticking out of a carton (*Samways v Westgate Engineers Ltd* (1962) 106 Sol Jo 937), a foundry-worker 40 per cent for not wearing goggles when exposed to metal splashes (*Bux v Slough Metals Ltd* [1974] 1 All ER 262, [1973] 1 WLR 1358), a young assistant at a meat slicer one-third to blame for not using a 'pusher' (*McGuinness v Key Markets Ltd* (1972) 13 KIR 249).

A railway guard was 20 per cent at fault for failing to apply the brakes, in accordance with standing orders, before trying to help the defendant on to the train: *Harrison v British Railways Board* [1981] 3 All ER 679 (the defendant was trying to get on when the train was moving and this resulted in the guard also being injured).

5 Breach of the workman's statutory duties

Most of the statutes providing for safety in factories and other places impose duties on the workmen as well as on the occupier.

A breach by the workman of his statutory duty, if it is a cause of the accident, is equivalent to contributory negligence: *Norris v Syndic Manufacturing Co* [1952] 2 QB 135 at 142, [1952] 1 All ER 935 at 939.

In considering how far a breach of the workman's statutory duty should reduce the damages, regard must be had, it is suggested, to the publicity given to the order, i.e. whether the employers have taken adequate measures to bring the order to the workman's notice and to see that he complies with it. A breach of regulations by a senior official is

---

11 On appeal to the House of Lords there was held to be no negligence by the defendants: [1959] 2 All ER 38.

obviously more serious than a breach by an ordinary workman. Another factor is the extent of the workman's knowledge, and whether he is a properly instructed and experienced workman. In *Laszczyk v National Coal Board* [1954] 3 All ER 205 orders having statutory force were clearly given to the plaintiff, a trainee miner, by the training officer of the mine: but he disobeyed them on the instructions of the deputy, his immediate superior. His damages were reduced by 5 per cent.

As in all cases where contributory negligence is pleaded, it must be shown that the default complained of was a cause of the accident. In *McGovern v James Nimmo & Co* (1938) 107 LJPC 82 there was a breach of the Coal Mines General Regulations, reg. 121, in that the pursuer, though an unauthorised person, had tampered with an electrical pump. The jury made no finding that this breach of regulations had any bearing on the happening of the accident: and the House of Lords declined to draw any inference from the other findings to supply their omission[12].

A general duty is now imposed on employees by the Health and Safety at Work Act 1974, s. 7 to take reasonable care for the safety of themselves and other people affected by their acts or omissions at work and to 'co-operate' with employers and others in carrying out the duties imposed on them.

This replaces earlier duties under the Factories Act and other specific legislation, which have been repealed, but case-law decided under these Acts is still relevant. General duties were imposed by s. 143 of the Factories Act 1961 on employees in factories and other places subject to the Act. By s. 143(1), they must not 'wilfully interfere with or misuse' appliances provided under the Act: and 'where any means or appliance for securing health or safety is provided for the use of' any such employee, 'he shall use such means or appliance'. This would extend, for instance, to guards on machines, push-sticks, respirators and safety belts, and also to other safety appliances. An appliance is *provided* if it is ready to hand and available, whether or not the workman is ordered to use it: *Norris v Syndic Manufacturing Co* [1952] 2 QB 135, [1952] 1 All ER 935; *Ginty v Belmont Building Supplies Ltd* [1959] 1 All ER 414 (boards for use on asbestos roof). *Aliter*, perhaps, with an appliance like a lamp which may serve many purposes; in such a case express instructions may be needed to earmark it for a particular purpose: *Gibby v East Grinstead Gas and Water Co* [1944] 1 All ER 358. 'Wilfully

---

12 Cf. *Westwood v Post Office*, p. 605, *ante*.

interfere with or misuse' does not include every intentional act, e.g. in moving a guard, but means something in the nature of 'perverse intermeddling': *Charles v S. Smith & Sons (England) Ltd* [1954] 1 All ER 499. Similar duties are imposed by many special regulations which have not been repealed. Indeed, it is normal for regulations to impose specific duties to make use of the safety equipment.

Failure to wear or use safety equipment, such as goggles when exposed to metal splashes, is not a mere technical breach but a substantial contributory factor to any accident: *Bux v Slough Metals Ltd* [1974] 1 All ER 262, [1973] 1 WLR 1358 (40 per cent).

By s. 143(2), no employee 'shall wilfully and without reasonable cause do anything likely to endanger himself or others'. An example is *Ginty v Belmont Building Supplies Ltd* [1959] 1 All ER 414 (stepping on fragile asbestos roof without using boards). But there is no breach where there is nothing 'wilful', e.g. neglecting to secure a ladder: *Geddes v United Wires Ltd* 1974 SLT 170.

More detailed duties are imposed by the various codes of special regulations, e.g. the Woodworking Machines Regulations 1974 (S.I. No. 903), Chapter 11, section 13, *ante*.

Under the Mines and Quarries Act 1954, s. 89 it is an offence for any person employed at a mine to contravene directions given for the safety of the mine; and any negligent or wilful act or omission likely to endanger safety is an offence under s. 90(1). Removal, alteration or tampering with any safety appliance is prohibited by s. 90(2) unless done by an official, or with the permission of an official.

In some cases the workmen are required to comply with a whole code of regulations, in common with their employers and the other persons responsible. For example, it was the duty of all persons employed to comply with Part IV of the former Docks Regulations 1934. Where the duties imposed are as sweeping as this, common sense must be used in applying the law. In *Jerred v Roddam Dent (T.) & Son Ltd* [1948] 2 All ER 104 a beam over a hatchway had not been firmly secured, and Atkinson J said:

> 'I cannot think it means that every man must personally look at and examine every bolt even if he is assured by his foreman that all is in order. If men reasonably believe that duties have been performed, they cannot be held blameworthy for not seeing to compliance.'

A fair interpretation of wide duties of this nature is, it seems, that they require the workman to observe the regulations so far as they impose specific duties on him. If any other requirement has not been carried out, the proper course for an ordinary workman to take would usually be to report the defect, rather than try to put it right.

Regulation 4 of the former Building (Safety, Health and Welfare) Regulations 1948 required every person employed 'to comply with the requirements of such regulations as relate to the performance of an act by him and to co-operate in carrying out Parts II to VII' of the regulations. The codes of Construction Regulations issued in 1961 ('General Provisions' and 'Lifting Operations') and 1966 ('Working Places'), which replace the 1948 regulations, contain wider requirements (to comply as to acts which he is to perform *or* refrain from; to co-operate; to report defects promptly): but decisions under the 1948 regulations are still helpful. The words 'relate to the performance of an act by him' are wide enough to cover acts which he has to do in the course of his work, and are not (as Hodson LJ thought in *Davidson's* case, *infra*) restricted to duties *specifically* imposed on particular employees. Thus they cover the choice by a foreman of the wrong type of scaffolding coupler where the right type is available (*Davison v Apex Scaffolds Ltd* [1956] 1 QB 551, [1956] 1 All ER 473), the duty to 'use' crawling boards when provided (*Ginty v Belmont Building Supplies Ltd* [1959] 1 All ER 414; *Jenner v Allen West & Co Ltd* [1959] 2 All ER 115), the duty to fasten the top of a ladder (*Boyle v Kodak Ltd* [1969] 2 All ER 439, where the House of Lords must be taken to have approved the earlier cases). But an employee's duty extends only to his own acts, and he has no responsibility for a breach of regulations (e.g. to 'construct' properly) which is due to material supplied by the employers: *Quinn v J. W. Green (Painters) Ltd* [1966] 1 QB 509, [1965] 3 All ER 785.

Many of the special regulations made under the Factories Act expressly require the workmen to report any defects which they 'discover'.

6 Breach of employer's statutory duty caused by plaintiff alone

Difficulty has arisen in one special type of case where the defendants are in breach of their statutory duty, but this has occurred by reason only of the conduct of the plaintiff, perhaps by removing the fence from a machine contrary to express orders and warnings. In these extreme cases it would be unreasonable to attribute any legal liability to the defendants.

Now an employer cannot be vicariously liable to his servant for that servant's own negligence: see the remarks of Alderson B at p. 8, *ante*. But a statutory duty is different, because it rests directly on the employer, and the mere non-performance, if it is a contributory cause of the accident, normally establishes liability. Before 1945 these special cases were no different from other cases of contributory negligence—which always defeated the claim—except that they were unusually strong cases. An example is *Vincent v Southern Rail Co* [1927] AC 430 where failure by a railway foreman to appoint a look-out man, as required by statute, was treated as contributory negligence, and the expression used in one speech that a plaintiff 'could not recover for the consequences of his own default' was at that date no more than a way of describing contributory negligence, which totally defeated the claim. (Cf. Lord Atkin at p. 603, *ante*). The Law Reform (Contributory Negligence) Act 1945 has altered this position. In *Stapley v Gypsum Mines Ltd* [1953] AC 663, [1953] 2 All ER 478 Lord Oaksey said, at 679, 484:

> 'The doctrines of common employment and of contributory negligence having been abolished, the only question is whether, under the Law Reform (Contributory Negligence) Act 1945, Stapley's death was "the result partly of his own fault and partly of the fault of" Dale, for whose fault the respondents are responsible.'

Yet the House of Lords has decided that there are still exceptional cases, where the fact that breach of statutory duty has occurred, and contributed to the accident, does not make the defendant liable. This happens when the breach occurred *solely* through the plaintiff's conduct, without any failure on the part of the defendant or any other person for whom he is responsible: *Ross v Associated Portland Cement Manufacturers Ltd* [1964] 2 All ER 452; *Boyle v Kodak Ltd* [1969] 2 All ER 439. The emphasis is on the word 'solely'. If there is any failure to provide necessary equipment, or to give instructions (including instructions as to safety regulations), the defendant is not exonerated: he must have done everything in his power. In both the above cases, the defendant did not succeed in showing this, and it was irrelevant that his failure was not negligent. There is no difference between cases where the duty rested on the defendant alone, or on both parties, except that a breach of a duty imposed on the plaintiff personally is equivalent to contributory negligence.

These two decisions have settled the law, and are the only ones which should be referred to for the correct principles in future. Previously there had been some rather unsatisfactory case-law. In these earlier cases the courts had not entirely shaken off the pre-1945 approach of looking for the 'substantial' or 'decisive' cause, but disguised this either by using the term 'sole cause' in a rhetorical sense or by somewhat artificial doctrines.

Obsolete approaches

(i) The 'delegation' cases

A defendant upon whom a statutory duty is imposed cannot delegate the *duty* to another person, but he can delegate the *performance* of the duty. If the duty is not performed by the delegate, the defendant is in breach of statutory duty, and is in general liable to all persons who sustain consequential injury. It was nevertheless held (citing the *Vincent* case as authority), that the person to whom performance of the duty was delegated could not recover damages, because the defendant's breach of duty was due to the plaintiff's own default: *Smith v A. Baveystock & Co Ltd* [1945] 1 All ER 531; *Barcock v Brighton Corpn* [1949] 1 KB 339, [1949] 1 All ER 251; *Johnson v Croggon & Co Ltd* [1954] 1 All ER 121; *Man-waring v Billington* [1952] 2 All ER 747; *Stapley v Gypsum Mines Ltd* [1952] 2 QB 575, [1952] 1 All ER 1092, reversed on other grounds [1953] AC 663, [1953] 2 All ER 478. But this special defence did not succeed if the plaintiff was not a skilled and experienced man: *Vyner v Waldenberg Bros Ltd* [1946] KB 50, [1945] 2 All ER 547; nor if the duty was of a purely negative character: *Gallagher v Dorman, Long & Co Ltd* [1947] 2 All ER 38 (overloading of crane); nor if the defendants failed to prove express delegation: *Beal v E. Gomme, Ltd* (1949) 65 TLR 543; *Hilton v F. H. Marshall & Co Ltd* [1951] WN 81.

After the *Stapley* case, 'delegation' argument was tacitly abandoned in favour of other approaches such as 'sole cause'[13].

---

13 In an *obiter dictum* in *Imperial Chemical Industries Ltd v Shatwell* [1965] AC 656, [1964] 2 All ER 999 Lord Pearce appears to resuscitate the 'delegation' principle. However, the *Ross* case, which is inconsistent with it, had just been decided by a House differently constituted but not yet reported.

(ii) Predisposition to find a 'sole cause'

That the plaintiff was the sole cause of the accident is undoubtedly a defence, but there was a tendency to stretch the term to mean 'the main cause'. The best example is the *Stapley* case, p. 613, *ante*, where two men disobeyed orders to make a mine roof secure and one of them, returning alone, was injured by a fall of rock. The Court of Appeal held that the plaintiff, by returning alone, took the decisive step and was the sole cause. The House of Lords reversed this and held there must be an apportionment of fault.

(iii) Ex turpi causa non oritur actio

This maxim states the general rule of law that a criminal act cannot be made the foundation of an action: *Holman v Johnson* (1775) 1 Cowp 341. The delegation cases were said to depend upon this maxim in *Cakebread v Hopping Bros (Whetstone) Ltd* [1947] KB 641, [1947] 1 All ER 389, followed in *Johnson v Croggon & Co Ltd, supra.*

However, the House of Lords decided that a breach of safety regulations is not a criminal act within the meaning of this maxim. In *National Coal Board v England* [1954] AC 403, [1954] 1 All ER 546 an accident was caused partly by the plaintiff's own breach of the shotfiring regulations: it was held that the maxim *Ex turpi causa* had no application, and that the fault must be apportioned under the Law Reform (Contributory Negligence) Act 1945.

(iv) 'Fault' as criterion when statutory duties are co-extensive

The decision in *Ginty v Belmont Building Supplies Ltd* [1959] 1 All ER 414 was approved by the House of Lords in the two leading cases, but the principle which they enunciate is different, or at least far better stated[14]. A workman was injured through failing to use a crawling board provided by his employers, the duty to 'use' being imposed on both parties. Pearson J held that since the employers' breach of statutory duty 'consisted of, and was co-extensive with, that of the plaintiff', the action must totally fail, on the ground that the accident 'was solely due to the fault of the plaintiff'. The peculiarity of the case (he said) was that there was one identical statutory fault, not 'using' the board, for which both

14 In the meantime the case had been approved by the Court of Appeal in *Jenner v Allen West & Co Ltd* [1959] 2 All ER 115 (crawling boards) and *McMath v Rimmer Bros (Liverpool) Ltd* [1961] 3 All ER 1154 (not having man at foot of ladder) but in both cases the employer's default was held to be more than the plaintiff's.

parties were equally responsible. Therefore you could not apply the 1945 Act but had to go behind it and see where the 'fault' lay. It had to be shown that the employers' 'fault' went beyond the workman's. Lord Reid, commenting on this in the *Ross* case, said it must be remembered that 'fault' includes statutory fault. The danger of using the term is to imply that *negligence* must be proved against the employer. Similarly the objection to such phrases as 'in substance and reality' the plaintiff was solely at fault is the same as the objection to the use of the phrase 'sole cause' in *Stapley's* case: by describing the *major* factor as the *sole* factor, they circumvent the Act of 1945 and bring back the old law by a side-wind.

(v) Scottish cases

The 'delegation' cases were not discussed in Scotland until *Nicolson v Patrick Thomson Ltd* 1964 SLT 171 where the court said that, if they were accepted, an express delegation must be proved, and accordingly the defence failed although the pursuer was the chief maintenance engineer. The question was raised again in *Crowe v James Scott & Sons Ltd* 1965 SLT 54, but in the meantime the *Ross* case had been decided and the rejection of the pursuer's claim was justified by that decision.

Liability excluded where breach brought about by plaintiff alone

The two House of Lords' decisions quoted above establish that a defendant is not liable for a breach of statutory duty if he has done everything within his power to carry out the duty, and has failed by reason of the plaintiff's conduct and nothing else. Both cases show that *prima facie* where a breach of statutory duty has caused an accident there is liability, and it is for the defendant to negative this and show that he took all necessary steps but in spite of these the plaintiff himself caused the breach. In both cases the House looked very critically indeed at the facts and refused to allow the defence.

In *Ross v Associated Portland Cement Manufacturers Ltd* [1964] 2 All ER 452, the plaintiff's husband had been killed in a fall from a ladder at the second defendant's factory. He was a chargehand steel erector whose services had been supplied on a permanent basis by his own employers, but by the time the appeal reached the House of Lords the original employers were out of the case; and in the claim against the occupiers for breach of s. 26 of the Factories Act 1937 (safe means of access and place of work) it did not matter whether Ross was their temporary servant or not.

Ross had been instructed with two other men, of whom he was in charge, to repair the supports of a wire safety net, suspended about 20 feet above the ground to catch objects falling from an overhead ropeway. The net was held up at intervals by brackets, from which cables ran at each side to fixed pylons. The first task was to replace the cables. It was an unusual job, not within the normal routine experience of a steel erector. The chief engineer of the factory simply told Ross to do the job without specific instructions, or encouragement to come back if in difficulty. The only equipment available without being specially asked for was a long ladder. Ross and his mates started working from the ladder propped against a pylon. Later this was not possible, and after a discussion they decided to continue with the ladder propped against a bracket and cable. While Ross was on the ladder, something gave way and he was thrown to the ground and killed. The expert witness said that it was an obviously unsafe method to work from an unstable ladder, and a movable platform should have been provided. It was common ground in all the courts that the occupiers had failed to provide safe means of access and safe place of work and were in breach of the statute. Yet the Court of Appeal, affirming Nield J, held that the deceased man, having chosen his own method, was the only person at fault for the accident, the occupier's breach being 'coterminous and co-extensive with the deceased man's own fault'. The trial judge, said Willmer LJ, had given 'the only possible answer . . . there is no other conclusion open to us'. This emphatic language reads strangely in the light of the unanimous decision of the House of Lords to reverse the decision. Lord Reid described the defence accepted by the courts below as 'quite unrealistic'.

He conceded that an occupier, though in breach of statutory duty, 'can avoid civil liability to the actual offender if he can show that the conduct of this offender was the sole cause of the breach and resulting injury to him'. He referred to *Manwaring v Billington* [1952] 2 All ER 747 (use of a ladder without fixing it) as an example where a workman had deliberately disobeyed express instructions; and similarly to *Ginty v Belmont Supplies Ltd* [1959] 1 All ER 414 where the workman had been told to use boards on an asbestos roof and had not done so. After quoting the suggested test of Pearson J, 'Whose fault was it?', Lord Reid said:

'If the question is put in that way one must remember that fault is not necessarily equivalent in this context to blameworthiness. The question really is whose conduct caused the accident, because it is now well-established that a breach of statutory duty does not give rise to civil liability unless there is proved a causal connection between the breach and the plaintiff's injury.'

Looking at the question on this basis—simply as one of causation—he said that where an occupier has provided proper equipment and given proper instructions he cannot make provision against disobedience. But in this case proper equipment and instructions had not been given, and a chargehand could not be treated as an expert with full authority. Accordingly the defendants must be held partly responsible, and two-thirds of the blame must be apportioned to them. The other Lords treated the case as a straight issue of causation: the occupier's failure to provide safe means of access was a contributory cause of the accident, and Ross's use of makeshift apparatus did not make him the 'sole cause' as he had not disobeyed orders and was not a specialist with full authority. By itself, therefore, the *Ross* case could be taken as deciding no more than that disobedience to explicit orders would sever the causal connection between the breach of statutory duty and the accident.

Boyle v Kodak Ltd [1969] 2 All ER 439 confirmed and amplified the opinion of Lord Reid in the *Ross* case, and decided that it is not just a matter of causation, that there is indeed a special exception to liability for breach of statutory duty where, in spite of all necessary equipment being supplied and instructions given, the breach is brought about by the plaintiff's own act. Both Lord Reid and Lord Diplock gave a good rational explanation for this exception. Liability for a breach, they said, is imposed by the common law, not by the statute, so the common law can qualify it, and ought to do so where the alternative would be to give a plaintiff a right of action founded on his own actions *and nothing else.* *Prima facie* the breach establishes liability: the defendants have to show that they did everything in their power by way of supplying equipment and giving instructions, and that their efforts were defeated by the plaintiff alone. It is not enough (as was explicitly decided) to prove absence of negligence.

In the *Kodak* case, the plaintiff had to paint the upper part of a large oil-tank from a ladder, and by statutory regulations which imposed a duty on both plaintiff and defendants, the top of the ladder should have been tied to the structure. The plaintiff went up the ladder to tie it, but it fell before he could do so. He could have used a stairway to reach the top and tie the ladder. There was no negligence by either party, but both were in breach of statutory duty. Lord Diplock said:

> 'The plaintiff establishes a prima facie cause of action . . . by proving the fact of non-compliance with a . . . regulation and . . . injury as a result. He need prove no more. No burden lies on him to prove what steps should have been taken . . . But if the employer can prove that the only act or default of anyone which caused or contributed to the non-compliance was the act or default of the plaintiff himself, he establishes a good defence.'

He continued that since the employer normally performs his duties through others, it is his responsibility to see that those others, including the plaintiff, know what is required by statutory regulations, and he is not entitled to assume that a man has this knowledge just because he is skilled and experienced. As the employers produced no evidence that they had given such instructions, they could not be exonerated, and liability was divided equally[15].

Injured person held to be sole cause of the breach
In the following cases the injured person was held to be the sole cause of the breach: those decided before *Boyle v Kodak Ltd*, and indeed some decided since, are open to question if and so far as they decide that it was sufficient that the plaintiff's act brought about the accident, without investigating what instructions were given. In some of them the plaintiff was sole cause of the accident, i.e. the breach of statutory duty was *not* one of the causes, independently of the present rule:

Lane v Gloucester Engineering Co Ltd [1967] 2 All ER 293 (failed to put light on before crossing floor).

Kirk v Scaffolding (Great Britain) Ltd 1969 SLT (*Notes*) 64 (scaffold tube fell when hoisted, injured man had failed to tie securely).

McMullen v Alexander Findlay & Co Ltd 1966 SLT 146 (ladder rested against stanchion, which gave way: man himself should have secured stanchion).

Anderson v Gaskell and Chambers (Scotland) Ltd 1969 SLT (*Notes*) 88

15 The passage in Lord Diplock's speech at pp. 446 D to 447 D is particularly valuable, and if this is taken as the key statement of the law, the vague ambiguities of the past such as 'whose fault was it', 'who was in truth and substance the cause', should be avoided.

(man used trestle scaffold to fire nail gun into concrete, overbalanced with recoil: own choice of scaffold).

Richardson v Stephenson Clarke Ltd [1969] 3 All ER 705 (foreman rigger chose unsafe shackle: no need for instructions, ample equipment available).

Crowe v James Scott & Sons Ltd 1965 SLT 54 (electrician removed lid of bus bar chamber without switching off).

Horne v Lec Refrigeration Ltd [1965] 2 All ER 898 (trapped when machine started while unfenced: disobeyed instructions to turn off all switches, turned off only one which he accidentally caught).

Allison v Alex. Cowan & Sons 1970 SLT (Notes) 46 (removed fence and switched on machine). But there is certainly no general rule that to take the fence off and start the machine makes a man the sole cause. It may be a natural thing to do, e.g. to test after repair, or after making an adjustment or clearing blockage. Unless clear instructions have been given to the contrary, it will be a case of contributory negligence or inadvertence, as in *Thornton v Swan Hunter (Shipbuilders) Ltd* [1971] 3 All ER 1248n, [1971] 1 WLR 1759.

Injured man held not to be sole cause of the breach
In the following cases the injured man was held not to be the sole cause of the breach:

Keaney v British Railways Board [1968] 2 All ER 532 (sub-inspector sent three men—all required for the job—on railway line where unscheduled trains possible: ganger failed to appoint look-out, not sole cause).

Leach v Standard Telephones and Cables Ltd [1966] 2 All ER 523 (man used wrong machine for metal cutting, failed to adjust fence close enough, but even if adjusted fence insufficient).

Donaghey v Boulton and Paul Ltd [1968] AC 1, [1967] 2 All ER 1014 (man failed to use crawling-board: sub-contractor's foreman had discouraged use of it).

Quinn v J. W. Green (Painters) Ltd [1966] 1 QB 509, [1965] 3 All ER 785 (foreman painter selected trestle, but there was a *latent* defect for which employers were automatically liable under regulations).

Aitken v John R. Bryson Ltd 1966 SLT 234 (joiner—working director in company—injured through failure to secure uprights of scaffold: not sole cause because co-director had taken part in supervising erection).

Denyer v Charles Skipper and East Ltd [1970] 2 All ER 382 (young person supposed to clean roller when stationary put hand in before stopped: not sole cause because contrary to s. 20 of Factories Act to put him on this work).

Stocker v Norprint Ltd (1970) 10 KIR 10 (youth had to oil guillotine machine as well as collect tags coming out: put hand too far up orifice in collecting tags. Court of Appeal held could not be sole cause when the breach of s. 14 by the inadequate guard was not due to his act).

Geddes v United Wires Ltd 1974 SLT 170 (ladder not secured at top or held at foot—employees not given instructions to do this. Lord Robertson, in a valuable judgment, said to exclude liability in these cases it has to be shown that instructions were given and disobeyed).

Chapter 24

Voluntary assumption of risk

1 The maxim *'volenti non fit injuria'*

Sometimes the maxim *volenti non fit injuria*—'No injury is done to one who consents'—may afford a defence to an action founded on negligence: but in practice this defence is rarely successful.

The maxim has two branches:

In its first and most immediate application, it means that an act done to the plaintiff with his consent cannot be complained of as a legal wrong. A boxer, for example, cannot claim damages for being knocked out by his opponent.

In a second and inaccurate sense, the maxim is quoted where a plaintiff has voluntarily taken the *risk* of injury inherent in some activity, but not arising from anyone's negligence. This sort of case arises when a spectator is injured by some misadventure at an organised sport. There is no liability when a participant, doing his best to win, moves fast or makes some misjudgment, because these risks are inherent in the sport and there is no negligence: *Wooldridge v Sumner* [1963] 2 QB 43, [1962] 2 All ER 978 (photographer at horse show injured when horse deviated from course)[1]. Similarly it has been held both in Canada and in England

---

1 A competitor going all out to win must not, however, act in disregard of the spectators: *Wilks v Cheltenham Home Guard Motor Cycle and Light Car Club* [1971] 2 All ER 369, [1971] 1 WLR 668. Similarly, even competitors in a physical contact game must not act in disregard of one another's safety: *Condon v Basi* [1985] 2 All ER 453, [1985] 1 WLR 866 (dangerous football tackle). The duty of care is there, but it takes into account the necessities of the event. The same principle applies when a film is being shot and no doubt in other cases.

that a spectator at an ice-hockey match has no right of action if he is hit by the puck: *Elliott v Amphitheatre Ltd* [1934] 3 WWR 225; *Murray v Harringay Arena Ltd* [1951] 2 KB 529, [1951] 2 All ER 320 n. In *Cutler v United Dairies London Ltd* [1933] 2 KB 297 it was held that a bystander who, without being under any duty to do so, tried to stop a bolting horse, could not claim damages for his injuries.

There are some risks incidental to most employments. The risk of explosion in an explosives factory, and the risk that a sailor may fall while climbing a mast, are familiar examples. The employer must take reasonable care to protect his employees against all hazards of the employment, including inherent risk of this kind: *Ellis v Ocean SS Co Ltd* [1958] 2 Lloyd's Rep 373 (seaman falling overboard): but provided that due care is taken, the employee necessarily accepts the inherent risks. For example, a stockman in charge of a bull could not complain if, notwithstanding the exercise of due care by the farmer, he is injured by the bull: *Rands v McNeil* [1955] 1 QB 253, [1954] 3 All ER 593[2]. This, however, is not a true case of *volenti non fit injuria*. The maxim does not begin to apply until it is proved that, *prima facie*, the employer is negligent, e.g. by failing to provide a proper system, or proper equipment, or a proper place of work, and the defence is then put forward that the servant consented to run the risk which was thus negligently created. The same problem may arise where a workman brings his action against a third party. In all cases it must be shown that consent was given to the risk of *negligence*: so, where the plaintiff was permitted to walk along a private railway track, she necessarily took the risk of injury through railway operations conducted without negligence, but that did not mean that she accepted the risk of negligence, e.g. by failure to slow down and whistle when entering a tunnel: *Slater v Clay Cross Co Ltd* [1956] 2 QB 264, [1956] 2 All ER 625. In *Titchener v British Railways Board* [1983] 3 All ER 770 [1983] 1 WLR 1427, a case under the Occupiers' Liability (Scotland) Act 1960 where the defence that the risks were accepted is incorporated in s. 2(3), the House of Lords held that the railway owed no duty as occupiers to a person who went through a fence to cross the line: but they approved the decision in

---

2   But the position in England and Wales is now different under the Animals Act 1971 which states expressly that an employee is not deemed to accept the risk. Under the Animals (Scotland) Act 1987 voluntary acceptance of the risk is a defence, but the Act is silent on the position of an employee: see Chapter 2, section 6.

the *Clay Cross* case that the risk is accepted on the assumption that the trains will operate in the 'ordinary and accustomed way' and would not extend to a case of negligent driving[3].

Where a person takes a risk in the course of duty or for some other good reason, for example a fireman going to fight a blaze, he does not thereby consent to any *antecedent* negligence which may have created the danger: *Flannigan v British Dyewood Co Ltd* 1969 SLT 223[4].

Volenti non fit injuria is not a defence to a breach of the employer's own statutory duty (*Baddeley v Granville (Earl)* (1887) 19 QBD 423; *Wheeler v New Merton Board Mills Ltd* [1933] 2 KB 669). But it is a defence to an employer's *vicarious* liability for the breach of a servant's statutory duty, at any rate if the servant was not a person of superior rank whose orders the plaintiff was bound to obey: *Imperial Chemical Industries Ltd v Shatwell* [1965] AC 656, [1964] 2 All ER 999. (This was an extreme case where the plaintiff, one of two shotfirers in a quarry, consented to and actually took part in a deviation from regulations, strictly enforced by the employers[5].)

As a starting point, a servant must have full knowledge of the risk to which he is said to have consented. In *Olsen v Corry and Gravesend Aviation Ltd* [1936] 3 All ER 241 an aircraft apprentice was injured owing to a negligent system of starting aircraft engines, and it was held that as an inexperienced apprentice could not appreciate the risk, the defence of *volenti non fit injuria* failed *in limine*. So, too, the defence failed when a fireman was exposed to exceptional risk of explosion through the presence of aluminium dust of which he had not been told: *Merrington v Ironbridge Metal Works Ltd* [1952] 2 All ER 1101.

Knowledge, however, is not enough. The mere fact that a servant continues at work, with full knowledge of a risk to which he has been exposed by the negligence of his master or of fellow-servants, does not mean that he consents to the risk. This was finally settled by the decision

---

3   Though it could hardly arise in an employer's liability case, the *volenti* defence succeeded where the plaintiff was a passenger in a car driven by the defendant whom he knew to be under the influence of drink, and who was driving wildly to escape a police chase after a burglary: *Ashton v Turner* [1981] QB 137, [1980] 3 All ER 870.
4   On appeal 1970 SLT 285 this point did not arise.
5   Claims were similarly rejected where, in breach of regulations forbidding 'disorderly conduct' in the mine, colliers jumped off moving trams and raced to the pit shaft to get the best places in the cage: *Hugh v National Coal Board* 1972 SC 252.

of the House of Lords in *Smith v Baker & Sons* [1891] AC 325. In *Smith v Baker* a gang of navvies were working in a railway cutting, and stones were swung overhead by crane. No warning was given before the stones were swung over, nor were the workmen cleared out of the way. Thus the employers were negligent in adopting an unsafe system of work, and eventually a stone fell and injured the plaintiff, who was a member of the gang. The House of Lords held that the plaintiff's continuance at work—though he knew of the risk and had complained about it—did not establish that he had consented to take the risk.

It is evident, then, that *in all cases* consent in the full sense of the word must be proved. As between master and servant, continuance at work does not by itself alone manifest consent to run a known risk; and the Court of Appeal, in *Bowater v Rowley Regis Corpn* [1944] KB 476, [1944] 1 All ER 465 have expressed the opinion that there are very few cases where, as between master and servant, the defence of *volenti* can succeed[6]. In this case a corporation dustman had taken an unruly horse after protesting that it was unsafe. It was held that the maxim *volenti non fit injuria* did not apply. Even where the claim is against a third party, *volenti* does not apply unless the plaintiff consented to run the risk with full freedom to refuse, and an employee carrying out his duties does not have this freedom: thus a notice that a dock authority excluded liability for the negligence of their staff was no defence to a claim by a lighterman on a barge moving into the dock, who was injured by a breaking rope: *Burnett v British Waterways Board* [1973] 2 All ER 631, [1973] 1 WLR 700[7].

In practice, in many cases where it is contended that the maxim applies, it is found that the risk was not one which was created by the defendant's negligence, and that there is not even a *prima facie* liability.

While knowledge does not prove acceptance of the risk, it may go a long way towards establishing contributory negligence. *Prima facie*, disregard of an obvious danger amounts to contributory negligence. Moreover, a defendant may in some cases be under no duty to a plaintiff

6 This view was accepted in Scotland in *Keenan v City Line Ltd* 1953 SLT 128 where, however, it was said that the defence might succeed if a servant deliberately continued at work with knowledge of his own incompetence (e.g. to drive truck).

7 The position is different where warning of a risk is a sufficient discharge of the third party's duty: *London Graving Dock Co Ltd v Horton* [1951] AC 737, [1951] 2 All ER 1. In such a case the fact that the workman has no choice does not concern the third party. But *quaere* whether warning can be a sufficient discharge of a duty in many cases; see p. 183, *ante*.

who has full knowledge of a danger: *London Graving Dock Co Ltd v Horton* [1951] AC 737, [1951] 2 All ER 1.

Finally, even if the plaintiff did voluntarily take a risk, this is no defence if he acted in pursuance of a moral duty to save life or prevent injuries to some other person (*Haynes v Harwood* [1935] 1 KB 146); or if he is a person such as a fireman, whose duty compels him to face risks which other persons have negligently created (*Merrington v Ironbridge Metal Works Ltd* [1952] 2 All ER 1101 at 1103); or a doctor, who is called to assist workmen overcome by poisonous fumes in a well (*Ward v T. E. Hopkins & Son Ltd, Baker v T. E. Hopkins & Son Ltd* [1959] 3 All ER 225). *A fortiori*, a defendant employer cannot put forward the defence where the plaintiff has taken a risk in his employer's interests, as in *Neil v Harland and Wolff Ltd* (1949) 82 Ll L Rep 515 CA, where a workman, with his eyes open, took the risk of working at electrical cables without removing the fuses, knowing that if the fuses were removed the factory would have to come to a standstill. Within the same principle fall several cases where a servant has acted for his master's benefit in an emergency, such as the outbreak of fire, even though the servant has done the wrong thing: *D'Urso v Sanson* [1939] 4 All ER 26; *Steel v Glasgow Iron and Steel Co Ltd* 1944 SC 237. But where workmen have deliberately agreed to disobey safety regulations which impose a direct duty on them, contrary to the employer's orders, the defence will succeed although they took a short cut to get on with their work: *Imperial Chemical Industries Ltd v Shatwell* [1965] AC 656, [1964] 2 All ER 999; *McMullen v National Coal Board* [1982] ICR 148 (man jumped off man-rider in breach of s. 89 of the Mines and Quarries Act and in disobedience to standing orders).

2 Liability to a volunteer worker

While the doctrine of common employment was in force, the extent of an employer's liability to a person who had volunteered, without pay, to assist his servants with their work, was rather obscure. It is convenient first of all to examine the older cases—mixed up as they were with the obsolete doctrine of common employment—and then to consider what are now the true principles of law.

In *Degg v Midland Rly Co* (1857) 1 H & N 773 the plaintiff ran to assist some railway servants who were trying to move a turntable, and was injured by a railway engine. It was held that he could claim no higher rights than the servants he was assisting, and that his claim was subject to the defence of common employment. In the later case of *Potter v Faulkner* (1861) 1 B & S 800 where this principle was affirmed, Erle CJ said:

> 'This is the case of one who volunteers to associate himself with the defendant's servant in the performance of his work, and that without the consent or even the knowledge of the master. Such a one cannot stand in a better position than those with whom he associates himself in respect of their master's liability.'

On the other hand, the rights of a person who intervened to help with the unloading of cattle which were consigned to him, and was therefore assisting with the work on his own account, were governed by ordinary common law principles, and he was awarded damages as an invitee: *Wright v London and North Western Rly Co* (1876) 1 QBD 252.

Degg's case was followed in *Bass v Hendon Urban District Council* (1912) 28 TLR 317 and in *Heasmer v Pickfords* (1920) 36 TLR 818 where McCardie J said:

> 'I myself feel that the true explanation of *Degg's* case and of *Potter v Faulkner* may be that a plaintiff who volunteers to assist the servants of another and who is injured by the negligence of those servants finds himself in a legal dilemma. For if he was engaged, or requested to help, on the authority of the master, then he becomes a fellow-servant with the other servants of the master. If, on the other hand, he was engaged or requested to help without any authority at all from the master, then he is, in legal strictness, a trespasser.'

This dictum was followed in *Bromiley v Collins* [1936] 2 All ER 1061, where a boy had volunteered to help in moving a heavily laden trailer, and it was held that he was either in common employment with the other men, or a trespasser.

On the other hand, a plaintiff could succeed even under the old law if he could show that he was present in some capacity which created a common law duty towards him. In *Hayward v Drury Lane Theatre and Moss' Empires* [1917] 2 KB 899 the plaintiff was injured at a theatre where she was attending rehearsals with a view to engagement as a dancer. It was held that she was entitled to recover damages as an invitee. In *Lomas v Jones (M.) & Son* [1944] 1 KB 4, [1943] 2 All ER 548 the defendants had delivered a heifer to the plaintiff's farmyard, and the plaintiff was helping to close the doors of the van when he was injured, owing to the driver's negligence. It was held that the defendants were liable, as the plaintiff was lawfully present in his own farmyard, and the defendants owed him a duty of care.

The rights of an *infant* volunteer were considered by the Court of Appeal in *Holdman v Hamlyn* [1943] KB 664, [1943] 2 All ER 137 where a boy of ten was allowed to help with work on a threshing machine, and was injured while doing so. The court held that the boy was entitled to succeed[8]. After referring to the various cases quoted above, du Parq LJ said at pp. 667 and 141:

> 'The true ground of all these decisions seems to be that the volunteer was a trespasser in the sense that he officiously and illegally meddled with what was no concern of his . . . the late Sir Frederick Pollock regarded them as illustrations of the principle *volenti non fit injuria*.'

So far as these various cases depend on the doctrine of common employment, they are obsolete since the Law Reform (Personal Injuries) Act 1948, which abolished the defence. The following suggestions are believed to be in accordance with the fundamental principles of the common law, and consistent with the cases decided before 1948:

(1) There is no reason why the relationship of master and servant should not be established between a master and an unpaid volunteer: but before this relationship is established, it must be shown that the master, either personally or through his servants, invited the volunteer to work for him, and that the volunteer agreed to obey the master's orders in doing the work.

(2) If the relationship of master and servant is established, even on an unpaid basis, the master is under normal common law liabilities towards the volunteer: he must take reasonable care for the safety of the place of work, and system of work, and the equipment provided, and is vicariously liable for negligent conduct by fellow-servants.

(3) If no relationship of master and servant is established, the consequences are as follows:

(a) liability for the condition of the premises depends on whether

---

8 There may now be a breach of statutory duty where children are allowed on some farm machinery: the Agriculture (Avoidance of Accidents to Children) Regulations 1958 (S.I. No. 366).

the plaintiff is a lawful visitor, to whom a duty is owed under the Occupier's Liability Act 1957, or a trespasser to whom a lower duty is owed (in Scotland, the corresponding Act does not exclude trespassers);

(b) similarly there must be liability if activities are conducted negligently in the knowledge that the plaintiff is present and may be endangered;

(c) in both cases, if the plaintiff has interfered, without invitation, to do risky work in which he has no direct interest, he is liable to be met by the defence of *volenti non fit injuria*. This was the case, for instance, in *Cutler v United Dairies (London) Ltd* [1933] 2 KB 297 where the plaintiff took upon himself the task of stopping a runaway horse.

Proposition (3) is broadly supported by the Irish case of *Fitzgerald v Great Northern Railway (Ireland)* [1947] NI 1. In this case the plaintiff, a coal merchant's carter, called at the defendants' premises to take delivery of coal, and while there he was requested to assist in the handling, by means of a crane, of a load in which he had no interest. The defendants' servant handled the crane negligently and injured the plaintiff. The defendants were held liable on the ground that, even if the plaintiff, being initially an invitee, had exceeded the scope of his invitation and become a trespasser, the defendants were responsible for a dangerous operation conducted by their servant with knowledge of the plaintiff's presence.

Chapter 25

The liability of the Crown as an employer and otherwise

1 The general liability of the Crown

Before the Crown Proceedings Act 1947[1], the Crown was not liable in tort. Therefore, a servant of the Crown could not sue for damages for personal injuries caused by the negligence of the Crown or of his fellow-servants. Similarly, no action could be based on breach of statutory duty, even though the statute, like the Factories Act 1937, was binding on the Crown.

Section 2(1) of the Crown Proceedings Act 1947 provides as follows:

> 'Subject to the provisions of this Act, the Crown shall be subject to all those liabilities in tort to which, if it were a private person of full age and capacity, it would be subject:—
>
> (a) in respect of torts committed by its servants or agents;
> (b) in respect of any breach of those duties which a person owes to his servants or agents at common law by reason of being their employer;
>   and
> (c) in respect of any breach of the duties attaching at common law to the ownership, occupation, possession or control of property.'

Section 2(1)(b) clearly makes the Crown liable to its servants for negligence in failing to provide a safe system of work, a safe place of work and safe appliances, in the same way as other employers; and s. 2(1)(a), in conjunction with the Law Reform (Personal Injuries) Act 1948, makes the Crown liable for the torts of its servants to one another,

---

1   8 Halsbury's Statutes, 3rd Edn., 844.

or to other persons[2]. Under head (c), both the Occupiers' Liability Act 1957 (by s. 6) and the Occupiers' Liability (Scotland) Act 1960 (by s. 4) are binding on the Crown. So, under head (b), is the Employer's Liability (Defective Equipment) Act 1969.

Breach of statutory duty is dealt with by s. 2(2):

> 'Where the Crown is bound by a statutory duty which is binding also upon persons other than the Crown and its officers, then, subject to the provisions of this Act, the Crown shall, in respect of a failure to comply with that duty, be subject to all those liabilities in tort (if any) to which it would be so subject if it were a private person of full age and capacity.'

By s. 4[3], the law on indemnity and contribution between tortfeasors, and on division of damages in cases of contributory negligence, is applied to the Crown.

These provisions, broadly, place the Crown in the same position as a private employer, but care must be taken, in bringing an action for breach of statutory duty, to see that the statute is one which is binding on the Crown. The prerogative rights of the Crown are saved under s. 11[4], but it is difficult to see how these could have any bearing on a claim by an injured employee.

The Act binds the Crown only so far as it is acting in relation to the Government of the United Kingdom; that is, it does not enable Governments in other parts of the Commonwealth which are still ruled by the Crown (though in a different capacity) to be sued in United Kingdom courts. Proceedings against such Governments must therefore be taken in their own courts, if authorised by the law in force there.

2 The special case of the armed forces

These provisions did not, when the Act was first passed, apply to the armed forces (which include the women's services and the nursing

---

2   A person such as a police officer, who is appointed to a public office in which he 'serves' the Crown, is not a 'servant' of the Crown so as to enable the Crown to claim damages for the loss of his services: *A.-G. for New South Wales v Perpetual Trustee Co (Ltd)* [1955] AC 457, [1955] 1 All ER 846. It is not clear whether this limitation of the meaning of servant applies for other purposes, nor how far the concept of a 'public office' extends.

3   8 Halsbury's Statutes, 3rd Edn., 848.

4   8 Halsbury's Statutes, 3rd Edn., 855.

services): their special position was dealt with in rather an elaborate manner in s. 10[5]. Section 10 has been repealed by the Crown Proceedings (Armed Forces) Act 1987 except where a claim arises for an act or omission before 15 May 1987. But the Secretary of State may make an order bringing it into force either in case of national emergency or in the case of warlike operations outside the United Kingdom: so it is necessary to say something about the section.

In substance, s. 10(1) provided that a soldier[6] could not in general sue the Crown for injuries caused by the negligence or other tort of a fellow-soldier, if he sustained the injuries while on duty, or while on land or premises, or on a ship, aircraft or vehicle, used for military purposes, provided that the accident was certified as attributable to service for the purposes of pension entitlement. In general, too, it was not possible to sue the fellow-soldier, unless he was off duty at the time.

Thus an airman being flown as a passenger from one place to another could not sue the pilot if he negligently crashed the aircraft, nor could he sue the Crown; nor could a soldier sue a medical officer for alleged negligent treatment in a military camp, though when a soldier was sent to a civil hospital without a note of explanation it was held that the resulting damage occurred outside the camp: *Bell v Secretary of State for Defence* [1986] QB 322, [1985] 3 All ER 661 as explained in *Pearce v Secretary of State for Defence* [1988] AC 755, [1988] 2 All ER 348. If a soldier drove a vehicle off duty and without authority, and ran down another soldier, whether he was on duty or off duty, or inside or outside the camp, the negligent soldier could be sued, but there was still no action against the Crown, because the negligence did not arise in the course of the negligent soldier's employment. On the other hand, if an authorised despatch rider, for instance, collided with another soldier, who was both off duty and outside the camp, the injured soldier could sue both the despatch rider and the Crown.

To put the matter very tersely, then, a soldier could not sue the Crown for injuries inflicted on him by a fellow-soldier on duty, unless he himself was off duty at the time, and was not on land or premises, or on any aircraft, ship or vehicle, which was being used for military purposes.

Section 10(2) dealt with injuries caused by defects in land, premises,

---

5   8 Halsbury's Statutes, 3rd Edn., 854.
6   This term is used here for the sake of brevity to include any member of the armed forces.

ships, aircraft or vehicles used for military purposes, or in military equipment or supplies, and declared that no proceedings should lie against the Crown in such cases, so long as it was certified that the injuries were attributable to service for the purpose of pension entitlement.

In relation to soldiers, therefore, the Crown was clearly under no duty to provide a safe place of work or safe appliances; and if a soldier was injured by the bursting of a defective rifle, for example, he had no common law remedy.

What brought s. 10 into operation was a certificate by the Ministry of Defence that there was a pension entitlement arising out of the accident, or, to be more accurate, that the accident 'will be treated as attributable to service' for the purpose of determining pension entitlement[7]. If this certificate was withheld in any case, a common law action could be brought as against an ordinary employer. But if a certificate was given, no action can be brought, even though a pension was refused: *Adams v War Office* [1955] 3 All ER 245. Moreover a certificate could validly be given although in fact no one would qualify to receive a pension: *Bell v Secretary of State for Defence* [1986] QB 322, [1985] 3 All ER 661.

Where negligence was alleged against the Atomic Energy Authority in the supervision of atomic bomb tests in the Pacific, s. 10 did not afford a defence although the liabilities of the Authority were transferred to the Ministry of Defence: *Pearce v Secretary of State for Defence* [1988] AC 755, [1988] 2 All ER 348.

---

7   Actual entitlement to a pension depends on other factors besides attributability to service.

Chapter 26

Pleading and practice

1 Pleading

Only one action can be brought against the same person in respect of the same injuries: *Brunsden v Humphrey* (1884) 14 QBD 141. If, therefore, an action can be founded both on breach of statutory duty and on negligence, the proper course is to plead both causes of action, although this may sometimes cause additional expense in obtaining expert witnesses, as the burden of proving a common law claim is usually a heavy one. The two causes of action are distinct and must be pleaded separately: *London Passenger Transport Board v Upson* [1949] AC 155, [1949] 1 All ER 60 per Lord Wright at 169, 67–8. A single payment into court may nevertheless be made in satisfaction of both causes of action, since they are alternative ways of claiming the same damages: *Graham v C. E. Heinke & Co Ltd* [1959] 1 QB 225, [1958] 3 All ER 650.

In common law claims, there is no need to set out in detail the duties which rest on the employer at common law. No doubt where there is an unusual duty it is necessary to allege it, but the law of employer's liability is so well established that it is sufficient to allege that the plaintiff was at the material time in the employment of the defendant, and to give details of the negligence charged.

Since the Occupiers' Liability Act 1957, the duty of care which rests on an occupier has sometimes been pleaded as a 'breach of statutory duty'. But this statute merely restated in an improved form the occupier's common law liability for negligence, and it is pedantic to treat it as similar to a breach of the Factories Act. It is sufficient to allege that the defendant was an occupier, the plaintiff a visitor, and to give particulars of negligence.

Where a defect in plant or machinery is alleged, it is undesirable to give elaborate technical details, so long as the substance of the matter is explained: technical details can always be supplied when further particulars are requested. Similarly in alleging an accident such as a fall from a scaffold or ladder, it is sufficient to allege the substance of what happened, without setting out the whole of the story.

Where the claim is based on an unsafe system of work, it has been said that the statement of claim must show clearly what is said to have been wrong with the system, and indicate what would have been a proper system: per Viscount Simon in *Colfar v Coggins and Griffiths (Liverpool) Ltd* [1945] AC 197, [1945] 1 All ER 326. This, however, is in conflict with *Manchester Corpn v Markland* [1936] AC 360 where it was held that a plaintiff is not required to show what exact precautions the defendant ought to have taken. It seems, therefore, that it is enough if the statement of claim shows what was unsafe or dangerous in the method of work: see *General Cleaning Contractors Ltd v Christmas* [1953] AC 180 at 190–1, [1952] 2 All ER 1110 at 1114–1115; *Buckingham v Daily News Ltd* [1956] 2 QB 534 at 538; *Dixon v Cementation Co Ltd* [1960] 3 All ER 417; *Harnett v Associated Octel* [1987] CLY 3072 (particulars of measures necessary to suppress fumes refused).

The above comments are offered with a view to simpler pleading in employer's liability cases: the pleadings in these cases have tended to be longer and more complex than is really necessary. A statement of claim should give the court a clear and concise picture of the facts which are said to establish liability.

Where a breach of statutory duty under the Factories Act is alleged, the statement of claim must show that the plaintiff was employed in a factory (or other premises subject to the Act) of which the defendant was the occupier. Similarly facts must be shown to make other special Acts applicable.

It is important to formulate a claim on the right basis from the start: an amendment at the trial to allege a totally different case may be refused if the defendant has been prejudiced (*Rawding v London Brick Co Ltd* (1970) 10 KIR 207); or the expense of a new trial may be incurred where the judge has been influenced by a new case put forward at the trial (*Lloyde v West Midlands Gas Board* [1971] 2 All ER 1240).

Contributory negligence must be specifically pleaded as a defence, with particulars: if it is not, the court has no power to make a finding of contributory negligence or to reduce damages: *Fookes v Slayter* [1979] 1 All ER 137, [1978] 1 WLR 1293.

2 Evidence and interlocutory proceedings

Evidence and interlocutory proceedings in employer's liability cases follow the same general lines as in other cases of personal injuries.

It is a matter of paramount importance to take full statements from the witnesses before their memories become blurred, as this happens very quickly after an accident. It may seem superfluous to mention so obvious a point, but in practice there is often unjustifiable delay, especially where it seems likely that the claim will be settled. Care must also be taken to obtain full evidence on the issue of damages, including the special damages if they have not been agreed.

Where the injuries are alleged to have been caused by defective or unfenced machinery, inspection is usually allowed by agreement between the parties, but if there is any difficulty the court may make an order for inspection under Order 29, rule 2. The costs of such an inspection may be allowed in either case: *Ashworth v English Card Clothing Co (No. 1)* [1904] 1 Ch 702. The same rule enables 'preservation' to be ordered, e.g. of a ladder involved in an accident, or a broken guard. The court may order facilities to be given for a video of moving machinery to be shown at the trial: *Ash v Buxted Poultry Ltd* (1989) Times, 29 Nov. At the discovery stage, it should be kept in mind that records have to be kept under the Factories and Mines Acts of periodical inspections of machinery, and that records will also be available of any previous accident on the same machine. If there is good ground for believing that there are reports in the employer's possession or control of similar accidents within a reasonable time limit and at a place reasonably near, discovery may be ordered: *Edmiston v British Transport Commission* [1956] 1 QB 191; but unlimited discovery of similar accidents will not be allowed. Reports and statements made for the specific purpose of helping the employer's solicitors if a legal claim is made are privileged and cannot be inspected (*Seabrook v British Transport Commission* [1959] 2 All ER 15); but privilege does not extend to the report of an inquiry whose purpose was to establish the true cause of an accident, although this may also assist the solicitor in legal claims (*Longthorn v British Transport Commission* [1959] 2 All ER 32). At mines, quarries and offshore installations, special rules or standing orders adapted to local conditions or the system of operation are required, and these should be inspected.

Under the Supreme Court Act 1981 ss. 33–35, replacing the Administration of Justice Act 1969, s. 21 and the Administration of Justice Act 1970 ss. 31 and 32, the court has power to order both inspection of property and discovery of documents before an action is started, and after an action has started it may make such orders against a person who is not a party to the action[1].

Under the Civil Evidence Act 1968, s. 11, a certificate of a conviction for an offence (e.g. under the Factories Act) may be given in evidence in a civil action and is presumed correct until the contrary is proved: *Stupple v Royal Insurance Co Ltd* [1971] 1 QB 50, [1970] 3 All ER 230.

In dock and shipping cases, witnesses such as seamen or ship's officers may be away at sea when the action comes to trial, and it is desirable to arrange for their evidence to be taken on deposition under Order 39, rule 1.

Under the Civil Evidence Act 1972, s. 2, rules of court may be made to facilitate the use of an expert's report in evidence without necessarily calling him personally; while on the other hand an expert may be prevented from giving evidence at all if exchange of reports has been

---

1   Discovery before action cannot be ordered unless a claim is 'likely' to be made, but an order is not precluded merely because the documents are material in deciding whether a claim should be pressed: *Dunning v Liverpool Hospital Board* [1973] 2 All ER 454, [1973] 1 WLR 586. It is not necessary to show that the documents are essential for the plaintiff's case: *O'Sullivan v Herdmans Ltd* [1987] 3 All ER 129, [1987] 1 WLR 1047. While the court is reluctant to allow 'fishing' tactics where a plaintiff is trying to find something on which he can pin a claim, discovery of documents about an alleged defect in a machine was allowed because the documents, if adverse, were likely to dispose of the claim: *Shaw v Vauxhall Motors Ltd* [1974] 2 All ER 1185, [1974] 1 WLR 1035. The court has no power to order disclosure restricted to medical advisers: *McIvor v Southern Health and Social Services Board* [1978] 2 All ER 625, [1978] 1 WLR 757.

refused. The object is to induce the parties to save expense by putting their cards on the table, especially in medical issues[2].

At the trial, if the judge inspects the machine or *locus in quo*, what he sees is part of the evidence from which he is entitled to draw his own conclusions, e.g. as to safe system: *Buckingham v Daily News Ltd* [1956] 2 QB 534[3].

3 Third-party proceedings

Third-party proceedings under Order 16 are often taken in employer's liability cases when the defendant claims contribution or indemnity from some other person. In general, where two persons are liable to the plaintiff for the same injuries, they may claim contribution *inter se* under the Civil Liability (Contribution) Act 1978, which replaces the Law Reform (Married Women and Tortfeasors) Act 1935. Contribution will be awarded to such an extent as the court thinks just, and may amount to a complete indemnity.

There are three main possibilities to be taken into account:

(1) The defendant may be liable for breach of his common law duties as employer, but some other person may be liable on other grounds. Thus a manufacturer or repairer of machinery or plant may be liable under the principle of *Donoghue v Stevenson* [1932]

2 For details see R.S.C. Order 38, rr. 35–44. Normally expert reports are exchanged simultaneously. Exceptionally, in a case about exposure to excessive noise in railway workshops, the defendants were allowed to postpone their reports until they had seen the plaintiffs', because otherwise they would have had to make very widespread inquiries without knowing what particular workshops and working conditions were in issue: *Kirkup v British Railway Engineering Ltd* [1983] 3 All ER 147, [1983] 1 WLR 1165. Reports exchanged should give the 'substance' of the expert's intended evidence, which means not merely the facts but also his opinion on them: *Ollett v Bristol Aerojet Ltd* [1979] 3 All ER 544n, [1979] 1 WLR 1197n.
3 The major fault in our litigation procedure today is that it still preserves the mentality of Dickens' day. It is a 'fight', in which cunning surprises are kept back. The tactical skirmishing which results is responsible for much of the expense and delay. My view is that there should be *one good try* before action to compromise: if that fails, both sides should co-operate to bring the matter as quickly as possible before the court, where they should *not* think of fighting, but of each putting his side to the arbitrator. It would be a useful innovation if, at the summons for directions, the registrar interviewed each side separately to see if there was any ground for compromise.

AC 562, or, where the workman was away from his employer's premises at the time of the accident, the occupier of the premises where he was working may be liable. The converse applies where the action has been brought against a manufacturer or other person instead of against the employer.

(2) Some other person, as well as the defendant, may be liable under the statutes or statutory regulations. Under the old Docks Regulations, for example, defective equipment was the responsibility of both the owner of the equipment and the employer who uses it.

(3) An express indemnity may have been given, as where a contractor undertakes building operations in the factory premises (*Hosking v De Havilland Aircraft Co Ltd* [1949] 1 All ER 540); or where stevedores use the ship's gear, and obtain an indemnity in case of defects (*Maltby (T. F.) Ltd v Pelton S.S. Co Ltd* [1951] 2 All ER 954n)[4].

---

4   *Some cases on indemnity.* (1) A servant employed as a driver is liable to indemnify his employer against claims arising out of his negligent driving (*Lister v Romford Ice & Cold Storage Co Ltd* [1957] AC 555, [1957] 1 All ER 125); but not unless driving is part of his normal duties (*Harvey v O'Dell* [1958] 2 QB 78, [1958] 1 All ER 657).

(2) Indemnity against 'claims at common law' includes breach of statutory duty (*Hamilton v Anderson* 1953 SC 129); but in an indemnity by a contractor to the occupier against claims 'under any statute or at common law . . . from any cause other than the negligence of' the occupier, personal negligence only is excepted (*Murfin v United Steel Companies Ltd* [1957] 1 All ER 23).

(3) Where a servant is hired out with equipment, the hirer to be 'responsible for his actions as though the driver were in the hirer's direct employ', this gives full indemnity against vicarious liability for negligent operation (*Herdman v Walker (Tooting) Ltd* [1956] 1 All ER 429); indemnity against 'all claims arising out of use' also covers negligence by the owners' own servant (*Blake v Richards and Wallington Industries Ltd* (1974) 16 KIR 151; for a similar decision in Scotland see *Clark v Sir Wm. Arrol & Co* 1974 SLT 90: the real purpose of these clauses is to say who should take out insurance); 'indemnity for claims in connection with the operation of the plant by the driver' includes the fall of an excavator bucket which the driver had left in suspension, having also failed to service the brakes properly (*Arthur White (Contractors) Ltd v Tarmac Civil Engineering Co Ltd* [1967] 3 All ER 586—House of Lords regarded maintenance as part of 'operation'); an accident arose 'directly or indirectly out of hiring or use of' a crane though caused by movement of the vehicle being loaded and not by the crane (*Wright v Tyne Improvement Commissioners* [1968] 1 All ER 807); where the users expressly undertook to service a crane properly, the owners were not liable under implied warranty for a faulty adjustment existing when it was handed over (*Hadley v Droitwich Construction Co Ltd* [1967] 3 All ER 911); an indemnity against accidents during the 'use' of a crane did not extend to accidents during dismantling: *Murray v Caledonian Crane & Plant Hire* 1983 SLT 306; indemnity to plant owners ineffective where their crane driver not 'competent' as contracted: *McCarkey v Amec* (1990) Times, 28 February.

All these possibilities must be considered, but their detailed examination is beyond the scope of this book.

The Employers' Liability (Compulsory Insurance) Act 1969 requires employers, with certain exceptions, to take out insurance against liability to their own employees (excluding certain close relatives, and overseas employees unless in the United Kingdom for a minimum of 14 days)[5]. If an employer (or any defendant) becomes insolvent while insured (whether compulsorily or not) having incurred a liability, under the Third Parties (Rights against Insurers) Act, 1930 his rights under the policy as respects that liability are tranferred to the claimant who is not

---

(4) Indemnity by scaffolders to builders against 'liability [for] injuries . . . by reason of any act, default or omission' of the scaffolders covered the builders' liability for danger created by their own servant because the scaffolders had failed to protect their own men by complaining and this 'omission' actuated the indemnity: *Smith v Vange Scaffolding and Engineering Co Ltd* [1970] 1 All ER 249 (this seems dubious).

(5) Condition in insurance against accident liability requiring 'reasonable precautions' is broken only by wilful neglect, not mere negligence: *Fraser v B. N. Furman (Productions) Ltd* [1967] 3 All ER 57; *Duncan Logan (Contractors) Ltd v Royal Exchange Assurance* 1973 SLT 192.

(6) Where under a contract cleaners had to indemnify factory occupiers against a claim for injuries to one of their men caused by one of the factory employees, they were not entitled by way of subrogation to require the factory owners to sue the employee: *Morris v Ford Motor Co Ltd* [1973] QB 792, [1973] 2 All ER 1084.

(7) However wide the wording of an indemnity is, it will not extend to damage caused by the claimant's own negligence unless such negligence is expressly mentioned: *Smith v South Wales Switchgear Ltd* [1978] 1 All ER 18, [1978] 1 WLR 165.

(8) Where liabilities are shifted by agreement as between contractors, e.g. on the hire of plant, this is not an 'exclusion' of liability so as to be invalidated by s. 2 of the Unfair Contract Terms Act 1977: *Thompson v Lohan (Plant Hire) Ltd* [1987] 2 All ER 631, [1987] 1 WLR 649.

5   The Act was brought into force by S.I. 1971 No. 1116 on 1 January 1972. Section 3 exempts nationalised industries and local authorities; exemption regulations (S.I. 1971 No. 1933 amended by S.I. 1974 No. 208 and 1981 No. 1489) extend this to various other authorities or persons covered by public funds; also shipowners covered by mutual insurance and (as regards nuclear risks otherwise covered) nuclear installation operators. The Employers' Liability (Compulsory Insurance) General Regulations 1971 (S.I. No. 1117, amended by S.I. 1974 No. 208 and 1975 No. 194) require the issue of certificates of insurance available for inspection: they also invalidate conditions in policies making liability conditional on reasonable care by the employer or performance of statutory duties, or on acts or omissions after a claim has arisen (e.g. giving prompt notice to insurers, making no admissions), but it is permissible to claim repayment from the employers in such cases after claims have been met. There are also the Employers' Liability (Compulsory Insurance) (Offshore Installations) Regulations 1975 (S.I. No. 1443).

required to pay arrears of premiums (*Murray v Legal and General Assurance Society Ltd* [1970] 2 QB 495) but was formerly bound by conditions in the policy e.g. as to giving notice of claims (*Farrell v Federated Employers Insurance Association Ltd* [1970] 3 All ER 632). Regulations under the compulsory insurance system (footnote 5, *supra*) now invalidate such conditions as against the injured claimant. Unfortunately a serious deficiency has come to light in this Act: the House of Lords have held that there are no 'rights' which can pass to the injured person until liability is determined by judgment or agreement: so the insurers are not liable if this does not happen before the company is dissolved: *Bradley v Eagle Star Insurance Co Ltd* [1989] AC 957, [1989] 1 All ER 961. But s. 141 of the Companies Act 1989 now allows the court to restore a company to the register where there is a claim for damages for injuries or death.

4 Limitation periods

The limitation period for actions for personal injuries—the time limit within which such actions must be brought—has had an unfortunate history of ill-conceived changes and pedantic law reform. Originally (under the Limitation Act 1939) the time limit was six years from the date when the cause of action accrued, but there was a shorter period of only one year for actions against public authorities. In the late 1940s when various industries (mines, transport, hospitals, etc.) were nationalised, a time limit of three years was fixed as against the new boards. In 1954, the 1939 Act was amended to fix a uniform period of three years in all cases. Around this time the courts began to allow claims for exposure to dust which caused silicosis, often many years later, as it was found that the time limit for many claims had expired before the plaintiff even knew he had the disease. In *Cartledge v E. Jopling & Sons Ltd* [1963] AC 758, [1963] 1 All ER 341 the House of Lords declined to adopt the simple solution that damage was not sustained, and therefore no cause of action accrued, until the disease 'manifested itself'. The Limitation Act 1963 was then passed, giving a plaintiff the right to apply to the court for leave to bring an action after the time limit had expired, if the delay was due to lack of knowledge: but the conditions which a plaintiff had to satisfy were very elaborate and gave rise to conflicting case-law.

All this was replaced by an entirely new code in the Limitation Act 1975, now included in a consolidation Act, the Limitation Act 1980: ss. 11 to 14 and s. 33 replace ss. 2A, 2B, 2C and 2D which the Act of 1975 inserted in the Act of 1939.

Under s. 11(4), the period is still three years, but it now runs from either '(a) the date on which the cause of action accrued, or (b) the date of knowledge (if later) of the person injured'. If, before that period expires, the injured person dies, a claim on behalf of his *estate* under the Law Reform (Miscellaneous Provisions) Act 1934 may be brought within three years from the date of death or of the personal representative's knowledge (whichever is later). But claims under the Act of 1934 are no longer important since the Administration of Justice Act 1982, under which claims for loss of future earnings and loss of expectation of life can no longer be made on behalf of the estate.

Under the Fatal Accidents Act—which gives the dependants the right to substantial damages on death—the time limit is three years from the death, or from the date of knowledge by the dependant who is claiming: but if the time limit has already expired at the death, the claim of the dependants is barred: s. 12(1), (2). 'Knowledge' is elaborately defined to mean knowledge that there was a 'significant' injury and of the facts which make the defendant responsible for causing it—but if there is knowledge of the *facts*, time will run against the defendant whether or not he knew that they would establish legal liability: s. 14. It is enough if the plaintiff knows in broad terms, that his injury (more usually a disease) was due to 'unsafe working conditions' though he cannot specify exactly what was wrong: *Wilkinson v Ancliff (BLT) Ltd* [1986] 3 All ER 427, [1986] 1 WLR 1352. A 'belief' or suspicion—as distinct from knowledge—that the injury or disease was due to working conditions is not enough: *Davis v Ministry of Defence* [1985] CLY 2017. (but how do you differentiate between 'knowledge' and 'belief'?) Once there is knowledge, mistaken legal advice that there is no claim does not stop time running: *Farmer v National Coal Board* [1985] CLY 2018. However, lack of knowledge of the correct company to sue in the group which employed the plaintiff (all of which had similar names) prevented time from running when the plaintiff and his solicitor were given no indication that they were using the wrong name: *Simpson v Norwest Holst Southern Ltd* [1980] 2 All ER 471, [1980] 1 WLR 968.

Section 33 gives the court a discretion to override the normal time limits and allow an action to proceed if it would be 'equitable' to do so, having regard to a number of specified factors, in particular the prejudice to a defendant if a claim is raised at so late a stage that evidence is no longer available to resist it.[6] This gives the court an unrestricted power to allow the action to proceed, after balancing the disadvantage to the defendant against the injustice to the plaintiff if his claim is barred: *Firman v Ellis* [1978] 2 All ER 851 [1978] 2 WLR 1. This discretion is entrusted to the judge of first instance who will not be overruled on appeal if he has applied the right criteria: *Conry v Simpson* [1983] 3 All ER 369[7]. It is not limited to exceptional cases: *Simpson v Northwest Holst Southern Ltd, supra*. The fact that the plaintiff had a cast-iron case against an uninsured defendant, whose liability would in practice be met by the Motor Insurers' Bureau, was a sufficient reason for refusing to allow another defendant to be added out of time: *Liff v Peasley* [1980] 1 All ER 623, [1980] 1 WLR 781. The existence of a potential claim for negligence against solicitors if the application is refused is a factor to be taken into account against allowing the plaintiff to proceed, but is not conclusive, because there is always some prejudice in having to start a second action: *Thompson v Brown Construction (Ebbw Vale) Ltd* [[1981]] 2 All ER 296. Conversely, the fact that a defendant is always to some extent at a disadvantage if the evidence is stale does not preclude the exercise of discretion in favour of a plaintiff if he had a good reason for delay: *McCafferty v Metropolitan Police District Receiver* [1977] 2 All ER 756, [1977] 1 WLR 1073. On the other hand, the plaintiff has not been prejudiced by the limitation period if he started an action within the time limit but it became abortive through discontinuance, want of prosecution, failure to renew the writ or any other reason, and s. 33 cannot be applied to such cases: *Walkley v Precision Forgings Ltd* [1979] 2 All ER 548, [1979] 1 WLR 606; *Chappell v Cooper* [1980] 2 All ER 463. In the *Walkley* case the House of Lords did indeed leave the door open for exceptional cases where failure to pursue the action was

---

6   Even though the claim was made within the three-year limitation period: *Donovan v Gwentoys Ltd* (1990) Times, 23 March, (HL).
7   An application for leave to proceed under s. 33 may be made to a judge in chambers as a preliminary point: *Firman v Ellis, supra*, at p. 863.

due to misrepresentation or other conduct of the defendant (or his insurers) but such exceptional facts would have to be alleged distinctly and proved: *Deerness v Keeble & Son* [1983] 2 Lloyd's Rep 260.

If, to explain his delay, the plaintiff says he did not know he had a good claim until the last minute, he may be required to disclose what advice he originally received, though this is normally privileged: *Jones v G. D. Searle & Co Ltd* [1978] 3 All ER 654, [1979] 1 WLR 101.

When time has run out against a potential defendant, he cannot be added as a defendant to an existing action so as to deprive him of his defence, unless of course the court extends the time under s. 33: *Liff v Peasley* [1980] 1 All ER 623, [1980] 1 WLR 781. Similarly if a writ has been issued but not served within the limitation period, the time for service will not be extended to defeat the defence: but in this case, since an action has been started, s. 33 does not apply and the plaintiff is finally barred: *Chappell v Cooper* [1980] 2 All ER 463, [1980] WLR 958.

In calculating the time allowed under the Limitation Act, the day when the cause of action arose is omitted; so that where, for example, an accident occurred on 8 November 1954, the last day for starting an action was 8 November 1957 (*Marren v Dawson Bentley & Co Ltd* [1961] 2 QB 135, [1961] 2 All ER 270); but if the court office is closed on the last day of the period, the writ may be issued on the first open day afterwards (*Pritam Kaur v S. Russell & Sons* [1973] QB 336, [1973] 1 All ER 617). In cases of disability such as infancy and unsoundness of mind time does not run until the disability ceases: Limitation Act 1980, s. 28. The former rule that time ran against a person under disability while in the custody of a parent was repealed by the 1975 Act, ss. 2(2), 4(5) and Schedule 2. 'Unsoundness of mind' is a matter of fact, so may arise from head injuries due to the accident if they render a plaintiff incapable of managing his affairs: *Kirby v Leather* [1965] 2 QB 367, [1965] 2 All ER 441 (further proceedings [1965] 3 All ER 927, HL).

When the limitation period has expired, and a writ has been issued in time, it must be served within four months, unless renewed, and it cannot be renewed after the limitation period has expired (*Chappell v Cooper* [1980] 2 All ER 463, [1980] 1 WLR 958); in particular the fact that negotiations are in progress is no excuse for failure to serve the writ (*Easy v Universal Anchorage Co Ltd* [1974] 2 All ER 1105, [1974] 1 WLR 889). Renewal of a writ is not allowed as a matter of course: good reason must be shown for failure to serve it in time, and if there is no such reason hardship to the plaintiff is irrelevant: *Waddon v Whitecroft-Scovill Ltd* [1988] 1 All ER 996, [1988] 1 WLR 309[8]. Amendment of a writ or pleading after the limitation period has expired is now regulated by the new Order 20, r. 5, under which the court has discretion to allow amendment even of the name of a party or a cause of action where no one has been misled and there is no change of substance: see e.g. *Sterman v E. W. & W. J. Moore Ltd* [1970] 1 QB 596, [1970] 1 All ER 581. A defendant may be allowed to amend his defence to allege that some other person was at fault although it is too late for the plaintiff to sue that person: *Turner v Ford Motor Co Ltd* [1965] 2 All ER 583; but such cases are less likely to occur under the present Limitation Act where time runs from the plaintiff's knowledge of the facts which bring in the third party and in any event there is discretionary power to allow extra time: see *Firman v Ellis* [1978] 2 All ER 851 at 860–1.

An action started within the time allowed may be dismissed for want of prosecution if there is excessive delay which prejudices the defendant; but this course will not normally be taken if the limitation period is still running so that the plaintiff could start a fresh action: *Birkett v James* [1978] AC 297, [1977] 2 All ER 801.

Under s. 8 of the Maritime Conventions Act 1911 there is a special time limit of two years for bringing an action against a vessel or 'its owners' in respect of injuries or death of a person on board another vessel, where caused by the fault of the first vessel (not necessarily through collision)[9]: but the court has a discretion to enlarge the time: *The Alnwick* [1965] P 357, [1965] 2 All ER 569. This section does not apply to a claim against the ship on which the dead or injured person was travelling: *The Niceto de Larrinaga* [1965] 2 All ER 930.

8 Unfortunately claims for negligence against solicitors for failing to issue or serve a writ in time have become very common. If there is a claim of any substance, a writ should be issued *and* served well before time expires, unless the defendants agree *in writing* that this shall not be done pending negotiation and that time bar will not be pleaded. More often, however, it is a weak or hopeless claim where delay occurs, because the solicitor is reluctant to abandon it yet is not confident enough to issue a writ. Such claims should be 'killed' before it is too late, by informing the client in writing that there is no chance and adding that there is a three-year limit—either with or without first making an unsuccessful application for legal aid.

9 *The Norwhale* [1975] QB 589, [1975] 2 All ER 501 (barge swamped by discharge of water from larger vessel alongside).

Limitation in Scotland   The Prescription and Limitation (Scotland) Act 1984, amending the earlier Act of 1973, contains provisions broadly similar to the English Act, but in a simpler form more acceptable to Scottish taste. Section 2 substitutes new ss. 17 and 18 for ss. 17 to 19 in the 1973 Act. Under s. 17 the normal time limit in an action for personal injuries is three years, running from the date of the act or omission to which the injuries were due, or the date of cessation if it was a continuing act or omission (for example continuing exposure to dust: *Wilson v Morrinton Quarries* 1979 SLT 82). Alternatively, under s. 17(2)(b), it may run from the date, if later, when the pursuer actually knew the following facts or when, 'in the opinion of the court, it would have been reasonably practicable' for him to become aware of them: (i) that the injuries were sufficient to justify an action against a solvent person who did not dispute liability; (ii) that they were attributable to some act or omission; (iii) that the defender was a person to whom that act or omission was attributable, or the employer or principal of such a person. Item (iii) supersedes a previous decision—*Love v Harant Sealant Services* 1979 SLT 89—that lack of knowledge of the right person to sue did not prevent time from running. The previous decision that it is irrelevant whether the pursuer knew that an act or omission gave rise to legal liability is however confirmed: new s. 22(3) introduced by s. 3, confirming *McIntyre v Armitage Shanks Ltd* 1980 SLT 112. Cases where s. 17(2)(b) is invoked are not to be tried by jury: new s. 22(4).

Section 17 applies not only to an action by the injured person but also to actions by other persons based on his injuries (such as a tutor or curator claiming on behalf of the injured person). If a claim has been assigned (surely an unusual situation) only the knowledge of the assignor is relevant: new s. 22(2).

The new s. 18 applies where a claim is brought after the death of the injured person, whether it is based on the death or is a 'survival' claim for the injuries. Here too the primary period is three years, but running from the death; the alternative is that it may run from the date, if later, when the pursuer actually knew the following facts, or when 'in the opinion of the court, it would have been reasonably practicable' for him to become aware of them: (i) that the injuries were due to some act or omission and (ii) that the defender was the person responsible for that act or omission, or was the employer or principal of such a person. Here too lack of knowledge of legal liability is irrelevant, and jury trial is excluded where extension on the ground of lack of knowledge is required.

Subject to the overriding power of the court to extend all the time limits under s. 19A (considered below) an action cannot be brought after death if time ran out for the injured person while still alive.

Whether the claim is for injuries or for death, any period while a claimant was under disability due to being under full age or to unsoundness of mind is disregarded. It will be noted that in the case of a death claim some relatives may be barred and others not, owing to either lack of knowledge or disability.

Under s. 19A of the 1973 Act (introduced by s. 23 of the Law Reform (Miscellaneous Provisions) (Scotland) Act 1980) the court has a discretionary power to override all these time limits and allow an action to proceed after they have expired, 'if it seems . . . equitable to do so'. The onus is on the pursuer to convince the court that an extension would be equitable, and it has been said that the power will be exercised 'sparingly and with reluctance': *Whyte v Walker* 1983 SLT 441. As in England, the potential prejudice on both sides is balanced. Thus a late action was allowed for noise-induced deafness when the pursuer did not realise he might have a claim and the defenders were not prejudiced by delay: *Black v British Railways Board* 1983 SLT 146. The possibility of an alternative claim against the solicitor for delay is a relevant factor but not conclusive. The need to bring a second action is itself inconvenient and prejudicial, and extension was allowed in one such case where the defenders were not prejudiced: *Henderson v Singer* 1983 SLT 198. It was refused where the insurers would be prejudiced: *Whyte v Walker, supra*; also in *Donald v Rutherford* 1984 SLT 70, reversing the court below on appeal, on the ground that although the insurers had completed their inquiries and even made an interim payment, the delay was entirely due to the solicitor. It was also refused in *Williams v Forth Valley Health Board* 1983 SLT 376 where at an early stage, after legal advice, the pursuer decided that the claim was not worth pursuing and his interest was not revived until much later when he was called as a witness in a similar action brought by another person.

Where an accident occurs overseas and the English and foreign law are both taken into account, the foreign limitation period is now regarded as an intrinsic part of the course of action and not as a procedural matter: so a claim outside that period is, *prima facie*, barred: Foreign Limitation Periods Act 1984. This applies to England and Wales only. However, under s. 2(2) the court may override the Act on grounds of public policy if it would cause 'undue hardship'.

Explanation of legal terms[1]

Action.   Proceedings in a court, commenced usually by a Writ of Summons, to claim damages (or other relief).

A fortiori.   Literally 'even more strongly'. A phrase used where the argument in favour of a point is stronger than for one which is conceded to be correct.

Aliter.   'Otherwise': often used to introduce the second of two cases where there have been conflicting decisions by different courts.

Case.   (Early 19th century.) An old form of action where injuries had not been caused by a direct act of the defendant, but had resulted indirectly from his conduct (especially negligence). In the old days actions for direct interference with either person or property were started by a Writ of Trespass. This was extended by degrees to damage done indirectly by allowing a Writ of Trespass 'on the Case', which was abbreviated to an action of Case: see p. 6, note 4, p. 63, note 12.

Causa causans.   A cause which effectively brings about some result, as distinct from pre-existing circumstances which were the necessary setting (condition *sine qua non*).

Causa directa non remota spectatur.   'You look at the most immediate cause, not the one farther away.' (This maxim is correct only for

---

1   By special request from non-legal readers. Academic lawyers have thought this appendix should be omitted. I know, however, that many readers have found it useful: a legal subject can be followed with surprising ease when a few elementary terms are explained. In the 10th edn. I amplified it to include all Latin phrases at the request of the Safety Engineer at Reeds' Colthorp Board Mills (Mr. D. Wilson).

insurance law: in employer's liability and other claims for damages for injuries it requires considerable modification.)

Cause of action.   The set of facts which, if proved, will establish legal liability.

Common law.   The traditional unwritten law of the country as opposed to statutes: it includes the law of torts (and the right to damages for breach of a statute).

Condition sine qua non.   Literally, 'without which not'. A pre-condition without which an event could not happen, though not an active cause of it, such as the fact that there is a road on which two cars are travelling when they collide.

Construction.   Interpreting the meaning of (e.g.) an Act of Parliament.

Contributory negligence.   Carelessness by an injured person which has contributed to cause his injuries.

Courts.   In England and Wales, actions are brought in the High Court (small claims in the county court). Appeals go to the Court of Appeal.

In Scotland, actions are brought in the Outer House of the Court of Session (small claims in the sheriff court). Appeals go to the Court of Session, Inner House.

Ultimate appeals from both countries go to the House of Lords (where they are heard by five Lords of Appeal). The same Lords sit on the Judicial Committee of the Privy Council which, by agreed constitutional arrangements, hears occasional appeals from such countries as New Zealand.

Damages.   Compensation in money for personal injuries and other loss or damage.

Defence.   (1) Facts which, if proved, will free the defendant from liability or reduce the amount of damages; (2) a formal document in an action embodying the defence.

Defendant.   The person against whom an action is brought (defender, in Scotland).

Ejusdem generis.   'Of the same kind'. A maxim used in interpretation where there is a list of particular things followed by general words—e.g. 'steamers, yachts and other craft'—the general words include only items within the same class, in this case 'sea-going' craft.

Indemnity.   A right (arising usually by agreement) to require another person to pay a debt or damages for which one is liable.

In pari materia.   'On equivalent subject-matter': used to refer to a previous decision on a similar point.

Liability.   An obligation to pay damages (or a debt) which can be enforced by an action.

Negligence.   Failure to take reasonable care when a duty to do so is imposed by law.

Novus actus interveniens.   A new cause intervening: fully explained at pp. 65–67.

Obiter dictum.   'Said in passing'. Remarks made by a judge which were not necessary for the decision of the case and therefore need not be followed by other judges: nevertheless treated with respect, especially if the judge had a high reputation.

Per incuriam.   'By an accidental oversight' (in giving judgment).

Plaintiff.   The person who brings an action.

Pleadings.   The formal documents (Statement of Claim and Defence) in an action. *Not* the oral arguments in court.

Post hoc ergo propter hoc.   'After this, therefore because of it'. The logical fallacy of supposing that because something preceded an event, it must be a cause of it.

Prima facie.   'On first impression'. A *prima facie* case is one which should succeed unless counteracted by contrary evidence.

Pursuer.   The plaintiff in a Scottish action.

Quaere.   Literally, 'question'. Used to express doubt about the accuracy of a decision or opinion.

Qui sentit commodum, sentire debet et onus.   'Whoever takes the benefit of a thing should also be subject to the burden.'

Res ipsa loquitur.   'The thing speaks for itself'—the situation when the happening of an accident is in itself evidence of negligence.

Statement of Claim.   A formal document in an action setting out the facts alleged to establish liability (*condescendence* in Scotland).

Statute.   An Act of Parliament or a rule made under its authority.

Statutory duty.   A duty imposed by a statute.

Third party.   (1) Colloquially, a person other than the injured man, his employer and his fellow-servants; (2) in procedural law, a person who is brought into an action by the defendant on the ground that he is liable to pay to the defendant the whole or a part of the damages awarded against him.

Tort.   Conduct which gives rise to an action for damages: e.g. negligence, breach of statutory duty, libel, etc.

Explanation of legal terms 659

Trespass. (Early 19th century.) A form of action where the defendant, by a direct and personal act, had injured the plaintiff or his property. (Now usually limited to interference with land.)

Vicarious liability. Liability for the conduct of another person, especially a servant.

Volenti non fit injuria. A phrase meaning that a plaintiff cannot complain of an injury if he deliberately took the risk upon his own shoulders.

Appendix II

Note on employer's liability for loss of property

This book is concerned only with employer's liability for personal injuries, but it will be useful to mention three cases where liability for loss of property has been considered.

In *Deyong v Shenburn* [1946] KB 227, [1946] 1 All ER 226 it was argued that an employer was liable at common law for failing to have a proper system for the protection of his servants' clothing. This contention was rejected by the Court of Appeal: and there can be no liability at common law unless the relationship of bailor and bailee is established between a workman and his employer, or unless, as Tucker LJ suggested in his judgment, the circumstances give rise to some special duty of care within the broad principles explained by Lord Atkin in *Donoghue v Stevenson* [1932] AC 562. Similarly a hospital were under no liability for the theft of a doctor's property from his room in a hostel provided by them, although he was required to leave the key in the door: the hospital did not owe any duty of care like that of a boarding-house proprietor: *Edwards v West Herts Group Hospital Management Committee* [1957] 1 All ER 541.

On the other hand, in *McCarthy v Daily Mirror Newspapers Ltd* [1949] 1 All ER 801 the Court of Appeal had to consider s. 43 of the Factories Act 1937[1], which provides that:

'There shall be provided and maintained for the use of employed persons adequate and suitable accommodation for clothing not worn during working hours.'

1 Now s. 59 of the Act of 1961.

The court held that, in deciding whether accommodation is 'suitable', regard must be had to the risk of theft: and accordingly in appropriate cases an action for the loss of clothing through a breach of s. 43 (now s. 59) may be successful.

Index

Unloading
  meaning, 417–418
Unsafe method of work
  negligently adopting, 156

Vehicles
  manoeuvring or driving, 199
Ventilation, 152, 373
Vertical spindle moulding machines,
  365
Vibration, 153–154
Vicarious liability, 1
  Admiralty Court, and, 4–5
  extension of, 5
  fellow-servants, and, 95
  final rationalisation of doctrine, 5
  history, 4–5
  independent contractor, and, 102–
    103
  meaning, 659
  outrider, and, 5
  Scotland, 11–12
  system of work, and, 142
  temporary loan of servant, and, 91
Volenti non fit injuria, 14–15, 85, 630–
  634
  breach of statutory duty, and, 17–18,
    223, 632
  consent, 632–633
  contributory negligence, and 633–634
  knowledge of risk, 632
  meaning, 659
  negligence, and, 631–632
  risk taken in pursuance of moral duty,
    634
  risks, and, 630–634
  two branches of maxim, 630
Voluntary assumption of risk, 630–637
Volunteer worker
  common law duty to, 635–636
  common law principles, 636–637
  infant, 636
  liability to, 634–637
Volunteers
  employer's duty of care, and, 92

War risks
  place of work, and, 127
Warehouses, 267, 418–420
  meaning, 419
Washing facilities, 153, 388

Water pumping stations, 258
Weights
  excessive, lifting, 386
Wet docks
  meaning, 401
Wild animals
  strict liability, and, 77
Window-cleaners, 148
Women
  cleaning machinery, 356–357
Woodworking machines, 359–366
  adjustment, 362
  alternative safeguards, 361–362
  circular sawing machines, 363–364
  cleaning, 362
  duties of persons employed, 363
  gap between guards, 366
  general conditions of work, 360–361
  guards for cutters, 361
  hire of, 362
  instruction on dangers, 362
  light, 361
  narrow band saws, 366
  noise, 361
  planing machines, 365–366
  sale of, 362
  space, 360
  stability, 361
  state of floor, 360–361
  stopping and starting devices, 361
  surface of ground, 360–361
  temperature, 361
  training, 362
  types, 360
  vertical spindle moulding machines, 365
Work of engineering construction
  meaning, 429–430
Working operations, 154–156
Working place
  meaning, 484
Workmen's Compensation Acts, 15–16
  application, 16
  automatic compensation, 15
  common law, and, 16
  procedure, 16

Young persons
  cleaning machinery, 356–357
  dangerous machinery, working at
    supervision, 357–358
    training, 357–358